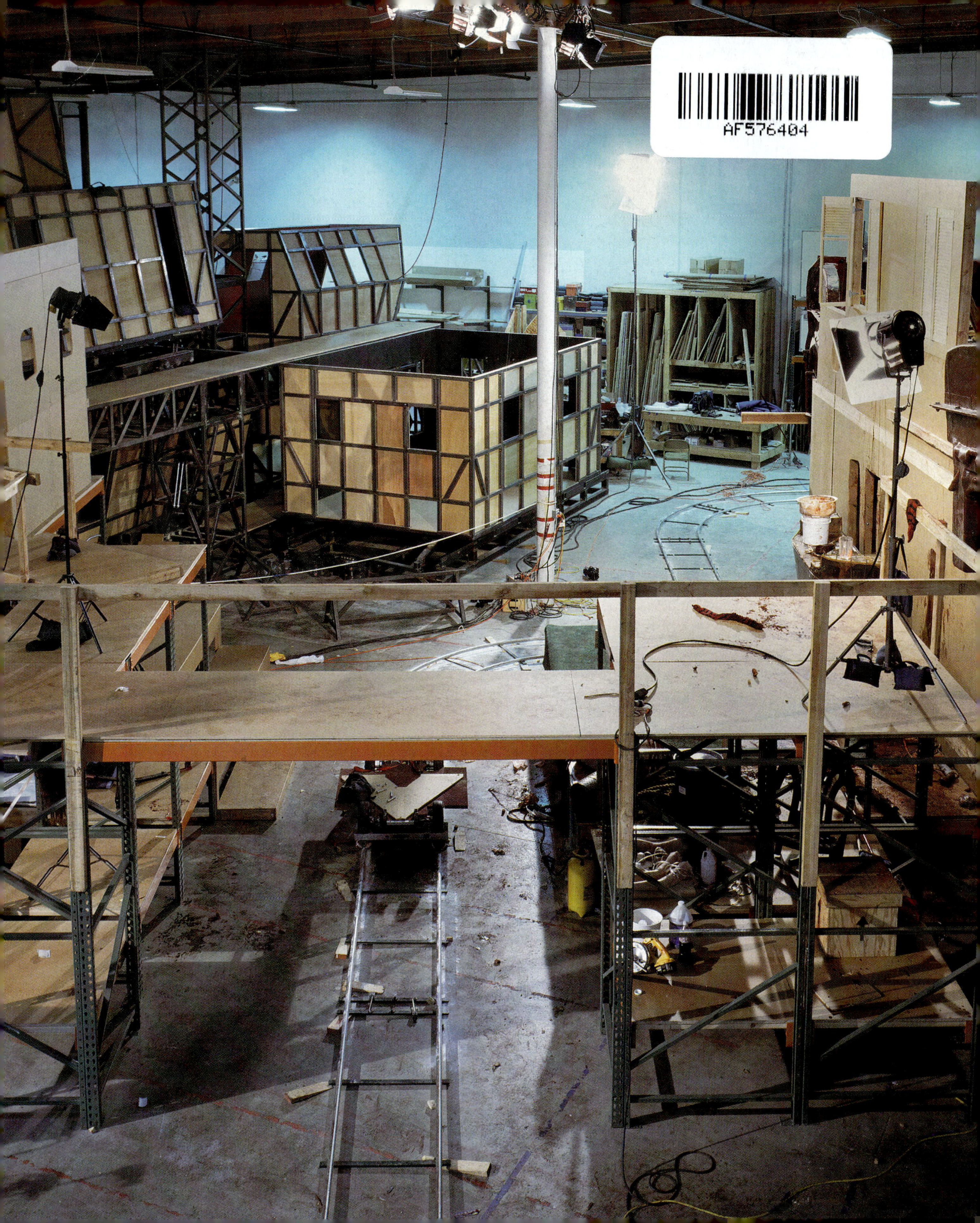

DIE PARKETT-REIHE MIT GEGENWARTSKÜNSTLERN / THE PARKETT SERIES WITH CONTEMPORARY ARTISTS

Book Series with contemporary artists in English and German, published three times a year. Each volume is created in collaboration with artists, who contribute an original work specially made for the readers of Parkett. The works are reproduced in the regular edition and available in a limited and signed Special Edition.

Buchreihe mit Gegenwartskünstlern in deutscher und englischer Sprache, erscheint dreimal im Jahr. Jeder Band entsteht mit Künstlern oder Künstlerinnen, die eigens für die Leser von Parkett einen Originalbeitrag gestalten. Diese Werke sind in der gesamten Auflage abgebildet und zusätzlich in einer limitierten und signierten Vorzugsausgabe erhältlich.

PARKETT NR. 74 ENTSTEHT IN COLLABORATION MIT • **BERNARD FRIZE, KATHARINA GROSSE, RICHARD SERRA** • WILL BE COLLABORATING ON PARKETT NO. 74

JAHRESABONNEMENT (DREI NUMMERN) / ANNUAL SUBSCRIPTION (THREE ISSUES) SFR. 116.– (SCHWEIZ), € 78 (D), € 82 (ÜBRIGES EUROPA), US$ 80 (USA AND CANADA ONLY)

ZWEI- UND DREIJAHRESABONNEMENTPREISE SIEHE GELBE BESTELLKARTE IM HEFT / FOR TWO & THREE YEAR RATES, PLEASE CONSULT YELLOW ORDER FORM.

Zürichsee Druckereien AG (Stäfa) Satz, Litho, Druck / Copy, Printing, Color Separations

PARKETT-VERLAG AG ZÜRICH MAI 2005 PRINTED IN SWITZERLAND ISBN 3-907582-33-0 ISSN 0256-0917

Cover / Umschlag: ELLEN GALLAGHER, MOBY DICK (DeLuxe), 2004/2005, photogravure, aquatint, oil, collage, cut paper, laser cutting, 13 x 10 1/8" / Photogravüre, Aquatinta, Öl, Collage, Laserschnitt, Papier, 33 x 35,7 cm. (PHOTO: TWO PALMS PRESS, NEW YORK)
Cover flap / Umschlagklappe: ANRI SALA, UNTITLED, 2004, still from 7 min. color video with sound / Videostill.
Inner cover flap: ANRI SALA, NOW I SEE, 2004, still from 9 min. 35-mm color film in Dolby SR-D / JETZT SEHE ICHS, Filmstill.
Page / Seite 1: PAUL McCARTHY, PIRATE PROJECT (UNDERWATER WORLD), 2001–2005, part of the stage set for "Lalaland – Parodie Paradies," Haus der Kunst, Munich, 12 June to 28 August 2005 / Bauten für die grosse Werkschau im Haus der Kunst, München, vom 12. Juni bis 28. August 2005.
Back cover / Rückseite: PAUL McCARTHY, PIRATE PROJECT, 2001–2005, film still.
(All images slightly cropped / Alle Bilder leicht beschnitten.)

PARKETT Zürich New York

Bice Curiger Chefredaktorin / Editor-in-Chief; **Jacqueline Burckhardt** Redaktorin / Senior Editor; **Cay Sophie Rabinowitz** Redaktorin USA / Senior Editor US; **Suzanne Schmidt** Textredaktion und Produktion / Editing and Production; **Hanna Koller · Simone Eggstein** Graphik / Design, **Trix Wetter** Graphisches Konzept / Founding Designer (–2001); **Catherine Schelbert** Englisches Lektorat / Editorial Assistant for English; **Claudia Meneghini Nevzadi** Korrektorat / Proof Reading

Beatrice Fässler Vorzugsausgaben, Inserate / Special Editions, Advertising; **Nicole Stotzer** Buchvertrieb, Administration / Distribution, Administration; **Mathias Arnold** Abonnemente / Subscriptions; **Jeremy Sigler** Redaktionsassistenz USA / Assistant Editor US; **Monika Condrea** Vorzugsausgaben, Inserate und Abonnemente USA / Special Editions, Advertising, and Subscriptions US; **Charlotte Marra** Praktikantin USA / Intern US

Jacqueline Burckhardt – Bice Curiger – Dieter von Graffenried Herausgeber / Parkett Board;
Jacqueline Burckhardt – Bice Curiger – Dieter von Graffenried – Walter Keller – Peter Blum Gründer / Founders

Dieter von Graffenried Verleger / Publisher

www.parkettart.com

PARKETT-VERLAG AG, QUELLENSTRASSE 27, CH-8031 ZÜRICH, TEL. 41-44-271 81 40, FAX 41-44-272 43 01
PARKETT, NEW YORK, 155 AV. OF THE AMERICAS, N.Y. 10013, PHONE (212) 673-2660, FAX (212) 271-0704

VOM ÖFFENTLICHEN SPRECHEN

EDITORIAL

Die «alte Zeitung» auf der Titelseite spielt auf kontrastreiche Spannungsfelder an. Denkbar, dass sich jemand sorgfältig einen Einband fürs Parkett gebastelt hätte: Die Zeitung, die sprichwörtlich bloss einen Tag überdauert, als Schutz um eine Kunstpublikation mit sogenanntem Ewigkeitsanspruch geschlagen? Doch wer waren die Leserinnen und Leser dieser Tageszeitung, die offensichtlich älter ist als der Parkettband und sich an ein nichtweisses Publikum richtete?

Zeitungen stehen für Wirklichkeit. Aber gerade in Ellen Gallaghers Interventionen, so minimal sie sich ausnehmen mögen, entsteht im Bild eines erbarmungslos determinierten Daseins eine verspielte und phantastische Gegenwelt.

Paul McCarthys Kunst hingegen setzt auf Kräftiges, auf den Exzess, den Ausbruch, auf räumlich und mental weit ausgreifende Dimensionen. Dabei bezieht er alles mit ein – das gängige Menschenbild ebenso wie sein eigenes Ich oder mythische Figuren. Das geht so weit, dass sich auch in der Interviewsituation mit Jeremy Sigler die normale Frage- und Antwortsituation in der nachträglichen Überarbeitung verselbständigt (S. 120–144). Und wie im Fall der überarbeiteten Zeitung entsteht das Bild eines neu in den Raum gestellten Anspruchs.

«Interview» und «Zeitung» sind zwei Stichworte, die im Werk von Anri Sala, dem dritten Collaboration-Künstler dieser Parkettausgabe, ebenfalls eine wichtige Bedeutung haben: 2003 erschien sein Buch mit dem Titel *Thousand Windows – The World of the Insane.* Es enthält Photos von den unmittelbar nach dem Fall des sozialistischen Regimes zu Hunderten lancierten neuen Zeitungstiteln und den entsprechend zahlreichen improvisierten Verkaufsstellen in den Strassen von Tirana, Bilder, die der damals achtzehnjährige Künstler 1991 gemacht hat. Der Buchtitel setzt sich übrigens aus zwei Namen solcher Zeitungen zusammen.

In ihrem Gespräch mit Anri Sala spricht Lynne Cooke den Künstler unter anderem auch auf ein anderes bekanntes Werk an, INTERVISTA – FINDING THE WORDS (1998), und damit auf die Essenz seiner künstlerischen Tätigkeit: «Der Faden, den ich in deinen Arbeiten verfolge, hat nicht nur mit Schweigen im eigentlichen Sinn zu tun, sondern häufiger noch mit einem Nicht-Sprechen oder einer Unfähigkeit zu sprechen, oder aber mit einem Sprechen über Sprachrohre oder andere Kanäle.» (S. 79)

Auch Matthew Brannon wirft in seinem Insert quasi einen Metablick auf Druckerzeugnisse: Der Künstler als Sammler entwirft einen Abriss über menschliche Ängste in unserer Kultur, allein durch das prosaische Aneinanderreihen von Filmplakaten mit ihren Bände sprechenden Slogans und ihrer satten visuellen Sprache, von der er mühelos den Bogen zu Freud und Schopenhauer spannt, denn auch in diesen Plakaten liegt offen zutage: Das Unglück ist der Erfahrung leichter zugänglich als das Glück. «Von drei Seiten droht das Leiden, vom eigenen Körper her, der, zu Verfall und Auflösung bestimmt, sogar Schmerz und Angst als Warnungssignale nicht entbehren kann, von der Aussenwelt, die mit übermächtigen, unerbittlichen, zerstörenden Kräften gegen uns wüten kann, und endlich aus den Beziehungen zu anderen Menschen.» (Sigmund Freud, *Das Unbehagen in der Kultur,* engl. zit. im Insert, S. 161)

OF WORDS MADE PUBLIC

EDITORIAL

The tension generated by the "old newspaper" on the cover derives from several contrasting associations. Someone may have thoughtfully made a personal cover for Parkett: a newspaper that proverbially lasts but a single day protectively wrapped around an art publication to preserve its so-called claim to eternity. Who were the readers of this daily newspaper, which is obviously older than Parkett and once targeted non-white readers?

Newspapers stand for reality. Yet no matter how low-key Ellen Gallagher's interventions may be, they counter images of relentlessly determined existence with a world that is both playful and fantastic.

Paul McCarthy's art banks on brawn, excess, outbursts and sweeping spatial and mental dimensions, incorporating everything from the conventional image of humanity to his own ego and mythological figures. Here he has so thoroughly revamped the usual question and answer format of his interview with Jeremy Sigler that it is beyond legibility (pp. 112–134). And as in the modified newspaper, the resulting image makes new demands on readers.

The words 'interview' and 'newspaper' also loom large in the work of Anri Sala, the third Collaboration artist in this issue of Parkett. In 2003, Sala published a book titled *Thousand Windows – The World of the Insane.* It contains photos that the then 18-year-old artist took in 1991 of the untold newspapers that sprang up after the fall of the socialist régime as well as the improvised newsstands where they were sold on the streets of Tirana. The book takes its title from two such newspapers.

In her conversation with Anri Sala, Lynne Cooke inquires about another well-known work, INTERVISTA – FINDING THE WORDS (1998), and hence the essence of Sala's artistic concerns: "The strand that I'm tracing in your works has to do not only with actual silence but, more often, with not speaking or not being able to speak, or speaking via conduits or other channels." (p. 73)

In his Insert, Matthew Brannon also takes what might be called a meta-look at printed matter. The artist as collector traces the contours of human fear in contemporary civilization in his prosaic lineup of movie posters. Their telling slogans and compact visual language speak volumes, covering territory that ranges from Schopenhauer to Freud and cogently illustrating a truism of journalism: Unhappiness is a more easily accessible experience than that of happiness. "We are threatened with suffering from three directions: from our own body, which is doomed to decay and dissolution and which cannot even do without pain and anxiety as warning signals; from the external world, which may rage against us with overwhelming and merciless forces of destruction; and finally from our relations to other men." (Sigmund Freud, as quoted on p. 161)

BICE CURIGER

WO IST WICKERFINN LUTZ?

ANGELA ROSENBERG

Die Arbeit THE DISAPPEARANCE OF WICKERFINN LUTZ (Das Verschwinden des Wickerfinn Lutz, 2004) von Jason Dodge ist überraschend einfach angelegt. Der Künstler schickte Briefe an zahlreiche Adressen in verschiedenen Ländern, an die von ihm erfundene Person Wickerfinn Lutz. Da diese Person nicht existiert, dort ebenso wenig wie hier, gelangen die Briefe zurück an den Künstler, und was darin steht, bleibt mysteriös. In dem Zeitraum jedoch, in der ein Postbote an einem fremden Ort nach dieser Person sucht, existiert sie vielleicht doch, und sei es nur in der Phantasie des Postboten. Und so bleibt die Frage, ob jene Briefe, die nicht an den Absender zurückgingen, tatsächlich einen gleichnamigen Adressaten erreicht haben oder nur in einem von vornherein zum Scheitern verurteilten Spiel verloren gegangen sind. Aber wann ist die Geschichte zu Ende, das Ziel erreicht?

Dodge hat für die Präsentation dieser Arbeit in der Villa Arson in Nizza eine Auswahl der retournierten Briefe zu einem Tableau arrangiert. Die Umschläge tragen Spuren der Strecken, die sie zurückgelegt haben, und veranschaulichen die Distanz zwischen Absender und fiktivem Adressaten, die wiederum mit der realen Distanz zwischen Künstler und fiktivem Betrachter korrespondiert.

Dieser Briefwechsel mit einer imaginären Person, die unterschiedliche Grade von Konkretheit durchläuft, erinnert in seiner Aussichtslosigkeit an die Abenteuer von Don Quijote de la Mancha. In Cervantes' Satire auf die Ritterromane und Romanzen seiner Zeit glaubt der von ebendieser Literatur geblendete Held im Umgang mit alltäglichen Phänomenen wie Windmühlen, um nur das bekannteste Beispiel zu nennen, sagenhafte Abenteuer mit dunklen Mächten zu bestehen. Der «Ritter von der traurigen Gestalt», wie sich Don Quijote selbst nennt, lebt ausschliesslich in seiner eigenen Fiktion, in einer literarischen Parallelwelt aus Heldenepen und Liebesabenteuern, die heute nahezu in Vergessenheit versunken sind. Doch Don Quijote hat sich ihnen voll und ganz ergeben, er ist bereit alles zum Ruhme seiner grossen Liebe Dulcinea zu ertragen, obwohl er sie noch nie gesehen hat. Denn auch sie ist seine eigene Erfindung.

Die anscheinend planlose Suche nach Wickerfinn Lutz stellt ein Sinnbild der Suche nach einem Protagonisten dar. Dieser ist nun nicht mehr in der Phantasie des Betrachters angesiedelt, er existiert, wenn überhaupt, in der Phantasie eines Gesandten, eines

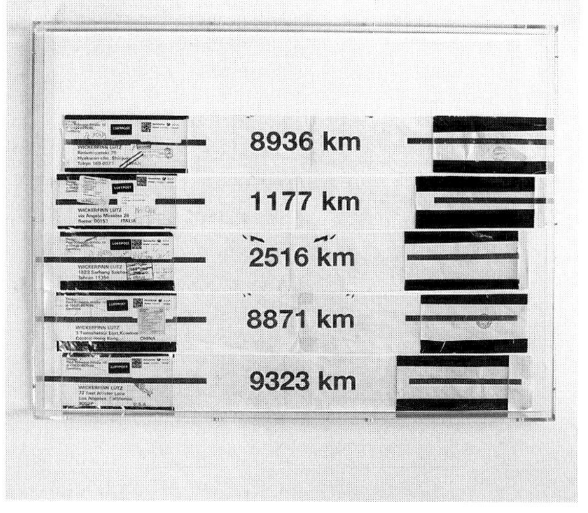

JASON DODGE, THE DISAPPEARANCE OF WICKERFINN LUTZ, 2004, mixed media, detail, Villa Arson, Nice, France / DAS VERSCHWINDEN DES WICKERFINN LUTZ, Teil der Mixed-Media-Installation, Villa Arson, Nizza. (PHOTO: J. BRASILLE)

ANGELA ROSENBERG ist Kunsthistorikerin und freie Kuratorin. Sie lebt in Berlin.

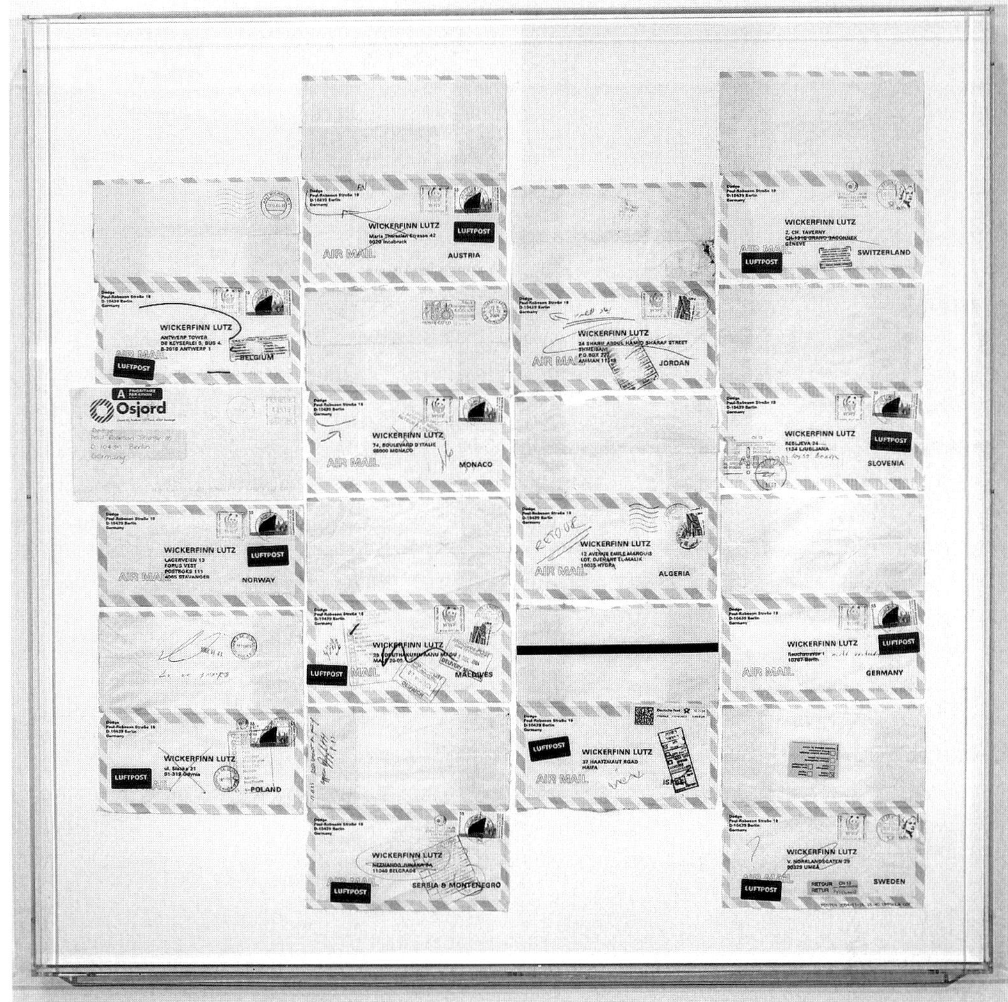

JASON DODGE, THE DISAPPEARANCE OF WICKERFINN LUTZ, 2004, installation detail, 13 Airmail envelopes, 36 x 36 x 2,5" / DAS VERSCHWINDEN DES WICKERFINN LUTZ, Bestandteil der Installation, 13 Luftpostbriefumschläge, 91,5 x 91,5 x 6,4 cm. (PHOTO: CASEY KAPLAN GALLERY, NEW YORK)

Agenten des Künstlers wie des Betrachters: des Briefträgers. Ständig gehen beim Künstler Briefe aus den unterschiedlichsten Winkeln der Welt ein, China, Israel, USA, Frankreich… Es gibt keine Grenzen, alle Länder stehen dem flüchtigen Protagonisten offen. Den Figuren, die in früheren Arbeiten von Jason Dodge auftauchen, etwa Anders Contrave, ist Wickerfinn Lutz in seiner Flüchtigkeit zwar verwandt, aber er ist auch vollkommen verschieden.

Wie konkret können Paralleluniversen sein? Die visuellen Fragmente, die Jason Dodge im Ausstellungsraum verteilt und locker miteinander in Beziehung zu setzen versteht, produzieren Szenarien einer ebenso beiläufigen wie beunruhigenden Künstlichkeit. Es sind alltäglich erscheinende Gebrauchsgegenstände, welche die Präsenz von Menschen vermitteln, Spuren einer Geschichte darstellen. Jason Dodges Doppelausstellung «Anders Contrave: Part 1», 1999 in Basel, und «Anders Contrave: Part 2, Your description of an impossible scenario of how we could be together is what made me love you and broke both our hearts» (Teil 2, Deine Beschreibung eines unmöglichen Szenarios, wie wir zusammen sein könnten, hatte zur Folge, dass ich dich liebte, und brach uns beiden das Herz), 1999 in Stockholm, basiert auf Ideen, die kaum in linearen Entwicklungen nachvollziehbar sind, sondern eher als Akkumulationen. Brüchige, spröde Tableaus teilen eine Faszination mit, die es dem Betrachter erlaubt, den Faden der Geschichte an einem attraktiven Punkt aufzunehmen und weiterzuspinnen. Das Porträt von Anders Contrave hängt an einem verlassenen, halb verwüsteten Basler Messestand. Die mit einem Monogramm mit den Initialen SQ versehene Tenniskleidung einer geheimnisvollen Spielerin liegt verstreut in der zur exklusiven Tennishalle uminterpretierten alten Pfarrei des Moderna Museet Projekt. Das exklusive Ambiente, in dem sich Elemente von luxuriösem Lebensstil und Corporate Design vermischen und sich als Referenzen von Stil und kulturellem Gepräge auflösen, stellt hier weniger einen Hintergrund dar, sondern eine Situation, in der alle Details wie Indizien gelesen werden können: ein narrativer Zusammenhang – allein für das Auge des Betrachters arrangiert und produziert.

Auf einem konzeptuellen Ansatz beruhend erzählen diese Dinge von Konsum, von Produkten und ihrer Gestaltung, als Ensemble jedoch von Leidenschaft und unerwiderter Liebe, und zeichnen so das Bild eines rätselhaften Protagonisten. Glätte und Emotionen vermischen sich, man betritt einen Moralstrudel. Nebensächliches erfüllt die Luft, alles ist zufällig und wie hingeworfen. Kann eine Geschichte überhaupt innerhalb eines Objekts existieren? Bleiben nicht vielmehr die Spuren der Geschichte an den Dingen hängen? Und werden nicht die Geschichten dadurch erzählt, wie die Dinge zueinander in Beziehung stehen?

Die verschiedenen Ebenen dieser Geschichten überlappen und bedingen einander, in Glamourwelten selbst erfundener Marken spielt Jason Dodge seinen präzisen Sinn für Design als Sprache und deren Bedeutungsebenen aus – und inszeniert seine Geschichten mit viel Liebe zum Detail aus nur scheinbar vorgefundenen Dingen. Vertraut anmutende Alltagsgegenstände, Objekte, Bettwäsche – jeder wichtige Aspekt dieser Erzählungen ist konstruiert, vom Monogramm bis zum Möbel. Jason Dodge verleiht dieser Welt Leben und Logik durch seine erfundenen Details und wandelt dabei auf einem feinen Grat zwischen Realität und Satire.

In seinen Objekten spiegeln sich kulturelle Kontexte als Qualität ästhetisch aufgeladener Gebrauchsgegenstände. Dabei kommen unterschwellig Wertvorstellungen ins Spiel: Ästhetische Werte, die eine moralische Dimension in sich bergen, treten in einen Gegensatz zum repräsentativen Wert, der durch hochwertige Materialien und sorgfältige Bearbeitung ablesbar wird; betont durch die inszenierte Nähe zu billigen Wegwerfprodukten, entrückt dies die Protagonisten in eine Gesellschaftsschicht von ausgeprägter Exklusivität. Der Betrachter kommt nicht nur zu spät, er gehört sowieso nicht dazu, und als uneingeladenem Besucher bleibt ihm nichts anderes übrig, als in diesen Überresten, nach den Ruinen des Moments zu suchen.

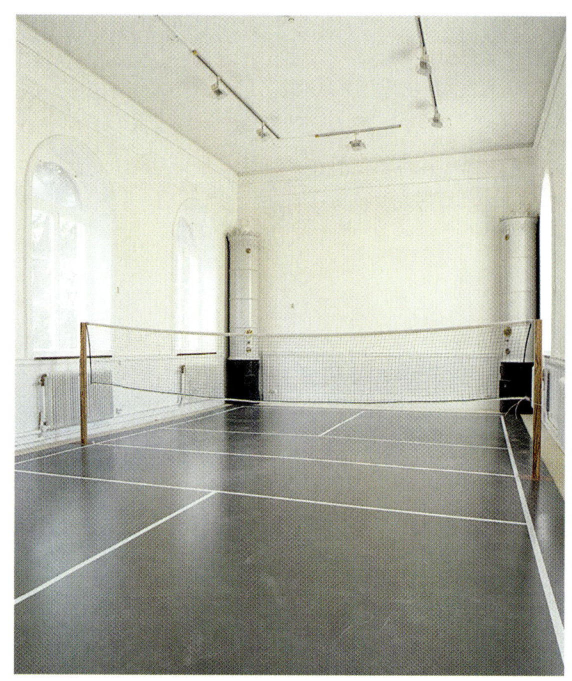

Statt des charmant Zerstreuten dieser Arbeiten, die von der emotionalen Verfassung ihrer nicht anwesenden Akteure vorangetrieben werden und den Betrachter zur «forensischen» Rekonstruktion einla-

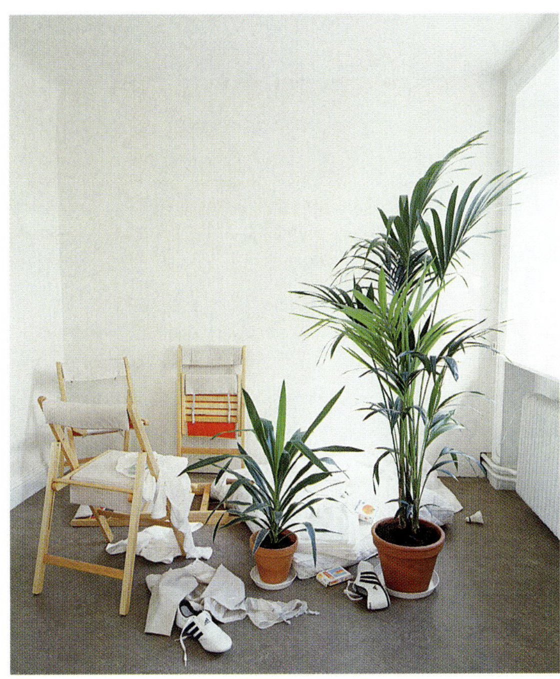

JASON DODGE, "ANDERS CONTRAVE: PART 2," 1999, exhibition views, Moderna Museet Projekt, Stockholm / Ausstellungsansichten. (PHOTOS: ANNA KLEBERG / CASEY KAPLAN GALLERY, NEW YORK)

den (wie Nancy Spector in ihrem Katalogtext zur Ausstellung «Anders Contrave: Part 2» im Moderna Museet, Stockholm, 1999, bemerkte), muss der Betrachter heute Definitionen aushalten: Die Bühne ist ein Wörterbuch geworden, ein Lexikon, dem Jason Dodge nun mit jeder Ausstellung neue Bestandteile seiner Arbeit angliedern will.

Eine fiktive Logik ist genauso gut wie jede andere. Im Dialog mit einem Gegenüber werden die Möglichkeiten und Reibungsflächen, die sich zwischen scheinbar objektiver Konnotation und subjektiver Assoziation ergeben, besonders deutlich. Zwischen der direkten sinnlichen Erfahrung, der subjektiven Wahrnehmung und einer im sozialen Austausch, im ästhetischen Diskurs zu erfahrenden Wirklichkeit entsteht ein spannender Dialog, vergleichbar mit der Auseinandersetzung zwischen dem literarisch verblendeten Don Quijote und dem bedauerlichen Sancho Pansa, der erfolglos versucht ihm seine Realität zu vermitteln.

So können die Arbeiten von Jason Dodge als Reflexionen zur Verhandelbarkeit von Kunst und Realität gesehen werden. Die Aktivierung der Vorstellungskraft erzeugt eine simultane Existenz an einem anderen Ort auf dieser Welt und stellt damit eine Einladung an den Betrachter dar, das Unvereinbare zusammenzubringen, in dem Sinne, dass jeder Erzählung eine wesentliche Vorraussetzung entgegengebracht werden muss: der absichtsvolle Verzicht auf mögliche Zweifel.

Wie überzeugend muss ein Objekt sein, wie echt muss etwas aussehen, damit man der Attrappe glauben will – um wie Don Quijote schliesslich auf Windmühlen loszugehen? Für seinen Installationsbeitrag mit dem kryptischen Titel 12. OKT. 1982 – zur Ausstellung «Formalismus. Moderne Kunst, heute» (2004) – hatte Jason Dodge den Hamburger Kunstverein mit einer Reihe von Aschenbecherobjekten aus Messing ausgestattet, die wie repräsentatives Corporate Design der 60er Jahre aussehen oder so, als ob der Künstler kurz entschlossen einige Elemente aus *Stack*-Arbeiten von Donald Judd recycelt hätte. Natürlich durften die Skulpturen nicht als Aschenbecher benutzt werden, so provokativ sie auch platziert waren.

Die Installation POSSIBILITY OF ROSE COLORED LIGHT (Möglichkeit von rosafarbenem Licht, 2004) in der Villa Arson, Nizza, besteht aus siebzig Messinglampen für Leuchtstoffröhren, die – zusätzlich zur vorhandenen Beleuchtung gleichmässig über die Decke eines Raumes verteilt – aussehen, als ob sie funktionieren könnten, jedoch nicht ans Stromnetz angeschlossen sind. Neben Kartons lehnen zwei Stapel Leuchtstoffröhren an der Wand, mit rosa Folie umwickelt und bereitgestellt, um den Raum in rosa Licht zu tauchen. Aber die sprichwörtliche rosarote Brille wird nur vor das innere Auge des Betrachters gesetzt, es ist eine individuelle Anstrengung, sich das Bild dieses weissen Raums in Rosa getaucht vorzustellen. Darin schwingt eine gewisse Melancholie, wenn nicht sogar Resignation, die der Betrachter – interpretiert er die Arbeit politisch – als sarkastisch auffassen kann. Am Eröffnungstag der Ausstellung, dem 1. November 2004, fiel der Entscheid über die Wiederwahl von George W. Bush, in einer Zeit, in der Frankreich in den USA als Speerspitze des «alten Europa» angesehen wurde, als Vertreter eines dekadenten Systems, das sich einem unaufhaltsamen Fortschritt in den Weg stellt. Die Möglichkeit einer rosa Erleuchtung kann da als ironisches, doppeldeutiges und kritisches Plädoyer gegen zu einfache Erklärungsmodelle und repressives Schwarzweissdenken gelesen werden.

COMPLETE SOLAR ECLIPSE SIERRA LEONE 1982 (Totale Sonnenfinsternis Sierra Leone 1982) aus dem Jahr 2004 besteht aus Notizen von Reisedaten fiktiver, aber nicht näher benannter Personen, die von unterschiedlichen Orten aufbrachen, um die totale Sonnenfinsternis im Jahre 1982 in Sierra Leone zu beobachten. Das Naturereignis, das ohne Absicht geschieht, ist Ausgangspunkt eines kollektiven Erlebnisses vor dem Hintergrund des extrem grausamen Bürgerkriegs, der das afrikanische Land in diesen Jahren besonders unsicher machte. Die aufwändige Reise zu diesem exotischen und gefährlichen Ort, um Zeuge eines Naturereignisses zu sein, legt nahe, dass die ignoranten Sonnenfinsternisbegeisterten kein anderes Interesse teilten, ausser jenem für das sie zusammenführende Naturschauspiel, das sich jenseits moralischer Kategorien vollzieht, jenseits von Grausamkeit, Brutalität und Mord. Dennoch ist auch die Sonnenfinsternis für den Betrachter nicht ganz ungefährlich: Man kann sie nicht direkt betrachten ohne sich die Augen zu verletzen. Sie ist also nur mittelbar, durch eine geschwärzte Glasscheibe oder eine Spezialfolie zu verfolgen. In diesem ebenso exotischen wie speziellen Kontext drängt sich die Frage auf, an welcher Stelle die Erfindung des Künstlers eigentlich ihren Anfang nimmt und wo sie endet, wenn sie überhaupt endet – und endet sie dann zwangsläufig in der Realität, in der wir uns befinden? Hätte der Künstler die erfundenen Betrachter nicht mit Fähigkeiten ausstatten können, die es ihnen erlaubten, direkt in die Sonne zu sehen? Oder hätte die Fiktion sanft mit dem vom Bürgerkrieg gebeutelten Land umgehen können? Die Arbeit wird zum Bilderrätsel, das wie eine verschachtelte, unauflösbare Allegorie von Kunst und Gesellschaft erscheint.

PERPETUAL LIGHT (BETWEEN SUNSET AND SUNRISE IN GREENLAND) – Ewiges Licht (zwischen Sonnenuntergang und -aufgang in Grönland), 2005 – kann als Gegenstück zu diesen beiden Arbeiten gesehen werden, denn Sonnenlicht und Kunstlicht treten an zwei unterschiedlichen Orten in einen Austausch. Wie in einer Fabrikhalle sind normale Standardleuchtstoffröhren im Orange County Museum in Reihen montiert. Wenn in Nuuk, Grönland, die Sonne untergeht, werden im Orange County Museum die Lampen eingeschaltet, bei Sonnenaufgang erlöschen sie wieder. Da sich im Ausstellungsverlauf die Lichtverhältnisse in Nuuk aufgrund der exponierten Lage in der Nähe des Polarkreises dramatisch verändern, werden Besucher, je nachdem, wann sie die Ausstellung gesehen haben, unterschiedliche Erinnerungen davon mit nach Hause nehmen. Die Arbeit lässt sich also im imaginierten Dialog zwischen zwei Besuchern weiterführen, die diese Arbeit zu verschiedenen Zeiten gesehen haben.

Die Vorstellung von anderen Welten und ihren Parallelen zu unserer ähnelt dem Versuch einen Sinn in Dingen zu finden, die über logische Erklärungen hinausgehen, wie die Vorstellung, dass – egal, wo man sich gerade befindet – an einem anderen Ort der Welt gerade Heerscharen von Menschen aus dem Bett springen um zur Arbeit zu eilen, während an wieder einem anderen Ort gerade die Lichter ausgehen, genau jetzt.

In der Installation YOU ALWAYS MOVE IN REVERSE (Du bewegst dich immer im Rückwärtsgang, 2004) sieht man einen 1-Kilogramm-Silberbarren, der durch eine Fensterscheibe geworfen wurde, inmitten von Glassplittern auf dem Boden liegen, die zerschlagene Glasscheibe sitzt noch im Fensterrahmen. Die Umkehrung des Konzepts von Diebstahl im Allgemeinen und Kunstdiebstahl im Besonderen bedeutet, dass etwas Wertvolles nicht gewaltsam entfernt, sondern hinzugefügt wurde, in einem Akt von invertiertem Vandalismus. Das scheint beinahe schon als Definition von Kunst zu taugen. Aber wer würde so etwas tun? Es wird wohl Wickerfinn Lutz gewesen sein, und der Künstler bemüht sich, ihm seinen Silberbarren zurückzugeben.

Aber das ist nur eine Vermutung, ich war nicht dabei.

WHERE IS WICKERFINN LUTZ?

ANGELA ROSENBERG

THE DISAPPEARANCE OF WICKERFINN LUTZ (2004), by Jason Dodge, takes a disarmingly simple approach. The artist sent letters to Wickerfinn Lutz, a person of his own invention, to a number of addresses in various countries. Since this person does not exist, neither there nor here, many letters were returned to the artist and their contents remain a mystery. However, for as long as there is a mailman out there looking for such a person, he may exist after all, even if only in the mailman's imagination. And what about the letters that were not returned to the sender? Did they actually reach an addressee of the same name or did they get lost in a game that was doomed from the start? And when will the story end, what is the ultimate goal?

For the presentation of this piece at Villa Arson in Nice, Dodge made a tableau of selected letters that had been returned to their sender. The envelopes show traces of the journeys they have been through, illustrating the distance between sender and fictive addressee, which corresponds, in turn, to the real distance between the artist and the fictive viewer.

The futility of corresponding with an imaginary person in a venture that undergoes varying degrees of concreteness recalls the adventures of Don Quixote de la Mancha. In Cervantes' satire on the romances of his time, the hero, blinded by the very literature the writer parodies, believes that he is engaging in extraordinary adventures with dark powers in his dealings with the mundane paraphernalia of everyday life, such as windmills, to name the most famous example. The "Knight of the Sad Face," as Don Quixote calls himself, lives entirely in a fiction of his own making, in a parallel literary world of heroic epics and amorous adventures, a world that has now sunk into almost complete oblivion. But Don Quixote succumbs to that world heart and soul; he is prepared to suffer all for the sake of honoring his great love Dulcinea, whom he has never seen face to face—for she, too, is of his own invention.

The seemingly haphazard search for Wickerfinn Lutz proves to symbolize the search for a protagonist per se, but this protagonist is no longer a fiction of the viewer's imagination. He exists, if at all, in the imagination of an emissary, an agent of both artist and viewer, namely, the mailman. The artist keeps receiving letters from all corners of the world, from China, Israel, U.S.A., France... The possibilities are legion; every country is open to the escapee protagonist and, as an escapee, he is related to—although entirely different from—figures, like Anders Contrave, that crop up in Dodge's earlier work.

How concrete can parallel universes be? The visual fragments that Dodge lays out in exhibition spaces, where they are loosely interrelated, yield scenarios of a casual, and yet disturbing, artificiality. We are familiar with the objects of use that communicate the presence of human beings and offer clues to a narrative. Dodge's double exhibition, "Anders Contrave: Part 1" (Basel, 1999) and "Anders Contrave: Part 2, Your description of an impossible scenario of how we could be together is what made me love you and broke both our hearts" (Stockholm, 1999), is based on ideas that can not be read as linear developments but as accumulations. Dilapidated, aloof

ANGELA ROSENBERG is an art historian and a freelance curator. She lives in Berlin.

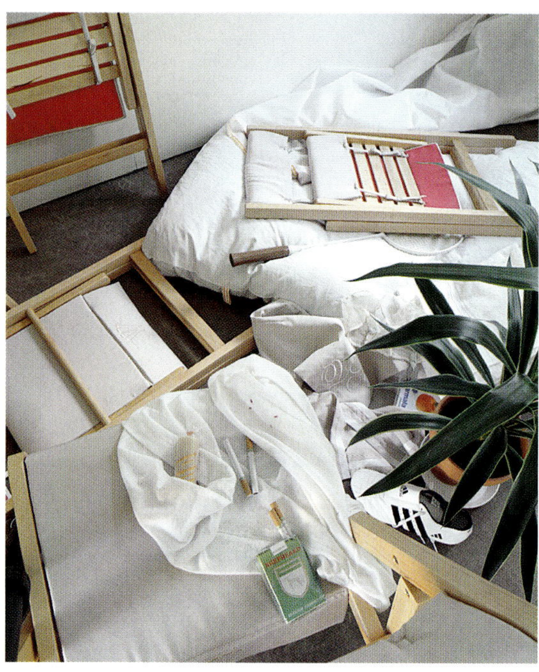

JASON DODGE, "ANDERS CONTRAVE: PART 2," 1999, exhibition view, Moderna Museet Projekt, Stockholm / Ausstellungsansicht.
(PHOTOS: ANNA KLEBERG / CASEY KAPLAN GALLERY, NEW YORK)

tableaus exert a fascination, allowing viewers to take up the thread of the story and elaborate on it wherever they please. The portrait of Anders Contrave is hanging on an abandoned, semi-trashed Basel trade-fair stand. The tennis clothes of a mysterious woman with the monogram SQ lie scattered about in the old rectory of the Moderna Museet, which has been converted into an exclusive tennis court. The exclusive ambiance, in which elements of luxury living and corporate design blend into a referential fabric of style and culture, does not provide the backdrop but rather a situation in which all of the details can be read as indexical signs: a narrative arranged and produced only for the sake of the viewer.

Taking a conceptual approach, these props speak of consumption, of products and their design. But as an ensemble, they speak of passion and unrequited love, hence conveying the image of an enigmatic protagonist. Polish and emotions mingle; we enter a moral maelstrom. The air is filled with inconsequentials, everything is accidental, as if casually cast about. Can a story even exist within an object? Or conversely, aren't the traces of a story attached to things? And don't plots develop by the way in which things relate to each other?

The levels of these stories overlap and mutually determine each other. Within the glamorous framework of invented labels, Dodge plays out his precise sense of design on the semantic level of language in stories that he stages, with great devotion to detail, using exquisitely faked found objects. All of the familiar items of daily life (including bed linens)—every important aspect of these narratives is constructed, from monogram to furniture. Dodge invests his world with life and logic, all his invented details walking the fine line between reality and satire.

His objects are aesthetically charged items of use that mirror cultural contexts. Under the surface, notions of value come to play: aesthetic values with moral implications are pitted against status symbols, flaunting top-of-the-line materials and manufacturing excellence. Juxtaposed with a contrasting scenario of cheap, flimsy disposables, the protagonists reside in a social limbo of conspicuously exclusive luxury. The viewers have come too late and they don't belong there anyway. As uninvited guests, all they can do is rummage through the remains looking for the ruins of the moment.

The charming distraction of these works is buoyed by the emotional state of their absent actors and invites viewers to attempt a "forensic" reconstruction—as Nancy Spector remarks in her catalogue essay on the exhibition, "Anders Contrave: Part 2." But now the viewer has to endure definitions. The stage has become a dictionary, an encyclopedia, to which Dodge plans to add new components with every successive exhibition. Fictional logic is just as good as any other. The use of dialogue makes especially conspicuous the potential and the friction that mark the relationship between supposedly objective connotation and subjective associations. Direct sensual experience, subjective perception, and the reality of social intercourse and aesthetic discourse provide the wherewithal for an exciting exchange, comparable to the conflict between Don Quixote, blinded by literature, and the unfortunate Sancho Pansa, who tries in vain to communicate his reality.

In this respect, Dodge's works can be interpreted as reflections on the negotiability of art and reality. By activating the imagination, he generates a simultaneous existence somewhere else in the world and invites viewers to unite incompatibles inasmuch as every narrative rests on one essential prerequisite: the purposeful waiver of possible doubts.

How convincing does an object have to be, how authentic does it have to look, to make us believe in the mock up—and join Don Quixote in chasing after windmills? For the exhibition "Formalismus. Moderne Kunst, heute" (2004) at the Hamburger Kunstverein, Jason Dodge created an installation cryptically entitled 12. OCT. 1982. It consisted of a number of brass ashtray objects placed around the venue (memories of sixties corporate design), as if he had simply lifted and recycled elements from Donald Judd's *stack* sculptures. Obviously they could not be used as ashtrays despite their provocatively convenient placement.

The installation POSSIBILITY OF ROSE COLORED LIGHT (2004) in the Villa Arson, Nice, consists of seventy brass lamps for fluorescent lighting evenly distributed on the ceiling of the gallery, in addition to the regular lighting. The lamps look perfectly functional although they are not wired. Two stacks of neon tubes are propped against the wall next to cardboard boxes; they are wrapped in pink film, ready to bathe the gallery in "rose colored light." But only the viewer's inner eye can peer through the proverbial rose-colored glasses; it takes individual effort to imagine this white room suffused with a pink glow. One senses a certain melancholy and possibly even resignation, which might be interpreted as sarcastic, given a political reading of the work. The exhibition opened on November 1, 2004, the day that George W. Bush was reelected, and a time when the United States viewed France as the spearhead of "old Europe," as the representative of a decadent system attempting to obstruct irrepressible progress. The potential of rose colored illumination might then be read as a pun, an ironic critique of oversimplification and repressive black-and-white thinking.

COMPLETE SOLAR ECLIPSE SIERRA LEONE 1982 (2004) lists the traveling day of fictional, but unnamed, people who set out from different places to watch the eclipse of the sun that took place in Sierra Leone in 1982. This natural event, which occurs with no ulterior motive, is the point of departure for a collective experience against the background of a particularly horrific civil war, which made the African country extremely unsafe at the time. The arduous journey to this exotic and dangerous place in order to witness a natural event indicates that the ignorant enthusiasts were only interested in the shared experience, in a natural spectacle that lies beyond moral categories, beyond cruelty, brutality, and murder. But the eclipse is not entirely without dangers of its own: if you look at it directly, your eyesight will be permanently damaged. The eclipse can therefore be seen only through a filter, a blackened pane of glass, or a special film. In this exotic and especial context, the question arises as to where the artist's invention actually begins and where it ends, if it ends at all—and does it necessarily have to end in the reality in which we happen to be? Couldn't the artist have equipped his invented viewers with abilities that

JASON DODGE, YOU ALWAYS MOVE IN REVERSE, 2004, 1 kilo silver bullion, window, Villa Arson, Nice, France. / DU BEWEGST DICH IMMER IM RÜCKWÄRTSGANG, 1-Kilogramm-Silberbarren, Fenster, Villa Arson, Nizza. (PHOTO: J. BRASILLE)

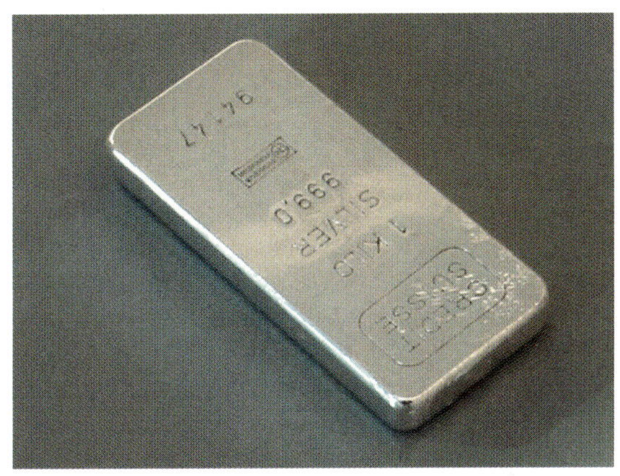

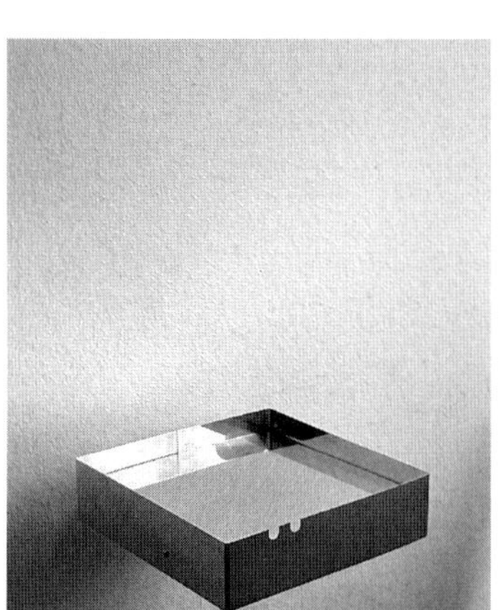

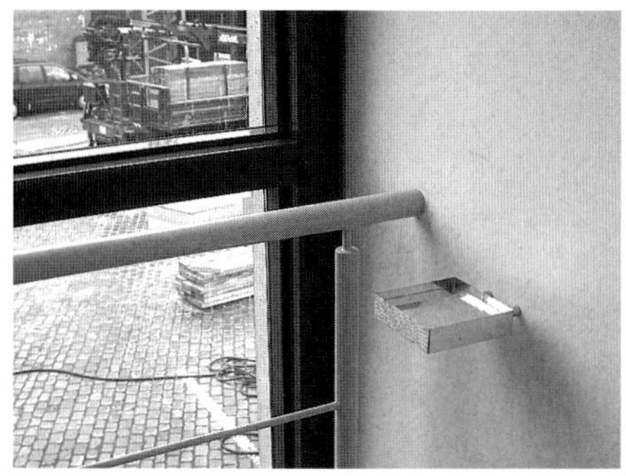

JASON DODGE, 12 OCTOBER 1982, installation views, exhibition "Formalism. Modern Art Today," Hamburger Kunstverein, 2004 / 12. OKTOBER 1982, Ausstellung «Formalismus. Moderne Kunst heute» im Hamburger Kunstverein.

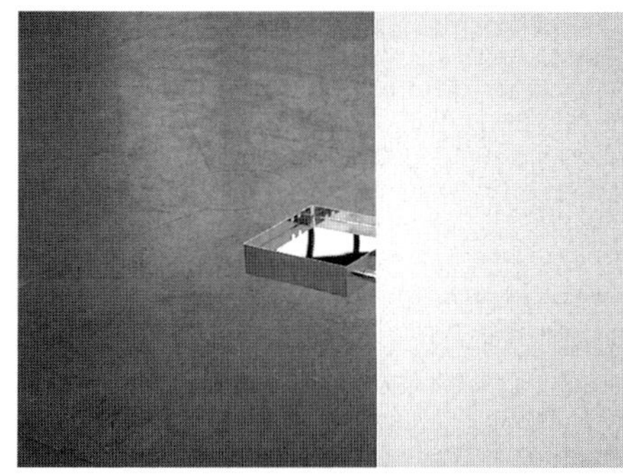

would allow them to gaze directly at the sun? Or could his fiction have quietly coped with a country crippled by civil war? Dodge's piece is a puzzle, a convoluted, impenetrable allegory of art and society.

PERPETUAL LIGHT (BETWEEN SUNSET AND SUNRISE IN GREENLAND) (2005) might be seen as a counterpoint to these two works; it establishes an exchange between sunlight and artificial light in two different geographical locations. Standard commercial neon lights have been mounted in rows at the Orange County Museum as if in an ordinary factory. When the sun sets in Nuuk, Greenland, the lights come on in the Orange County Museum, and they go out again at sunrise. Since Nuuk is so close to the Arctic circle, the light changes dramatically in the course of the exhibition so that viewers who see the exhibition at different times will have entirely different memories of it. The work can therefore be extended into an imaginary dialogue between two visitors who saw the piece at different times.

The idea of different worlds and their parallel existence resembles the attempt to understand things that go beyond logical explanation. Regardless of where we happen to be at the moment, somewhere else in the world masses of people are jumping out of bed and hurrying off to work while, somewhere else, the lights are going out.

In the installation YOU ALWAYS MOVE IN REVERSE (2004), a one-kilogram bar of silver is lying on the floor in a pool of splintered glass; the broken pane through which it was thrown is still in its frame. Dodge has reversed the concept of theft, in general, and art theft, in particular: instead of violently removing something of value, he has added something in an act of inverted vandalism. That could almost be a viable definition of art. But who would do something like that? It was probably Wickerfinn Lutz, and the artist is trying to give the bar of silver back to him. But that's only conjecture; I wasn't there.

(Translation: Catherine Schelbert)

Ellen Gallagher, born 1965 in Providence, Rhode Island, USA, lives and works in New York City / geboren 1965 in Providence, Rhode Island, USA, lebt und arbeitet in New York.

Paul McCarthy, born 1945 in Salt Lake City, Utah, USA, lives and works in Los Angeles, California / geboren 1945 in Salt Lake City, Utah, USA, lebt und arbeitet in Los Angeles, Kalifornien.

Anri Sala, born 1974 in Tirana, Albania, lives and works in Berlin, Germany / geboren 1974 in Tirana, Albanien, lebt und arbeitet in Berlin, Deutschland.

Ellen Gallagher

ELLEN GALLAGHER, ISAAC, 2004/2005, *4-color lithograph, drypoint, laser cutting, crystals, gold leaf, and velvet, 13 x 10" (slightly cropped) / 4-Farben-Lithographie, Kaltnadel, Laserschnitt, Glasperlen, Blattgold und Samt, 33 x 25,4 cm (leicht beschnitten).* (PHOTO: D. JAMES DEE / TWO PALMS PRESS, NEW YORK)

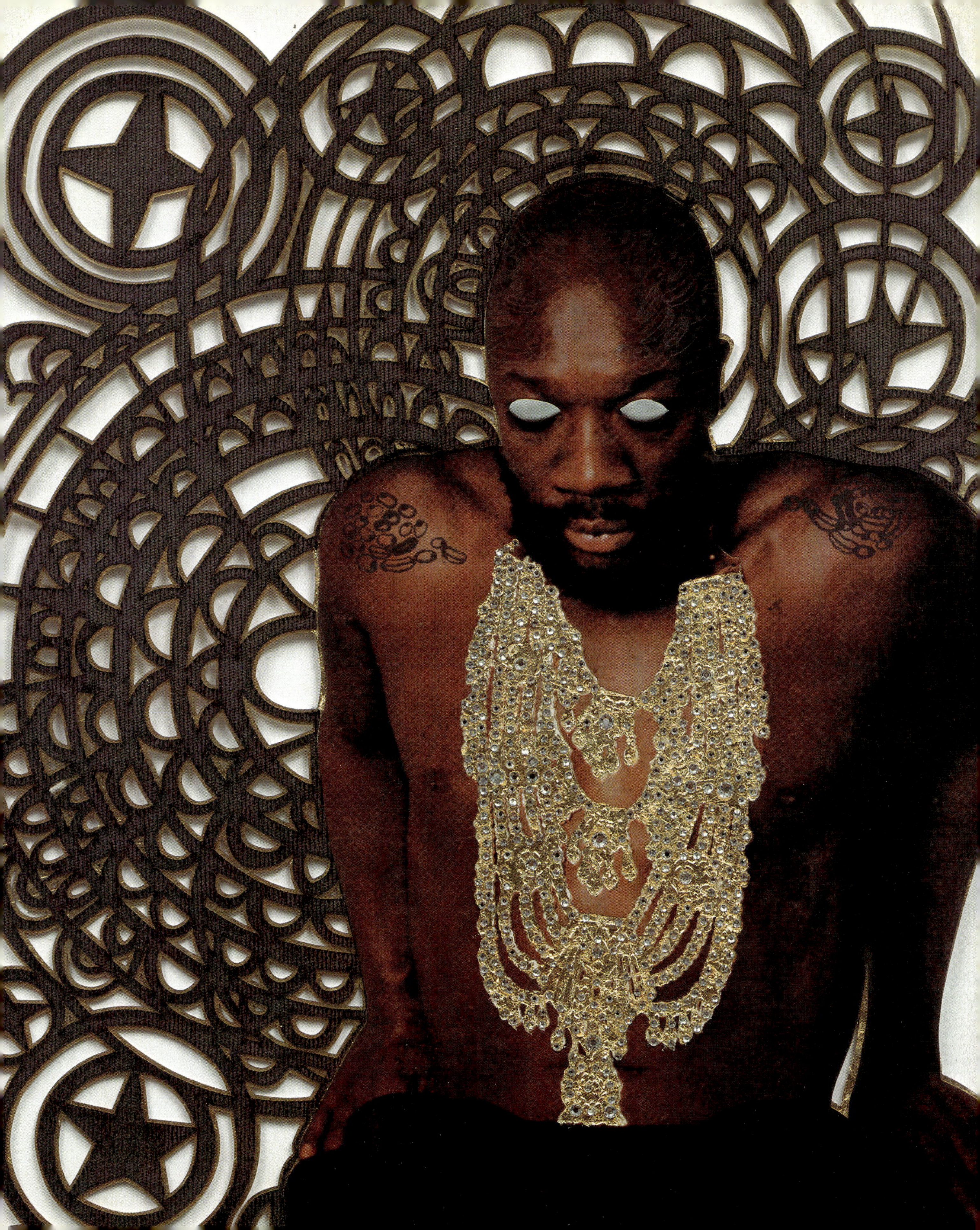

Ellen Gallagher

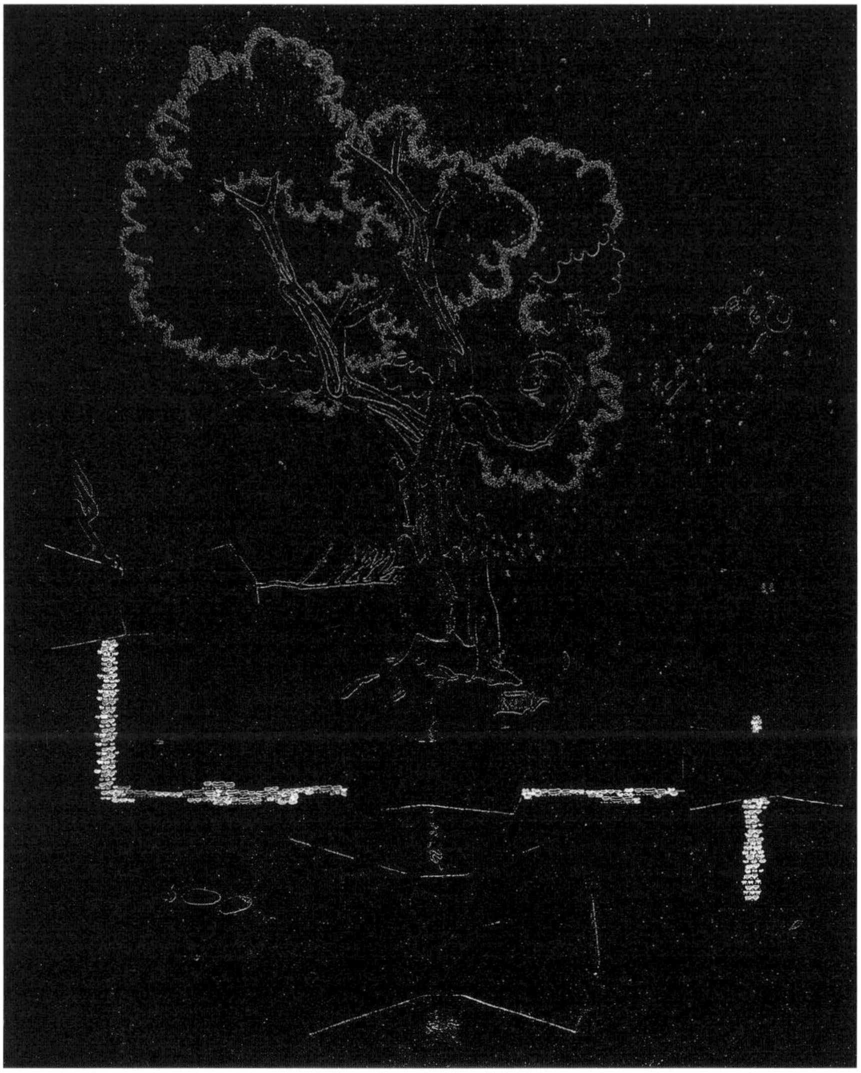

OBLIQUE BRILLIANCE

MICHELLE CLIFF

I. On a Plane on the Way to Houston/I Identify Myself

On a plane on the way to Houston, I overhear a conversation between two men. Actually, it's more of a monologue. The speaker is American, holding forth to a European about Texas History: Sam Houston, Santa Ana, the Battle of San Jacinto.

MICHELLE CLIFF's novel *Free Enterprise* was reissued by City Lights Books, San Francisco, in 2004. Her most recent works are translations of poetry by Pier Paolo Pasolini and Federico García Lorca.

Houston's troops—he says—killed "six hundred goddamn Mexicans." The Texans were able to accomplish this because the Mexicans were taking a siesta (caught napping) and Santa Ana was "fucking this little mulatto gal from one of the plantations."

The "little mulatto gal became known as the yellow rose of Texas."

This little mulatto gal adds that bit of lore to her store of a million items. In the words of Bessie Head (another little mulatto gal): I am "the collector of such treasures."

(Michelle Cliff, "In My Heart Is a Darkness")[1]

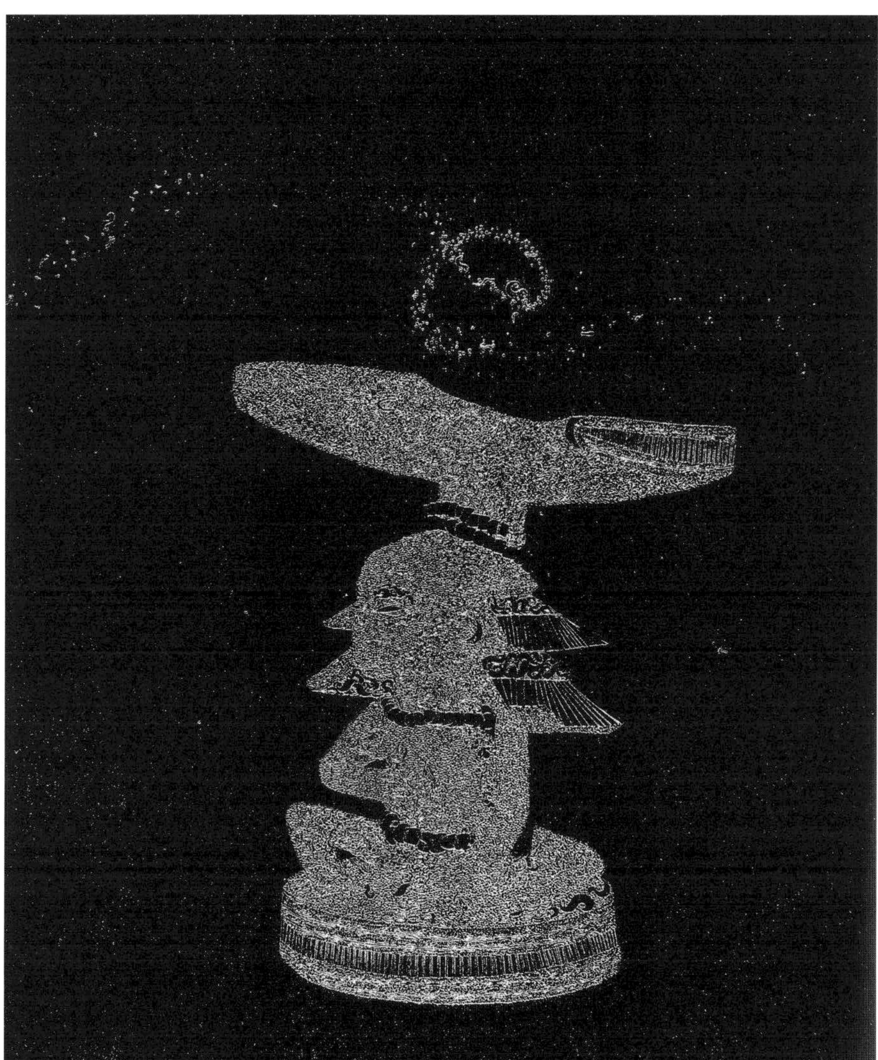

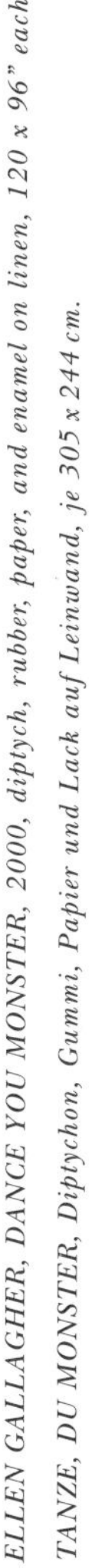

ELLEN GALLAGHER, DANCE YOU MONSTER, 2000, diptych, rubber, paper, and enamel on linen, 120 x 96" each / TANZE, DU MONSTER, Diptychon, Gummi, Papier und Lack auf Leinwand, je 305 x 244 cm.
(PHOTO: PRUDENCE CUMMING ASSOCIATES, LONDON)

Ellen Gallagher is another collector of treasures.

II. 20,000 Leagues Under the Sea: Ellen Gallagher's BLUBBER (2000)

The ocean closed its books, darkness revealing nothing... Underneath, underneath right now the painting came to life. The stunning fish, the brown limbs, the chain.

In the darkness, in the silence at the bottom, bones comminuted into sand, midden becoming hourglass. Here and there a golden guinea shone, the coin minted fresh for the Trade, surface impressed by an African elephant. Bone into sand, into coral, alive, glancing against gold, growing into it, into the African elephant.

The sunlight on the surface of the water bathed her face. She felt everyone behind her. In the here and now.

(Michelle Cliff, *Free Enterprise*)

The history of African-American people begins in the Atlantic Slave Trade, the Middle Passage. The painting referred to above is J.M.W. Turner's SLAVERS THROWING OVERBOARD THE DEAD AND DYING, TYPHON COMING ON (1840), the artist's depiction of the real-life case of the slaveship Zong, whose captain, as a storm bore down on the slaver, threw overboard the dead and dying slaves, in order to collect insurance on his cargo. The white turmoil in the background is an evocation of white supremacy, which destroys those in its path. This white turmoil can be linked to Melville and his great white whale: the idea whiteness, destructive force again. And what of Melville's narrator: Ishmael. Is the narrator, and survivor, of the pursuit African-American?

In the Bible, Ishmael is the son of Hagar—an African woman, Sarah's maid—and Abraham. Ishmael is cast into the wilderness with his mother. African-Americans came to be known as "Aunt Hagar's Children." (See the marble statue by the African/Native-American sculptor, Wildfire/Edmonia Lewis: HAGAR, 1875; also W.C. Handy's "Aunt Hagar's Children Blues," 1922.)

Both the whaling industry and the slave trade center around capture, removal, apprehension. There is a connect between Turner's painting and Gallagher's work: the floor of the Atlantic Ocean—Boneyard or Black Atlantis? The overpopulated, unvoiced, unheard undersea evoked by Ellen Gallagher's PURGATORIUM (2000). Endless repetitions of mouths. Side by side. From these mouths: sound or no sound. Nearly four centuries of slave trade. Between thirty and sixty million lost on the way, by suicide or murder or a slow death along the Middle Passage. The living chained to the dead in the belly of the beast. Not Jonah's whale but slaver.

It gave me heart when I found that mirages could be photographed, that they resulted from the bending of light and were imaginary only insofar as every real thing was imaginary.

The Fata Morgana was one of these. The work of the witch Morgan le Fay.

I wanted to find the island on the map that was not there.

So I followed her under the water.

... We were greeted by the mermaids of the unfathomable deep, those responsible for language.

When I came to I was washed ashore.

Apocalypso.

(Michelle Cliff, *Into the Interior*)

Or do the drowned slide into another dimension, transmuting themselves, suffering "a sea-change, into something rich and strange," as Ariel sings in *The Tempest.*[2] In Aimé Césaire's version of *The Tempest*, Ariel, like Caliban, is a slave.

In Ellen Gallagher's BLUBBER I may glimpse the other dimension I suggest at the end of *Into the Interior:*

A myriad of mermaids, a floating world beneath, beyond the Middle Passage, beneath the ocean an island where beings learn the gift of taking oxygen from water.

Apocalypso.

In the torture and chaos which was the Middle Passage, the barracoons, the holding pens, the seasoning stations of the Caribbean, the auction block, bondage itself, diverse African groups collided, African culture did not perish, language and imagery and music were reconfigured, recombined, African-American culture began.

BLING BLING (2001)—the title of another of Ellen Gallagher's pieces; the term coined by the New Orleans rap family Cash Money Millionaires, in the song "Bling Bling"—meaning diamonds, glittery jewelry, showy style. *Bling bling.*

Light scattered against pitch blackness. Am I underwater; is the pitch ocean, the spots of light clouds of krill, plankton floating along ocean currents, to be devoured by whales, who will be captured by whalers.

Or am I looking up into the night sky from the deck of a slaver, the crow's nest of a whaler.

I go underneath again, to the pitch-black depths of a South African diamond mine, where the rock face trembles as African miners labor, harvesting *bling bling.*

III. DANCE YOU MONSTER (2000)

As I gaze at Gallagher's piece, my mind flashes back to a trading card. On the backside the legend:

MILLIE CHRISTINE!
8th WONDER OF THE WORLD
THE FAMOUS TWO-HEADED LADY

On the front of the card, in full color, the "RENOWNED TWO-HEADED LADY," two African-American women, joined back to back, in evening dress. The

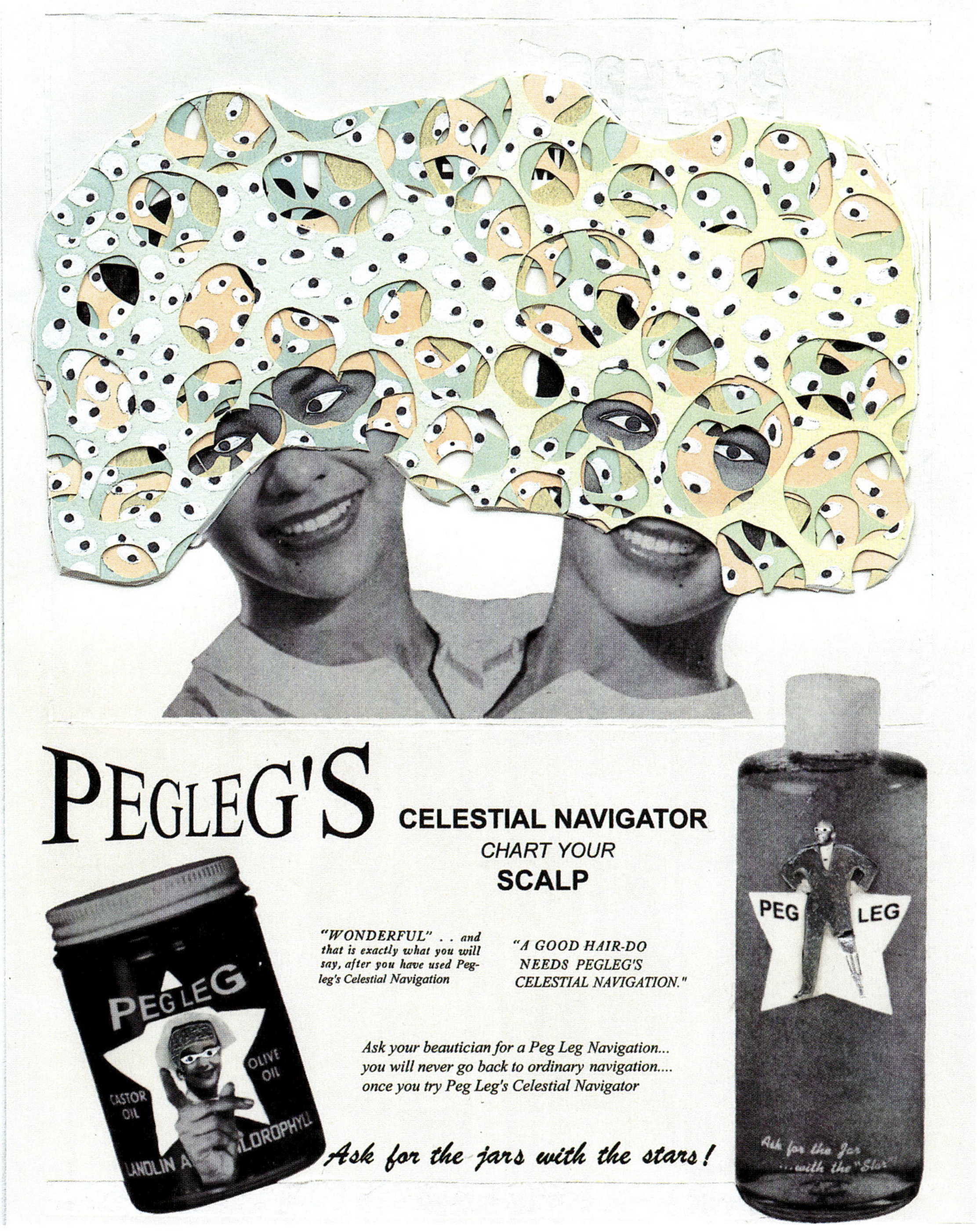

ELLEN GALLAGHER, MILLIE-CHRISTINE (DELUXE), 2004/2005, photogravure, collage, watercolor, laser cutting, and oil, 13 x 10"/ Photogravüre, Collage, Aquarell, Laserschnitt und Öl, 33 x 25,4 cm. (PHOTO: D. JAMES DEE / TWO PALMS PRESS, NEW YORK)

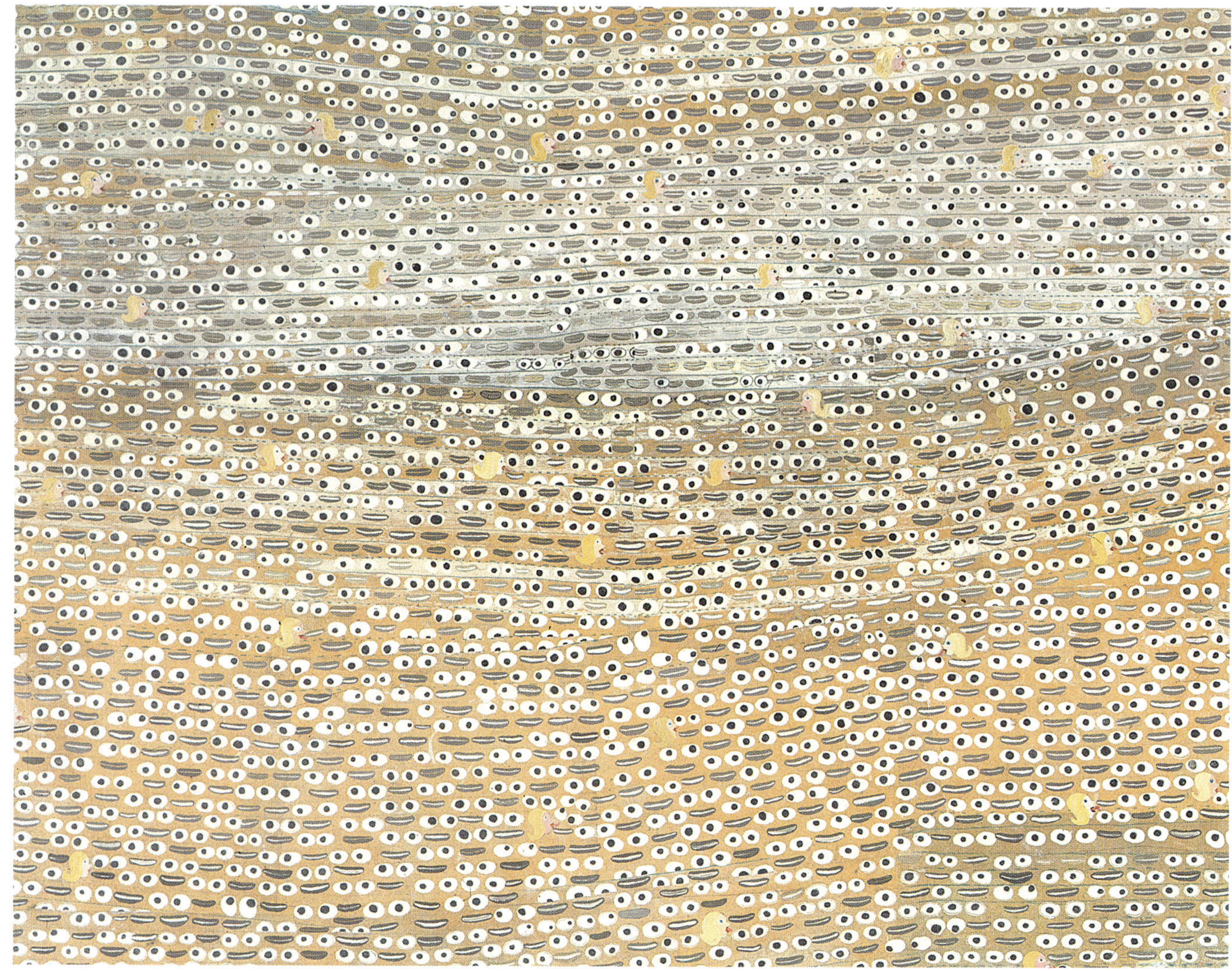

ELLEN GALLAGHER, OH! SUSANNA, 1993, oil, pencil, and paper on canvas, 60 x 36", detail /
Öl, Farbstift und Papier auf Leinwand, 152,4 x 91,4cm, Ausschnitt.
(ALL PHOTOS, IF NOT INDICATED OTHERWISE: GAGOSIAN GALLERY, NEW YORK)

card resides in the collection of the Mütter Museum at the College of Physicians of Philadelphia, an institution dedicated to the preservation of "medical monstrosities." (You can read all about it on the roadsideamerica.com website.)

Millie Christine McCoy were billed also as the Two-Headed Nightingale: born into slavery in 1851, the sisters were connected at the lower spine and had two heads, four arms, four legs. In the course of their lives they were sold, traded and stolen, displayed at fairs and freak-shows. Doctors were called upon to conduct public physical examinations to prove Millie Christine were authentic.

The sisters taught themselves to dance sideways, on four legs. They performed in public, with their two-voiced song and four-legged dance act. Once stolen, they performed in private: available to small, private groups. One can only imagine the make up of these small, private groups. They danced for Queen Victoria, who gave them diamond earrings. *Bling bling.*

IV. eXelento (2004)

Tu pelo es tu personalidad: Someone sends me a postcard from Bucles, a hairdresser in Madrid. These words are printed across the face of Marilyn Monroe. Only her blond hair and dark eyebrows are visible. Her eyes and nose and mouth are concealed by this dictum.

The iterative process of fractal formation, working with sound: from St. Louis Blues to *Birth of the Cool.* The recombination of notes, the call and response of instruments, the unexpected where the expected, the ordinary once was.

The iterative process of fractal formation working with image: Take something ordinary and work with it, add to it, distort it, so that something extraordinary is created. Repeat and repeat and repeat this process.

The frames in Ellen Gallagher's eXelento pile one defaced, recombined image upon another. They exist as fractals. In many of the images the artist begins with advertisements from African-American publications like *Jet* and *Ebony.* Ads for hair straighteners, wigs, wiglets, pomades, beauty parlors, etcetera—familiar newsprint of a certain time and place. These are overlaid with yellow plasticine, perhaps referencing the title product—eXelento—"LOOK FOR THE YELLOW CAN AT ALL FINE COSMETIC COUNTERS." Yellow can, blondness as apotheosis, the blues(t) eye.

Note X in eXelento: X is for Malcolm, who in his autobiography describes the process of conking. "I took the little list of ingredients [Shorty] had printed out for me and went to a grocery store, where I got a can of Red Devil lye, two eggs, and two medium-sized white potatoes. Then at a drugstore near the poolroom, I asked for a large jar of vaseline, a large bar of soap, a large-toothed comb and a fine-toothed comb, one of those rubber hoses with a metal spray-head, a rubber apron, and a pair of gloves."[3]

Malcolm begins to mix the homemade congolene, which turns pale yellowish, the Mason jar in which it is held is alive with heat.

"...then my head caught fire."[4] (But not the fire with which it would later burn.) In *The Autobiography,* Malcolm returns again and again to the process of black self-mutilation for an absurd goal.

To my own shame, when I say all of this I'm talking first of all about myself—because you can't show me any Negro who ever conked more faithfully than I did. I'm speaking from personal experience when I say of any black man who conks today, or any white-wigged black woman, that if they gave the brains in their heads just half as much attention as they do their hair, they would be a thousand times better off. [5]

In and around the ads for eXelento, etcetera, what of the news of the day:

The salesman had tied the stacks of Jets *tightly, and Rosalind had to work the knife under the string, taking care not to damage the cover of the magazine on top. The string gave way and the stack slid apart. The faces of Jackie Wilson, Sugar Ray Robinson, and Dorothy Dandridge glanced up at her. A banner across one cover read EMMETT TILL, THE STORY INSIDE. She arranged herself on a wicker chaise on the verandah and began her return to the world she'd left behind.*

She took the photographs—they were photographs—released by his mother—he was an only child—his mother was a widow—he stuttered—badly—these were some details—she took the photographs into her—into herself—and she would never let them go (...)

The mother had insisted on the pictures, so said Jet. *This is my son. Swollen by the beating—by the waters of the River Pearl—misshapen—unrecognizable-monstrous.*

(Michelle Cliff, "Transactions")

1) Here and further down Cliff quotes from her own works: "In My Heart Is a Darkness" in *Some of My Best Friends,* ed. by Emily Bernard (New York: Harper & Collins, 2004), p. 117; *Free Enterprise* (San Francisco: City Lights Books, 2004), p. 210; *Into the Interior,* unpubl. manuscript, 2002, p. 136; "Transactions" in Cliff, *The Store of a Million Items* (Boston: Houghton Mifflin, 1998), p. 17.

2) William Shakespeare, *The Tempest,* act I, scene ii.

3) Malcolm X, *The Autobiography of Malcolm X* (New York, Grove Press, 1964), p. 52.

4) Ibid., p. 53.

5) Ibid., p. 55.

VERBORGENER GLANZ

MICHELLE CLIFF

I. Unterwegs nach Houston / Ich weise mich aus

In einem Flugzeug unterwegs nach Houston höre ich zufällig ein Gespräch zwischen zwei Männern mit. Eigentlich ist es eher ein Monolog. Der Sprecher ist Amerikaner und hält einem Europäer einen Vortrag über die Geschichte von Texas: Sam Houston, Santa Ana, die Schlacht von San Jacinto.

Houstons Truppen – sagt er – haben «sechshundert gottverdammte Mexikaner» getötet. Die Texaner waren dazu in der Lage, weil die Mexikaner Siesta hielten (also im Schlaf überrascht wurden) und Santa Ana, «gerade dabei war, diese kleine Mulattin von einer der Plantagen zu ficken».

Die «kleine Mulattin wurde später als Gelbe Rose von Texas bekannt».

Die kleine Mulattin steckt dieses Stück Legende in ihren millionenschweren Vorrat an solchen Stücken. Mit den Worten von Bessie Head (einer anderen kleinen Mulattin): Ich bin «die Sammlerin solcher Schätze».

(Michelle Cliff, «In My Heart Is a Darkness»)[1]

Ellen Gallagher ist auch so eine Schatzsammlerin.

MICHELLE CLIFF ist Schriftstellerin und lebt in den USA. Auch in deutscher Übersetzung erhältlich ist *Kein Telefon zum Himmel* (Unionsverlag, Zürich 2000).

II. 20 000 Meilen unter den Meeren: Ellen Gallaghers BLUBBER (2000)

Der Ozean schloss seine Bücher, die Dunkelheit enthüllte nichts… Darunter, darunter wurde genau jetzt das Gemälde lebendig. Die verblüffenden Fische, die braunen Glieder, die Kette.

In der Dunkelheit, in der Stille am Grund, zersplitterte Gebein zu Sand, das Weggeworfene wurde zur Sanduhr. Hie und da leuchtete eine goldene Guinee, eine für den Handel frisch geprägte Münze mit einem afrikanischen Elefanten darauf. Gebein wird zu Sand, zu Korallen, lebendig, gegen Gold stossend, in es hineinwachsend, in den afrikanischen Elefanten hinein.

Das Sonnenlicht auf der Wasseroberfläche überflutete ihr Gesicht.

Sie spürte sie alle hinter sich. Im Hier und Jetzt.

(Michelle Cliff, *Free Enterprise*)

Die Geschichte der Schwarzen in Amerika beginnt mit dem transatlantischen Sklavenhandel, der sogenannten Mittelpassage. Das oben erwähnte Gemälde ist J. M. W. Turners SLAVERS THROWING OVERBOARD THE DEAD AND DYING, TYPHON COMING ON (Sklavenhändler, Tote und Sterbende über Bord werfend, anbrechender Taifun, 1840), in welchem der Künstler ein tatsächliches Ereignis an Bord des Sklavenschiffs Zong schildert, dessen Kapitän bei nahendem Sturm die toten und sterbenden Sklaven ins Meer warf, um später die Versicherungsprämie für die verlorene Ladung kassieren zu können. Der weisse Aufruhr im Hintergrund deutet auf die weisse Vorherrschaft, die jene zerstört, die ihr im Weg stehen. Man kann diesen weissen Tumult auch mit Melville und seinem grossen weissen Wal in Verbindung bringen: die Idee des Weissen, einmal mehr als zerstörerische Kraft. Und Melvilles Erzähler, Ismael? Ist der Erzähler und Überlebende der Hetzjagd am Ende ein Schwarzer?

In der Bibel ist Ismael der Sohn von Hagar, Sarahs afrikanischer Magd, und Abraham. Ismael wird mit seiner Mutter in die Wüste verbannt. Die schwarzen Amerikaner wurden auch «Tante Hagars Kinder» genannt. (Beispiele dafür sind die Marmorstatue des afrikanisch-indianischen Bildhauers Wildfire / Edmonia Lewis, HAGAR (1875), oder W.C. Handys «Aunt Hagar's Children Blues» (1922).)

Sowohl in der Walfangindustrie wie beim Sklavenhandel geht es ums Einfangen, Wegschleppen, Festnehmen. Es gibt eine Verbindung zwischen Turners Gemälde und Gallaghers Arbeit: Der Boden des Atlantiks – Grabstätte oder schwarzes Atlantis. Die überbevölkerte, stimmlose, ungehörte Welt unter dem Meeresspiegel, die Ellen Gallaghers PURGATORIUM (2000) heraufbeschwört: endlose Repetition von Mündern. Seite an Seite. Aus diesen Mündern: Ton oder kein Ton. Fast vier Jahrhunderte Sklavenhandel. Zwischen dreissig und sechzig Millionen gingen unterwegs verloren, durch Selbstmord oder Mord oder langsames Dahinsiechen im Lauf der Mittelpassage. Die Lebenden an die Toten gekettet im Bauch des Ungeheuers. Nicht Jonas' Wal, sondern ein Sklavenschiff.

Es machte mir Mut, als ich entdeckte, dass man Fata Morganas photographieren konnte, dass sie aus Lichtspiegelungen entstehen und nur so weit imaginär sind, wie jedes existierende Ding imaginär ist.

Die Fata Morgana war eines von ihnen. Die Arbeit der Hexe Morgan le Fay.

Ich wollte die Insel auf der Karte finden, die nicht da war.

Also folgte ich ihr unter Wasser.

… Wir wurden begrüsst von den Meerjungfrauen der unergründlichen Tiefe, jenen, die für die Sprache verantwortlich sind.

Als ich zu mir kam, wurde ich an die Küste gespült.

Apokalypso.

(Michelle Cliff, *Into the Interior*)

Oder gleiten die Ertrunkenen in eine andere Dimension und verwandeln sich, so dass nichts an ihnen ist, «das nicht wandelt Meereshut in ein reich und seltnes Gut», wie Ariel in *Der Sturm* singt?[2)] In Aimé Césaires Version des Stückes ist Ariel ein Sklave wie Caliban.

In Ellen Gallaghers BLUBBER kann ich vielleicht einen Blick auf diese andere Dimension erhaschen, die ich am Ende von *Into the Interior* beschrieben habe:

Myriaden von Meerjungfrauen, eine schwebende Unterwelt, unter der Mittelpassage, eine Insel unter dem Ozean, wo Lebewesen lernen, Sauerstoff aus dem Wasser zu ziehen.

Apokalypso.

ELLEN GALLAGHER, BLING BLING, 2001, enamel, rubber, and paper on linen, over-all measurements 96 x 120", detail / Lack, Gummi und Papier auf Leinwand, 244 x 305 cm, Ausschnitt. (PHOTO: TOM POWEL)

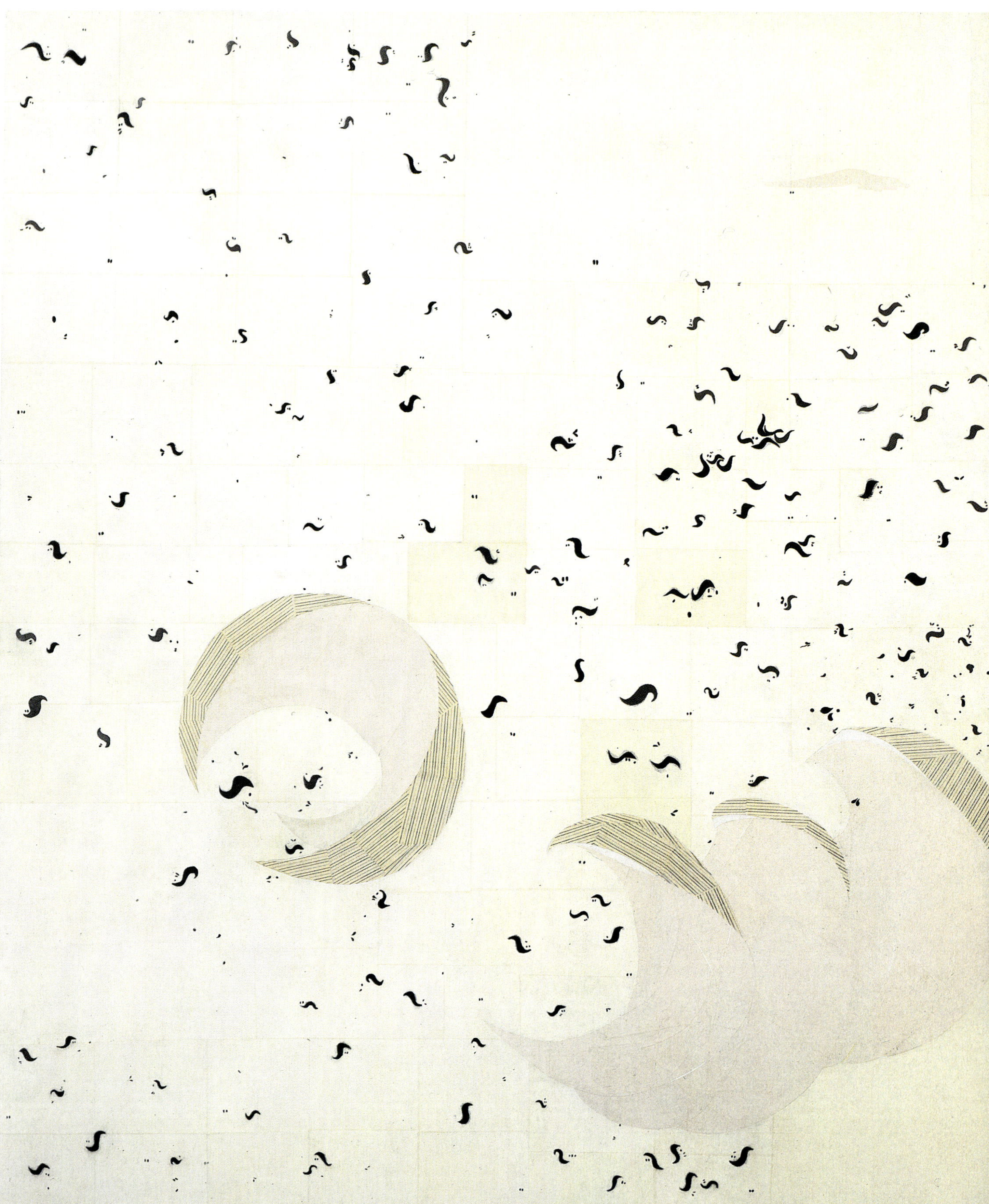

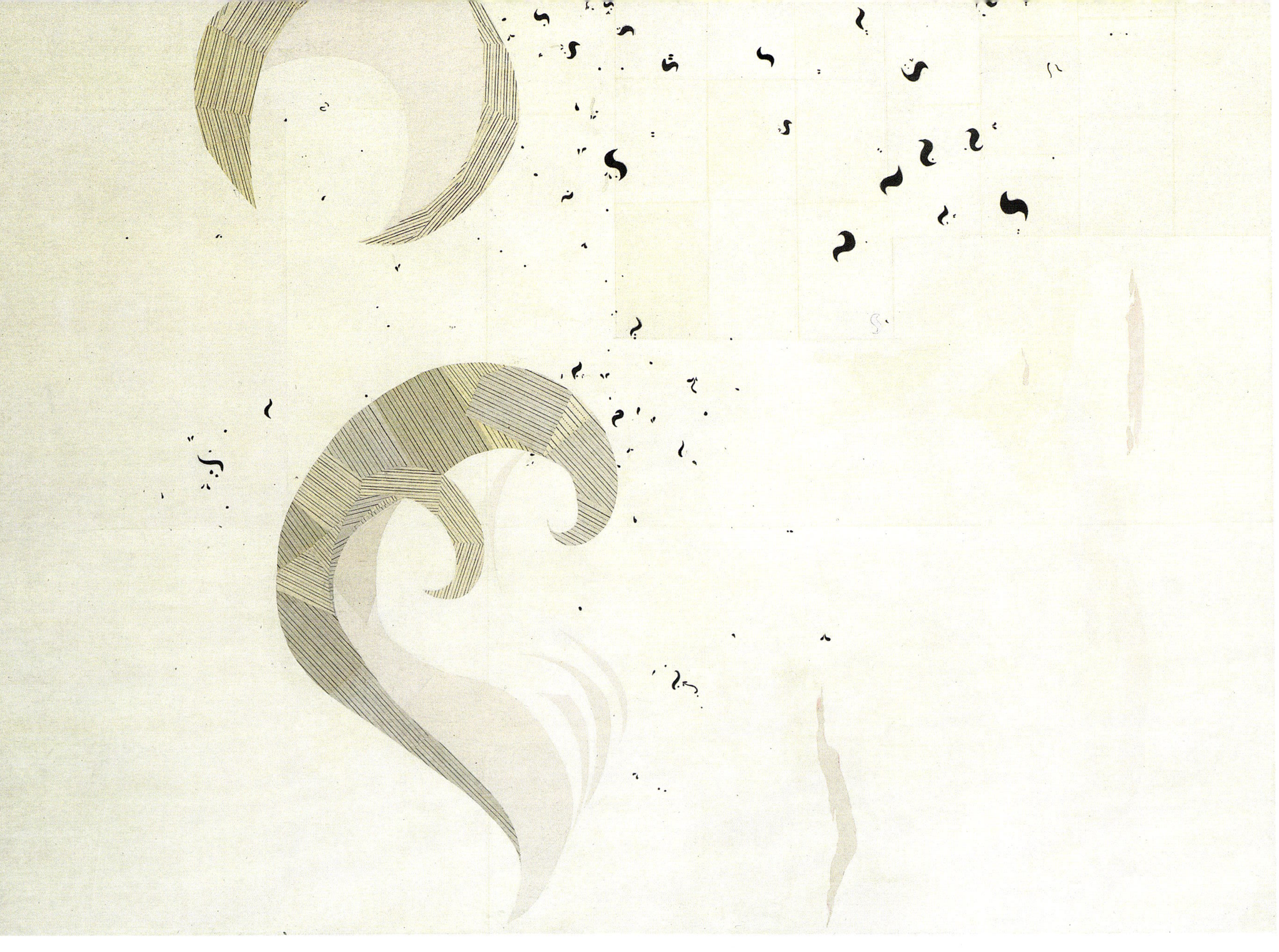

ELLEN GALLAGHER, BLUBBER, 2000, ink, pencil, and paper on linen, 120 x 192" / Tusche, Farbstift und Papier auf Leinwand, 305 x 488 cm. (PHOTO: TOM POWEL)

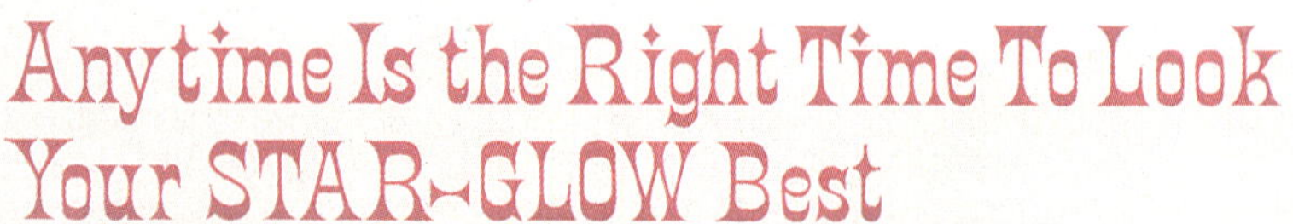

Immediate Delivery on This Elegant
New Collection—in Kanekalon
Don't Put It Off; Put It On.
ORDER TODAY!

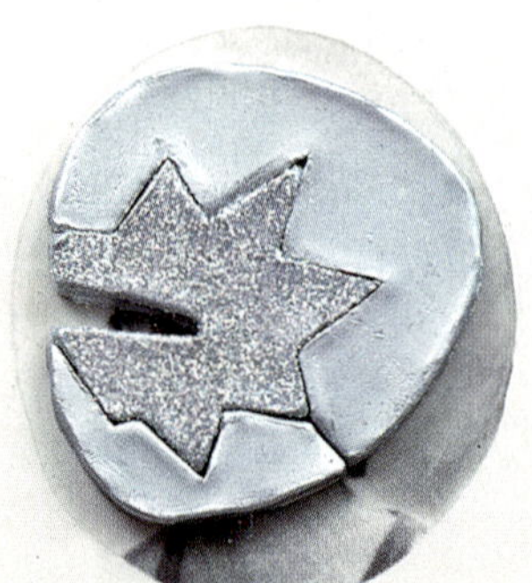

34T—"BOSS LADY." Take charge. Manage yourself. Be the leader of your set. $28.00

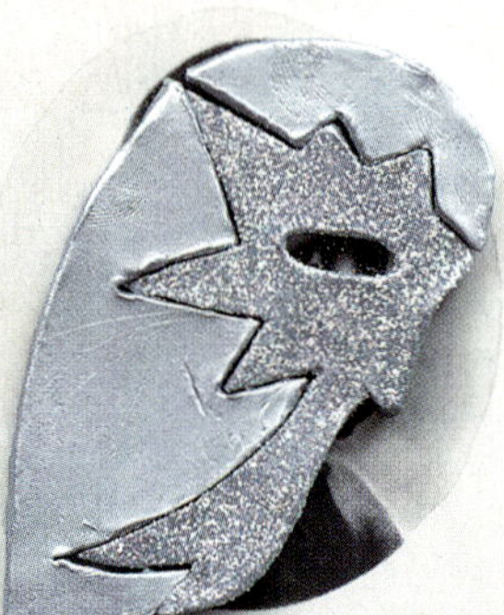

3… …ATE SECRETARY." From nine to five you'll know you're alive. For your evening appointments too. A fall for all occasions. $19.00

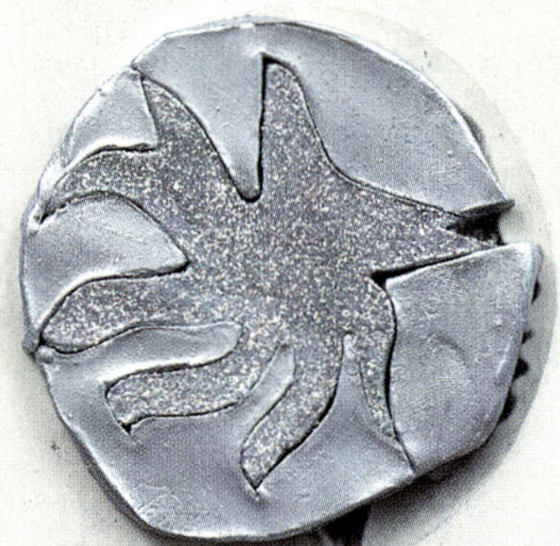

32T—"BRAIDS OF HEAVEN." The assessory that's a necessity. Priced right. $8.00

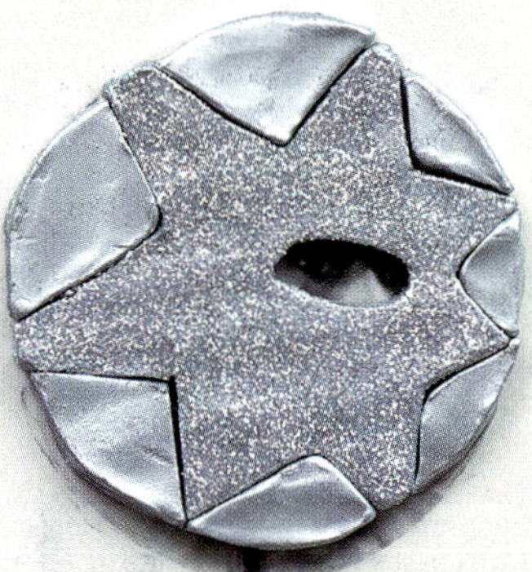

37T—"SHOW STOPPER." Steal the scene. Get rave reviews whenever you wear it. $25.00

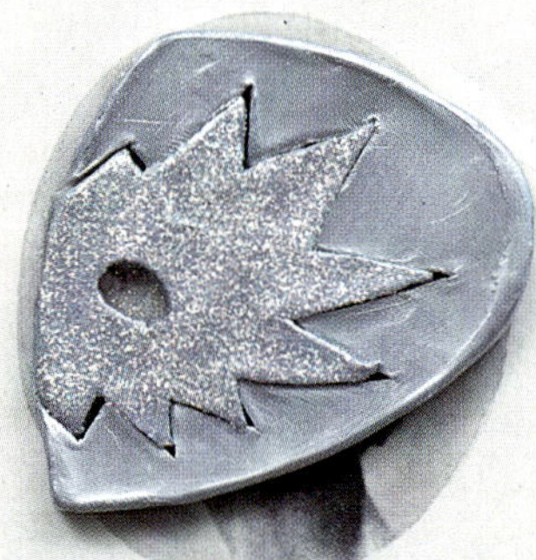

36T—"DOUBLE TAKE." When you're looking good, you'll feel good. Keep 'em watching—and watch yourself! $25.00

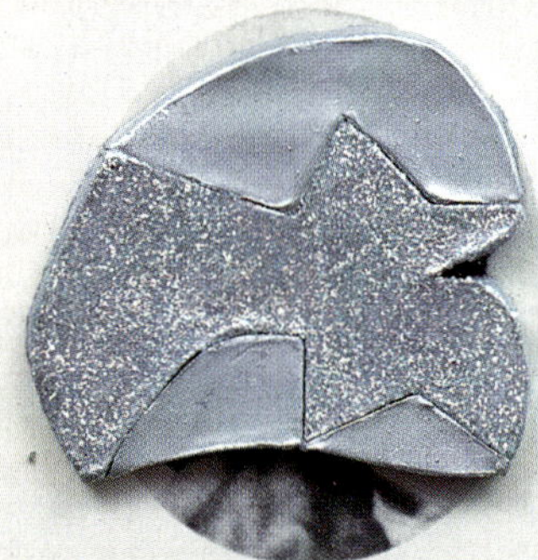

35T—"KISS 'N CURL." Add a new twist to your charm and personality. But don't tell. $18.00

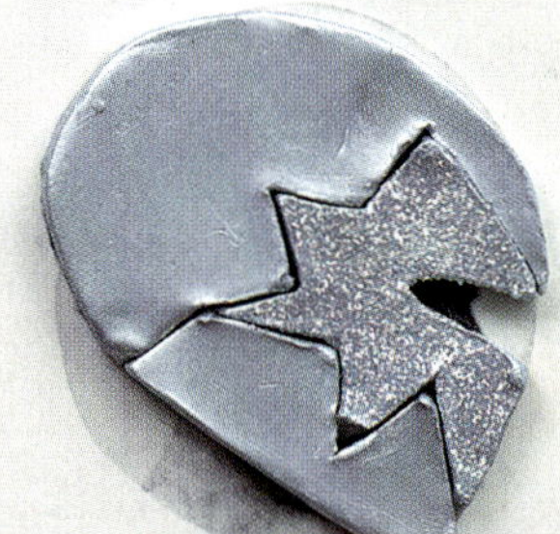

40T—"UPKEEP." Simplicity is the keynote with this one-piece bun. For the woman on the go. $10.00

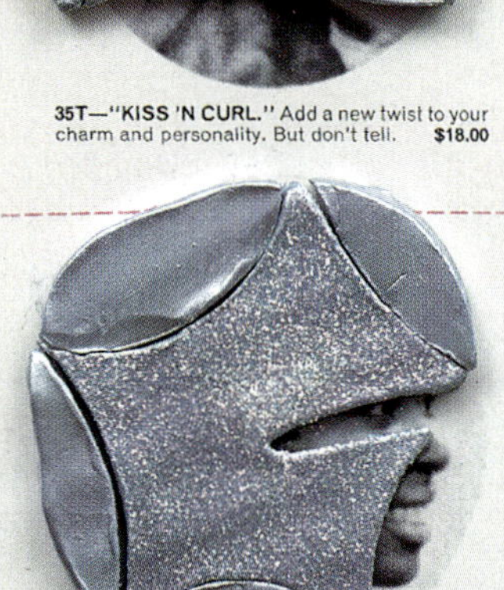

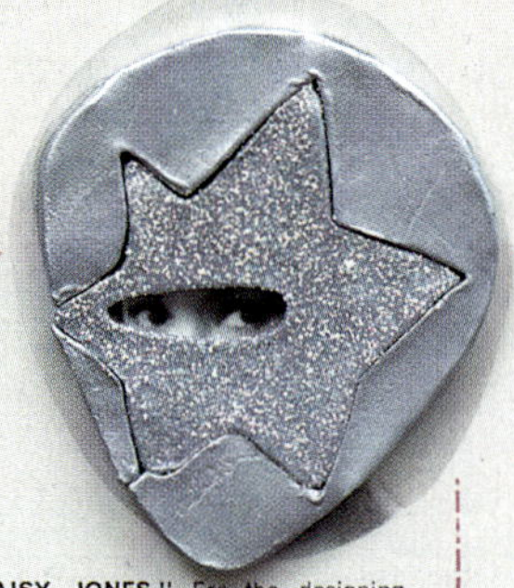

STAR-GLOW WIGS

39T—"DAISY JONES." For the designing woman of the "Roaring Seventies." Lift prohibition on your own good looks. $25.00

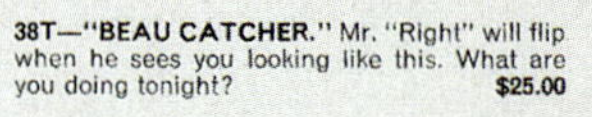

38T—"BEAU CATCHER." Mr. "Right" will flip when he sees you looking like this. What are you doing tonight? $25.00

ELLEN GALLAGHER, *STARGLOW WIGS (DELUXE)*, *2004/2005, photogravure, plasticine, aluminum powder, and glitter, 13 x 10"* /
STARGLOW-PERÜCKEN, Photogravüre, Knetmasse, Aluminiumstaub und Glimmer, 33 x 25,4 cm. (PHOTOS: D. JAMES DEE / TWO PALMS PRESS, NEW YORK)

ELLEN GALLAGHER, MR. TERRIFIC (DeLuxe), 2004/2005, photogravure and plasticine, 13 x 10 1/8" / Photogravüre und Knetmasse, 33 x 25,7 cm.

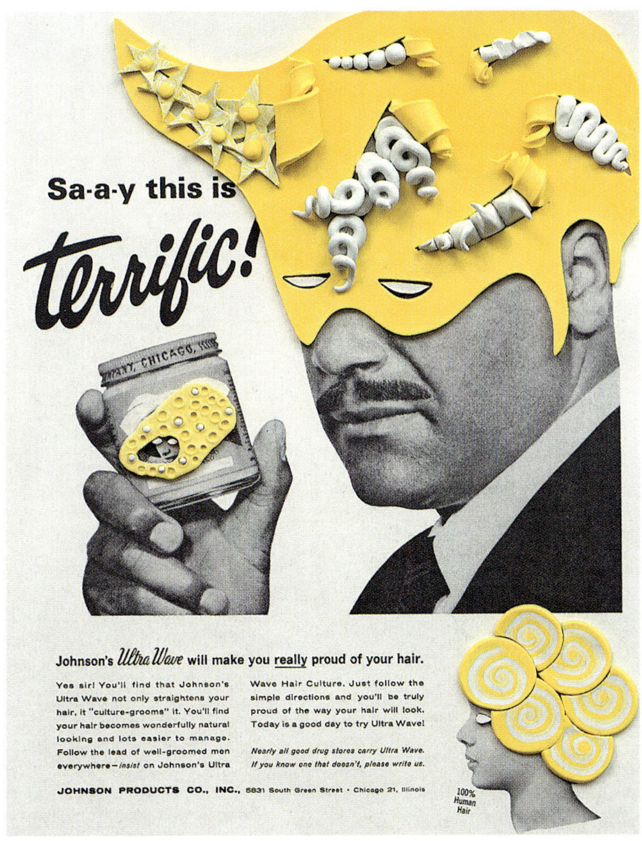

Im Chaos und den Qualen der Mittelpassage, den Barracken, dem Eingepferchtsein, den «Eingewöhnungs»-Stationen in der Karibik, dem Auktionspodest, dem Gefesseltsein überhaupt, gerieten verschiedene afrikanische Stämme aneinander, doch die afrikanische Kultur ging nicht zugrunde, Sprache, Bildsprache und Musik erhielten eine neue Gestalt und Zusammensetzung: Die schwarzamerikanische Kultur nahm ihren Anfang.

BLING BLING (2001) heisst ein anderes von Ellen Gallaghers Werken; der Ausdruck wurde von der Rap-Familie Cash Money Millionaires aus New Orleans geprägt, die einen ihrer Songs so nannte, «Bling Bling», was so viel bedeutet wie Diamanten, glitzernde Juwelen, aufwändiger Stil. *Bling bling.*

Verstreute Lichtpunkte vor pechschwarzem Grund. Bin ich unter Wasser, ist das Pechschwarze der Ozean, die Flecken, helle Krillwolken, Planktonteilchen, die der Meeresströmung folgen und von Walen verzehrt werden, die wiederum von Walfängern gefangen werden?

Oder schaue ich vom Deck eines Sklavenschiffes zum Nachthimmel empor? Oder aus dem Mastkorb eines Walfangschiffes?

Ich steige wieder tief hinab, in die pechschwarzen Tiefen einer südafrikanischen Diamantmine, wo die Felsfront erbebt, während die afrikanischen Minenarbeiter am Schürfen sind und *Bling bling* abbauen.

III. DANCE YOU MONSTER (Tanz, du Monster, 2000)
Während ich Gallaghers Arbeit betrachte, erinnere ich mich an eine alte Ansichtskarte. Auf deren Rückseite stand:

MILLIE CHRISTINE!
8. WELTWUNDER
DIE BERÜHMTE DAME MIT ZWEI KÖPFEN

Vorn auf der Karte war «Die berühmte Dame mit zwei Köpfen» in Farbe abgebildet, zwei am Rücken zusammengewachsene schwarze Amerikanerinnen im Abendkleid. Die Ansichtskarte befindet sich in der Sammlung des Mütter Museums am Medizinkolleg in Philadelphia, eine Institution, die sich der Konservierung «medizinischer Monstrositäten» widmet. (Auf www.roadsideamerica.com kann man alles darüber nachlesen.)

Millie und Christine McCoy wurden auch als «Nachtigall mit zwei Köpfen» gehandelt: 1851 als Sklaven geboren, waren die beiden Schwestern an

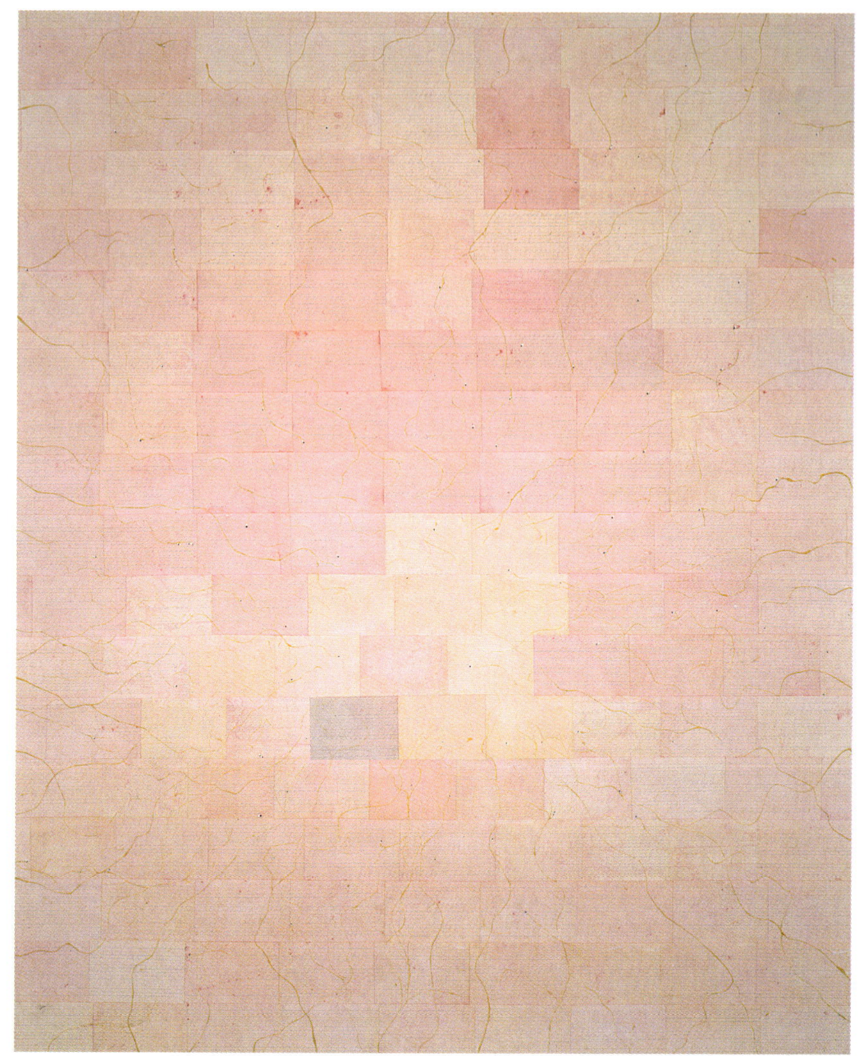

ELLEN GALLAGHER, THEY COULD STILL SERVE, 2001, oil, pigment, paper, and glue on linen, 120 x 96", detail / SIE KÖNNTEN NOCH IMMER DIENEN, Öl, Pigment, Papier und Leim auf Leinwand, 305 x 244 cm, Ausschnitt.
(PHOTO: TOM POWEL)

der unteren Wirbelsäule zusammengewachsen und hatten zusammen zwei Köpfe, vier Arme und vier Beine. Im Lauf ihres Lebens wurden sie verkauft, weiterverkauft, gestohlen und auf Jahrmärkten und Freakshows präsentiert. Es wurden Ärzte beigezogen um öffentliche Untersuchungen durchzuführen und zu bestätigen, dass Millie Christine kein Schwindel war.

Die Schwestern brachten sich selbst bei, mit ihren vier Beinen seitwärts zu tanzen. Sie traten mit ihrer zweistimmigen und vierfüssigen Gesangs- und Tanznummer öffentlich auf. Nachdem sie einmal entführt worden waren, traten sie nur noch im Verborgenen auf: vor kleinen, privaten Gesellschaften. Man kann nur mutmassen, wie diese kleinen, privaten Gesellschaften zusammengesetzt waren. Sie tanzten für Königin Victoria, die ihnen diamantene Ohrringe schenkte. *Bling bling.*

IV. eXelento (2004)

Tu pelo es tu personalidad: Jemand sendet mir eine Ansichtskarte von Bucles, einem Friseur in Madrid. Die Worte sind quer über das Gesicht von Marilyn Monroe gedruckt. Nur ihr blondes Haar und ihre dunklen Augenbrauen sind sichtbar. Augen, Nase und Mund sind unter diesem Satz versteckt.

Der schrittweise Prozess fraktaler Gestaltung auf musikalischer Ebene: vom St.-Louis-Blues bis zu *Birth of the Cool.* Die Neukombination von Noten, das Rufen und Antworten von Instrumenten, das Unerwartete, wo einst das Erwartete, das Gewöhnliche war.

Der schrittweise Prozess fraktaler Gestaltung auf der Bildebene: etwas Gewöhnliches nehmen und damit arbeiten, hinzufügen, verzerren, bis etwas Aussergewöhnliches entsteht. Und diesen Prozess wiederholen und wiederholen und wiederholen.

Die Einzelbilder in Ellen Gallaghers eXELENTO häufen ein entstelltes und wieder neu zusammengesetztes Bild auf das andere. Sie existieren als Fraktale. In vielen dieser Bilder beginnt die Künstlerin mit Anzeigen aus schwarzamerikanischen Zeitschriften wie *Jet* und *Ebony*. Anzeigen für Haarstreckmittel, Perücken, Haarteile, Pomaden, Schönheitssalons usw. – eine zeitlich und örtlich definierte, vertraute Zeitungsrealität. Darüber wurde gelbe Knetmasse gelegt, vielleicht ein Verweis auf das im Titel genannte Produkt, eXelento.

«LOOK FOR THE YELLOW CAN AT ALL FINE COSMETIC COUNTERS» (Suche nach der gelben Dose bei jeder guten Kosmetikverkaufsstelle).

Die gelbe Dose, das Blonde als Apotheose, das blaue(ste) Auge (oder Blues-Auge).

Man achte auf das X in eXELENTO: X steht für Malcolm, der in seiner Autobiographie das «Entkrausen» des Haars beschrieben hat – «Ich nahm die kleine Liste von Ingredienzen, die [Shorty] für mich aufgeschrieben hatte, und ging zu einem Gemüsehändler, wo ich eine Büchse *Red-Devil*-Lauge und zwei mittelgrosse weisse Kartoffeln kaufte. In einem Drugstore in der Nähe des Billardsalons verlangte ich einen grossen Topf Vaseline, ein grosses Stück Seife, einen grobzinkigen und einen feinzinkigen Kamm, einen jener Gummi-Sprühbehälter mit metallenem Sprühkopf, eine Gummischürze und ein Paar Gummihandschuhe.» [3]

Malcolm beginnt die hausgemachte Haarpaste anzurühren, sie nimmt eine bleichgelbe Farbe an, die Maurerschale, in der sie sich befindet, ist siedend heiss geworden.

«... dann fing mein Kopf Feuer.»[4] (Aber noch nicht das Feuer, das später darin lodern sollte.) In seiner Autobiographie kommt Malcolm X wiederholt auf den Prozess der Selbstverstümmelung der Schwarzen um eines absurden Zieles willen zurück.

Zu meiner eigenen Schande muss ich gestehen, dass ich, wenn ich dies sage, zuallererst von mir selber spreche – denn Sie werden keinen Schwarzen finden, der sich je die Haare sorgsamer entkräuselte, als ich es tat. Ich spreche aus persönlicher Erfahrung, wenn ich sage, dass jeder Schwarze, der sich heute entkräuselt, und jede Schwarze mit heller Perücke tausendmal besser dran wären, wenn sie dem Hirn in ihren Köpfen nur halb so viel Zeit widmen würden wie ihrem Haar.[5]

Und wie lautet die Meldung des Tages in den und um die Anzeigen von eXelento etcetera herum:

Der Händler hatte die Jet-*Stapel eng zusammengebunden und Rosalind musste mit dem Messer sorgfältig unter die Schnur fahren, damit das Titelblatt des obersten Heftes nicht beschädigt wurde. Die Schnur gab nach und der Stapel glitt auseinander. Die Gesichter von Jackie Wilson, Sugar Ray Robinson und Dorothy Dandridge schauten zu ihr empor. Auf einem Balken über einer der Titelseiten hiess es EMMETT TILL, THE STORY INSIDE. Sie richtete sich auf einem Korbstuhl auf der Veranda ein und begann ihre Rückkehr in eine Welt, die sie hinter sich gelassen hatte.*

Sie nahm die Photographien – es waren Photographien – von seiner Mutter freigegeben – er war ein Einzelkind – seine Mutter war Witwe – er stotterte – schwer – das waren einige der Details – sie nahm die Photographien in sich hinein – in sich selbst auf – und sie würde sie nie mehr loslassen (...).

Die Mutter hatte grossen Wert auf die Bilder gelegt, schrieb Jet. *Dies ist mein Sohn. Aufgedunsen durch die Schläge – durch das Wasser des Pearl River – deformiert – nicht wiederzuerkennen – monströs.*

(Michelle Cliff, «Transactions»)

(Übersetzung: Wilma Parker)

1) Hier und im Folgenden zitiert die Autorin aus einigen ihrer eigenen Werke: «In My Heart Is a Darkness», in: *Some of My Best Friends,* hg. v. Emily Bernard, Harper & Collins, New York 2004, S. 117; *Free Enterprise,* City Lights Books, San Francisco 2004, S. 210; *Into the Interior,* unveröff. Manuskript, 2002, S. 136; «Transactions», in: Cliff, *The Store of a Million Items,* Houghton Mifflin, Boston 1998, S. 17.

2) William Shakespeare, *Der Sturm,* 1. Akt, 2. Szene, zit. nach der Übers. Schlegel/Tieck.

3) Malcolm X, *The Autobiography of Malcolm X* (Grove Press, New York 1964, S. 52. Deutsch in mehreren Ausgaben erschienen, zuletzt: *Die Autobiographie,* überarb. Neuaufl., hg. und mit einem Nachwort v. Alex Haley, Atlantik Verlag, Bremen 2003. Die Zitate in diesem Text wurden direkt aus dem Engl. übersetzt.

4) Ebenda, S. 53.

5) Ebenda, S. 55.

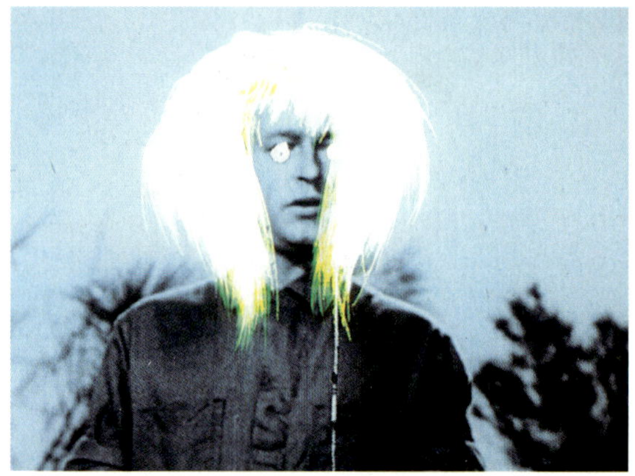

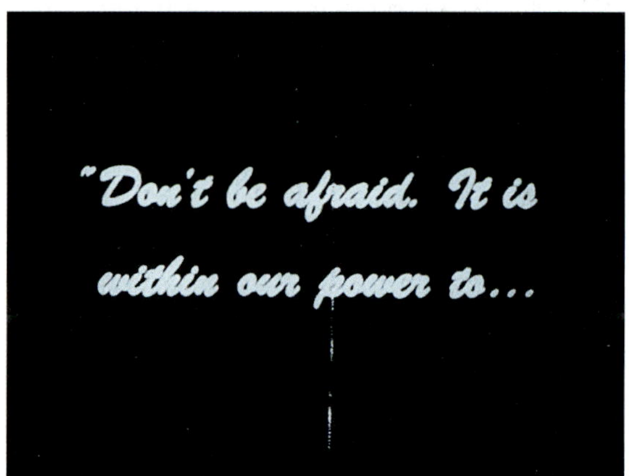

The Racial Colorist

BEN OKRI

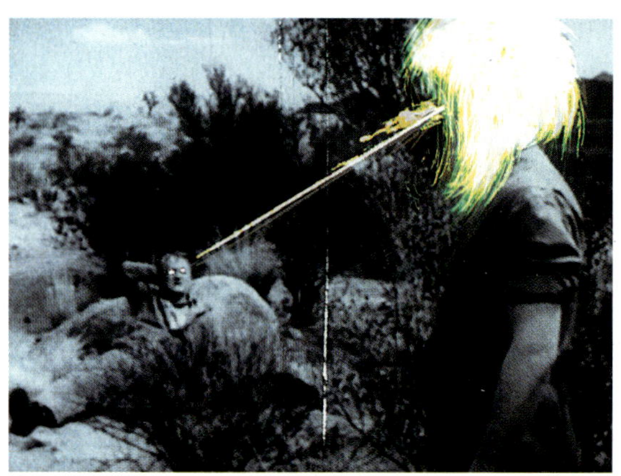

This was during the war. We were in a line, sitting on a wall, and I was trying to get these two people, these two men, to know one another. I was trying to get them to meet. But one of them was a racial colorist and he had a chart in one hand and a paste on his fingertips and he said to me that there was no way he could shake hands with a second class white man. I was surprised—because this chap too was white, and he would take a hug from me but he wouldn't accept a touch from another white man whom he believed was inferior to him in color purity. I tried but he refused; and the supposedly second class white man was so hurt and offended that he stormed away. I went after him, but he

BEN OKRI was born in Minna, Nigeria, and lives in London. He is the author of the Booker Prize winning novel *The Famished Road* (1991) and has published numerous books, among them two books of poems, *Mental Fight* (1999) and *An African Elegy* (1992), as well as a collection of non-fiction, *A Way of Being Free* (1997). His most recent novel is *In Arcadia,* published in 2002. He is a Fellow Commoner in Creative Arts at Trinity College, Cambridge, and a Fellow of the Royal Society of Literature.

walked so fast he disappeared. And, as I went back to the group, I became aware for the first time of the danger of my position.

I had no way of telling who was a racial colorist. I rejoined the group. The first white man, who had begun it all, had gone. He too had vanished. I stood among the rest, ill at ease. Then I noticed a white youth amongst the men. He wore little round glasses. And he was looking at me in a peculiar way. I tried to ignore him. A white girl went past, and waved hello to me. She was someone I knew. The youth with glasses consulted his color chart and then made an immediate call with a walkie-talkie to someone.

"Yes, sir. He said hello to one of ours. Yes, yes, sir."

It was clear he was monitoring the contact I had with people of accepted racial purity. I became aware that he belonged to a shadowy organization. What else do they do? Do they assassinate people like me? I felt unsafe. I hurried away from the group. I went down the road. The bespectacled youth, with his chart, and his walkie-talkie, got up and came after me. I crossed the field, at a near run. He picked up speed. Where was I running to, where could I run to, where was safe for me? It grew dark. The chap kept on my tail, pursuing me. I lost him across a maze of fields. Soon it was dark. Then suddenly I could see him in the distance, with a torch in his hand. He was coming at me. He walked alongside a field. Behind him was a quaint provincial town, almost a village. A voice in me said:

"Go towards him. Don't run away from him, go at him, menacingly, purposefully. He's more scared of you than you think."

So I stopped running away and with a mean purpose in me I made towards him, striding. As I went towards him he appeared to hesitate. I continued. He too continued towards me. When I neared him I gazed into his face. It was an ordinary face, a harmless, scared, timid face which I didn't have the heart to hurt in any way. I went past him in the dark, and he went past me. I went on towards the village, and I didn't look back, I couldn't be bothered. I didn't care anymore.

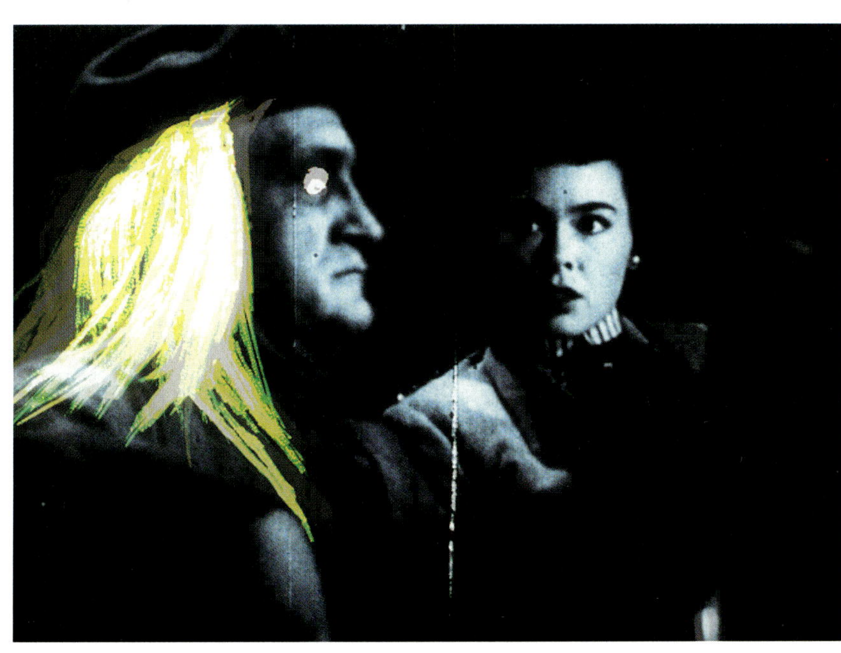

ELLEN GALLAGHER & EDGAR CLEIJNE, MONSTER (MURMUR), 2003, 16-mm film stills / MONSTER (RAUNEN), 16mm-Filmstills.

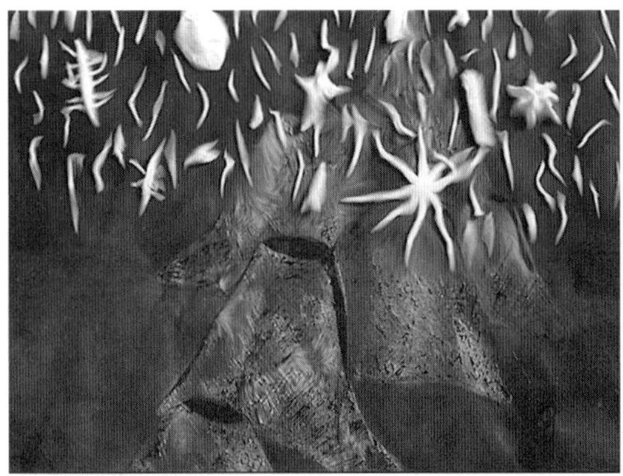

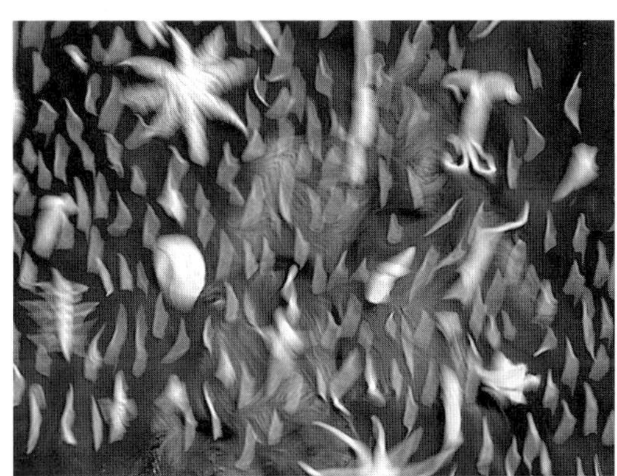

Der rassistische Kolorist

BEN OKRI

Es war während des Krieges. Wir sassen in einer Reihe auf einer Mauer und ich versuchte diese beiden Leute, diese zwei Männer, dazu zu bringen, einander kennen zu lernen. Ich wollte sie miteinander bekannt machen. Aber einer von ihnen war ein rassistischer Kolorist und hatte in der einen Hand eine Karte und Paste an den Fingerspitzen, und er sagte zu mir, dass er auf keinen Fall einem zweitklassigen Weissen die Hand geben könne. Ich war verblüfft – denn der Kerl war selber auch weiss und liess sich von mir umarmen, duldete jedoch nicht, dass ein anderer Weisser ihn berührte, weil er glaubte, dieser wäre ihm in Sachen Rassenreinheit nicht ebenbürtig. Ich versuchte es, doch er weigerte sich; und der anscheinend zweitklassige Weisse war derart verletzt und beleidigt, dass er wütend weglief. Ich ging ihm nach, aber er lief sehr schnell und verschwand. Und auf dem Weg zurück zur Gruppe wurde mir zum ersten Mal die Gefährlichkeit meiner Lage bewusst.

Ich konnte nicht wissen, wer ein rassistischer Kolorist war. Ich stiess wieder zur Gruppe. Der erste Weisse, mit dem alles angefangen hatte, war gegangen. Auch er war wie vom Erd-

---

BEN OKRI ist Schriftsteller. Er stammt aus Minna, Nigeria, und lebt in London. Mit dem Roman *Die hungrige Strasse* gewann er 1991 den Booker Preis; auf Deutsch erschienen sind u.a. der Gedichtband *Afrikanische Elegie* (1999), der Erzählband *Maskeraden* (2001) sowie *Vögel des Himmels – Wege zur Freiheit,* ein Band mit 12 Essays und einem Gedicht (2000). Er ist Fellow Commoner in Creative Arts am Trinity College in Cambridge und Fellow der Royal Society of Literature.

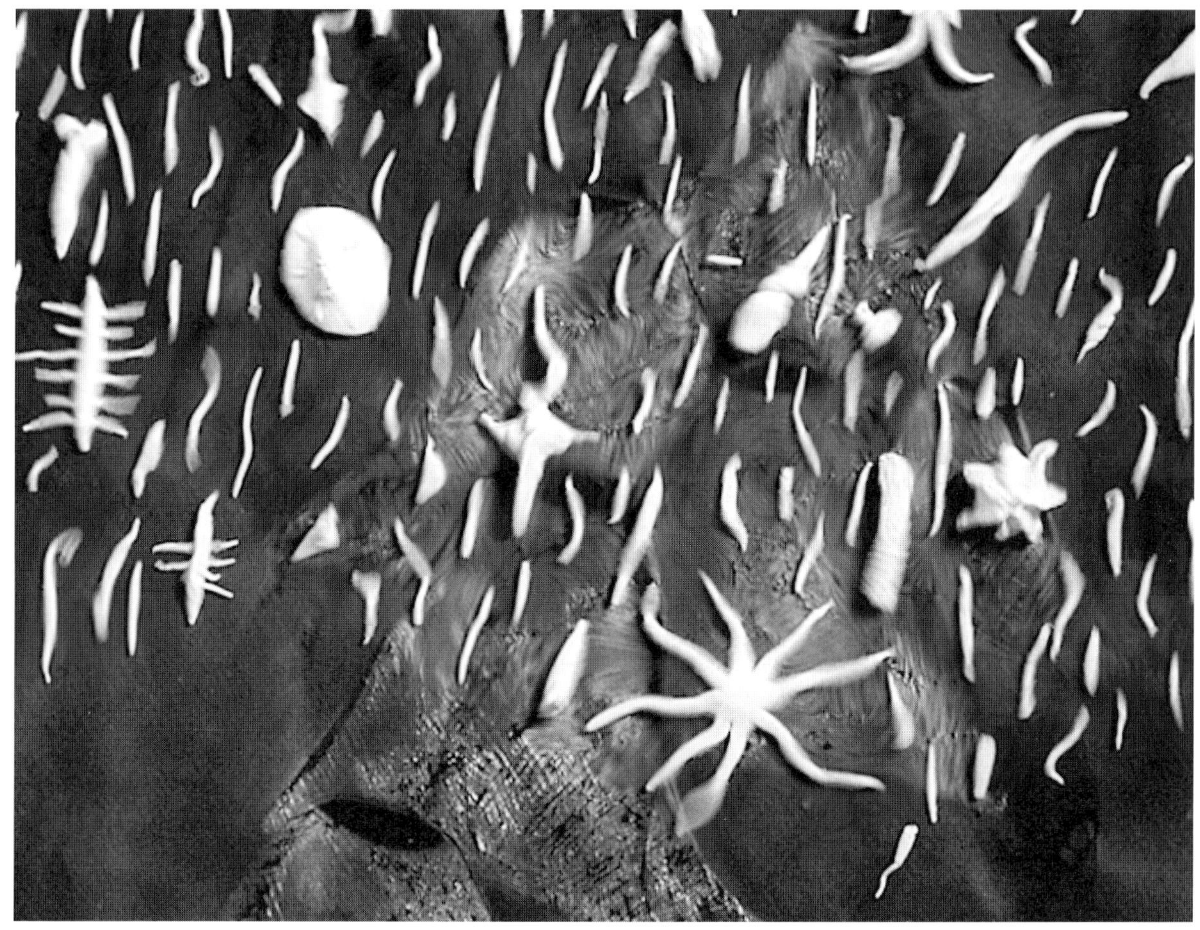

ELLEN GALLAGHER & EDGAR CLEIJNE, BLIZZARD OF WHITE (MURMUR), 2003, 16-mm film stills / WEISSER SCHNEESTURM (RAUNEN), 16mm-Filmstills.

boden verschwunden. Unbehaglich stand ich bei den anderen. Dann fiel mir unter den Männern ein weisser Jugendlicher auf. Er trug eine Brille mit kleinen runden Gläsern. Und er schaute mich seltsam an. Ich versuchte ihn nicht zu beachten. Ein weisses Mädchen ging vorbei und winkte mir zu. Eine Bekannte. Der Junge mit der Brille konsultierte seine Farbtabelle und rief dann sofort mit seinem Walkie-Talkie jemanden an.

«Jawohl. Er hat eine von uns gegrüsst. Ja, jawohl.»

Es war eindeutig, dass er meine Kontakte mit Leuten von anerkannter Rassenreinheit überwachte. Mir wurde klar, dass er einer zwielichtigen Vereinigung angehören musste. Was tun die sonst noch? Bringen sie Leute wie mich um? Ich fühlte mich nicht mehr sicher. Schnell ging ich weg von der Gruppe. Ich ging die Strasse hinunter. Der Brillenträger mit seiner Tabelle und seinem Walkie-Talkie erhob sich und folgte mir. Ich überquerte das Feld,

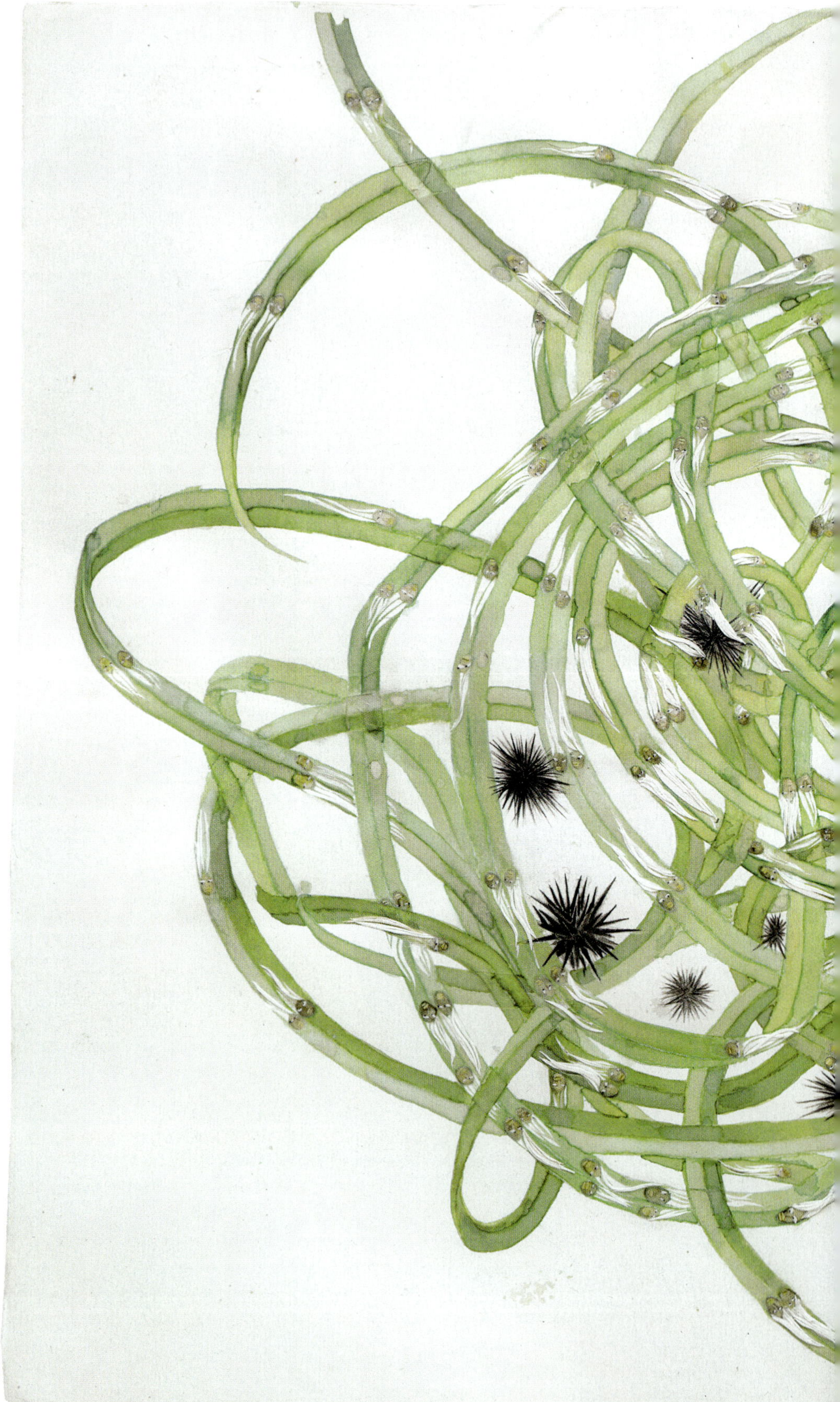

ELLEN GALLAGHER, UNTITLED (WATERY ECSTATIC SERIES), 2003, watercolor, pencil, varnish, and cut paper on paper, 27 1/2 x 40 1/2" / OHNE TITEL (SERIE: WÄSSERIG VERZÜCKT), Aquarell, Farbstift, Firnis und ausgeschnittenes Papier auf Papier, 69,8 x 102,9 cm. (PHOTO: TOM POWEL)

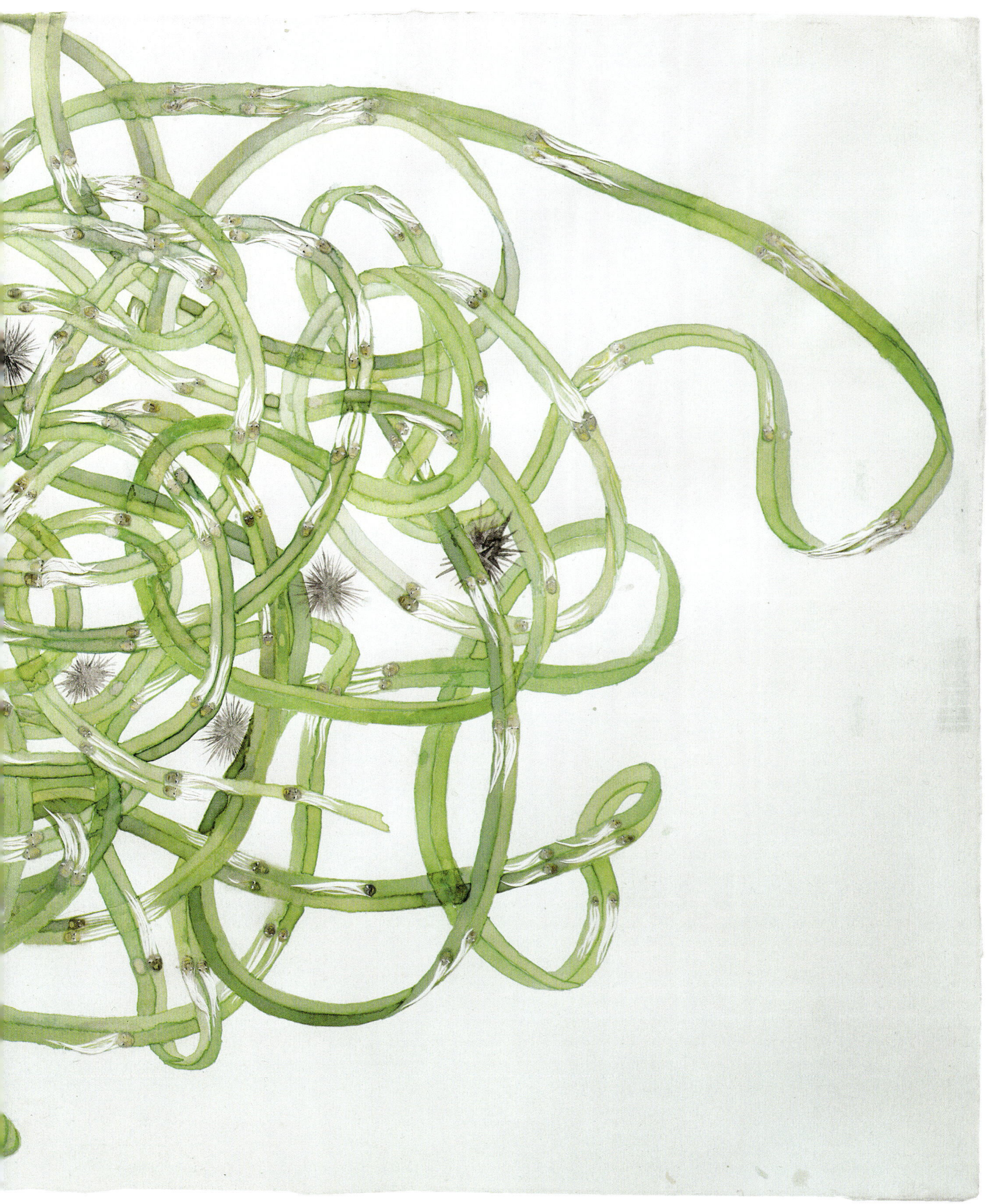

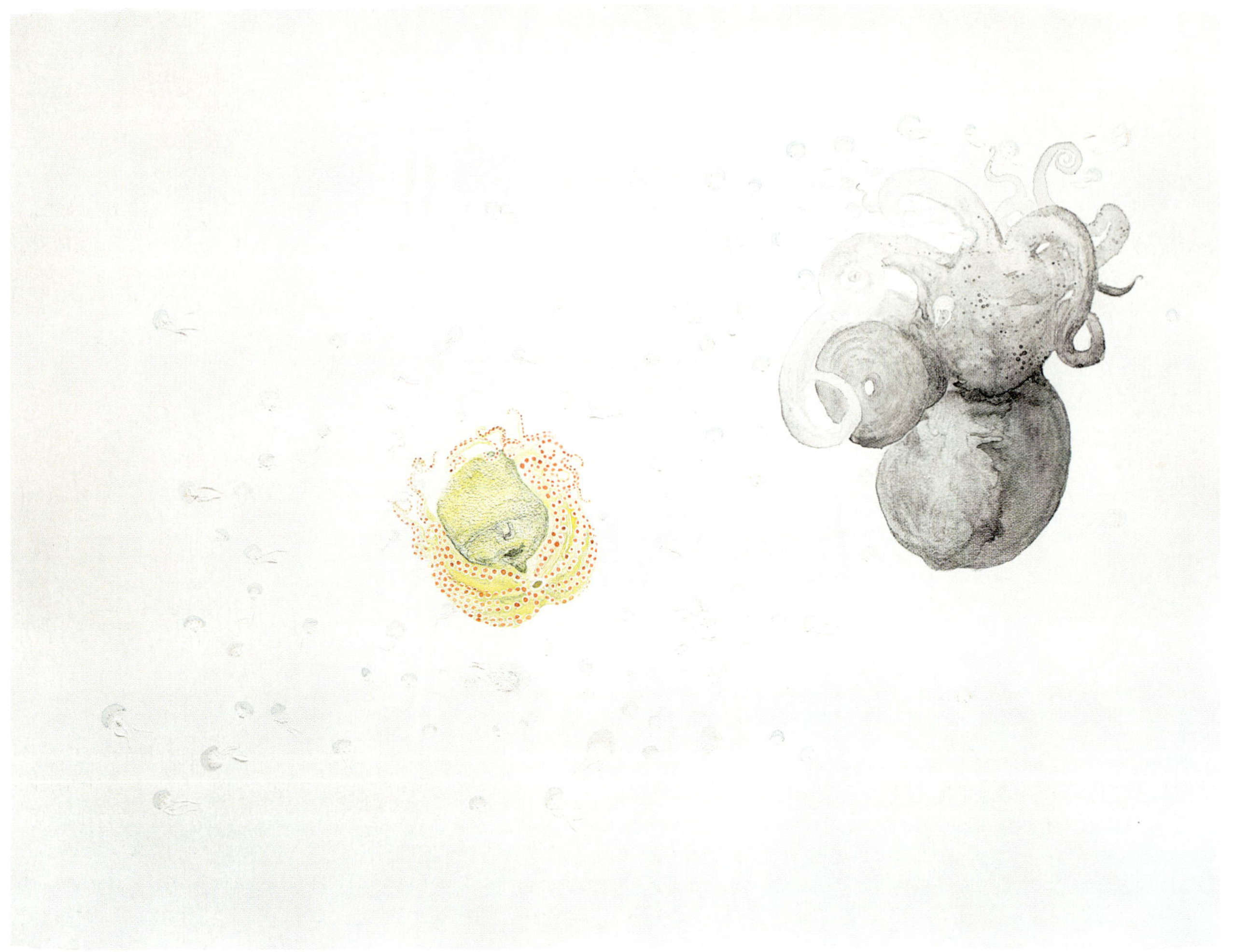

ELLEN GALLAGHER, UNTITLED (WATERY ECSTATIC SERIES), 2004, watercolor and cut paper on paper, 30 1/4 x 39 1/2" / OHNE TITEL (SERIE: WÄSSERIG VERZÜCKT), Aquarell und ausgeschnittenes Papier auf Papier, 77 x 100,5 cm. (PHOTO: TOM POWEL)

nun fast im Laufschritt. Er ging schneller. Wohin rannte ich eigentlich, wohin konnte ich fliehen, wo war ich sicher? Es wurde dunkel. Der Kerl blieb mir auf den Fersen, verfolgte mich. Ich durchquerte ein Labyrinth von Feldern und verlor ihn aus den Augen. Plötzlich sah ich ihn, weit weg, mit einer Fackel in der Hand. Er kam auf mich zu. Er ging am Rand eines Feldes entlang. Hinter ihm lag ein hübsches Provinzstädtchen, beinah ein Dorf. Eine innere Stimme sagte mir:

«Geh zu ihm hin. Lauf nicht vor ihm weg, geh auf ihn zu, drohend, zielgerichtet. Er hat mehr Angst vor dir, als du glaubst.»

Also hörte ich auf wegzulaufen und bewegte mich mit bösem Vorsatz und festen Schritten auf ihn zu. Als ich näher kam, schien er zu zögern. Ich ging weiter. Auch er kam weiter auf mich zu. Als ich ganz nahe war, schaute ich ihm ins Gesicht. Es war ein ganz gewöhnliches Gesicht, ein harmloses, ängstliches, schüchternes Gesicht, dem ich überhaupt nichts hätte antun können. Ich ging im Dunkeln an ihm vorbei und er ging an mir vorbei. Ich ging weiter auf das Dorf zu und schaute nicht mehr zurück, mich konnte man nicht belästigen. Es machte mir nichts mehr aus.

(Übersetzung: Suzanne Schmidt)

The History Lesson
FLESH IS A TEXTURE AS MUCH AS A COLOR

THYRZA NICHOLS GOODEVE

...one feels not a tooth-gritting, dogma-driven politics, but the verve and exuberance of mind that accompanies creative indignation.

– Adrienne Rich[1]

Properly practiced creativity can make one ad do the work of ten.

– William Bernbach[2]

When one enters the Dictionary.com website to find a definition of the word "creative," one reads, "the ability or power to create: Human beings are creative animals." The word creative is also "characterized by originality and expressiveness; imaginative: creative writing." This is hardly earth-shattering news for an art audience. But as the definition continues, the visual artist is oddly excluded: "One who displays productive originality: the creatives in the advertising department."

THYRZA NICHOLS GOODEVE is a writer living in Brooklyn, New York. Her essay "Ellen Gallagher: A Painter in Three Acts" appears in *Ellen Gallagher,* published by Anthony d'Offay Gallery, 2001.

This wouldn't surprise Ellen Gallagher, since she has been talking back to the "creatives" in the advertising departments of black popular magazines from the thirties through to the seventies for several years. Talking back and reconstituting, she has certainly given these creatives a run for their money, working with creativity in its most basic and literal form. Hers is not the creativity of genius, bred of the nothing of Yahweh, but of the indignant child of a first principle called Chaos (by the pre-Socratics). In this model, in the beginning was not nothing but Chaos.[3] In fact, for Gallagher, in the beginning is the already made, or ready-made, of minstrelsy and the shamrock. Her major motif has long been tiny bits of popping eyeballs, hotdog lips, hair flips, and four-leaf clovers. She carves part-creatures (at times from rubber but often in paper, paint, and plasticine) and situates them in a world where Bert Williams, Agnes Martin, and surrealism procreate with the doodle, visual jazz, and the sensibility of Langston Hughes. This is art that takes a lot of work; hours of hand labor go into Gallagher's intricately detailed and layered prints and canvases. And when they are finished, they insist that you be there to feel them as skins—tattooed and scarred by new possibilities, not tired, craggy

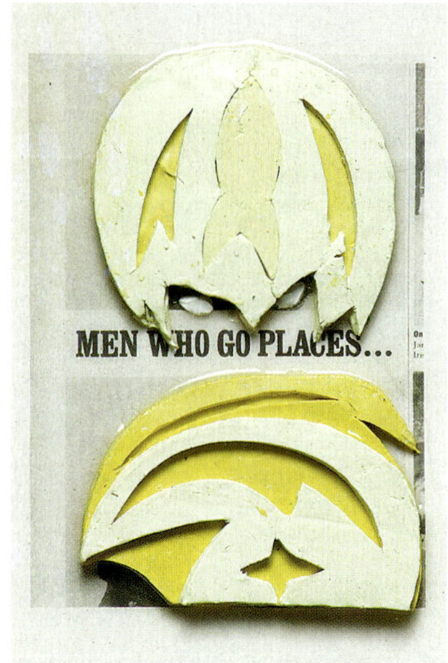

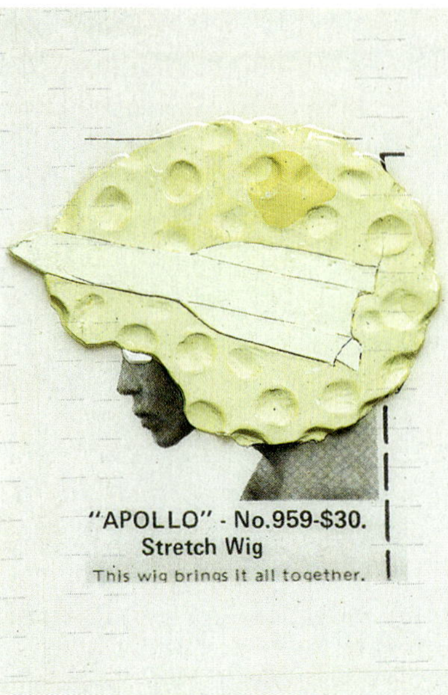

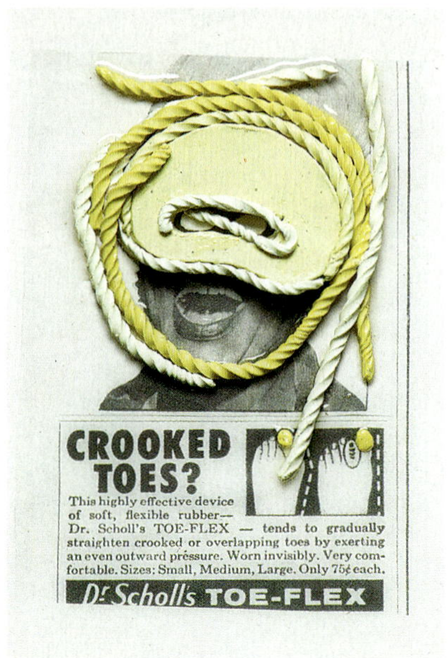

ELLEN GALLAGHER, AFRYLIC, 2004, 3 of 396 'pages', plasticine, ink, and paper on canvas, over-all measurements 96 x 192" / 3 von 396 «Seiten», Knetmasse, Tusche und Papier auf Leinwand, Masse der ganzen Bildtafel: 244 x 488 cm. (PHOTO: TOM POWEL)

stereotypes. In other words, for Gallagher, reproduction doesn't work. Everything is hand-made.

And yet, DeLuxe (2004–2005), like her 2004 exhibition "eXelento," is predicated on reproduction. Her matter—first principle—is: chaos as advertising—specifically magazine advertising, directed at the black culture of the "Negro self-improvement" movement of the fifties and sixties.

As is well documented, popular culture and advertising are the handmaidens of racism. Ethnic stereotypes and ethnic notions of the nineteenth and twentieth century continue to riddle the African American unconscious like perpetually returning bullet wounds that never go away. Marlon Riggs' 1987 documentary film essay *Ethnic Notions* explores the deep rewiring of the unconscious wrought by such images as the happy Coon, Step 'n' Fetchit, and the ever-smiling Mammy. Working within popular culture, Spike Lee's feature film *Bamboozled* (2000) is merciless in its criticism of those who draw on the stereotypes of old for identity and profit, but he is equally contrite about the simplicity of thinking you can just walk away. Why is this so difficult? Because the African American identity and unconscious has had to be i n v e n t e d apart from its past, as much as it has had to be rediscovered. As Alain Locke put it in his introduction to the 1925 anthology, *The New Negro*: "The Old Negro, we must remember, was a creature of moral debate and historical controversy. He has been a stock figure perpetuated as an historical fiction... the Negro has been more a formula than a human being..."[4)]

When African American culture entered into modernism, there was no "Old Negro" to rediscover or reclaim, only historical fictions produced in the vacuum of violence and dehumanization that defined African (and Caribbean) identity in America under slavery. Black modernism sought to create a "new negro" at the very moment minstrelsy was moving from the aura-drenched halls of vaudeville to the increasingly simulacrum-bound imagery of cinema.[5) Within this context of the intensification of mass and image-defined culture, where people of color are forced to "claim an identity they taught me to despise,"[6) is the very creation of "self"—an act of radical creativity, not sentimental recollection. Alain Locke's anthology hails a modernism of the flesh and mind, as much as a modernism of the palette and the pen, where "Desire destroys, consumes my mortal fears / Transforming me into the shape of flame."[7) Where, as Charles S. Johnson says:

New emotions accompany these new objectives. Where there is ferment and unrest, there is change. Old traditions are being shaken and rooted up by the percussion of new ideas. In this year of our Lord, 1925, extending across the entire country are seventeen cities in violent agitation over Negro residence areas, where once there was acquiescence, silent or ineffectually grumbling, there are now in evidence new convictions which more often prompt to resistance.[8)

And here is where Gallagher's work cuts across the categorizations of art and cultural history. Her voracious biting, gulping, digesting, and expulsing of the ready-made political unconscious, splices historically constructed streams of modernisms into a "Combine" (to use Rauschenberg's term). For simplicity's sake, we will call them American black modernism (often reduced to the Harlem Renaissance) and Anglo-European modernism, which bifurcates across Freud's dream work, the Surrealists' objective chance, the radical juxtaposition of Viktor Sklovskij's *ostranie* ("making strange"), Cubism's appropriated primitivism, Futurism, and Dada. DELUXE, is a teeming gene pool of these histories and critical strategies.

Gallagher—the daughter of a Cape Verdian father and a white Irish mother from Rhode Island—crosshatches the "isms" of high modernism with those of black cultural modernism. DELUXE is her *Une semaine de bonté,* but where Max Ernst used scientific and medical textbooks to construct a haunting world of hybrid melodrama, Gallagher lays over the medical

ELLEN GALLAGHER, AFRYLIC, 2004, 3 of 396 'pages', plasticine, ink, and paper on canvas, over-all measurements 96 x 192" / 3 von 396 «Seiten», Knetmasse, Tusche und Papier auf Leinwand, ganze Bildtafel: 244 x 488 cm. (PHOTO: TOM POWEL)

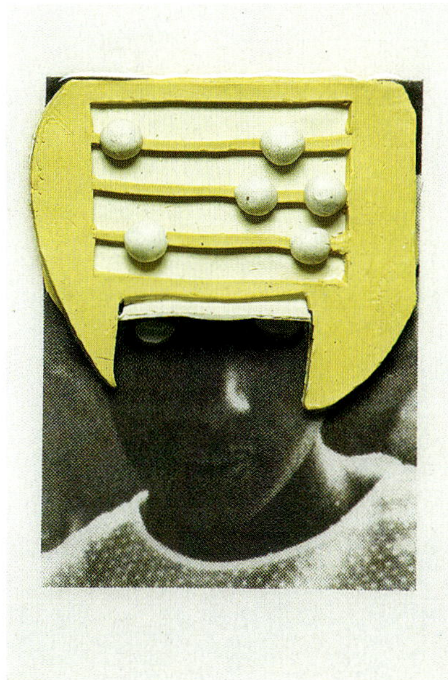

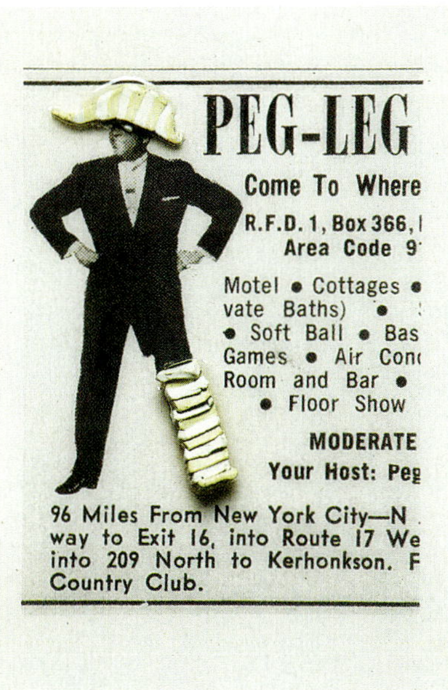

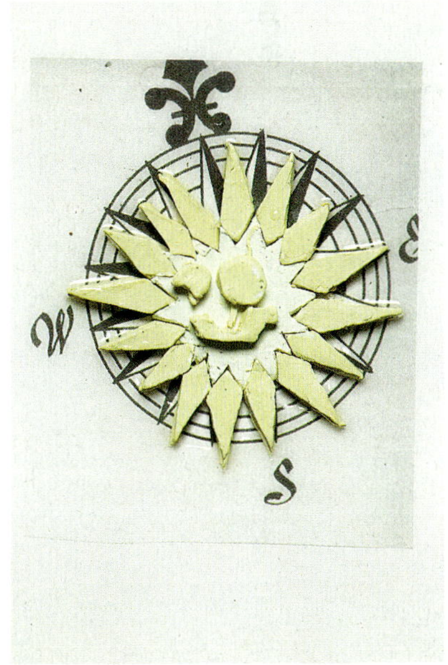

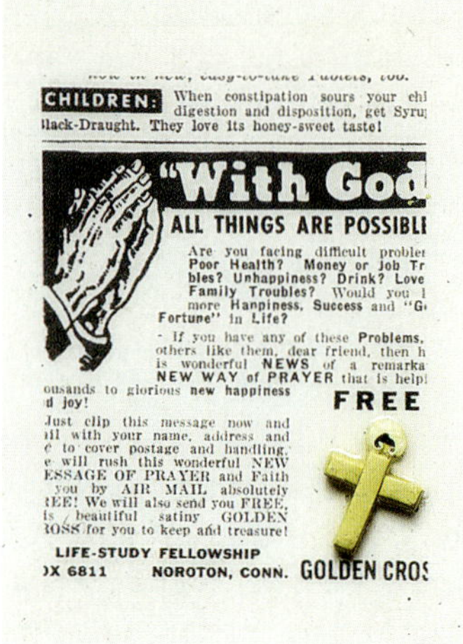

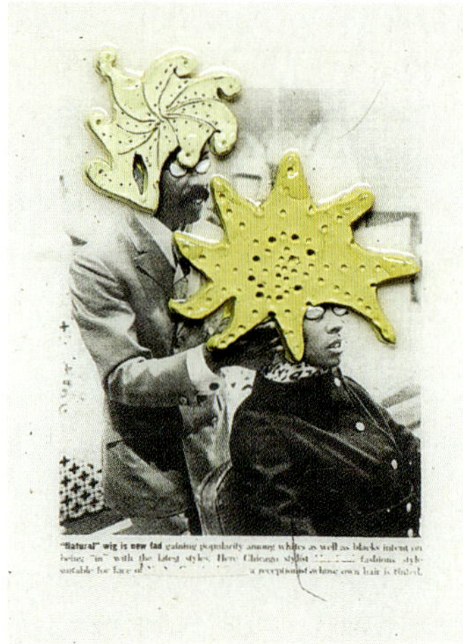

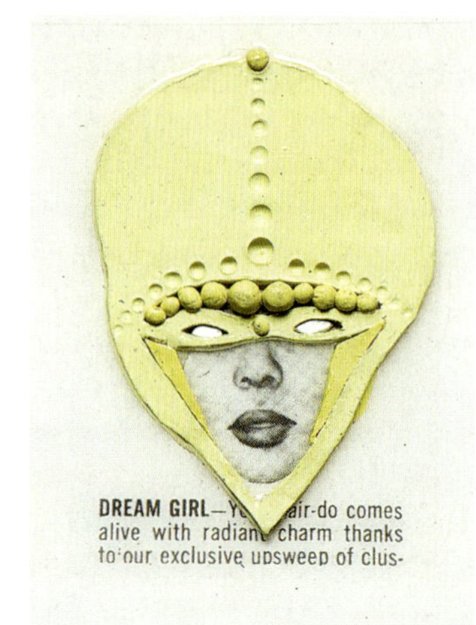

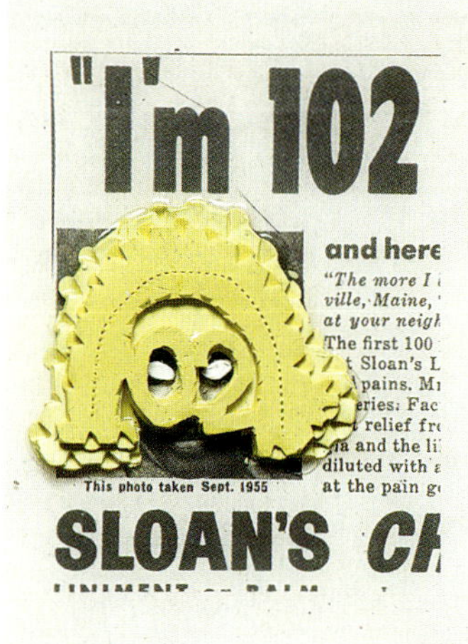

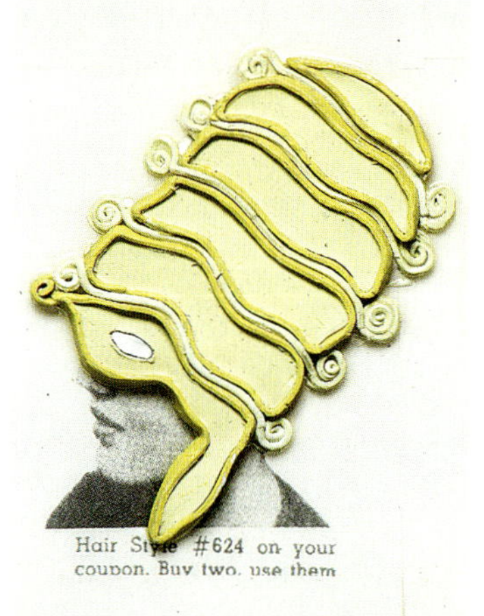

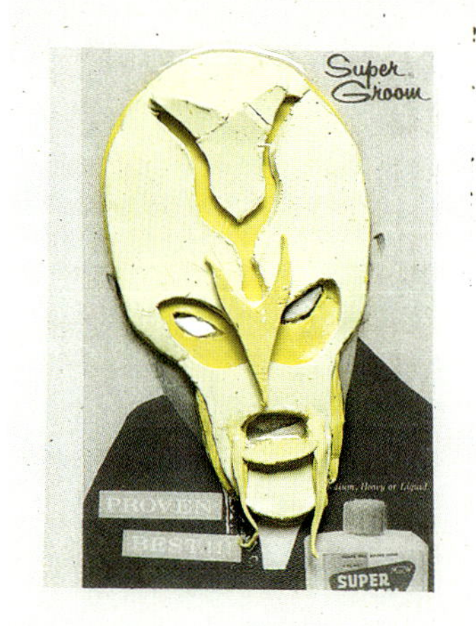

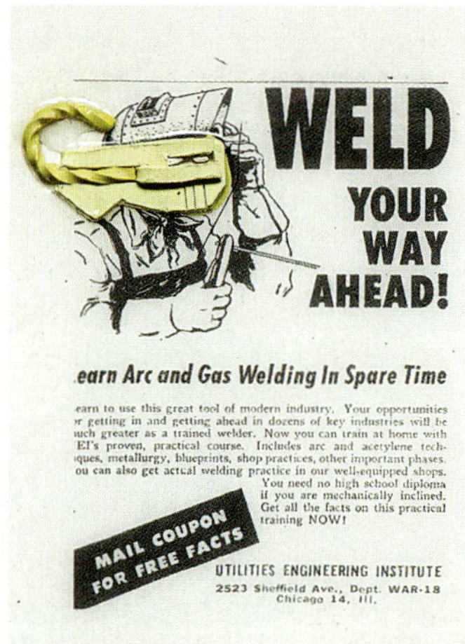

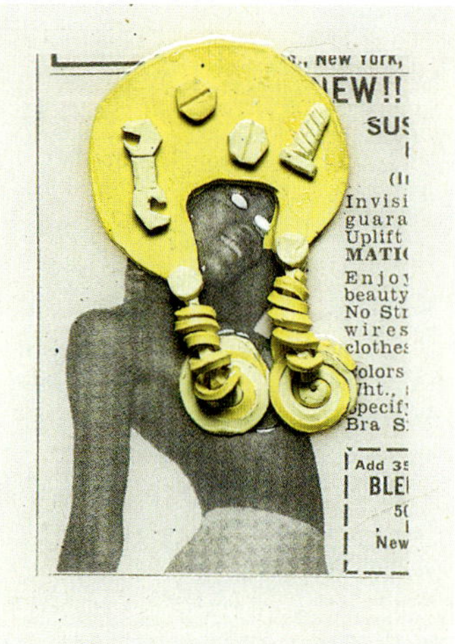

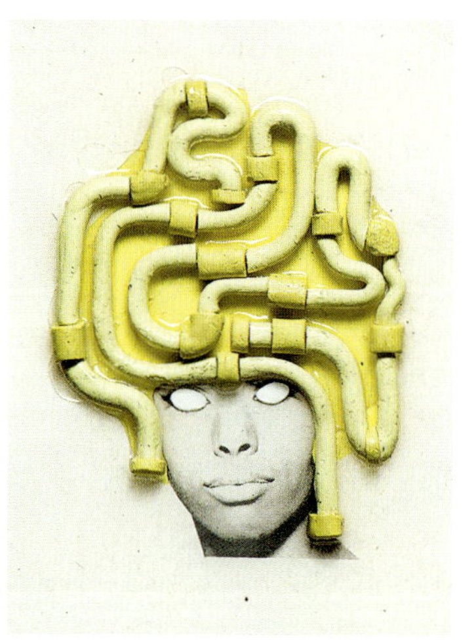

ELLEN GALLAGHER, *details from* AFRYLIC *and* eXELENTO, *2004. The works each consist of a panel with a grid of 396 'pages'; here you see 7 'pages' from* eXELENTO, *and 2 from* AFRYLIC *(middle row: middle and right image) / Ausschnitte aus* AFRYLIC *und* eXELENTO. *Beide Werke bestehen je aus einer Bildtafel mit einem Raster von 396 «Seiten»; hier sind 7 solche «Seiten» aus* eXELENTO *und 2 aus* AFRYLIC *abgebildet (mittlere Reihe: mittleres und rechtes Bild).* (PHOTO: TOM POWEL)

report from the Tuskegee Study (THE MAN WHO KEPT HARLEM COOL, 2004–2005), putting a simple sketch of a face under a massive swirling plasticine Afro. (According to Gallagher, the Afro "becomes this important way of taking up space in the city."[9]) There are layers to this image, both materially and historically, such as its reference to the celebrated NYPD officer and professor, Lloyd Sealy.

This brings us to Gallagher's methods, that, for the most part, you can't see. When viewed in art magazines or on the pages of catalogues, DELUXE looks like great collage, touched by the mad whimsy of Play-doh. Which it is; but this is only the beginning. As mentioned, Gallagher is a hardworking, hand laborer (she spent time, in her youth, in Alaska working in canneries). The production of a simple, flat, engaging image is never her sole purpose. This is why she works in print, as well as in painting and in drawing. Process, layers, materials—physicality is everything to her. Flesh is a texture as much as a color. DELUXE is collage (paper), photomontage (digital), photogravure (the process of printing from an intaglio plate, etched according to a photographic image); it is mounted, built-up and -upon by: abrasion, aquatint, burnishing, drypoint, embossing, etching, laser cutting, stenciling, tattoo-machine engraving (yes, for skin)—adding blue varnish, crystals, cut paper, toy eyeballs, white spaces, glitter, gold leaf, pomade… and this is not even the half of it. And yet, in tandem with this virtuoso exploration of material and technique, DELUXE is, in some ways, a book—a disemboweled book that carries its past life in pages that have been cut out, splayed onto a grid, and hung on a wall for display.[10] One does not look at DELUXE so much as read it. And what you read are textures as much as information.

Ultimately, DELUXE is a vast history lesson—a history of modernism(s), of black popular culture, of fashion and race in mid-century America, of advertising, of racial tensions lost in a history of popular culture that must be pointed to, felt, and pulled apart. Imagine a class of young children sitting before it with their teacher pointing at Peg Leg and saying, do you know who this is? And why is Moby Dick here? And look at all these wigs, why do you think they are that color, those shapes? What is a "Freedom Wig"? And look at Lustre Cream—what kind of a face is that? And who was Lloyd Sealy? And why does the artist incorporate the phrase "externally caused" in an ad claiming to give advice for bad skin? And the children will stand up and move closer to see the glitter, the gold, the plastic ice cube and cut paper mingled with black nurses and black celebrities, and, as "Each new painting is becoming its own universe," they will question and wonder.[11]

Coda

Many of McKay's published sonnets betray the terms of his search for an ideal racial self.[12] The day I go to see DELUXE at the Whitney Museum of American Art, a guard who has watched me taking notes on the work approaches me and says, "Come here. You must see this." He takes me to the wall where Gallagher's painting hangs, accompanied by a long list of multiple techniques. "These are the things that she uses in the piece. I don't know what 'spitbite' is, do you?" I don't. We talk. He likes the piece. He tells me he is from Jamaica, which is evident from his speech. And then he asks, "Do you know who Claude McKay was?" I answer, yes, although I am actually misremembering, mixing Claude McKay with Claude Brown, whose novel *Manchild in a Promised Land* was influential in my early life. "He was my uncle," the guard says, and I look down and see the name "Claude McKay" on his Whitney Museum identification badge. "And you're named after him!" "Yes, I am." He smiles one of those wide, warm, full-of-pride smiles. "And I am a poet too." He takes my name and address and says he will send me a book of his poems.

When I return home I am embarrassed by the fact that I don't really have a clear idea who Claude McKay is. I am even more amazed when I check the contents of Locke's anthology to find his poem "Baptism" a few pages away from "Jazzonia" by Langston Hughes. I turn to Google and surf websites and read his biography, and discover that he was a scion of the Harlem Renaissance—a one-time editor of *The Liberator,* whose most famous sonnet "If We Must Die" (1919) was written in response to an epidemic of lynchings and mass white assaults on black neighborhoods traveling across post-World-War-I America. The poem was a call to fight back, an act of creative indignation, which was a source of great inspiration to the black community. A perfect coda: for here is this guard who becomes a guide to Gallagher's work—a quiet legacy of the Harlem Renaissance—making sure I see the detail in her work. Gallagher's creativity draws us together. DELUXE has not only made "one ad do the work of ten" but, via an encounter of two—a white female writer and a black poet guard discussing her work—transformed a simple moment of synchronicity, across art and life, into a history lesson.[13]

1) Adrienne Rich, Preface to *Manifesto: Three Classic Essays on How to Change the World* (New York: Ocean Press, 2005), p. 2. (The three essays are by Karl Marx, Rosa Luxemburg, and Che Guevara.)
2) William Bernbach (1911–1982), US advertising executive, copywriter who pioneered the subtle, low-pressure advertising that became a hallmark of the agency which he founded, Doyle Dane Bernbach, Inc. The quote can be found on several Internet sites.
3) I have spoken elsewhere of the appearance of creation myths in Gallagher's generation (for example: Matthew Barney, Matthew Ritchie). See, "The Myth is A Muscle" in *Art Becomes You. Parody, Pastiche and the Politics of Art. Materiality in a Post-material Paradigm,* edited by Henry Rogers (London: ARTicle Press, 2005).
4) Alain Locke, "The New Negro" in *The New Negro,* edited by Alain Locke (New York: Atheneum Press, 1986), p. 3.
5) It is no minor coincidence that cinema's two celebrated rites of passage, one into narrative, and the other into sound coincide with spectacular examples of racism. Did narrative cinema have to be invented through a tale featuring the Ku Klux Klan? Did the human voice first have to be heard in cinema as the sound of "Mammy" sung by a Jew in blackface on bended knee?
6) The title of a collection of essays by Michelle Cliff: *Claiming An Identity They Taught Me to Despise* (New York: Norton, 1980).
7) Claude McKay, "Baptism" in *The New Negro,* edited by Alain Locke (New York: Antheneum Press, 1986), p. 133.
8) Charles S. Johnson, "The New Frontage on American Life" in ibid, p. 296.
9) Ellen Gallagher, "1000 Words," *Artforum,* April 2004, p. 128.
10) For her show "eXelento" at Gagosian Gallery (September 2004), Gallagher published *eXelento,* a compendium of the Gallagher-made characters from that mammoth piece and POMP-BANG (2003). EXELENTO like DELUXE takes its name from the company names of the products advertised. There is as well the company "Humania."
11) Ellen Gallagher, "1000 Words," *Artforum,* April 2004, p. 128.
12) Marcellous Blount: http://www.english.uiuc.edu/maps/poets/m_r/mckay/mustdie.htm
13) The wig is a major motif and source of information in her work. In "1000 Words" she notes that in the thirties wigs were called "transformations."

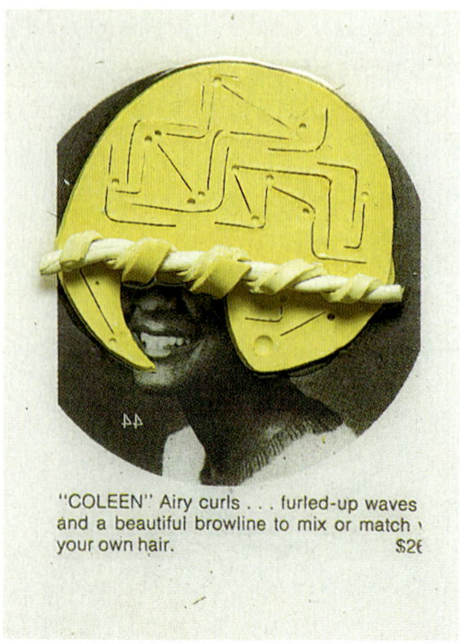

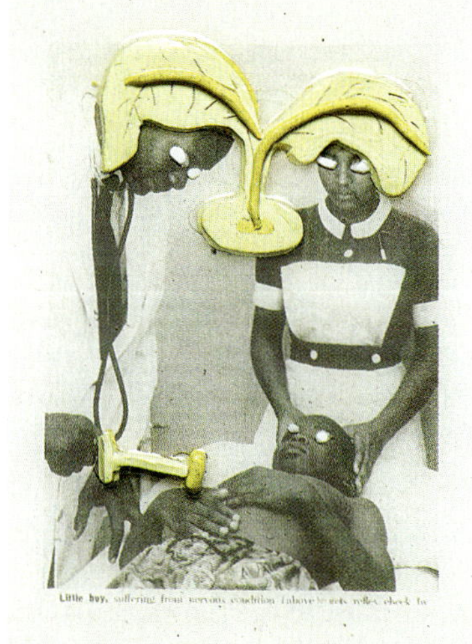

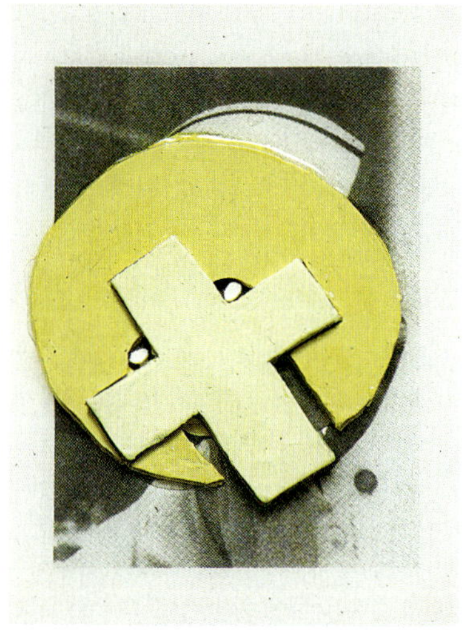

ELLEN GALLAGHER, EXELENTO, 2004, plasticine, ink, and paper on canvas, over-all measurements 96 x 192", details / Knetmasse, Tusche und Papier auf Leinwand, ganze Bildtafel: 244 x 488 cm, Ausschnitte. (PHOTO: TOM POWEL)

Die Geschichtslektion

FLEISCH IST NICHT NUR EINE FARBE, SONDERN AUCH EINE TEXTUR

THYRZA NICHOLS GOODEVE

... man spürt keine zähneknirschende, dogmatisch bestimmte Politik, sondern den geistigen Elan und Überschwang einer kreativen Empörung.

– Adrienne Rich[1)]

Wird Kreativität richtig angewandt, kann eine Anzeige die Wirkung von zehn entfalten.

– William Bernbach[2)]

Sucht man die Website Dictionary.com auf, um eine Definition des englischen Wortes *creative* zu finden, so liest man da (sinngemäss übersetzt): «die Fähigkeit oder Kraft zu schaffen: Menschen sind kreative Tiere.» Das Wort *creative* bezeichnet auch «Originalität und Ausdrucksfähigkeit; phantasievolles: kreatives Schreiben.» Das wird für ein Kunst gewohntes Publikum nicht gerade weltbewegend neu sein. Doch im Fortgang der Definition bleibt der bildende Künstler seltsamerweise aussen vor: «Leute, die produktive Originalität an den Tag legen: die Kreativen in der Werbeabteilung».

Dies ist für Ellen Gallagher natürlich keine Überraschung, denn sie übt seit Jahren Kritik an den «Kreativen» in den Werbeabteilungen der populären Zeitschriften für Schwarze der 50er und 60er Jahre. Mit ihrer Kritik und Richtigstellung hat sie diesen Kreativen gewiss nichts geschenkt, wobei sie selbst Kreativität in ihrer ursprünglichsten und buchstäblichsten Form einsetzte. Gallaghers Kreativität ist nicht die eines Genies, die aus Jahwes Nichts hervorgeht, sondern die eines zornigen Kindes des (vorsokratischen) Urprinzips namens Chaos. Nach diesem Modell war am Anfang nicht nichts, sondern das Chaos.[3)] Tatsächlich stand für Gallagher am Anfang das «bereits Geschaffene» (das Readymade) der gesungenen Balladen und des Kleeblattes. Lange Zeit waren ihre wichtigsten Motive winzige Partikel, die Glupschaugen, Hotdog-Lippen, Haarknoten und vierblättrige Kleeblätter darstellen. Sie schnitzelt Teilwesen (manchmal aus Gummi, aber öfter aus Papier, Farbe und Knetmasse) und versetzt sie in eine Welt, in der Bert Williams, Agnes Martin und der Surrea-

---

THYRZA NICHOLS GOODEVE schreibt und lebt in Brooklyn, New York. Ihr Essay «Ellen Gallagher: A Painter in Three Acts» erschien im Katalog *Ellen Gallagher,* Anthony d'Offay Gallery, London, 2001.

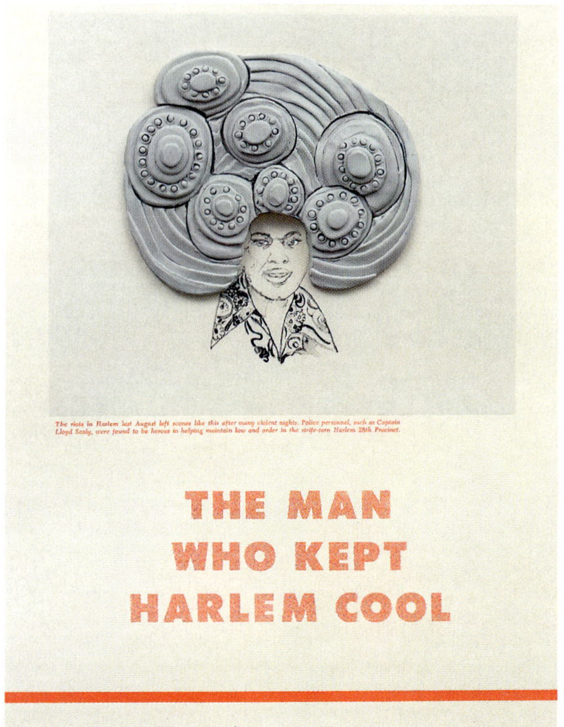

ELLEN GALLAGHER, *THE MAN WHO KEPT HARLEM COOL* (DELUXE), 2004/2005, *photogravure, aquatint, chine collé, and plasticine, 13 x 10" / Photogravüre, Aquatinta, Chine collé und Knetmasse, 33 x 25,4 cm.* (PHOTO: D. JAMES DEE / TWO PALMS PRESS, NEW YORK)

lismus sich zu Doodle-Zeichnungen, visuellem Jazz und der Sensibilität eines Langston Hughes gesellen. Es ist eine Kunst, die sehr arbeitsintensiv ist; in den verzwickten Details der mehrschichtigen Drucke und Arbeiten auf Leinwand stecken viele Stunden Handarbeit. Und wenn sie fertig sind, verlangen sie unbedingt, dass man vor Ort ist und ihren Hautcharakter spürt: übersät mit den Tätowierungen und Narben neuer Möglichkeiten, nicht mit schlaffen, schroffen Stereotypen. Mit anderen Worten, Reproduktion ist nichts für Gallagher. Alles ist von Hand gefertigt.

Und doch beruht DELUXE (2004–2005), wie die Ausstellung «eXelento», 2004, auf Reproduktion. Ihr Stoff oder Grundprinzip ist das Chaos in Gestalt der Werbung – insbesondere der Zeitschriftenwerbung, die sich an die schwarze Kultur der so genannten «Selbstverbesserung der Neger» seit den 30er bis in die 70er Jahre des zwanzigsten Jahrhunderts richtete.

Wie zahlreiche Dokumente belegen, sind Populärkultur und Werbung eifrige Handlanger des Rassismus. Ethnische Stereotype und Vorstellungen aus dem neunzehnten und zwanzigsten Jahrhundert belasten das Unbewusste der Schwarzamerikaner noch immer wie ewig wiederkehrende Schusswunden, die nie verheilen. Marlon Riggs' dokumentarischer Filmessay *Ethnic Notions* (1987) untersucht die Wiederbelebung dieser Verletzungen in der Tiefe des Unbewussten durch Bilder des «fröhlichen Negers», des *Step 'n' Fetchit*[4] und der ewig lächelnden schwarzen Mammy. Spike Lees innerhalb der Populärkultur angesiedelter Spielfilm *Bamboozled* (2000) ist erbarmungslos in seiner Kritik derer, die ihre Identität und ihren Profit aus diesen alten Stereotypen beziehen, aber der simplen Haltung, man könne sich einfach davonmachen, steht er nicht minder zähneknirschend gegenüber. Warum ist dies so schwer? Weil die schwarzen Amerikaner ihre Identität und ihr kollektives Unbewusstes unabhängig von ihrer Vergangenheit erfinden, aber genauso auch wieder entdecken mussten. Wie Alain Locke in seiner Einleitung zu der 1925 erschienenen Anthologie, *The New Negro,* schrieb:

> *Der «alte Neger», das dürfen wir nicht vergessen, war ein Resultat moralischer Auseinandersetzung und historischer Kontroversen. Er war eine feste Grösse, die als geschichtliche Fiktion am Leben erhalten wurde… der Neger war eher eine Formel als ein menschliches Wesen…*[5]

Als die schwarzamerikanische Kultur in die Moderne eintrat, gab es keinen «alten Neger» mehr, den man wieder entdecken oder auf den man sich zurückbesinnen konnte, sondern nur noch geschichtliche Fiktionen, erzeugt in dem Vakuum von Gewalt und Entmenschlichung, das in Amerika die Identität der aus Afrika und der Karibik stammenden Menschen zur Zeit der Sklaverei bestimmte. Die Schwarze Moderne wollte einen «neuen Neger» erschaffen, genau zu dem Zeitpunkt, als das Minstrelvarieté aus den atmosphärisch allzu belasteten Theatersälen des Vaudeville auszog und zu der noch stärker dem Bild verhafteten Sprache des Kinos hinüberwechselte.[6] Im Kontext dieser immer stärker vom Bild bestimmten Massenkultur, in der Leute mit dunkler Hautfarbe gezwungen sind eine Identität zu behaupten, die man sie zu verachten gelehrt hat,[7] ist schon die Erschaffung eines «Selbst» ein Akt radikaler Kreativität und nicht etwa sentimentale Rückschau. Alain Lockes Anthologie feiert neben der Moderne von Pa-

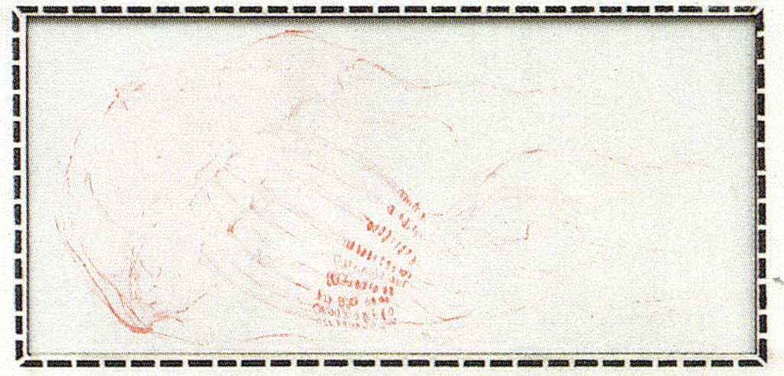

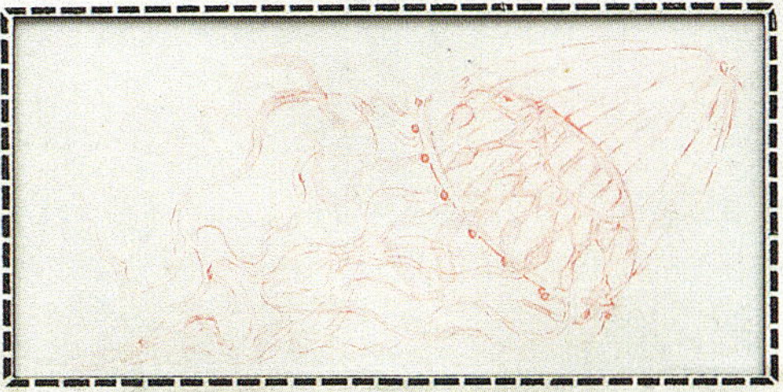

FILL OUT THE COUPON ABOVE
AND I WILL RUSH TO YOU...

FREE NURSES BOOKLET
AND SAMPLE
LESSON PAGES

LEARN PRACTICAL NURSING AT
HOME IN ONLY 10 SHORT WEEKS

THIS IS THE HOME STUDY COURSE
security, independence and freedom
good times

accept your case

YOUR AGE AND EDUCATION ARE NOT IMPORTANT common sense
desire

future
now!

HUNDREDS OF ADDITIONAL PRACTICAL NURSES WILL SOON BE NEEDED
opportunity
happiness, contentment and prestige

BUT THE IMPORTANT THING is to get FREE

FREE

FREE

12R81

ELLEN GALLAGHER, *FREE NURSES* (DELUXE), *2004/2005, photogravure, aquatint, collage, laser cutting, and cut paper, 13 x 10" / Photogravüre, Aquatinta, Collage, Laserschnitt und ausgeschnittenes Papier, 33 x 25,4 cm.* (PHOTO: D. JAMES DEE / TWO PALMS PRESS, NEW YORK)

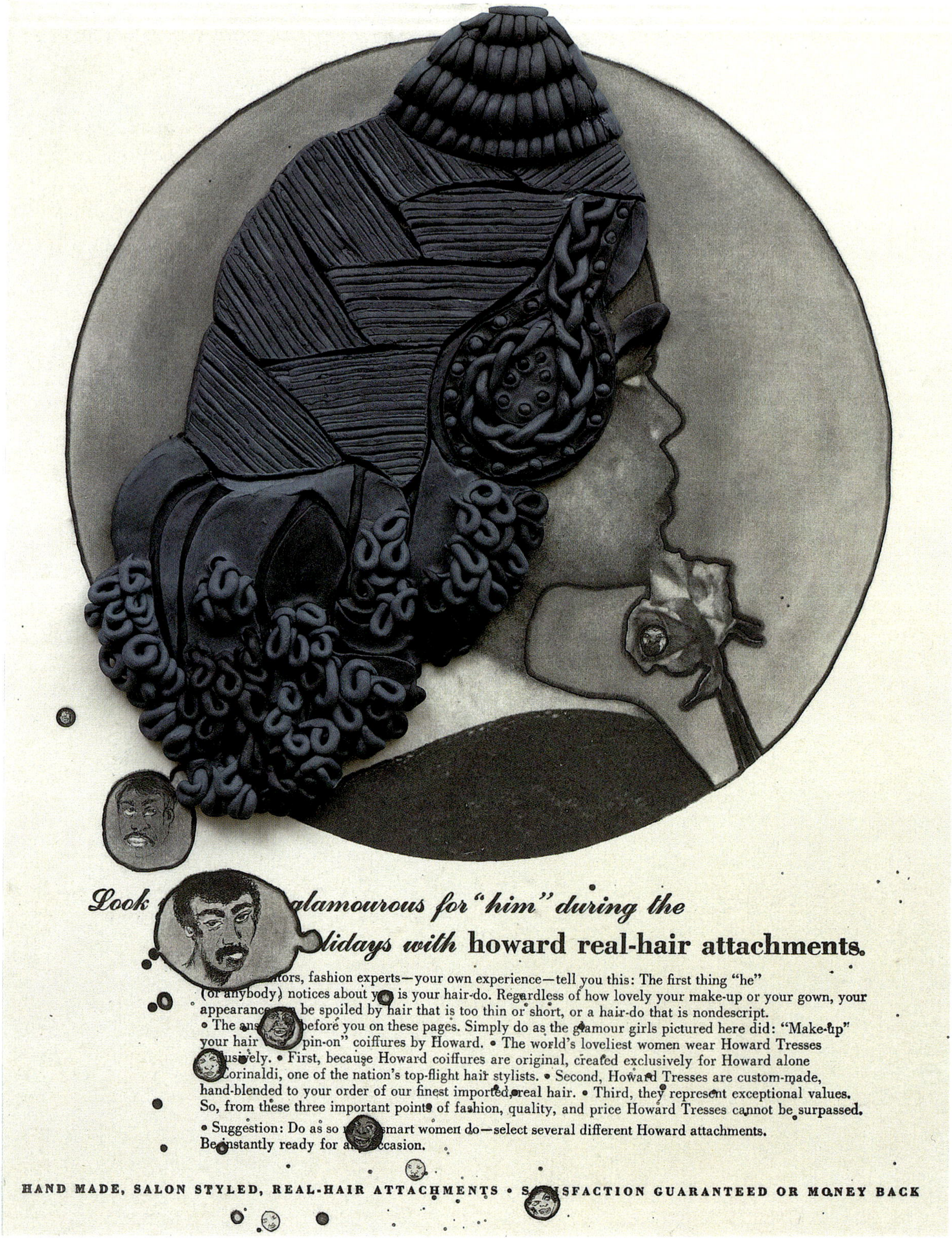

ELLEN GALLAGHER, AMERICAN BEAUTY (DELUXE), 2004/2005, photogravure, aquatint, spitbite, and plasticine, 13 x 10" / Photogravüre, Aquatinta, Pinselätzung und Knetmasse, 33 x 25,4 cm. (PHOTO: D. JAMES DEE / TWO PALMS PRESS, NEW YORK)

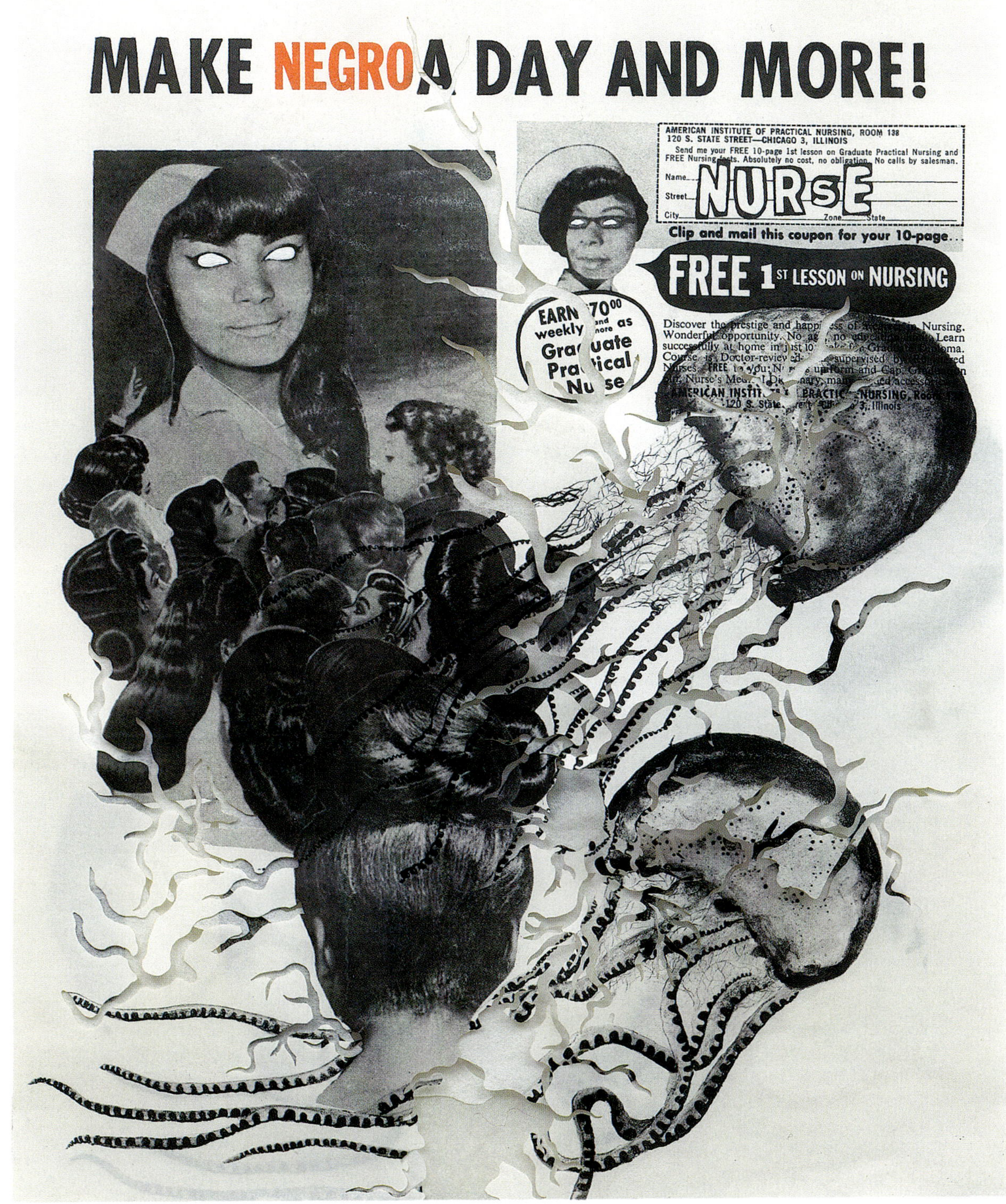

ELLEN GALLAGHER, NEGRO A DAY (DeLuxe), 2004/2005, photogravure, aquatint, laser cutting, and gouache, 13 x 10" / Photogravüre, Aquatinta, Laserschnitt und Gouache, 33 x 25,4 cm. (PHOTO: GAGOSIAN GALLERY, NEW YORK)

lette und Feder auch eine Moderne des Fleisches und des Geistes, in der «das Begehren meine sterblichen Ängste zerstört, aufzehrt / und mich in die Flammengestalt verwandelt».[8] Oder wie Charles S. Johnson sagt:

Mit den neuen Zielen sind neue Gefühle verbunden. Wo es gärt und unruhig ist, da findet Veränderung statt. Alte Traditionen werden erschüttert und entwurzelt dank der Stosskraft neuer Ideen. In diesem Jahr unseres Herrn, 1925, finden über das ganze Land verteilt in siebzehn Städten gewaltsame Auseinandersetzungen um die Wohngebiete der Schwarzen statt; wo man einst einwilligte, obwohl man im Stillen oder erfolglos murrte, da werden nun neue Überzeugungen offen kundgetan und führen immer häufiger zum Widerstand.[9]

Genau hier macht Gallaghers Werk den Schnitt mitten durch alle Kategorisierungen der Kunst und Kulturgeschichte. Ihr gieriges Abbeissen, Schlucken, Verdauen und Ausstossen des bereits bestehenden (engl.: *ready-made*) politischen Unbewussten verbindet die verschiedenen historisch bedingten Strömungen der Moderne zu einem kombinierten Werk (im Sinne von Rauschenbergs *Combine Painting*). Der Einfachheit halber seien hier nur Folgende genannt: die schwarzamerikanische Moderne (welche oft auf die Harlem Renaissance reduziert wird) und die anglo-europäische Moderne, innerhalb der sich wiederum unterscheiden lassen: Freuds *Traumdeutung*, der objektive Zufall der Surrealisten, der radikale Gegensatz von Viktor Sklovskijs *ostranie* (Verfremden), der vom Kubismus aufgegriffene Primitivismus und schliesslich Futurismus und Dadaismus. DELUXE ist gleichsam ein Genpool, der nur so wimmelt von diesen Traditionen und kritischen Strategien.

Ellen Gallagher, Tochter eines kapverdischen Vaters und einer weissen irischen Mutter aus Rhode Island, überkreuzt die Ismen aus der Blütezeit der Moderne mit jenen der Moderne der schwarzen Kultur. DELUXE ist Gallaghers *Une semaine de bonté* (Max Ernsts Collagen-Roman von 1934), doch wo Max Ernst naturwissenschaftliche und medizinische Bücher verwendete, um eine beunruhigende Welt von hybrider Melodramatik zu erzeugen, legt sie über den medizinischen Bericht aus der Tuskegee-Studie[10] nur die einfache Skizze eines Gesichts unter einer mächtigen krausen Afrofrisur aus Plastilin (THE MAN WHO KEPT HARLEM COOL / Der Mann, der Harlem cool hielt, 2004–2005). Laut Gallagher wird der Afro «zu dieser wichtigen Möglichkeit, in der Stadt Platz in Anspruch zu nehmen».[11] In diesem Bild gibt es mehrere Schichten, sowohl materiell wie historisch, darunter auch eine Anspielung auf den legendären Offizier und Professor des New York Police Departement, Lloyd Sealy.

Das bringt uns auf Gallaghers Arbeitsmethoden, die meistens unsichtbar bleiben. In Kunstzeitschriften oder auf Katalogseiten wirkt DELUXE wie eine grossartige Collage, die eine etwas schräge Knetgummi-Anwandlung erdulden musste. Das trifft zwar zu, aber es ist nur der Anfang. Wie bereits erwähnt, ist Gallagher eine fleissige und ausdauernde Handarbeiterin (in ihrer Jugend war sie eine Zeit lang in Alaska und arbeitete in diversen Konservenfabriken). Die Herstellung eines einfachen zweidimensionalen attraktiven Bildes ist bei ihr nie alleiniges Ziel. Deshalb arbeitet sie ebenso mit Drucktechniken wie malender und zeichnender Weise. Prozesse, Schichten, Materialien, stoffliche Sinnlichkeit bedeuten ihr mehr als alles andere. Fleisch ist nicht nur eine Farbe, sondern auch eine Textur. DELUXE ist sowohl Collage (Papier), Photomontage (digital) und Photogravüre (Photo-Tiefdruck-Prozess); es ist montiert und aufgebaut mit Hilfe von Abrasion, Aquatinta, Feilen, Kaltnadel, Prägung, Radierung, Laserschnitt, Schablonen, Tätowiernadeln (ja, für Hauttätowierungen) sowie Blaulack, Glasperlen, Zeitungsausschnitten, Puppenaugen, weiss abgedeckten Elementen, Glitter, Blattgold, Pomade ..., und das ist bei weitem noch nicht alles. Dennoch ist DELUXE, neben all dieser experimentellen Virtuosität im Umgang mit Materialien und Techniken, ein Buch, ein ausgeweidetes Buch, dessen früheres Leben noch in den Seiten steckt, die ausgeschnitten, auf ein Raster gespannt und zur Präsentation an die Wand gehängt wurden.[12] Man schaut sich DELUXE weniger an, als dass man es liest. Und was man da zu lesen bekommt, sind nicht nur Informationen, sondern vor allem auch Texturen.

Im Grunde ist DELUXE eine gewaltige Geschichtslektion: über die Geschichte der Moderne(n), der Schwarzen Populärkultur, der Moden und Rassen um die Mitte des zwanzigsten Jahrhunderts in Amerika, der Werbung und der Rassenkonflikte, die in die Entwicklung der populären Kultur eingegangen oder in ihr untergegangen sind und auf die man hinweisen muss, die gespürt und zerpflückt werden müssen. Stellt euch eine Schulklasse vor, kleine Kinder, die vor diesem Werk sitzen, während ihre Lehrerin auf Peg Leg zeigt und fragt: «Wisst ihr, wer das ist? Und warum ist hier Moby Dick? Und schaut mal, all diese Perücken, warum, glaubt ihr, haben sie diese Farbe und diese Form? Was ist eine ‹Freiheitsperücke›? Und schaut euch Lustre Cream an – was für ein Gesicht ist das? Und wer war Lloyd Sealy? Und warum verwendet die Künstlerin den Ausdruck ‹von aussen verursacht› in einer Anzeige, die ein Mittel gegen unreine Haut zu empfehlen scheint?» Die Kinder werden aufstehen und näher herangehen, um den Glitter, das Gold, den Plastik-Eiswürfel und die Zeitungsausschnitte mit den schwarzen Krankenschwestern und Berühmtheiten anzuschauen; sie werden Fragen stellen und staunen, denn: «Jedes Bild wird zu einem eigenen Universum.»[13)]

Coda

Viele der Sonette, die McKay veröffentlicht hat, zeugen von den Umständen seiner Suche nach dem idealen, durch seine Rasse geprägten Selbst.[14)] Am Tag, als ich mir DeLuxe im Whitney Museum in New York ansehen will, kommt ein Museumswärter, der bemerkt hat, dass ich mir Notizen mache, auf mich zu und sagt: «Kommen Sie. Das müssen Sie sehen.» Er führt mich zu der Wand, an der Gallaghers Bild hängt, begleitet von einer langen Liste verschiedenster Techniken. «Das sind die Dinge, die sie für die Arbeit verwendet hat. Ich weiss nicht, was ‹Pinselätzung› ist, Sie vielleicht?» Ich auch nicht. Wir reden miteinander. Das Bild gefällt ihm. Er erzählt, er stamme aus Jamaika, was mir sein Akzent schon verraten hat. Dann fragt er: «Wissen Sie, wer Claude McKay war?» Ich sage ja, obwohl ich ihn tatsächlich mit Claude Brown verwechsle, dessen Roman *Manchild in a Promised Land* mich in meiner Jugend tief beeindruckt hatte. «Er war mein Onkel», sagt der Wärter. Ich schaue auf sein Namensschild und lese den Namen «Claude McKay». «Und Sie sind nach ihm benannt!» – «Ja, genau.» Er zeigt mir dieses weite, herzliche, stolze Lächeln. «Und ich bin auch ein Dichter.» Er schreibt sich meinen Namen und meine Adresse auf und sagt, er werde mir ein Buch mit seinen Gedichten zuschicken.

Auf dem Heimweg ist es mir peinlich, dass ich nicht wirklich weiss, wer Claude McKay ist. Ich bin ziemlich verblüfft, als ich im Inhaltsverzeichnis von Lockes Anthologie sein Gedicht «Baptism» nur wenige Seiten von Langston Hughes «Jazzonia» entfernt finde. Ich nehme Google zu Hilfe und surfe durchs Netz, ich lese seine Biographie und entdecke, dass er ein Abkömmling der Harlem Renaissance war – ein ehemaliger Redaktor von *The Liberator*, dessen berühmtestes Sonett, «If We Must Die» (Wenn wir sterben müssen, 1919), als Reaktion auf eine sich nach dem Ersten Weltkrieg über ganz Amerika verbreitende Lynchjustiz-Welle und zunehmende Übergriffe weisser Horden auf die Wohnviertel der Schwarzen entstanden war. Das Gedicht war ein Aufruf, sich zur Wehr zu setzen, ein Akt kreativer Empörung, der für die Gemeinschaft der Schwarzen zur Quelle der Inspiration wurde. Ist das nicht ein perfekter Schluss? Da ist dieser Museumswärter, der zum Führer zu Gallaghers Werk wird – quasi ein stilles Vermächtnis der Harlem Renaissance – und sich vergewissert, dass ich alle Einzelheiten ihrer Arbeit beachte. Gallaghers Kreativität bringt uns zusammen. DeLuxe hat nicht nur «eine Anzeige die Wirkung von zehn entfalten» lassen, sondern über die Begegnung von zweien – einer weissen Schreiberin und eines schwarzen Dichters und Wärters, die über ihr Werk reden – einen einfachen Moment der Synchronität von Kunst und Leben in eine Geschichtslektion verwandelt.[15)]

(Übersetzung: Suzanne Schmidt)

1) Adrienne Rich in ihrem Vorwort zu *Manifesto: Three Essays on How to Change the World,* Ocean Press, Melbourne/New York 2005. (Die Essays sind von Karl Marx, Rosa Luxemburg und Che Guevara.)

2) William Bernbach (1911–1982), amerikanischer Werbefachmann und Texter, Pionier der subtilen, leisen Werbung, die zum Markenzeichen der von ihm gegründeten Agentur Doyle Dane Bernbach Inc. wurde. Das Zitat ist mehrfach im Internet zu finden.

3) Ich habe andernorts über das Auftauchen von Schöpfungsmythen in der Generation, der auch Ellen Gallagher angehört, gesprochen (etwa bei Matthew Barney oder Matthew Ritchie). Vgl. dazu «The Myth is a Muscle», in: *Art Becomes You. Parody,*

Pastiche, and the Politics of Art. Materiality in a Post-material Paradigm, hrsg. v. Henry Rogers, ARTicle Press, London 2005.
4) Von der Sklavenzeit in den Südstaaten geprägte und in den Minstrelshows noch lange danach aufrechterhaltene stereotype Bilder des «Negers». *Step 'n' Fetchit:* Klassische Varietényummer (wörtlich: Komm rein und hol's dir).
5) Alain Locke, «The New Negro», Aufsatz im gleichnamigen, vom Autor herausgegebenen Band, *The New Negro,* Atheneum Press, New York 1986, S. 3.
6) Es ist kein unbedeutender Zufall, dass zwei berühmte Entwicklungsschritte des Kinos, der erste zum Erzählkino, der zweite zum Tonfilm, mit zwei eklatanten Beispielen von Rassismus zusammenfallen. Musste das Erzählkino mit einer Ku-Klux-Klan-Geschichte beginnen? Musste die erste menschliche Stimme im Film jene eines schwarz geschminkten Juden sein, der kniend «Mammy» sang?
7) So auch der Titel einer Essaysammlung von Michelle Cliff: *Claiming an Identity They Taught Me to Despise,* Norton, New York 1980.
8) Claude McKay, «Baptism», in: *The New Negro,* vgl. Anm. 5, S. 133.
9) Charles S. Johnson, «The New Frontage on American Life», in: ebenda, S. 296.
10) Eine Studie über unbehandelte Syphilis bei schwarzen Männern: Seit den 30er Jahren hatten sich 399 Männer beim U.S. Public Health Service zur kostenlosen Behandlung angemeldet. Tatsächlich wurde eine Studie über die Auswirkungen von Syphilis auf den menschlichen Körper durchgeführt. Die Männer erfuhren nie, dass sie Syphilis hatten, man sagte ihnen, sie hätten «schlechtes Blut», und die Behandlung wurde ihnen noch jahrelang verweigert, obwohl man seit 1947 mit Penicillin ein wirksames Mittel zur Verfügung hatte. Als die Studie 1972 bekannt wurde, waren 28 Männer an Syphilis gestorben, 100 weitere waren an damit verbundenen Komplikationen gestorben, mindestens 40 Ehefrauen waren angesteckt worden, 19 Kinder hatten sich bei der Geburt angesteckt.
11) Ellen Gallagher, «1000 Words», *Artforum,* April 2004, S. 128.
12) Zur Ausstellung «eXelento» in der Gagosian Gallery im September 2004 veröffentlichte Ellen Gallagher das Buch *eXelento,* ein eigentliches Kompendium der Figuren in ihrem gleichnamigen Mammutwerk. Wie DELUXE hat auch EXELENTO seinen Titel vom Markennamen der angepriesenen Produkte. Es gibt auch eine Firma Humania.
13) Ellen Gallagher, «1000 Words», *Artforum,* April 2004, S. 128.
14) Marcellous Blount:
www.english.uiuc.edu/maps/poets/m_r/mckay/mustdie.htm
15) Die Perücke ist ein zentrales Motiv und eine wichtige Informationsquelle ihrer Arbeit. In «1000 Words» weist sie darauf hin, dass Perücken in den 30er Jahren auch *transformations* (Verwandlungen) genannt wurden.

ELLEN GALLAGHER, UNTITLED (WATERY ECSTATIC SERIES), 2004, watercolor and cut paper, 16 x 19 3/4" /
OHNE TITEL (SERIE: WÄSSERIG VERZÜCKT), Aquarell und ausgeschnittenes Papier, 41 x 50 cm. (PHOTO: TOM POWEL)

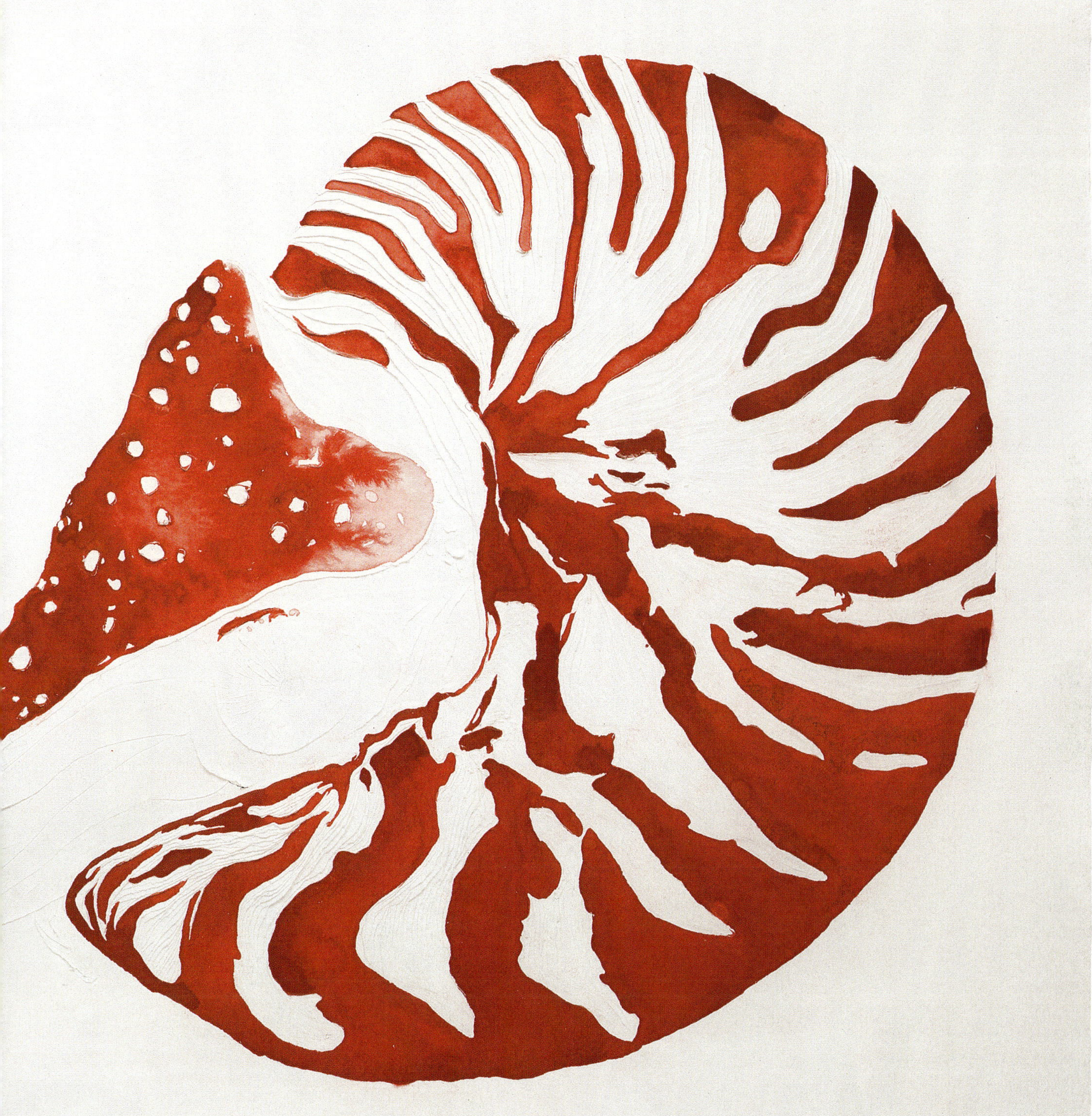

Edition for Parkett

ELLEN GALLAGHER
RUBY DEE, 2005
Two-plate photogravure with aquatint and unique hand-shaped plasticine elements (in three colors) on multilayered laminated paper, framed.
Image size 6 x 4 x 1/8", with frame 9 1/4 x 7 1/4 x 1 1/4".
Produced by Two Palms Press, New York.
Edition of 30/XV, signed and numbered.

Photogravüre, Aquatinta und Knetmasse (dreifarbig, handgeformt), auf mehrschichtigem, laminiertem Papier, gerahmt.
Bildformat: 15,2 x 10,2 x 0,3 cm, mit Rahmen 23,5 x 18,4 x 3,8 cm.
Hergestellt bei Two Palms Press, New York.
Auflage: 30/XV, signiert und nummeriert.

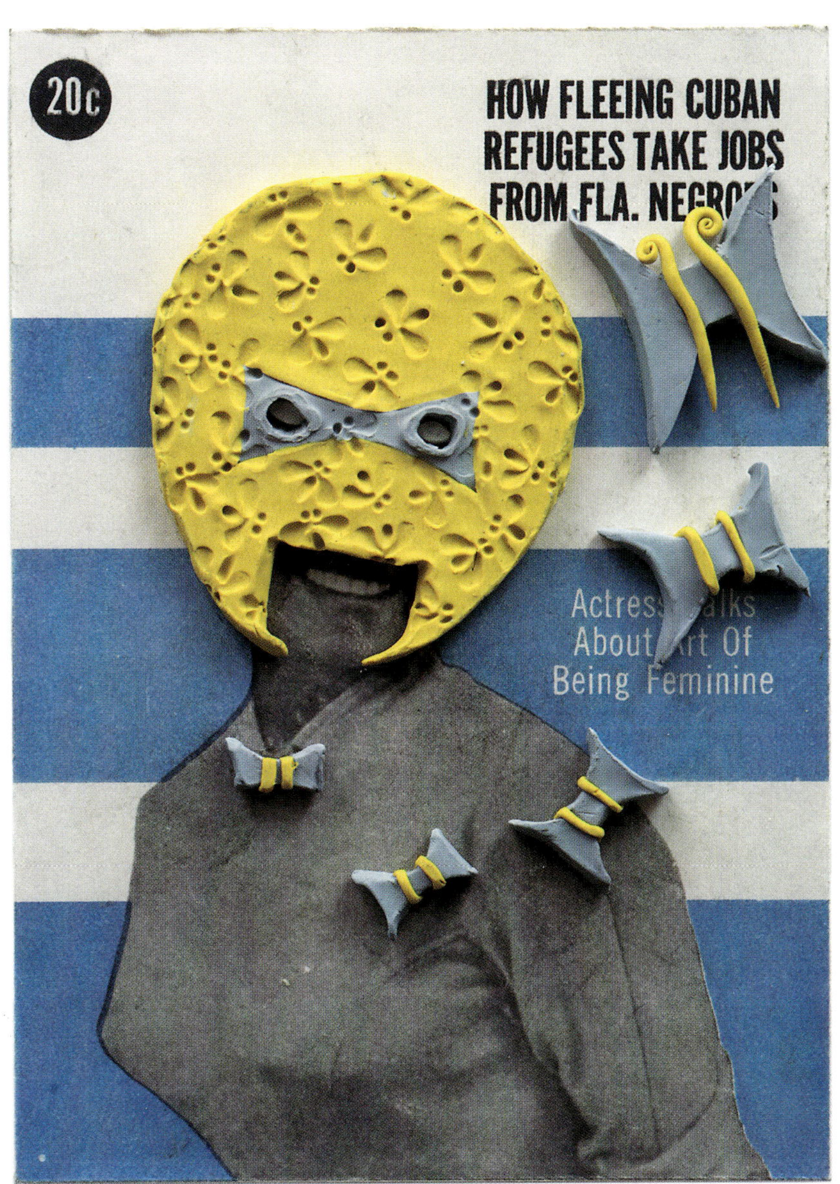
20c
HOW FLEEING CUBAN
REFUGEES TAKE JOBS
FROM FLA. NEGR
Actress alks
About rt Of
Being Feminine

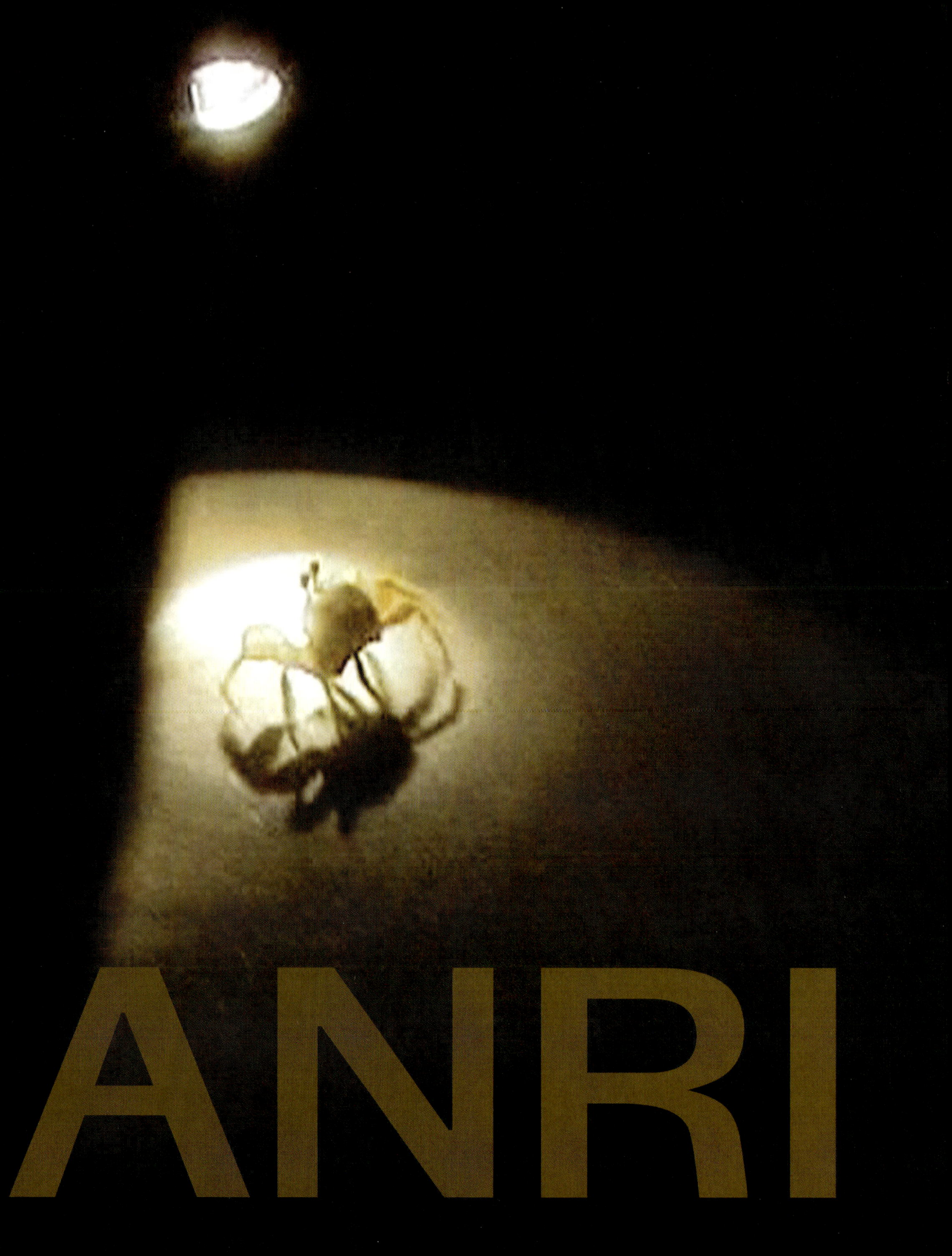

ANRI SALA, GHOST GAMES, 2002, 9 min. 15 sec. color film and sound, stills / GEISTERSPIELE, 9 Min. 15 Sek. Farbfilm mit Ton.

ANRI

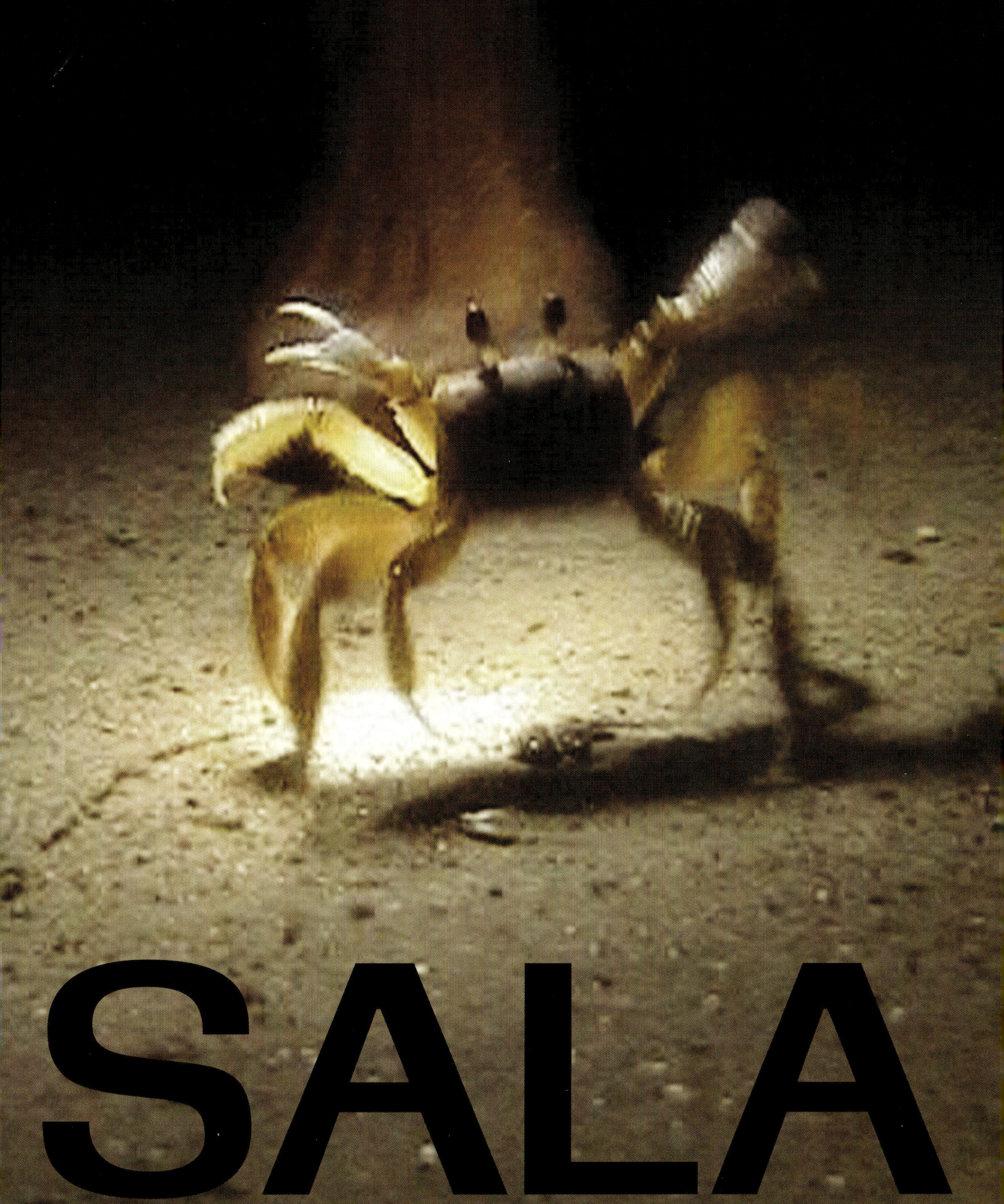
SALA

MARK GODFREY

Missing presences

ON ANRI SALA'S PHOTOGRAPHY

In 1992, when he was only eighteen, Anri Sala took to the streets of his hometown Tirana, camera in hand, to record an explosion of newspapers. Prior to this time, as he would later recall, the media in Albania had been strictly controlled: "The only TV program we had started at 18.00 and ended at 22.00, mainly airing the same news program and fiction film... Everything was so unreal that I remember the only realistic thing was the weather forecast."[1] After the first free elections in 1991, however, the information industry rolled into action, and Sala's street photographs showed vendors hawking countless different publications. Clearly there had been no time for anyone to manufacture plastic or metal racks, let alone establish chains of newsagents. Newspapers were displayed in the simplest way possible, spread across trestle tables, steps, upturned cardboard boxes, or simply laid on the pavement, held down by stones as if they were fabrics in a market.

Sala would often take photographs of the same stall, moments apart, showing different customers selecting their papers. Sometimes he would take successive shots as he moved around a stall, capturing its image from every necessary angle. He took over eighty photographs of the news sellers, rolls and rolls of camera film for stacks and stacks of newspapers. His photographs would seem to fulfill a documentary function, as if he had set out to record a moment in history as comprehensively as possible.

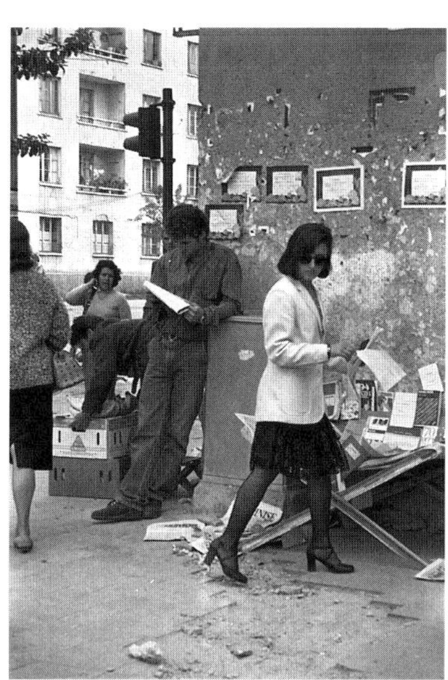

ANRI SALA, A THOUSAND WINDOWS—THE WORLD OF THE INSANE, 2003, images from the artist's book / TAUSEND FENSTER – DIE WELT DER WAHNSINNIGEN, Bilder aus dem Künstlerbuch.

MARK GODFREY is an art historian who teaches at the Slade School of Fine Art, University College, London.

To document and "celebrate" the very existence of news was good news, and this freedom of information much welcomed. Just look at the way the customers are "selecting"—not just grabbing a particular paper out of habit, but poring over what's on offer and gradually making their choices.

In 2003, some eleven years after they were taken, Sala gathered the photographs together in an artist's book, *A Thousand Windows—The World of the Insane* (2003), titled after two of the newspapers that were

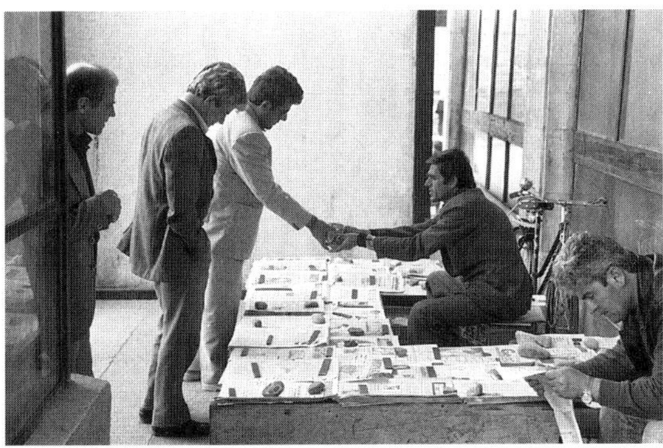

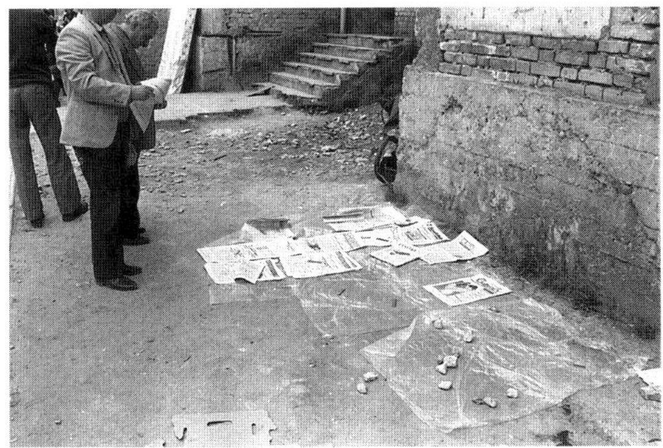

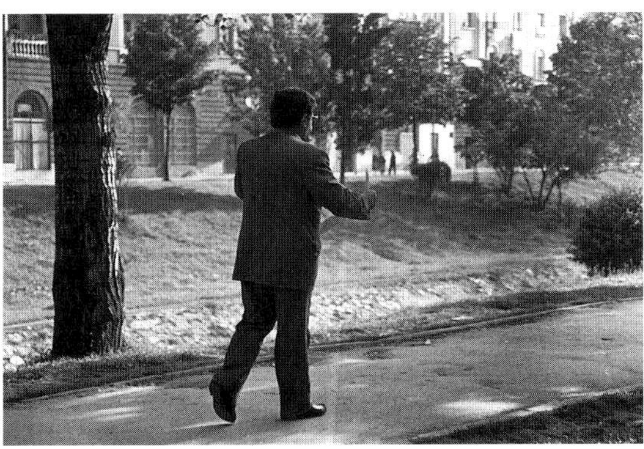

being sold. (The other titles were listed at the back of Sala's book and include *The Democratic Renaissance, The Fatherland, The Republic,* and *Sickle and Hammer.*) When you page through the book, the photographs soon become extremely repetitive, and through repetition their narrative facility slips away. You begin to attend to other features in the images—for instance, to the absence of women from most of the shots. As you go on and on, any celebratory mood is quickly deflated. The number of images begins to feel excessive, too much information producing a paucity of meaning. Or rather, the meaning of the whole enterprise flips one hundred and eighty degrees. The phenomenon of new newspapers no longer seems to be heralded, but represented with extreme scepticism. The deadening repetition of Sala's photographs mimes the deadening effect of too much media. The book tacitly acknowledges that these stalls merely initiate the commodification of information, and silently recognizes that the plethora of publications stands in the way of meaningful future knowledge. Newspapers seemed initially to offer "a thousand windows" onto a new world, but their proliferation engenders "a world of the insane."

Given what Sala has said about his training in a painting department at art school, it seems unlikely that these photographs were conceived as art when they were taken. But retrospectively they must have seemed the ideal material for an artist's book. Perhaps it was Sala's increasing awareness of the history of photo-conceptualism that enabled him to register the interest of these eleven-year-old shots. If they were amateurish, so too were those that Ed Ruscha had used for his photo books, similarly interspersed with blank facing pages. If Sala's project was a parody of photojournalism, so too were certain works by artists such as Robert Smithson and Douglas Huebler.[2] If Sala suggested the amnestic effect of too much information, so too had Gerhard Richter in his deployment of news images in *Atlas* (work in progress since 1962).[3] But these precedents could be irrelevant, for maybe it was Sala's own work that returned him to the 1992 photographs. After all, in 2003, videos like TIME AFTER TIME (2003) and MIXED BEHAVIOUR (2003) continued according to a dynamic that was central to the photo project. Both

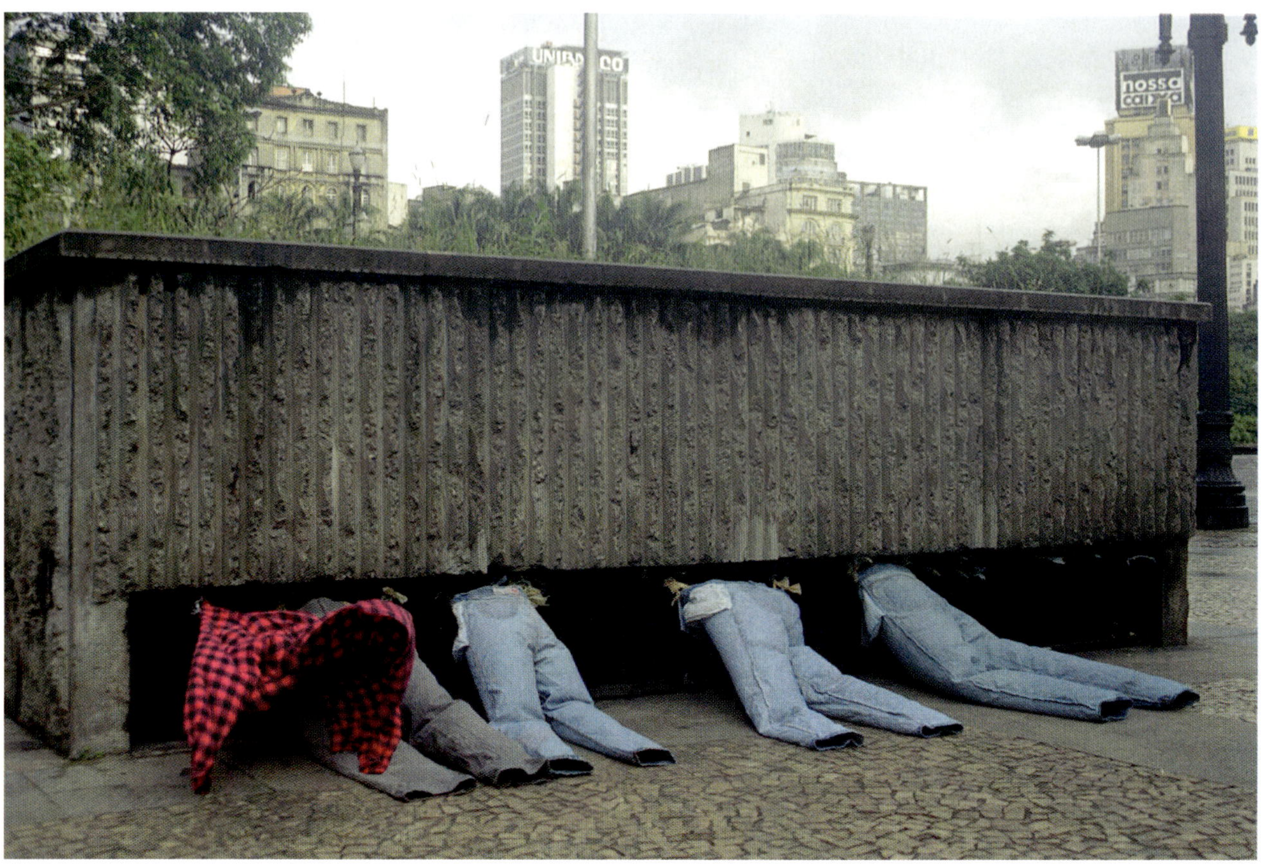

ANRI SALA, UNTITLED, 2002, color photograph, 43 1/4 x 61 3/4" / OHNE TITEL, Farbphotographie, 110 x 157 cm.

bear witness to a desire to record a changing moment in history, but in both, repetitive structures (formed by focusing and editing) cut against the documentary impulse by fragmenting linear time.[4)]

A couple of years before he published *A Thousand Windows,* Sala had retrieved another old photograph and declared it a work. Titled THE GIFT (2000), the work appears to be an enlargement of an old photograph taken of Sala as a child of about eight. The boy fills the foreground beaming with pleasure, his arms stretched out before the camera as if he were about to receive a present. Two other figures are in the background: a grandmother oblivious to the event, and Sala's older sister, clapping at what she watches. But unlike her, we cannot know what the excitement is all about, because the action is behind the camera, the focus of the scene missing. The photograph appears scratched and spotted, and the texture heightens its strangeness, for we cannot tell whether these are marks of excessive handling over the years, or the scratches accumulated while it was ignored at the bottom of some drawer or storage box. While in *A Thousand Windows* photography is deployed in a series, so that the more images there are, the less they tell, here, a single image becomes more enigmatic the more you look at it. You become ever more conscious that what's important lies outside the frame, and that the photograph won't let you know what it is.

One way to resolve the narrative, however, would be to suppose that the camera itself was "the gift" and that in taking the shot a parent was showing a child how the present worked. The instant captured in the image would therefore mark the very origin of Sala's involvement with photographic media. The publication of the image as the frontispiece of Sala's catalogue for his Paris exhibition "Entre Chien et Loup" would seem to endorse this supposition, as would a comment he made in 2001 where he referred to photography as "a gift." ("Now that I'm also working with photography, it feels as if I could have that gift back again, I mean this possibility of negotiating meanings all through one image.")[5] This solution would also explain why THE GIFT became important only retrospectively, not so much because of what the image showed at the time, but because of the activity it could later be seen to have initiated. Sala has spoken of some places as "condensations of time, like time-clouds"[6] but this "photograph" is also a kind of time-cloud, and one which only rained years after it was taken. In this way, THE GIFT is like the reel of film that Sala found of his mother speaking at a Communist rally that initiated the work INTERVISTA (1998) for which he became well known.

When INTERVISTA began to gain recognition in the circuits of the art world in the late nineties, photography itself no longer seemed crucial to Sala's project—and yet his oeuvre is scattered with pictures. For the most part, they work like THE GIFT: singular, compressed, and enigmatic. It's not the information they contain, but the lack of it that makes them perplexing. Take for example 31–131° (2002), which shows a site where something seems to have taken place, something that has left a trace in the flatten-

ANRI SALA, HOUSE WITH HORIZON, 2002, color photograph, 43 1/4 x 61 3/4" /
HAUS MIT HORIZONT, Farbphotographie, 110 x 157 cm.

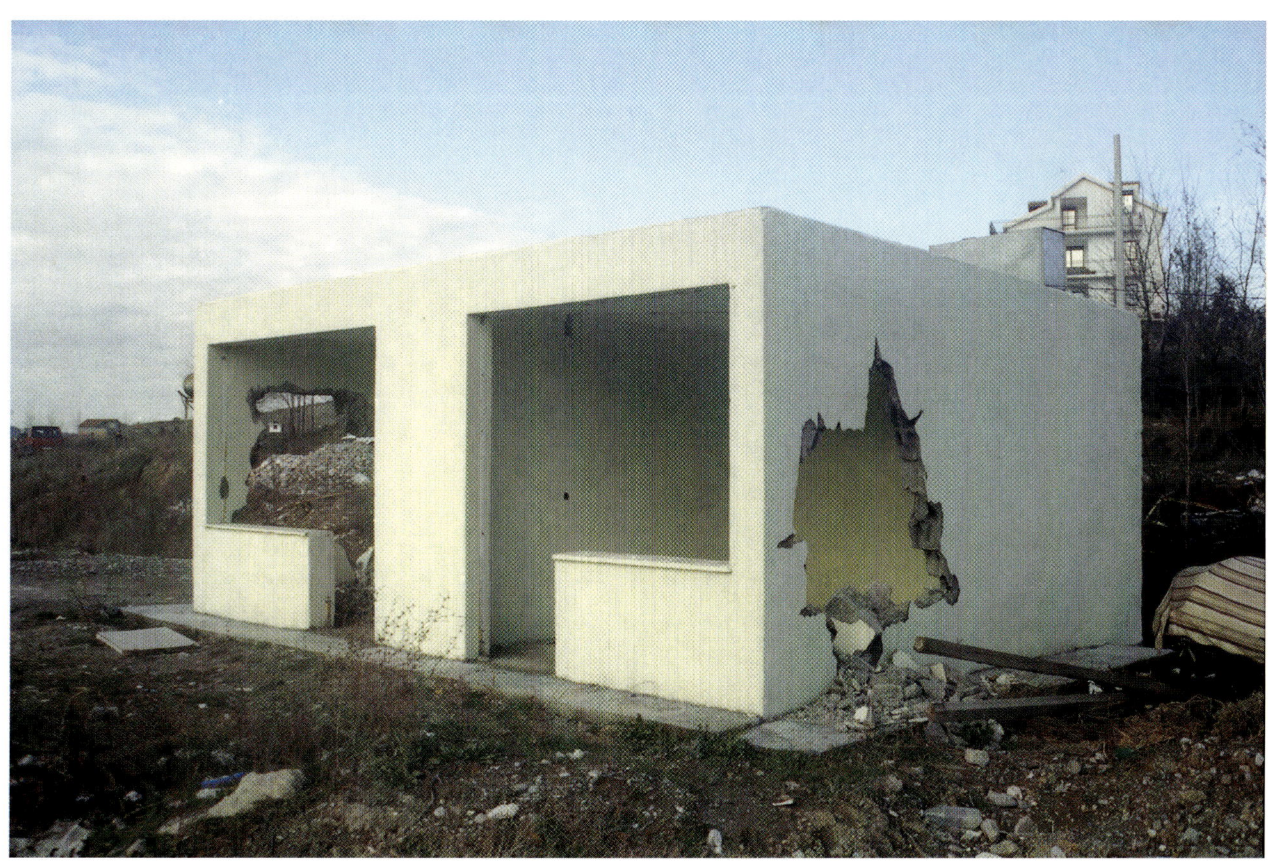

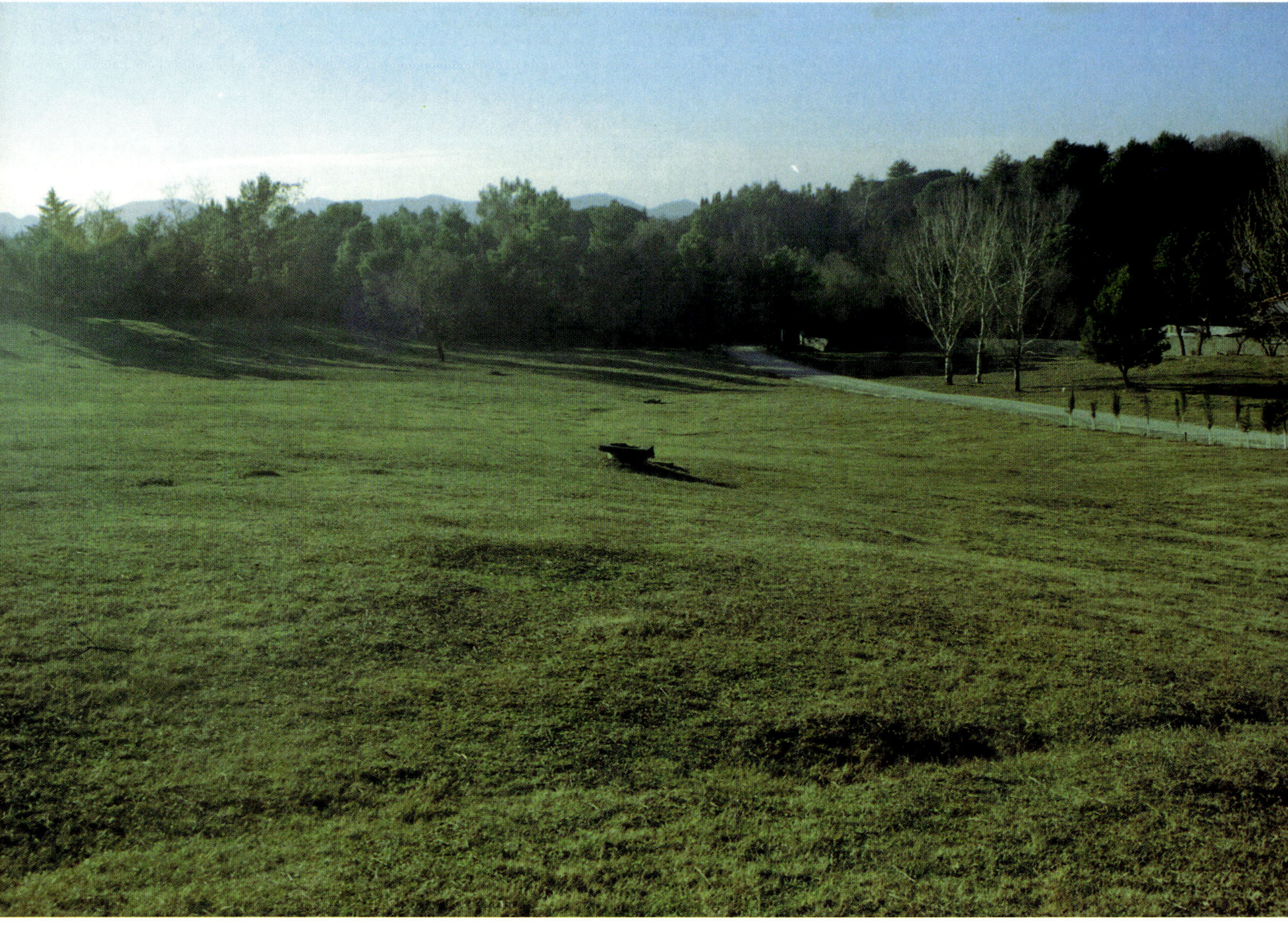

ANRI SALA, LANDSCAPE WITH UNDERGROUND, 2002, color photograph, 43 1/4 x 61 3/4" / LANDSCHAFT MIT UNTERGRUND, Farbphotographie, 110 x 157 cm.

ing of a clearing. The title indicates exactly where this site is (South Japan), but its precision only serves to underscore the absence of information in the image itself. It seems a belated photograph, one that has failed to record what "has been." LANDSCAPE WITH UNDERGROUND (2002), meanwhile, appears to picture a site were something might happen. Shot on a calm, sunny day, it shows a field pierced by an opening that, we assume from the title, is a tunnel entrance. But this photograph seems to have come too soon—nothing is emerging from below.

Sala has commented that what interests him about photography is "the relation between the *cadre* and *hors cadre*"[7)]—what is inside and outside the frame. While a video camera can move around to show the fullness of a scene, a camera necessarily compresses a scene into its view. In 31–131° and LANDSCAPE WITH UNDERGROUND, what is missing is not so much a visual piece of information beyond the frame of the image, but an event beyond the time of its exposure. However, it is the controlled elimination of surrounding information that powers the poetry of WE HAVE OTHER CONCERNS (2001). The image pictures two young men on the beach, both with a ball at their feet, a pretty mundane sight at first. Between them, right at the center of the photograph, are two children, closer to the shore, playing together. Once you notice them, your eyes return to the outer parts of the image and you begin to realize what's odd: unlike the younger pair, the men face away from each other, not passing a ball back and forth, as one would expect. Probably, both were simply involved in different games, playing with people behind the camera, but the way Sala frames the image means that they are joined only by repetition, both seeming utterly private, both appearing to have "other concerns" than the game. Sala has commented that the title could be thought about in two ways: either it suggests that these men want to travel to a place outside the frame, namely to Italy, across the sea from this Albanian beach, a place directly in front of the camera but way beyond its view; or the title emphasizes their absent-minded contentedness in Albania. Though fellow Europeans might presume they are desperate to leave their country, they have other concerns.

HOUSE WITH HORIZON (2002) is another image characterized by doubling. A half-finished, yet already ruined house made up of two identical sections is photographed at an oblique angle. Each section only contains a single room and has a large opening at the front, a space where you assume a door and window were planned. Oddly, there is no interconnecting door, but odder still, the outer side walls of both halves are ruptured, yet in such a way that the force managed not to penetrate the inside walls. Far from disturbing the symmetry of the structure, the holes emphasize it. If we wonder first what caused its destruction, what becomes more puzzling, eventually, is how the structure was supposed to function had it not been damaged. Nothing that might have been in Sala's peripheral vision when he made the image, would necessarily answer these questions. We do not miss what is physically exterior to the shot, yet the absence of information is palpable. Sala has spoken of how throughout his work "the missing thing becomes so obvious that it becomes like a presence,"[8] and this observation could characterize the operation of an even more haunting photograph from 2002, this one taken in São Paulo. UNTITLED (2002), like HOUSE WITH HORIZON, simply records a situation Sala chanced upon. Four pairs of jeans and a coat are seen billowing in front of the exterior vent of a building, the hot air drying them out. What's "missing" here are the owners of the clothes who have discovered this ingenious way around laundromat costs. The photograph manages to represent homelessness without recourse to the "expressionist liberalism of the find-a-bum school of concerned photography" that Allan Sekula once criticized,[9] and it does so in a way that is as resourceful and economical as the activity it captures. The image comes to represent both the tendency to blank out from sight the people we see daily on the street, and the possible consequence of such blindness, for by evoking other photographs of bloated bodies in devastated war zones, it causes us to think about so many needless deaths.

The inflated empty volumes in UNTITLED recall Gabriel Orozco's photograph TWO TRASH CANS UP (1998), but where Orozco's photograph shows a sculptural situation he set up, Sala just came by his scene. Set-up photographs are rare for Sala, but the exception is NO BARRAGÁN NO CRY (2002), which shows a white horse stuck on top of a metal cylinder on an otherwise empty rooftop. This was a carefully planned image, and Sala designed the cylinder especially to prevent any discomfort to the animal during the shoot. Sala made the photograph on top of a building in Guadalajara during a show of his work in the artist's space OPA which occupied one of its top floors, but the set-up was inspired by an earlier event during this trip to Mexico. Before he traveled, Sala had consulted a website showing simulated views around the Barragán House at Calle Ramírez in Mexico City because he planned to visit the building. Barragán was famously fascinated by horses and the image on the website that struck Sala showed an equine sculpture on a plinth against a pink wall. But when Sala arrived at Calle Ramírez, the sculpture was missing. It transpired that the horse had disappeared during the house's restoration. Few visitors would have noticed this, yet for Sala it was a dramatic absence. Looking at his rooftop photograph in the light of all this, we could suppose that Sala was staging a bizarre return of the missing animal, as if the plinth in Mexico City had fired the horse into the stratosphere so that it landed hundreds of miles away, transforming from wood to flesh en route. Sala told Hans-Ulrich Obrist that a photograph can be a "compression of a story,"[10)] and this is certainly the case here, yet the photograph is no less bizarre if we do not know the narrative just recounted. It doesn't conform to any kind of image to which we are accustomed: it's neither an image of a building, nor of the view from a roof; nor is it a typical shot of a horse which would tend to show the animal in motion (Barragán's wooden horse was mid-gallop). Benjamin Buchloh wrote that "hardly an image could proclaim the final loss of the natural more tragically, more comically"[11)] than Orozco's photograph PERRO EN TLAPAN (1992), which shows a dog gazing out from a kind of concrete plinth. Sala's photograph could also proclaim this loss, so removed is the horse from its environment, but its obvious set-up quality produces more questions than answers. The more we look at the photograph, the greater its enigma—like the animal suspended in its center.

In 2004, Sala returned to making photographs in series, taking eight images of moths in a room in Dakar, Senegal. The creatures line the junction of two right-angled walls and the ceiling, marking out the straight lines of the architecture and breaking them up at once. Even in day time (when the photographs were taken), the insects go to these joints and corners, presumably because they are the safest places in the room, but the camera has searched them out, repetitively disturbing their peace. The background is bleached out by the flash, but the moths remain like a residue of the night, irregular stains against the white ground. When Europeans first took photographs in such places and brought images of the "dark continent" back home, they hoped photography would illuminate the worlds they saw and to which they returned. Sala's images present a darker view of illumination. Photography here hunts out its subjects, chasing them into corners. Yet photography remains imprecise and fumbling—nothing much can be told about the moths, no details on their wings, no delicate tentacles. All the camera sees are black marks against the whiteness.

1) Massimiliano Gioni and Michele Robecchi, "Anri Sala: Unfinished Histories," *Flash Art*, July–September 2001, p. 107.
2) Jeff Wall, "'Marks of Indifference': Aspects of Photography In, Or As, Conceptual Art" in Ann Goldstein and Anne Rorimer (eds.), *Reconsidering the Object of Art 1965–1975* (Los Angeles: Museum of Contemporary Art, 1995).
3) Benjamin Buchloh, "Gerhard Richter's *Atlas*: The Anomic Archive," *October* 88, Spring 1999, pp. 117–145.
4) I discuss these works in my article "Anri Sala," *Art Monthly*, July–August 2004, pp. 18–20.
5) Massimiliano Gioni and Michele Robecchi, op. cit., p. 107.
6) Gerald Matt, "An Interview with Anri Sala," *Anri Sala* (Vienna: Kunsthalle, 2003), p. 52.
7) Ibid., p. 75.
8) Conversation with the author at Tate Modern, November 2004.
9) Allan Sekula, "Dismantling Modernism, Reinventing Documentary (Notes on the Politics of Representation)" in *Dismal Science: Photo Works 1972–1996* (Normal: University Galleries, Illinois State University, 1999), p. 126.
10) Hans Ulrich Obrist, *Interviews*, vol. 1 (Milan: Charta, 2003), p. 831.
11) Benjamin Buchloh, "Cosmic Reification: Gabriel Orozco's Photographs" in *Gabriel Orozco* (London: Serpentine Gallery, 2004), p. 88.

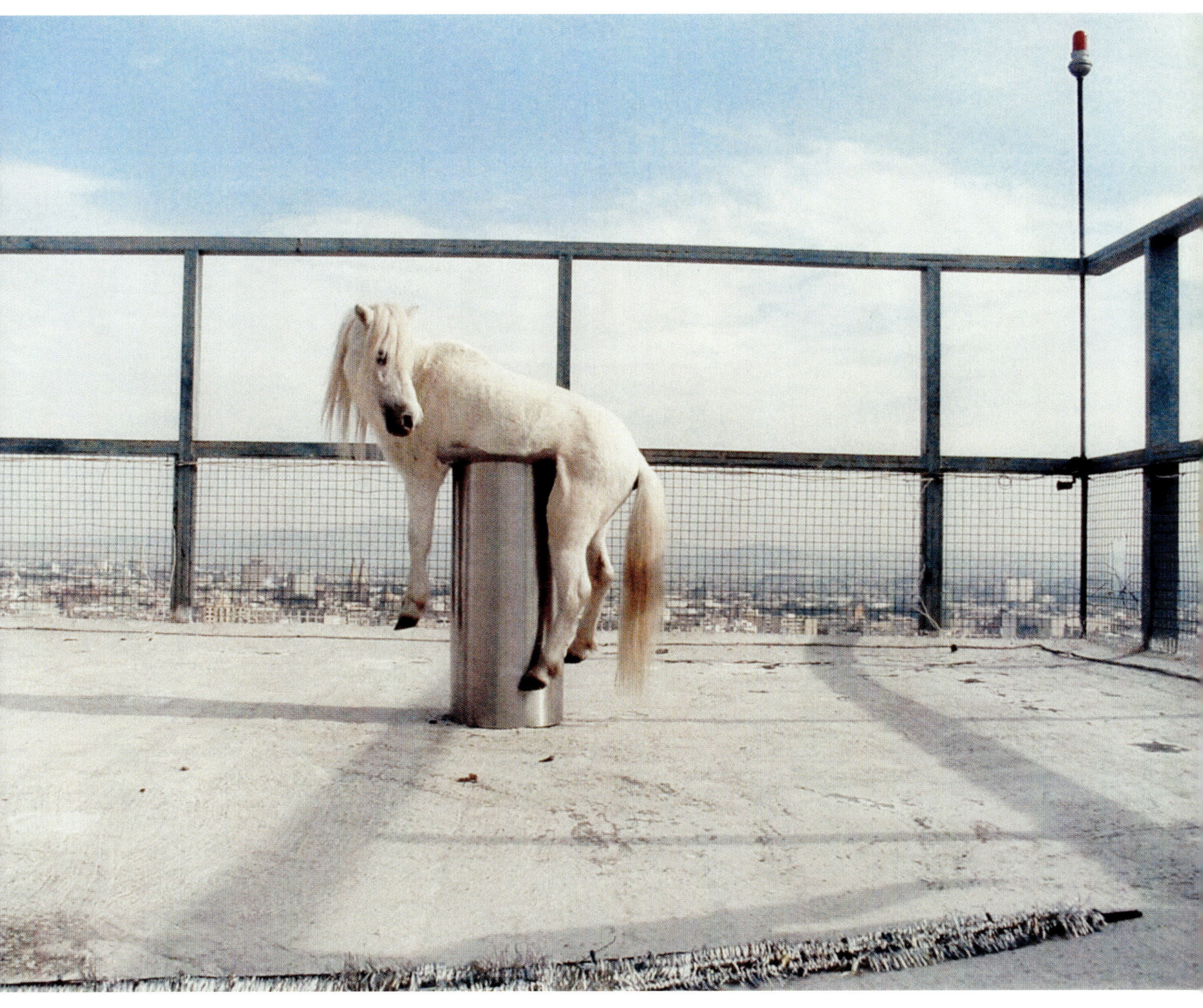

ANRI SALA, NO BARRAGÁN NO CRY, 2002, color photograph, 24 3/4 x 30 3/4 x 1 1/8" / Farbphotographie, 63 x 78 x 3 cm.

MARK GODFREY

Abwesend präsent

ÜBER DIE PHOTOGRAPHIE ANRI SALAS

Im Jahr 1992 zog es den erst achtzehnjährigen Anri Sala hinaus auf die Strassen seiner Heimatstadt Tirana, um mit der Kamera in der Hand die explosionsartige Entwicklung des Zeitungswesens zu dokumentieren. Bis zu diesem Zeitpunkt hatten die Medien in Albanien, wie er sich später erinnern sollte, einer strengen Kontrolle unterlegen: «Das damals einzige Fernsehprogramm begann um 18 Uhr und endete um 22 Uhr. Es zeigte eigentlich immer dieselbe Nachrichtensendung und denselben Spielfilm... Alles war dermassen unwirklich – das einzig Realistische, dessen ich mich entsinne, war die Wettervorhersage.»[1] Nach den ersten freien Wahlen, 1991, setzte sich jedoch die Informationsmaschinerie in Bewegung und Salas Strassenphotos zeigten Verkäufer, die unzählige Blätter feilboten. Offensichtlich hatte niemand Zeit gehabt, Ständer aus Plastik oder Metall herzustellen, geschweige denn ein Netz von Zeitungshändlern aufzubauen. Die Zeitungen wurden auf denkbar einfache Art und Weise ausgelegt, auf Stelltischen, Treppenstufen und umgedrehten Kartons ausgebreitet, oder einfach aufs Pflaster gelegt und mit Steinen beschwert wie Stoffe auf einem Markt.

MARK GODFREY ist Kunsthistoriker und lehrt an der Slade School of Fine Art, University College, London.

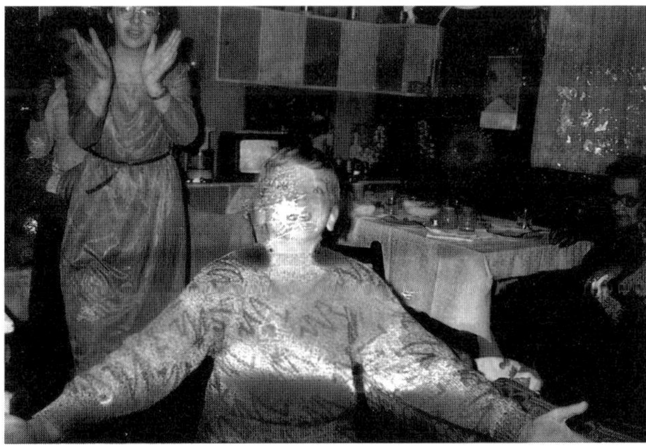

Sala machte oft in kurzen zeitlichen Abständen Aufnahmen desselben Verkaufsstandes, auf denen verschiedene Kunden beim Aussuchen ihrer Zeitung zu sehen sind. Manchmal photographierte er auch in schneller Folge, während er um einen Stand herumging, und fing so dessen Bild aus jedem wichtigen Blickwinkel ein. Er machte mehr als achtzig Aufnahmen von den Zeitungsverkäufern, verbrauchte eine Rolle Film nach der anderen für die nicht enden wollenden Zeitungsstapel. Seine Photos schienen eine dokumentarische Funktion zu erfüllen, als hätte er sich vorgenommen, einen bestimmten Augenblick der Zeitgeschichte möglichst umfassend festzuhalten; als gälte es, zu dokumentieren und zu feiern, da das

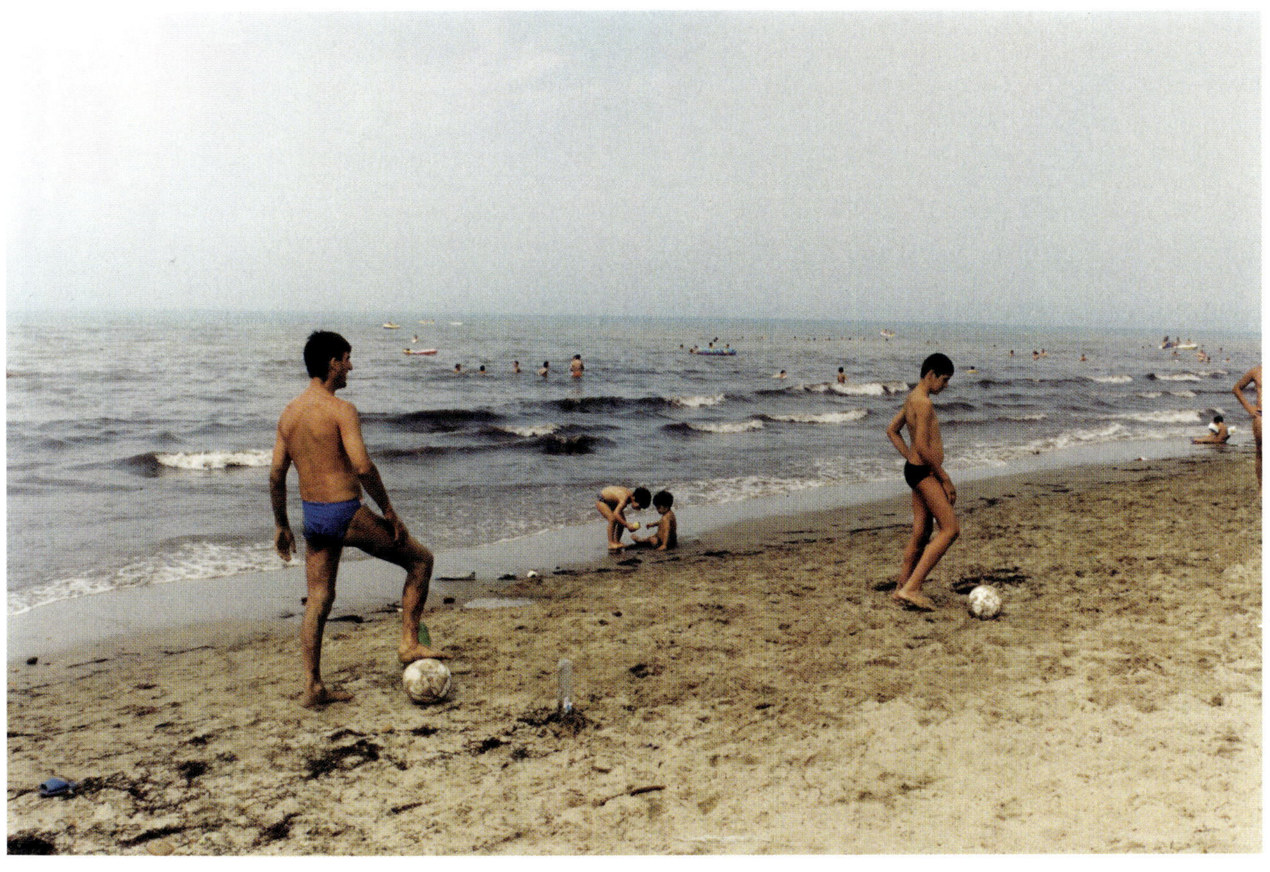

On the left / Links:
ANRI SALA, THE GIFT, 2000, black-and-white photograph on baryte paper, 19 11/16 x 23 5/8" / Schwarzweissphotographie auf Baryt-Papier, 50 x 60 cm.

ANRI SALA, WE HAVE OTHER CONCERNS, 2001, color photograph mounted on aluminum, 31 1/2 x 47 1/4" / WIR SIND MIT ANDEREN DINGEN BESCHÄFTIGT, Farbphotographie auf Aluminium aufgezogen, 80 x 120 cm.

schiere Vorhandensein von Nachrichten eine gute Nachricht war und diese Informationsfreiheit begeistert begrüsst wurde. Man achte bloss darauf, wie die Kunden ihre Zeitung aussuchen: Sie greifen nicht einfach gewohnheitsmässig nach einem Blatt, sondern studieren das Angebot und entscheiden sich erst nach reiflicher Überlegung.

Im Jahr 2003, rund elf Jahre, nachdem sie entstanden waren, fasste Sala die Photos zu einem Künstlerbuch zusammen, mit dem Titel *A Thousand Windows – The World of the Insane*, so benannt nach zwei der zum Kauf angebotenen Blätter. (Eine Auflistung der übrigen Zeitungstitel, darunter *Die Demokratische Renaissance, Das Vaterland, Die Republik* sowie *Sichel und Hammer*, fand sich auf der Rückseite des Bandes.) Beim Durchblättern wirken die Aufnahmen bald extrem repetitiv, und durch die Wiederholung verflüchtigt sich das narrativ Eingängige der Bilder. Man beginnt anderen Besonderheiten Beachtung zu schenken, etwa der Tatsache, dass auf den meisten Bildern keine Frauen vorkommen. Blättert man weiter, so weicht alsbald jede Festtagsstimmung. Die schiere Zahl der Bilder wirkt allmählich exzessiv; zu viel Information bringt zu wenig Sinn hervor. Oder besser gesagt: Der Sinn des ganzen Unterfangens dreht sich um 180 Grad. Das Phänomen der neuen Zeitungen wird hier, so scheint es, nicht mehr freudig begrüsst, sondern mit äusserster Skepsis dargestellt.

Die abstumpfende Wiederholung in Salas Photographien widerspiegelt die abstumpfende Wirkung der Medienflut. Der Photoband räumt stillschweigend ein, dass diese Zeitungsstände lediglich die Degradierung der Information zur Ware einläuten und dass die Fülle von Publikationen einer sinnvollen Informiertheit in Zukunft tatsächlich im Wege stehen wird. Die Zeitungen schienen zunächst Tausend Fenster auf eine neue Welt zu öffnen, doch ihre Flut erzeugt eine Welt der Wahnsinnigen.

In Anbetracht dessen, was Sala über sein Malstudium an der Kunstakademie gesagt hat, scheint es eher unwahrscheinlich, dass diese Photos zum Zeitpunkt ihrer Aufnahme als Kunst gedacht waren. Im Rückblick müssen sie ihm jedoch als idealer Stoff für ein Künstlerbuch erschienen sein. Vielleicht war es seine zunehmende Vertrautheit mit der Geschichte der konzeptuellen Photokunst, die es Sala ermöglichte, die Bedeutung dieser elf Jahre alten Aufnahmen zu erfassen. Waren es auch Amateurphotos, so gilt dasselbe für die Aufnahmen, die Ed Ruscha für seine Photobüchlein verwendet hat, in denen ebenfalls die jeweils den Photos gegenüberliegenden Seiten leer gelassen sind. Falls Sala eine Parodie der Photoreportage im Sinn hatte, so gilt dasselbe für gewisse Arbeiten eines Robert Smithson oder Douglas Huebler.[2] Und wenn er auf den Gedächtnisschwund anspielte, den ein Zuviel an Information bewirkt, so hatte Gerhard Richter mit seiner Verwendung von Nachrichtenbildern in *Atlas* dies auch getan.[3] Es ist aber auch denkbar, dass diese Vorläufer überhaupt keine Rolle spielten, denn möglicherweise war es die eigene Arbeit, die Sala auf die Photos aus dem Jahr 1992 zurückkommen liess. Immerhin sind die Videoarbeiten TIME AFTER TIME (Ein ums andere Mal) und MIXED BEHAVIOUR (Gemischtes Verhalten), beide aus dem Jahr 2003, noch derselben Dynamik verpflichtet, die das Photoprojekt bestimmt hatte. Beide zeugen von einem Bedürfnis, einen Wendepunkt in der Geschichte festzuhalten, doch bei beiden konterkarieren die (durch Einstellung und Schnitt) erzeugten repetitiven Strukturen den dokumentarischen Impuls, indem sie den linearen zeitlichen Ablauf aufbrechen.[4]

Einige Jahre vor der Veröffentlichung des Photobandes *A Thousand Windows* hatte Sala ein anderes altes Photo wieder entdeckt und zum Kunstwerk erklärt. Die Arbeit mit dem Titel THE GIFT (Das Geschenk, 2000) wirkt wie die Vergrösserung eines alten Photos, das Sala im Alter von etwa acht Jahren zeigt. Der freudestrahlende Junge nimmt den ganzen Vordergrund ein und breitet vor der Kamera die Arme aus, als wolle er gleich ein Geschenk entgegennehmen. Im Hintergrund sind zwei weitere Personen zu sehen, eine Grossmutter, die vom Geschehen nichts mitbekommt, und Salas ältere Schwester, die beklatscht, was sie sieht. Im Unterschied zu ihr wissen wir jedoch nicht, was der Anlass für die Aufregung ist, weil sich alles hinter der Kamera abspielt, das Zentrum des Geschehens also gar nicht im Bild ist. Das Photo wirkt zerkratzt und fleckig, und dieser Zustand lässt es noch merkwürdiger erscheinen, wissen wir doch nicht, ob es sich um Spuren eines allzu häufigen Zur-Hand-Nehmens im Lauf der Jahre handelt, oder aber um Kratzer, die entstanden sind, während das Photo zuunterst in einer Schublade oder einer Schachtel vergessen war. Tritt in *A Thousand Windows* die Photographie in einer Serie auf, in welcher die Bilder immer weniger aussagen, je zahlreicher sie werden, so wird dagegen hier das Einzelbild immer rätselhafter, je länger man es anschaut. Allmählich begreift man, dass das, worauf es ankommt, ausserhalb des Bildausschnitts angesiedelt ist, und dass das Photo nicht verraten will, was es ist.

Ein möglicher Schlüssel zur Erklärung des Handlungszusammenhangs wäre allerdings die Annahme, dass die Kamera selbst «das Geschenk» war und dass ein Elternteil dem Kind mit der Aufnahme zeigen wollte, wie das Geschenk funktioniert. Der festgehaltene Augenblick würde in diesem Fall den eigentlichen Beginn von Salas Beschäftigung mit dem Medium Photographie markieren. Die Tatsache, dass das Bild auf dem Frontispiz des Katalogs zu Salas Ausstellung «Entre Chien et Loup» in Paris abgebildet wurde, scheint ebenso für diese Annahme zu sprechen wie eine Aussage Salas aus dem Jahr 2001, im Zuge derer er die Photographie als «Geschenk» bezeichnete. («Jetzt, da ich auch photographisch arbeite, ist es, als bekäme ich diese Gabe noch einmal geschenkt, ich meine die Möglichkeit, mit einem einzigen Bild Inhalte zu vermitteln.»)[5] Dies würde auch erklären, weshalb THE GIFT erst nachträglich wichtig wurde: nicht auf Grund dessen, was das Bild zeigte, sondern auf Grund der Tätigkeit, die es – im Rückblick – ausgelöst hatte. Sala hat von manchen Orten als «Zeitkondensaten, gleichsam Zeitwolken»[6] gesprochen; auch diese Photographie bildet eine Art Zeitwolke, und zwar eine, aus der es erst Jahre nach ihrer Aufnahme zu regnen begann. In diesem Sinn gleicht THE GIFT der von Sala aufgestöberten Filmrolle mit Aufnahmen seiner Mutter während der Ansprache vor einer kommunistischen Versammlung; diese bildete den Ausgangspunkt der Arbeit INTERVISTA (1998), durch die Sala einem breiteren Kreis bekannt wurde.

Gegen Ende der 90er Jahre, als INTERVISTA in der Kunstszene allmählich Anerkennung fand, war die Photographie als solche für Salas Arbeit nicht mehr zentral, dennoch ist sein Schaffen gespickt mit Bildern. Meist funktionieren sie ähnlich wie THE GIFT; sie sind etwas Besonderes, weisen eine extreme Verdichtung auf und wirken rätselhaft. Es ist nicht die in ihnen enthaltene Information, die Verwirrung auslöst, sondern der Mangel an Information. Nehmen wir zum Beispiel die Arbeit 31–131° (2002). Sie zeigt einen Ort, an dem etwas stattgefunden haben muss, irgendetwas, das in einer Lichtung eine Spur, einen Abdruck hinterlassen hat. Der Titel gibt zwar genau an, wo sich dieser Ort befindet, nämlich in Südjapan, doch diese Genauigkeit unterstreicht nur den Mangel an Information im Bild selbst. Es wirkt, als sei das Photo zu spät geknipst worden, als sei versäumt worden, festzuhalten, was «gewesen ist». Das Photo LANDSCAPE WITH UNDERGROUND (Landschaft mit Untergrund, 2002) wiederum scheint einen Ort zu zeigen, an dem etwas stattfinden könnte. Aufgenommen an einem ruhigen, sonnigen Tag zeigt es ein Feld, in dem sich eine Öffnung auftut; dabei handelt es sich wohl, wie der Titel nahe legt, um einen Tunneleingang. Dieses Photo scheint jedoch zu früh gemacht worden zu sein: Es kommt nichts von unten herauf.

Nach eigener Aussage interessiert Sala an der Photographie «das Verhältnis zwischen *cadre* und *hors cadre*»[7]: dem, was sich innerhalb, und dem, was sich ausserhalb des Bildausschnitts befindet. Während eine Videokamera beweglich ist und den gesamten Schauplatz erfassen kann, wird dieser von der Photokamera zwangsläufig im Rahmen ihres Blickwinkels zusammengedrängt. Was bei 31–131° und LANDSCAPE WITH UNDERGROUND fehlt, ist weniger eine visuelle Information, die sich ausserhalb des Bildausschnitts befände, als vielmehr ein Ereignis, das nicht in den Belichtungszeitraum fiel. Wie dem auch sei, WE HAVE OTHER CONCERNS (Wir sind mit anderen Dingen beschäftigt, 2001) verdankt seine poetische Ausstrahlung exakt dieser gezielten Ausklammerung ergänzender Informationen. Das Bild zeigt zwei junge Männer am Strand, jeweils mit einem Ball zu ihren Füssen – ein ganz alltäglicher Anblick, wie es zunächst scheint. Genau in der Bildmitte zwischen den beiden Männern, aber etwas näher am Wasser, spielen zwei Kinder miteinander. Hat man sie einmal bemerkt, wandert der Blick wieder zurück gegen die Bildränder, und es geht einem allmählich auf, was an dem Bild merkwürdig ist: Im Unterschied zu den beiden Kindern stehen die beiden Männer voneinander abgewandt, ohne sich, wie zu erwarten wäre, gegenseitig den Ball zuzuspielen. Vermutlich waren beide einfach an einem je anderen Spiel mit Mitspielern ausserhalb des Bildausschnitts beteiligt. Der von Sala gewählte Ausschnitt bewirkt jedoch, dass das Verbindende zwischen den Männern lediglich in einer Wie-

ANRI SALA, 31–131°, 2002, black-and-white photograph on baryte paper, 43 5/16 x 63" / Schwarzweissphotographie auf Baryt-Papier, 110 x 160 cm.

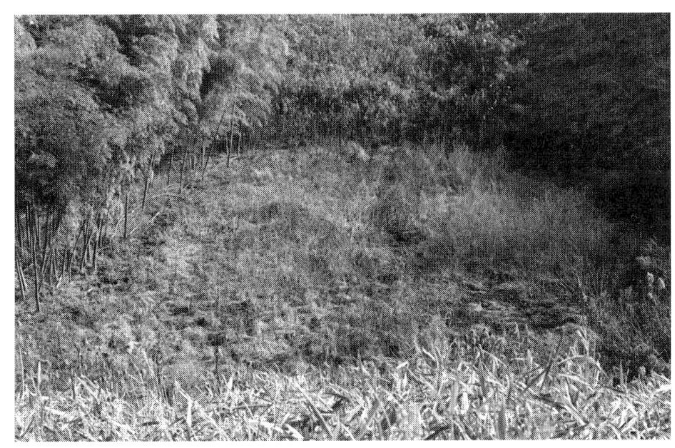

derholung besteht, sind doch beide scheinbar ganz für sich und «mit ganz anderen Dingen beschäftigt» als dem Spiel. Laut Sala kann der Titel auf zweierlei Art verstanden werden: entweder als Hinweis auf die Sehnsucht der Männer, an einen Ort zu gelangen, der ebenfalls, aber auf andere Weise ausserhalb des vorgegebenen Rahmens liegt, nämlich an das diesem albanischen Strand gegenüberliegende Ufer, nach Italien, das zwar im Blickwinkel der Kamera, aber ausserhalb ihrer Sichtweite liegt; oder aber als Hinweis auf ihre gedankenverlorene Zufriedenheit in Albanien. Auch wenn andere Europäer ihnen unterstellen, dass sie ihre Heimat lieber heute als morgen verlassen wollen, sind sie mit ganz anderen Dingen beschäftigt.

HOUSE WITH HORIZON (Haus mit Horizont, 2002) ist ein weiteres Bild, das sich durch eine Verdoppelung auszeichnet. Ein halb fertiges, aber bereits verfallenes Gebäude, das aus zwei identischen Hälften besteht, wurde über Eck aufgenommen. Jeder Teil weist lediglich einen einzigen Raum und an der Vorderseite eine grosse Öffnung auf, die wohl einst für Tür und Fenster gedacht war. Seltsamerweise gibt es keine Verbindungstür, noch seltsamer aber ist, dass die äusseren Seitenmauern auf beiden Seiten aufgebrochen sind, jedoch so, dass der Wucht der Einwirkung zum Trotz ein Durchbruch der Innenwände vermieden wurde. Die Offnungen stören keineswegs die Symmetrie des Gebäudes, sondern unterstreichen diese sogar noch. Wundern wir uns zunächst, was diese Zerstörung herbeigeführt haben mag, so drängt sich alsbald die noch verwirrendere Frage auf, wie das Bauwerk überhaupt hätte funktionieren sollen, wenn es nicht beschädigt worden wäre. Was auch immer sich während der Aufnahme in Salas peripherem Blickfeld befunden haben mag, würde wohl keine Antwort auf diese Fragen liefern. Was hier fehlt, ist nichts, was physisch ausserhalb des Bildausschnitts liegt, und doch ist der Mangel an Information offenkundig. Sala hat davon gesprochen, wie in seinem Werk immer wieder «das Abwesende derart ins Auge fällt, dass es zu einer spürbaren Präsenz wird»,[8)] und diese Formulierung trifft auch auf die Wirkungsweise einer vielleicht noch beklemmenderen Photographie zu, die 2002 in São Paolo entstand. UNTITLED (2002) dokumentiert wie HOUSE WITH HORIZON einfach eine Situation, auf die Sala zufällig stiess. Vier Paar Jeans und ein Mantel bauschen sich vor einem Lüftungsabzug an der Aussenseite eines Gebäudes, wo sie durch die ausströmende heisse Luft getrocknet werden. Was hier «abwesend ist», sind die Besitzer der Kleider, die diese einfallsreiche Methode zur Einsparung der Kosten für den Waschsalon erfunden haben. Dem Bild gelingt es, Obdachlosigkeit darzustellen, ohne Zuflucht zu nehmen zum «expressionistischen Liberalismus des ‹Such-dir-einen-Penner›-Zweigs der engagierten Photographie», gegen die Allan Sekula einst zu Felde gezogen war,[9)] und es tut dies auf eine Weise, die genauso einfallsreich und ökonomisch ist wie die Aktivität, die es einfängt. Das Bild steht am Ende gleichzeitig für unsere Neigung, die Augen vor den Menschen zu verschliessen, die wir täglich auf der Strasse sehen, und für die mögliche Folge einer solchen Blindheit; denn indem es an andere Photos von aufgeblähten Leichen in verwüsteten Kriegsgebieten erinnert, bringt es uns dazu, über so viel sinnloses Sterben nachzudenken.

Die aufgeblähten leeren Hüllen in UNTITLED erinnern auch an Gabriel Orozcos Photo TWO TRASH CANS UP (Zwei Mülltonnen höher, 1998), doch während Orozcos Aufnahme eine eigens inszenierte skulpturale Situation zeigt, kam Sala an seinem Sujet zufällig vorbei. Inszenierte Photographien sind bei Sala die Ausnahme. Eine solche Ausnahme ist NO BARRAGÁN NO CRY (2002), ein Bild, das auf einem sonst leeren Dach eines Gebäudes ein anscheinend bäuchlings auf einem zylindrischen Metallsockel gestrandetes weisses Pferd zeigt. Dieses Bild wurde sorgfältig geplant und Sala gestaltete den Sockel eigens so, dass das Tier nicht leiden musste. Die Aufnahme entstand auf dem Dach eines Gebäudes in Guadalajara, während in einer der oberen Etagen des Gebäudes, im Kunstraum OPA, eine Ausstellung von Salas Werk stattfand. Die Inspiration zu dieser Arbeit geht auf ein Ereignis zu einem früheren Zeitpunkt seiner Mexikoreise zurück. Vor Antritt der Reise hatte Sala sich eine Website mit Trickaufnahmen des Hauses Barragán in der Calle Ramírez in Mexiko City angeschaut, weil er das Gebäude besichtigen wollte. Barragán war bekanntlich ein grosser Pferdenarr, und die Aufnahme auf der Website, die

Sala im Gedächtnis haften blieb, zeigte eine Pferdeskulptur auf einem Sockel vor einer rosafarbenen Wand. Als Sala jedoch in der Calle Ramírez eintraf, war von der Skulptur nichts zu sehen. Es stellte sich heraus, dass das Pferd während der Restaurierung des Gebäudes verschwunden war. Nur wenigen Besuchern dürfte dies aufgefallen sein, für Sala stellte es jedoch eine dramatische Absenz dar. So besehen, könnte man mutmassen, dass Sala mit der von ihm photographierten Szene auf dem Dach eine bizarre Rückkehr des fehlenden Tieres inszenieren wollte, so, als habe der Sockel in Mexiko City das hölzerne Pferd in die Stratosphäre gefeuert, es unterwegs in Fleisch und Blut verwandelt und hundertfünfzig Kilometer entfernt landen lassen. Sala erklärte gegenüber Hans Ulrich Obrist, ein Photo könne «Verdichtung einer Geschichte» sein,[10] und das ist hier ohne Frage der Fall. Doch auch wenn wir von der erwähnten Geschichte nichts wüssten, wäre das Photo nicht weniger bizarr. Es entspricht keiner gewohnten Bildgattung, ist weder eine Architekturphotographie, noch eine Aussicht von einem Dach, noch eine typische Pferdephotographie, die das Tier eher in Bewegung zeigen würde (Barragáns Holzpferd war in vollem Galopp dargestellt). Benjamin Buchloh meinte, es sei «kaum ein Bild denkbar, das auf tragischere und komischere Weise vom endgültigen Verlust der Natürlichkeit kündet» als Orozcos Photo PERRO EN TLAPAN (1992), das einen Hund zeigt, der von einer Art Betonsockel aus in die Ferne blickt.[11] Salas Photo könnte ebenso von diesem Verlust künden, so sehr ist das Pferd seiner Umgebung entrückt, doch die Offensichtlichkeit der Inszenierung wirft eher Fragen auf, als dass sie Antworten gibt. Beim Betrachten des Photos bekommt man mehr und mehr das Gefühl, selbst festzusitzen wie das in der Bildmitte festhängende Tier.

Sala machte 2004 erneut Photos in Form einer Serie, diesmal acht Aufnahmen von Nachtfaltern in einem Raum in Dakar, Senegal. Die Kreaturen säumen die Stelle, an der zwei Wände und die Decke im rechten Winkel zusammentreffen, und zeichnen dort die geraden Linien der Architektur nach, brechen sie aber zugleich auf. Selbst bei Tage (als die Photos gemacht wurden) halten sich die Insekten an diesen Naht- und Schnittstellen auf, vermutlich weil das die sichersten Stellen im Raum sind. Die Kamera hat sie jedoch aufgespürt und stört wiederholt ihre Ruhe. Der Hintergrund ist durch das Blitzlicht ausgebleicht, doch die Nachtfalter verharren wie Relikte der Nacht, unregelmässige Flecken auf weissem Grund. Als Europäer erstmals an Orten wie diesem photographierten und Bilder vom schwarzen Kontinent mit nach Hause brachten, hegten sie die Hoffnung, dass die Photographie sowohl ein Licht auf die Welt, die sie gesehen hatten, werfen würde als auch auf die Welt, in die sie zurückkehrten. Salas Aufnahmen bieten eine düsterere Auffassung des Lichtes. Hier stöbert die Photographie ihr Sujet auf und treibt es in die Ecke. Dennoch bleibt sie unpräzise und tastend – von den Nachtfaltern ist nicht viel zu erkennen, keine Details ihrer Flügel, keine feinen Fühler. Die Kamera registriert lediglich schwarze Tupfer auf Weiss.

(Übersetzung: Bram Opstelten)

1) Massimiliano Gioni und Michele Robecchi, «Anri Sala: Unfinished Histories», *Flash Art,* (Juli–September 2001), S. 107.
2) Jeff Wall, «‹Marks of Indifference›: Aspects of Photography in, or as, Conceptual Art», in: *Reconsidering the Object of Art 1965–1975,* hrsg. v. Ann Goldstein und Anne Rorimer, Ausstellungskatalog, Museum of Contemporary Art, Los Angeles, MIT Press, Cambridge Mass. 1995.
3) Benjamin Buchloh, «Gerhard Richter's *Atlas*: The Anomic Archive», *October* 88 (Frühjahr 1999), S. 117–145.
4) Näheres zu diesen Arbeiten in meinem Beitrag «Anri Sala», *Art Monthly* (Juli–August 2004), S. 18–20.
5) Gioni und Robecchi (vgl. Anm. 1), S. 107.
6) Gerald Matt, «An Interview with Anri Sala», in: *Anri Sala,* Ausstellungskatalog, Kunsthalle Wien, 2003, S. 52.
7) Ebenda, S. 75.
8) Der Künstler im Gespräch mit dem Autor in der Tate Modern Gallery, London, November 2004.
9) Allan Sekula, «Dismantling Modernism, Reinventing Documentary (Notes on the Politics of Representation)», in: *Dismal Science: Photo Works 1972–1996,* Ausstellungskatalog, University Galleries, Illinois State University, Normal (Ill.) 1999, S. 126.
10) Hans Ulrich Obrist, *Interviews,* Vol. 1, Charta, Mailand 2003, S. 831.
11) Benjamin Buchloh, «Cosmic Reification: Gabriel Orozco's Photographs», in: *Gabriel Orozco,* Ausstellungskatalog, Serpentine Gallery, London 2004, S. 88.

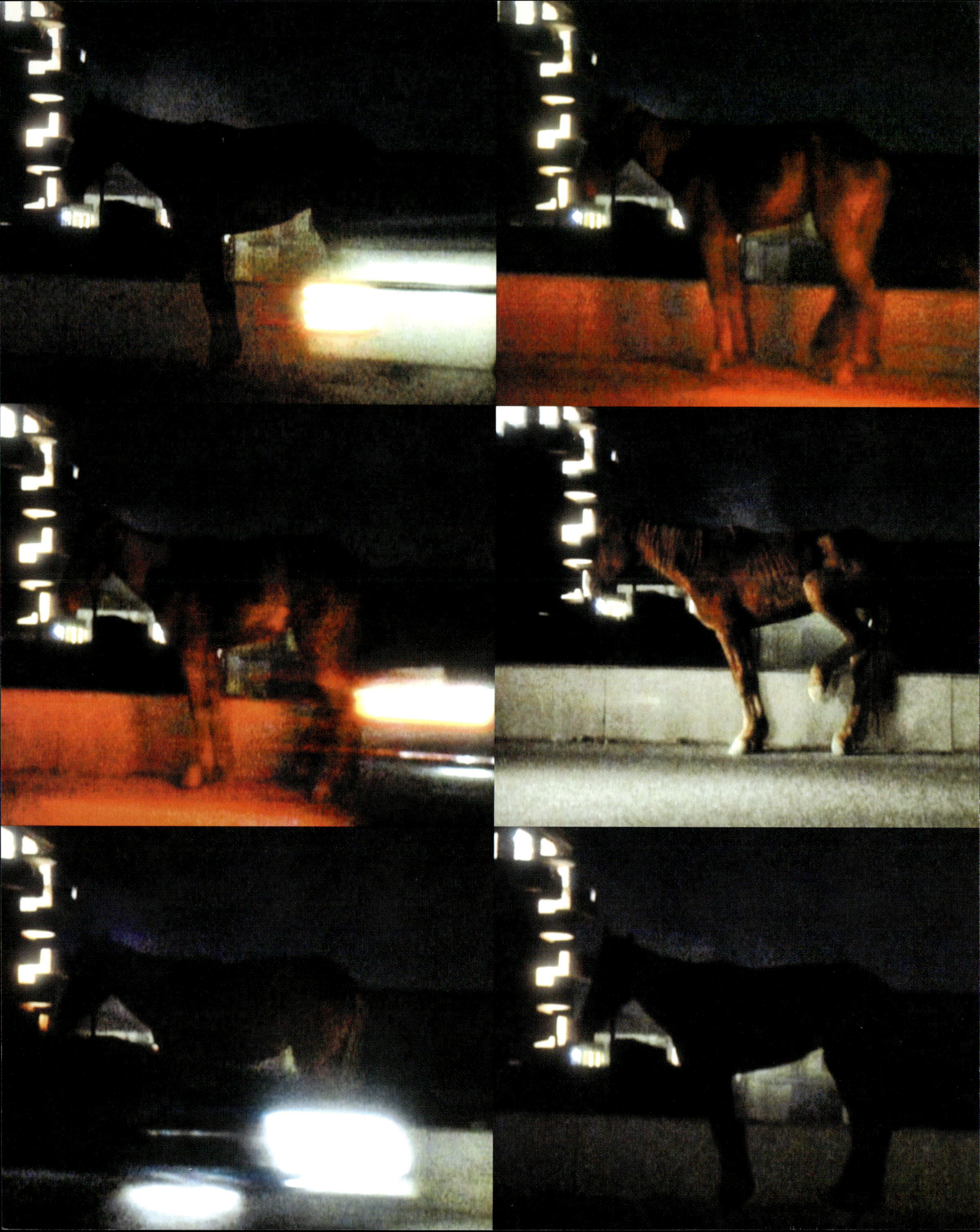

LYNNE COOKE & ANRI SALA

From Silence to Language and Back Again

Lynne Cooke: I'd like to begin this dialogue with a question about silence. Silence—a loaded silence even—seems to play a crucial role in a number of your works. In INTERVISTA (1998) there's the silence of your mother vis-à-vis her political past, which you dissolved by having her speeches deciphered by someone who read her lips. Then there's the almost uncanny silence of the man who so carefully tends the fish in NOCTURNES (1999). That strange, intense relationship contains no aural communication of the kind that happens between most owners and their pets. Such a haunting silence reminds me of TIME AFTER TIME (2004) in which a horse is shown standing stoically on the edge of the highway as traffic streams by. Its steadfast presence seems to mask a kind of silent panic. Whether lost or abandoned, it's transfixed by fear.

In concert, or contrast, with these works, I think of the group of men sitting together speaking in clichés taken from movies. Their "tough guy" talk is clearly borrowed: it's not their own words. They seem to need to speak through, to rehearse or imitate the speech of others to create an identity. Finally, there is the little boy in LÀK-KAT (2004), the work you made in Senegal, who tries to imitate the correct pronunciation of a word that conveys a highly charged meaning about which he seems to be (and, given his age, should be) completely oblivious.

The strand that I'm tracing in your works has to do not only with actual silence but, more often, with not speaking or not being able to speak, or speaking via conduits or other channels. Do you recognize this as a recurring thematic?

Anri Sala: This silence is, for me, a substitute for language. It's a quiet syntax, a syntax abandoned by words that would have made sense a while ago or, maybe, will make sense again sometime in the future. A mute syntax may absorb details or signs that language cannot yet name. It often goes with situations where you sense that something is wrong, but you are unable to name it, or resolve it.

I am aware that even those few times that language is present in my work, it's there either as a "malaise" or as a promise of something which is be-

LYNNE COOKE has been curator at Dia Center for the Arts, New York, since 1996. She is also a writer and a faculty member for Curatorial Studies at Bard College, Annandale-on-Hudson.

ANRI SALA, TIME AFTER TIME, 2003, video transferred to DVD, sound; realized for "Point of View: an Anthology of the Moving Image" / auf DVD übertragenes Video. (BICK PRODUCTIONS; ILENE KURTZ-KRETZSCHMAR, CAROLINE BOURGEOIS; NEW MUSEUM OF CONTEMPORARY ART, NEW YORK)

coming but not yet settled. In INTERVISTA the malaise of my mother in front of her recovered speech was not connected to the ideological content (which neither she nor I found surprising) but rather to the syntax of her speech. Her first reaction to what she said thirty years ago was: "I cannot believe that. It doesn't make sense." What didn't make sense to her was not the message of her past ideals (since, later in the film, she says she still believes in most of them) but the syntax that linked her thoughts. That's what became interesting to me. A gap of thirty years makes not just a rupture in content but it may also bring a change of syntax. What happens when a system changes, especially in the case of totalitarian regimes which exercise great control over language, is that the syntax of the language breaks—like a pot that cannot resist the temperature changes of the liquid inside. In the case of PROMISES (2001), as you say, it seems that these men needed to rehearse to create an identity. This actually happened at a time when the streets in Albania became violent and the country was so lawless that many people (myself included) had to create an outdoor self, or identity, in order to survive, to make their public life easier and less vulnerable. When I shot PROMISES I wanted to see where my closest friends still living in Albania now stood, and to guess how I would have evolved if I had never left. It was like trying to discover the pitch of my voice in a possible but different world. In LÀK-KAT, the malaise is situated not only in the difficulties the children have with pronunciation but also in the translation/adaptation of the words into the target languages of British English, American English, French, and German (each of those languages representing countries which had different histories and practices of colonization). One possible source of salvation, for the audience and for me, from the probable malaise caused by the meaning of the words when pronounced in Wolof lies in their musicality when repeated. I'm reminded of my first experience with repetition when I was a kid. I would repeat my name—Anri, Anri, Anri—so often until it lost its meaning and came to mean something else which sounded unfamiliar to me. The choice is ours: we can deal with the meaning, or through repetition we can enjoy the musicality and forget all else.

LC: I was very struck by your account of what your mother found so difficult in the reconstruction of her speech at the rally. You describe it beautifully with the notion of a "mute syntax." I was reminded of a passage from Merleau Ponty's *The Phenomenology of Perception* about a certain dissembling of the usual modes of speech processes, about the fact that it is not merely the utility and efficiency of words, but their materiality that forms the ground upon which our subjectivity is created in relation to others. "The essence of normal language is that the intention to speak can reside only in an open experience. It makes its appearance like the boiling point of a liquid, when in the density of being, volumes of empty space are built up and move outward. 'As soon as [a person] uses language to establish a living relation with himself or with his fellows, language is no longer an instrument, no longer a means—it is a manifestation, a revelation of intimate being and of the psychic link which unites us to the world and to our fellows.'"[1)] If I understand you correctly your mother seems to have sensed a certain dissembling, or irreality, in these modes of speaking that parallels the mis-registration, the mis-fit, between a concept in one language and in another that is for me at the heart of LÀK-KAT. The shift from language as an instrument to what Merleau Ponty calls "language as a manifestation, a manifestation of intimate being" seems here to connect to the making of sound as much as of sense. A young baby makes sounds partly in order to surround itself with a comforting or secure ambience, an ambience that, although self-generated, nonetheless provides a cocoon of well-being. I wonder to what extent those children try to fit the words that they are struggling to learn back into their own "sound systems," their own aural matrix, as a way of negotiating the unfamiliar—like your incantatory repetition of your name when you were a child... This in turn connects these works, for me, to MIXED BEHAVIOUR (2003) where a solitary musician plays on a rooftop in a tremendous storm...

AS: Well, the DJ filling with music a space without an audience, in order to surround himself with a comforting ambience, must have been a baby who once surrounded himself with sounds to provide a cocoon of well-being. But now as a man he is not vulnerable in the same way; now there is also a sense of desolation. He returned to sounds as if making or playing sounds could be more remedial than making sense of fucked up situations that don't make much sense anyway. Speaking of the DJ, I speak of myself. When I asked him to play music just for us during that stormy New Year's Eve, I was thinking about shooting my film but we were also trying to negotiate that particular night in our lives. We couldn't bear the fireworks—maybe because we remembered that some years earlier a number of people had been found dead but no one had noticed the shots amidst the blasts from the fireworks.

If we follow this idea of sound becoming meaning and meaning becoming sound, we can trace a line between INTERVISTA, LÀK-KAT, and NATURALMYSTIC (2002)—where the guy whispers the tomahawk sound as if it could almost become a word. Perhaps this relation keeps on changing. Sometimes the words become meaningless and sometimes the sounds become meaningful.

LC: I recently learned from Mark Godfrey that some of your first forays into photography arose from salvaging images you made much earlier in your life, and turning them into art works. Do you feel you have kept the same attitude to the making of an image—what is essentially a snapshot technique or style—that you had years ago? Today, it would place you in a lineage stretching from, say, Ed Ruscha or Robert Smithson onwards, a lineage that responds to the particulars of the everyday world in a direct even "dumb" fashion, a lineage that privileges the finding of the image over any technical finesse involved in its representation.

AS: I'm thrilled by the moment when, hunting for a potential image, you first frame it, and so help it leave the context in which it was born and gained its independence. "What it was" becomes "what it will be forever." The time that was before and the time that would have been after it was taken become a past continuous and future continuous that will never leave the image.

Initially, I was more interested in the making of an image than its final result. At that time things started to radically change in Albanian society. The tranquility that had accompanied my school classes and

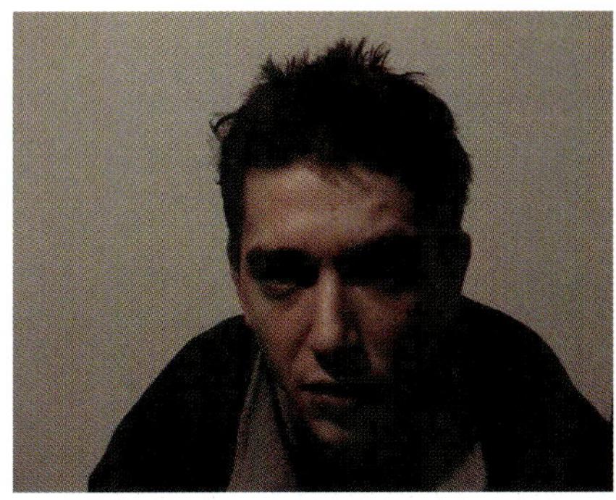

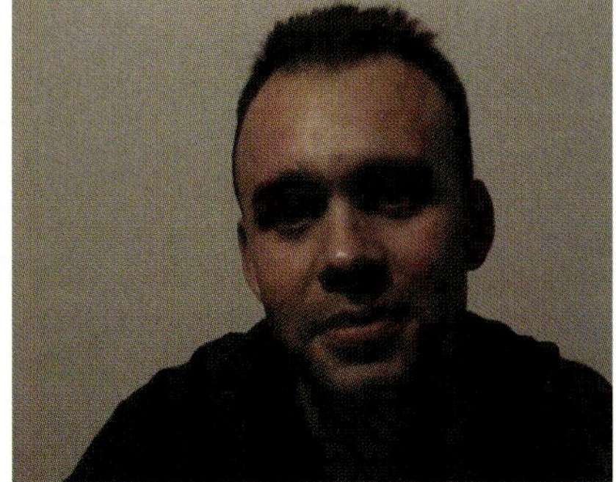

ANRI SALA, PROMISES, 2001, color film and sound / VERSPRECHEN, Farbfilm mit Ton.

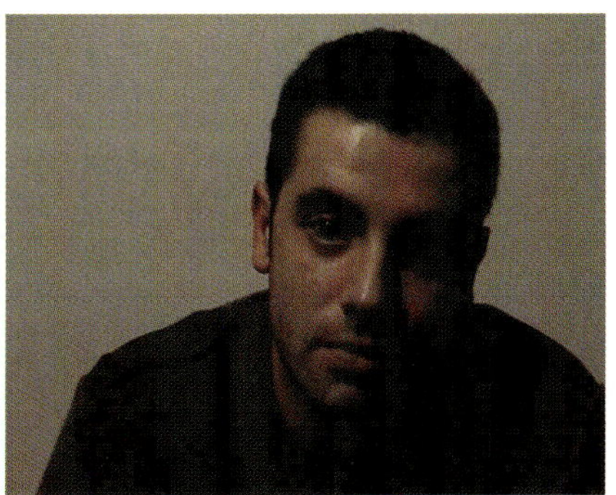

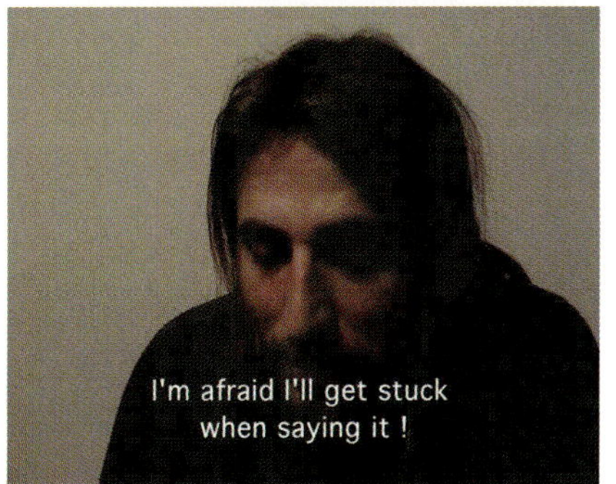

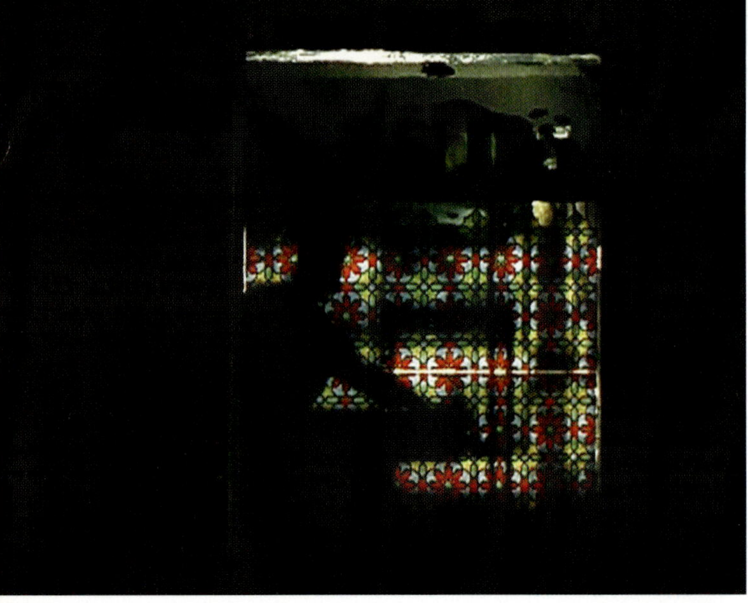

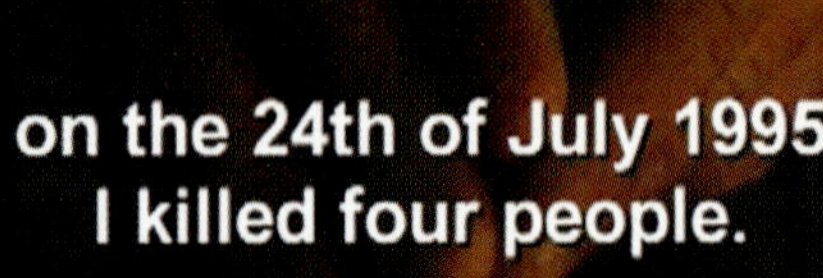

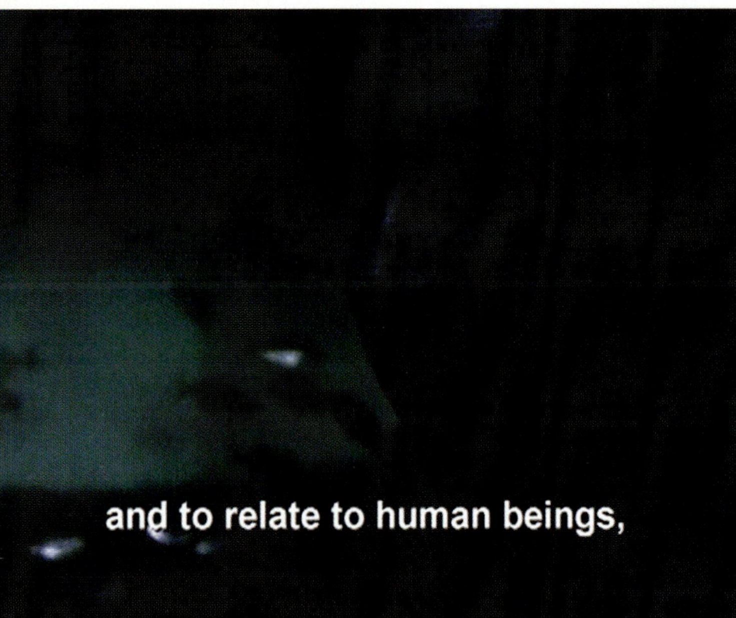

everyday life at large was shaken. I started to lose interest in painting, as many people did with other things that until then had been important to them. I realized that I was perhaps spending too much time elaborating answers rather than asking the most urgent questions. I started to get interested in something that was bigger than the image, something that prints the image rather than something that is printed in the image—something that answers to a necessity, an urgency, a drive that enables you to set up the world again through an image, even if only for one minute. Such precise moments make you feel right; they make you feel connected.

I remember when I was fourteen and had to choose between starting art studies or continuing general studies at high school (which postponed the choice of career for later).

It seemed a difficult choice. One day I went to see a close friend, an artist named Edi Rama, who at that time had just started as professor at the art academy. After a long discussion he told me that this choice had to be mine, and that he couldn't answer for me. But, he said, at the end of the day the choice wasn't about whether I would make paintings or study math later in life; the choice lay somewhere else. He said that if I were to go to art school then I would have my first sexual relations during the second year, while if I were to go to the high school, it would happen only a year later. This could sound banal, if you don't know that at that time everyone was living almost the same life, with the same small events happening at the same time. So such a 'small' difference would have a deeper significance. It revealed a truth that was more decisive for me than the choice of wanting to be surrounded by colors or numbers the rest of my life. It didn't offer me an answer, but it affected my attitude towards questioning things ever since.

LC: The second part of my question concerns whether your approach to photography parallels that

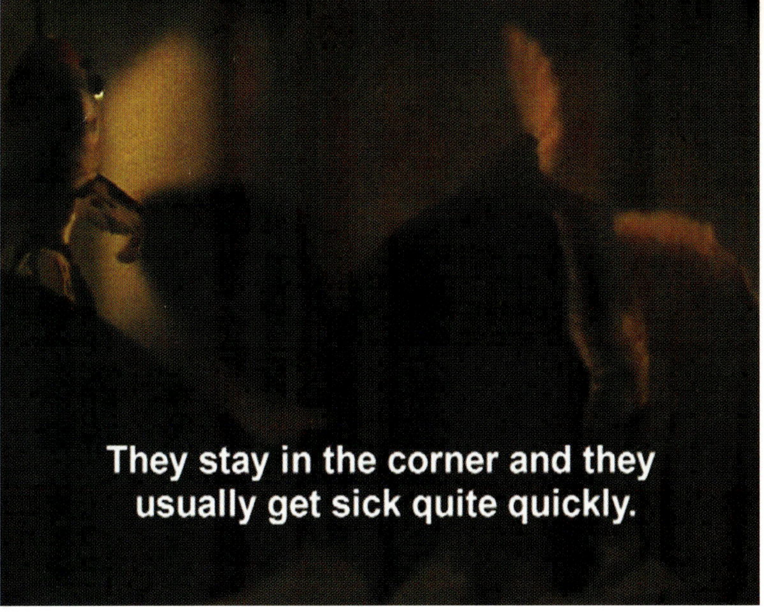

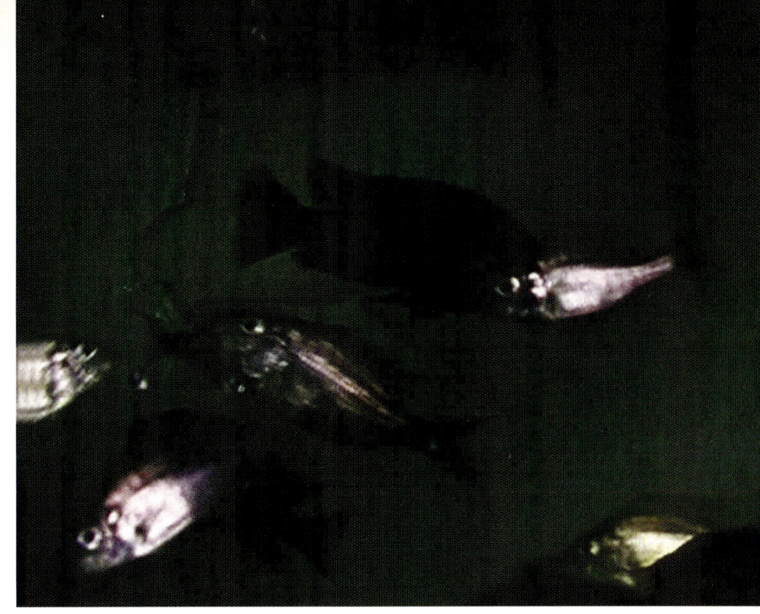

ANRI SALA, NOCTURNES, 1999, 11 min. 28 sec. 16-mm film transferred to video / 11 Min. 28 Sek. auf Video übertragener 16mm-Film.

you now employ with video, even though time necessarily operates differently in each medium. Do you feel that the video camera works for you as a temporal extension of the still camera? Is this why you so often choose a static shot, one that allows the passage of time to be more easily registered because the frame is fixed? Things change within the frame, people walk in and out, the sun rises, etcetera, but it remains constant. I realize that there are some works in your oeuvre, such as the piece with ghost crabs, in which a sequence of shots sets up a quasi narrative but they seem largely the exception. Mostly, relations to time take precedence over questions of space: they become a means to engage ideas of history and memory.

AS: There's a similar approach to these media in terms of attitude, of being curious and letting my unconscious play a role. Through my work I'm interested in approaching those dark areas where culture meets nature, the rule meets the unconstrained, the rational meets the irrational, the wish to control meets the loss of control, or the never intended. Given the role time plays in video, there is always a danger of saying too much, of erring on the side of "making sense." It's a fascinating but far from easy task. It's like time-coding a darkness where there are no codes and time is not yet known. I try to move on without needing to know—wanting not to know. I want to deal with what I don't know yet, and try to evacuate what I'm starting to know too well. I'm interested in what haunts versus what makes sense in the world. We often struggle to evacuate what haunts us by trying to make sense of everything, by controlling our environment, giving everything efficiency, a role, a function, a normality, and isolating whatever is dark and makes us feel insecure, whatever is uneasy to name. This might explain why language plays such an important role, why it takes precedence over the visual and the aural. Language names, neutralizes, and makes safe. My interest in language is not based in a relation of trust but rather of wariness. I don't trust the narrative of language, especially when syntax plays a bigger role than the words themselves.

1) Maurice Merleau-Ponty, *Phenomenology of Perception*, trans. Colin Smith (London/New York: Routledge 1962), p. 196. The "quote within the quote" is from Kurt Goldstein, "L'analyse de l'aphasie et l'essence du langage" in *J. Psychol.* vol. 30 (1933), pp. 430–496.

Vom Schweigen zur Sprache und wieder zurück

LYNNE COOKE & ANRI SALA

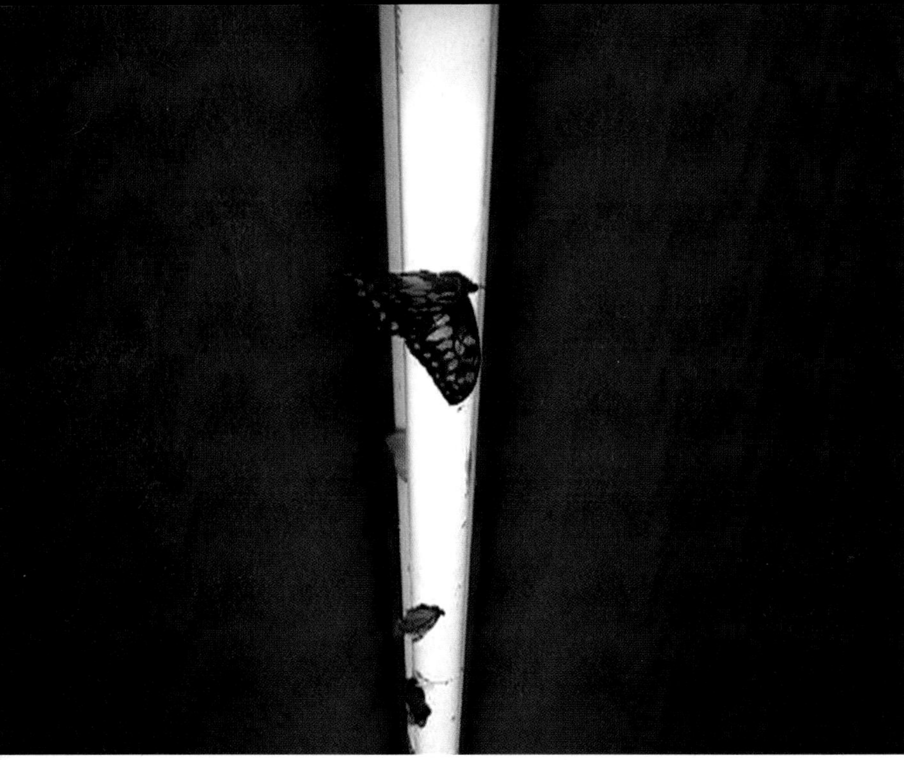

ANRI SALA, LÀK-KAT, 2004,
video and sound / Video mit Ton.

Lynne Cooke: Ich möchte dieses Gespräch gerne mit einer Frage über das Schweigen eröffnen. Das Schweigen – selbst das bedeutungsschwangere Schweigen – scheint in einigen deiner Arbeiten eine Schlüsselrolle zu spielen. In INTERVISTA (Interview, 1998) ist es das Schweigen deiner Mutter über ihre politische Vergangenheit, das du aufgelöst hast, indem du ihre auf Film festgehaltenen Reden von jemand hast entziffern lassen, der Lippen lesen konnte. Dann ist da auch das fast unheimliche Schweigen des Mannes in NOCTURNE (1999), der sich so rührend um seine Fische kümmert. In dieser merkwürdigen, intensiven Beziehung findet keine hörbare Kommunikation statt, wie das sonst oft zwischen Mensch und Haustier der Fall ist. Dieses beängstigende Schweigen wiederum erinnert mich an TIME AFTER TIME (Ein ums andere Mal, 2004), in welchem man ein Pferd nachts stoisch am Rand einer Schnellstrasse stehen sieht, während der Verkehr vorbeiströmt. Hinter seinem standhaften Ausharren scheint sich eine Art stumme Panik zu verbergen. Ob es sich verlaufen hat oder hier ausgesetzt wurde: Es ist vor Angst erstarrt.

LYNNE COOKE ist seit 1996 Kuratorin am Dia Center for the Arts in New York. Sie schreibt über Kunst und lehrt am Bard College, Annandale-on-Hudson.

Eine Übereinstimmung mit diesen Arbeiten – oder auch einen Kontrast dazu – sehe ich bei PROMISES (Versprechen, 2001) in der Gruppe von Männern, die beisammensitzen und in Klischees reden, die aus der Welt des Kinos stammen. Ihr «Harte-Männer»-Gerede ist eindeutig geklaut: Das sind nicht ihre eigenen Worte. Es scheint, dass sie die Sprechweise anderer einüben oder nachahmen müssen, um sich mit ihrer Hilfe eine Identität zu verschaffen. Schliesslich ist da noch der kleine Junge in LÀK-KAT (2004), der Arbeit, die du in Senegal gemacht hast: Er versucht die richtige Aussprache eines Wortes nachzuahmen, das eine ziemlich deftige Bedeutung hat, von welcher er jedoch keine Ahnung zu haben scheint (und angesichts seines Alters auch nicht haben sollte).

Der Faden, den ich in deinen Arbeiten verfolge, hat nicht nur mit Schweigen im eigentlichen Sinn zu tun, sondern häufiger noch mit einem Nicht-Sprechen oder einer Unfähigkeit zu sprechen, oder aber mit einem Sprechen über Sprachrohre oder andere Kanäle. Siehst du das selbst als wiederkehrendes Thema in deinem Werk?

Anri Sala: Dieses Schweigen ist für mich ein Sprachersatz. Es ist eine lautlose Syntax, eine Syntax, der die Worte abhanden gekommen sind, die vor kurzer Zeit noch einen Sinn ergeben hätten oder, wer weiss, irgendwann in der Zukunft wieder einen Sinn haben werden. Eine stumme Syntax kann Einzelheiten oder Zeichen in sich aufnehmen, für die es noch keine Wörter gibt. Häufig kommt sie in Situationen vor, bei denen man spürt, dass etwas nicht stimmt, jedoch nicht zu sagen vermag, was es ist, geschweige denn, es auflösen kann.

Ich bin mir darüber im Klaren, dass Sprache selbst in den seltenen Fällen, in denen sie in meiner Arbeit tatsächlich vorkommt, entweder in Gestalt eines «Unbehagens» auftritt oder als etwas, was im Entstehen begriffen, aber noch nicht abgeschlossen ist. In INTERVISTA hatte das Unbehagen meiner Mutter angesichts ihrer wieder aufgestöberten und rekonstruierten Ansprache nichts mit deren ideologischem Inhalt zu tun (der weder sie noch mich überraschte), sondern vielmehr mit der Syntax ihrer Rede. Ihre erste Reaktion auf das, was sie vor dreissig Jahren gesagt hatte, war: «Das kann ich nicht glauben. Es macht überhaupt keinen Sinn.» Was für sie keinen Sinn machte, war nicht etwa die Botschaft ihrer früheren Ideale (denn später im Film sagt sie, dass sie an die meisten nach wie vor glaubt), sondern die logische Syntax, welche die einzelnen Gedanken miteinander verband. Das war es, was mir interessant erschien. Ein Sprung von dreissig Jahren bedeutet nicht nur einen inhaltlichen Bruch, sondern kann auch eine Veränderung der Syntax mit sich bringen. Wenn sich ein System verändert, besonders, wenn es sich um totalitäre Systeme handelt, die auch die Sprache streng kontrollieren, so zerbricht die Syntax der Sprache – wie ein Krug, der den schnellen Temperaturwechsel der Flüssigkeit in seinem Innern nicht aushält. Wie du sagst, wirkt es im Fall von PRO-

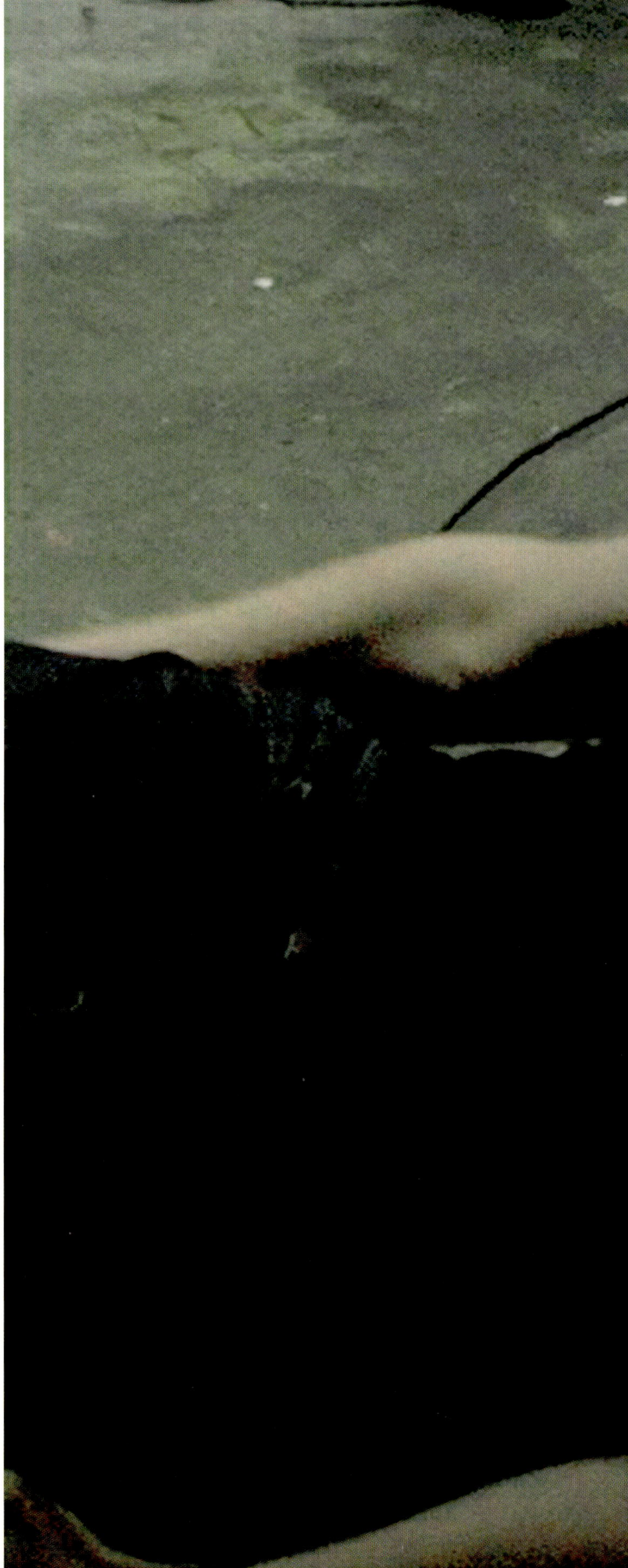

ANRI SALA, NOW I SEE, 2004, 9 min. 35-mm color film in Dolby SR-D / JETZT SEHE ICHS, 9 Min. 35mm-Farbfilm in Dolby SR-D.

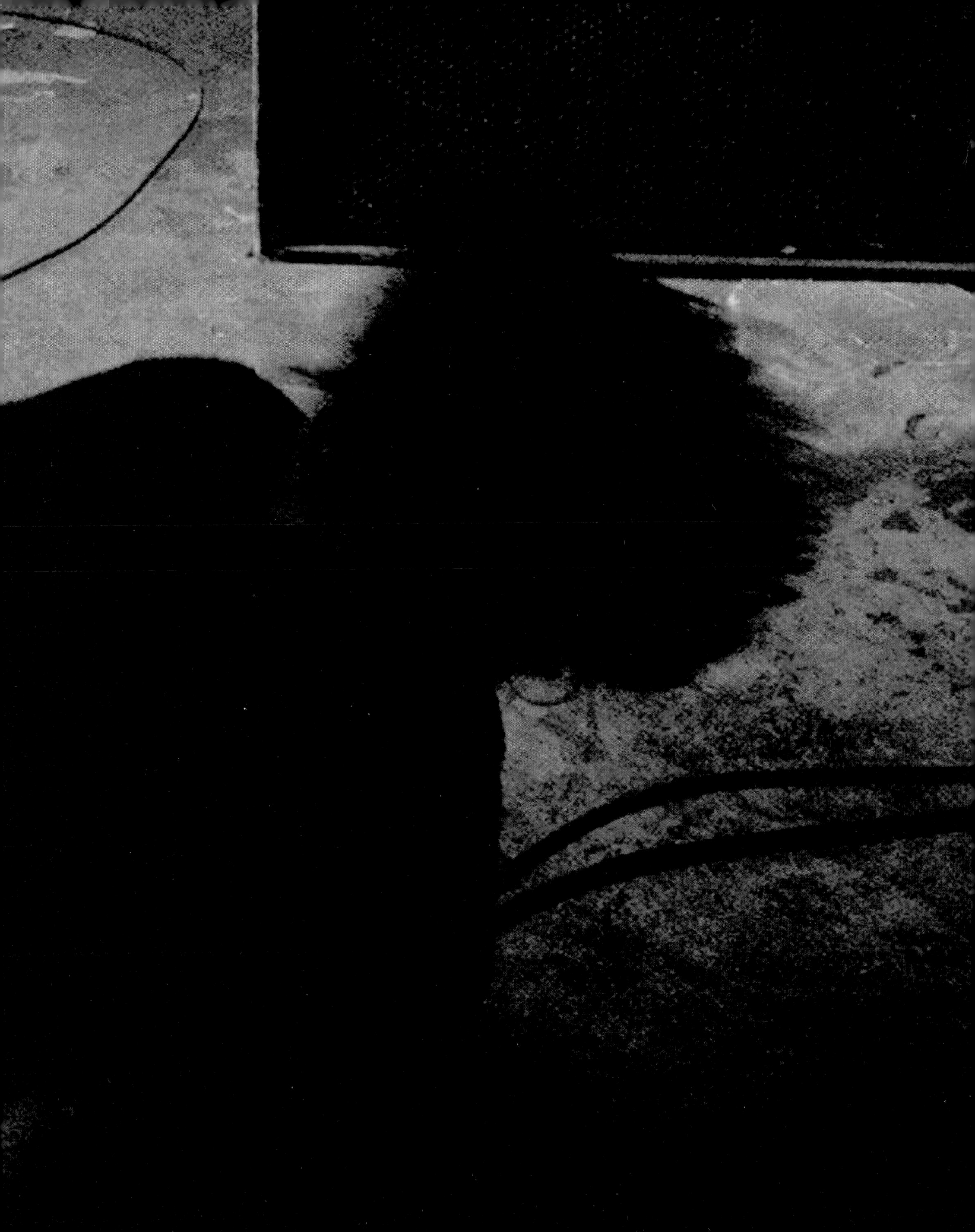

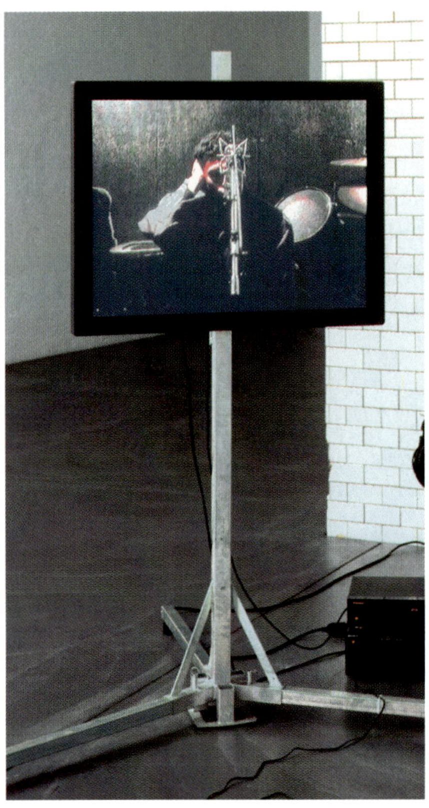

ANRI SALA, NATURAL MYSTIC (TOMAHAWK #2), 2002, 2 min. 8 sec. color video and sound, installation view, Hauser & Wirth, Zürich / NATURMYSTIKER, 2 Min. 8 Sek. Farbvideo mit Ton.

MISES so, als ob diese Männer eine Identität erst einüben müssten. Dies ist tatsächlich der Fall gewesen, als die Gewalt in den Strassen von Albanien um sich griff und eine Gesetzlosigkeit herrschte, dass viele Leute (einschliesslich meiner selbst) sich ein spezielles Ich oder eine Identität für die Aussenwelt zulegen mussten, um überleben zu können, um sich das Leben in der Öffentlichkeit zu erleichtern und weniger verletzbar zu sein. Als ich PROMISES drehte, wollte ich sehen, wo meine nächsten, noch immer in Albanien lebenden Freunde jetzt standen, und versuchte herauszufinden, wie ich mich wohl entwickelt hätte, wenn ich nicht weggegangen wäre. Es war, als wollte ich erforschen, wie meine Stimme in einer möglichen, aber anderen Welt klingen würde. In LÀK-KAT liegt das Unbehagen nicht nur in den Schwierigkeiten, die die Kinder mit der Aussprache haben, sondern auch in der Übersetzung und Einpassung der Wörter in die Zielsprachen Britisch Englisch, Amerikanisch, Französisch und Deutsch (da jede dieser Sprachen für ein Land stand, das eine eigene Geschichte und ein eigenes Kolonialverhalten hatte). Für das Publikum und mich liegt ein möglicher Ausweg aus dem Unbehagen, das die Bedeutung der in Wolof ausgesprochenen Wörter wahrscheinlich auslösen würde, in der Musikalität, welche die Wörter entwickeln, wenn sie wiederholt ausgesprochen werden. Das erinnert mich an mein erstes Wiederholungserlebnis, als ich noch ein Kind war. Ich wiederholte meinen Namen – Anri, Anri, Anri – so lange, bis er seine Bedeutung verlor und etwas anderes zu bedeuten beziehungsweise fremd zu klingen begann. Die Entscheidung liegt bei uns: Wir können uns mit der Bedeutung befassen oder mittels Wiederholung die Musikalität der Wörter geniessen und alles andere vergessen.

LC: Was du darüber erzählt hast, was deine Mutter an der Rekonstruktion ihrer Rede an der Versammlung befremdete, hat mich sehr beeindruckt. Du umschreibst das sehr schön mit dem Begriff der «stummen Syntax». Es erinnert mich an eine Passage aus Merleau-Pontys *Phänomenologie der Wahrnehmung* über eine gewisse «Falschheit» der üblichen Redevorgänge, über die Tatsache, dass es nicht nur der Nutzen und die Effizienz der Worte ist, die den Boden bilden, auf dem unsere Subjektivität in Beziehung auf andere entsteht, sondern ihre Materialität. «... das Wesen der normalen Sprache: die Intention des Sprechens erfordert eine offene Erfahrung, dem Sieden einer Flüssigkeit gleich tritt sie auf, wenn inmitten der Dichte des Seins offene Sphären sich bilden und nach aussen drängen. ‹Wo der Mensch sich der Sprache bedient, um in ein lebendiges Verhältnis zu sich selbst und seinen Mitmenschen zu treten, ist die Sprache nicht mehr nur Instrument, nicht mehr nur Mittel, sondern Bekundung und Offenbarung seines innersten Seins und des seelischen Bandes, das mit der Welt und unseren Mitmenschen uns verbindet.›»[1] Wenn ich dich recht verstehe, hat deine Mutter in dieser Art zu sprechen eine gewisse Falschheit oder Unwirklichkeit gespürt, die dieser leichten Verzeichnung, diesem nicht ganz Ineinanderpassen der Begriffe in verschiedenen Sprachen entspricht, das für mich den Kern von LÀK-KAT ausmacht. Die Verlagerung von der Sprache als Werkzeug zu dem, was Merleau-Ponty (mit Goldstein) die «Sprache als Bekundung und Offenbarung des innersten Seins» nannte, scheint sich hier sowohl auf die Erzeugung von Lauten wie von Sinn zu beziehen. Ein kleines Kind gibt zum Teil auch Laute von sich, um eine beruhigende oder geborgene Atmosphäre um sich herum zu erzeugen, eine Atmosphäre die, obwohl sie selbst erzeugt ist, für das Kind eine Art Kokon der Geborgenheit darstellt. Ich frage mich, wie weit die Kinder versuchen, die Wörter, die sie zu lernen bemüht sind, in dieses eigene Lautsystem zu integrieren, um sich das nicht Vertraute anzueignen – wie du es als Kind mit der inkantierenden Wiederholung deines eigenen Namens getan hast... Das wiederum verbindet diese Arbeiten mit MIXED BEHAVIOUR (Gemischtes Verhalten, 2003), wo ein einsamer Musiker, während eines fürchterlichen Sturms, auf einem Dach spielt...

AS: Nun ja, der DJ, der einen Raum ohne Publikum mit Musik ausfüllt, um sich selbst mit einer tröstlichen Atmosphäre zu umgeben, muss einst solch ein Baby gewesen sein, das sich selbst mit einem Lautkokon der Geborgenheit umgeben hat. Aber jetzt, als erwachsener Mann, ist er nicht mehr auf dieselbe Weise verletzlich; jetzt kommt ein Gefühl von Trostlosigkeit hinzu. Er ist wieder zu den Lauten und Klängen zurückgekehrt, wie wenn ihm das Erzeugen oder Spielen von Tönen heilsamer vorkäme, als irgendeinen Sinn in verfahrenen Situationen zu suchen, die letztlich keinen Sinn machen. Wenn ich vom DJ rede, meine ich mich selbst. Als ich ihn bat, in jener stürmischen Silvesternacht nur für uns zu spielen, habe ich schon an meinen Film gedacht, aber es ging auch darum, jene besondere Nacht in unserem Leben zu überstehen. Wir konnten Feuerwerk nicht ausstehen – vielleicht weil wir uns daran erinnerten, dass ein paar Jahre zuvor einige Leute tot aufgefunden wurden, aber, inmitten der allgemeinen Silvesterknallerei, niemand die Schüsse gehört hatte. Wenn wir dieser Idee folgen, dass der Laut Bedeutung wird und die Bedeutung Laut, können wir eine Verbindungslinie erkennen zwischen INTERVISTA, LÀK-KAT und NATURALMYSTIC (2002); dort flüstert der Typ den Laut, den das Tomahawk erzeugt, fast wie wenn er Wort werden könnte. Vielleicht verändert sich diese Beziehung laufend. Manchmal verlieren die Wörter jede Bedeutung und manchmal gewinnen blosse Laute einen Sinn.

LC: Vor kurzem habe ich von Mark Godfrey erfahren, dass einige deiner ersten Ausflüge in die Photographie sich daraus ergeben haben, dass du auf Bilder gestossen bist, die du in deiner Jugend aufgenommen und jetzt nachträglich zu Kunstwerken gemacht hast. Glaubst du, dass deine Auffassung vom Bildermachen – im Wesentlichen eine Schnappschuss-Technik oder ein Schnappschuss-Stil – noch immer dieselbe ist wie früher? Damit würdest du heute in einer Tradition stehen, die sich, sagen wir, von Ed Ruscha oder Robert Smithson herleitet, eine Tradition, die auf die Besonderheiten der Alltagswelt reagiert, auf eine direkte, ja «dumme» Art, eine Tradition, die das «Finden» des Bildes über alle technischen Finessen seiner Darstellung stellt.

AS: Auf der Jagd nach einem potenziellen Bild finde ich den Moment spannend, in dem man es zum ersten Mal eingrenzt und ihm so dazu verhilft, seinen «ursprünglichen» Kontext zu verlassen und unabhängig zu werden. «Was es war» wird «was es für immer sein wird». Die Zeit, die davor lag, und die Zeit, die danach gekommen wäre, werden zu einer kontinuierlichen Vergangenheit und einer kontinuierlichen Zukunft, die sich niemals vom Bild lösen werden.

Zu Beginn interessierte mich die Aufnahme des Bildes mehr als das Endergebnis. Damals begann sich die albanische Gesellschaft radikal zu verändern. Die Ruhe, die meine Schulzeit und meinen Alltag begleitet hatte, wurde erschüttert. Ich begann das Interesse an der Malerei zu verlieren, wie viele Leute das Interesse an den Dingen verloren, die ihnen bis dahin wichtig gewesen waren. Mir wurde bewusst, dass ich vielleicht zu viel Zeit damit verbrachte, Antworten auszuarbeiten, statt die wirklich drängenden Fragen zu stellen. Ich begann mich für etwas zu interessieren, was grösser war als das Bild, etwas, was das Bild selbst prägt, statt etwas, was im Bild ausgeprägt ist – etwas, was auf eine Notwendigkeit, eine Dringlichkeit antwortet, ein Impetus, der einem erlaubt, die Welt in einem Bild noch einmal zu erschaffen, und wenn es nur für eine Minute ist. Diese präzisen Momente geben einem ein gutes Gefühl; ein Gefühl des Verbundenseins.

Ich kann mich daran erinnern, als ich vierzehn war und mich entscheiden musste, ob ich ein Kunststudium beginnen oder die allgemeine Ausbildung an der Mittelschule fortsetzen sollte (was die Berufswahl etwas hinausgeschoben hätte). Die Wahl fiel mir schwer. Eines Tages besuchte ich einen guten Freund, einen Künstler namens Edi Rama, der damals eben als Professor an der Kunstakademie zu arbeiten begonnen hatte. Nach einem langen Gespräch sagte er zu mir, dass ich diese Wahl selbst treffen müsse und dass er mir die Verantwortung nicht abnehmen könne. Aber, sagte er, letztlich gehe es nicht darum, ob ich Bilder malen oder später Mathematik studieren würde; es gehe um etwas anderes. Er sagte, wenn ich gleich mit der Kunstschule begänne, so würde ich im zweiten Jahr meine ersten sexuellen Erfahrungen machen, wenn ich jedoch zur Mittelschule ginge, würde dies erst ein Jahr später der Fall sein. Das mag banal klingen, wenn man nicht weiss, dass damals alle fast dasselbe Leben führten, mit denselben kleinen Ereignissen zur selben Zeit. Also hatte solch ein «kleiner» Unterschied eine tiefere Bedeutung. Darin lag eine Wahrheit, die für mich entscheidender war als die Entscheidung, ob ich für den Rest meines Lebens mit Farben oder Zahlen zu tun haben würde. Es war keine wirkliche Antwort, aber es veränderte meinen Umgang mit Fragen nachhaltig.

LC: Im zweiten Teil meiner Frage geht es darum, ob es in deinem Umgang mit der Photographie eine Parallele gibt zu deiner jetzigen Verwendung von Video, obwohl die Zeit in den beiden Medien jeweils eine andere Funktion hat. Ist die Videokamera für dich eine zeitliche Erweiterung des Photoapparates? Und wählst du deshalb so häufig eine statische Einstellung, eine die erlaubt, das Verstreichen der Zeit besser wahrzunehmen, weil der Bildausschnitt fixiert ist? Die Dinge innerhalb des Ausschnitts verändern sich, Leute treten ins Bild und verlassen es wieder, die Sonne geht auf und so weiter, aber das Bild bleibt konstant. Mir fällt auf, dass es in deinem Werk einige Arbeiten gibt, etwa jene mit den Ghost-Krabben (GHOST GAMES, 2002), in denen eine Bildsequenz mit handlungsähnlicher Struktur vorkommt, aber das scheint die grosse Ausnahme zu sein. Meistens sind zeitliche Beziehungen wichtiger als räumliche Fragen, und sie geben Anlass dazu, über Geschichte und Erinnerung zu reflektieren.

AS: Was die allgemeine Einstellung angeht, ist das Vorgehen bei beiden Medien ähnlich: Neugier und das Einbeziehen meines eigenen Unterbewusstseins. Ich bin daran interessiert, mich in meiner Arbeit jenen dunklen Regionen zu nähern, in denen Kultur und Natur aufeinander treffen, wo die Regel auf das Zwanglose, das Rationale auf das Irrationale, der Wunsch nach Kontrolle auf den Wunsch nach Kontrollverlust oder nach dem Nicht-Gewollten trifft. Angesichts der Rolle, welche die Zeit im Video spielt, besteht immer die Gefahr zu viel zu sagen, auf die Seite der «Herstellung von Sinn» abzudriften. Es ist eine faszinierende, aber alles andere als leichte Aufgabe. Es ist, als müsste man eine dunkle Zone, in der es keine Codes gibt und man noch nicht weiss, was Zeit ist, nach einem Zeitcode einteilen.

Ich versuche mich weiterzubewegen ohne wissen zu müssen – ohne wissen zu wollen. Ich will mich mit dem befassen, was ich noch nicht kenne, und versuche beiseite zu räumen, was ich allmählich zu gut kenne. Was die Welt plagt, interessiert mich mehr, als was in ihr Sinn macht. Wir geben uns oft grosse Mühe, das, was uns plagt, beiseite zu räumen, indem wir einen Sinn in allem finden wollen, indem wir unsere Umgebung kontrollieren und allem einen Nutzen, eine Rolle, eine Funktion, eine Normalität zuschreiben und andrerseits alles ausschliessen, was dunkel ist, uns verunsichert und mit dessen Benennung wir uns schwer tun. Das erklärt vielleicht, warum die Sprache eine so wichtige Rolle spielt, warum sie Vorrang hat vor dem Bild oder Ton. Die Sprache benennt, neutralisiert und gibt Sicherheit. Mein Interesse an der Sprache beruht nicht auf Vertrauen, sondern eher auf Vorsicht. Ich traue dem, was die Sprache erzählt, nicht mehr, sobald die Syntax wichtiger wird als die Worte selbst.

(Übersetzung: Suzanne Schmidt)

1) Maurice Merleau-Ponty, *Phänomenologie der Wahrnehmung*, § 38: Das Wunder des Ausdrucks in Sprache und Welt, De Gruyter & Co, Berlin 1966, S. 232. Merleau-Ponty zitiert hier einen Artikel von Kurt Goldstein, «L'analyse de l'aphasie et l'essence du langage», *J. Psychol.*, vol. 30 (1933), S. 430–496.

ANRI SALA, MIXED BEHAVIOUR, 2003, 8 min. 17 sec. color video and sound / GEMISCHTES VERHALTEN, 8 Min. 17 Sek. Farbvideo mit Ton.

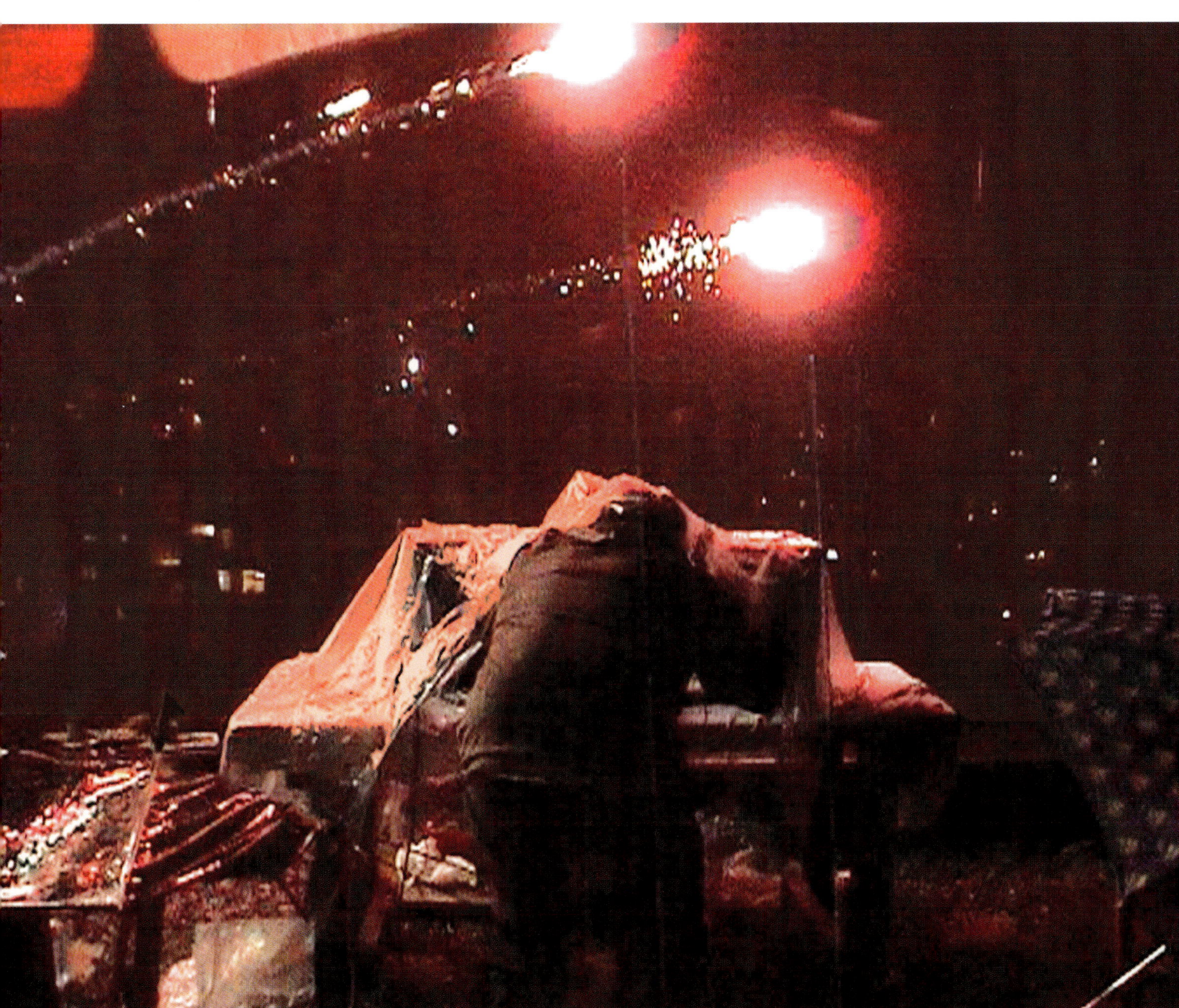

VON DEN RÄNDERN DER GESCHICHTE

JAN VERWOERT

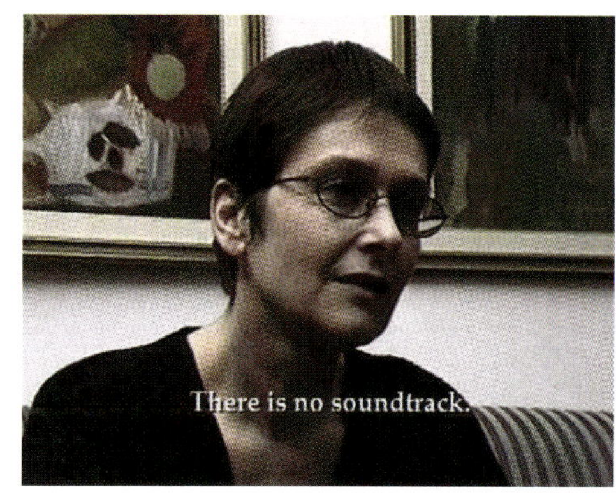

Die Geschichte von ihren Rändern her denken heisst die Grenze des Horizonts historischer Erfahrung zu ergründen. Diese Grenze ist eine Bewusstseinsschwelle, an der gegenwärtige Geschehnisse als Ereignisse erlebt werden, die potenziell einmal Geschichte sein könnten, es aktuell aber noch nicht sind. Etwas geschieht, aber was es bedeutet haben wird, ist noch nicht klar. Der Entstehungsmoment historischer Erfahrung ist so zugleich ein Zustand ahistorischen Erlebens. Dieser Zustand geht der Geschichte nicht etwa zeitlich voraus, er stellt sich vielmehr unmittelbar im Moment ihres Vollzugs ein, dann etwa, wenn im Zuge tiefgreifender politischer Umwälzungen einer Gesellschaft jeder Begriff von Geschichte abhanden kommt. Jeder spürt, dass sich alles verändert, aber niemand findet Worte, um diese Veränderung zu beschreiben. Die Ränder der Geschichte verlaufen im Zentrum des historischen Prozesses.

In seinen Videofilmen arbeitet Anri Sala an einer Beschreibung dieser Erfahrung der Latenz des Historischen. Er befragt, überdenkt und verändert dabei fortlaufend die formalen Mittel der filmischen Annäherung an seinen Gegenstand. In INTERVISTA (FINDING THE WORDS) (Interview – Das Auffinden der Worte, 1998) nutzt er die Mittel der biographischen Erzählung und dokumentarischen Darstellung, um die ungeklärte Situation des gegenwärtigen historischen Umbruchs der albanischen Gesellschaft nachzuvollziehen. In GHOST GAMES (Geisterspiele, 2002) löst er den Rahmen der Geschichtserzählung dagegen auf zugunsten der Freistellung der Aufnahme von umherirrenden Krebsen am Strand als atmosphärisches Bild. Die geisterhafte Bewegung der Tiere in einem zeit- und ortlosen Raum vergegenwärtigt hier eben den Zustand des reinen Lebens und Erlebens, der den Horizont historischer Erfahrung zugleich radikal begrenzt und – aufgrund der Bedeutungsfülle des Erlebnisses – neu eröffnet. Aus der Perspektive dieses entrückten Blicks auf einen geisterhaft fremden Gegenstand zeigt Sala in DAMMI I COLORI (Gib mir die Farben, 2003) daraufhin eine Stadt, Tirana, das Zentrum des Landes, als Ort, der in einem Zustand der historischen Latenz auf der Schwelle zwischen einer unbewältigten Vergangenheit und einer versprochenen Zukunft existiert. Die Diskussion dieser drei Videos soll im Folgenden exemplarisch wesentliche Problemstellungen von Salas Arbeit erschliessen.

JAN VERWOERT lebt in Hamburg, er ist Contributing Editor der Zeitschrift *frieze* und veröffentlicht unter anderem in *Afterall, Metropolis M, Camera Austria* und *springerin*. Er ist Gastprofessor für zeitgenössische Kunst und Theorie an der Akademie von Umeå in Schweden.

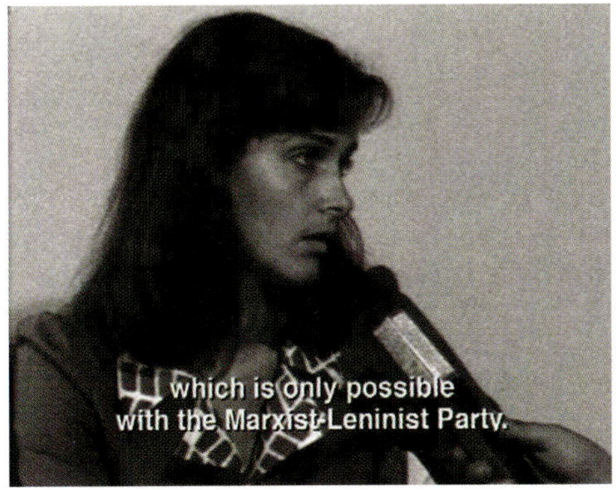

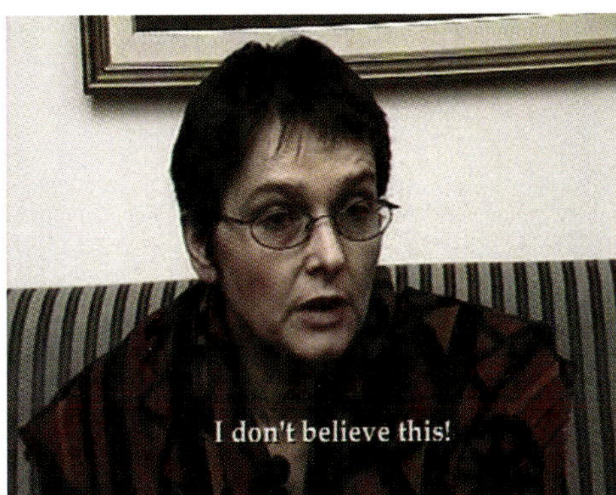

ANRI SALA, INTERVISTA—FINDING THE WORDS, 1998, 26 min. video and sound / INTERVIEW – DAS AUFFINDEN DER WORTE, 26 Min. Video mit Ton.

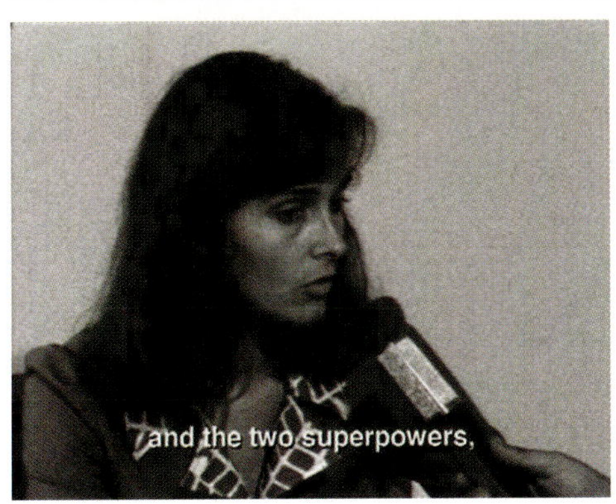

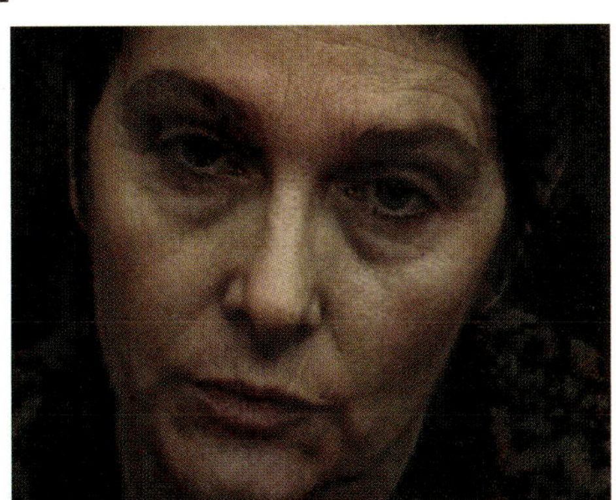

1. Erzählung, Biographie, Geschichte

Die Geschichte von INTERVISTA (FINDING THE WORDS) beginnt damit, dass Sala in einem Umzugskarton eine Reihe von Filmspulen findet. Einige der Aufnahmen zeigen seine Mutter, Valdete Sala, als junge Frau, wie sie als Vertreterin der Jugendbewegung der kommunistischen Partei unter Enver Hoxha im albanischen Staatsfernsehen ein Interview gibt. Der Ton des Interviews fehlt. Sala reist nach Tirana und versucht im Gespräch mit Mitgliedern des damaligen Fernsehteams und zwei ehemaligen Parteigenossen etwas über den Inhalt und politischen Kontext des Interviews zu erfahren. Aber erst mit Hilfe einer gehörlosen Lippenleserin gelingt die Rekonstruktion der Rede. Konfrontiert mit deren Wortlaut, reagiert die Mutter verunsichert. Ihre damaligen Worte ergeben für sie keinen Sinn mehr. Die Begriffe sind ihr fremd und im wortwörtlichen Sinne unverständlich geworden. Sie distanziert sich von ihrer damaligen Sprache, bekennt sich aber weiterhin zu ihren Idealen. Sie sind Teil ihres Lebens.

INTERVISTA vermittelt so eine intensive Vorstellung davon, wie der geschichtliche Wandel die Sprache, in der eine Gesellschaft zuvor ihr historisches Selbstverständnis formulierte, entwertet. Um diesen geschichtlich bedeutsamen Moment des Sprachverlusts überhaupt beschreiben zu können, erzählt Sala selbst eine Geschichte. Er nutzt die Form einer einfachen biographischen Erzählung vom Verlust und Fund der Worte als Vehikel zur Erschliessung eines überpersönlichen gesellschaftlichen wie geschichtlichen Zusammenhangs.[1] Diese Öffnung erhält die Erzählung des Films gerade dadurch, dass sie keine konventionelle kathartische Auflösung erfährt. Exemplarisch wirkt Valdete Salas Biographie ja eben deshalb, weil sie ein Gefühl

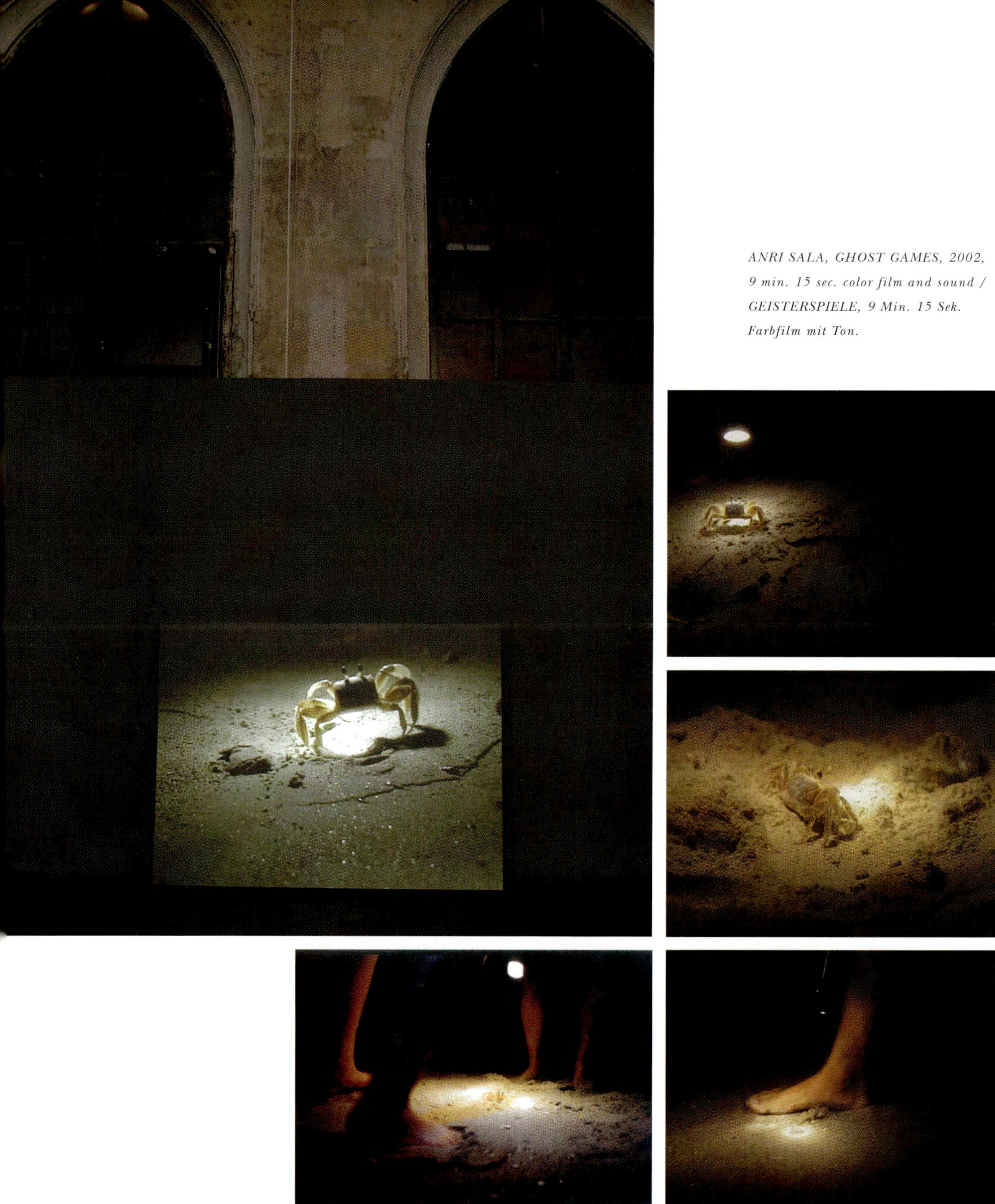

ANRI SALA, GHOST GAMES, 2002, 9 min. 15 sec. color film and sound / GEISTERSPIELE, 9 Min. 15 Sek. Farbfilm mit Ton.

für den unauflöslichen Widerspruch von Identifikation und Distanznahme vermittelt, der potenziell das gespaltene Verhältnis einer ganzen Generation zur Geschichte des albanischen Staatssozialismus wiedergibt. Die Filmerzählung schildert ein wirkliches als ein mögliches Leben. Dieses Leben erscheint dabei als Grenze des Horizonts historischer Erfahrung. Valdete Sala ist gerade deshalb Zeitzeugin, weil sie die Geschichte überlebt. Die Geschichte des Regimes ist zu Ende. Ihr Leben geht weiter. INTERVISTA vermittelt so ein Gefühl für die Komplexität des Verhältnisses von Biographie und Historie: Die Geschichte holt das Leben immer wieder ein, vereinnahmt es jedoch nie gänzlich, weil das Leben die Geschichte immer wieder überdauert.

Die visuelle Textur von INTERVISTA ist dabei durch eine Vielzahl von Exkursen und Aussetzern bestimmt: Während der Autofahrten zu Drehorten streut Sala unkommentiert Bilder aus Tiranas Stadtraum ein. Zuweilen schwenkt er im Verlauf eines Interviews die Kamera unvermittelt weg von der interviewten Person, um den Blick durch das Fenster gleiten und auf der Fassade des gegenüberliegenden Gebäudes ruhen zu lassen. Diese Bilder haben keine Funktion für den Fortgang der Erzählung. Sie geben ihr eine gewisse Dichte, indem sie ein Gefühl für Ort und Zeit vermitteln. Zugleich verweisen sie jedoch auch auf das, was jenseits der Erzählung liegt, insofern sie einen Eindruck davon geben, was bleibt, wenn der Film endet: die stumme Besonderheit von Orten. Der Film erzählt von der Stadt, aber die Stadt weiss nichts von dem Film. Diese Bilder markieren die Grenzen der Narration, indem sie auf eine Realität hindeuten, die ihrer Interpretation durch die Geschichte gleichgültig gegenübersteht.

2. Freigestellte Bilder, ortloser Raum, verräumlichte Zeit

Auf die methodische Freistellung eben solcher Bilder stummer Realität konzentriert sich das Video GHOST GAMES (2002).[2] Die Bilder des Videos sind gespenstisch: An einem nächtlichen Strand huschen zahllose Krabben, getrieben von den Lichtkegeln mehrerer Taschenlampen, in grotesk ziellosen Bewegungen durch den Sand. Das Geschehen scheint an einem Ort jenseits von Raum und Zeit stattzufinden. Dass es sich um ein Spiel handelt, bei dem es darum geht, mithilfe des Lichts der Taschenlampen eine Krabbe zwischen den Beinen des Gegenspielers hindurchzujagen, erschliesst sich erst allmählich aus den gelegentlichen «Goal»-Rufen der ansonsten schweigend agierenden Spieler, von denen man nie mehr sieht als die Füsse. Der latent sadistische Charakter des Spiels vermittelt dabei ein bedrohliches Gefühl, denn das stupide Gefangensein im berechenbaren Reiz-Reaktions-Schema macht die Tiere im wahrsten Sinne des Wortes zum Spielball menschlicher Willkür.

Der konzeptuelle Ansatz von GHOST GAMES ist die gezielte Reduktion der Erzählung auf das Spiel. Sala sagt dazu: «In GHOST GAMES ist die nächtliche Szene mit den Krabben am Strand eindeutig mehr Spiel als Geschichte. Beim Spielen entstehen Spielfelder und Aktionen, Beziehungen und Szenarien, aber keine Geschichten (...).»[3] Diese Reduktion der Erzählung auf das Spiel verändert die Wahrnehmung der Videobilder entscheidend. Der Erfahrungshorizont der Geschehnisse ist der einer verräumlichten Zeit: Alles, was es zu sehen gibt, geschieht auf einem Stück Strand irgendwo im Nirgendwo. Die Zeit an diesem Ort ist nicht die lineare Zeit der Erzählung, Handlung und Geschichte, sondern die zirkuläre Zeit der ständigen Wiederholung von Spielzügen, welche die immer gleichen Reaktionsmuster der Tiere abrufen. Die Einstellung der Wahrnehmung auf eine verräumlichte Zeit der offenen Dauer bewirkt eine Freistellung der Bilder: Der Blick geht in ein leeres Schauen über. Man schaut auf Körper im Raum, die im freien Spiel, aber doch getrieben von Notwendigkeit (die Krabben können nicht anders) umeinander kreisen.

Die Suspendierung der Erzählung löst die Bilder aus ihrer Einbindung in gängige Deutungsmuster. Zugleich verdichten sich die Bilder der Videos in der Anschauung jedoch zu einem einzigen eindringlichen Vorstellungsbild: gejagte Krabben am Strand. Dieses Bild kann man als Metapher verstehen: Die unkoordinierten, zwanghaften Bewegungen der flüchtenden Krabben vermitteln ein Gefühl für die Verengung des Horizonts auf den Erhalt des nackten Lebens in einem Zustand existenzieller Bedrängnis, den ein Mensch angesichts von Gewalt, Krieg oder einer schwerwiegenden gesellschaftlichen Krise erfahren würde. Entscheidend ist aber, dass diese metaphorische Deutung zwar nahe liegt, aber de facto nicht in die Videobilder eingeschrieben ist. Zu sehen sind Tiere, die sich den Gesetzen ihrer eigenen – und nicht der menschlichen – Natur entsprechend verhalten. Die Krabben wissen nichts vom Menschen. Sie reagieren nur auf Licht. Sie sind uns ebenso fremd wie wir ihnen. Und gerade diese Fremdheit des Tieres stellt das Video ja unter Beweis. Die Fremdheit des Tieres markiert erneut eine Grenze, welche die Konturen der menschlichen historischen Erfahrung, von der Schwelle des nicht mehr menschlichen aus betrachtet, in Erscheinung treten lässt.

3. Geisterhafte Stadt, zukünftige Gegenwart und kommende Gesellschaft

Die Atmosphäre, die DAMMI I COLORI (2003) vermittelt, ist nicht weniger gespenstisch als die von GHOST GAMES, mit dem Unterschied jedoch, dass dieser Eindruck des Geisterhaften von einer nicht näher benannten Stadt ausgeht. Das Video zeigt Bilder von einer nächtlichen Autofahrt. In fliessender Bewegung ziehen Häuserzeilen an der Kamera vorbei. Im grellen Licht eines im Fahrzeug installierten Scheinwerfers erstrahlen die Fassaden der Häuser. Sie sind in leuchtenden Farben mit abstrakt geometrischen Mustern bemalt. Bei den Gebäuden handelt es sich meist um ansonsten schmucklose Bauten, funktionale Mietskasernen älteren Datums. Die Bemalung lässt ihren Bauzustand kaum erahnen. Vor den Gebäuden sieht man unbefestigte Gehwege und Schutthalden. Der Eindruck, den die Bilder vermitteln, ist zutiefst widersprüchlich. Die unwirklich hell leuchtenden Farbmuster auf den Fassaden lassen es so erscheinen, als seien die kühnsten Träume der modernistischen Architektur-Avantgarden Wirklichkeit geworden. Das Fehlen von Gehwegen und Strassenbeleuchtung erzeugt dagegen eher die Atmosphäre einer Krise mit ungeklärtem Ausgang.

Die Bilder werden begleitet von einem überwiegend aus dem Off gesprochenen Kommentar. Der Sprecher erzählt von den anfänglichen Zweifeln der Bevölkerung gegenüber der Fassadenbemalung und der anschliessenden breiten Unterstützung. Er betont die grosse Bedeutung der durch die Farben erzeugten Veränderung der allgemeinen Stimmung zum Positiven, auch hinsichtlich der Realisierung der anstehenden Modernisierungsmassnahmen. Dass es sich bei der Stadt um Tirana und beim Sprecher um den Bürgermeister Edi Rama handelt, ist eine Information, die das Video aus guten Gründen zurückhält. DAMMI I COLORI zeigt und kommentiert die spezifische Realität einer Stadt, tut dies aber gerade nicht im konventionellen Stil einer (vorgeblich) informativen Reportage. Die Pointe des Videos ist vielmehr zuallererst ein Staunen angesichts der Unwirklichkeit der dargestellten Realität. (In diesem Sinne zitiert Sala Liam Gillick im Vorspann des Films mit den Worten: «Anri, sag mir die Wahrheit. Sag mir, dass diese Stadt nicht existiert.») In dem Masse, wie der Charakter der Stadt dadurch bestimmt ist, dass ihr aktuelles Erscheinungsbild eine potenzielle Zukunft vorwegnimmt, wirkt die Stadt wie ein ort- und zeitloses, in die Gegenwart zurückprojiziertes Abbild einer zukünftigen Realität. Was DAMMI I COLORI somit dokumentiert, ist nicht eine faktische Wirklichkeit, sondern die Existenz eines Versprechens: das noch unrealisierte Potenzial einer kommenden Gesellschaft.

Was hier wiederkehrt, ist das aus INTERVISTA und GHOST GAMES bekannte Gefühl der Fremdheit einer Wirklichkeit, die von ihrem Betrachter nichts weiss – in Gestalt einer Stadt, die sich trotz ihrer grellen Ausleuchtung der Betrachtung verschliesst. Es ist eine Stadt, die in einer der Vergangenheit abgerungenen und in der Gegenwart vorweggenommenen Zukunft zu existieren scheint und somit als stummer Zeuge der Geschichte zugleich auch jenseits der historischen Zeit, in einem Zustand leerer Dauer fortbesteht. Eine Erfahrungsdimension, die Salas Videos so aus der dokumentarischen Darstellung herausschälen, ist das Gefühl für das zeitlose Fortdauern von Existenzen, Städten oder Instinkten mitten im Horizont des Geschichtlichen. Es ist ein Sinn dafür, dass sich gerade im Moment gesellschaftlicher Umbrüche und historischer Krisen das Gefühl einstellt, dass das Leben weitergeht. Salas Arbeiten entwickeln einen Blick für ein gerade im Moment der Suspendierung von Deutungskategorien zutage tretendes Leben.[4] Es ist ein Leben, das in INTERVISTA in der Differenz zwischen dem Biographischen und dem überpersönlich Historischen aufscheint, in GHOST GAMES an der Schwelle zwischen der gesellschaftlich geschichtlichen Existenz des Menschen und der nicht mehr menschlichen, ort- und zeitlosen Existenz des Tiers spürbar wird, und in INTERVISTA und DAMMI I COLORI im Spannungsfeld einer Gegenwart Gestalt gewinnt, die in gleichem Masse von einer unversöhnten Vergangenheit und versprochenen Zukunft geprägt und gespalten wird. Das dokumentarische Bild deutet in Salas Arbeiten somit auf eine Schwelle der unhistorischen Existenz hin, von deren Erfahrung her sich die Dimension des historischen gesellschaftlichen Wandels erst ermessen lässt.

1) Catherine Russell beschreibt die hier von Sala angewandte Methode der Verwendung einer biographischen Erzählung als Mittel zur Darstellung gesellschaftlicher Zusammenhänge prägnant als «Autoethnographie»: «Die Autobiographie wird in dem Moment ethnographisch, wo Film- oder Videoautor(-inn)en ihre persönliche Geschichte auf dem Hintergrund grösserer gesellschaftlicher Gebilde und historischer Prozesse sehen. Identität ist nicht mehr ein transzendentales oder wesentliches Selbst, das sich offenbart, sondern eine ‹Inszenierung der Subjektivität› – eine Darstellung des Selbst als Performance. In der Politisierung des Persönlichen kommen Identitäten oft in verschiedenen kulturellen Diskursen zum Ausdruck, seien diese ethnisch, national, sexuell, radikal und/oder schichtspezifisch bestimmt. Das Subjekt wird ‹in der Geschichte› als ein aus dem Gleichgewicht geratenes, inkohärentes dargestellt, als ein Ort vielfältiger Spannungen und Artikulationen.» Catherine Russell, «Autoethnography: Journeys of the Self», in: Russell, *Experimental Ethnographies,* Duke University Press, Durham 1999, S. 276 (Übers. des Zitats: *Parkett*).

2) Sala erzählt, dass die Arbeit auf die Erfahrung eines nächtlichen Strandspaziergangs zurückgeht. Der Strand war von zahllosen Krabben, sogenannten *Ghost-Crabs* bevölkert, die auf das Licht von Taschenlampen instinktiv mit sofortiger Flucht reagierten.

3) «... in GHOST GAMES the scene with crabs on a beach at night definitely has more to do with games than with narrative. Games create territory and action, relations and scenarios but no narratives (...)», in: «What's the difference?» (Jörg Heiser und Jan Verwoert im Gespräch mit Yael Bartana, Annika Eriksson, Anri Sala und Gitte Villesen), *frieze* 84 (Juni–August 2004), S. 72–77, Zitat S. 74.

4) Im Rückgriff auf eine Passage aus Gilles Deleuze' «Die Immanenz: ein Leben...» definiert Agamben diese Schwelle eines überpersönlichen, überhistorischen und nicht mehr nur menschlichen Lebens wie folgt: «Dieses indefinite Leben hat selbst keine Augenblicke, so nahe sie auch beieinanderliegen mögen, sondern nur Zwischen-Zeiten, Zwischen-Momente. Es bricht nicht herein und folgt nicht nach, sondern bietet die Unermesslichkeit der leeren Zeit, in der man das Ereignis noch als künftiges und schon als geschehenes sieht, und zwar im Absoluten eines unmittelbaren Bewusstseins.» Giorgio Agamben, «Die absolute Immanenz», in: Agamben, *Bartleby oder die Kontingenz gefolgt von Die absolute Immanenz,* Merve Verlag, Berlin 1998, S. 111. Dies erscheint mir eine wunderschöne Beschreibung der Zeit- und Erfahrungsdimension zu sein, deren Beschreibung Salas Arbeiten anstreben. Gleichermassen erscheint mir das Bild der Geisterkrabben in GHOST GAMES den Geist der Idee vom Leben des Tieres als apokalyptischer Schwelle der menschlichen historischen Existenz zu artikulieren, die Agamben in *Das Offene – der Mensch und das Tier* (Suhrkamp, Frankfurt am Main 2002) in Begriffe zu fassen versucht.

When I first showed the city footage
in Poughkeepsie,
Liam Gillick said to me,
"Anri, tell me the truth.
Tell me that this city does not exist.
Please tell me that you do not have
an artist - Mayor friend?"

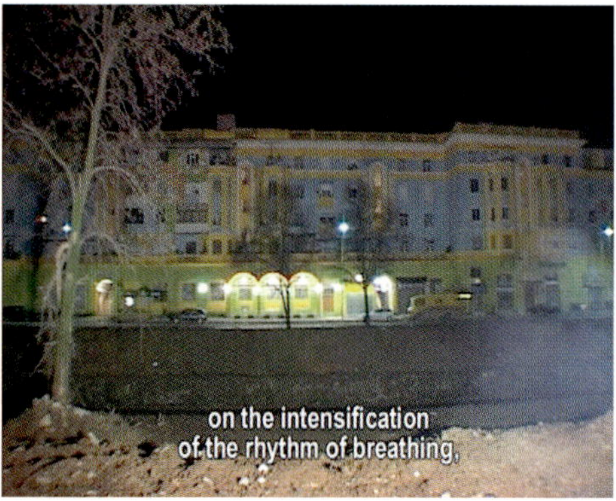

ANRI SALA, DAMMI I COLORI, 2003: GIVE ME THE COLORS, 15 min. 24 sec. video projection and sound / HER MIT DEN FARBEN, 15 Min. 24 Sek. Videoprojektion mit Ton.

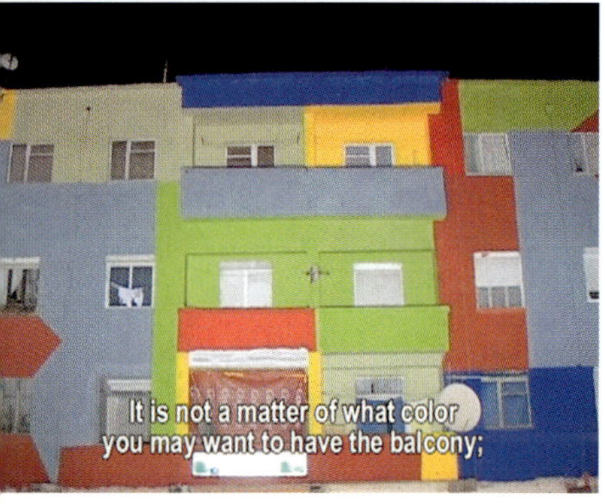

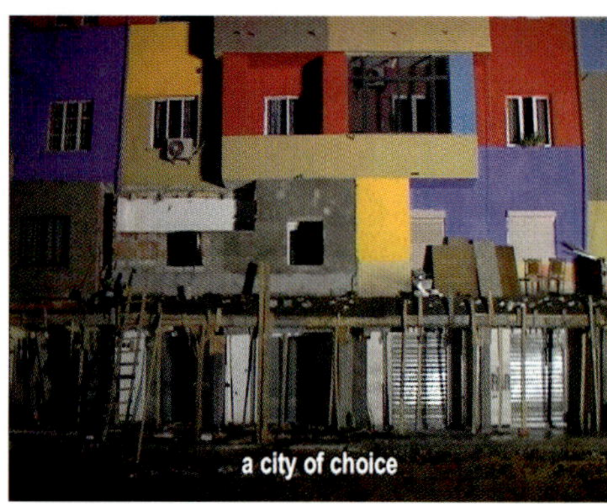

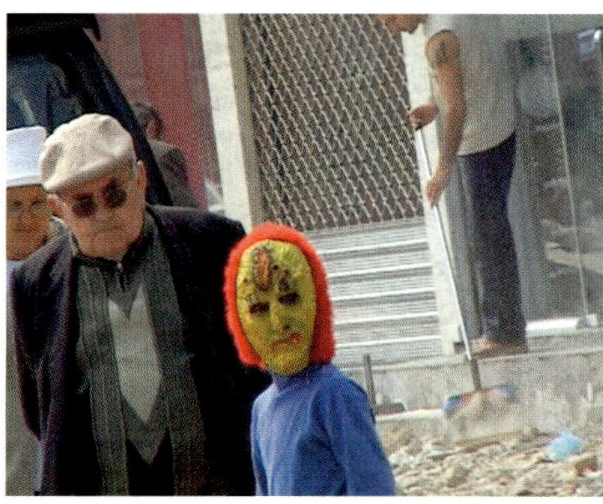

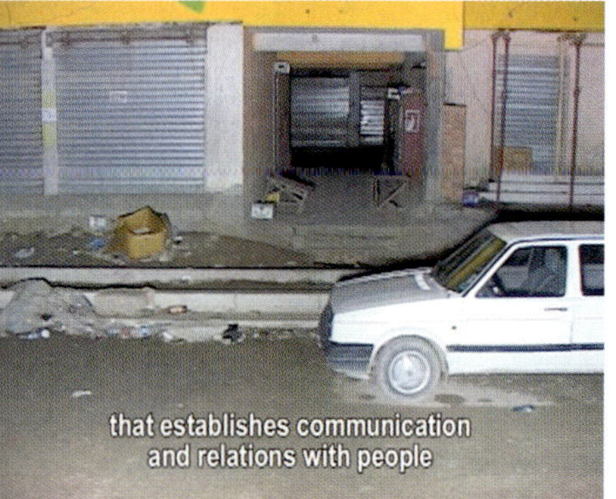

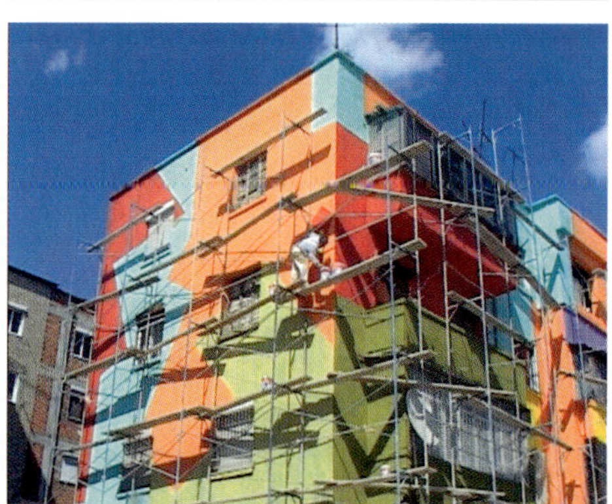

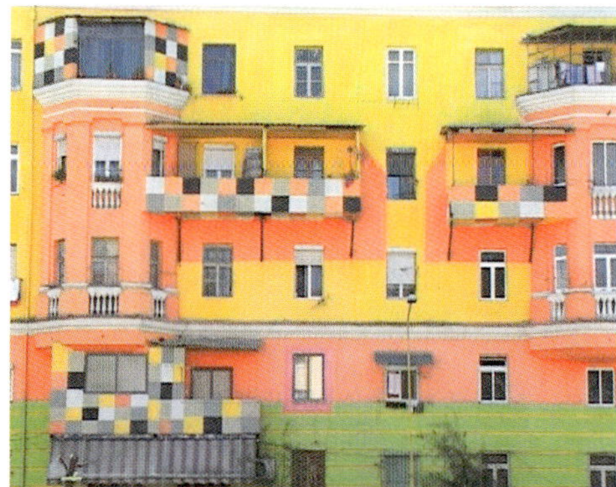

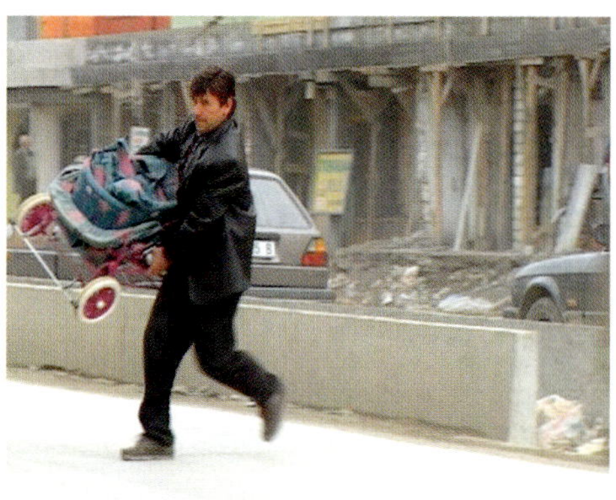

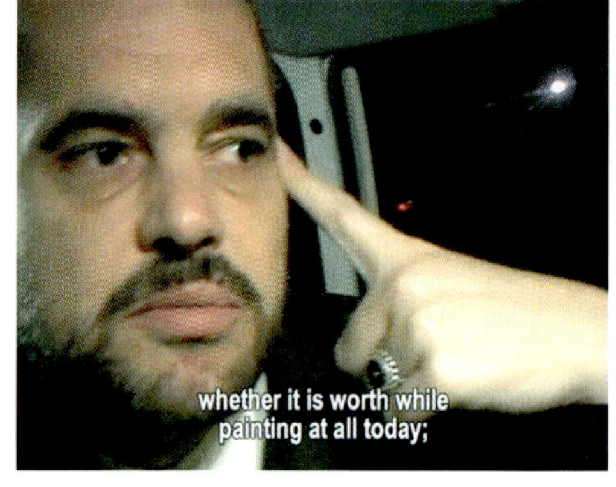

ON THE MARGINS OF HISTORY

JAN VERWOERT

To approach history from its margins means to explore the horizons of historical experience. Their limits lie on the threshold of historical consciousness where present occurrences are perceived as events that could potentially, but have not yet actually, become history. Something is happening, but what it might once have meant, is not yet clear. The origin of historical consciousness is at the same time a state of ahistorical experience. This state does not precede history in time; on the contrary, it rather occurs in the process of its unraveling, for instance, when, in the course of fundamental social upheaval, all the established concepts for explaining history no longer serve. People sense that everything is changing but no one can find the words to describe the change. The margins of history thus cross the very center of the historical process.

In his videos Anri Sala works to describe this experience of historical latency. He consistently questions and reformulates the formal means of approaching his subject. In INTERVISTA (FINDING THE WORDS)(1998), he explores the capabilities of the biographical narrative and the documentary image to portray the complex situation of current historical change in Albanian society. In GHOST GAMES (2002), however, he eliminates the narrative frame in favor of atmospheric images of crabs scuttling across a beach at night. The spectral presence of these animals in placeless space and empty time visualizes a state of bare life and basic experience, which both radically delimits and opens up the horizon of historical experience due to the depth of meaning it implies. From the perspective of this remote gaze on a ghostlike phenomenon Sala then, in DAMMI I COLORI (2003), depicts a city, Tirana, the center of a country, as a place, which in a state of historic latency exists on the threshold between an unresolved past and a promised future. An analysis of these three videos in the following essay shall provide an overview of the issues that Sala addresses and explores in his work.

JAN VERWOERT lives in Hamburg, Germany. He is a contributing editor at *frieze* magazine and writes regularly for *Afterall, Metropolis M, Camera Austria, springerin,* and others. He is guest professor for Contemporary Art and Theory at the Academy of Umeå, Sweden.

1. Narrative, Biography, History

INTERVISTA (FINDING THE WORDS) is a documentary video based on a narrative structure. The video begins with the artist's discovery of film reels in a moving box. A few of the shots show his mother, Valdete Sala, as a young woman, giving an interview on Albanian state television as a representative of the Communist Party youth movement under Enver Hoxha. Since the soundtrack of the interview is missing, Sala travels to Tirana and, in conversations with former party associates and members from the crew who recorded the television program, tries to find out more about the content and political context of the interview. A reconstruction of the actual words, however, is not possible until a hearing-impaired lip-reader comes to his aid. On being confronted with her words, his mother reacts with disbelief. The words she once used do not make sense to her anymore. They have become strange and, in the most literal sense, incomprehensible to her. But even though she distances herself from the kind of language she used, she stands by the ideals she held back then. They are part of her life.

INTERVISTA thus conveys a strong sense of how the language in which a society once formulated its understanding of its own historical reality is jettisoned in the wake of historical change. To be able to describe this historically meaningful loss of a language, Sala tells a story himself. He uses the straightforward structure of biographical narrative as a vehicle for grasping a wider historical and social context.[1] The narrative is open to this more general perspective because it does not lead to conventional catharsis. The biography of Valdete Sala comes to be perceived as exemplary precisely because it communicates the insoluble contradiction between identification and distance, which potentially represents the ambivalent relationship of an entire generation to the history of Albanian state socialism. The narrative of the film portrays a real life as a possible one. At the same time this life marks the limits of historical experience. Valdete Sala is able to bear witness by very virtue of the fact that she has survived history. The history of the regime has come to an end. Her life goes on. INTERVISTA thus conveys the complex relationship of biography to history. History always catches up with life, but it never fully consumes it since life always outlasts history.

The visual texture of INTERVISTA is marked by detours and jump cuts. While driving to film locations, Sala intercuts scattered images of urban Tirana without comment. Sometimes, while interviewing, he may suddenly pan away from the person being interviewed, over to the window, for example, where the camera looks out and comes to rest on the façade of the building across the street. These images have no function; they do not further the plot. But they do provide a certain density by imparting a sense of local time and space. In addition, they refer to what lies beyond the story since they give an impression of what remains when the film ends: the silent singularity of places. The film gives an account of the city, but the city knows nothing about the film. These images mark the limits of narration by referring to a reality that remains indifferent to historical interpretation.

2. Released Images, Placeless Space, Spatialized Time

The video GHOST GAMES concentrates on methodically extracting and releasing just such pictures of mute reality.[2] The pictures of the video are ghostly: countless crabs are seen scrambling aimlessly across a sandy beach at night, driven by the beams of flashlights. The setting appears to be somewhere beyond space and time. All we hear in the silence is the

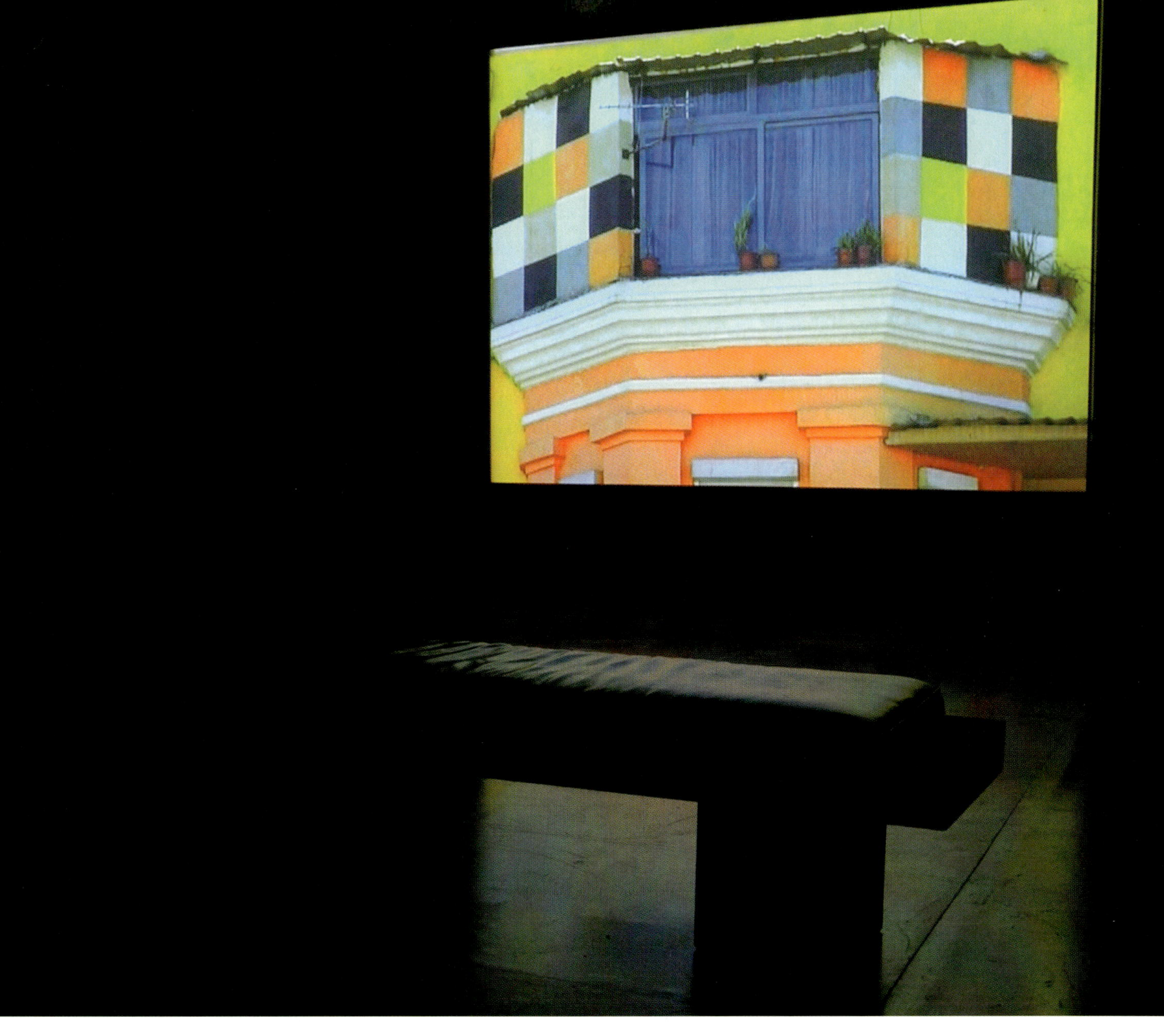

ANRI SALA, DAMMI I COLORI, 2003: GIVE ME THE COLORS, 15 min. 24 sec. video projection and sound, installation view, Galerie Chantal Crousel, Paris / HER MIT DEN FARBEN, 15 Min. 24 Sek. Videoprojektion mit Ton.

occasional cry of "goal," so that we gradually realize we are watching a game in which two players use the beam of their flashlights to force a crab to run between the legs of the opponent. Only the feet of the players are visible throughout. In addition, there is a sense of menace in the latently sadistic character of the action: animals, stupidly imprisoned in a predictable stimulus-response schema, are literally turned into game balls of human arbitrariness.

Conceptually, the narrative of GHOST GAMES is deliberately reduced to the game; it alone supplies the formal principle that determines the structure of the film. Sala himself remarks that "in GHOST GAMES the scene with crabs on a beach at night definitely has more to do with games than with narrative. Games create territory and action, relations and scenarios but no narratives ..."[3] Sala's reductive approach radically alters our perception of the video images. We experience what is happening within a context of spatialized time: all of the action, all we ever see, takes place on a section of beach located somewhere that is nowhere. It is a place where time does not correspond to the linear time of narrative, action, and plot but to the circular time of constantly repeated moves in a game that keeps activating the same response pattern in the animals. The adjustment of perception to a spatialized time of undefined length brings about the release of the images: the gaze shifts over into empty looking. We look at bodies in space, which circle around each other in an unconstrained game, though they are still driven by necessity (the crabs have no choice).

The suspension of narrative precludes conventional patterns of interpretation. Nonetheless, when we watch the video, the pictures coalesce into a single, powerful image: hounded crabs on a beach. This image could be understood as a metaphor. The uncoordinated, compulsive movements of the fleeing crabs create the impression of perceptual horizons abruptly narrowing down to the point of preserving bare life when existentially threatened, as one might be in the face of violence, war or profound social upheaval. It is significant, however, that even though this metaphorical reading of the image is potentially possible, it is not actually inscribed in the images of the video. What you see are animals that behave in consonance with the laws of their own nature. They know nothing of human beings. They only react to light. They are as strange to us as we are to them. And it is precisely this aspect of utter strangeness that the video brings to the fore. The radical otherness of the animal again marks the margins of historical consciousness, as it sets off the contours of the quintessentially human experience of history against the experience of forms that are no longer human.

3. Spectral City, the Future in the Present, and a Society to Come

The atmosphere, communicated by DAMMI I COLORI, is no less spectral than that of GHOST GAMES, but there is one important difference: the ghostly impression emanates from an unnamed city. The video shows pictures taken while driving through the city at night. The camera captures the flowing movement of buildings passing by, caught in the bright beam of a spotlight mounted on the car. Abstract geometrical patterns are painted on them in glowing colors. Most of the buildings are otherwise unembellished: they are functional, relatively old apartment buildings. Since they have been freshly painted, it is almost impossible to judge their condition. Dirt walkways and piles of rubble are seen in front of them. The pictures make an extremely ambivalent impression. The patterns of color on the façades, almost too bright to be real, look as if the most daring dreams of a modernist architectural avant-garde had come true. But without sidewalks or streetlights, the neighborhood seems to have suffered some unidentified crisis whose outcome remains a mystery.

A running commentary accompanies the pictures; the speaker talks about the painted façades, recalling how the initial skepticism of the urban populace gradually gave way to widespread support of the project. He points out that the colorful façades contributed to changing the overall atmosphere and that people now take a more positive view of pending measures to modernize the city. The fact that the city is Tirana and the speaker is its mayor, Edi Rama, is information that the video withholds for good reason. The point is that DAMMI I

COLORI shows and comments the specific reality of a city, but dismisses the form of conventional reportage and its claim to factual information. Instead, the video provokes astonishment at being confronted with the unreality of the reality it represents. (Sala tellingly quotes Liam Gillick in the opening credits of the video: "Anri, tell me the truth. Tell me that this city does not exist.") Inasmuch as the character of the city is determined by the fact that its current appearance anticipates a potential future, it conveys the impression of representing a timeless and placeless future reality, which has been projected back into the present. Hence, DAMMI I COLORI does not document a factual reality but the existence of a promise: the unrealized potential of a society to come.

As in INTERVISTA and GHOST GAMES, this video again confronts us with the familiar feeling of an alien reality that knows nothing about its viewers—now, however, in the shape of a city that withdraws into its own shell, as it were, in spite of the bright illumination. It is a city that seems to exist in a future wrested from the past and prefigured in the present, thereby becoming a mute witness to history, which also abides beyond historical time in a condition of emptiness and duration. The documentary form of Sala's videos succeeds in extracting from experience the sensation of the timeless continuation of lives, cities, or instincts in the midst of the aggregate of history. The films seem almost buoyed by the sense that life goes on, even in times of social upheaval and historical crisis. Sala's works offer insight into the life that emerges at the very moment when hermeneutic categories are suspended.[4)] In INTERVISTA, life surfaces in the spaces between biography and supra-personal history; in GHOST GAMES, it becomes palpable on the threshold between social, historical human existence and the no longer human existence of animals beyond place and time; and in INTERVISTA and DAMMI I COLORI, it acquires form within the context of a present, both marked and ruptured by an un-reconciled past and a promised future. The documentary image, in Sala's works, points toward a threshold of non-historical existence, the experience of which is actually a precondition for measuring the extent of historical and social change.

(Translation: Jan Verwoert & Catherine Schelbert)

1) Catherine Russell aptly describes this method of using biographical narrative to reveal wider social issues: "Autobiography becomes ethnographic at the point where the film- or videomaker understands his or her personal history to be implicated in larger social formations and historical processes. Identity is no longer a transcendental or essential self that is revealed, but a 'staging of subjectivity'—a representation of the self as a performance. In the politicization of the personal, identities are frequently played out among several cultural discourses, be they ethnic, national, sexual, radical, and/or class based. The subject 'in history' is rendered destabilized and incoherent, a site of discursive pressures and articulations." See "Autoethnography: Journeys of the Self" in Catherine Russell, *Experimental Ethnographies* (Durham, NC: Duke University Press, 1999), p. 276.

2) According to Sala, a night-time walk on the beach provided the initial impetus of the video. He discovered untold crabs inhabiting the beach, which instantly fled the beam of his flashlight, and learned that they were called ghost crabs.

3) Quoted from "What's the difference?" (Jörg Heiser and Jan Verwoert in conversation with Yael Bartana, Annika Eriksson, Anri Sala, and Gitte Villesen) in *frieze*, issue 84 (June–August 2004), pp. 72–77, here p. 74.

4) Giorgio Agamben bases his analysis of the threshold between supra-personal, supra-historical, and no longer human life on the following passage from Gilles Deleuze's last text, "Immanence: A Life...": "This undefined life does not itself have moments, however close to one another they might be; it has only inter-times [*entre-temps*], inter-moments [*entre-moments*]. It neither follows nor succeeds, but rather presents the immensity of empty time, where one sees the event that is to come and that has already happened in the absolute of an immediate consciousness." Quoted in Giorgio Agamben, *Potentialities: Collected Essays in Philosophy,* transl. and edited by Daniel Heller-Roazen (Stanford, CA: Stanford University Press, 1999), p. 233. This to me is a marvelous account of the dimensions of time and experience that Sala seeks to describe in his work. Similarly, the image of ghost crabs in GHOST GAMES seems to articulate the spirit of the idea of animal life as the apocalyptic threshold of historical human existence, which Agamben explores in *The Open – Man and Animal* (Stanford, CA: Stanford University Press, 2004).

Edition for Parkett

ANRI SALA
AIRPORT, 2005
C-print, paper size 20 ½ x 27 9/16", image size 16 ½ x 23 5/8".
Edition of 60/XX, signed and numbered certificate.

C-Print, Blattformat: 52 x 70 cm, Bildformat: 42 x 60 cm.
Auflage: 60/XX, signiertes und nummeriertes Zertifikat.

(PHOTO: MANCIA/BODMER, FBM-STUDIO, ZÜRICH)

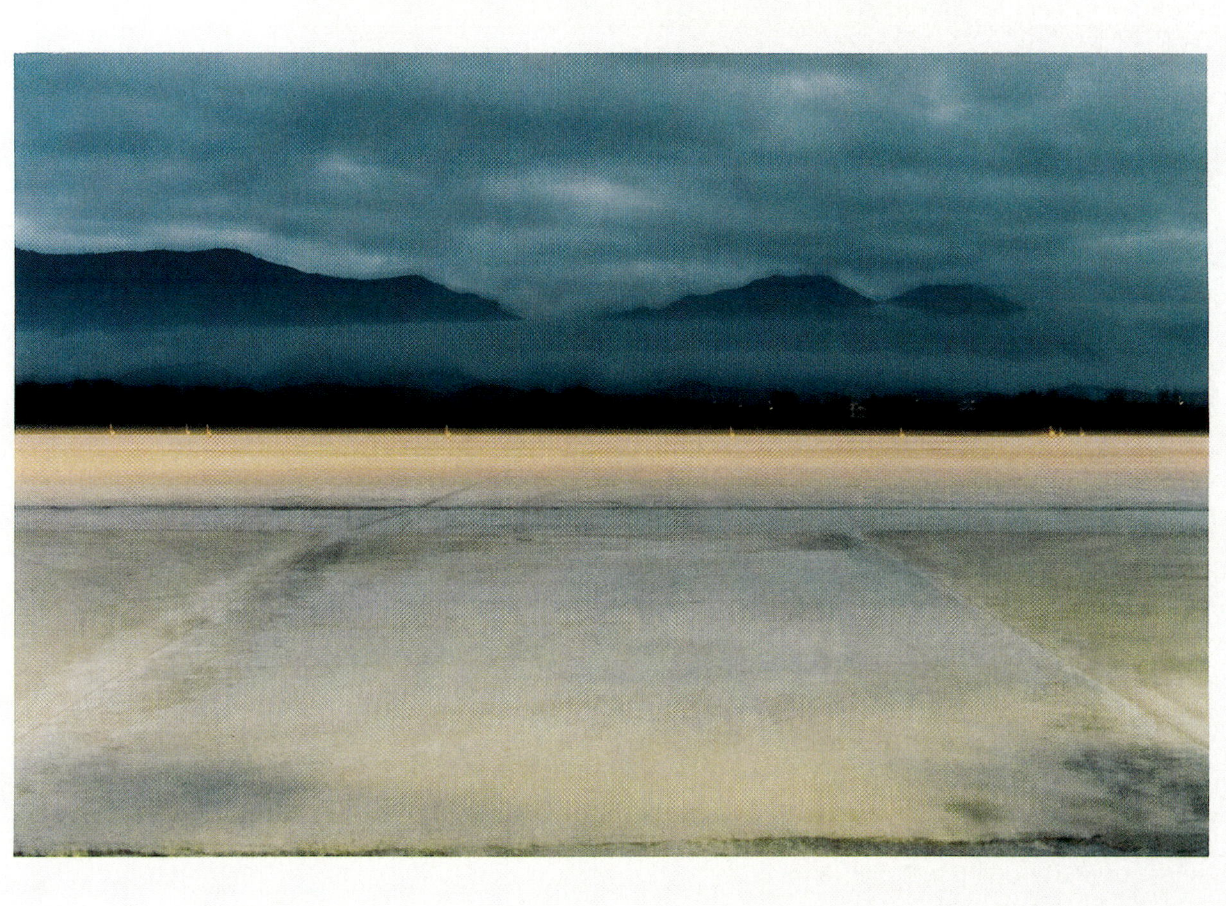

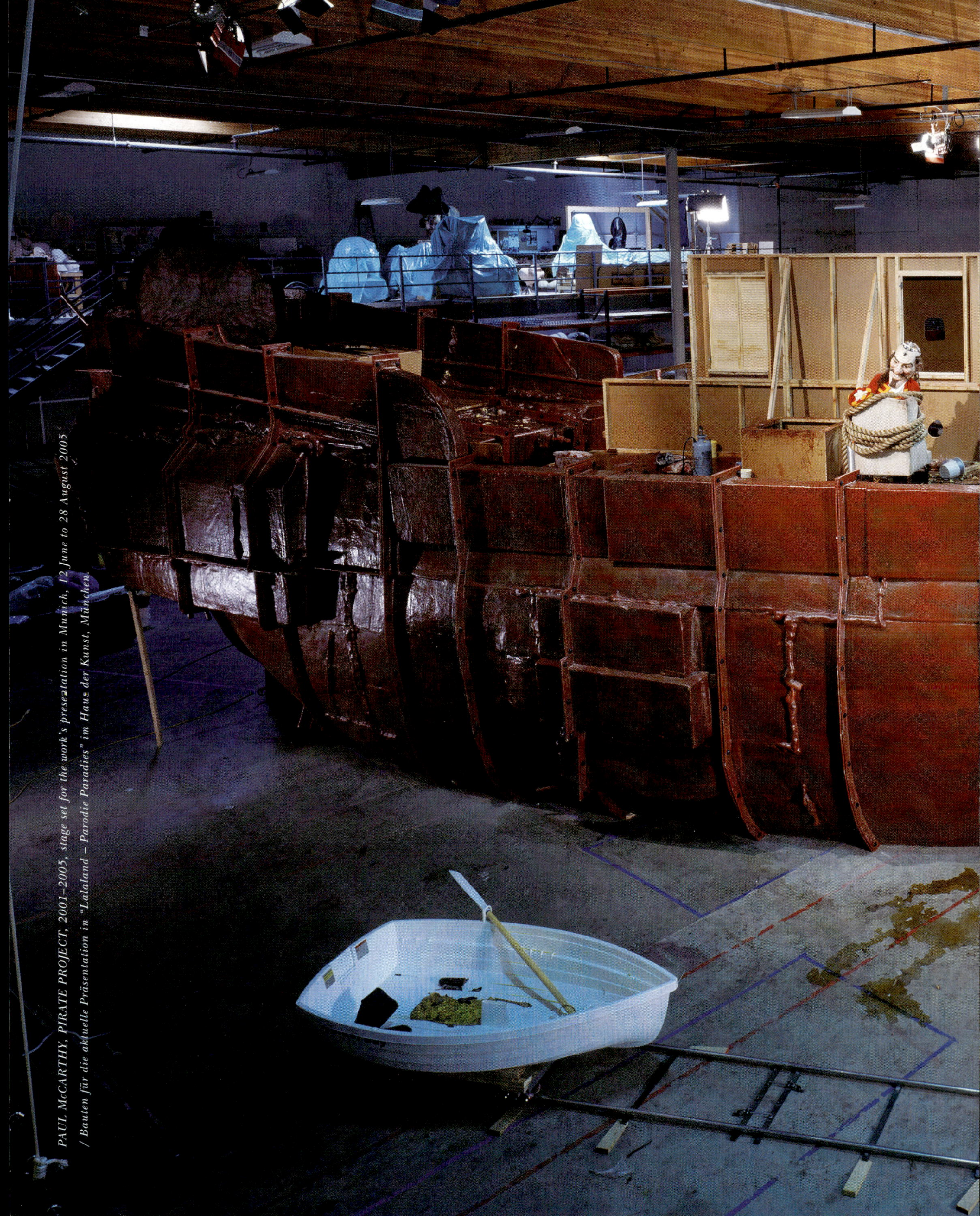

PAUL McCARTHY, *PIRATE PROJECT*, 2001–2005, stage set for the work's presentation in Munich, 12 June to 28 August 2005 / Bauten für die aktuelle Präsentation in "Lalaland – Parodie Paradies" im Haus der Kunst, München.

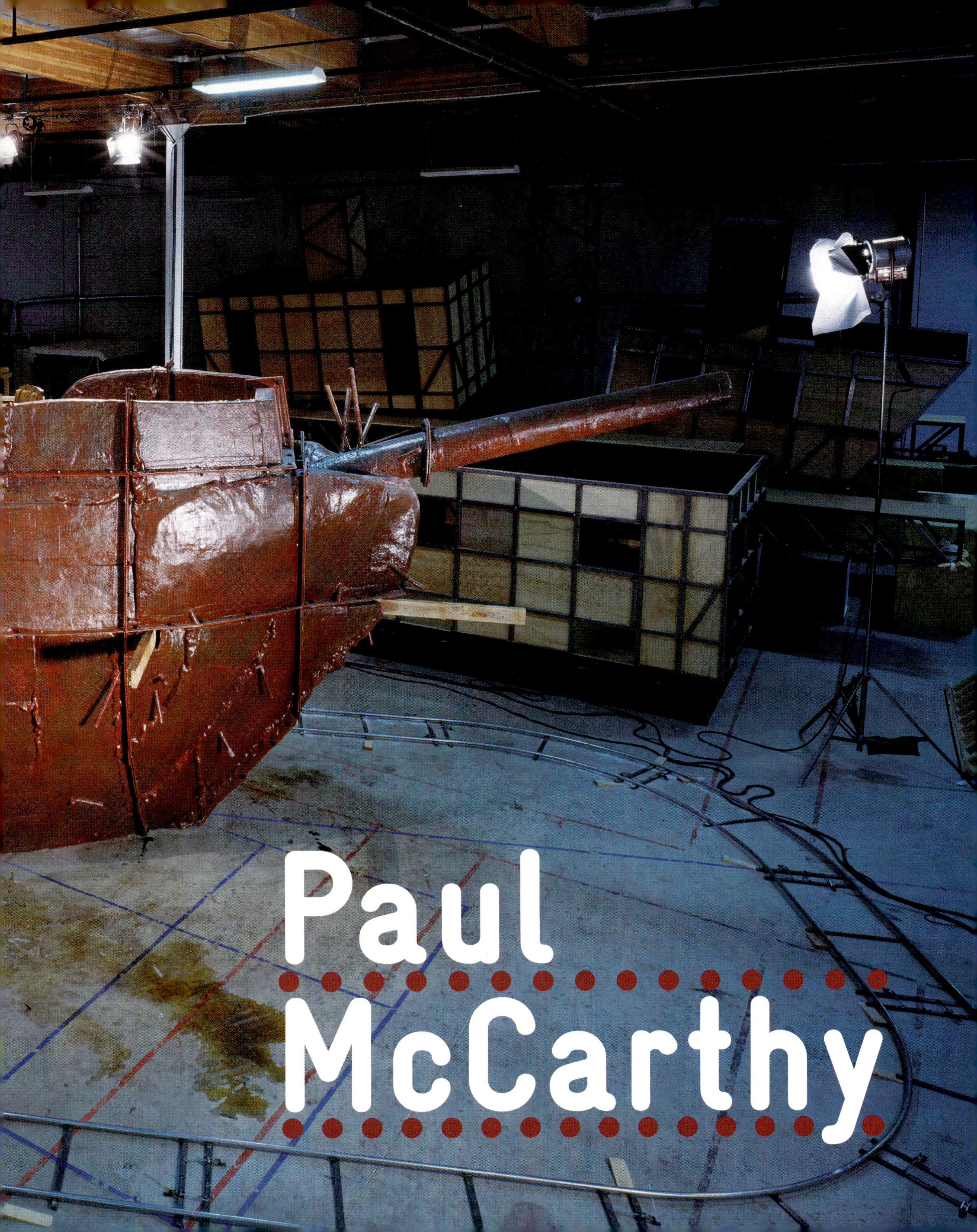
Paul
McCarthy

A Few Words for DEAD H

LANE RELYEA

In her introductory essay for the catalogue accompanying Paul McCarthy's 2000 retrospective at The New Museum in New York, Lisa Phillips labeled the artist's work "pop expressionism." 1) The phrase fits McCarthy's oeuvre surprisingly well, but only because the two terms—pop and expressionism—go together so uncomfortably. Expressionism is supposed to be about empowered subjectivity, creation, the artist as producer; pop is about product, commodities, the artwork as sales pitch. The former relies on the poetics of the private, lone individual, and how that individual achieves self-realization at the cost of social isolation and withdrawal. The latter turns instead to the public rhetoric of the marketplace, where social integration is won at the price of selling out, of self-alienation.

McCarthy gained much belated recognition in the early nineties as the art world lost enthusiasm for glossy spectacle in favor of the body, dissolution, and trauma (think Kiki Smith, Sue Williams, Cady Noland). But if there was a heyday of pop expressionism it would have to be the eighties, the era of Reagan, of recycled hero myths and untrammeled capitalism. This was when the poetics of self and the rhetoric of promotion were brought together in a crescendo of self-promotion, as a stampede of corporate-executive kitsch and grandstanding painter-geniuses overran the art galleries. Perhaps McCarthy's work exerted a subterranean influence then, the defiled pop personae and Wal-Mart props he'd been stockpiling since his seventies performances finding echoes in the Marlboro Men and New Shelton Wet/Drys of the eighties, with more pointed references cropping up in the Halloween masks Haim Steinbach would sometimes display, or, say, in the penis silhouettes, baby-bottle nipples, and other tokens of toilet humor that Meyer Vaisman affixed to his mid-eighties paintings. Pop expressionism also found exemplars in Jean-Michel Basquiat's canvases, with their Twombly scrawls routinely punctuated by copyright signs, and in Christopher Wool's action-painted billboards, with their Frankenstein mix of Franz Kline and Robert Indiana. All of these artists partake in a grim view of the publicly paraded private self, as does McCarthy, who always shoehorns his Dionysian outbursts in pop vernacular, enlisting as theater stages the discarded studio sets of canceled

LANE RELYEA is Assistant Professor of Art Theory and Practice at Northwestern University.

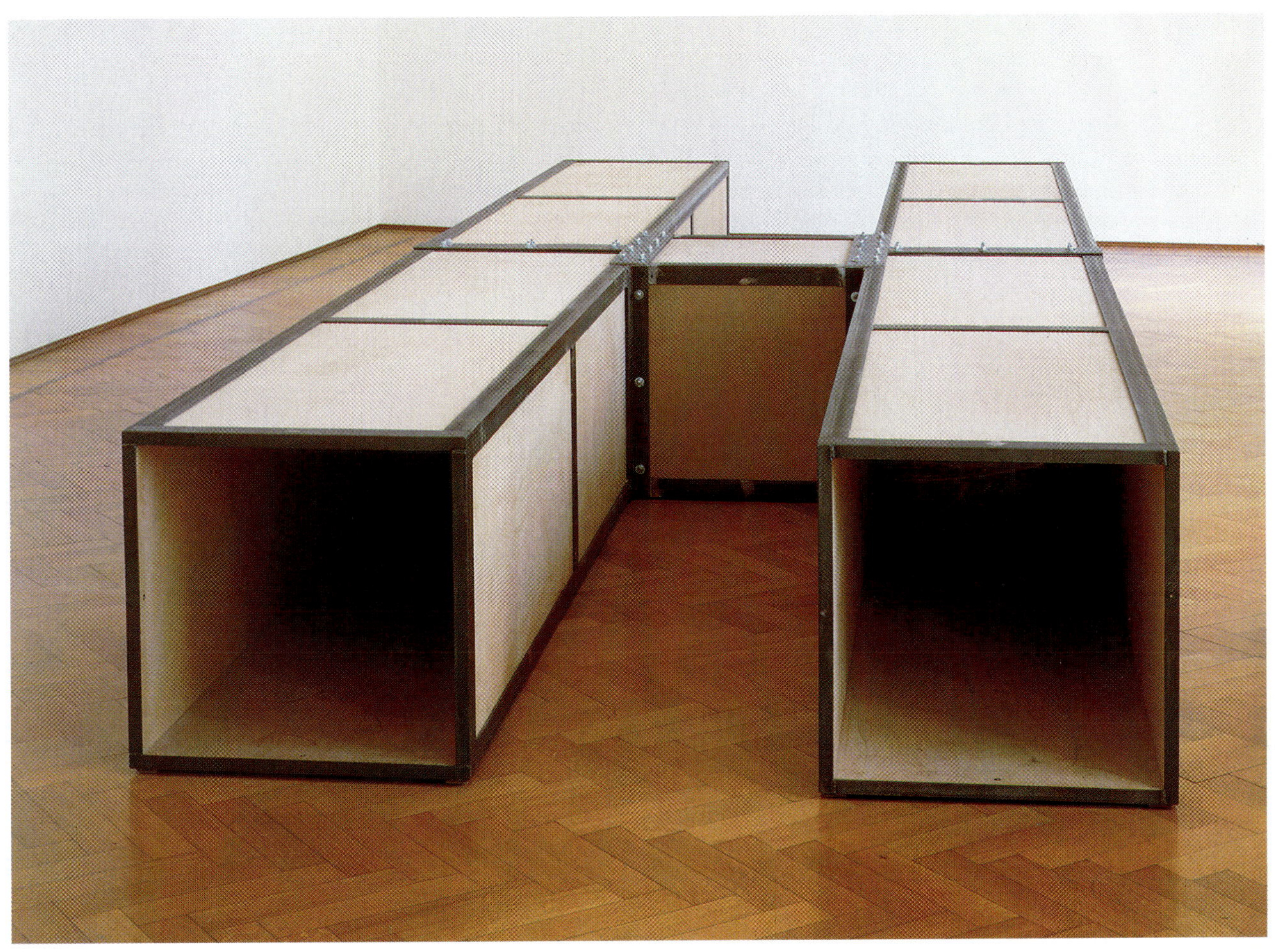

PAUL McCARTHY, DEAD H CRAWL, 1968/1999, wooden paneling, steel, bolts, 72 x 192"; tunnel to crawl through 24 x 24 x 192" / TOTES H AUF ALLEN VIEREN, Holzplatten, Stahl. Schrauben, 183 x 488 cm, Tunnel zum Hindurchkriechen 61 x 61 x 488 cm.

TV sitcoms, lubricating his rituals with neither bodily fluids, nor wine and wafers, but, rather, bargain-priced ketchup and mayonnaise, and who employs cultural icons like Santa Claus, Popeye, and Alfred E. Neuman as emcees. Every civilization gets the shaman it deserves.

Funny, then, that McCarthy started his career working in styles neither expressionist nor pop. Rather he began with, among other things, minimalism. But the paradox is only seemingly so: there is indeed a path that leads from minimalism to pop expressionism, and McCarthy is one of the pioneers who blazed it. Take, for example, DEAD H (1968), a skinny, six-foot-long geometric sculpture configured from metal furnace ducts. The piece holds an important place in McCarthy's career: as a ventilation system spreading along the floor rather than the ceiling, it anticipates the upside-down photographs of industrial interiors that the artist made in 1970. DEAD H was re-fabricated in 1975; two decades later, in 1999, McCarthy constructed an enlarged version, DEAD H CRAWL (1999), this time sixteen feet long, just big enough for a person to wriggle into. DEAD H can thus be seen as the stringing together of several of McCarthy's ongoing concerns: not only disorientation, enclosure, and visibility (or the lack thereof), but also—since it's both a big capital letter and a small hiding place—simultaneous display and withdrawal, declaration and secrecy.

Perhaps even the original DEAD H is too peculiar to be called minimalist. For starters, its size, symmetry, and four limbs make it insistently anthropomorphic. Recognizing it as a letter from the alphabet only heightens this figurative aspect: as semioticians like to profess, letters are not things but cultural forms, communicative building blocks with which we face, hail, and welcome each other. "As soon as you recognize a thing as a face," Leo Steinberg remarked in the sixties, "it is an object no longer, but one pole in a situation of reciprocal consciousness."[2] Modernists heartily agreed: "It's that quality of connection I'd like my colors to have," exclaimed Kenneth Noland.[3] Minimalists, on the other hand, tried to defeat such reciprocity in their quest to attain an art of utter indifference, of pure objectivity. "In most of my pieces there are no front or sides," confessed Donald Judd.[4] Critics concurred: minimalism, or "literalism" as many called it back then, seemed "impenetrable," possessed by "a menacing anonymity."[5]

So on which side of this debate does DEAD H stand? Actually, it doesn't stand at all, but rather looks like something that fell off a billboard or retail storefront, a bit of moribund, orphaned signage. Furthermore, it's impossible to tell which way it's turned, whether it lies face up or face down. It no longer returns our gaze, and that's why it seems dead. Ambiguously situated between modernist identification and minimalist indifference, DEAD H can be said to pervert both. What should be a compelling social sign (and a sign of socialization) now appears uncanny; what we once mastered is now too big, and we, in turn, feel smaller. The work enacts a regression by rendering language material and opaque. It returns us to a crisis point in our process of socialization: we experience both too much connection and too little; language is both too near to us—an

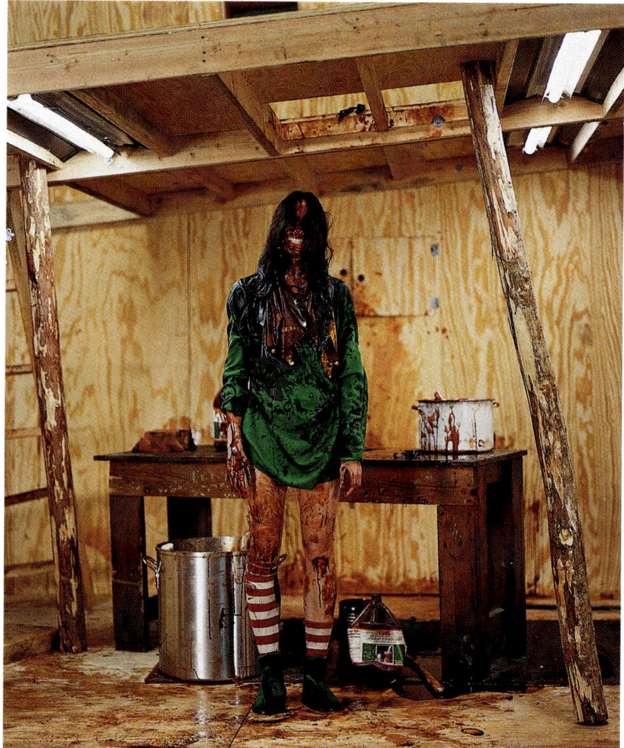

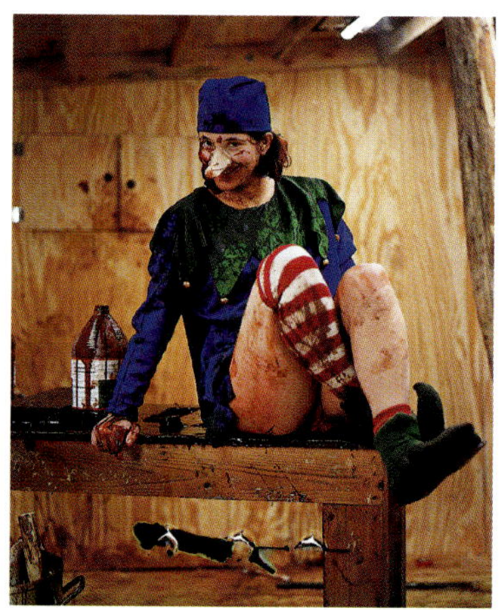

PAUL McCARTHY, SANTA CHOCOLATE SHOP, 1997, performance, video tape and installation, Los Angeles, California; with Lisa Auerbach, Larry Butler, Jerry Quinn, and Melinda Ring; laser discs and players, three-tube video projectors, speakers, amplifiers, and mixed media.

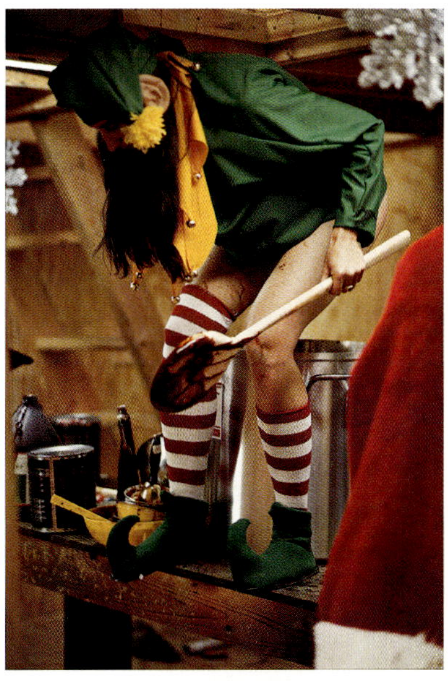

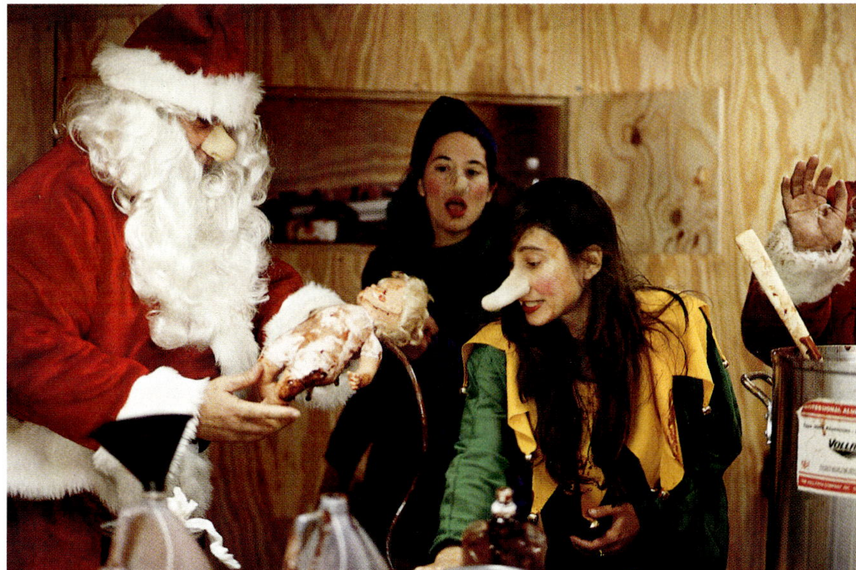

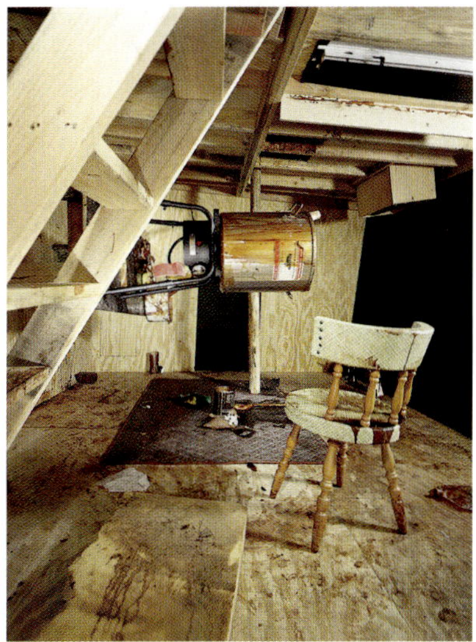

PAUL McCARTHY, SANTA CHOCOLATE SHOP, 1997, Performance, Video und Installation, Los Angeles, Kalifornien; mit Lisa Auerbach, Larry Butler, Jerry Quinn und Melinda Ring; Laserdisks und Abspielgeräte, Dreikanal-Videoprojektoren, Lautsprecher, Verstärker und diverse Materialien.

over-enlarged letter—and too far away—language that no longer speaks or breathes, that slips away, is gone forever.

"Literalism theatricalized the body, put it endlessly on stage, made it uncanny or opaque to itself, hollowed it out, deadened its expressiveness, denied its finitude and in a sense its humanness." This is Michael Fried grumbling, in what could serve as the perfect description of DEAD H, indeed of many of McCarthy's works. "There is ... something vaguely *monstrous* about the body in literalism." [6)]

Over- and under-identification, by the way, suggest the two moments that bracket the castration complex, as the little boy narcissistically expects to see his same penis when looking at the female other, only to then draw back and dress this narcissistic wound by re-possessing the other under his now objective, dispassionate, mastering gaze.

In his later performances, McCarthy again turns to embrace a public he simultaneously ignores. He faces the audience as both a subject (an artist making art) and as an object (the artist *as* art). The masks he dons provide not only pop personalities that gratify the viewer's desire for identification, but also dark, private spaces in which McCarthy can hide. He is at once the exposed post-studio artist and the lonely painter in his garret. And yet, the two sides of this equation never balance out; a reconciliation between audience and artist is never made. The more convincingly McCarthy coils into himself, the more he shuts out any awareness of a surrounding social field, including the immediate one inhabited by the viewer. The artist hides within himself—and that's what he puts on public display, what he carefully crafts for his audience to enjoy.

Much the same goes for DEAD H. It should be facing us but has turned away. Not because it's dead: we feel shunned because it has betrayed us, abandoned us, is no good to us anymore. The goal posts of DEAD H should avail themselves as a bit of language, a tool that articulates us within a communicative field, bridging us to the social world. But DEAD H refuses to do that, and that's why we want it dead. DEAD H has turned in on itself, its two posts face each other in narcissistic symmetry, it connects with itself at the groin, its identification with itself so complete as to shut us out entirely. If there's an Oedipal moment recreated here, it's the primal scene: the artwork breaking its promise to flatter and gratify us, like the two parents who once lavished us with attention, but now swing that attention sideways, toward each other, in total neglect of us. And, as so often happens when audiences confront McCarthy's work, we can only shake our heads. Enacted here is both modernist connection and minimalist indifference, but the two modes are unable to reconcile, to mend their split. The damage is done; this abstract artwork might compel fascination, but it will no longer compel our belief. We've become guarded, the promise is hollow, the wound won't heal. Just look at it, for chrissakes. DEAD H is a sculpture fucking itself in public.

PAUL McCARTHY, DEAD H CROOKED LEG, 1979, pencil drawings on paper, 11 x 8 1/2" (top), 8 1/2 x 11" (bottom) / TOTES H MIT VERWINKELTEN BEINEN, Bleistift auf Papier, 28 x 21,6 cm (oben) bzw. 21,6 x 28 cm (unten).

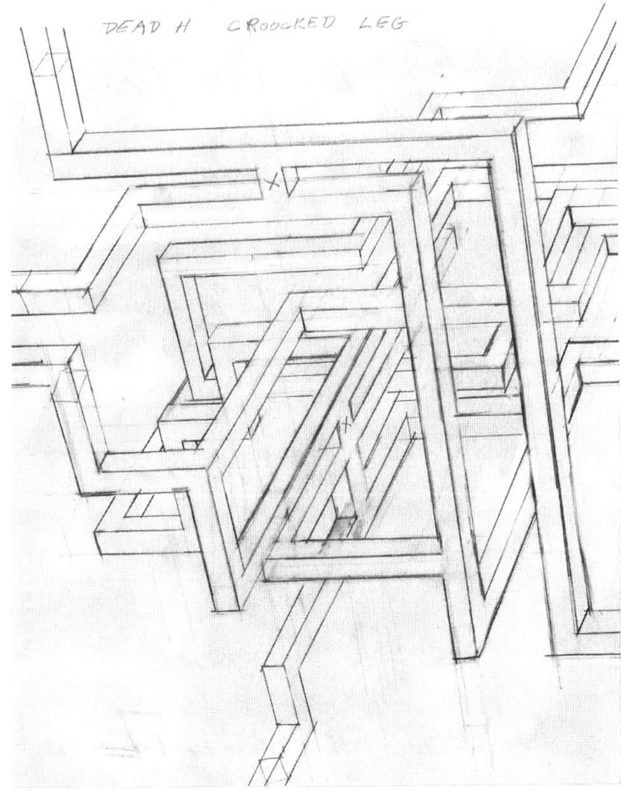

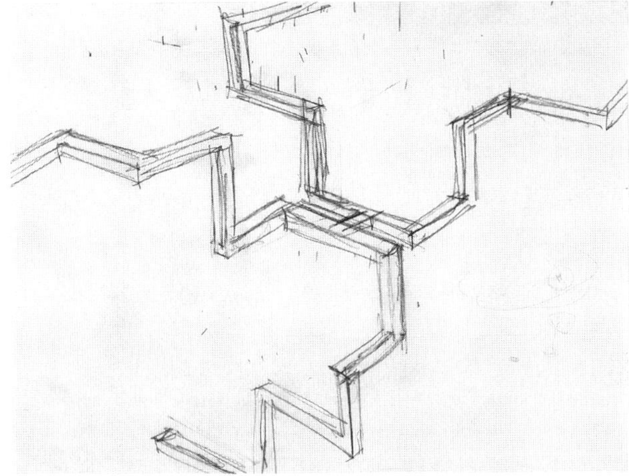

1) Lisa Phillips, "Paul McCarthy's Theater of the Body" in *Paul McCarthy* (New York: New Museum of Contemporary Art; and Ostfildern-Ruit: Cantz Verlag, 2000), p. 5.
2) Leo Steinberg, "Contemporary Art and the Plight of its Public" (1962) in *The New Art,* ed. Gregory Batcock (New York: E. P. Dutton, 1973), p. 222.
3) Quoted in Philip Leider, "The Thing in Painting Is Color," *The New York Times* (August 25, 1968), sec. 2, p. 21.
4) John Coplans, *Don Judd* (Pasadena, CA: Pasadena Museum of Art, 1970), p. 36.
5) Mel Bochner, "Systemic," *Arts Magazine,* vol. 41, no. 1 (November 1966), p. 40; Lucy R. Lippard, "Reviews," *Artforum,* vol. 2, no. 9 (March 1964), p. 19.
6) Michael Fried, "An Introduction to My Art Criticism" in *Art and Objecthood* (Chicago and London: University of Chicago Press, 1998), p. 42.

Ein paar Worte für das tote H

Paul McCarthys DEAD H

LANE RELYEA

In ihrer Einleitung zum Ausstellungskatalog der Paul-McCarthy-Retrospektive im New Yorker New Museum im Jahr 2000 bezeichnete Lisa Phillips das Werk des Künstlers als «Pop-Expressionismus».[1] Das Etikett passt erstaunlich gut zu McCarthys Œuvre, aber nur, weil die beiden Bezeichnungen Pop und Expressionismus eigentlich überhaupt nicht zusammengehen. Mit Expressionismus verbindet man ein ausdrucksstarkes Subjekt und einen ebensolchen kreativen Akt, kurz: den produktiven Künstler; beim Pop hingegen geht es um das Produkt, das Konsumgut, das Kunstwerk als Verkaufsschlager. Der Expressionismus beruht auf einer Poetik des privaten, einsamen Individuums und seiner Selbstverwirklichung, die durch gesellschaftliche Isolation und Rückzug erkauft ist. Pop dagegen bedient sich der gängigen Sprache eines Marktes, auf dem der Einzelne die gesellschaftliche Integration mit Selbstentfremdung und -verrat bezahlt.

McCarthy wurde erst sehr spät Anerkennung zuteil, erst als die Kunstszene Anfang der 90er Jahre das Interesse am glanzvollen Spektakel verlor und sich vermehrt dem Körper, der Auflösung, dem Traumatischen zuwandte (man denke an Kiki Smith, Sue Williams, Cady Noland). Wenn es eine Blütezeit des

LANE RELYEA ist Assistenzprofessor für Kunsttheorie und Praxis an der Northwestern University in Chicago.

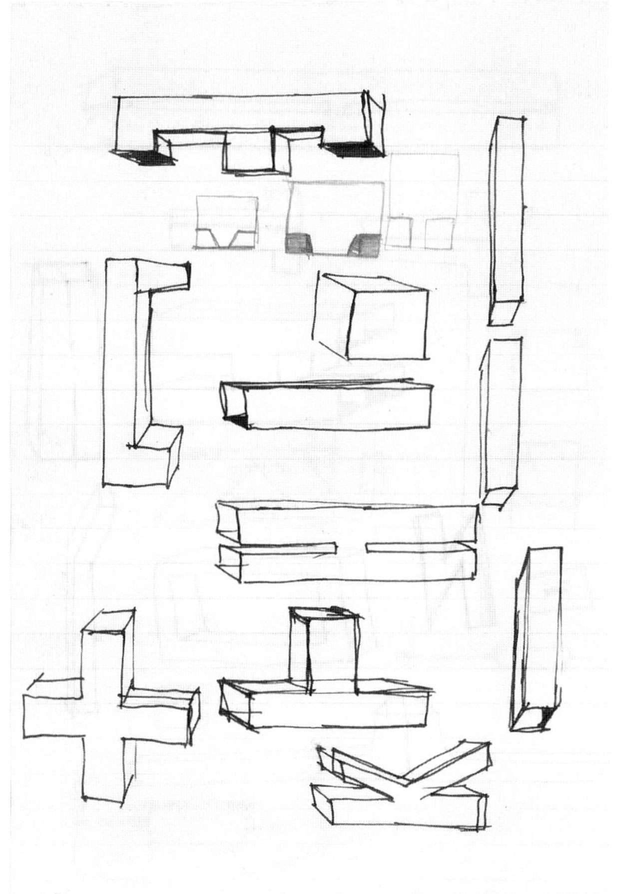

PAUL McCARTHY, drawing from DEAD H TEXT & DRAWING (VENT SCULPTURES INCLUDING DEAD H), 1968, marker on paper, 8 7/8 x 6" / Zeichnung aus TEXT UND ZEICHNUNG ZUM TOTEN H (LÜFTUNGSSKULPTUREN MIT TOTEM H), Filzstift auf Papier, 22,5 x 15,2 cm.

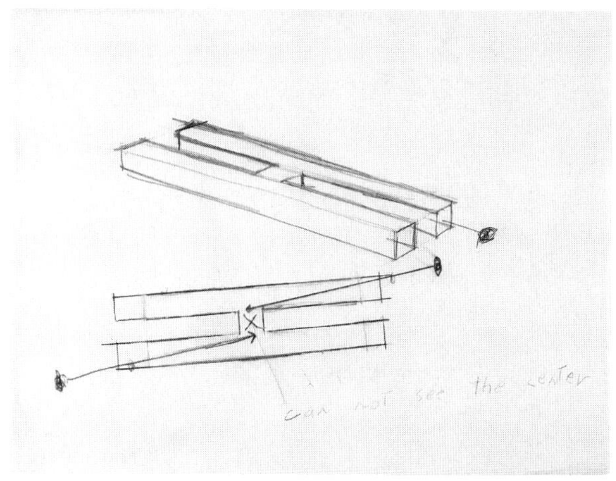

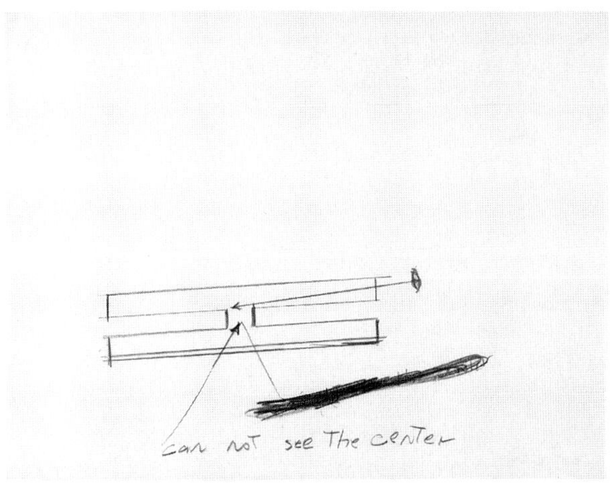

PAUL McCARTHY, DEAD H DRAWINGS, 1974, pencil on paper, 8 1/2 x 11" each / ZEICHNUNGEN ZUM TOTEN H, Bleistift auf Papier, je 21,6 x 28 cm.

Pop-Expressionismus gegeben hat, so in den 80er Jahren, während der Reagan-Ära, einer Zeit der wieder aufgewärmten Heldenmythen und des ungebremsten Kapitalismus. Damals verbündete sich die Poetik des Selbst mit der Rhetorik der Werbung zu einem Crescendo der Selbstvermarktung, während eine Welle von Konzernmanager-Kitsch und effekthascherischen Malergenies die Galerien überschwemmte. Vielleicht übte Paul McCarthys Werk schon damals insgeheim seinen Einfluss aus, und seine ramponierten Popgestalten und *Wal-Mart*-Versatzstücke, die er seit seinen Performances in den 70er Jahren gesammelt hatte, fanden ihren Nachhall in den *Marlboro*-Typen und *New-Shelton*-Saugreinigern der 80er Jahre. Noch deutlicher waren die Referenzen in Haim Steinbachs Halloween-Masken oder den Penis-Silhouetten, Schnullernippeln und anderen Elementen aus der Toiletten-Humorkiste, mit denen Meyer Vaisman seine Bilder Mitte der 80er Jahre versah. Beispiele für Pop-Expressionismus finden sich auch unter Jean-Michel Basquiats Leinwänden mit ihren routinemässig mit Copyright-Zeichen durchsetzten Twombly-Kritzeleien, oder auf Christopher Wools Plakattafeln im Stil der Aktionsmalerei und ihrer frankensteinschen Kreuzung aus Franz Kline und Robert Indiana. Alle diese Künstler werfen einen unbarmherzigen Blick auf die öffentlich inszenierte Privatperson, genau wie Paul McCarthy, der seine dionysischen Ausbrüche in ein gängiges Popvokabular presst und ausrangierte Studiokulissen abgesetzter Sitcoms als Theaterbühnen verwendet, nur ölt er seine Rituale nicht mit Körpersekreten, ja nicht einmal mit Wein und Oblaten, sondern mit Ketchup und Mayonnaise aus Aktionsangeboten. Dabei kürt er kulturelle Ikonen wie den Weihnachtsmann, Popeye und Alfred E. Neuman [2] zu seinen Zeremonienmeistern. Jede Kultur hat den Schamanen, den sie verdient.

Doch seltsamerweise arbeitete McCarthy am Anfang seiner Karriere weder im Stil der Pop Art noch expressionistisch. Vielmehr setzte er sich zu Beginn unter anderem mit dem Minimalismus auseinander. Aber das ist nur scheinbar paradox: In der Tat gibt es einen Weg, der vom Minimalismus zum Pop-Expressionismus führt, und McCarthy ist einer der Pioniere, die ihn freigelegt haben. Schauen wir uns DEAD H (1968/1975) an, eine karge, knapp zwei Meter lange geometrische Plastik aus Heizlüftungselementen. Der Arbeit kommt in der Laufbahn des Künstlers eine wichtige Rolle zu: Als Belüftungssystem, das sich nicht an der Decke, sondern am Boden ausbreitet, nimmt es die auf den Kopf gestellten Photographien industrieller Innenräume vorweg, die McCarthy 1970 machte. 1975 wurde DEAD H noch einmal neu angefertigt, und zwei Jahrzehnte später schuf der Künstler eine vergrösserte Version, DEAD H CRAWL (1999). Diese war fast fünf Meter lang, gerade gross genug, dass eine Person sich hineinzwängen konnte.

In DEAD H laufen also mehrere Dinge zusammen, die McCarthy schon seit längerem beschäftigt hatten: nicht nur Orientierungsverlust, Eingeschlossensein und Sichtbarkeit (oder fehlende Sichtbarkeit), sondern auch – schliesslich handelt es sich gleichzeitig um einen riesigen Grossbuchstaben und ein winziges Versteck – ein Zeigen und Verstecken, ein Erklären und Verschweigen, die miteinander Hand in Hand gehen.

Vielleicht ist das ursprüngliche DEAD H aber auch zu seltsam, um minimalistisch genannt zu werden. Zunächst einmal verleihen ihm seine Grösse, Symmetrie und vier Extremitäten einen ausgesprochen anthropomorphen Charakter. Dass man darin einen Buchstaben des Alphabets erkennen kann, verstärkt noch diesen figurativen Aspekt: Wie Semiotiker gern unterstreichen, sind Buchstaben keine Dinge, sondern kulturelle Formen, Bausteine der Kommunikation, mit deren Hilfe wir uns begegnen, grüssen und willkommen heissen. «Sobald man ein Ding als Gesicht erkennt», bemerkte Leo Steinberg in den 60er Jahren, «ist es kein Gegenstand mehr, sondern einer der Pole in einer Situation gegenseitiger Wahrnehmung.»[3] Die Künstler der Moderne stimmten dem gerne zu: «Genau diese Art von Verbindung sollen meine Farben bewirken», begeisterte sich Kenneth Noland.[4] Die Minimalisten hingegen wollten diese Reziprozität gerade ausschalten bei ihrer Suche nach einer Kunst der absoluten Indifferenz und reinen Objektivität. «In den meisten meiner Arbeiten gibt es weder vorne noch links oder rechts», gestand Donald Judd.[5] Und Kritiker pflichteten dem bei: Der Minimalismus oder «Literalismus», wie damals viele sagten, schien «unzugänglich» und von einer «bedrohlichen Anonymität» besessen zu sein.[6]

Wo aber steht DEAD H innerhalb dieser Debatte? Von Stehen kann eigentlich keine Rede sein, denn das Werk sieht eher aus, als wäre es von einer Reklametafel oder Ladenfassade heruntergefallen, ein Stück ausgediente, verwaiste Reklameschrift. Ausserdem lässt sich unmöglich sagen, ob es mit dem Gesicht nach oben oder unten liegt. Jedenfalls erwidert es unseren Blick nicht mehr, deshalb erscheint es uns als tot. Man könnte sagen, dass DEAD H zwischen modernistischer Identifikation und minimalistischer Indifferenz oszillierend beide in Frage stellt. Was eigentlich ein gesellschaftlich eindeutiges Zeichen sein sollte (und auch ein Zeichen der Sozialisation), wird plötzlich unheimlich; was wir einst beherrschten, ist jetzt zu gross, und wir fühlen uns entsprechend klein. Die Arbeit inszeniert eine Regression, indem sie die Sprache dinghaft und undurchdringlich werden lässt. Sie führt uns an einen kritischen Punkt in unserem Sozialisierungsprozess zurück: Wir erleben gleichzeitig zu viel und zu wenig Verbundenheit; die Sprache ist uns gleichzeitig zu nah – ein übergrosser Buchstabe – und zu weit weg: eine Sprache, die nicht mehr spricht oder atmet, sondern sich entzieht und für immer entschwindet.

«Der Literalismus hat den Körper theatralisch dargestellt, ihn pausenlos auf der Bühne exponiert, er hat ihn sich selbst unheimlich oder unzugänglich gemacht, hat ihn ausgehöhlt, seinen Ausdruck stumpf werden lassen, er hat ihm seine Endlichkeit und in gewissem Sinn auch seine Menschlichkeit abgesprochen.» So schimpft Michael Fried und liefert damit ungewollt eine perfekte Beschreibung von DEAD H und vielen anderen Arbeiten McCarthys. «Im Literalismus hat der Körper immer ... etwas leicht Monströses.»[7]

Über- und Unteridentifizierung erinnern, nebenbei gesagt, auch an die beiden Momente, die den Kastrationskomplex kennzeichnen. Betrachtet nämlich der kleine Junge sein weibliches Gegenüber, so tut er das in der narzisstischen Erwartung, bei ihm einen ebensolchen Penis zu sehen, wie er ihn selber hat, um sich darauf enttäuscht zurückzuziehen und die narzisstische Verletzung zu überwinden, indem er sein Gegenüber einer nunmehr kalten, gefühllosen, beherrschten Musterung unterzieht.

In seinen späteren Performances wendet sich McCarthy wieder einem Publikum zu, ignoriert es jedoch gleichzeitig. Er tritt dem Publikum sowohl als Subjekt (als Künstler, der Kunst macht) wie als Objekt (der Künstler als Kunst) gegenüber. Die Masken, die er sich aufsetzt, verweisen nicht nur auf Persönlichkeiten der Popkultur, die dem Wunsch des Betrachters nach Identifikation entgegenkommen, sondern auch auf dunkle, persönliche Räume, in denen sich McCarthy verstecken kann. Er ist sowohl ein exponierter Künstler, der nicht mehr nur auf das Atelier beschränkt ist, als auch einsamer Maler im

Dachkämmerchen. Und doch sind die beiden Seiten dieser Gleichung nie wirklich ausgeglichen; die Versöhnung zwischen Publikum und Künstler kommt nie zustande. Je überzeugender McCarthy sich auf sich selbst zurückzieht, desto mehr schliesst er jede Wahrnehmung des sozialen Umfeldes aus, das gilt auch für das unmittelbare Umfeld, in dem sich der Betrachter aufhält. Der Künstler verkriecht sich in sich selbst: Genau dies stellt er öffentlich aus und bereitet es sorgfältig für sein Publikum auf.

Dasselbe gilt weitgehend auch für DEAD H. Es sollte uns anblicken, hat sich jedoch abgewandt. Nicht, weil es tot ist: Wir fühlen uns vor den Kopf gestossen, weil es uns verraten und verlassen hat und zu nichts mehr zu gebrauchen ist. Die Torbögen von DEAD H sollten uns als Sprachpartikel dienen, als Werkzeug, das uns in einem kommunikativen Feld zum Ausdruck verhilft und mit der Gesellschaft verbindet. Aber DEAD H weigert sich, das zu tun, und deshalb wollen wir es lieber tot sehen. DEAD H hat sich in sich selbst zurückgezogen, seine beiden Balken sind einander in narzisstischer Symmetrie zugewandt. Und in Hüfthöhe ist es mit sich selbst verbunden; seine Identifikation mit sich selbst ist so vollkommen, dass wir nicht mehr zählen. Falls es sich dabei um einen ödipalen Konflikt handelt, ist es die Urszene: Das Kunstwerk bricht sein Versprechen, uns zu schmeicheln und zu beglücken, ähnlich wie unsere Eltern uns zuerst ihre ganze Aufmerksamkeit schenkten, um sich dann von uns abzuwenden und sich so ausschliesslich miteinander zu beschäftigen, dass wir uns vernachlässigt fühlten. Und wie das angesichts der Werke von Paul McCarthy häufig der Fall ist, können wir nur noch den Kopf schütteln. Hier kommt sowohl moderne Verbundenheit wie minimalistische Indifferenz zum Ausdruck, doch die beiden Methoden bleiben unversöhnlich, die Kluft ist nicht zu überbrücken. Der Schaden ist nicht rückgängig zu machen; das abstrakte Kunstwerk fasziniert uns vielleicht noch, aber wirklich daran glauben können wir nicht mehr. Wir sind auf der Hut, das Versprechen ist hohl, die Wunde will nicht heilen. Herrgottnochmal, schaut doch einfach mal genau hin! DEAD H ist eine Plastik, die sich in aller Öffentlichkeit selbst fickt.

(Übersetzung: Uta Goridis/Wilma Parker)

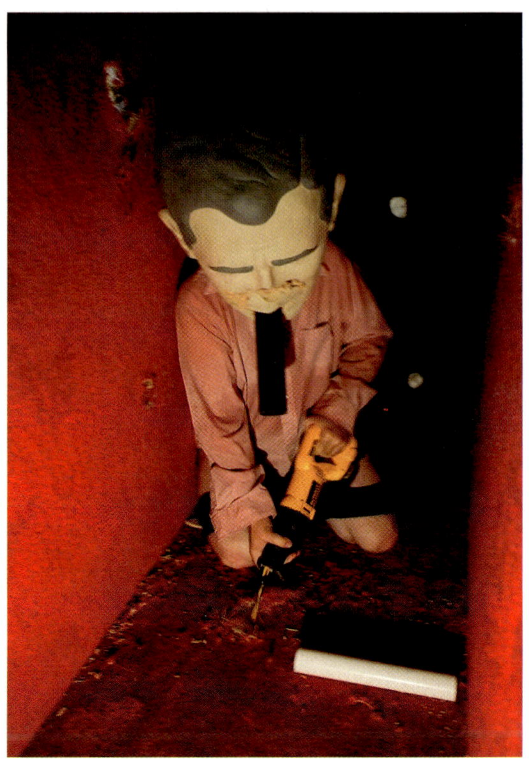

PAUL McCARTHY, PICCADILLY CIRCUS / BUNKER BASEMENT, 2003, video projection and installation, Hauser and Wirth Gallery, London / LUFTSCHUTZKELLER, Videoprojektion und Installation.
(PHOTOS: ANN-MARIE ROUNKLE)

1) Lisa Phillips, «Paul McCarthy's Theater of the Body», in: *Paul McCarthy,* New Museum of Contemporary Art, New York / Cantz Verlag, Ostfildern-Ruit 2000, S. 5. (Alle Zitate in diesem Essay wurden von der Redaktion aus dem Engl. übersetzt.)
2) Alfred E. Neuman: Protagonist der Satirezeitschrift *Mad Magazine.*
3) Leo Steinberg, «Contemporary Art and the Plight of its Public» (1962), in: *The New Art,* hg. v. Gregory Batcock, E. P. Dutton, New York 1973, S. 222.
4) Zitiert nach Philip Leider, «The Thing in Painting is Color», *New York Times,* 25. August 1968, S. 21.
5) Zitiert nach John Coplans, *Don Judd,* Pasadena Museum of Art, Pasadena 1971, S. 36.
6) Mel Bochner, «Systemic», *Arts Magazine,* vol. 41, No. 1 (November 1966), S. 40; Lucy R. Lippard, «Reviews» *Artforum,* vol. 2, No. 9 (März 1964), S. 19.
7) Michael Fried, «An Introduction to My Art Criticism», in: *Art and Objecthood,* University Press, Chicago/London, 1998, S. 42.

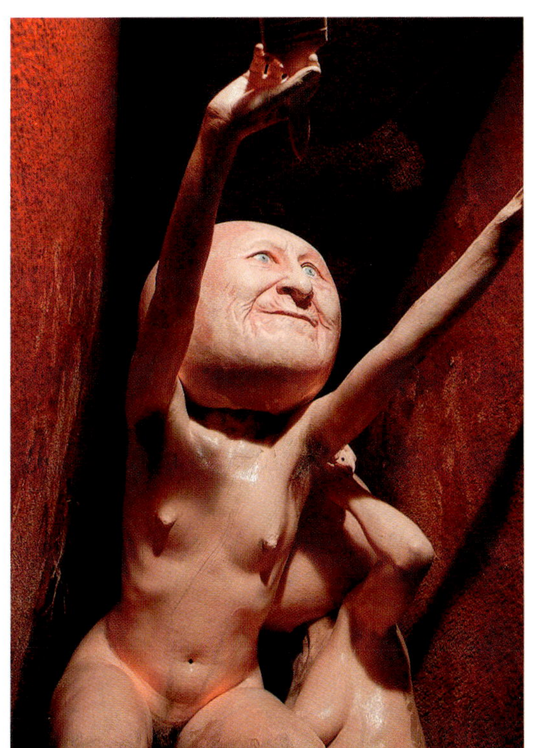

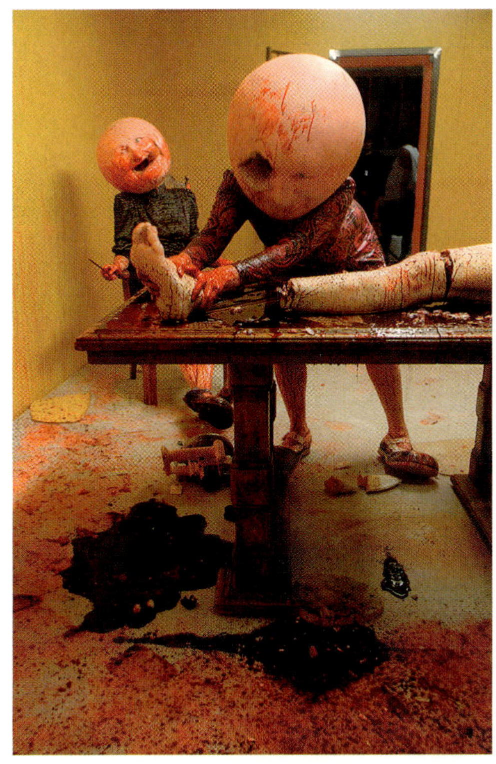

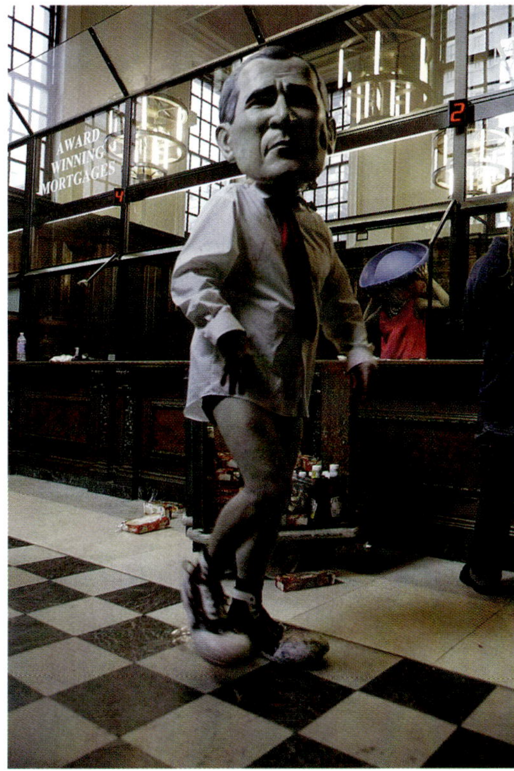
AWARD
WINNING
MORTGAGES
2

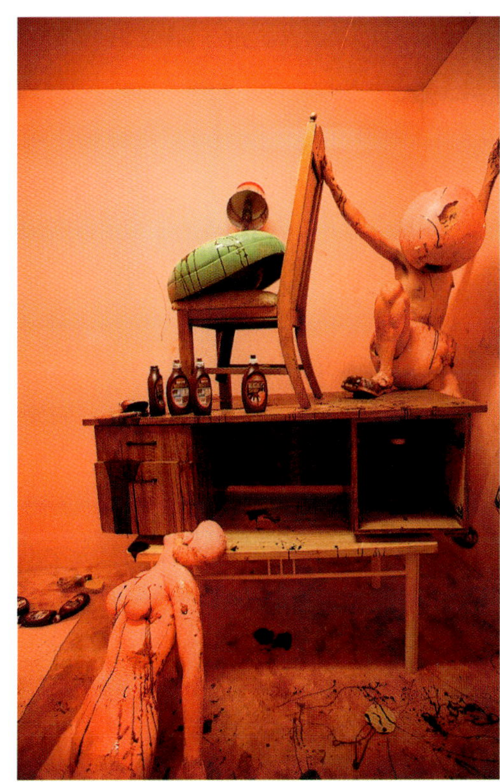

A Dialogue with Language Itself

JEREMY SIGLER & PAUL McCARTHY

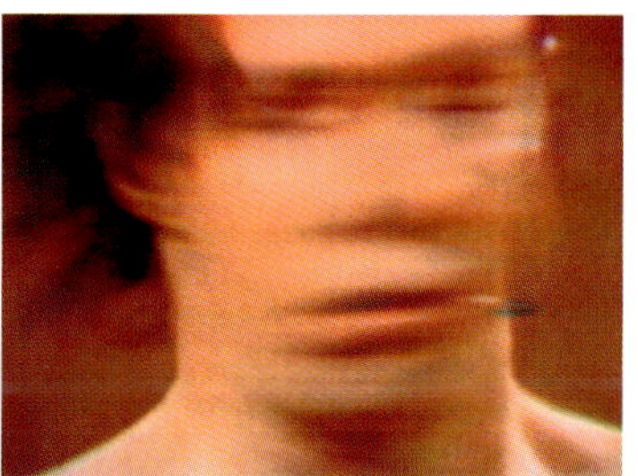

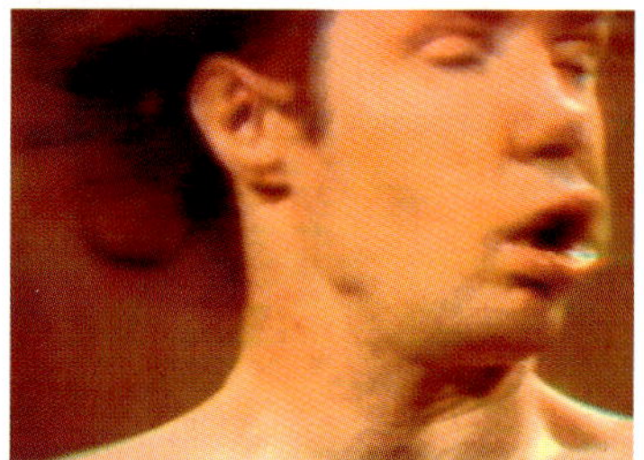

PAUL McCARTHY, RATTLE HEAD, 1974, 3 min. 27 sec. color video / RASSELKOPF, 3 Min. 27 Sek. Farbvideo.

When I recently sat down and talked on tape with Paul McCarthy in his studio, I continuously tried to steer the conversation toward poetry. I suppose, being a poet, it was for self-centered reasons. However, I didn't anticipate that when Paul got hold of the manuscript, he'd be compelled to work back into it, to hack it apart, to call each word and every syllable into question—to essentially re-write the damn thing! It was as if the spoken words we had shared in our pleasant studio discussion a week earlier had suddenly become, as written text, suspect, inaccurate—simply wrong. It became clear that Paul regarded the first version of the transcribed interview to be an exterior facade, a mere surface, inhibiting an alternative, more primary, loaded language. He sent back an impressive document that had transformed our rather conventional conversation into a messed-up, non-grammatical procedure, a dialogue, in other words, with language itself, unearthing—in typical Paul McCarthy fashion—a language all his own. Indeed a poem, in every sense of the word.

Jeremy Sigler

The final version of the artist's revised text follows. Please note that a facsimile of the (illuminating) original manuscript appears on pp. 120–134.

JS: And then there were ...
And then what? Did you do screen tests?
PM: I wrote these scenarios. Wenches being auctioned, "and you're frightened and you begin to cry."
JS: Did you give them lines?
PM: I realized I wasn't interested in the lines. I was interested in their body position, their faces when they were crying. It became about asking them to cry on all fours, or ... crawling while walking back and forth across the room ... like ten times, very slowly.
JS: It sounds pretty.
PM: You start with the genitals. I had auditioned this guy who I wanted to play a rich boat

---

JEREMY SIGLER is the author of two books of poetry, *To and To* and *Mallet Eyes.* He is *Parkett*'s assistant New York editor.

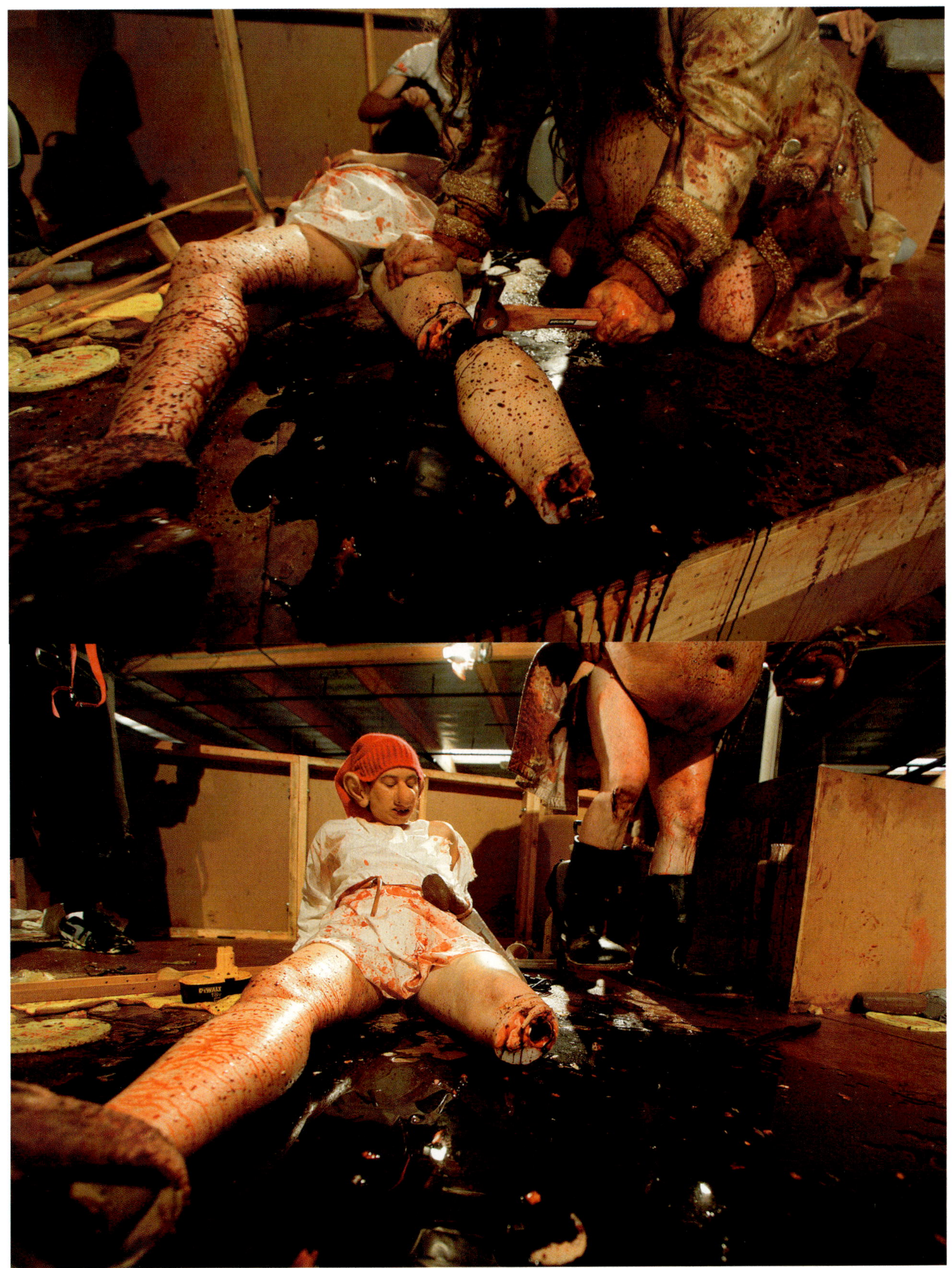

PAUL McCARTHY, PIRATE PROJECT, 2001–2005, performance scenes / Szenen aus der Performance. (PHOTOS: ANN-MARIE ROUNKLE)

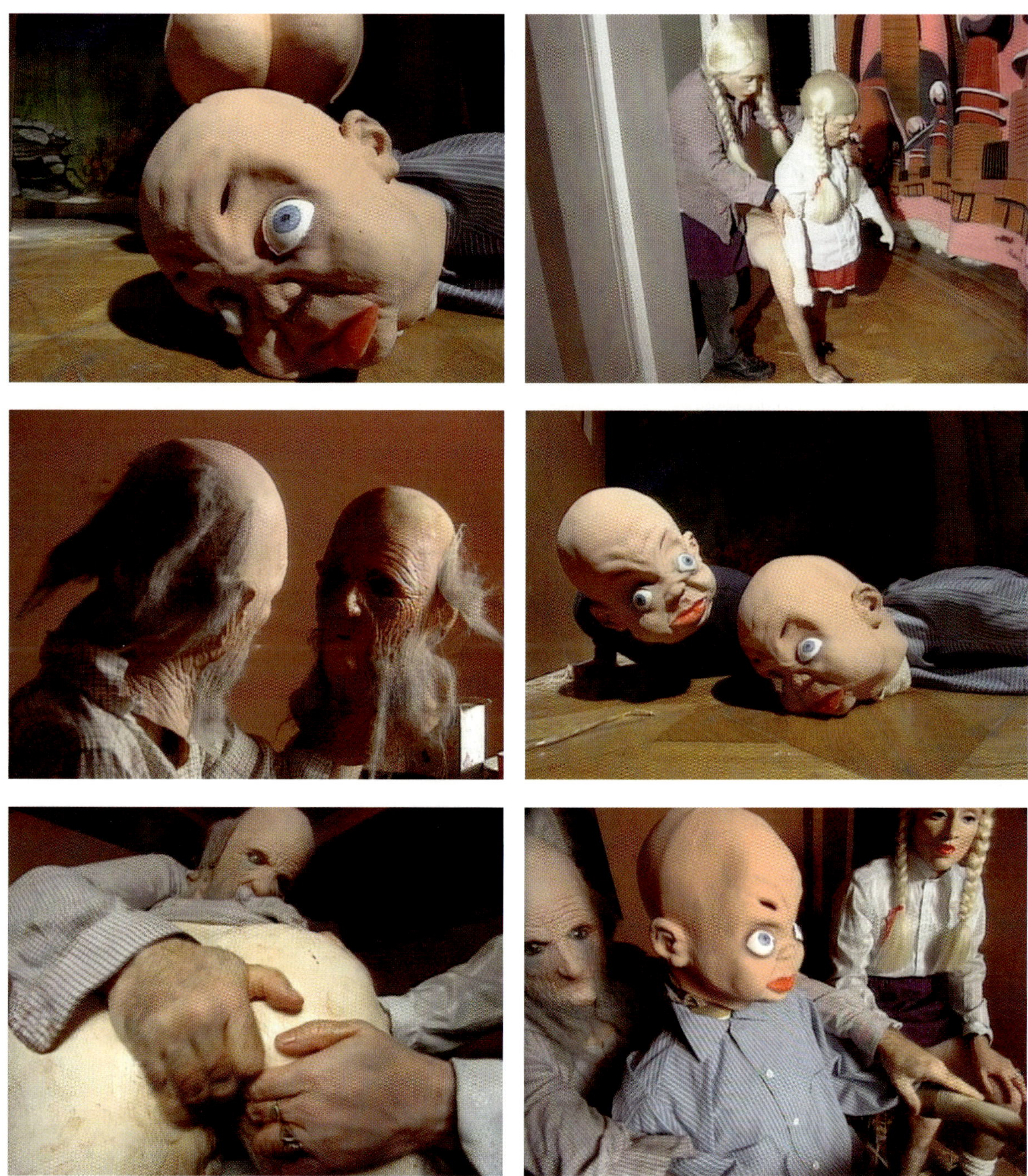

PAUL McCARTHY & MIKE KELLEY, HEIDI, MIDLIFE CRISIS TRAUMA CENTER AND NEGATIVE MEDIA-ENGRAM ABREACTION RELEASE ZONE, 1992, performance / HEIDI, MIDLIFE-CRISIS-TRAUMAZENTRUM UND FREISETZUNGSZONE ZUM ABREAGIEREN NEGATIVER MEDIEN-ENGRAMME.

owner who has these servants who abuses his power. At one point I realized still that what I was really interested in was his body. I spent all this time posing him on a table, a pedestal as if he was a Greek sculpture. It was about advertising and abusing power, one over another. Human but with this twist.

JS: The actors you audition need to be stuntmen?

PM: No.

JS: What about performing with materials. I get the feeling that something diabolical is about to occur.

PM: Realism, in the sixties you get shot where there's real danger. I was interested in the fake. Real blood, I began using ketchup. Though I did earlier where there were actions, let's step on glass, let's paint with shit.

JS: Falling from a rope.

PM: I cut a rope and fell.

JS: But when you are performing, you almost seem to leave your body.

PM: You mean NO?

JS: Exactly.

PM: It's more about focus, focus on a table, concentrating on something. I focus. To make a work of art the world can disappear. Yes, disappear but I don't think I'm—I'm in a trance. I made a videotape where I shook my head fast. It was called RATTLE HEAD (1974). When I did it my eyes rolled up and it looked trance-like. I made myself look like that on a … I also made these pieces, 1970, where I spun for 30 minutes at the same speed as the video tape reel.

PM: That word fuck (focus) reminds me of sports …

PM: I played baseball. It was my way of socially fitting in. Fingers of the mitt. *(This refers to the drawing in the original manuscript, see p. 121.)*

JS: Would you say there's quality to your …

PM: Yes and no. NO.

JS: I'm thinking of Yoko Ono. For her, it became a kind of style.

PM: In that type of singing there is a release, I'm sure. I was interested in therapy, and I talked about venting. I made a hollow box covered in—the type of bent metal hot rods (VENTED CUBE DRAWING, 1975). Then I wrote this poem about venting. Venting the subconscious. I want to vent a situation …

JS: Your work has gotten to be more collected and technical over the years with elaborate props and electronically animated, kinetic sculptures. You've come a long way from dipping your penis into buckets of black paint (PENIS DIP PAINTING, 1974).

PM: Yes, a while I made work solely by myself. I made the video tapes in … When the nineties came around I bent over with Mike Kelley, Jason Rhoades and Benjamin Weissman. I had the idea to have started working …

JS: And you call on experts …

PM: Yes … one point, I might fuck up the idea if I might not be able to make it. So I worked with fabricators, multiple types of work being done all at once. I had multiple interests. I was interested in abstract figures, in realistic figures, the mechanical figure, these different ideas of repression representation. That I became interested in Disney as sculpture. Mickey Mouse and Donald Duck attracted me.

JS: Did you aspire to create an entire theme park?

PM: Yes, there was this idea of creating. I was trying to create a town and also a production

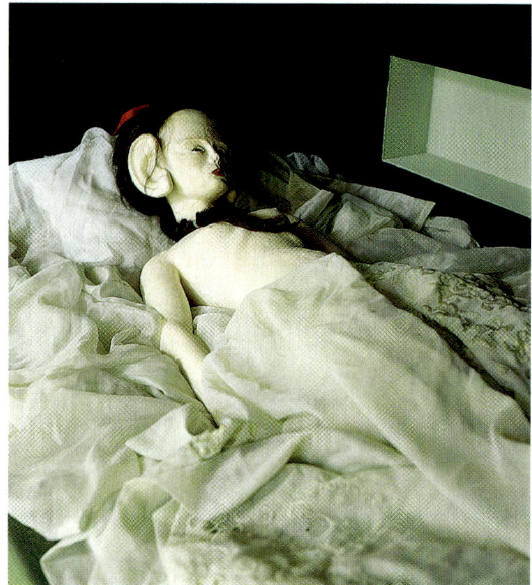

PAUL McCARTHY & MIKE KELLEY, HEIDI, 1992, installation detail.

company. In Los Angeles there are production companies. They're film industry. I wanted my studio to be a production.

JS: The studios share personnel so it's not unlikely that a guy who is working for you is working for Disney or some block ...

PM: My studio is made of people right now, I work closely, I have only a number of years with my son Damon. Friends came to Damon, his friend, it turns out, Disney, *Men in Black*.

JS: This makes you kind of like all the other Hollywood directors. Any directors in particular. I'm looking at—what about Mario Bava?

PM: Dario Argento. Was looking for something into Pasolini, I think I was seriously affected by Jack Smith films and Warhol where it's obvious the actors are pretending, pretending to be actors. We're going to get dressed up in costumes, and pretend we're on a boat.

JS: Russ Meyers and John Waters, there's this idea of the artist as some kind of pervert, to accept something that is in very bad taste, deeply humiliating.

PM: I want you to recognize what you just saw, but it doesn't fall into place. You can recognize the character, it's Pinocchio but the story isn't there. John Waters is a filmmaker because I'm not a filmmaker. I'm not a storyteller. I'm interested in the action situation being wrong theater.

JS: When I saw TOKYO SANTA (1996), I thought of *Bad Santa* (2004), which I'd just seen in the theater. I think Terry Zwigoff's Bad Santa (played by Billy Bob Thornton) and your "bad" Santa weren't too far apart from one another.

PM: Yes, very close.

JS: How aware were you? I'm thinking of this article he wrote on Jackson Pollock where he talks about painting but with all sorts of non-art, everyday materials.

PM: I think at the time I read that big fat brown book I was making these all red paintings influenced by Tony Smith. That is when I did the DEAD H (1968), Smith's DIE (1962) which was hollow. I didn't know of Acconci's work until I came to L.A.. His work was language—especially since he began as a poet. What about poetry. Were you interested?

JS: I wrote poetry in the seventies, hot a lot. Writing. You're right about the groans and moans—out of my mouth. That becomes poetry, not a written poetry, not a written script, just a verbalization.

JS: It reminds me of Dad.

PM: Or James Joyce.

JS: What about Cy Twombly? His paintings are scatological. They have the same idea of debauchery.

PM: Twombly, he uses shit and piss?

JS: No, I think he uses Crayola crayons, colored pencils and bits of smeared house paint.

PM: I think about Cy Twombly. In fact, DeKooning or DeKooning. I had gone and bought buy blond wig the day of the performance. I put the wig on. Before the taping I thought I would be Warhol. Then I looked DeKooning. The character DeKooning happened that day, it was not preconceived, Twombly and DeKooning.

PM: DeKooning also paints with Mayonnaise.

JS: What other painters have influenced you?

PM: —I liked. He divided the canvas into rooms. Like there was a big room above the small bedrooms across the bottom. This was the sixties which were very Byzantine-like—with smaller panels on the side and bottom. I painted them on the floor, they were stages. I'd be down on all fours on top of the painting. The problem was I never had enough, so I began to mix black paint with motor oil. And pour gasoline on them.

JS: Have those works been seen?

PM: Most were destroyed. When I came to L.A. in the ... in L.A. motor oil pieces—motor oil poured on paper and between sheets of glass. I also made pieces using butter and Vaseline. I covered the walls of a room with Vaseline and spray painted them red. I made a piece where I spread Vaseline in the cracks of the sidewalks with a rolled up newspaper on the corner of Wilshire and Santa Monica Boulevard.

JS: And then I guess you moved ketchup, always reminds me of Warhol ...

PM: Campbell's Soup, chicken noodle and ketchup were always part of my diet. I grew up with them. My father put ketchup on everything and ate Campbell's donut soup.

JS: Karen's body in a piece (KAREN'S KETCHUP DREAM, 1975)...

PM: A dream. So I turned it into. At that time I made video tapes and photographs that were never shown. They just went into cardboard boxes.

JS: How did people react to your early performance work?

PM: There was support. I didn't any work until I was outside on the porch of the gallery. There was a huge group who were not allowed in. You didn't expect love.

JS: Nowadays you have museum shows right out of grad school.

PM: The world.

JS: But not having a gallery must have fed you up experimental and resourceful. One of your videos in the operating room of some hospital?

PM: It was an autopsy. I wanted to make color. I had a friend who worked in the USC Medical Center late late at night.

JS: Gallery representation? You pull down your pants for the viewer and show your ass.

PM: There was always this, something had to be shown. Art world was interested, I think that it was work that was about Los Angeles. The L.A. art world wasn't interested in dirty little work. It would be categorized as "nasty work," European work, derivative.

JS: About L.A.?

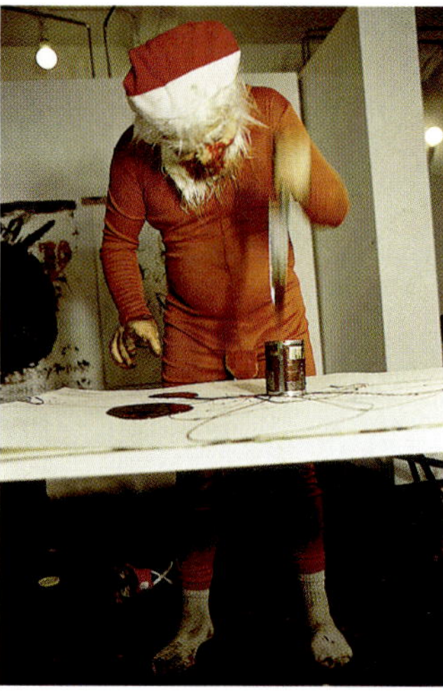

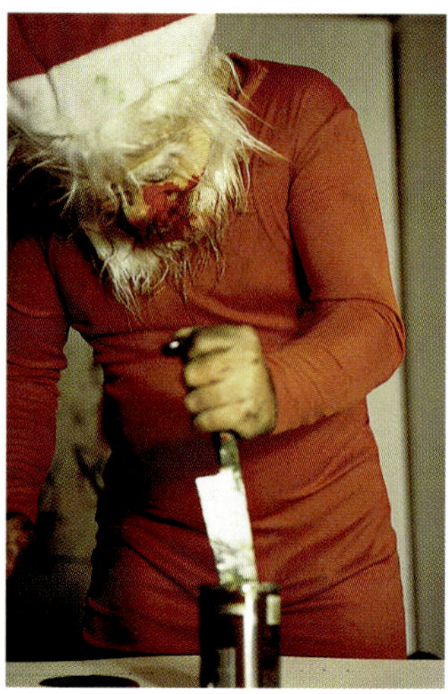

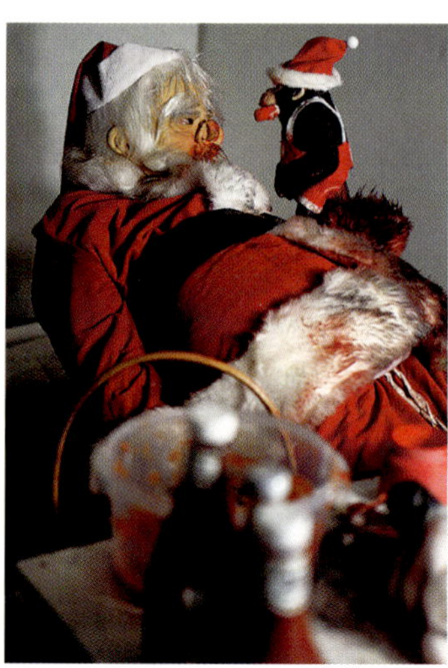

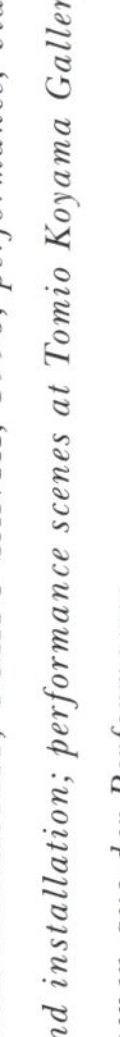

PAUL McCARTHY, TOKYO SANTA, 1996, performance, video tape and installation; performance scenes at Tomio Koyama Gallery, Tokyo / Szenen aus der Performance.

PM: I spent a lot of time in the streets in the early … bought a lot of. There used to be these fairly … with full of movie stills and you'd just thumb through images. I really liked this image I found, one from a film called *Europe in the Raw*, woman on a bed. (1963). When I did SAILOR'S MEAT, SAILOR'S DELIGHT (1975) the image on still was a … I mimic the pose from that movie still. At the time it was Russ Meyers discovered that later. The BOSSY BURGER set was a set for a family and, I think there was shocking sunny L.A. has an underbelly.
JS: But your European character.
PM: In the early eighties … something in France when they asked, I asked them to get me a chalet in the Alps to remake the story of *Heidi*. As a kid I was in the Alps. I wanted to be Swiss. I was really into having grown up near the mountains. I was totally into the boots, books, and parkas—the whole deal.
JS: So tell me about HEIDI (1991).
PM: The French government declined. In the end, HEIDI never got made and I talked about doing something together. Although the piece takes place in a small structure, one side a small chalet, the other side the American Bar and bedroom designed this Adolf Loos. It's a schizophrenic. You have Mike on one side and Paul on the other side. I always viewed it as a split melon by Adolf Loos.
JS: Your new project is also pretty.
PM: Four years ago Damon posed that we do a remake of *Pirates of the Caribbean*, the ride, starring Johnny Depp, and we started building a big fiber glass bloody boat, that houseboat we found. This announcement that Disney was going to do *Pirates of the Caribbean* starring Johnny Depp … they stole our idea. Beginning to envision The Museum of Munich came … asked to show the piece. The museum has enormous rooms. At the same time, we had begun working on which was a life size remake of the television show *F Troop*. F is for fuck. Its called FORT FUCK (2005) The museum was originally by Hitler to house degenerate by the Nazis' fascist invasion.
PM: A pirate boat invasion connects to the world today. A STRAIGHT LINE FROM HITLER'S BERLIN TO DISNEY'S DISNEYLAND (2005). It gets there by way of Berlin to Bavaria and Ludwig's, the Eiffel Tower, Las Vegas, and Disneyland. Adolf Hitler told me he wanted to build a straight road from Berlin to St. Petersburg with a German village every 100 kilometers.

JS: Speaking of roads, wagon train, I'm thinking of Hummers? A wagon train—

PM: Well, my original plan was to buy a piece of property in the California desert and go shooting. At one point I declined that maybe I should build a prairie schooner. My grandfather had a lamp wagon in his living room on the mantle, a little covered wagon, a prairie schooner made by a prisoner in Utah in the thirties or forties.

JS: But once it becomes actual ...

PM: It's fully functional, a convention—steel axles, bearings, and. The problem. My plan is to take them as a parade and then into the museum. Nazi, Disney parade.

JS: Would you say that your work has some relationships?

PM: I became a student from my dorm who considered myself a concrete poet. ("Oh, what's that?") His was to substitute the world for the action. At the time, I tried to steal a steam shovel, drive it on campus, dig a hole, and bury myself and the machine and the hole. A definition of poetry being equated to object or event, a huge effect.

JS: Poetry.

PM: When I went ... the university ... a year or so later, Yves Klein. He said, artist leaped from a ledge. Then that same year, I jumped out of a window. *(Laughs)* I didn't realize that Klein's leap had been a swan dive.

JS: He was like parallel to the ground—. And what about your leap?

PM: Pathetic jump. I found out that Klein's leap had been a photograph.

JS: I'm curious.

PM: My mother wanted to be an artist. It's a giant inflated bottle of rum. My smoking and drinking with her young brother who died of alcoholism.

JS: And your father. I recall a drawing you did of him before his death. And then there's that sculpture, the father helping his son suck a sheep or goat, or that's how I remember it.

PM: ... also about a father and his son. Ten years old, so I was reflecting on father. He worked seven days a week from seven morning until seven night. His job he was working. He expected to work.

JS: What was his occupation?

PM: Well, my father was a butcher. He worked in a grocery. One of my earliest memories of my father is of him in a white shirt.

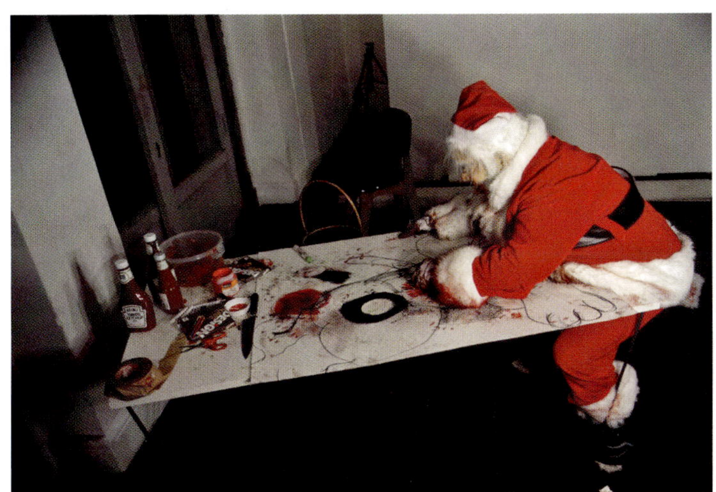

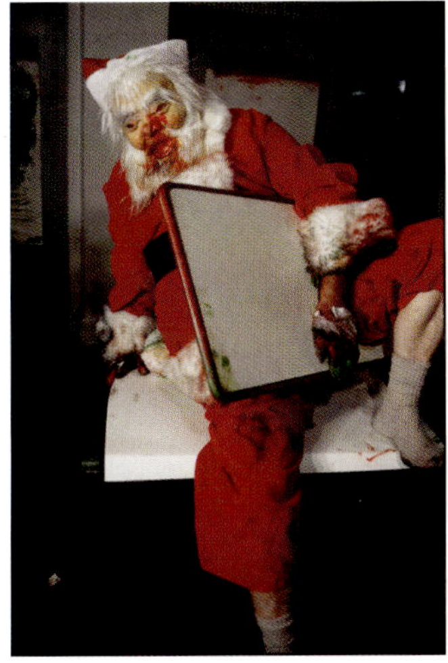

Paul McCarthy with Jeremy Sigler

JS: I imagine it would be fun to act in one of your pieces. Tell me about auditions.

PM: They come here and I don't quite know what to do with them.

JS: Are they professional actors?

PM: I didn't go to a casting agency. I put an ad in the *Hollywood Reporter* announcing that I was making films: a western and a type of pirate movie and I wound up with two hundred head shots. The description said that it might require nudity and that it was an unconventional film. We picked people from these head shots, and then there were a number of people from experimental theatre backgrounds.

JS: And then what? Did you do screen tests?

PM: I wrote these pretend scenarios. There's this scene where these wenches are being auctioned. So I tell them: "You're about to be auctioned and you don't quite know what that is, and you're frightened, and you begin to cry."

JS: Did you give them lines?

PM: I realized I wasn't interested in the lines; I was interested in the body position of crying. It became about asking them to cry in a particular position, like on all fours or... while walking back and forth across the room... like ten times, very slowly.

JS: It sounds pretty intuitive.

PM: You start with this premise. I had auditioned this guy who I wanted to play a rich boat owner who has these servants, and who abuses his power over them. Then I realized that what I was really interested in was his body. I spent all this time posing him as if on a pedestal.

JS: Don't the actors you audition need to be like stuntmen?

PM: I don't think I'm auditioning anybody for that purpose alone, but some of them are younger and stronger than me so they can perform longer then I can.

JS: What about the hazards of performing with materials. In BOSSY BURGER (1991), I get the feeling that something diabolical is about to occur.

PM: You're talking about the issue of realism: that definition of performance in the sixties where you get shot at—where there's an element of real danger. But I became interested in the fake. As opposed to using real blood, I began using ketchup. Though I did early performances where there were real actions, like stepping on glass.

JS: And falling from a rope.

PM: Well, I think it's just a matter of being aware of your body.

JS: But when you're performing, you almost seem to leave your body behind.

PM: Like going into a trance?

JS: Exactly.

PM: It's more about focus. It's about consciously attempting to make something—to make a work of art. So a lot of the world disappears in all that. But I don't think I'm pretending to be in a trance. I made a video tape years ago, where I shook my head really fast. It was called RATTLEHEAD (date?). When I did it, my eyes rolled up, and it looked real trance-like. I also made these pieces (SPINNING, EDIT #1, 1970) where I spun for thirty minutes. But I didn't think of it as being a whirling Dervish.

JS: That word "focus" reminds me of sports. Aren't you an athlete?

PM: I played baseball competitively growing up. It was my way of fitting it. I still play in a fast pitch softball league.

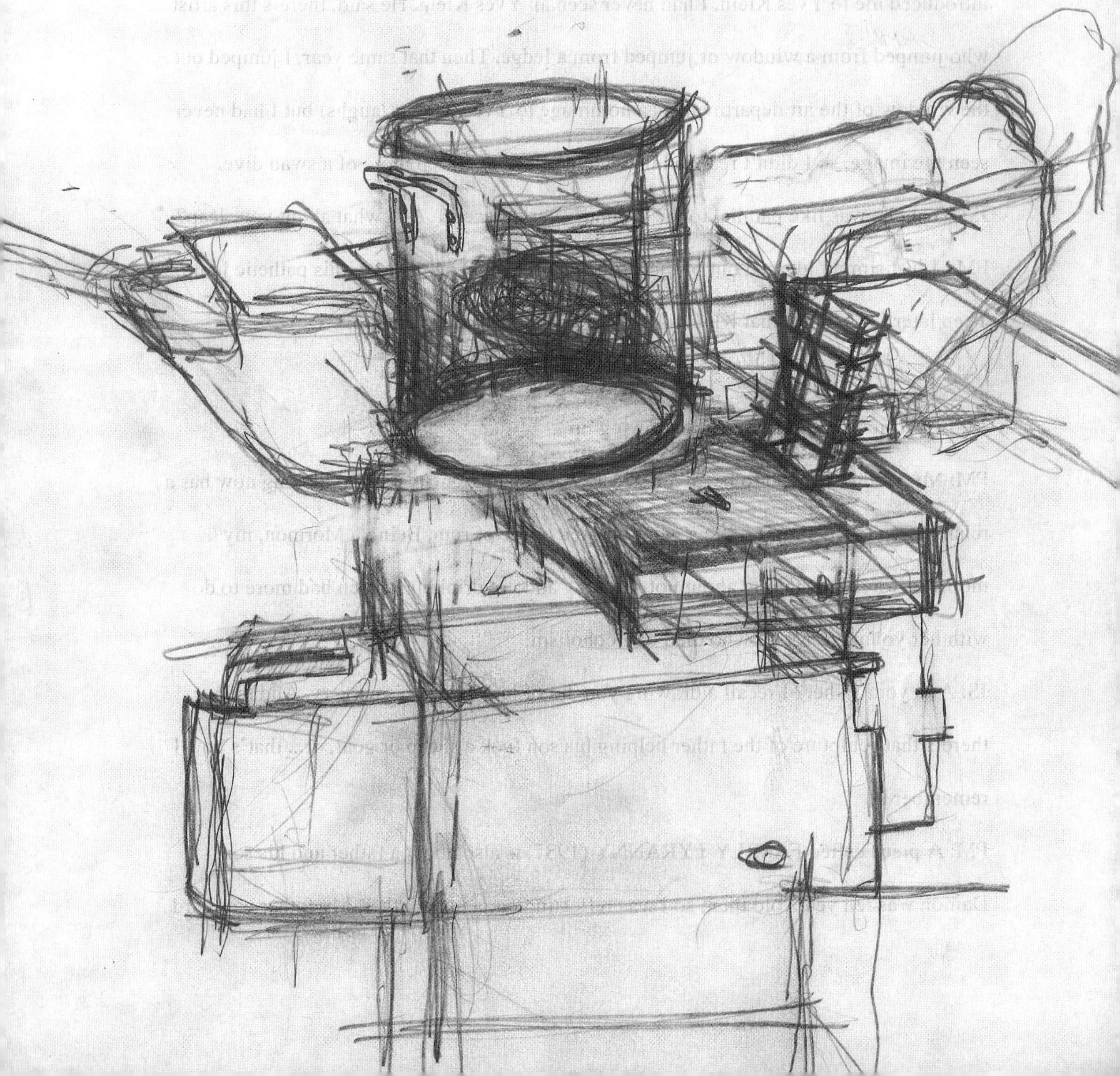

action. At the time, he was doing these pranks. He tried to steal a steam shovel, drive it on campus, dig a hole, and bury himself and the machine in the hole. That definition of poetry being equated to a real object or a real event had a huge effect on me.

JS: Did poetry then help form your idea of performance?

PM: When I went to the University of Utah a year or so later, I met another poet who introduced me to Yves Klein. I had never seen any Yves Klein. He said, there's this artist who jumped from a window or jumped from a ledge. Then that same year, I jumped out the window of the art department [illegible] (laughs) but I had never seen the image of him [illegible] of a swan dive.

[illegible] what [illegible]

PM: [illegible] his pathetic [illegible]

[illegible]

PM: M[illegible] now has a [illegible] Being Mormon, my [illegible] had more to do with [illegible] Catholicism.

JS: [illegible] there [illegible] one of the father helping his son [illegible] that's [illegible]

PM: A piece [illegible] (1987) is also [illegible] father [illegible]

Damon was [illegible]

JS: Would you say there's a cathartic quality to your performance work?

PM: No. It's not about setting up a situation for a catharsis.

JS: I'm thinking of Yoko Ono—the way she did scream therapy. For her, it became a kind of singing style.

PM: In that type of singing, it feels like there's a release. In the 70s, I was interested in primal therapy, and I talked about art as a venting. I made a hollow box with it's face covered in louvers—the type of bent metal louvers you'll see on hot rods (VENTED CUBE DRAWING, 1975). Then I wrote this poem about venting. In a way, I kind of vent the subconscious. I would, and I still do, talk about setting up a situation to get something unexpected to happen.

JS: Are you also trying to get something out of your system?

PM: It's more the opposite. You're in the present and you've brought these elements together and then you start forming them. It's in the forming that something begins to happen and you see something in it.

JS: Your work has gotten to be more collaborative, and technical over the years, with elaborate props and electronically animated, kinetic sculptures. You've come a long way from dipping your penis into bucket of black paint. (PENIS DIP PAINTING, 1974)

PM: For quite awhile I made work solely by myself, but even then when I made the video tapes in the seventies, there would be a crew. When the nineties came around, I collaborated with Mike Kelly and Jason Roads and Benjamin Weissmen. At one point in the eighties I had the idea to have something fabricated by an outside company. Some of those things got really technical.

JS: And you had to call on experts?

PM: I'd attempt to do it myself at times, but then at one point I realized, I might fuck up the idea if I fabricate it because I might not be able to make it well enough. So I worked with fabricators. Also I wanted to have multiple types of work being done all at once because I had multiple interests. For example, I was interested in an abstract figure. I was interested in a realistic figure. I was interested in a mechanical figure, these different ideas of representation. That was when I became interested in Disney as sculpture. The form of Mickey Mouse or Donald Duck is what attracted me. And that was when I made a clumsy attempt to mimic that kind of fabrication.

JS: Did you aspire to create an entire theme park?

PM: Early on, there was this idea of trying to creating a kind of full scale production company, or studio. In Los Angeles, these small production houses are very common. They're all sort of connected to the film industry in some way, either producing elements for film or for commercials.

JS: And I'd imagine that the studios share personnel. So it's not unlikely that a guy who is working for you is also making things for Disney or some blockbuster movie?

PM: My studio is made up of about thirty people right now, but I work really closely, and I have for a number of years, with my son, Damon. Then some of his friends came to work for me. It was like, "Damon, what does your friend do?" And his friend, it turns out, makes robotics for Disney and just worked on "Men in Black." (Robotic Pig, 2004)

JS: This makes you kind of like all the other Hollywood directors. Have you been influenced by any directors in particular. I'm looking at all those horror movie props (cast legs filled with blood)—what about Mario Bava?

PM: For awhile, I was really into Dario Argento. I was looking for something in all those films. In a way I found it, but in a way I didn't find it. I'm really into Pasolini, and have been for a long time. I think I was seriously affected by *Salo.* Lately I've been kind of interested in Jack Smith films where it's obvious there's something pretend going on... like we're going to get dressed-up in costumes, and pretend we're riding this raft. I've also watched a lot of westerns, all kinds: Italian, Spanish, Germany, and American.

JS: With Russ Myers and John Waters there's this idea of the artists as some kind of a pervert, who is pushing the audience, or society in general, to accept something that is really in bad taste, or in some way deeply humiliating.

PM: I want my work to be a snippet of that. Like somehow you know what you just saw, but it doesn't fall into place. Like you can recognize the character from pop culture, like Pinocchio, but can't put the story together. But I can't really compare myself to John Waters, because I'm not a filmmaker. I'm interested in taking it the whole distance, but not so much in making something meant to be seen in a blackened theater.

JS: When I saw TOKYO SANTA (1996), I thought of the recent release, *Bad Santa*, which I'd just seen in a theater. I think Terry Zweigoff's bad Santa (played by Billie Bob Thornton) and your "bad" Santa weren't too far apart from one another.

PM: [...]

JS: When you were an art student, how aware were you of the avant-garde. Had you read any of Allan Kaprow writing? I'm thinking of this article he wrote on Jackson Pollock where he talks about painting, but with all sorts of non-art, every day materials.

PM: I think at the time I read that big fat brown book on Assemblage. By 1968 I knew of Bruce Nauman. But I was really more interested in Minimalism. I was making these all black paintings influenced by Tony Smith. That was when I did the DEAD H (1968), which related to Smith's DIE (date?), which was hollow. I didn't know of Acconci's work until the 70s when I came to LA., although he was a huge influence in the art world. His work was so language-based, especially since he began as a poet.

JS: And yours, by comparison, must be grunt-based.

PM: I actually wrote some poetry in the 70s, not a lot. And the scores are another set of writing. You're right about the groans and moans—I didn't know how to get a word out of my mouth. Then in the performances, maybe from 1977 to 1983, I talked the whole time. That becomes poetry, not a written down poetry, not a written script, but just a spontaneous verbalizing.

JS: It reminds me of Dada poets like Hugo Ball or Kurt Schwitters.

PM: Or James Joyce. Now, I'm doing a lot of writing on the drawings. But it becomes obvious that I'm dyslexic and not able to spell.

JS: What about Cy Twombly? His paintings are really scatological; they have the same idea of debauchery and debasement.

PM: This is the first I ever heard of 'em. (laughs) Did he use shit and piss?

JS: No. I think he uses like Crayolo crayons, colored pencils, and bits of smeared house paint.

PM: I don't think about Cy Twombly at all. In fact, DeKooning comes up in PAINTER (1995), the video I made, but it was totally coincidental because I had gone and I bought a black wig, a brown wig, and a blonde wig, and the day of the performance, I put the blonde wig on, and when I put it on I said, "Oh Warhol, oh I'm Warhol." Then I looked in the mirror and went, "Oh no, I'm DeKooning."

JS: Didn't DeKooning also paint with Mayonnaise as a substitute for white paint?

PM: But the intention of that piece is not to be DeKooning; It's about this painter who's a fan of DeKooning and wants to be like DeKooning.

JS: What other painters have influenced you?

PM: Early on, I was really into British pop painting like Kataj and Peter Blake—I liked the way Blake's paintings were architectural. He divided the canvas into rooms. Like there was a big room above and smaller rooms across the bottom. This was the 60s, and I was working on black paintings, which were very Byzantine-like—triptychs, one with a big vertical column with divisions across the bottom like rooms. Then I started painting on the floor, and the supports were structured as platforms that were up off the floor like four inches. So they were almost like little stages. I'd be down on all fours on top of the painting smearing paint around with my hands. The problem was I never had enough black paint, so I began to mix my black paint with motor oil. And I would light the paintings on fire.

JS: Have those works been seen?

PM: No. A lot of them were destroyed. When I came to LA in the seventies, some of the first pieces I did were motor oil pieces—motor oil poured on paper and between sheets of glass. I also made a lot of pieces using butter and Vaseline. I covered a room or walls in Vaseline and spray painted them red. Then I made these pieces where I spread boiling Vaseline in the cracks of the sidewalks near Melrose.

JS: And then I guess you moved onto ketchup. Your ketchup, always reminds me of Warhol tomato soup.

PM: There is a correlation to the Campbell soup can. It was something that was so central to the dinner table. But the fact is my father put ketchup on everything.

JS: And didn't you spread ketchup all over your wife Karen's body in a piece (KAREN KETCHUP DREAM, EDIT #2, 1975).

PM: I had a dream and in the dream I had spread ketchup on Karen. So I turned it into a real piece. A lot of those video tapes were made, and the photographs were taken, and maybe a few friends saw them, and then they just went into boxes. There was kind of an erotic thing to it. It was this mix of something that was meant to feel good, but then there really was this stink.

JS: How did people react to your early performance work? Were they supportive or mortified?

PM: To a degree there was support within my community of artists, but I really didn't sell any work until 1990. At that time, I was just outside of the gallery art world. That's the way it was. There was a huge group of artists who were not showing. I think there was a certain acceptance of this. You didn't expect a show.

JS: Nowadays young artists have museum shows right out of grad school.

PM: I believed video might be a way of getting something out into the world.

JS: But not having a gallery, must have freed you up to be more experimental and resourceful. Didn't you film one of your videos in the operating room of some hospital?

PM: I wanted to make color video tapes, but at the time color equipment was much more difficult to get your hands on. I had a friend who worked in the USC medical center and we would work at night there using their color video equipment.

JS: But were you hoping for gallery representation? In one performance you pull down your pants for the viewer and show your ass, as if you're saying "kiss my ass." (ASS END I, 1972)

PH: There was always this hope that something would be shown. But the art world of Los Angeles was interested, even though I think it was work that was about Los Angeles. The LA art world wasn't interested in dirty work. It would be categorized as "messy work," like European work, derivative of Actionism or Happenings or Fluxus.

JS: In what way was your work about LA?

PM: I spent a lot of time in the streets of Hollywood during the early seventies and I bought a lot of movie stills. There used to be these stores that were fairly large, almost like a record store. The boxes were out, and you'd just thumb through images. I really liked this image I found from a film called *Europe and the Raw*, it was a woman on a bed. (EUROPE IN THE RAW PUBLICITY STILL, 1963)When I did SAILOR'S MEAT-SAILOR'S DELIGHT, EDIT #2 (1975) the image and the pose I used comes from that movie still. At the time I didn't even know it was a Russ Meyer film. I discovered that later. And of course, BOSSY BURGER's set was directly from a set for the sitcom, *Family Affair*. But generally, I think there was something about this place: sunny LA, there's an underbelly of a violence here.

JS: But your work also has European characteristics.

PM: In the early eighties I got an NEA grant to do something in France when they asked me what I would like to do, I asked them to get me a small chalet in the Alps where I proposed to remake the story of Heidi. Actually, as a kid I was really into the Alps because I wanted to be a Swiss mountain guide. I was really into rock climbing and mountaineering, having grown up right around ski resorts and mountains in the foothills of Salt Lake. I was totally into the boots, the packs, the parkas—the whole deal.

JS: So tell me more about HEIDI (1991).

PM: The French government declined. In the end, I never traveled to France and HEIDI never got made, until later when Mike (Kelly) and I talked about doing something together. Although the piece takes place in a kids version of a Swiss chalet, there is also this Adolph Loos aesthetic. It's like a schizophrenic building. You have Mike on one side and Paul on the other side. I always viewed it as a split piece.

JS: Your new project is also pretty schitzo?

PM: It's a long story. Like four years ago, Damon proposed that we do a remake of *Pirates of the Caribbean*, the ride, and we started working on building a big fiber glass boat that would float inside of, and be held up by, this houseboat we found. Then came this announcement that Disney was going to do *Pirates of the Caribbean* starring Johnny Depp (laughs) and I remember thinking, God they stole my idea. But my piece kept going; it sort of had its own life. We were also beginning to envision doing these forty foot sets but the problem was where to show them. Then the museum of Munich came along, saw the piece and asked to show it, and they had these enormous rooms. At the same time, there was another piece I had begun working on which was a life size remake of the fort from the television show *F Troop*. It's called FORT FUCK (date). Then there was the fact that the museum in Munich was originally commissioned by Hitler to house the art of the Third Reich.

JS: I think your art would have certainly been considered degenerate by the Nazis.

PM: But there's this idea of a pirate boat invasion that kind of connects to the situation of the world today. There's this piece I did a number of years ago which was called A STRAIGHT LINE FROM HITLER'S BERLIN TO WALT DISNEY'S DISNEYLAND (date?). It gets there by way of Bavaria and Ludwig's Castle, the World's Fair of the late 1800s in Paris when the Eiffel Tower was constructed, Las Vegas, and Disneyland. This person told me that Adolph Hitler wanted to build a straight road from Berlin to St. Petersburg, with a German village every so many kilometers along the road.

JS: Speaking of roads, can you talk about your wagon train piece? When I first saw them they made me think of Hummers?

PM: (Laughs) Well, my original plan with Damon was to buy a piece of property in the California desert and shoot this western/prairie film. At one point I decided that maybe I should build a wagon and then realized that my grandfather had a toy wagon in his living room on the mantle, this little covered wagon that was a lamp. It had been made by prisoners in Utah probably in the 30s or 40s, I'm not really sure. I decided that I would remake that toy wagon.

JS: But once the scale of the toy is blown up it becomes like the size of an actual wagon.

PM: It's fully functional, and very sturdy, it's built stronger then a conventional wagon, it has steel axles, bearings, and everything. The problem with these wagons is that they are actually stubbier and heavier then a conventional wagon. My plan is to take them on the road as a kind of parade and then into the museum.

JS: Would you say that your work has some relationship to pranks?

PM: In college, I became friends with this student from my dorm who considered himself a concrete poet. I said, "Oh, what's that?" His definition was to substitute the word for an action. At the time, he was doing these pranks. He tried to steal a steam shovel, drive it on campus, dig a hole, and bury himself and the machine in the hole. That definition of poetry being equated to a real object or a real event had a huge effect on me.

JS: Did poetry then help form your idea of performance?

PM: When I went to the University of Utah, a year or so later, I met another poet who introduced me to Yves Klein. I had never seen an Yves Klein. He said, there's this artist who jumped from a window or jumped from a ledge. Then that same year, I jumped out the window of the art department as a hommage to Yves Klein, (laughs) but I had never seen the image, so I didn't realized that Klein's leap had been more of a swan dive.

JS: Yeah, he was like parallel to the ground—very graceful. And what about your leap?

PM: I just simply jumped out of the window and landed on my feet, this pathetic jump. Then later I found out that Klein's leap had been a faked photograph.

[...]

JS: I'm curious. What was it like growing up?

PM: My mother wanted to be an artist. She was liberal. One piece I'm making now has a relationship to my mother. It's a giant inflated bottle of rum. Being a Mormon, my mother always had a thing about not smoking and not drinking, which had more to do with her younger brother who died of alcoholism.

JS: And your father? I recall a drawing you did of him before his surgery. And then there's that sculpture of the father helping his son fuck a sheep or goat, or... that's how I remember it.

PM: A piece called FAMILY TYRANNY (1987) is also about a father and his son. Damon was ten years old then, so I was reflecting on being a father. My father was hard

~~working~~; he worked seven days a week from seven ~~in the~~ morning until seven ~~at~~ night. ~~When he wasn't working at~~ his job he was working ~~at home~~. He expected ~~me~~ to work ~~around the house.~~

JS: What was his occupation?

PM: Well, I ~~think that's where it gets pretty interesting (laughs)~~ My father was a butcher. He worked in a grocery store. One of my earliest memories of my father is ~~an image~~ of him in a ~~bloody apron~~. white shirt.

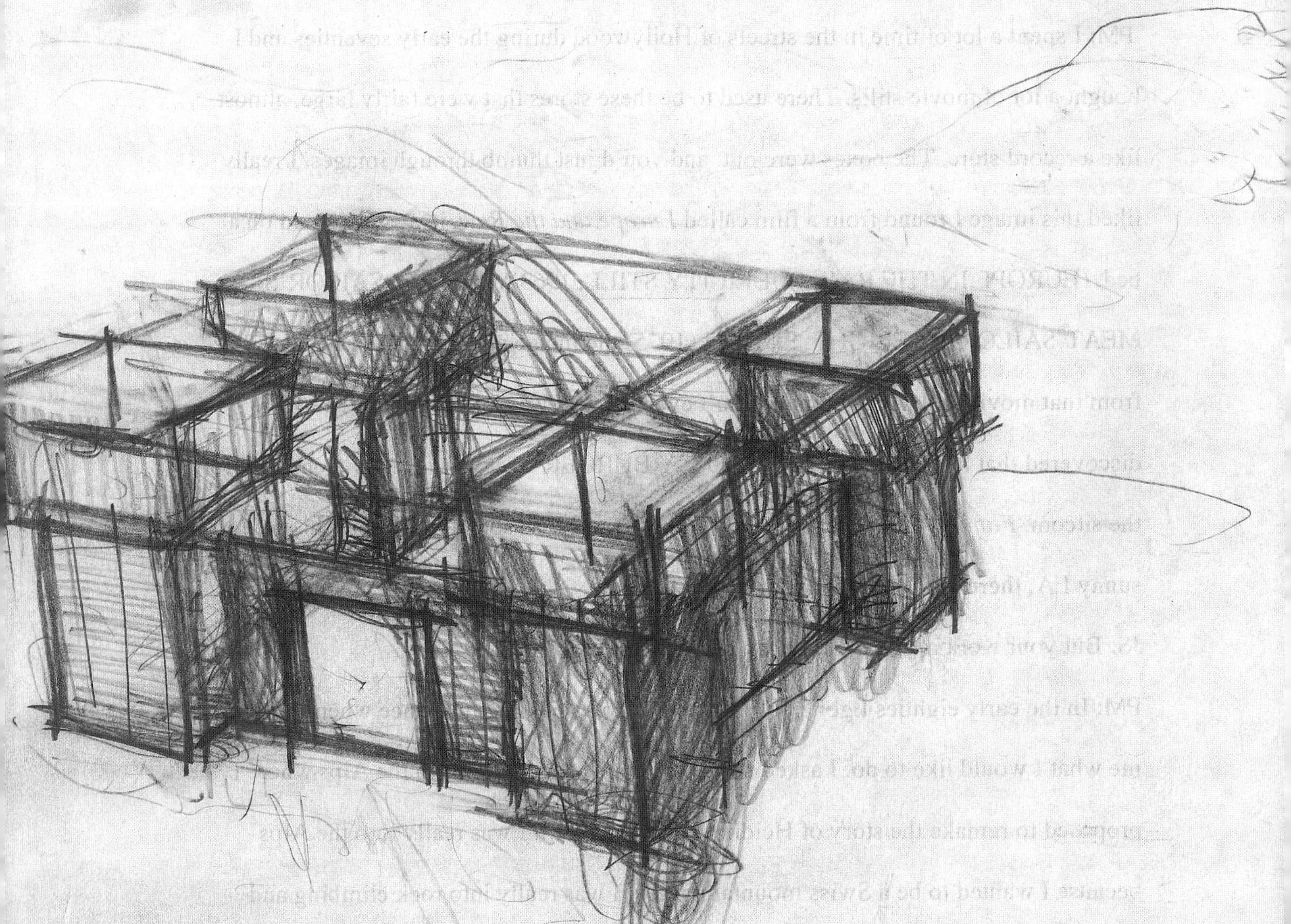

JS: But were you hoping for gallery representation? In one performance you pull down your pants for the viewer and show your ass, as if you're saying, "Kiss my ass." (ASS END I, 1972)

PM: There was always this hope that something would be shown. But the art world of Los Angeles wasn't interested, even though I think it was work that was about Los Angeles. The LA art world wasn't interested in that work. It would be categorized as "messy work," like European work, derivative of [illegible] Actionism or Happenings or Fluxus.

JS: In what way was your work about L.A.?

PM: I spent a lot of time in the streets of Hollywood during the early seventies and I looked a lot at movie stills. There used to be these stores that were fairly large, almost like a record store. The boxes were huge and you'd just thumb through images. I really liked this image I found from a film called [illegible] the [illegible] that had "ROCK [illegible] STILL [illegible]

MEAT SAL[illegible]

from that movie [illegible]

discovered that [illegible]

the sitcom [illegible]

sunny L.A. there [illegible]

JS: But your work [illegible]

PM: In the early eighties [illegible]

me what I would like to do. I asked [illegible]

proposed to remake the story of Heidi [illegible] was really [illegible]

because I wanted to be a Swiss mountain [illegible] was really into rock climbing and [illegible]

Im Dialog mit der Sprache selbst

JEREMY SIGLER & PAUL McCARTHY

Als ich mich in Paul McCarthys Atelier mit ihm zusammensetzte und unsere Unterhaltung auf Band aufnahm, versuchte ich immer wieder das Gespräch auf die Poesie zu bringen. Da ich selbst Gedichte schreibe wohl vornehmlich aus egoistischen Gründen. Ich rechnete jedoch nicht damit, dass Paul, sobald er das Manuskript in die Hände bekäme, sich erneut in das Gespräch hineinarbeiten, es zerpflücken und jedes Wort, jede Silbe in Frage stellen würde, um schliesslich das verdammte Ding komplett umzuschreiben! Es war, als wären die gesprochenen Worte, die wir in unserem freundlichen Ateliergespräch gewechselt hatten, durch das Niederschreiben suspekt und ungenau geworden, schlicht falsch. Es wurde deutlich, dass Paul die erste Version des transkribierten Interviews als äussere Fassade betrachtete, als blosse Oberfläche, die sich vor eine andere, ursprünglichere, tiefere Sprache geschoben hatte. Er schickte uns ein eindrückliches Dokument zurück, in dem unser konventionelles Gespräch in einen chaotischeren, nicht immer grammatikalisch korrekten Prozess verwandelt war. Mit anderen Worten: in einen Dialog mit der Sprache selbst, der – und das ist typisch für Paul McCarthy – eine ihm eigene Sprache freilegte. Im eigentlichen Sinn des Wortes: ein Gedicht.

Jeremy Sigler

Im Folgenden finden Sie die deutsche Übersetzung des vom Künstler bearbeiteten Manuskripts. Zum besseren Verständnis beachten Sie bitte auch das als Faksimile abgedruckte Original (S. 120–134).

JS: Und da waren auch …
Und dann? Wurden Probeaufnahmen gemacht?
PM: Ich schrieb diese Drehbücher. Mädchen, die feilgeboten werden, «und ihr habt Angst und beginnt zu weinen.»
JS: Hast du ihnen Text gegeben?
PM: Ich merkte, dass der Text für mich nicht wichtig war. Was mich interessierte, war ihre Körperhaltung, ihre Gesichter, wenn sie weinten. Es lief darauf hinaus, sie zu bitten auf allen vieren zu weinen, oder … zu kriechen, wenn sie im Raum hin und her gingen … so an die zehn Mal, ganz langsam.
JS: Das hört sich gut an.
PM: Man fängt mit den Genitalien an. Ich hatte diesen Typen vorsprechen lassen, der einen reichen Bootsbesitzer spielen sollte, der diese Bediensteten hat, seine Macht missbraucht. An einem bestimmten Punkt merkte ich wieder, dass es eigentlich sein Körper war, was mich

JEREMY SIGLER ist Autor von zwei Gedichtbänden, *To and To* und *Mallet Eyes*. Er ist Mitarbeiter der *Parkett*-Redaktion in New York.

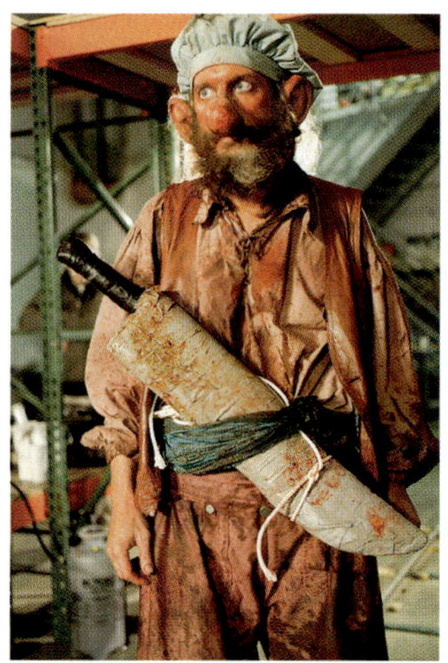

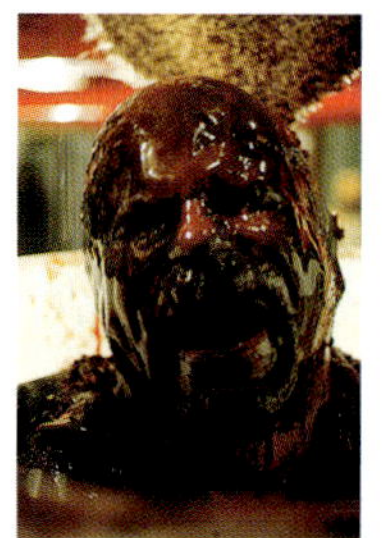

PAUL McCARTHY, PIRATE PROJECT, 2001–2005, performance scenes / Szenen aus der Performance.
(PHOTOS: S. DUENAS & A. ROUNKLE)

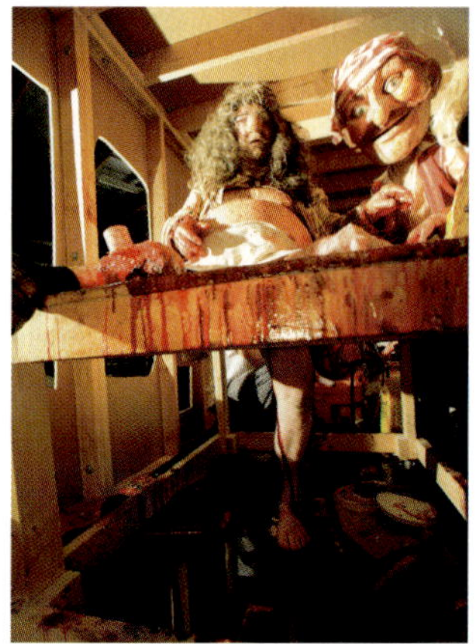

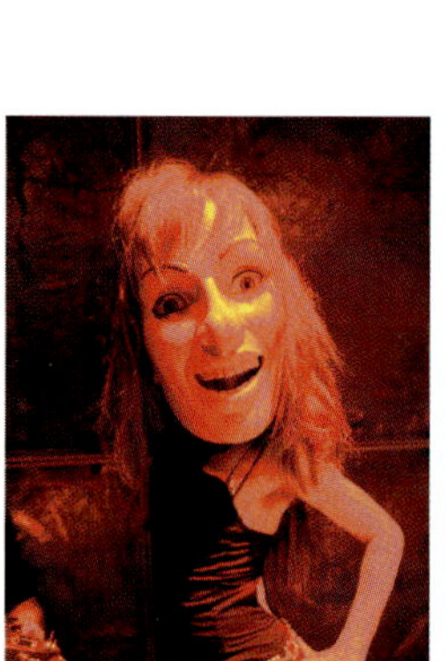

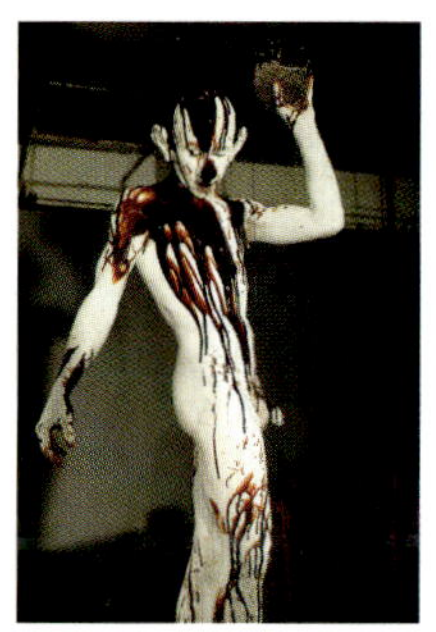

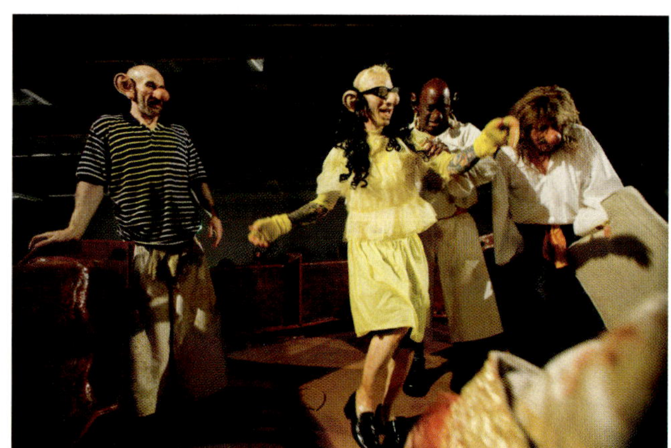

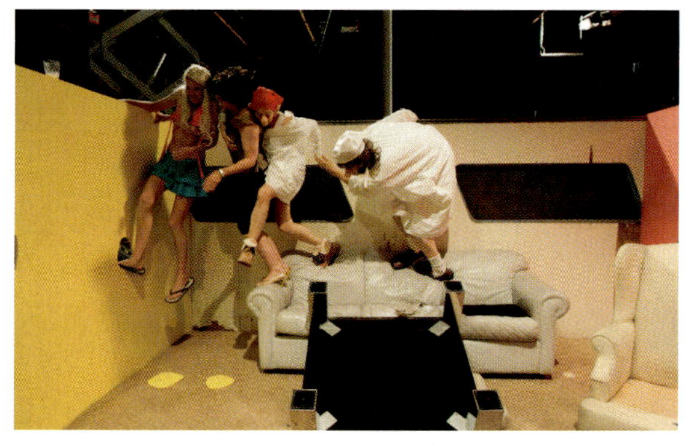

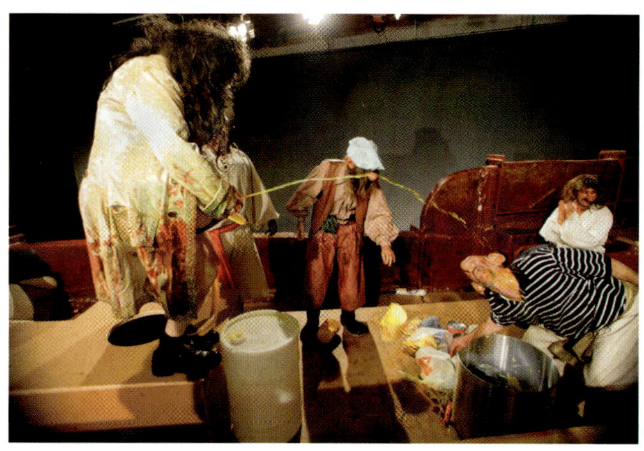

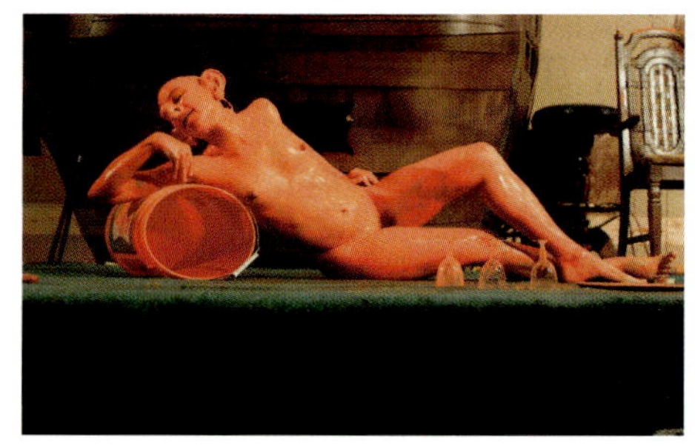

interessierte. Ich verbrachte die ganze Zeit damit, ihn auf diesem Tisch posieren zu lassen, einem Sockel, als wäre er eine griechische Skulptur. Es ging um das Demonstrieren und Missbrauchen der Macht des einen über den anderen. Menschlich, aber mit diesem gewissen Dreh.

JS: Die Darsteller, die du vorsprechen lässt, müssen Stuntmen sein?

PM: Nein.

JS: Wie stehts mit dem Spiel mit Materialien? In mir kriecht ein Gefühl hoch, dass gleich etwas Teuflisches vorfallen wird.

PM: Realismus, in den 60er Jahren schiesst man auf dich, wenn es wirklich gefährlich ist. Mich interessierte der Schwindel. Richtiges Blut, ich begann stattdessen Ketchup zu verwenden. Obwohl ichs früher fliessen liess, lass uns auf Glas treten, lass uns mit Scheisse malen.

JS: Von einem Seil stürzen.

PM: Ich zerschnitt ein Seil und fiel runter.

JS: Doch während einer Performance, scheinst du deinen Körper fast zu verlassen.

PM: Du meinst NO?

JS: Genau.

PM: Es ist eher eine Frage des Fokus, Fokus auf einen Tisch, Konzentration auf etwas. Ich fokussiere. Wenn ein Kunstwerk entstehen soll, kann die Welt verschwinden. Ja, verschwinden, aber ich glaube nicht, dass ich, dass ich in Trance bin. Ich drehte ein Video, in dem ich meinen Kopf unentwegt und schnell schüttelte. Es hiess RATTLE HEAD (1974). Während ich das tat, rollten meine Augen nach oben und es sah aus wie in Trance. Ich liess mich so aussehen auf einem ... Ich machte auch diese Arbeiten, in denen ich 30 Minuten lang im gleichen Tempo herumwirbelte wie die Videobandspule.

PM: Dieses Wort *fuck* (Fokus) lässt mich an Sport denken ...

PM: Ich spielte Baseball. Das war meine Art gesellschaftlich dazuzugehören. Finger des Fanghandschuhs. *(Erklärung zur Zeichnung im englischen Manuskript, Seite 121 unten.)*

JS: Würdest du sagen, es gebe eine Qualität in deinem ...

PM: Ja und nein. NO.

JS: Ich denke an Yoko Ono ... Bei ihr wurde es zu einer Art Stil.

PM: In dieser Art zu singen liegt eine Befreiung, da bin ich überzeugt, mich interessierten Therapien und ich habe übers Dampf Ablassen gesprochen. Ich machte einen hohlen Kasten bedeckt mit – diesen geschwungenen Karosserielüftungsschlitzen (VENTED CUBE – Belüfteter Kubus, Zeichnung, 1975). Dann schrieb ich dieses Gedicht übers Dampf Ablassen. Die Durchlüftung des Unterbewusstseins. Ich will eine Situation durchlüften.

JS: Deine Arbeiten sind über die Jahre immer gesammelter, technischer geworden, mit ausgefeilten Bauten und elektronisch animierten, kinetischen Skulpturen. Du hast einen weiten Weg zurückgelegt, seit du deinen Penis in Kübel voll schwarzer Farbe getaucht hast (PENIS DIP PAINTING, 1974).

PM: Ja, eine Zeit lang arbeitete ich allein. Ich machte die Videos in ... Als die 90er Jahre kamen, hängte ich mich mit Mike Kelley, Jason Rhoades und Benjamin Weissman rein. Ich hatte die Idee, dass ich beginnen müsste, arbeiten zu lassen.

JS: Und du zogst Fachleute bei?

PM: Ja. Ein Punkt, ich könnte die Idee versauen, wenn mir etwas misslingt. Also arbeitete ich mit Firmen zusammen, verschiedenste Arbeiten wurden alle gleichzeitig erledigt. Ich hatte vielfältige Interessen. Mich interessierte die abstrakte Figur, die realistische Figur, die mechanische Figur, diese verschiedenen Ideen der Darstellung von Unterdrückung. So dass ich mich für Disney als Skulptur zu interessieren begann. Mickey Mouse und Donald Duck faszinierten mich.

JS: Hattest du im Sinn, einen ganzen Themenpark zu kreieren?

PM: Ja, da war diese Idee etwas zu kreieren. Ich wollte eine eigene Stadt gründen und auch eine Produktionsfirma. In Los Angeles gibt es Produktionsfirmen. Sie gehören zur Filmindustrie. Mein Studio sollte eine Produktionsstätte sein.

JS: Die Studios beschäftigen zum Teil dasselbe Personal, also ist es nicht unwahrscheinlich, dass ein Typ, der für dich arbeitet, auch für Disney arbeitet oder für irgendeinen Klotz ...

PM: Mein Studio besteht momentan aus Leuten. Ich arbeite in der Nähe. Ich habe nur noch wenige Jahre mit meinem Sohn Damon. Freunde kamen zu Damon, sein Freund, wie sich herausstellt, Disney, *Men in Black*.

JS: Das macht dich irgendwie allen anderen Hollywoodregisseuren ähnlich. Manchen Regisseuren vielleicht besonders – wie stehts mit Mario Bava?

PM: Dario Argento. Suchte etwas in Pasolini hinein, ich glaube, ich bin stark beeinflusst von Jack Smiths Filmen und Warhol, wo es offensichtlich ist, dass die Schauspieler nur so tun, so tun, als ob sie Schauspieler wären. Wir werden uns verkleiden und so tun, als wären wir auf einem Schiff.

JS: Russ Meyers und John Waters ... da gibt es diese Idee des Künstlers als Perversling, um etwas zu akzeptieren, das sehr geschmacklos ist, eine schwere Demütigung.

PM: Ich wollte, dass man erkennt, was man eben sah, aber es funktioniert nicht. Man erkennt die Figur, es ist Pinocchio, doch die Geschichte steckt nicht drin. John Waters ist ein Filmemacher, denn ich bin kein Filmemacher, ich bin kein herkömmlicher Geschichtenerzähler. Ich interessiere mich für die Handlung/Situation als falsches Theater.

JS: Als ich TOKYO SANTA (Tokioter Sankt Nikolaus, 1996) anschaute, musste ich an *Bad Santa* (2004) denken, den ich eben im Kino gesehen hatte. Ich glaube Terry Zwigoffs böser Nikolaus (gespielt von Billy Bob Thornton) und dein «böser» Nikolaus liegen gar nicht so weit auseinander.

PM: Ja, sehr eng beisammen.

JS: Wie bewusst warst du? Ich denke an den Artikel, den er [Allan Kaprow] über Jackson Pollock schrieb, wo er vom Malen spricht, aber mit allerlei nichtkünstlerischen Alltagsmaterialien.

PM: Ich glaube, als ich dieses grosse dicke braune Buch las, machte ich diese ausschliesslich roten Bilder, beeinflusst von Tony Smith. Damals machte ich auch das tote H (DEAD H, 1968). Smiths DIE (Stirb, 1962) war innen hohl. Ich kannte Acconcis Werk nicht, bevor ich nach Los Angeles kam. Sein Werk war Sprache – schon, weil er als Dichter begonnen hatte. Wie ist es mit der Dichtkunst, hast du dich dafür interessiert?

JS: In den 70er Jahren hab ich Gedichte geschrieben, heiss, vieles. Schreiben. Du hast Recht mit dem Ächzen und Stöhnen – aus meinem Mund. Das wird zu Poesie, keine geschriebene Poesie, kein Manuskript, nur verbale Äusserung.

JS: Es erinnert mich an Dad.

PM: Oder James Joyce.

JS: Wie wärs mit Cy Twombly? Seine Bilder sind skatologisch. Sie haben auch diesen Hauch von Ausschweifung.

PM: Twombly, verwendet er Scheisse und Pisse?

JS: Nein, ich glaube er verwendet Crayola-Kreiden, Farbstifte und etwas verwischte Tünche.

PM: Ich überlege mir das mit Twombly. Eigentlich De Kooning. Ich ging und kaufte ...

kaufe eine blonde Perücke am Tag der Performance. Ich setzte die Perücke vor der Aufnahme auf und dachte, ich wäre Warhol. Dann sah ich aus wie De Kooning. Der Charakter De Kooning entstand an diesem Tag. Es war nicht vorbereitet, Twombly und De Kooning.

PM: De Kooning malt auch mit Mayonnaise.

JS: Haben dich noch andere Maler beeinflusst?

PM: Ich mochte ... Er unterteilte die Leinwand in Räume, als wäre da ein grosser Raum über den kleinen Schlafräumen darunter. Das war in den 60er Jahren, die sehr byzantinisch waren, mit kleineren Bildtafeln seitlich oder unter dem Hauptbild. Ich malte sie auf dem Boden, es waren Bühnen. Ich kroch auf allen vieren auf dem Bild herum. Das Problem war, dass ich nie genug bekam, also mischte ich schwarze Farbe mit Motorenöl und übergoss beides mit Benzin.

JS: Waren diese Arbeiten je zu sehen?

PM: Die meisten wurden zerstört. Als ich nach L.A. kam in den ... in den Arbeiten mit Motorenöl aus L.A. – auf Papier und zwischen Glasplatten gegossenes Motorenöl. Ich machte auch Arbeiten mit Butter und Vaseline. Ich bedeckte die Wände eines Raumes mit Vaseline und besprühte sie mit roter Farbe. Ich machte eine Arbeit, bei der ich mit einer zusammengerollten Zeitung Vaseline in die Risse der Gehsteige an der Ecke Wilshire und Santa Monica Boulevard verteilte.

JS: Und dann hast du Ketchup bewegt ... erinnert mich immer an Warhol.

PM: Campbell's Soup, Nudelsuppe mit Huhn und Ketchup gehörten schon immer zu meiner Diät. Ich bin mit ihnen aufgewachsen. Mein Vater übergoss alles mit Ketchup und ass Campbell's Raviolisuppe.

JS: In einer Arbeit Karens Körper (KAREN'S KETCHUP DREAM, 1975).

PM: Ein Traum. Also verwandelte ich ihn zu. Damals machte ich Videos und Photographien, die nie ausgestellt wurden. Sie wanderten einfach in Kartonschachteln.

JS: Wie reagierten die Leute auf deine frühen Performance-Arbeiten?

PM: Es gab Unterstützung. Ich arbeitete nichts, bis ich vor der Tür der Galerie stand. Da waren viele, die keinen Einlass fanden. Man erwartete nicht, geliebt zu werden.

JS: Heute hat man Museumsausstellungen, kaum ist die Schule abgeschlossen.

PM: Schön.

JS: Aber keine Galerie zu haben hat dir schliesslich gereicht ... experimentell und erfinderisch. Eines deiner Videos im Operationssaal eines Spitals?

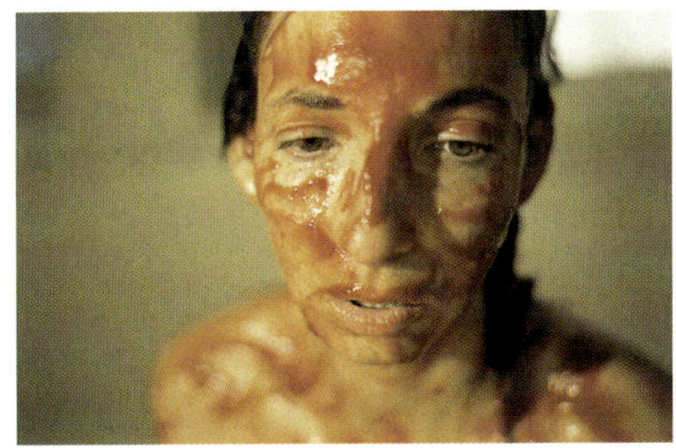

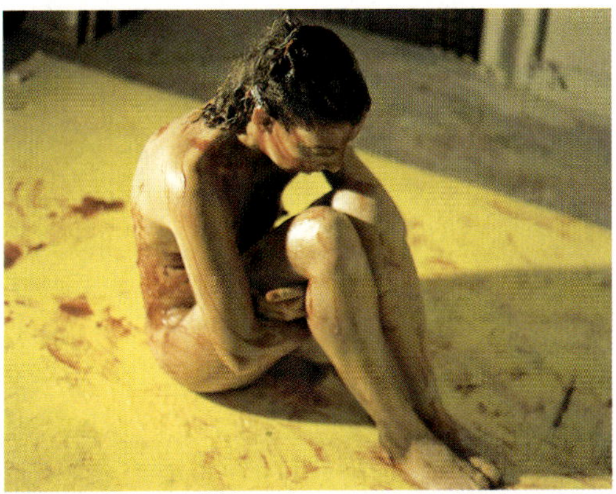

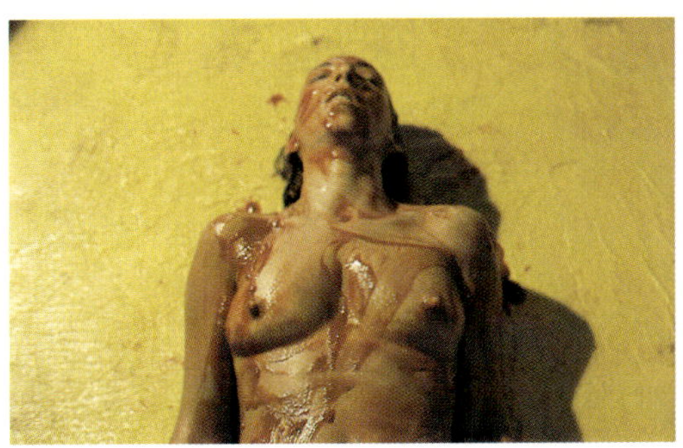

PAUL McCARTHY, KAREN KETCHUP DREAM, 1975, performance and video tape, Pasadena, California / Performance und Video.

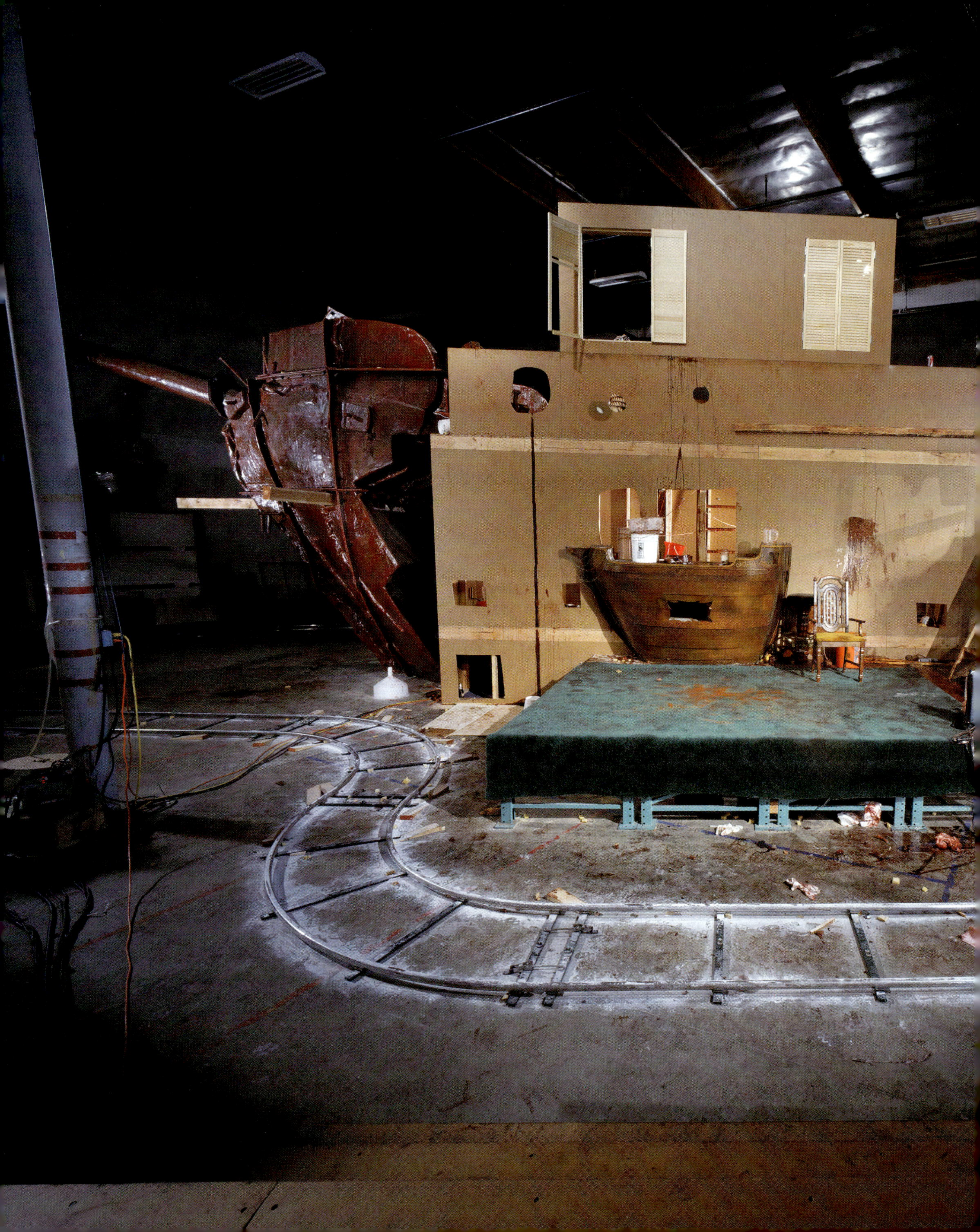

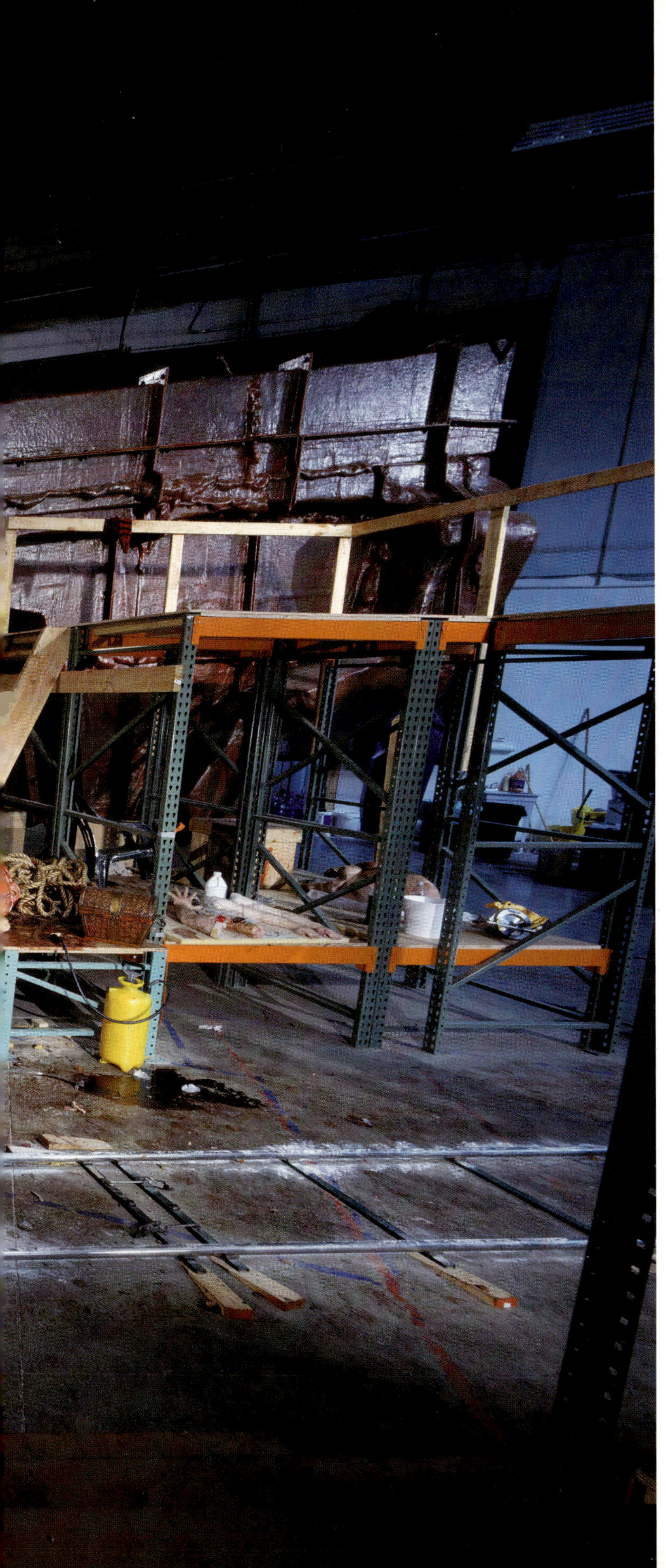

PAUL McCARTHY, PIRATE PROJECT (STAGE AND VILLAGE), 2001–2005, stage set for the work's presentation in "Lalaland – Parodie Paradies," Haus der Kunst, Munich, 12 June to 28 August 2005 / Bühne und Dorf, Bauten für die aktuelle Präsentation im Haus der Kunst, München.

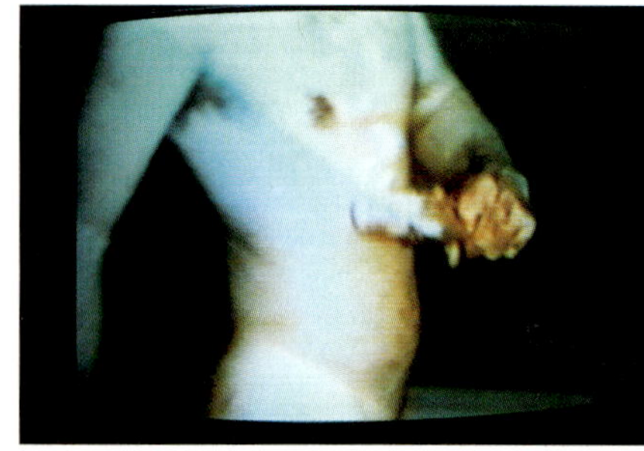

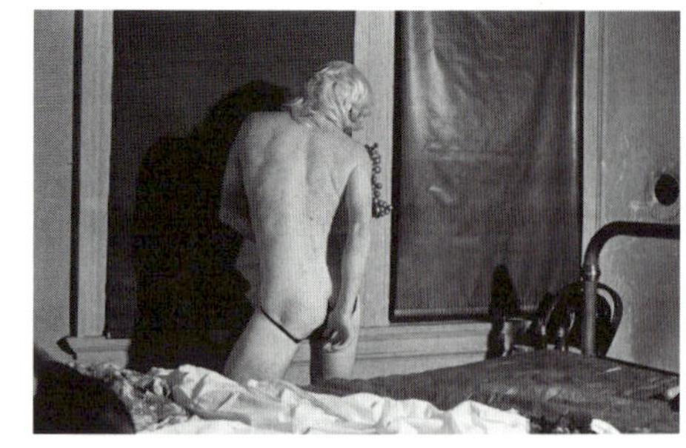

PAUL McCARTHY, SAILOR'S MEAT, 1975, *performance at the artist's studio in Pasadena* / SEEMANNSFLEISCH, *Performance im Atelier des Künstlers in Pasadena.*

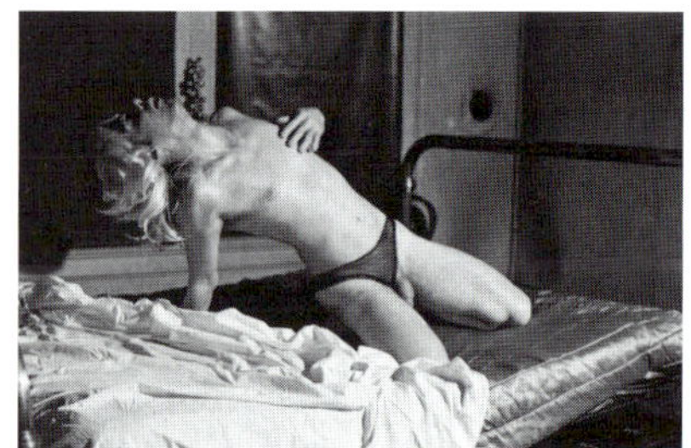

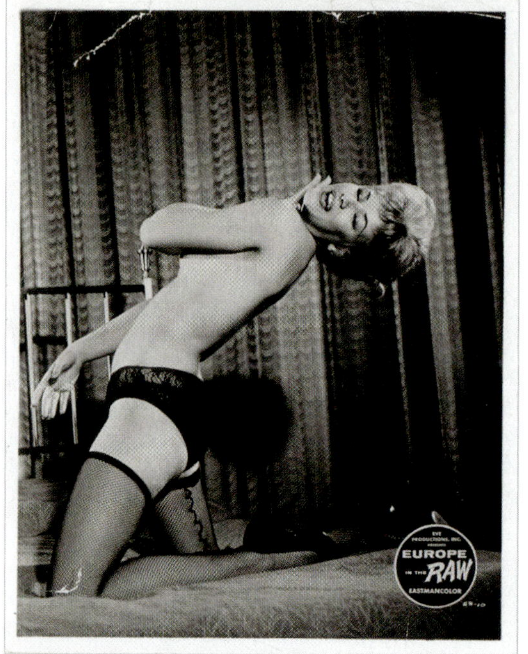

Publicity still for Russ Meyers' film "Europe in the Raw" / Kinoaushangphoto für Russ Meyers' «Europe in the Raw».

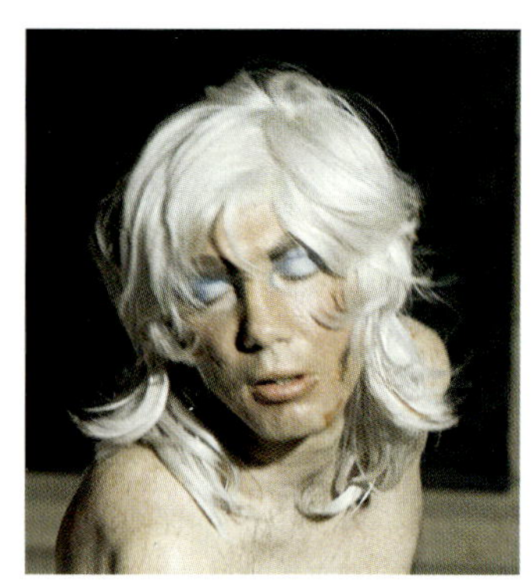

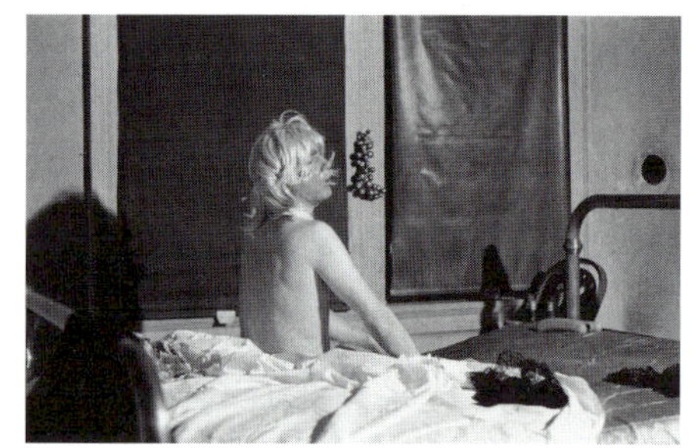

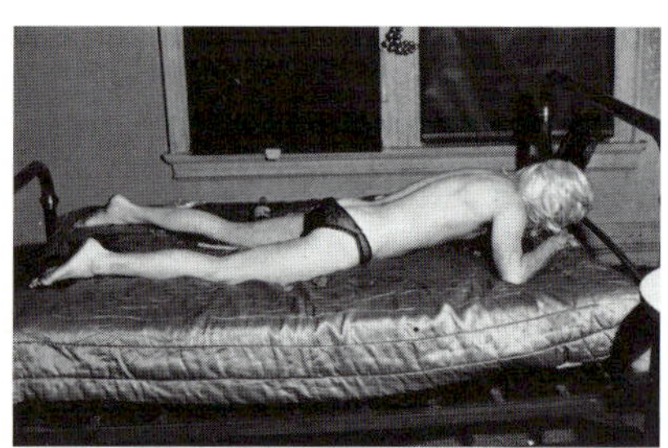

PM: Es war eine Autopsie. Ich wollte Farbe. Ich hatte einen Freund, der im USC Medical Center Nachtschicht hatte.
JS: Vertretung durch eine Galerie? Du lässt für den Zuschauer die Hosen runter und zeigst ihm deinen Arsch.
PM: Das war immer so etwas musste gezeigt werden. Die Kunstszene war interessiert, ich glaube, es waren Arbeiten, die von L.A. handelten. Die Kunstszene in L.A. hatte kein Interesse an schmutzigen kleinen Arbeiten. Es wurde als «hässliche Kunst, europäische Kunst» abqualifiziert, als nicht originell.
JS: Über L.A.?
PM: Ich verbrachte eine Menge Zeit auf den Strassen in den frühen ... Kaufte eine Menge. Da gab es damals ziemlich ... mit ... voll von Filmstills, und man blätterte die Bilder nur so durch. Ich mochte dieses Bild, auf das ich gestossen war, wirklich, eines aus einem Film mit dem Titel *Europe in the Raw* (Nacktes Europa), eine Frau auf dem Bett ... (1963). Als ich SAILOR'S MEAT, SAILOR'S DELIGHT (1975) ... war das Filmstill ein ... Ich ahme die Pose dieses Bildes nach. Zu der Zeit war das ... Russ Meyers entdeckte dies später. Die BOSSY BURGER-Kulisse war eine Familienkulisse, und ich glaube da war etwas schockierend ... das sonnige L.A. hat einen Unterleib.
JS: Aber dein europäischer Charakter ...
PM: In den frühen 80er Jahren etwas in Frankreich, als sie fragten, bat ich sie mir ein Chalet in den Alpen zu suchen, um ein Remake von *Heidi* zu machen. Als Kind bin ich in den Alpen gewesen. Ich wollte Schweizer sein. Ich hatte mich wirklich hineingesteigert, in der Nähe der Berge aufgewachsen zu sein, ich war besessen von den Büchern, Bergschuhen und Windjacken – dem ganzen Drum und Dran.
JS: Dann erzähl mir von HEIDI (1991).
PM: Die französische Regierung lehnte ab. Am Ende wurde HEIDI nie realisiert und ich redete davon, etwas gemeinsam zu machen. Obwohl das Stück in einem kleinen Raum spielt, auf der einen Seite ein kleines Chalet, auf der anderen die American Bar und das Schlafzimmer im Design dieses Adolf Loos ... Es ist ... ein Schizophrenes. Da ist Mike auf der einen Seite und Paul auf der anderen. Ich habe es immer als geteilte Melone von Adolf Loos betrachtet.
JS: Dein neues Projekt ist auch hübsch.
PM: Vor vier Jahren hat Damon vorgeschlagen, ein Remake von *Piraten der Karibik* zu machen, mit Johnny Depp in der Hauptrolle ... und wir begannen ein verdammt grosses Fiberglas-Schiff zu bauen, dieses Hausboot, das wir gefunden hatten. Diese Ankündigung, dass Disney *Piraten der Karibik* mit Johnny Depp drehen würde ... sie haben uns die Idee gestohlen. Als wir allmählich konkret werden wollten ..., kam das Haus der Kunst in München und

wollte die Arbeit ausstellen. Das Museum verfügt über riesige Räume. Gleichzeitig hatten wir mit etwas begonnen, was ein massstabgetreues Remake der Fernsehshow *F Troop* (F-Truppe) werden sollte. F steht für *fuck*. Der Titel ist FORT FUCK (2005). Das Museum war ursprünglich von Hitler gebaut worden, um durch die faschistische Invasion der Nazis Entartete zu beherbergen.

PM: Ein Überfall durch ein Piratenschiff hat etwas mit der heutigen Welt zu tun. A STRAIGHT LINE FROM HITLER'S BERLIN TO DISNEY'S DISNEYLAND (Eine direkte Linie von Hitlers Berlin zu Disneys Disneyland, 2005). Sie verläuft von Berlin über Bayern und Ludwig, den Eiffelturm und Las Vegas nach Disneyland. Adolf Hitler hat mir erzählt, er wolle eine direkte Strasse von Berlin nach Sankt Petersburg bauen und alle hundert Kilometer ein deutsches Dorf.

JS: Wenn wir von Strassen sprechen, Güterzug. Denke ich an Geländewagen? Ein Güterzug.

PM: Nun, ursprünglich wollte ich ein Stück Land in der kalifornischen Wüste kaufen und auf die Jagd gehen. An einem bestimmten Punkt weigerte ich mich, womöglich einen Prärieschoner zu bauen. Mein Grossvater hatte im Wohnzimmer eine Wagen-Lampe auf dem Kaminbord, ein kleiner gedeckter Wagen, ein Prärieschoner, den ein Gefangener in Utah in den 30er oder 40er Jahren angefertigt hatte.

JS: Aber wenn es einmal aktuell wird ...

PM: Ist es absolut funktionell, eine Konvention – Stahlachsen, Lagerung, etcetera. Das Problem. Mein Plan ist es, damit eine Parade abzuhalten und dann ins Museum zu fahren. Eine Nazi-, Disney-Parade.

JS: Würdest du sagen, dass dein Werk Beziehungen hat ...

PM: Ich wurde ein Student aus meinem Schlafsaal, der mich als konkreten Poeten betrachtete. («Oh, was ist das?») Er wollte die Welt an die Stelle der Tat setzen. Damals versuchte ich einen dampfbetriebenen Bagger zu stehlen, ihn auf den Campus zu fahren, ein Loch auszuheben und mich selbst samt Maschine und Loch zu begraben. Eine Definition von Poesie, die diese mit einem Objekt oder Ereignis gleichsetzt, ungeheuer wirkungsvoll.

JS: Poetisch.

PM: Als ich ging ... die Universität ... etwa ein Jahr später, Yves Klein. Er sagte, der Künstler sei von einem Sims gesprungen. Darauf sprang ich noch im selben Jahr aus einem Fenster *(lacht)*. Ich wusste nicht, dass Kleins Sprung ein Schwanensprung gewesen war.

JS: Er war quasi parallel zum Boden ... Und was war mit deinem Sprung?

PM: Ein erbärmlicher Satz. Ich fand heraus, dass Kleins Sprung eine Photographie war.

JS: Da bin ich neugierig.

PM: Meine Mutter wollte Künstlerin werden. Es ist eine gigantische aufgeblasene Rumflasche. Mein Rauchen und Trinken mit ihrem kleinen Bruder, der am Alkohol zugrunde ging.

JS: Und dein Vater. Ich erinnere mich an eine Zeichnung von ihm, die du vor seinem Tod gemacht hast. Und dann diese Skulptur, der Vater, der seinem Sohn hilft einen Schaf- oder Ziegenbock zu lutschen oder so habe ich es jedenfalls in Erinnerung.

PM: Auch über einen Vater und seinen zehnjährigen Sohn. So dachte ich über Vater nach. Er arbeitete an sieben Tagen von sieben Uhr morgens bis sieben Uhr abends. Seine Arbeit, er arbeitete. Er wollte ... arbeitete.

JS: Was war sein Beruf?

PM: Mein Vater war Metzger. Er arbeitete in einem Lebensmittelgeschäft. Eine meiner frühesten Erinnerungen an ihn ist das Bild meines Vaters im weissen Hemd.

(Übersetzung: Suzanne Schmidt)

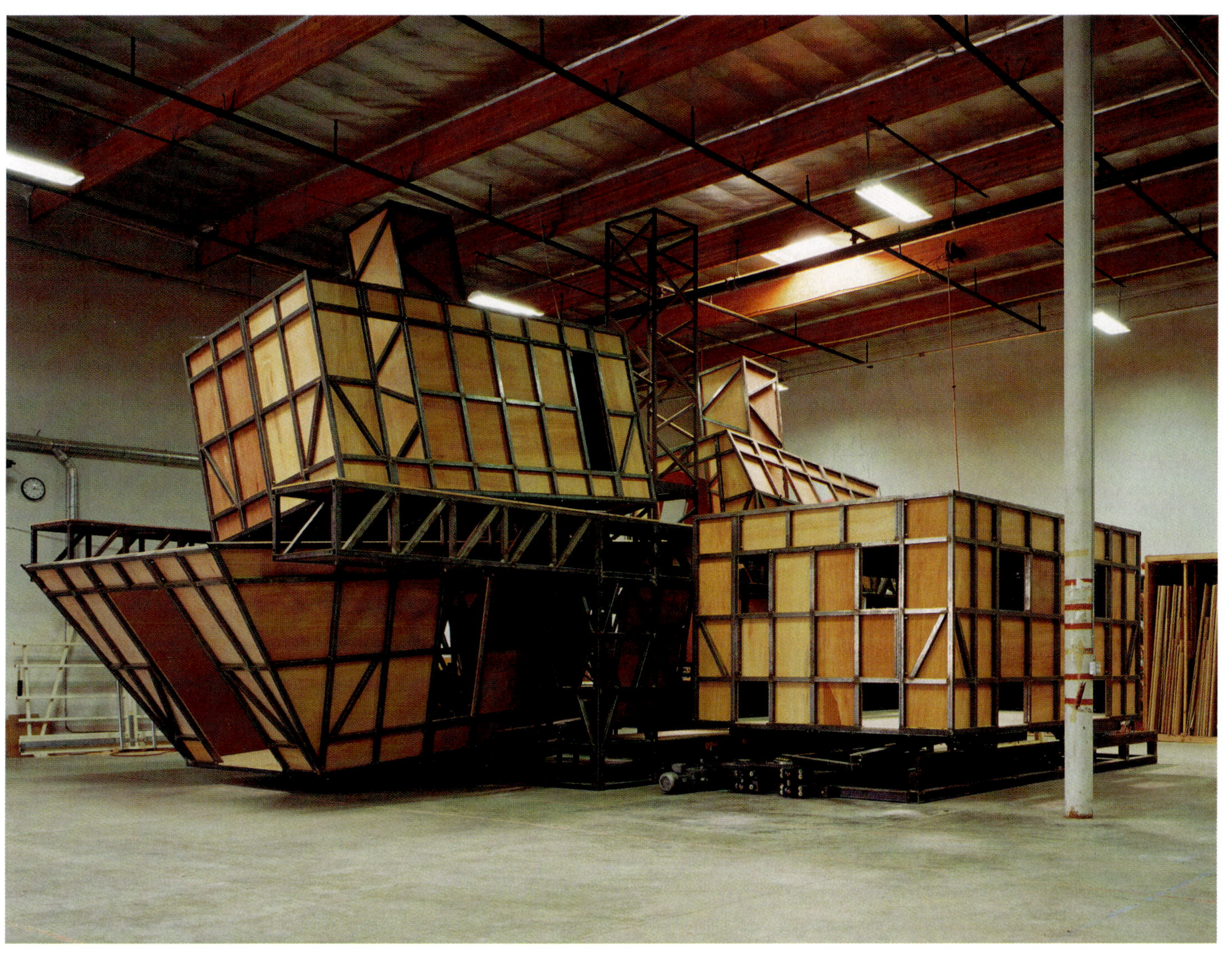

PAUL McCARTHY, PIRATE PROJECT (UNDERWATER WORLD), 2001–2005. The entire PIRATE PROJECT is part of the show "Lala-land – Parodie Paradies," Haus der Kunst, Munich, 12 June to 28 August 2005 / Das gesamte Projekt ist Teil der grossen Werkschau im Haus der Kunst, München, vom 12. Juni bis 28. August 2005.

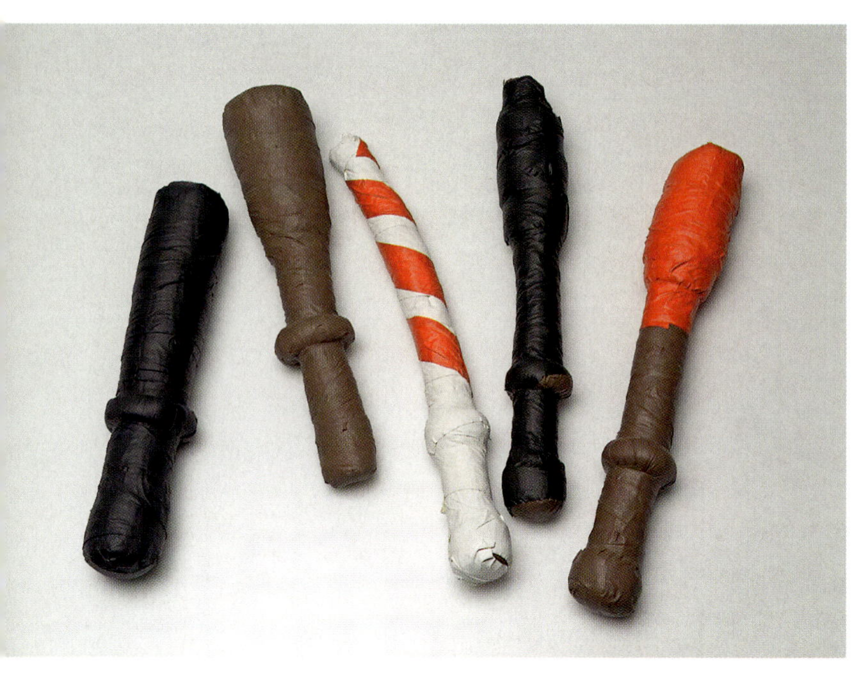

Editions for Parkett

BILLY CLUB, 2005
Unique sculptural object, PVC,
rubber foam, gaffers tape,
variable dimensions, ca. 20 x 4 x 4”.
Edition of 36/XII,
signed and numbered certificate.

Skulpturales Objekt, Unikat, PVC,
Schaumstoff, Gaffers Tape,
unterschiedliche Grössen, ca. 55 x 10 x 10 cm.
Auflage: 36/XII,
signiertes und nummeriertes Zertifikat.

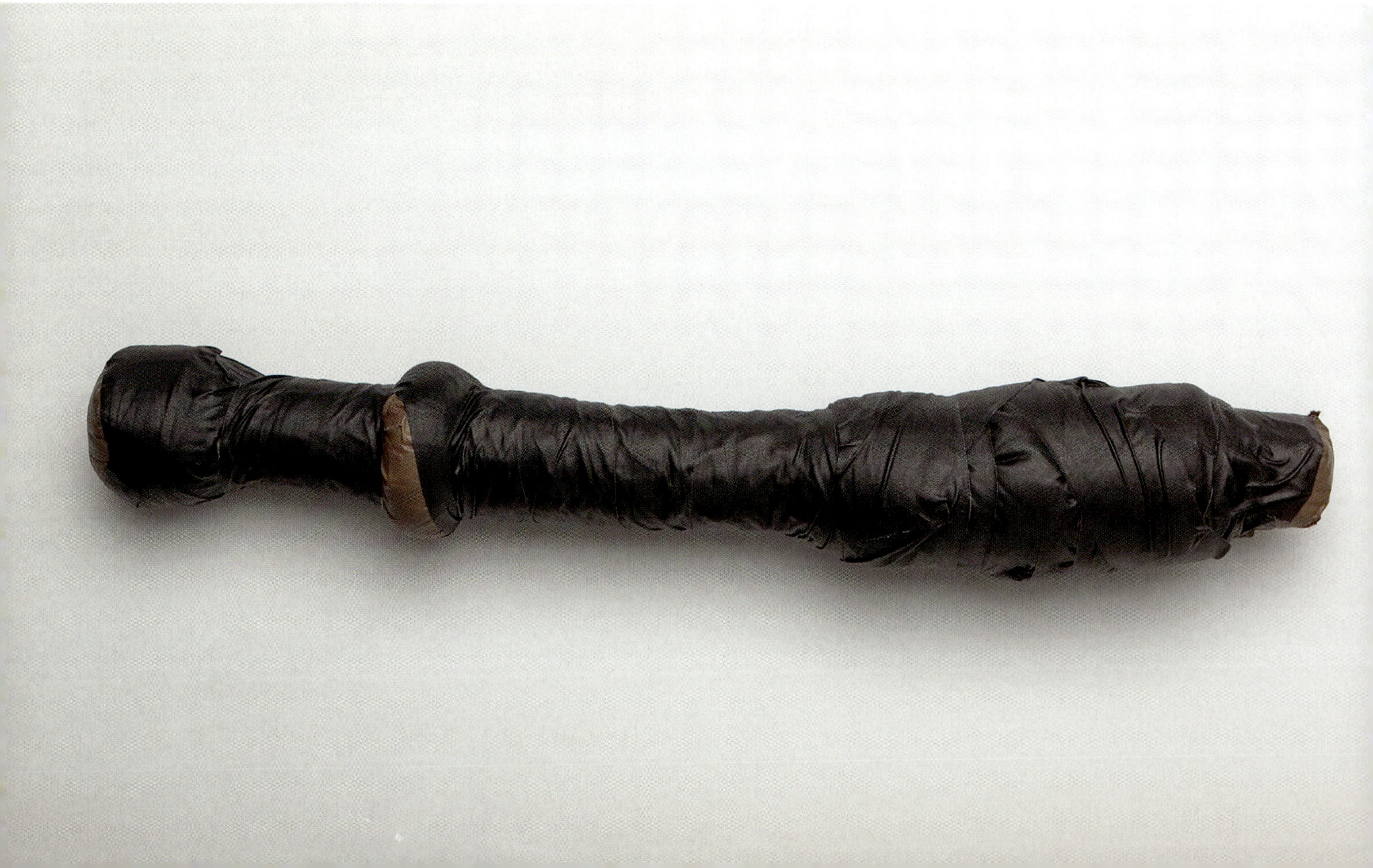

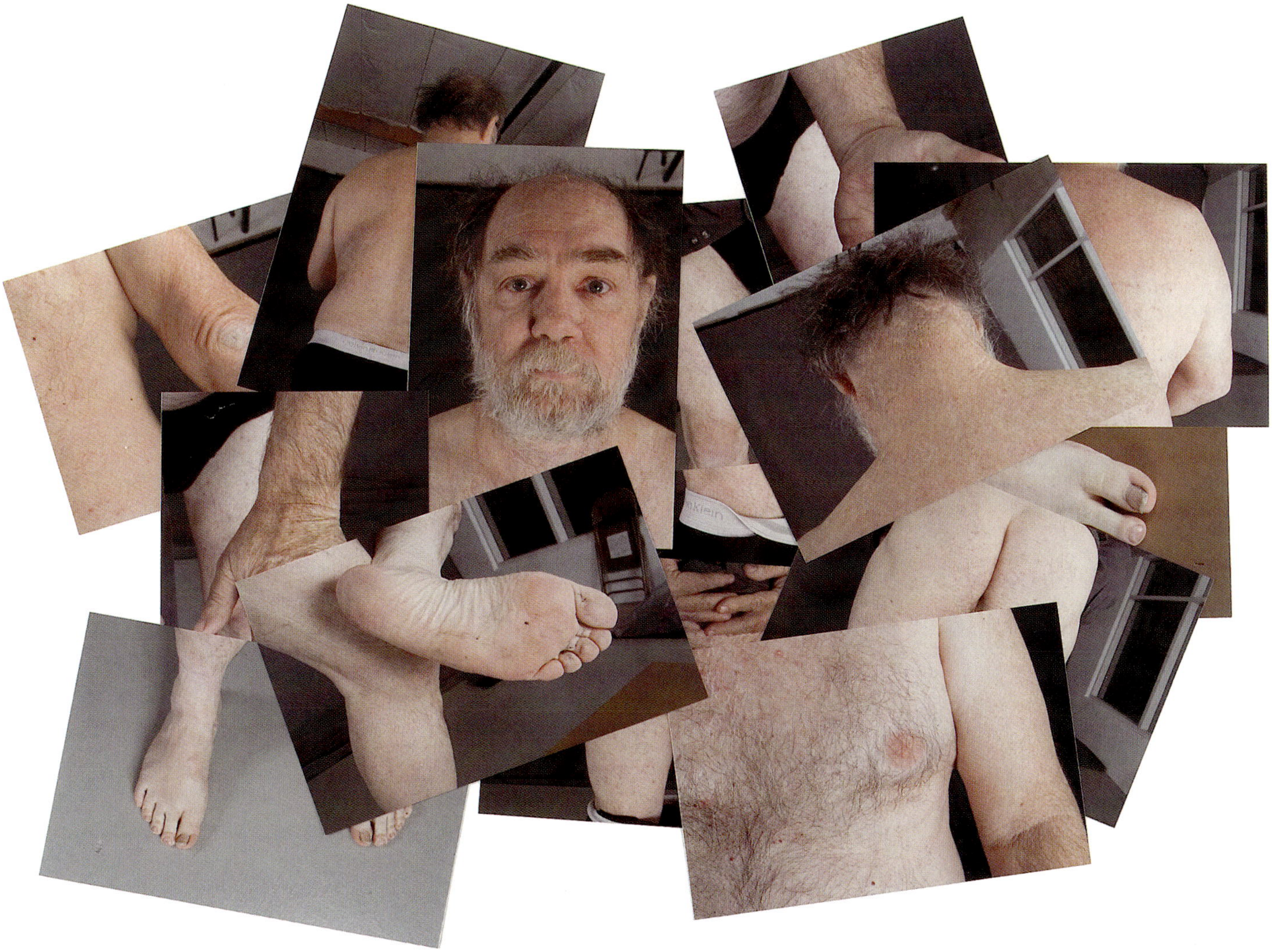

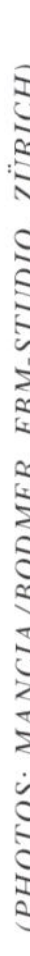
(PHOTOS: MANCIA/BODMER, FBM-STUDIO, ZÜRICH)

Editions for Parkett

PAUL McCARTHY
PETER PAUL SKIN SAMPLE, 2005
15 color photographs (digital laser prints) in cardboard box, 6 5/8 x 10" each.
Edition of 36/XII, signed and numbered certificate.

15 Farbphotos (digitale Laserprints) in Kartonschachtel, je 16,8 x 25,4 cm.
Auflage: 36/XII, signiertes und nummeriertes Zertifikat.

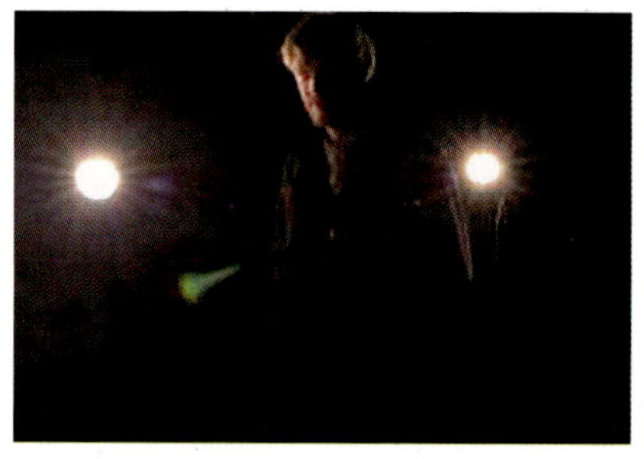
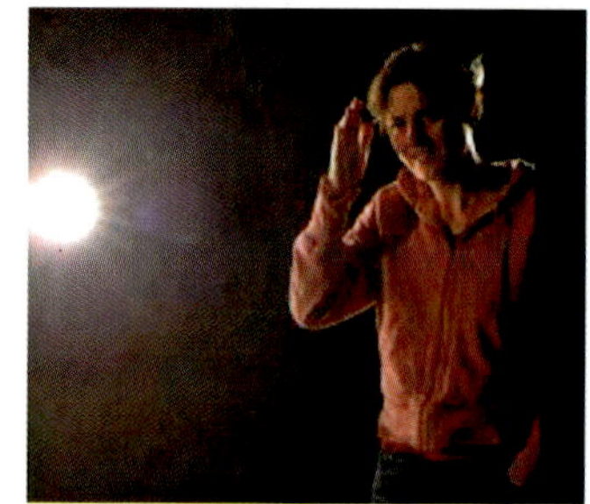
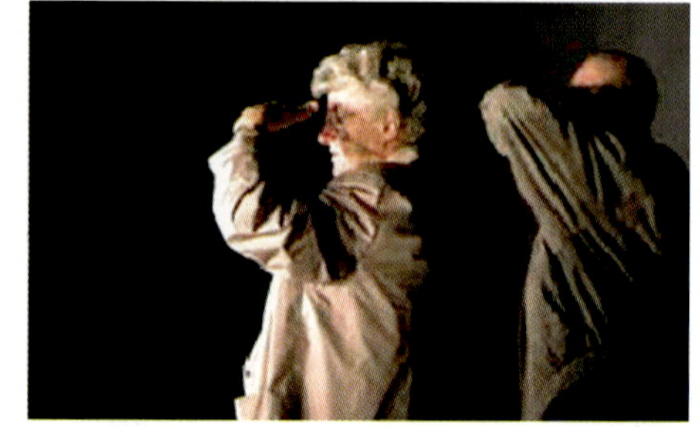

TANIA BRUGUERA

Dreaming in Cuban

ROSELEE GOLDBERG

When Tania Bruguera was introduced to Fidel Castro in 1975 at age seven by her proud father, Miguel Bruguera, who told the revolutionary leader that his young daughter was learning French, Castro stooped slightly to talk directly to the little girl and said, "You need to learn English." It's an incident that remains vivid in Bruguera's mind. "Can you believe it? Castro said 'learn English,'" she recalled. "It was confusing. Why would he tell me to speak the language of the enemy?" Even now, she finds it puzzling. But for Bruguera, this memory is symbolic of Castro—the consummate politician—of his understanding of the globalization to come, and the place of English (not Russian, which her peer group studied in Cuba) as the language of international communication. The incident is also an indication of Bruguera's proximity to the political machine that her parents' position in the upper echelons of the party afforded—her father was the Cuban Ambassador to Beirut, and later to Panama; her mother, Argelia, was a Spanish-English translator—and which Bruguera has worked so cleverly to interpret and to reveal for almost two decades.

Returning to Cuba at age twelve in 1980, the artist attended an art high school and continued making drawings, as she had done endlessly on long days alone in the family apartment when she found herself confined to home as war raged in the streets of Beirut. Back in Havana, drawing once more provided an outlet for coping, this time with her parents' divorce. "I associate being in Cuba with being an

ROSELEE GOLDBERG, art historian, critic, and curator, pioneered the study of performance art with her seminal books and writing, including *Performance Art: from Futurism to the Present* (London: Thames & Hudson, 1988) and *Laurie Anderson* (New York: Abrams, 2000).

TANIA BRUGUERA, UNTITLED (KASSEL 2002), 2002, performance and installation for Documenta 11, Germans, guns, light, sound / Performance und Installation, Deutsche, Gewehre, Licht und Ton.

TANIA BRUGUERA, UNTITLED (HAVANA, 2000), 2000, performance and installation, Cubans, sugar cane, video monitor and video / OHNE TITEL (HAVANNA, 2000), Performance und Installation, Kubaner, Zuckerrohr, Videomonitor und Video. (ALL PHOTOS: RHONA HOFFMAN GALLERY, CHICAGO)

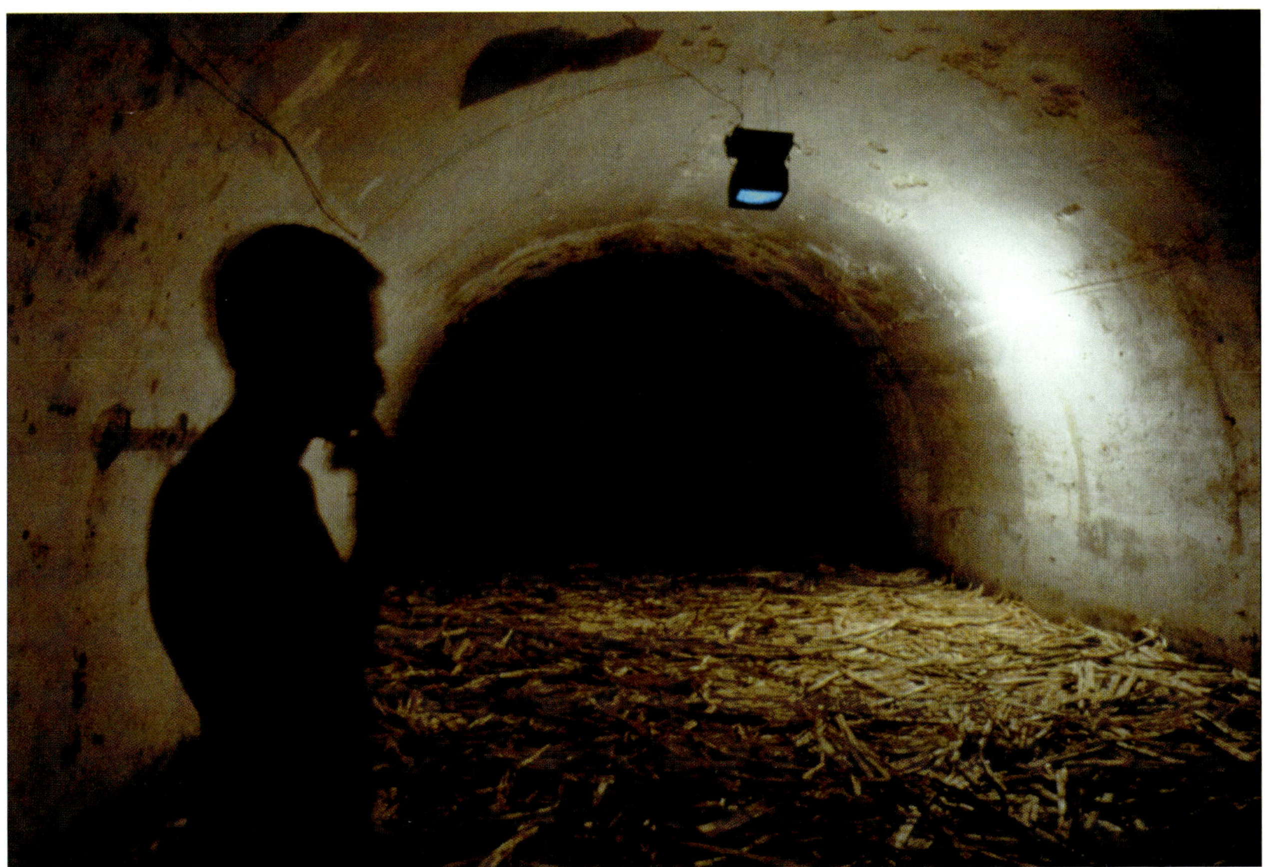

artist," Bruguera says. She also pointed out that the accoutrements of a charged political atmosphere, with its banners, slogans, ceremonies, parades, and seven-hour-long speeches by a formidable leader, with his studied gestures and energetic proclamations, were the engine that drove her creativity. "A country that knows how to use politics as metaphor is a good place to be an artist," Bruguera says of the frequent opportunities she encountered on a daily basis to respond to the pageantry, pomp, and hidden meanings of revolutionary culture. Cuba, today, provides rich source material for her work. "Cuba is a place where everything is political," she explains, "and nobody understands the symbolic value of the gesture better than the State." For Bruguera, whose work is all about political gesture seen from different angles, Cuba is a "socialist theme park," in which ideology itself is a tourist attraction. It is, she says, a place where the very strategies of the avant-garde have been co-opted by those in control. Provocation, for example, long the métier of the artist, is used as a course of action in statewide advertising campaigns, while censorship, as applied by the government, takes the form of a kind of art criticism. "The aesthetic strategies of an artwork are often censored over and above a work's content," Bruguera explains.

It is from afar that Bruguera sees Cuba most clearly. Since 1997, she has also lived in Chicago. She divides her year into three parts: one part Cuban (December, January, May, and September in Havana), one part American (Winter and Spring semesters teaching at the School of the Art Institute of Chicago), and one part travel (in 2004 she visited China, Canada, England, and Argentina). She shuttles back and forth on a Cuban passport, frequently delayed by last minute stays on her visa, but almost always transporting a work that has been presented in her homeland first, on the principle that Cuban soil—its history and the distinct sounds and sentiments of its daily life—provides the yardstick for her ideas. Even as her international reputation grows, it is this to and fro, between countries, ideologies, and time zones ("between past and future"), that sharpens Bruguera's understanding of the real task at hand: how to make work that is relevant both locally and internationally. "Can I use the same model inside Cuba as outside Cuba?" she asks. "I am very aware that this is a paradox I must solve. It's too easy to be exoticized [as a Cuban artist]." Hence a performance installation, UNTITLED (Kassel, 2003),

TANIA BRUGUERA, EYE STUDY FOR UNTITLED (KASSEL 2002), 2002, charcoal on paper, 40 x 60" / AUGENSTUDIE ZU OHNE TITEL (KASSEL 2002), Kohle auf Papier, 101,6 x 152,4 cm. (PHOTO: KAT PARKER)

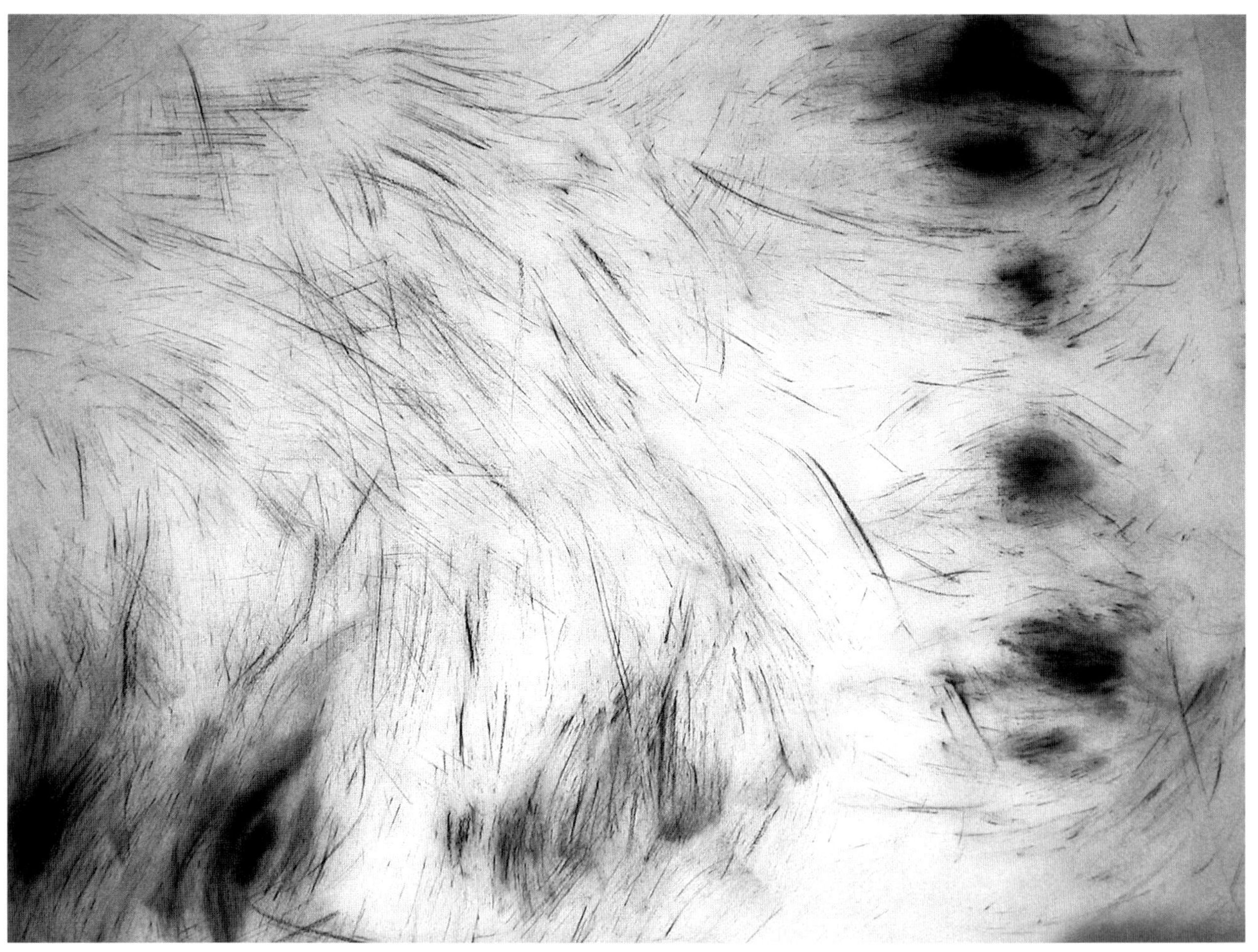

which she presented at Documenta 11, confronts the problem head-on; its ominous pitch-black room and alternating bright white lights, and its earsplitting amplification of marching footsteps and guns being cocked, speaks just as plainly of violence and terror in Cuba as it does of countless other countries where massacres have occurred in the name of politics, whether by government or freedom fighters. A video projection on one wall showed the names of towns and the years from 1945 until 2002 where such atrocities occurred, while on a raised platform on the opposite side of the room, two gun-toting performers, barely visible in the blackout, marched back and forth with military gaits. The blinding light caused all who entered to instinctively raise their hands to shield their eyes, initiating an unexpected action performed by the viewers.

The work in Kassel was a translation, from local to international, of a performance installation, UNTITLED (Havana, 2002), shown the previous year at the Havana Biennale. Also presented in total darkness—this time in the bowels of a seventeenth century Spanish fortress used for centuries for the incarceration of political prisoners, with a focal point of an almost invisible video monitor installed in the ceiling showing clips of Castro—both works carried the underlying message that people generally choose to remain in the dark, despite an overload of information on one hand, and a notorious lack of it on the other. Both works triggered visceral responses to noise, harsh lighting, total darkness, and to the smell of rotting sugar cane, which lined the floor of the Havana installation. And both were structured to generate specific experiences that would be uncomfortable and emotionally affecting. In Havana, visitors inside the dark fortress had to stand on tiptoe and strain their necks to watch the tiny video monitor high above their heads, an action which none would sustain for long since it was simply too painful to do so. "I want my work to be more and more about experience. I want to make 'feeling pieces' not merely 'looking pieces,'" Bruguera says of installations that force viewers to pay attention to the moment. "Looking at art is the only time that people are isolated from reality. Just about all other activities allow one to do one thing and still think about another."

Engagement, social responsibility, ethics, and aesthetics comprise a checklist of considerations that Bruguera brings to each work, while her biography provides the narrative matrix for each piece and the powerful imagery which remains. BURDEN OF GUILT (1997), a performance presented in Havana, culminated in a series of startlingly beautiful images which show Bruguera wearing only a "shield" of a lamb's carcass, with one hand raised to her mouth, filling it with dirt. Yet this stark self-portrait originated in a distressing history, both political and personal, that transforms BURDEN OF GUILT into an iconic symbol of an artist and her times. This work was made in the late nineties, during an especially restrictive economic period in Cuba, "when submission [to the system] was a way of surviving," and shortly after Bruguera had been called before a committee of censors to answer questions about an art newspaper she had produced, which she was subsequently instructed to destroy. "It was a traumatic moment for me and I stopped making art for a while because I didn't know how to make work under those circumstances," she says. "This piece was my way of saying: I'm being submissive, yet also expressing my personal point of view. It was about being submissive in order to survive." For Bruguera, this experience related directly to a story about Cuba's native Indians who inhabited the island before the Spanish invasion, many of whom, in a notoriously horrific incident, committed suicide *en masse* by eating dirt, rather than submitting to a colonial power.

The burden of guilt of the survivor is an especially self-critical and poignant aspect of Bruguera's artistic process. Or perhaps it comes with the territory of growing up in a totalitarian regime, where the most ordinary rites of daily life are determined by restrictive, and often absurd, regulations. Those who are able to live or work successfully outside of the system, or in spite of it, frequently carry the weight of their invisible chains, long after they have been removed. Likewise, Marina Abramovic, William Kentridge, or Anri Sala, who each came of age in dark periods of national strife (in Yugoslavia, South Africa, and Albania respectively), create work with a powerful moral undertow. They seem driven to make good with their art, or at least to suggest it, no matter the distance, in

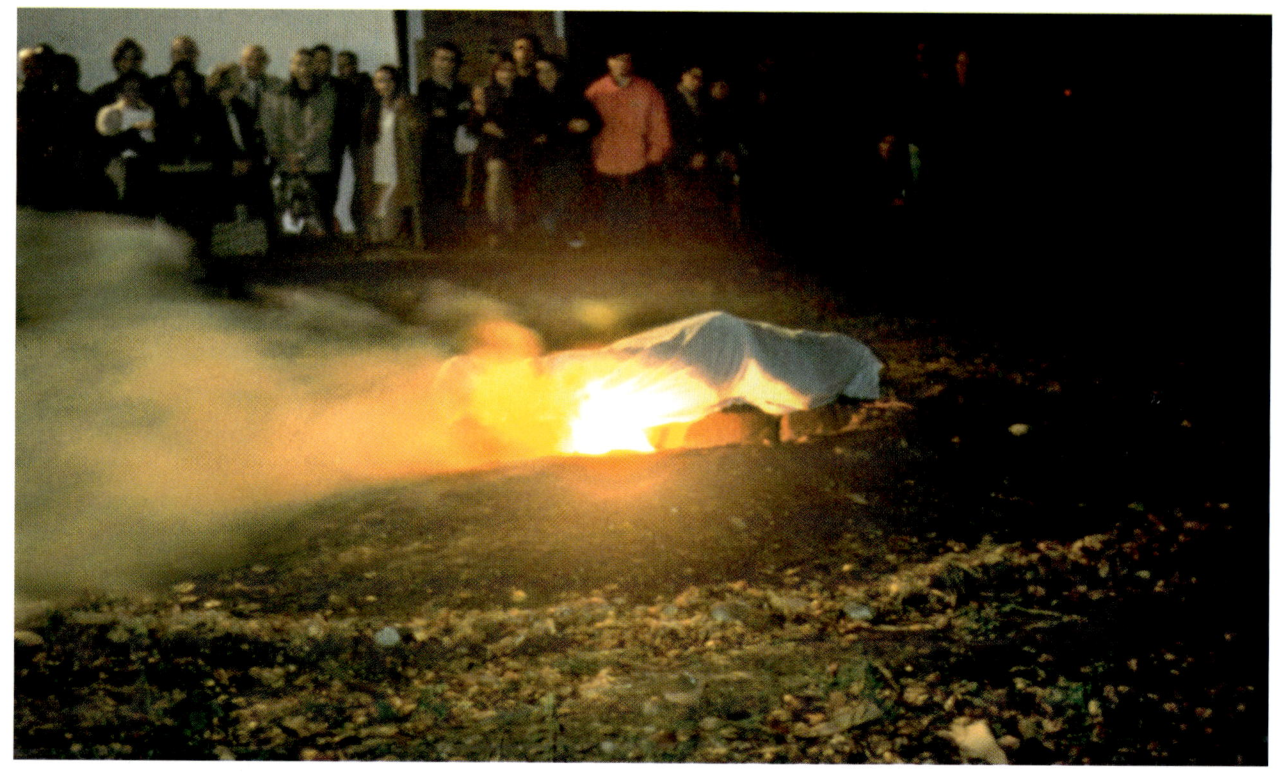

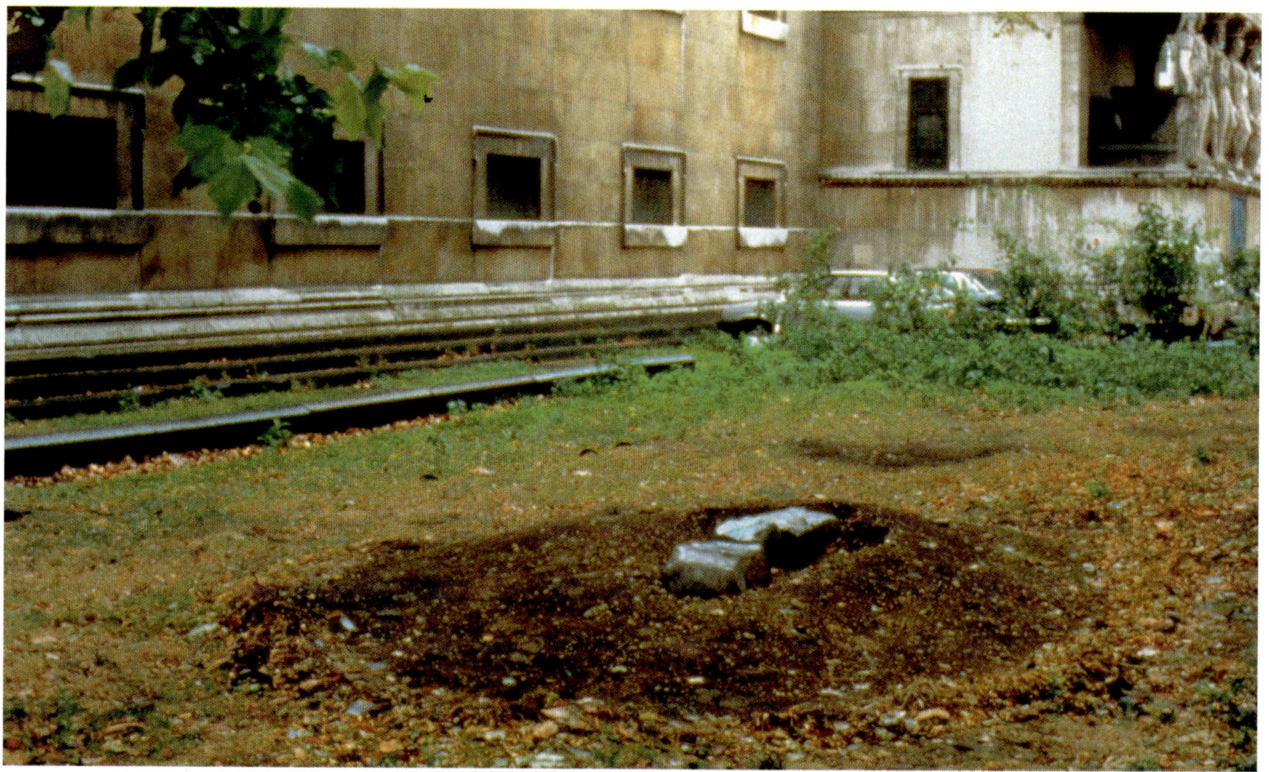

TANIA BRUGUERA, *ANIMA (HOMAGE TO ANA MENDIETA)*, 1996, *performance details* / *ANIMA (HOMMAGE AN ANA MENDIETA)*.

years or miles, from their earlier lives. The machinations at work within the creative minds of such socially responsible souls result in materials that are highly emotional. "I always thought of politics as something very stiff, as in a political speech," Bruguera says, "but now I understand how much of this material is emotional. Political ideas are injected into our systems as emotional agents." Teaching provides yet another outlet for Bruguera's conundrum of divided loyalties—to herself on an international stage, where it is expected of her that she will express herself without inhibition, and to a family of friends, students, parents, siblings, and cousins, in Cuba, who remain imbedded in the system she left behind, and who look to her as a model for their own survival. Thus, the school for performance which she recently established in Havana gives her a real foot in her country, allowing her to return home again, in unexpected, yet comforting ways.

That Bruguera began her career in Cuba in 1986, recreating works of Ana Mendieta's that had been performed in Iowa or in Mexico (but never before on native soil), was an intuitive act of understanding the power of home. "When you leave, you leave. They edit you from history, you no longer exist. So I decided to bring Ana back to Cuba, in a metaphorical way, but also in a very real sense," Bruguera says. It was also the starting point for her to keep tabs on the distances she would travel, from home-base to places far away, and back again. It is an elastic journey she cannot do without, for it is the energy and spirit which the connectedness provides for her. "Marx said that history is a tragedy and then a comedy. Cuban History is a tragedy and eventually a party, with singing and dancing. We call it *pachanda,* which means dancing, having a great time, and being together with lots of people."

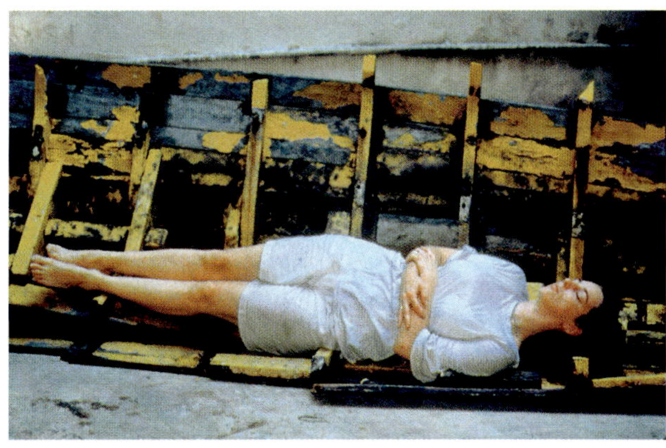

TANIA BRUGUERA, FEAR, 1994, performance from the series MEMORY OF THE POSTWAR / ANGST, aus der Performancereihe ERINNERUNG AN DIE NACHKRIEGSZEIT.

TANIA BRUGUERA, THE BURDEN OF GUILT, 1997–1999, performance scenes; decapitated lamb, rope, water, salt / DIE LAST DER SCHULD, Szenen aus der Performance mit enthauptetem Lamm, Strick, Wasser, Salz.

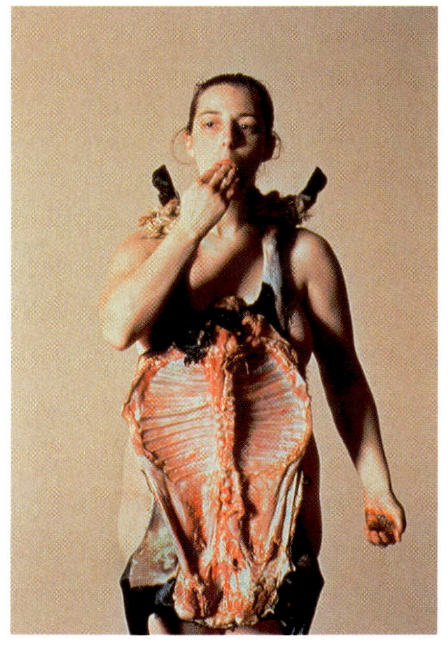

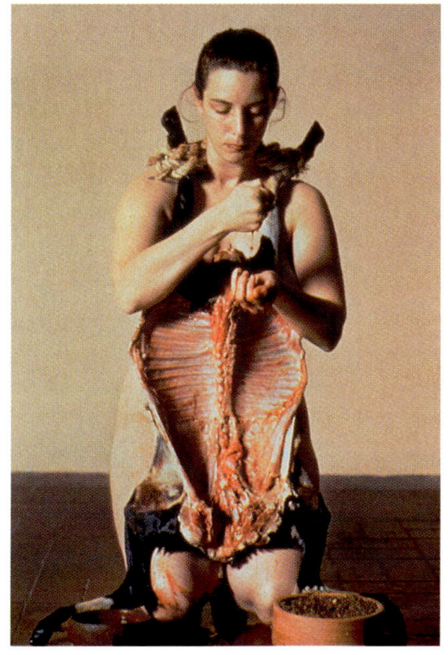

Träumen auf Kubanisch

TANIA BRUGUERA

Als Tania Bruguera 1975 im Alter von sieben Jahren Fidel Castro vorgestellt wurde und ihr stolzer Vater Miguel Bruguera den Revolutionsführer wissen liess, dass sein Töchterchen Französisch lernte, beugte sich Castro zu der Kleinen hinunter und meinte: «Lern lieber Englisch, Kind.» Der Vorfall ist Tania Bruguera in lebhafter Erinnerung geblieben. «Ist es zu fassen? Castro sagte, ‹Lern Englisch.› Es machte einfach keinen Sinn. Warum riet er mir, die Sprache des Feindes zu lernen?» Es ist ihr bis heute ein Rätsel geblieben. Gleichzeitig findet sie diese Erinnerung charakteristisch für den Vollblutpolitiker Castro und seine richtige Einschätzung der bevorstehenden Globalisierung und damit der Rolle, die dem Englischen (und nicht etwa dem Russischen, das ihre Altersgenossen in Kuba studierten) als Sprache der internationalen Verständigung zukommen würde. Die Episode zeigt auch, wie nahe sie aufgrund der Stellung ihrer Eltern dem Machtapparat stand – ihr Vater war kubanischer Botschafter in Beirut und später in Panama, ihre Mutter Argelia übersetzte aus dem Spanischen ins Englische –, ein Umstand, dessen Bruguera sich fast zwei Jahrzehnte lang geschickt für ihre Interpretationen und Enthüllungen bediente.

Als sie 1980 mit zwölf Jahren nach Kuba zurückkehrte, besuchte Bruguera eine Kunstschule und fuhr fort zu zeichnen, wie sie es schon damals in Beirut unermüdlich getan hatte, als sie lange Tage allein in der elterlichen Wohnung verbrachte, während in den Strassen der Stadt Krieg herrschte. Auch in Havanna wird das Zeichnen zum Rettungsanker, diesmal um mit der Scheidung der Eltern fertig zu werden. «In Kuba sein heisst für mich Künstlerin sein», sagt Bruguera. Sie unterstreicht auch, dass das ganze Drum und Dran der politisch aufgeladenen Atmosphäre – die Fahnen, Slogans, Feiern, Paraden, nicht zu vergessen die siebenstündigen Ansprachen des imposanten Diktators mit seinen einstudierten Gesten und energischen Proklamationen – ihre Kreativität stimulierte. «Ein Land, das mit Politik wie mit einer Metapher umgehen kann, ist ein guter Ort für Künstler», meint Bruguera mit Blick auf die sich praktisch täglich bietenden Gelegenheiten, sich mit Prunk, Pomp und tieferer Bedeutung der revolutionären Kultur auseinander zu setzen. Das Kuba von heute liefert reichlich Stoff für ihre Arbeit. «Kuba ist ein Ort, wo alles politisch ist», erklärt sie, «und nie-

ROSELEE GOLDBERG ist Kunstwissenschaftlerin, Kritikerin und Kuratorin und hat u. a. mit Büchern wie *Performance Art from Futurism to the Present* (1988) und *Laurie Anderson* (2000) wesentlich zum Verständnis der Performancekunst beigetragen.

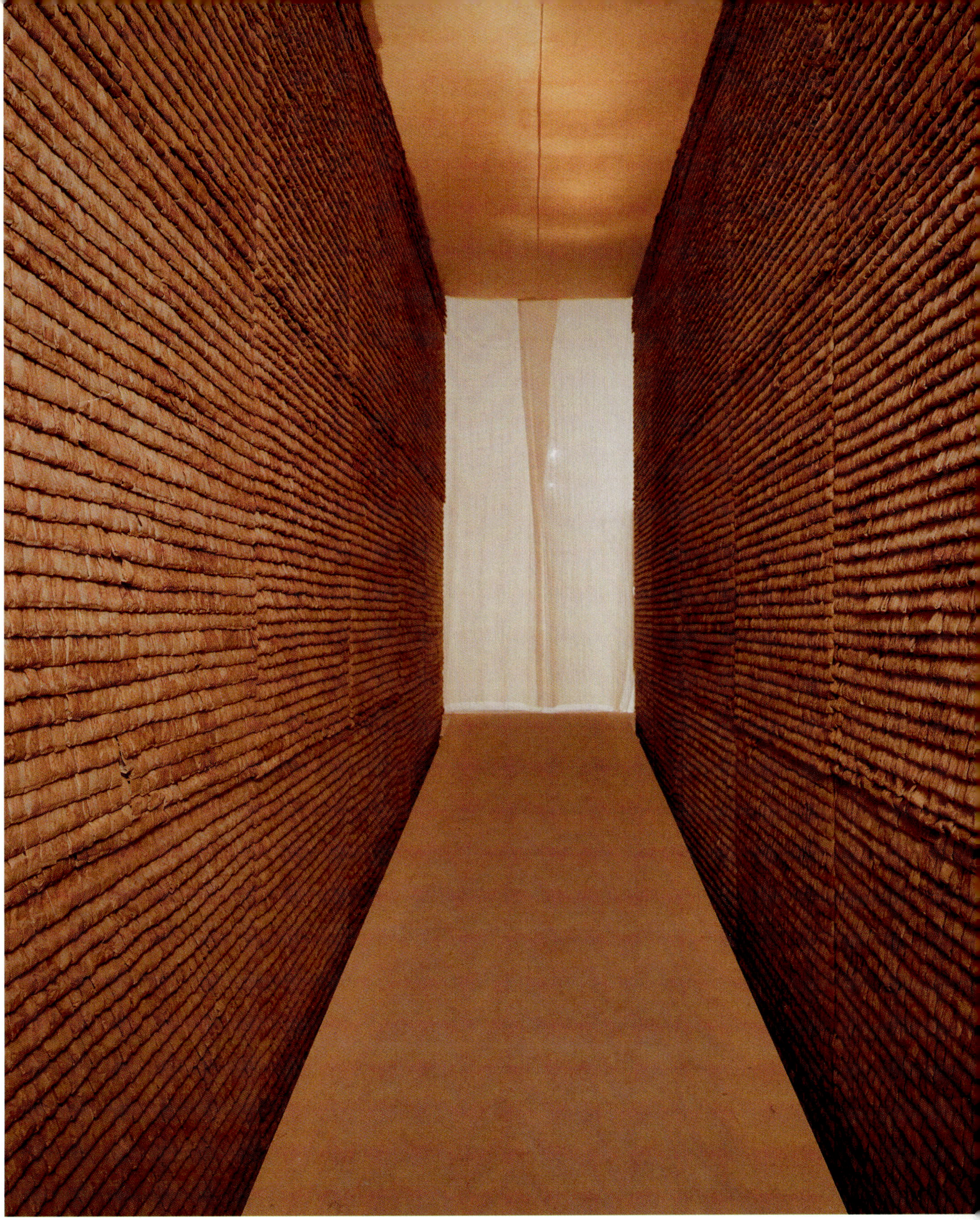

TANIA BRUGUERA, POETIC JUSTICE, 2002–2003, used teabags stitched on canvas, wood, small LCD monitors and DVDs, installed at Rhona Hoffman Gallery, spring 2004 / POETISCHE GERECHTIGKEIT, auf Leinwand aufgenähte, gebrauchte Teebeutel, Holz, LCD-Monitore, DVDs. (PHOTO: MICHAEL TROPEA)

mand versteht den symbolischen Wert der Geste besser als der Staat.» Für Bruguera, in deren Werk es allein um diesen politischen Gestus unter verschiedensten Blickwinkeln geht, ist Kuba ein «sozialistischer Themenpark», in dem sogar die Ideologie eine Touristenattraktion ist. «Es ist ein Ort, wo selbst die Strategien der Avantgarde von den politischen Machthabern übernommen wurden. Zum Beispiel arbeiten staatliche Werbekampagnen mit Provokationen – lange das Mittel der Kunst par excellence –, während die Zensur, so wie sie von der Regierung praktiziert wird, eher die Form einer Art Kunstkritik annimmt: «Die ästhetischen Strategien eines Kunstwerks werden häufig noch vor oder unabhängig von seinem Inhalt zensiert.»

Für Bruguera wird Kuba aus der Ferne am deutlichsten sichtbar. Seit 1997 lebt sie auch in Chicago. Sie unterteilt das Jahr in drei Teile: Einen Teil verbringt sie auf Kuba (Dezember, Januar, Mai und September in Havanna), einen in den USA (Winter- und Sommersemester als Dozentin am Art Institute of Chicago), und der dritte ist für Reisen reserviert (2004 besuchte sie China, Kanada, England und Argentinien). Sie kommt und geht mit ihrem kubanischen Pass, oft verlängert sie ihre Aufenthalte kurzfristig und überschreitet dadurch auch hin und wieder ihr Visum. Aber immer hat sie eine Arbeit dabei, die zuerst in ihrer Heimat ausgestellt worden ist, denn der kubanische Boden – seine Geschichte und sein Alltag mit all den besonderen Geräuschen und

TANIA BRUGUERA, VIDEO STUDY III FOR UNTITLED (KASSEL 2002), Documenta 11, charcoal on paper, 40 x 60" / VIDEOSTUDIE FÜR OHNE TITEL (KASSEL 2002), Kohle auf Papier, 101,6 x 152,4 cm. (PHOTO: KAT PARKER)

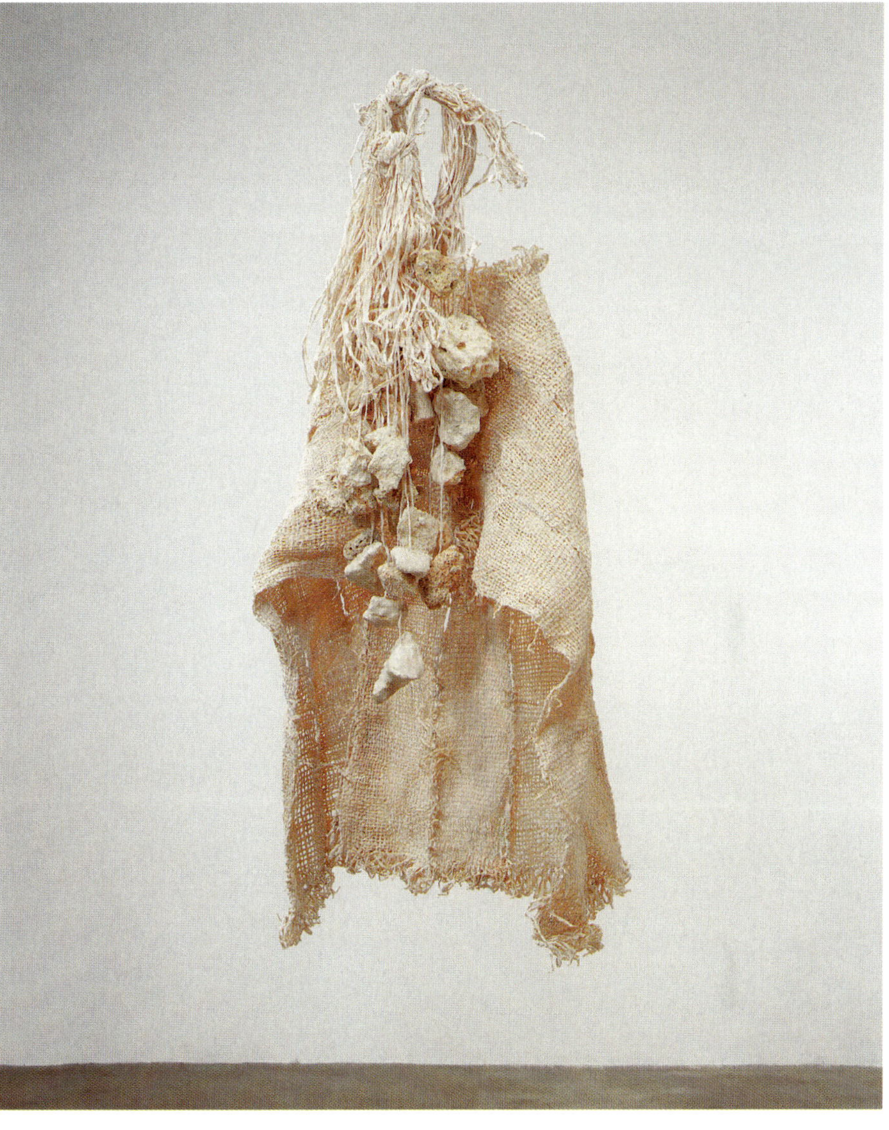

TANIA BRUGUERA, DATED FLESH I, 2003, cow guts, sea salt, stones, 58 x 24 x 24" / ALTMODISCHES FLEISCH I, Kuhdarm, Mehrsalz, Steine, 147,3 x 61 x 61 cm.
(PHOTO: MICHAEL TROPEA)

Gefühlen – ist für sie noch immer das Mass aller Dinge. Trotz Brugueras wachsender Bekanntheit im Ausland, ist es doch dieses Hin und Her zwischen Ländern, Ideologien und Zeitzonen («zwischen Vergangenheit und Zukunft»), das ihren Blick für die eigentliche Herausforderung schärft: eine Kunst zu machen, die lokal und international relevant ist. «Kann ich in Kuba dasselbe Modell benutzen wie ausserhalb?», fragt sie. «Mir ist klar, dass ich dieses Paradox lösen muss. Denn eh man es sich versieht, bekommt man das Etikett des Exotischen verpasst.» In einer Performance-Installation, UNTITLED (2003), an der Documenta 11 in Kassel, setzt sie sich direkt mit dem Problem auseinander: Der bedrohliche pechschwarze Raum mit den ab und zu aufblitzenden grellen Scheinwerfern, der ohrenbetäubende Lärm von marschierenden Stiefeln und Maschinengewehren, die entsichert werden, sprechen von Gewalt und Terror, nicht nur in Kuba, sondern auch in zahllosen anderen Ländern, in denen im Namen der Politik Massaker begangen wurden, egal ob von Seiten der Regierung oder von Freiheitskämpfern. Eine Videoprojektion an der Wand zeigte die Jahreszahlen und Ortsnamen der Greuel, die zwischen 1945

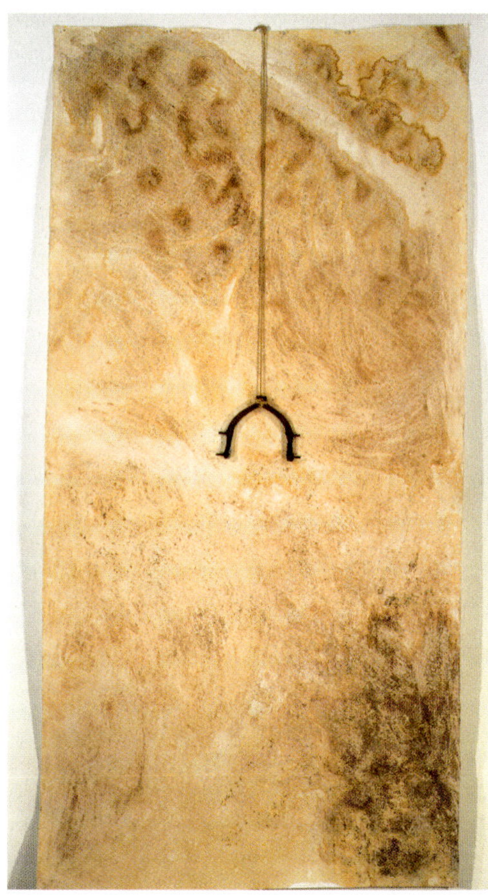

TANIA BRUGUERA, UNTITLED (16), 1998–99, coffee, iron, linen paper, 118 x 47 1/4" / Kaffee, Eisen, Leinenpapier, 300 x 120 cm.

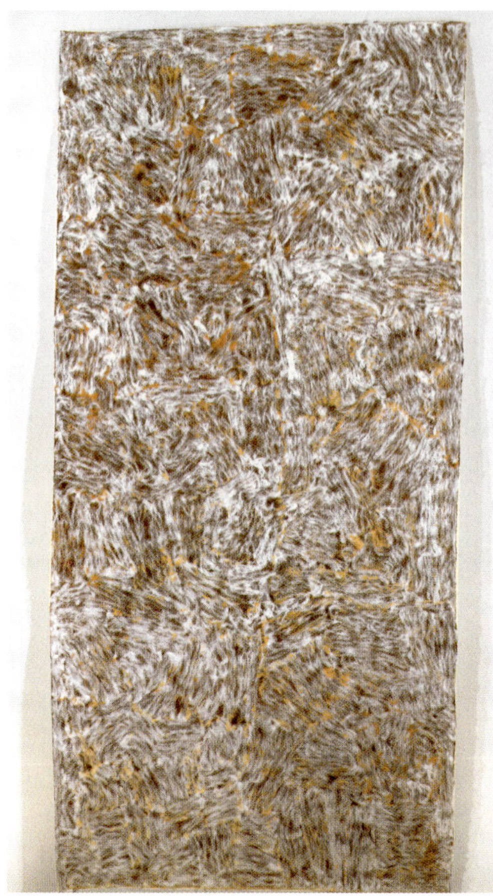

TANIA BRUGUERA, UNTITLED (18), 1998–99, coffee, cotton, linen paper, 118 x 47 1/4" / Kaffee, Baumwolle, Leinenpapier, 300 x 120 cm.

und 2002 verübt wurden, während auf einer erhöhten Plattform auf der gegenüberliegenden Seite des Raums zwei im Dunkel kaum erkennbare Schauspieler mit geschulterten Gewehren zackig auf und ab marschierten. Das gleissende Licht liess alle Eintretenden instinktiv die Hände schützend vor die Augen halten und machte so unversehens die Betrachter zu Akteuren.

Die Installation in Kassel war eigentlich eine Übertragung der im Jahr zuvor auf der Biennale in Havanna gezeigten Arbeit UNTITLED (2002) von der lokalen auf die internationale Ebene. Auch beim ersten Mal war die Performance in völliges Dunkel getaucht gewesen, doch spielte sich das Ganze im Innern einer spanischen Festung aus dem siebzehnten Jahrhundert ab, die jahrhundertelang als Gefängnis für politische Gefangene gedient hatte. Zentrales Element war ein kaum sichtbarer, in der Decke eingelassener Videomonitor, der Filmausschnitte von Castro zeigte. Der Subtext beider Werke war, dass die Menschen im Allgemeinen lieber im Dunkeln verharren, trotz Informationsüberflutung auf der einen und chronischem Informationsmangel auf der anderen Seite. Beide Arbeiten provozierten heftige Reaktionen auf den Lärm, das grelle Licht, die Finsternis und den Geruch des faulenden Zuckerrohrs, das den Boden der Installation in Havanna bedeckte. Und beide waren so konzipiert, dass sie bestimmte Empfindungen auslösten, die ebenso unangenehm wie aufrüttelnd waren. In Havanna mussten sich die Betrachter in der dunklen Festung auf die Zehenspitzen stellen und den Hals verrenken, um den winzigen Monitor hoch über ihren Köpfen zu sehen, und das hielt niemand lange aus, weil es einfach zu anstrengend war. «Der Erfahrungsaspekt wird in meinen Arbeiten immer wichtiger, ich will ‹Arbeiten zum Anfühlen und Erleben› und nicht nur ‹zum Anschauen› machen», bemerkt Bruguera zu ihren Installationen, die den Betrachter zwingen, sich auf den Moment einzulassen. «Nur beim Betrachten von Kunst ist man von der Wirklichkeit losgelöst. Bei fast allen anderen Tätigkeiten kann man eine Sache tun und dabei an eine andere denken.»

Engagement, gesellschaftliche Verantwortung, Ethik und Ästhetik sind die Punkte, die Bruguera regelmässig in ihre Arbeiten einbringt, während ihre Biographie die narrative Grundlage liefert und auch die starke, einprägsame Bildsprache. Die in Havanna gezeigte Performance BURDEN OF GUILT (Last der Schuld, 1997) gipfelte in einer Reihe überwältigend schöner Bilder, auf denen Bruguera, nur mit einem Lammkadaver bedeckt, die Hand zum Munde führt und ihn mit Erde füllt. Doch auch dieses schockierende Selbstporträt beruht auf einer politischen und menschlichen Tragödie, was BURDEN OF GUILT in ein bildhaftes Symbol für die Künstlerin und ihre Zeit verwandelt. Die Arbeit entstand in den späten 90er Jahren, einer Zeit, in der die wirtschaftlichen Zustände auf Kuba besonders erdrückend waren und «die Unterwerfung [unter das System] eine Frage des Überlebens». Bruguera musste vor einem Zensurkomitee erscheinen und Fragen über eine von ihr publizierte Kunstzeitschrift beantworten, die sie danach wieder einstampfen lassen musste. «Es war eine traumatische Erfahrung und eine Zeit lang hab ich überhaupt keine Kunst mehr gemacht, weil ich nicht

TANIA BRUGUERA, DISPLACEMENT, 1998–1999, performance, soil, glue, nails, fabric / VERTREIBUNG, Performance, Erde, Klebstoff, Nägel, Stoff.

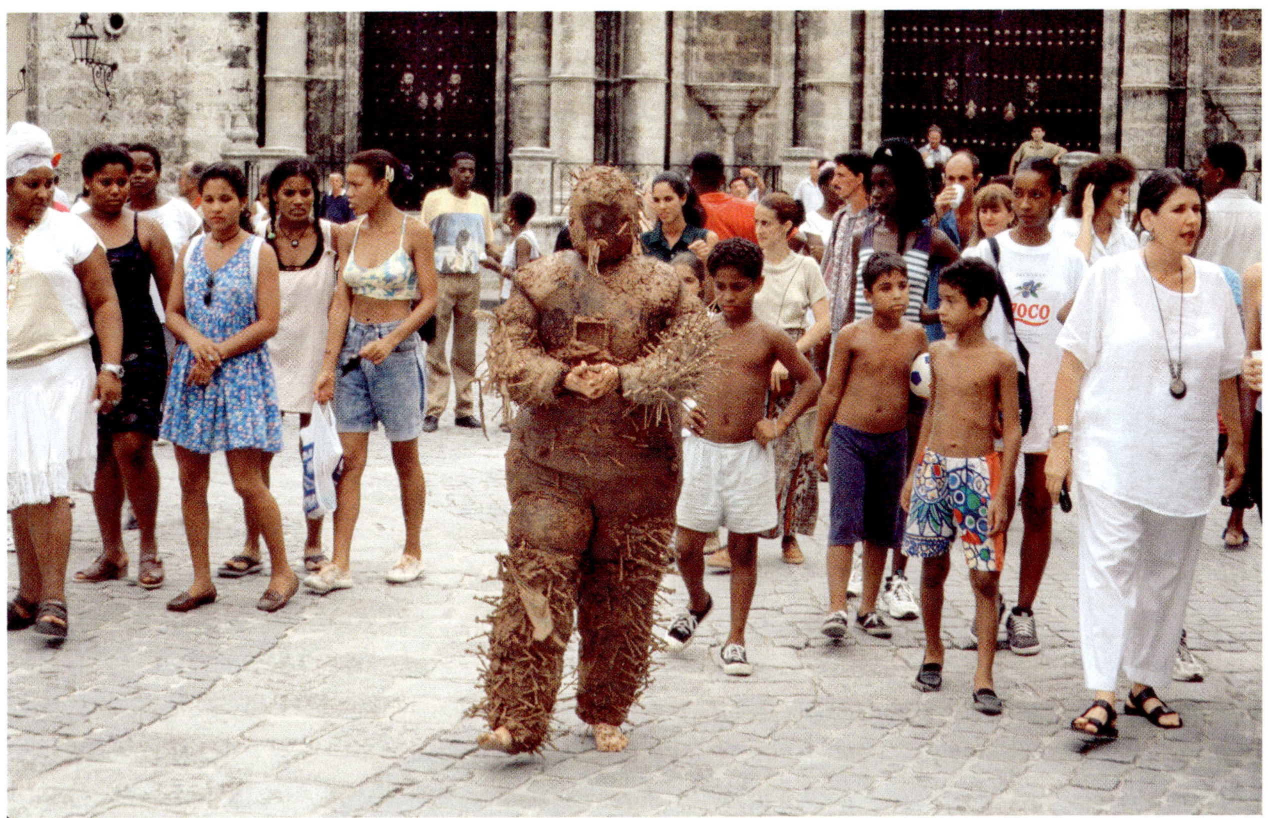

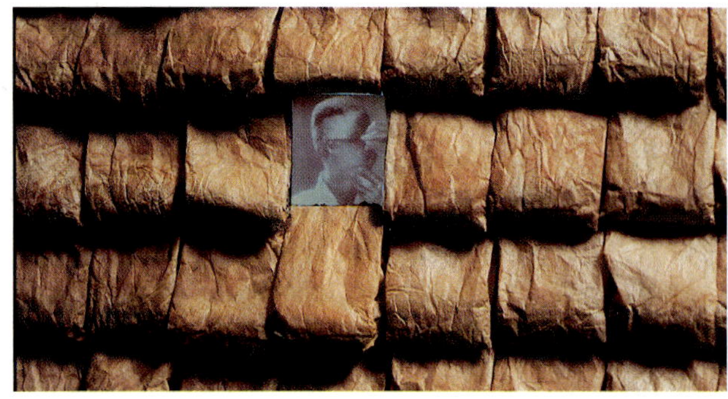

TANIA BRUGUERA, POETIC JUSTICE, 2002–2003.
Installation detail with LCD monitor, for over-all view see page 155 /
POETISCHE GERECHTIGKEIT, Detail mit LCD-Monitor,
ganze Installation Seite 155. (PHOTO: MICHAEL TROPEA)

wusste, wie ich unter solchen Umständen arbeiten sollte. [...] Diese Arbeit war meine Art zu sagen, dass ich mich unterwerfe, machte aber gleichzeitig auch meinen Standpunkt klar. Nämlich, dass es um Unterwerfung um des Überlebens willen ging.» Bruguera verband ihre eigene Erfahrung mit einer Geschichte über Kubas Ureinwohner, die vor der Eroberung durch die Spanier auf der Insel gelebt hatten. Die meisten von ihnen wollten lieber sterben als sich der Kolonialmacht beugen, was zu dem berüchtigten, entsetzlichen Massenselbstmord führte, bei dem sie sich selbst töteten, indem sie Dreck und Erde assen.

Die Schuld, die auf den Überlebenden lastet, ist ein besonders selbstkritischer und auffälliger Aspekt von Brugueras Kunst. Vielleicht kommt dies auch einfach daher, dass sie in einem totalitären Regime aufgewachsen ist, wo die einfachsten und alltäglichsten Vorgänge durch restriktive, oft absurde Regeln bestimmt wurden. Wer es dennoch schafft, ausserhalb oder trotz des Systems erfolgreich zu leben und zu arbeiten, trägt oft noch lange Zeit schwer an den unsichtbaren Ketten. So haben auch die Arbeiten von Marina Abramovic, William Kentridge oder Anri Sala, die alle in schweren Zeiten nationaler Konflikte aufgewachsen sind (in Jugoslawien, Südafrika beziehungsweise Albanien), einen unwiderstehlichen moralischen Zug. Sie scheinen mit ihrer Kunst etwas gutmachen zu wollen oder zumindest darauf anzuspielen, egal wie gross der zeitliche oder geographische Abstand zu ihrem früheren Leben ist. Wenn zum kreativen Verstand eine derart sozial verantwortungsbewusste Seele hinzukommt, kommen höchst emotionale Stoffe dabei heraus. «Für mich war Politik immer etwas Steifes, wie in einer Ansprache», sagt Bruguera, «inzwischen hab ich aber begriffen, wie viele Emotionen damit verbunden sind. Politische Ideen werden uns als emotionale Wirkstoffe eingeimpft.» Auch das Unterrichten ist für Bruguera ein Ausweg aus ihrem Loyalitätszwiespalt: Ihr selbst bietet es eine internationale Bühne, auf der sie sich frei und ungehindert ausdrücken kann, und ihrer Familie von Freunden, Studierenden, Verwandten, Geschwistern und Cousinen in Kuba, die noch in dem System, das sie verlassen hat, eingebettet sind, liefert es ein Vorbild für das eigene Überleben. Die Performanceschule, die sie vor kurzem in Havanna gegründet hat, ermöglicht ihr, in ihrer Heimat wieder Fuss zu fassen und auf unerwartete, aber tröstliche Weise immer wieder nach Hause zurückzukehren.

Als Bruguera zu Beginn ihrer Karriere 1986 in Kuba Performances von Ana Mendieta zeigte, die zwar in Iowa oder Mexiko, aber noch nie auf heimatlichem Boden aufgeführt worden waren, hatte sie instinktiv die Macht der Heimat erkannt. «Wenn man weggeht, ist man weg, man wird aus der Geschichte gestrichen und existiert nicht mehr. Deshalb wollte ich Ana nach Kuba zurückbringen, metaphorisch, aber auch ganz real», sagt Bruguera. Gleichzeitig fing sie damit an, die Distanzen zu registrieren, die sie zwischen ihrem Zuhause und ihren weit entfernten Zielen zurücklegte. Es ist eine Art Jo-Jo-Bewegung, ohne die sie nicht leben kann, denn die Verbundenheit liefert ihr Energie und geistige Nahrung. «Marx sagte, die Geschichte sei zunächst eine Tragödie und dann eine Komödie. Die Geschichte Kubas ist eine Tragödie, die sich in ein Fest verwandelt, bei dem gesungen und getanzt wird. Wir nennen das eine *pachanga,* was so viel heisst wie Tanzen, Spass und jede Menge Leute.»

(Übersetzung: Uta Goridis)

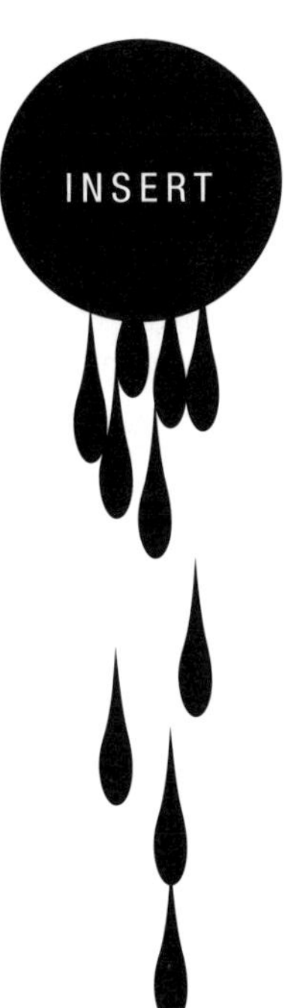

MATTHEW BRANNON

•

Unhappiness is much less difficult to experience.
We are threatened with suffering from three directions: from our own body, which is doomed
to decay and dissolution and which cannot even do without pain and anxiety as warning signals;
from the external world, which may rage against us with overwhelming and merciless forces of destruction;
and finally from our relations to other men.

•

Sigmund Freud, Civilization and Its Discontents, 1930

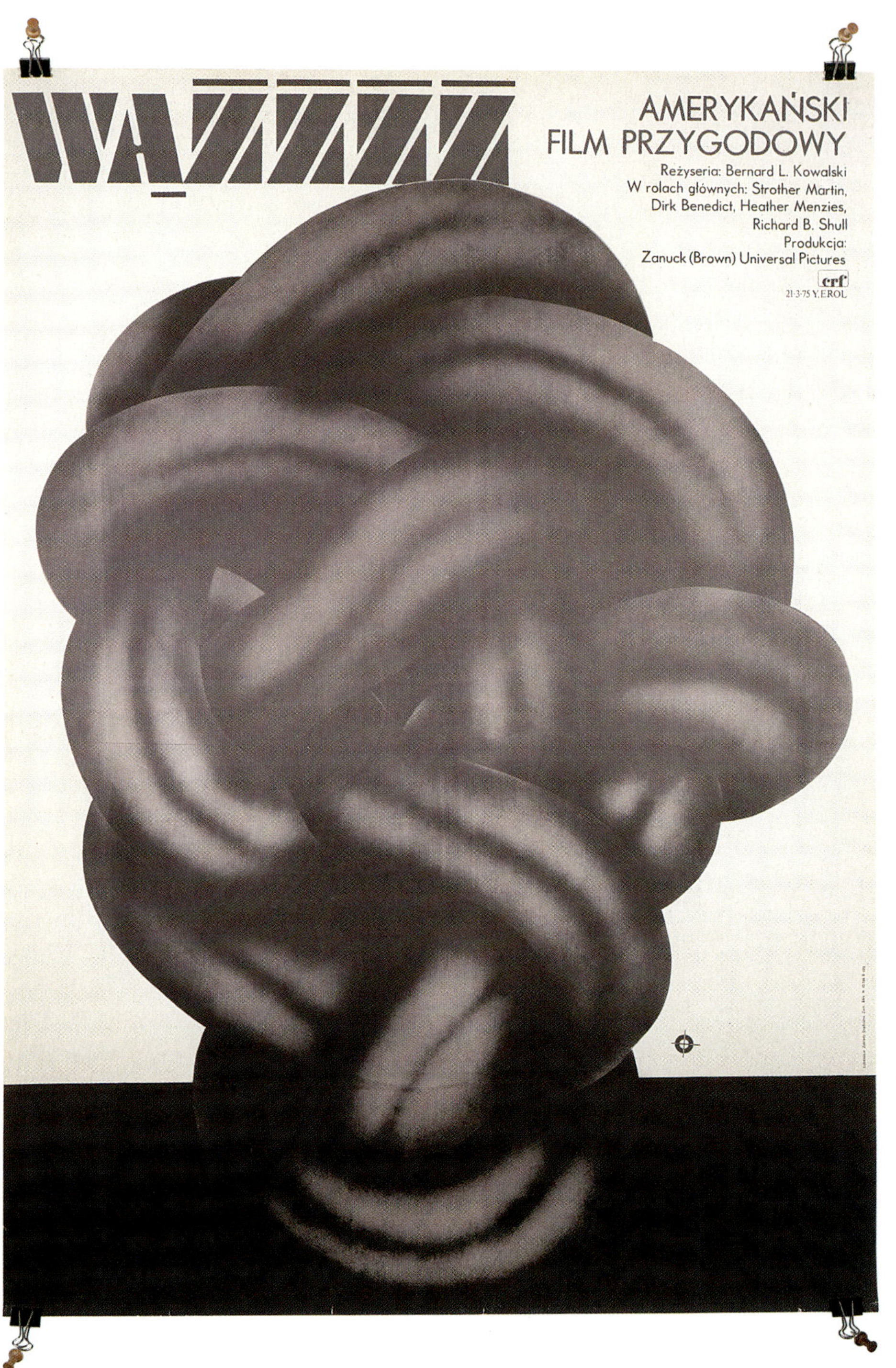
WĄŻŻŻŻ
AMERYKAŃSKI
FILM PRZYGODOWY
Reżyseria: Bernard L. Kowalski
W rolach głównych: Strother Martin,
Dirk Benedict, Heather Menzies,
Richard B. Shull
Produkcja:
Zanuck (Brown) Universal Pictures
crf
21·3·75 Y. EROL

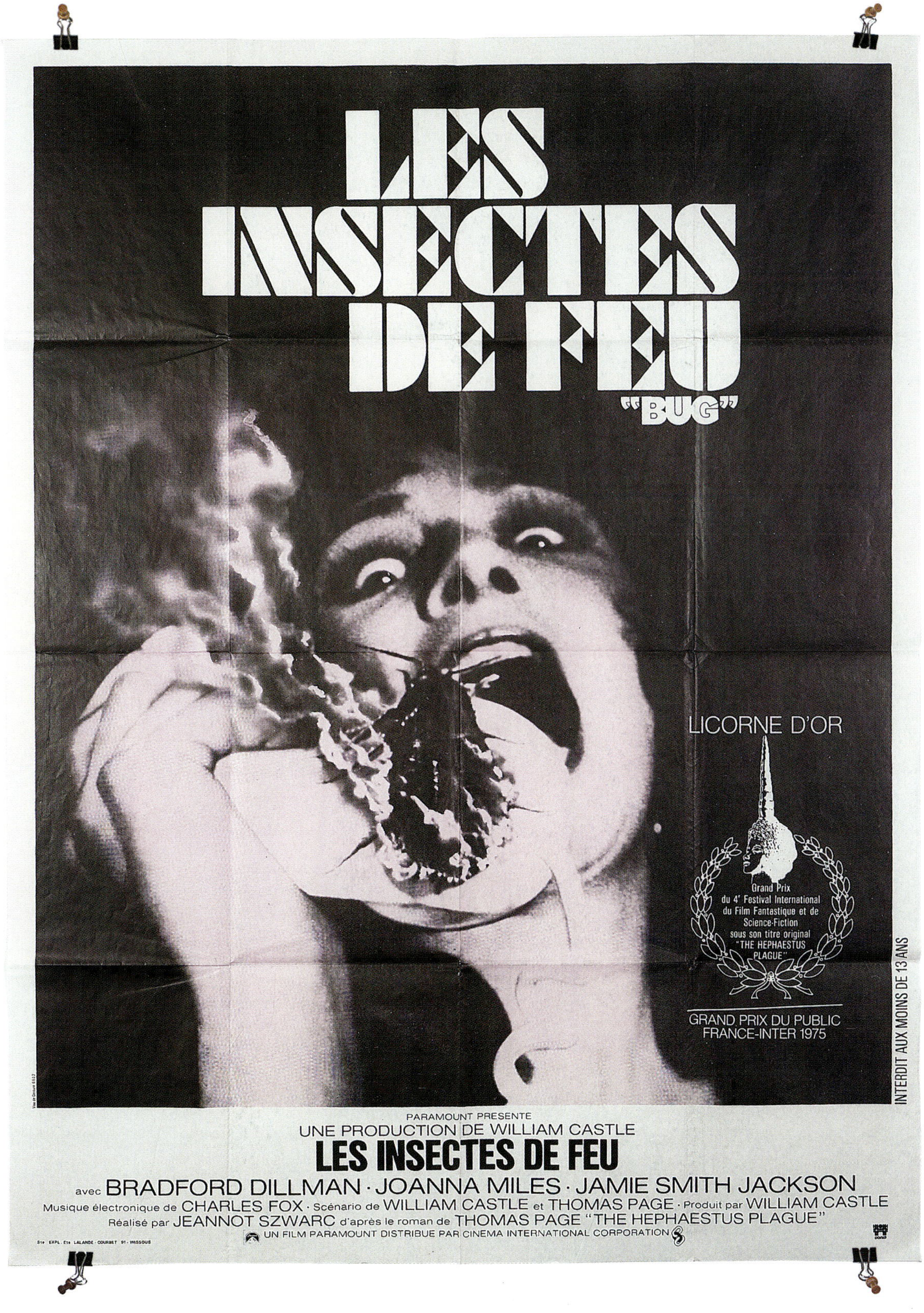

LES
INSECTES
DE FEU
"BUG"

LICORNE D'OR

Grand Prix
du 4e Festival International
du Film Fantastique et de
Science-Fiction
sous son titre original
"THE HEPHAESTUS
PLAGUE"

GRAND PRIX DU PUBLIC
FRANCE-INTER 1975

INTERDIT AUX MOINS DE 13 ANS

PARAMOUNT PRESENTE
UNE PRODUCTION DE WILLIAM CASTLE
LES INSECTES DE FEU
avec BRADFORD DILLMAN · JOANNA MILES · JAMIE SMITH JACKSON
Musique électronique de CHARLES FOX · Scénario de WILLIAM CASTLE et THOMAS PAGE · Produit par WILLIAM CASTLE
Réalisé par JEANNOT SZWARC d'après le roman de THOMAS PAGE "THE HEPHAESTUS PLAGUE"
UN FILM PARAMOUNT DISTRIBUE PAR CINEMA INTERNATIONAL CORPORATION

Ste EXPL. Ets LALANDE - COURBET 91 - WISSOUS

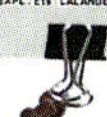

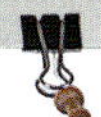

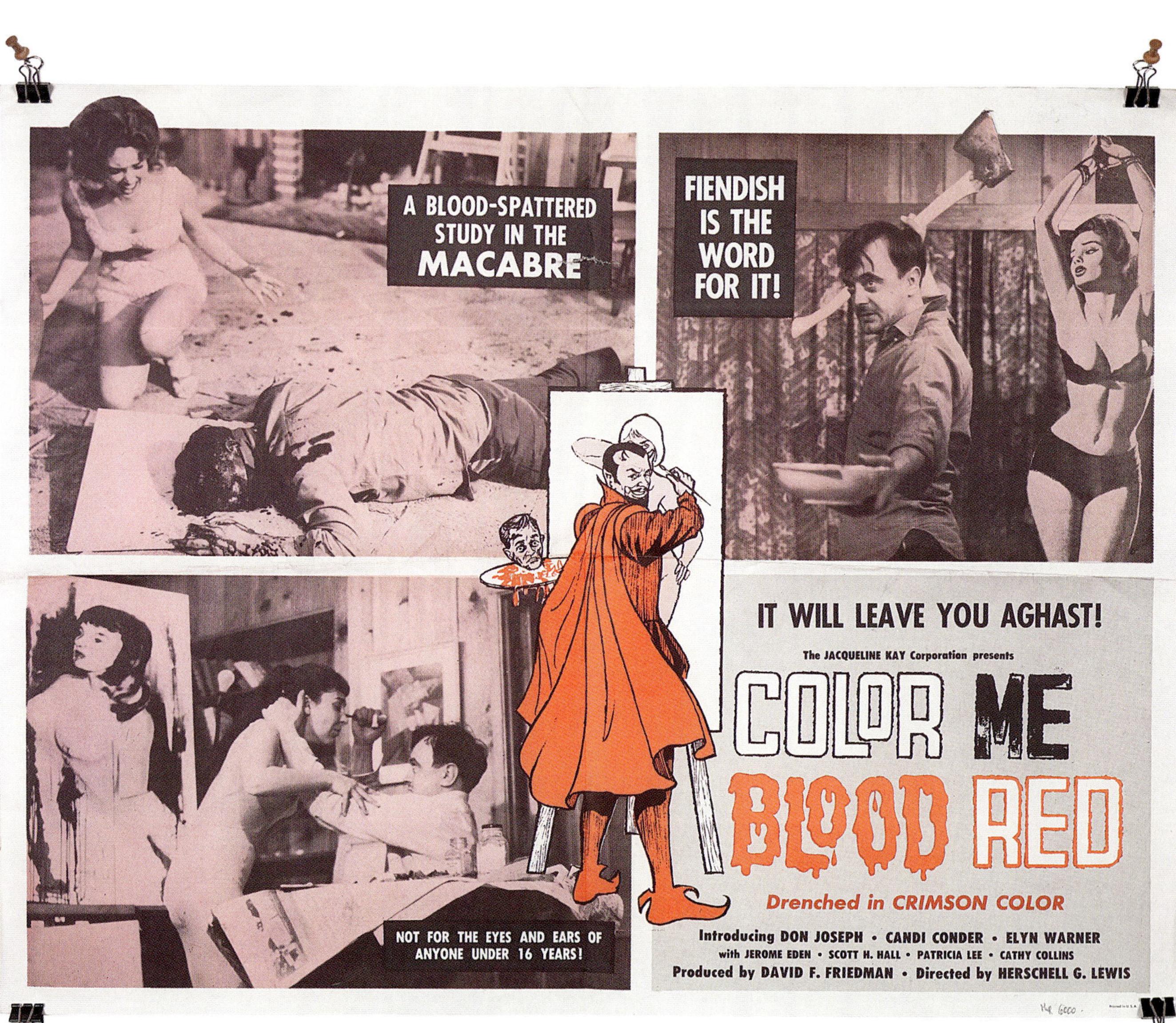
A BLOOD-SPATTERED STUDY IN THE MACABRE
FIENDISH IS THE WORD FOR IT!
IT WILL LEAVE YOU AGHAST!
The JACQUELINE KAY Corporation presents
COLOR ME BLOOD RED
Drenched in CRIMSON COLOR
Introducing DON JOSEPH • CANDI CONDER • ELYN WARNER
with JEROME EDEN • SCOTT H. HALL • PATRICIA LEE • CATHY COLLINS
Produced by DAVID F. FRIEDMAN • Directed by HERSCHELL G. LEWIS
NOT FOR THE EYES AND EARS OF ANYONE UNDER 16 YEARS!

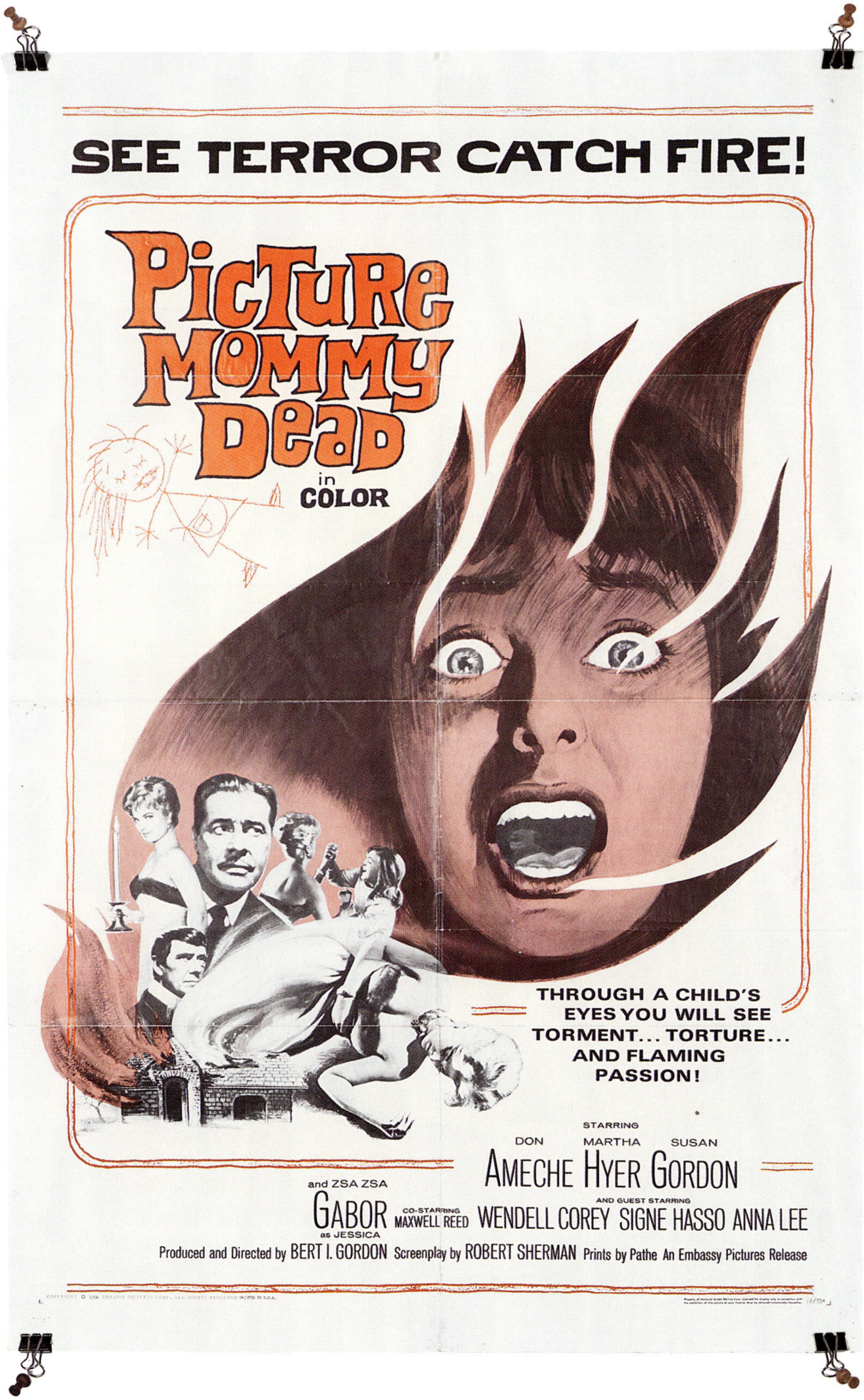

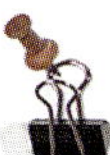
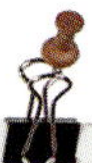

SEE TERROR CATCH FIRE!

PICTURE MOMMY DEAD

in COLOR

THROUGH A CHILD'S EYES YOU WILL SEE TORMENT... TORTURE... AND FLAMING PASSION!

STARRING

DON AMECHE MARTHA HYER SUSAN GORDON

and ZSA ZSA GABOR as JESSICA

CO-STARRING MAXWELL REED

AND GUEST STARRING WENDELL COREY SIGNE HASSO ANNA LEE

Produced and Directed by BERT I. GORDON Screenplay by ROBERT SHERMAN Prints by Pathe An Embassy Pictures Release

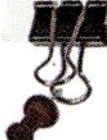
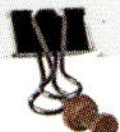

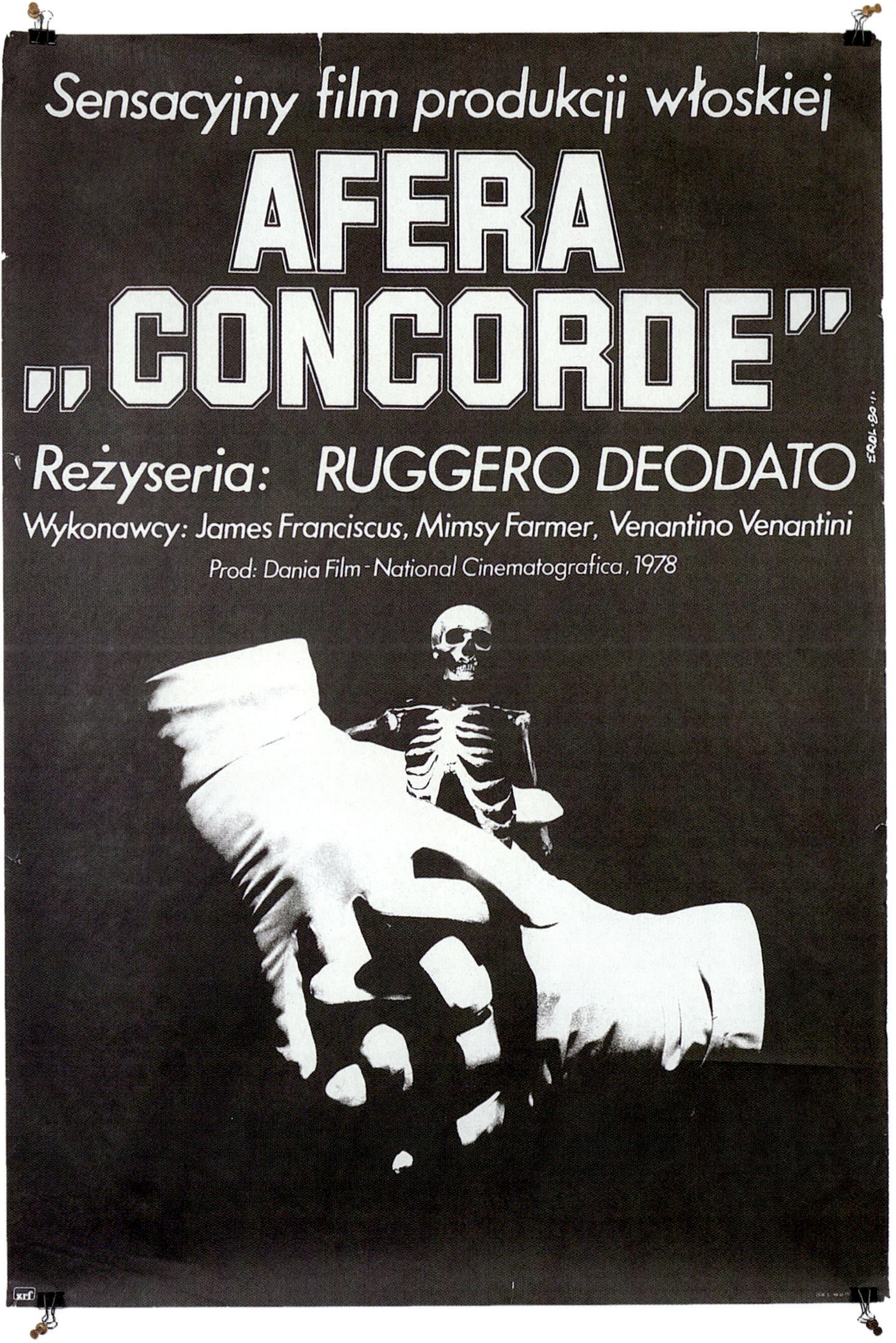
Sensacyjny film produkcji włoskiej
AFERA
„CONCORDE"
Reżyseria: RUGGERO DEODATO
Wykonawcy: James Franciscus, Mimsy Farmer, Venantino Venantini
Prod: Dania Film - National Cinematografica, 1978

Eurogroup Film ET Femina Distribution PRESENTENT

CANNIBAL HOLOCAUST

un film de **RUGGERO DEODATO**

AVEC
ROBERT KERMAN
FRANCESCA CIARDI
PERRY PIRKANEN
LUCA GIORGIO BARBARESCHI

S. E. LALANDE - COURBET 91 - WISSOUS

FAUGÈRE

PRODUIT PAR
Franco Palaggi
et
Franco di Nunzio

MUSIQUE COMPOSEE et DIRIGEE par
RIZ ORTOLANI
COULEURS

interdit aux moins de 18 ans

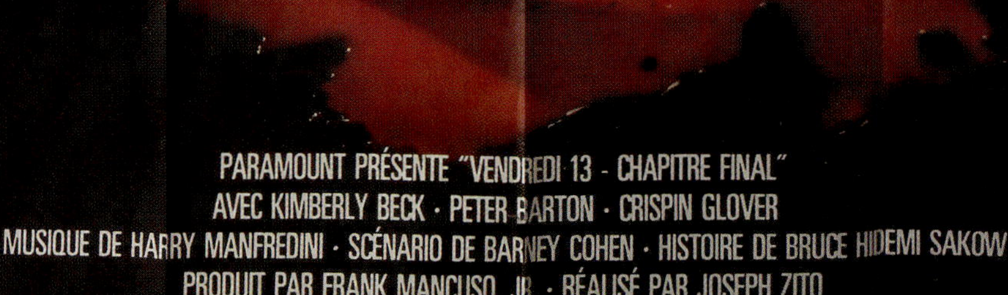
Vous avez connu la peur.
Maintenant
vous allez vivre la terreur.
VENDREDI 13
CHAPITRE FINAL
PARAMOUNT PRÉSENTE "VENDREDI 13 - CHAPITRE FINAL"
AVEC KIMBERLY BECK · PETER BARTON · CRISPIN GLOVER
MUSIQUE DE HARRY MANFREDINI · SCÉNARIO DE BARNEY COHEN · HISTOIRE DE BRUCE HIDEMI SAKOW
PRODUIT PAR FRANK MANCUSO, JR. · RÉALISÉ PAR JOSEPH ZITO
UN FILM PARAMOUNT DISTRIBUÉ PAR CINEMA INTERNATIONAL CORPORATION
© 1984 By Paramount Pictures Corporation. All Rights Reserved

"Oh my God, that's my daughter."

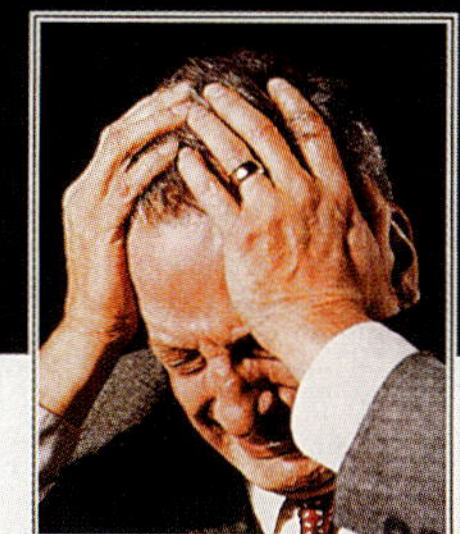

HARDCORE

COLUMBIA PICTURES PRESENTS
GEORGE C. SCOTT in
an A-TEAM PRODUCTION of a PAUL SCHRADER FILM
HARDCORE
starring PETER BOYLE
co-starring SEASON HUBLEY • EXECUTIVE PRODUCER JOHN MILIUS
PRODUCED BY BUZZ FEITSHANS • MUSIC BY JACK NITZSCHE
WRITTEN AND DIRECTED BY PAUL SCHRADER

Columbia Pictures

790010

HARDCORE

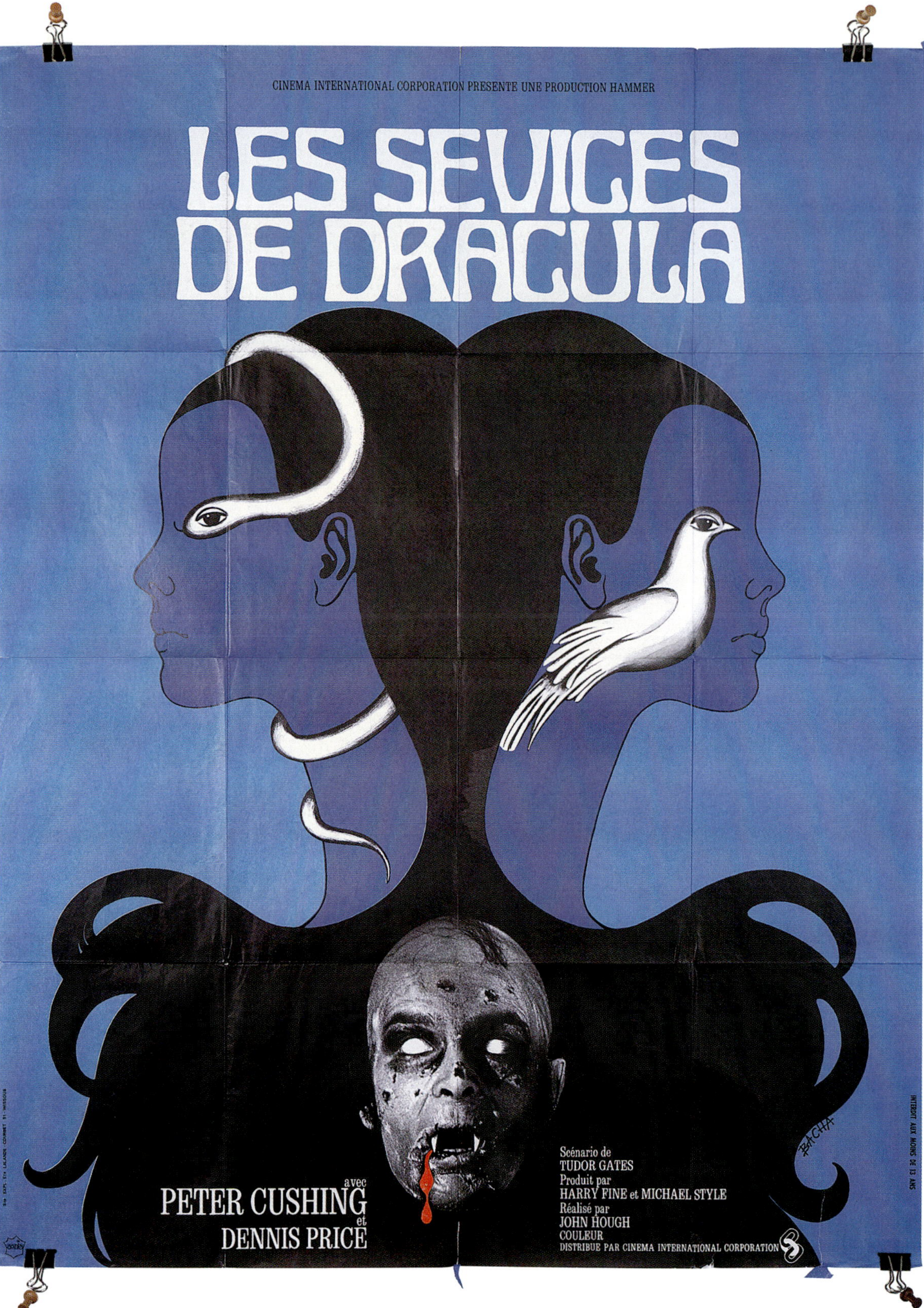
CINEMA INTERNATIONAL CORPORATION PRESENTE UNE PRODUCTION HAMMER
LES SEVICES DE DRACULA
avec
PETER CUSHING
et
DENNIS PRICE
Scénario de
TUDOR GATES
Produit par
HARRY FINE et MICHAEL STYLE
Réalisé par
JOHN HOUGH
COULEUR
DISTRIBUE PAR CINEMA INTERNATIONAL CORPORATION
BACHA
INTERDIT AUX MOINS DE 13 ANS

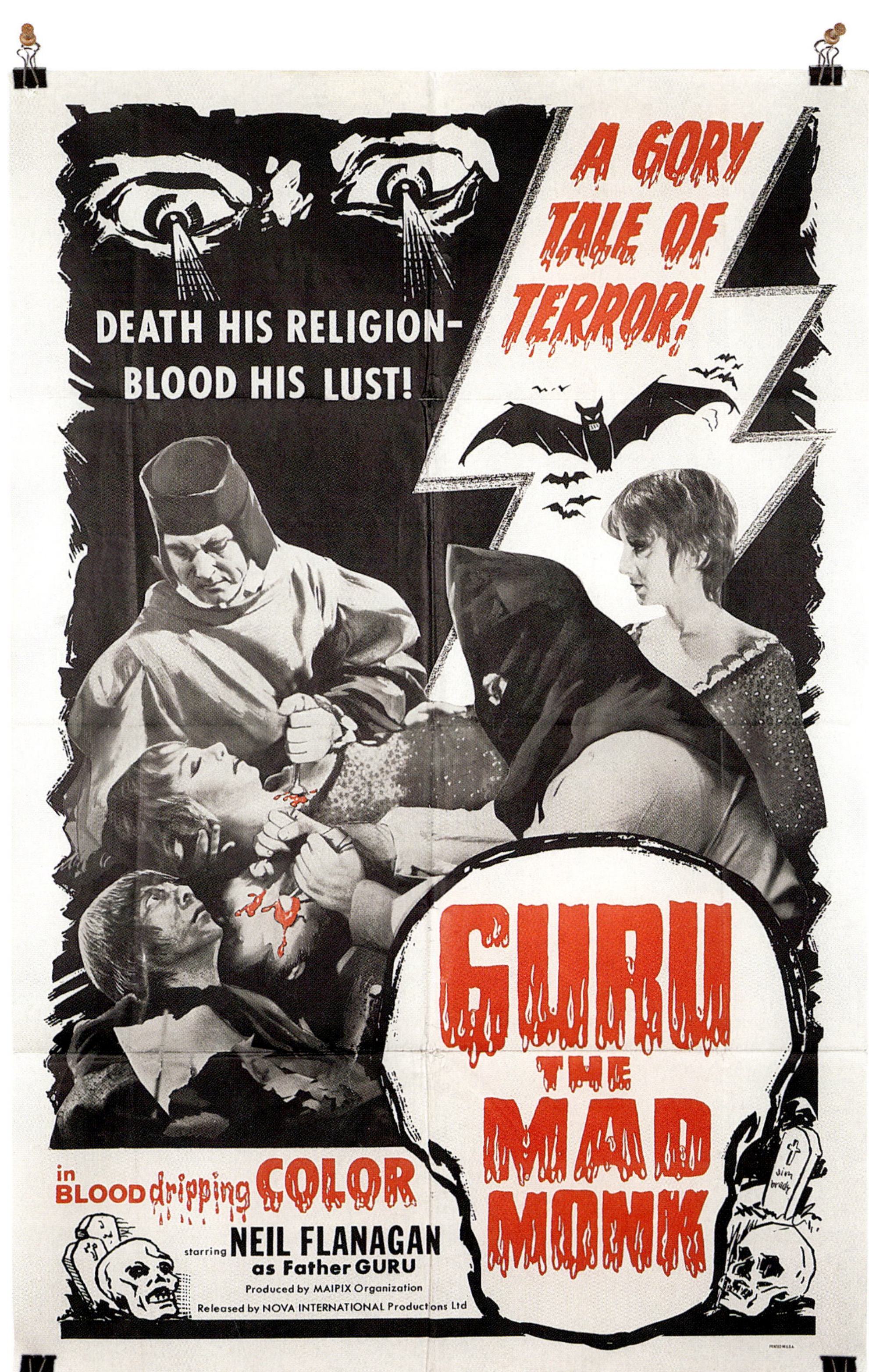
A GORY TALE OF TERROR!
DEATH HIS RELIGION-
BLOOD HIS LUST!
GURU THE MAD MONK
in BLOOD dripping COLOR
starring NEIL FLANAGAN
as Father GURU
Produced by MAIPIX Organization
Released by NOVA INTERNATIONAL Productions Ltd

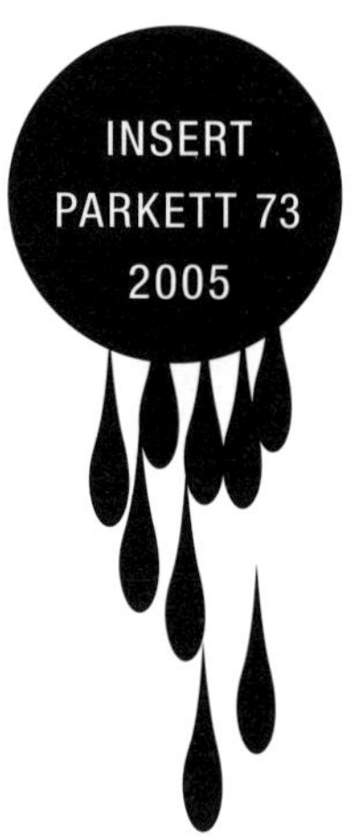

THE FEAR WHICH ORGANIZES YOUR GUILT

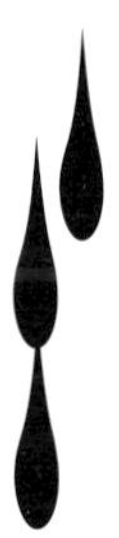

Film posters from the collection of the artist.
"Wazzzz," ("SSSSSSS") Polish, 1973, 57 x 80 cm | "Les Insectes De Feu," ("Bug") French 1975, 120 x 160 cm
"Color Me Blood Red," USA 1965, 71 x 56 cm | "Picture Mommy Dead," USA 1966, 69 x 104 cm
"Afera Concorde," (The Concorde Affair) Polish, 1979, 67 x 98 cm | "Cannibal Holocaust," French 1980, 120 x 160 cm
"Vendredi 13," (Friday the 13th, The Final Chapter) French 1984, 120 x 160 cm | "Hardcore," USA, 1979, 67 x 104 cm
"Les Seviges de Dracula," (Twins of Evil), French 1971, 120 x 160 cm | "Guru the Mad Monk," British 1970, 69 x 104 cm
Photographs by Noah Sheldon.

•

Each individual misfortune, to be sure, seems an exceptional occurance; but misfortune in general is the rule.

•

Arthur Schopenhauer, Parerga and Paralipomena, 1851

NATÜRLICHES PATHOS

HARALD SZEEMANN

TOBIA BEZZOLA

(1933–2005)

Anfang der 60er Jahre war Harald Szeemann klar, dass Bewegungen der Kunst längst auch die Arbeit ihrer Betreuer hätten verändern müssen. Ausstellungen fragten immer wieder: «Was ist Kunst?» Die Kunst fragte sich längst: «Was ist eine Ausstellung?» Eine Kunst, die seit Futurismus und Dada mit ihrer Geschichte, und seit Duchamp und Picabia mit Geschmack und ästhetischem Urteil gebrochen hatte, verlangte neue Weisen der Vermittlung. Historische und ästhetische Zugriffe wurden ihr nicht mehr gerecht. Zudem war ein Ausstellungsbetrieb herangewachsen. Nun unterschieden sich Museumsleiter – wie Manuel Gasser in der *Weltwoche* schon 1952 feststellte – kaum noch von Theater- und Revuedirektoren, Kino- und Zirkusbesitzern und was der öffentlichen Schausteller mehr sind. Indem sich in der Nachkriegszeit ein avantgardistisch verflüssigter Kunstbegriff durchsetzt und die ahistorischen und anästhetischen Avantgarden den Spielplan des Kunstbetriebs zunehmend besetzen, verschwimmen die Berufsbilder. Eine neue Schaustellerei wird institutionell möglich. An die Seite des historisch gebildeten Konservators – Hüter der Schätze – und des ästhetisch gebildeten Kritikers – Hüter der Schwelle – tritt eine neue Figur: der ahistorisch und geschmacksungebunden agierende Inszenierer, ein *metteur en scène*, ein reiner Aussteller, oder, wie man seit den 70er Jahren sagt: ein «Ausstellungsmacher». Harald Szeemann hat diese Neudefinition des Metiers des Organisators von Ausstellungen moderner und zeitgenössischer Kunst in der zweiten Hälfte des zwanzigsten Jahrhunderts fast im Alleingang in Theorie und Praxis vorangetrieben.

Der «gesunde Hang zum Exhibitionismus», den er sich gern selbst nachsagte, reichte dazu noch nicht aus. Der Bruch der Kunst mit ihrer Geschichte und mit der Ästhetik erforderte ein neues Prinzip der Auswahl und der Präsentation. Szeemann, noch Student der Kunstgeschichte, fand es für sich in den 50er Jahren in der Auseinandersetzung mit den drei «Initialgesten» der Moderne: Kandinsky, Malewitsch, Duchamp. Als das Gemeinsame so unterschiedlicher Kunstrevolutionen identifiziert er das Prinzip der «Intensität». Die Intensität der Kreation, statt der Stilqualität der Produkte, ist für Szeemann fortan letztmögliche Basis des Urteils über Kunst, der Auswahl und der Präsentation von Kunst. Eine subjektive, sinnlichkeitsgeleitete «Erregungslogik» löst die allgemein verbindliche Verstandeslogik ab. Weder historische noch ästhetische Gründe und Argumente sind gefragt, gesucht wird vielmehr die unmittelbare Übertragung intensiver Erlebnisse. (Theoriegeschichtlich gesehen ein Rückgriff auf eine reiche Tradition der Enthusiasmus-Ästhetik, und gewiss kein Zufall, dass ein Mann des Theaters diese in der bildenden Kunst wieder aktualisiert.) Die damit implizierte «Hypersubjektivität» rettet den absoluten und utopischen Anspruch der Avantgarde ins Refugium der «individuellen Mythologie». Der von Intensitätserlebnissen inspirierte und begeisterte Beobachter der Kunst löst sich von der Bindung an die akademische Historie, die dem traditionellen Konservator die Prinzipien seiner Auswahl und seiner Kommentierungen vorgibt. Er löst sich auch von Bünd-

---

TOBIA BEZZOLA ist Kurator am Kunsthaus Zürich.

nissen und Bekenntnissen – zu einem Stil, einer Schule, einem Künstler (was dem Kritiker seine Autorität kraft Intimität verschafft hatte). Er löst sich von der Bindung an die Stilkunst überhaupt. Öffnungen, nicht nur zu abwegigen kulturellen Produktionen hin, sondern zu überhaupt fast jeder enthusiastischen und enthusiasmierenden menschlichen Tätigkeit, werden möglich. Der Kosmos des Ausstellbaren wird grenzenlos, bis hin zur «Obsession» – so Szeemanns Selbstbeschreibung –, «Dinge zu zeigen, die es eigentlich gar nicht gibt».

Harald Szeemann hat fast fünfzig Jahre lang Ausstellungen organisiert. Das Werk – so kann man es getrost nennen – zerfällt dabei in drei Teile. In den 60er Jahren erarbeiten die Ausstellungen an der Kunsthalle Bern den Fonds einer neuen Methodologie und einen enormen Fundus an Wissen, Ressource für alles Spätere. Das in Bern Geleistete findet 1972 in der Documenta 5 seine Synthese: Dazu gehören die Öffnung gegenüber der Kunst von Aussenseitern (Bildnerei der Geisteskranken/art brut/«Insania pingens», 1963), gegenüber der Volkskunst («ex voto», 1964), gegenüber der Kommerz-, Populär- und Trivialkultur («Science Fiction», 1967) sowie ein Interesse für verschrobene Individualisten abseits und jenseits der Stilkunst (wie Etienne Martin, 1964). Und dazu gehört vor allem, in Einklang mit der Werkauffassung der damals jüngsten Generation, dass Werke überhaupt erst für einen Ausstellungsraum, im Ausstellungsraum, als Ausstellung geschaffen werden («12 Environments», 1968; «When Attitudes Become Form», 1969), sowie dass begleitende Happenings und Performances die Ausstellung zum permanenten Ereignis machen.

Im Anschluss an den Documenta-Rummel zieht sich Szeemann ins Tessin zurück. Dort erfindet er für sich das Metier des selbständigen Ausstellungsmachers. Er gründet dazu in pataphysischem Unternehmergeist das Vehikel der «Agentur für Geistige Gastarbeit» im Dienste des (imaginären) «Museums der Obsessionen». Die Agentur beauftragt fortan ihren einzigen Mitarbeiter, Harald Szeemann, spekulative Ausstellungskonzepte zu entwickeln, mit immensem Forschungsaufwand Material zu sichten und im Archiv der Agentur zu sichern, alsdann eine internationale Tour zu organisieren und die Ausstellung schliesslich an jeder Station bis zum letzten Nagel selbst einzurichten und zu promoten. Dabei entsteht eine neue Art von Ausstellung. «Ich konnte den Museen und Kunsthallen natürlich nicht einfach eine weitere Duchamp-Ausstellung oder so etwas anbieten; darauf konnten sie ja auch noch selbst kommen ...» Die neue Organisationsform erlaubt es vielmehr, neue, im Rahmen eines traditionellen institutionsverankerten Ausstellungswesens nicht denkbare Konzepte tatsächlich zu realisieren. Und Szeemann dehnt in der Folge das Medium bis an die Grenze. Er geht thematisch-historische Komplexe auf der Basis akribischer Recherche mit den Mitteln der assoziativ-poetischen Inszenierung von Artefakten, Dokumenten und Kunstwerken an und nimmt für dieselben eine poetische Kraft und eine Wahrheit ganz eigener Art in Anspruch. «Grossvater» (1974), «Junggesellenmaschinen» (1975) und «Monte Verità» (1978) definieren den Typus.

Die dritte Karrierephase ist geprägt von regelmässigen Engagements am Kunsthaus Zürich und einem nomadischen Leben mit weltweiten Gastspielen als bekanntester Meister einer von ihm erfundenen Zunft. Es entstehen beinahe hundert Ausstellungen in Dutzenden von Ländern. In den 80er Jahren steht die auratische Inszenierung grosser Skulpturenausstellungen – gern in erstmals für die Kunst erschlossenen Räumen – im Vordergrund («De Sculptura», 1986; «Zeitlos», 1988; «Einleuchten», 1989). Bevor er damit als Skulpturenregisseur selbst wieder in Stil und Geschmack zurückverfällt, bringen die 90er eine erneute Anarchisierung: Sie äussert sich als Öffnung gegenüber der allerjüngsten Kunst, auch nichtwestlicher Provenienz, sowie als Rückkehr zur spektakulär ahistorischen Aufbereitung kulturhistorischer Themen («Visionäre Schweiz», 1991; «Austria im Rosennetz», 1996; «Geld und Wert – Das letzte Tabu», 2002; «Visionäres Belgien», 2005).

Als «Verzauberung auf Zeit» charakterisierte Szeemann einmal den Zweck seines Tuns. Verzauberung ist Sache eines Zauberers, und ein solcher muss viele Talente vereinen. «Natürlich habe ich mich geängstigt, ob ich das alles mal zusammenbringen kann ...», bemerkte er im Rückblick auf die Jugendjahre, wo er in Bern und Paris gleichzeitig als Schauspieler, Autor, Regisseur, Bühnenbildner, Werbegrafiker und Kunsthistoriker beschäftigt war. Wie bei jedem guten Zauberer erschienen seine Fähigkeiten immer unbeschränkt. Die Ausstellungen unterschieden nicht nur mit Verstand und Urteilskraft, sondern vor allem führten sie mit Witz und Scharfsinn das Unterschiedene überraschend wieder neu zusammen. Szeemann stellte schlagfertig aus; mit präzisem Plan zwar, aber es war nie zu spät oder zu anstrengend, auf eine neue Situation oder einen besseren Einfall mit einer überraschenden Volte zu reagieren. So viel Kontrolle bei so viel Lässigkeit erfordern viel Energie, ein gutes Gedächtnis, grosse Geduld und vor allem ein grosses Herz: um jahrzehntelang in einem zuweilen auch lästigen und albernen Betrieb immer geradeaus, über die Köpfe von Intriganten und Schmeichlern hinweg, voll Liebe und Hingabe nur auf die Sache zu blicken; sich mit Fehden und Bestechungsversuchen nicht abzugeben, den Alleingang in völliger Unabhängigkeit und ohne Sicherheitsnetz, unerschrocken, geschickt und mutig bis ans Ziel zu gehen. Harald Szeemann hatte dieses grosse Herz. Und daraus floss in Hunderte von Ausstellungen ein, was er von Anfang an immer selbst gesucht hatte und seine Inszenierungen zu schaffen verstanden: «natürliches Pathos».

Die Zitate stammen aus fünf mehrstündigen, unpublizierten Interviews, die Roman Kurzmeyer und der Verfasser im Sommer 1996 mit Harry Szeemann führten.

Im Herbst 2005 erscheint der Band: *Harald Szeemann, with / by / through / because / towards / despite. Catalogue of all Exhibitions,* hg. v. Tobia Bezzola und Roman Kurzmeyer, ca. 800 S. und 1000 Ill., Edition Voldemeer, Zürich, und Springer Verlag, Wien, New York.

NATURAL PATHOS

HARALD SZEEMANN

(1933–2005)

TOBIA BEZZOLA

By the beginning of the sixties, Harald Szeemann knew that art movements should long since have exerted an influence on the work of its agents as well. Exhibitions were always asking, "What is art?" But art had already taken the lead by asking, "What is an exhibition?" Art, which had broken with its history since Futurism and Dada, and with taste and aesthetic judgment since Duchamp and Picabia, required new modes of transmission. Historical and aesthetic avenues of approach no longer sufficed. And exhibition operations were burgeoning. One could hardly distinguish anymore between the director of a museum and theater and vaudeville directors, movie and circus owners and, in fact, showmen in general, as Manuel Gasser observed in the *Weltwoche* back in 1952. After the war, the avant-garde meltdown of the concept of art took center stage and an ahistorical and anesthetic avant-garde increasingly monopolized the repertoire of art institutions, hence blurring job descriptions in art and paving the way for new forms of institutional presentation. A third figuree merged alongside the historically trained curator—guardian of the treasure—and the aesthetically trained critic—guardian of the threshold: the ahistorical, taste-independent presenter, the *metteur en scène*, the pure exhibitor or the "exhibition maker," as it has been called since the seventies. Almost single-handed, Harald Szeemann advanced and redefined both the theory and practice of organizing exhibitions of modern and contemporary art in the second half of the twentieth century.

This achievement required more then the "healthy penchant for exhibitionism," which he often ascribed to

TOBIA BEZZOLA is a curator at the Kunsthaus Zürich.

himself. The rupture between art and its history and aesthetics called for a new principle of selection and presentation. Szeemann found one for himself in the fifties while studying art history and especially the three "initial gestures" of modernism: Kandinsky, Malevich, and Duchamp. He identified the principle of "intensity" as the common factor in these extremely divergent artistic revolutions. From then on, Szeemann's ultimate criterion for judging, selecting, and presenting art was the intensity of creation rather than the stylistic quality of the products. A subjective, sensually motivated "logic of excitement" replaced the generally binding logic of reason. Neither historical nor aesthetic explanations and arguments were in demand but rather the immediate communication of intense experiences. (In terms of the history of ideas, this signifies a return to the rich tradition of an aesthetics of enthusiasm and it is most certainly no accident that a man of the theater updated this tradition in the fine arts.) This implied "hyper subjectivity" rescued the avant-garde's utopian claim to the absolute by offering the refuge of "individual mythologies." The observer of art, inspired and enthused by the intensity of experience, loosened his ties to academic history, which hitherto dictated the principles of selection and analysis for traditional curators. He also loosened his ties to the alliances and commitments—to a style, a school, an artist (an intimacy that had lent the critic authority). In fact, he broke all ties with art styles. The embrace not only of deviating cultural productions but of practically every enthusiastic and enthusing human activity became possible. The universe of things that can be exhibited became unbounded to the point of becoming "obsessed with showing things that don't actually exist"—as Szeemann himself described it.

Harald Szeemann organized exhibitions for close to fifty years. His oeuvre—a well-deserved designation—can be divided into three phases. The exhibitions of the sixties at the Kunsthalle Bern led to a new methodology and the acquisition of an enormous inventory of knowledge, providing the resources for everything that was to follow. The achievements in Bern found their synthesis at Documenta 5 in 1972: these included the recognition of art by outsiders ("Bildnerei der Geisteskranken—Art Brut—Insania pingens," 1963), folk art ("ex voto," 1964), the products of commerce and popular culture ("Science Fiction," 1967) as well as interest in eccentric characters positioned beside and beyond official styles ("Etienne Martin," 1964). Above all, it meant embracing the approach of young art practitioners in those days, who pioneered the creation of art specifically for or in exhibition spaces ("12 Environments," 1968; "When Attitudes Become Form," 1969) as well as the attendant Happenings and Performances, which turned the exhibition into a nonstop event.

Following the brouhaha of Documenta 5, Szeemann retired to Ticino and there invented his own profession as an independent exhibition maker. In a spirit of pataphysical enterprise, he founded the "Agency for Spiritual Guest Labor" as a subsidiary of the (imaginary) "Museum of Obsessions." The agency commissioned its one employee, Harald Szeemann, to work out speculative proposals for exhibitions, to conduct extremely elaborate research and file it in the archives of the agency, to organize an international tour, and, finally, to install and promote the entire exhibition at every stop of the tour. The outcome was a new kind of exhibition. "I couldn't simply offer museums and kunsthalles another Duchamp exhibition or something like that; they could come up with such an idea themselves..." The new form of organization enabled him to implement new ideas that would have been inconceivable within the context of traditional, institutionally defined exhibition operations. Szeemann proceeded to push the medium to extremes. Meticulous study of selected themes and historical issues fed into his associative and poetic scenarios of artifacts, documents, and works of art, in turn requiring them to generate great poetic power and a distinctive truth of their own. "Grossvater" (1974), "Junggesellenmaschinen" (1975), and "Monte Verità" (1978) have become classical exemplars of this entirely new type of exhibition.

The third phase of Szeemann's career is marked by regular productions at the Kunsthaus Zürich and the life of a nomad with guest performances all over the world as the most famous master of the guild he had himself invented. He chalked up close to 100 more exhibitions in dozens of countries. The eighties saw large-scale, auratically mounted exhibitions of sculpture, often inaugurating new spaces for art, as in "De Sculptura" (1986), "Zeitlos" (1988), and "Einleuchten" (1989). But the director of sculpture did not lapse into style and taste; instead the nineties saw a renewed period of anarchy, thanks once again to the unabashed embrace of the most recent art—not only from the West—as well as a return to the spectacular ahistorical

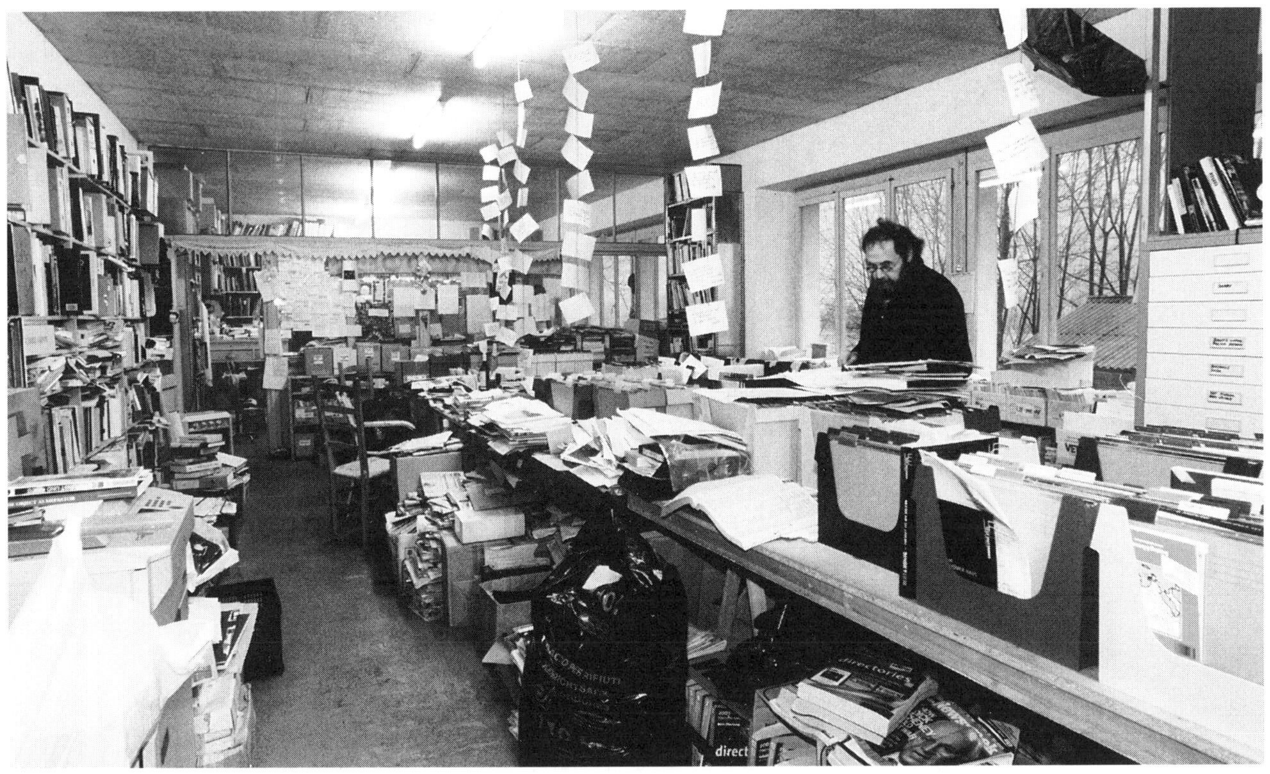

Harry Szeemann in seinem Archiv in Tegno, Tessin / in his archives in Tegno, Ticino, Switzerland. (PHOTO: ANDREA STAPPERT)

treatment of cultural and historical issues, as in "Visionäre Schweiz" (1991), "Austria im Rosennetz" (1996), "Geld und Wert—Das letzte Tabu" (2002), and "Visionäres Belgien" (2005).

Szeemann once described his purpose as "enchantment pro tem." Enchantment is the job of a magician and magicians must be possessed of many talents. "Obviously I worried about being able to bring everything together," he remarked, looking back on his early years in Bern and Paris, when he was working simultaneously as an actor, writer, director, stage-set designer, commercial artist, and art historian. Like a good magician, his skills always seemed unlimited. The exhibitions not only revealed and refined distinctions with intelligence and discriminating verve; they also wittily and wisely showed a startling unity of the discrete. Szeemann was not only sharp but also quick-witted; though his plans were always precise, it was never too late or too laborious to react to a new situation or a better idea with astonishing dexterity. So much control and so much nonchalance require substantial energy, a good memory, exceptional patience, and, above all, a big heart—in order to succeed for decades in an occasionally annoying and sometimes even inane art world, immune to intrigues and flattery, fully and lovingly focusing on subject matter alone, oblivious to feuds and attempted bribery, walking a solitary path in complete independence and without a safety net, fearlessly, skillfully, courageously pursuing his aims. Harald Szeemann had a large heart and, into hundreds of exhibitions, flowed what he himself had always sought and successfully injected into his productions: "natural pathos."

(Translation: Catherine Schelbert)

Harald Szeemann is quoted from five unpublished interviews of several hours each, conducted by Roman Kurzmeyer and the writer in the summer of 1996.

Forthcoming in autumn 2005:
Harald Szeemann, with / by / through / because / towards / despite. Catalogue of all Exhibitions, ed. by Tobia Bezzola and Roman Kurzmeyer, ca. 800 p., ca. 1000 ill. (Zürich: Edition Voldemeer; Wien & New York: Springer Verlag).

CUMULUS

From America

IN EVERY EDITION OF PARKETT, TWO CUMULUS CLOUDS, ONE FROM AMERICA, THE OTHER FROM EUROPE, FLOAT OUT TO AN INTERESTED PUBLIC. THEY CONVEY INDIVIDUAL OPINIONS, ASSESSMENTS, AND MEMORABLE ENCOUNTERS—AS ENTIRELY PERSONAL PRESENTATIONS OF PROFESSIONAL ISSUES.

OUR CONTRIBUTORS TO THIS ISSUE ARE DEBRA SINGER, EXECUTIVE DIRECTOR AND CHIEF CURATOR OF THE KITCHEN, NEW YORK, AND FORMER ASSOCIATE CURATOR OF CONTEMPORARY ART AT THE WHITNEY MUSEUM OF AMERICAN ART, AND NATAŠA PETREŠIN, AN INDEPENDENT CURATOR AND WRITER BASED IN LJUBLJANA.

A POST-BIENNIAL POST-SCRIPT

DEBRA SINGER

As one of the three co-curators of the 2004 Whitney Biennial, the better part of my 2003 was spent in airports, automobiles, and, thankfully, artists' studios in various cities across the United States. If life on the road is *modus operandi* for most art curators, it goes into hyperdrive when Biennial deadlines loom. The endeavor, at least at the Whitney, becomes a thirteen-month, warp-speed sprint against the clock (and the budget) to come up with a list of artists that somehow reflects trends in American art-making in the last two years. With the exhibition having come-and-gone, I've recently found some blurred aspects of this intensely compressed experience coming into focus. One in particular keeps resurfacing, which is: a noticeable return, particularly by younger artists, to politically-engaged work that addresses difficult realities through nuanced rhetorical strategies and allegorical approaches, in lieu of strategies of didactic critique or ironic statement. There were many artists in the Biennial—and myriad more outside of the exhibition—whose work represents this type of outlook; however, three quite distinct figures from the show seem aptly representative of this continuing, bubbling trend: Harrell Fletcher, Wynne Greenwood (a. k. a. Tracy & the Plastics), and Christian Holstad. These three artists seem paradigmatic of a range of current artistic practices that communicate, with refreshing sincerity, new, modest possibilities for social

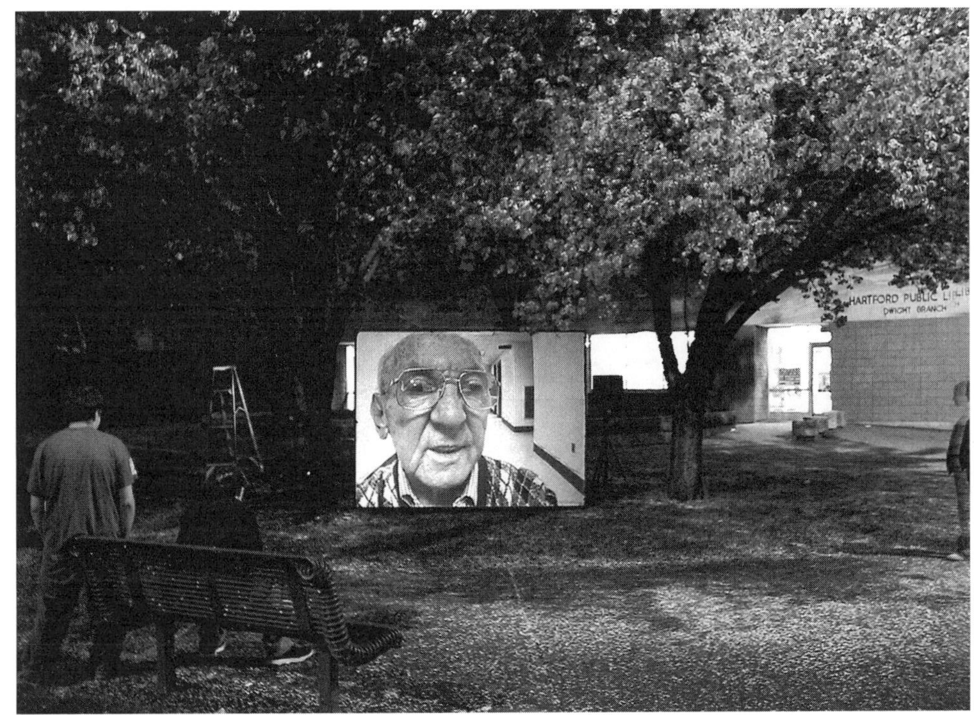

HARRELL FLETCHER, THE PROBLEM OF POSSIBLE REDEMPTION, 2003, video installation view, Parkville Senior Center, Hartford, Connecticut / DAS PROBLEM DER MÖGLICHEN ERLÖSUNG, Videoinstallation.

connectedness, personal empowerment, and positive political change.

The Oregon-based artist Harrell Fletcher produces work inside and outside museums and gallery spaces predicated on harnessing the creativity of diverse groups of people who do not necessarily identify themselves as artists. Through rather simple participatory structures, Fletcher enables groups of people to both create and exhibit work, fostering new relationships through cooperative processes along the way. In the 2004 Whitney Biennial, for instance, Fletcher exhibited several works clustered around one kiosk-like station. The first was a video project, BLOT OUT THE SUN (2002), that came about through Fletcher's acquaintance with a gas station owner in his Portland neighborhood. The two created a movie together out of the owner's favorite book, James Joyce's *Ulysses.* Filming at the gas station, mechanics and customers alike read selected excerpts of the novel off of cue cards, resulting in an alternative narrative focused on themes of death, love, and social inequality. A second related video, titled THE PROBLEM OF POSSIBLE REDEMPTION (2003), was created at a senior citizens center in Hartford, Connecticut. This time, Fletcher worked with elderly people, who read aloud different passages from the same Joyce text, meditating society, war, and mortality. Both were rather enchanting works created with a great economy of means, and were remarkable for their unusual contrast between the settings, protagonists, and breadth of content.

Two other exhibited works included a stack of take-away free newspapers, which were part of his project titled THIS CONTAINER ISN'T BIG ENOUGH (2004). The newspaper described and illustrated artwork by ten people whom Fletcher had met from around the country. It also functioned as a map for locations throughout the city, ranging from furniture stores to cafes to recreational centers where Fletcher had organized exhibits of this artwork. Featured alongside the newspapers was his collaborative project with artist Miranda July and designer Yuri Ono, titled LEARNING TO LOVE YOU MORE (2002–ongoing), which is a website dedicated to presenting artwork made by the general public in response to unusual, creative assignments crafted by Fletcher and July: they post and archive both the assignments and the results on the site as well as regularly exhibiting the original works at various venues when oppor-

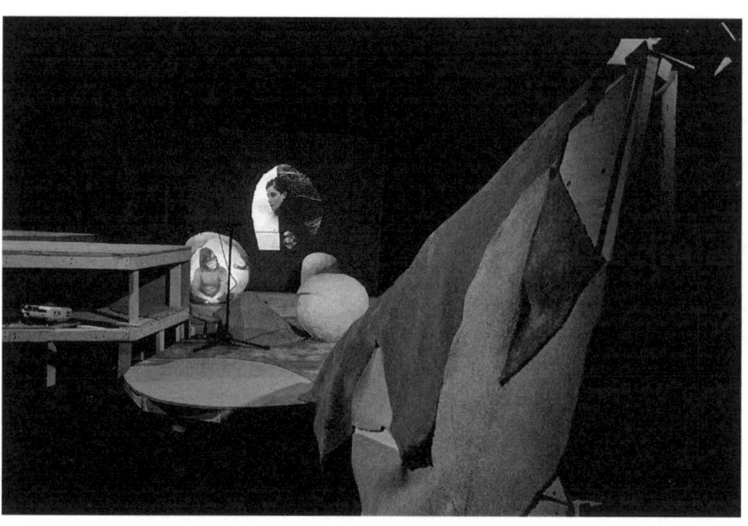

TRACY & THE PLASTICS on stage / in Aktion.

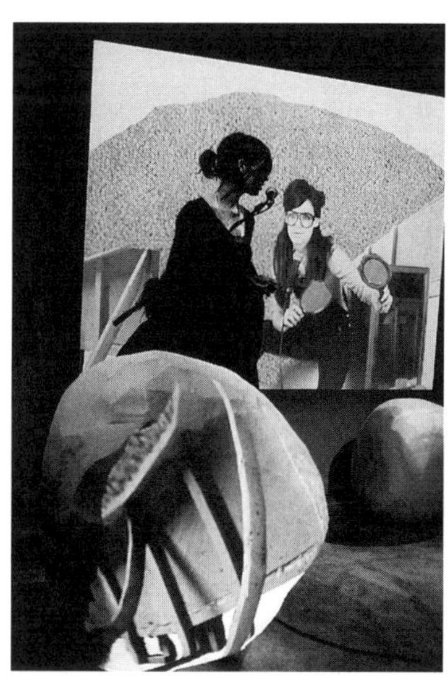

tunities arise. The assignments range from something as simple as, "Take a photograph of the sun," to more complex endeavors such as, "Make an audio recording of a choir (real or constructed)." The basic assumption is that by giving out assignments, Fletcher and July offer the chance to bypass the often daunting challenge of coming up with an idea on your own. Reflecting an unusual combination of high-tech and low-tech, the project taps into the internet's potential to initiate new forms of virtual community with a parallel dimension of hands-on art-making. What perhaps is most refreshing about this ongoing collaborative project is the enthusiastic level of participation from individuals living all over the globe.

Like Fletcher's other endeavors, LEARNING TO LOVE YOU MORE emphasizes inclusiveness through do-it-yourself approaches, creating, along the way, improbable connections between otherwise completely unrelated people. While the nature of his artistic practice is in a lineage of Beuysian social sculpture, and is reminiscent of modes of community-engagement that became particularly popular in the seventies, part of what distinguishes Fletcher's work is its consistent adaptability to generate poignant, site-responsive projects that succeed in a wide variety of contexts through noticeably ordinary and simple means.

In many respects, community and participatory social exchange are also at the crux of work by a very different Biennial artist, Wynne Greenwood, in her ongoing project *Tracy & the Plastics. Tracy & the Plastics* is a feminist-lesbian, art-punk band, in which Greenwood assumes the roles of all three band members, performing live on stage as Tracy, while also appearing as both Nikki and Cola in the form of pre-recorded video projections. Until recently, *Tracy & the Plastics* had performed mostly in clubs and underground music venues around the country. "Band practice" is often the guise of presentation during the performances, which establishes both an air of informality between performer and audience, as well as the rationale for frequent conversational interactions between Tracy and her band-mates on the video screen behind her. Throughout the show, interruptions in-between songs—or even smack in the middle of them—recur, as the trio discusses any number of topics that, while playfully humorous, allude to more serious concerns: like Nikki voicing a complaint about how she thinks the band's name upholds the "traditional hierarchy of the rock band," or explaining how to "do things like a lesbian," like drinking tea or holding a baby. Such deliberate "disruptions" and "technical difficulties" result in synapses in the evening's flow, creating unusual opportunities for Tracy to talk directly to the audience, to literally give them space to respond and participate in her world.

Recently, at The Kitchen, *Tracy & the Plastics* produced their first installation and full-length evening performance titled ROOM (2005), which was created in conjunction with the sculptor Fawn Krieger. The gallery installation was a kind of "utopian living room" made from cheap carpet, wood, and foam-mirroring, in a sense, the low-tech aesthetic of the video projections. The band performed in this built environment, which was designed so that musicians and audience members could share the same physical space, and was intended to re-imagine settings for feminist, consciousness-raising groups from the seventies. The project demonstrated how Greenwood weaves an idiosyncratic post-Seattle Slacker/post-Riot Grrrl sensibility with queer-punk politics and a surprising dose of pop-music virtuosity into an intensely engaging exploration of sexuality, collective identification, community, and home.

Offering up an equally hand-crafted but completely distinct style of work is Christian Holstad, who uses the popular aesthetics of sixties psychedelia, kitsch, camp, and seventies glam rock and disco styles to create vibrantly lavish installations composed of many disparate handmade objects, drawings, and collages. Strongly influenced by the films and performances of Jack Smith, Holstad often creates installations that are flamboyant memorials, dedicated either to real individuals or invented characters, made from wonderfully intricate hand-sewn quilts and soft-sculptural forms as well as erased newspaper drawings, pornographic collages, papier-mâché balloons, and transformed found objects.

His installation at the Whitney, for example, was comprised of three distinct works, which conjured a fantastical graveyard vigil. It centered around a campfire made from stitched fabric logs and crocheted flames as well as a thirties-style funeral basket made primarily from re-sewn roller skates, whimsically decorated with mirrored testicle-like shapes. Other elements included a wool-felt funeral wreath ornamented with Venus flytraps, men's leather underwear, and absurdly long red, white, and blue metallic pompoms. Incorporating camp's embrace of opposite sensibilities, Holstad's works paradoxically also conveyed an elegiac aura, as the setting was equally tinged with tenderness and longing for the lost "days of disco"—a more liberating, and liberal bygone era. The specificity and theatricality of the installation at once parodied recent over-the-top patriotic displays, while also expressing a celebratory affirmation of gay sexuality, which, in Holstad's words, served also as a tribute to a "rebellious spirit everywhere."

Within a broad spectrum, Fletcher, Greenwood, and Holstad represent different facets of a much broader trend among younger artists and art collectives based in New York and beyond, who, in an attempt to advocate for new possibilities for social transformation, are favoring tactics of deeply committed, hopeful engagement, rather than perspectives of overt protest. Theirs is a lyrical politics filled with generous gestures and an optimistic spirit. In a world currently scarred by pervasive fear, prejudice, and violence, it's certainly a welcome and productive respite.

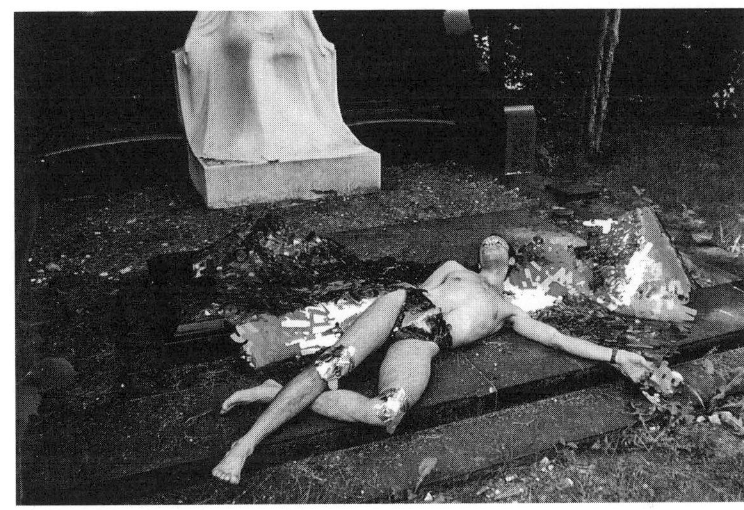

CHRISTIAN HOLSTAD, PRINCESS MIDDLEFINGER DRYING WINGS IN A SUNNY CEMETERY, 2004, color photograph, 11 x 14" / PRINZESSIN MITTELFINGER LÄSST IN EINEM SONNIGEN FRIEDHOF DIE FLÜGEL TROCKNEN, Farbphotographie, 28 x 35,6 cm.
(PHOTO: DANIEL REICH GALLERY, NEW YORK)

POSTSKRIPTUM

NACH DER WHITNEY-BIENNALE

DEBRA SINGER

In meiner Eigenschaft als Co-Kuratorin der Whitney-Biennale 2004 verbrachte ich den grössten Teil des Jahres 2003 auf Flughäfen, in Autos und zum Glück auch in Künstlerateliers in diversen Städten der Vereinigten Staaten. Das Reisen gehört für die meisten Kuratoren zum beruflichen Alltag, doch es wird zu einer einzigen Hetzerei, sobald die Termine für die Biennale bedrohlich näher rücken. Der Kraftakt wird, zumindest im Fall des Whitney, zu einem dreizehnmonatigen Rennen in *Warp*-Geschwindigkeit gegen die Uhr (und den Etat), mit dem Ziel, eine Liste von Künstlern vorzulegen, welche die Tendenzen des amerikanischen Kunstschaffens der vergangenen zwei Jahre mehr oder weniger widerspiegelt. Nachdem die Ausstellung glücklich stattgefunden hat und vorbei ist, stelle ich fest, dass eher schleierhaft gebliebene Elemente dieser äusserst komplexen Erfahrung im Rückblick an Deutlichkeit gewinnen. Besonders etwas sticht immer wieder hervor, und das ist, insbesondere bei jüngeren Künstlern, eine offensichtliche Rückbesinnung auf eine politisch engagierte Kunst, die sich weniger didaktisch kritisch oder ironisch als vielmehr in differenzierten rhetorischen und allegorischen Ansätzen mit komplexen Realitäten auseinander setzt. Diese Haltung kommt im Werk zahlreicher an der Biennale vertretener Künstlerinnen und Künstler zum Ausdruck – aber auch bei unzähligen, die nicht dabei waren; besonders repräsentativ für diesen anhaltend quicklebendigen Trend scheinen mir drei ganz unterschiedliche Ausstellungsteilnehmer zu sein, nämlich Harrell Fletcher, Wynne Greenwood (alias *Tracy & the Plastics*) und Christian Holstad. Diese drei scheinen für eine aktuelle, vielseitige künstlerische Praxis zu stehen, die mit wohltuender Aufrichtigkeit neue Möglichkeiten des gesellschaftlichen Engagements, der Stärkung des Einzelnen und einer politischen Veränderung zum Besseren vermitteln.

Die Arbeiten, die der in Oregon lebende Künstler Harrell Fletcher in und ausserhalb von Museen und Galerieräumen inszeniert, nutzen die Kreativität unterschiedlicher Gruppen von Menschen, die sich nicht unbedingt als Künstler verstehen. Durch ganz einfache, auf Partizipation ausgerichtete Strukturen bietet Fletcher gewissen Gruppen von Leuten die Möglichkeit, Werke zu schaffen und auszustellen, wobei durch die Zusammenarbeit gleichzeitig neue Beziehungen gefördert werden. So zeigte Fletcher an der Whitney-Biennale 2004 eine Reihe von Arbeiten, die um eine Art Kiosk herum angeordnet waren. Die erste war ein Videoprojekt, BLOT OUT THE SUN (Die Sonne verdunkeln, 2002), das sich durch Fletchers Bekanntschaft mit einem Tankstellenbesitzer aus seiner Nachbarschaft in Portland ergab. Die beiden machten gemeinsam einen Film aus dem Lieblingsbuch des Tankwarts, James Joyces *Ulysses.* Drehort war die Tankstelle, und Mechaniker wie Kunden lasen ausgewählte Stellen des Romans von Texttafeln ab. Daraus ergab sich eine etwas andere Erzählung, die um Themen wie Tod, Liebe und soziale Ungleichheit kreiste. Eine zweite, darauf Bezug nehmende Videoarbeit mit dem Titel THE PROBLEM OF POSSIBLE REDEMPTION (Das Problem der möglichen Erlösung, 2003) entstand in einem Seniorenzentrum in Hartford im US-Bundesstaat Connecticut. Hier arbeitete Fletcher mit älteren Leuten, welche verschiedene Passagen aus dem Roman von Joyce vorlasen, die Gedanken über Gesellschaft, Krieg und Sterblichkeit enthielten. Beide Arbeiten hatten etwas Bezauberndes und bestachen durch die äusserste Sparsamkeit der Mittel und den ungewöhnlichen Kontrast zwischen Schauplätzen, Protagonisten und inhaltlicher Bandbreite.

Bei zwei weiteren Arbeiten in der Ausstellung spielte ein Stapel Gratiszeitungen zum Mitnehmen eine Rolle; sie

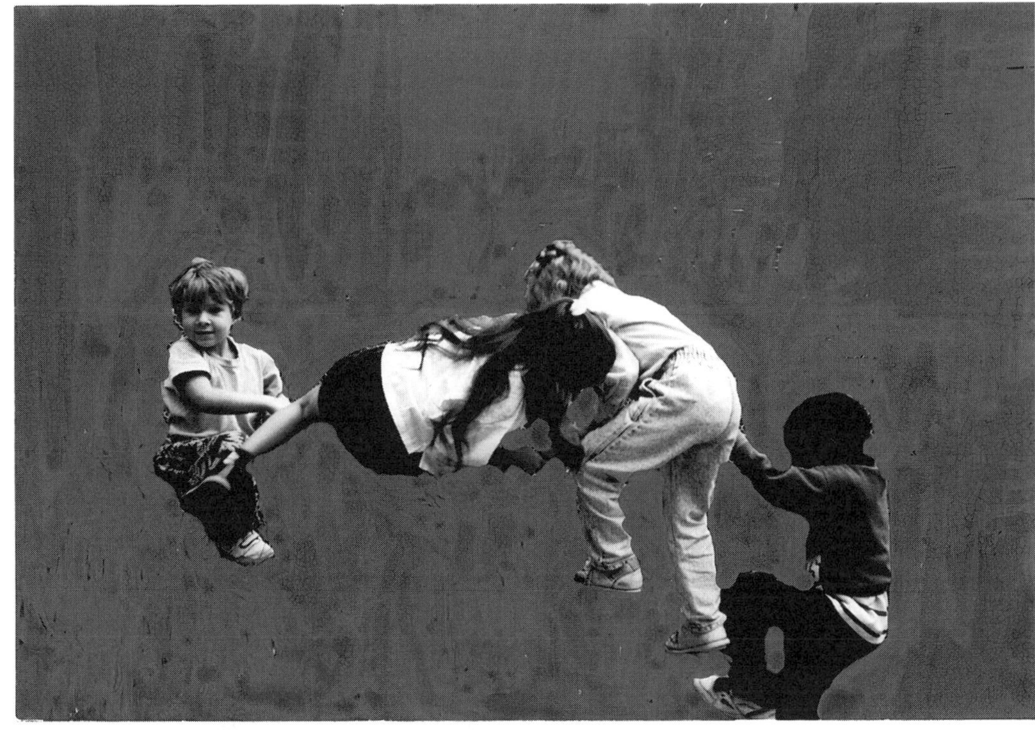

HARRELL FLETCHER, BROWN CHILDREN, 2004, painted found photograph from the exhibition "A Moment of Doubt," Christine Burgin Gallery, New York / gefundene Photographie, bemalt.

waren Teil des Projekts THIS CONTAINER ISN'T BIG ENOUGH (Dieser Behälter ist nicht gross genug, 2004). In der Zeitung waren die künstlerischen Arbeiten von zehn Leuten aus dem ganzen Land beschrieben und illustriert, die Fletcher kennen gelernt hatte. Sie diente gleichzeitig als Stadtplan mit Angaben zu verschiedenen Orten in der ganzen Stadt – von Möbelgeschäften über Cafés bis zu Freizeitzentren –, an denen Fletcher Ausstellungen der beschriebenen Kunstwerke organisiert hatte. Neben den Zeitungen stellte Fletcher sein Gemeinschaftsprojekt mit der Künstlerin Miranda July und dem Designer Yuri Ono vor, LEARNING TO LOVE YOU MORE (Dich noch mehr lieben lernen, seit 2002 laufendes Projekt). Dabei handelt es sich um eine Website, auf der künstlerische Arbeiten eines breiten Publikums vorgestellt werden, die auf ungewöhnliche, kreative Aufgabenstellungen von Fletcher und July hin entstanden sind. Aufgabenstellung und eingegangene Ergebnisse werden auf der Website präsentiert und archiviert, ausserdem werden die Originalarbeiten regelmässig an verschiedenen Orten ausgestellt, wenn sich die Gelegenheit bietet. Die Aufgaben reichen von ganz einfachen Dingen wie: «Mach ein Photo von der Sonne», bis zu komplexeren Unterfangen wie: «Mach eine Tonaufzeichnung eines Chores (egal ob echt oder konstruiert)». Dem Ganzen liegt die Annahme zu Grunde, dass die Aufgaben, die Fletcher und July vergeben, den Leuten die Möglichkeit bieten, die häufig bestehende Schwellenangst davor, eine eigene Idee zu entwickeln, auszuschalten. Das Projekt, das sich durch eine ungewöhnliche Verbindung von *Hightech*- und *Lowtech*-Mitteln auszeichnet, nutzt das Potenzial des Internets, neue Formen einer virtuellen Gemeinschaft zu schaffen, parallel zur ganz praktischen künstlerischen Handarbeit. Das vielleicht Erfrischendste an diesem laufenden Gemeinschaftsprojekt ist die begeisterte Teilnahme zahlloser Leute aus aller Welt.

Wie bei Fletchers übrigen Projekten geht es auch bei LEARNING TO LOVE YOU MORE vor allem um das Miteinbeziehen möglichst vieler Leute über einen *Do-it-yourself*-Ansatz. Dabei entstehen unerwartete Beziehungen zwischen Leuten, die sonst nicht das Geringste miteinander zu tun haben. Während Fletchers Kunst im Prinzip an die Tradition der sozialen Plastik von Beuys anknüpft und an Gemeinschaftsprojekte erinnert, wie sie vor allem in den 70er Jahren beliebt waren, besteht das Besondere seiner Arbeit nicht zuletzt darin, dass sie die nötige Flexibilität bewahrt, um immer wieder eindrucksvolle, situationsbezogene Projekte hervorzubringen, die dank auffallend einfacher und alltäglicher Mittel in ganz unterschiedlichen Kontexten funktionieren.

In vielerlei Hinsicht bilden Gemeinschaftlichkeit und sozialer Austausch durch Publikumsbeteiligung auch ein zentrales Moment der Arbeit einer ganz anderen Biennale-Künstlerin, Wynne Greenwood. In ihrem laufenden Projekt, *Tracy & the Plastics,* geht es um eine feministisch-lesbische Art-Punk-Band gleichen Namens, in der sie selbst den Part aller drei Bandmitglieder übernimmt. Greenwood steht als Tracy live auf der Bühne und tritt gleichzeitig in Form vorher aufgezeichneter Videoprojektionen als Nikki und Cola auf. Bis vor kurzem traten *Tracy & the Plastics* überwiegend in Nachtklubs und an Underground-Musikveranstaltungen im ganzen Land auf. Die Auftritte sind häufig als «Proben» getarnt, was eine ungezwungene Atmosphäre erzeugt und zugleich den Vorwand liefert für die ständigen Diskussionen zwischen Tracy und ihren Partnerinnen auf der Projektionswand hinter ihr. Im Lauf der Show ergeben sich immer wieder Unterbrechungen zwischen den Songs – oder auch mitten drin –, während derer sich das Trio zu allen möglichen Themen äussert, die trotz aller verspielten Komik durchaus auf ernste Anliegen Bezug nehmen: etwa wenn Nikki sich darüber beschwert, dass der Name der Band ihrer Ansicht nach die «traditionelle Hierarchie der Rockband» aufrechterhalte, oder wenn sie erklärt, wie «man Dinge wie eine Lesbe tut», Tee trinken, zum Beispiel, oder ein Baby im Arm halten.

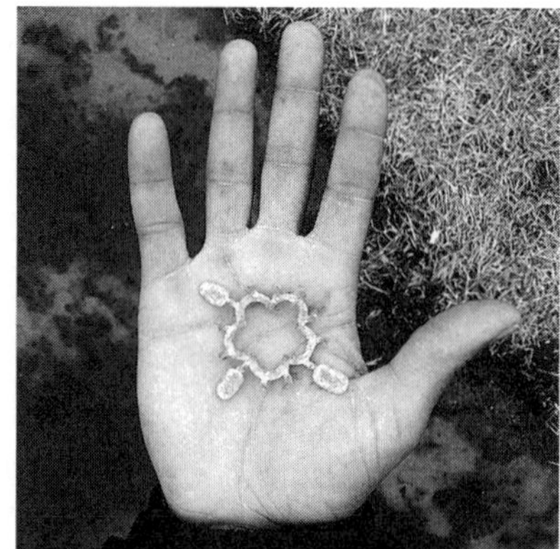
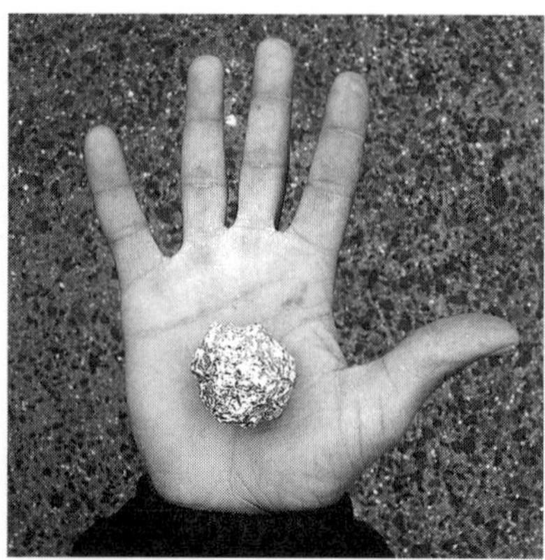
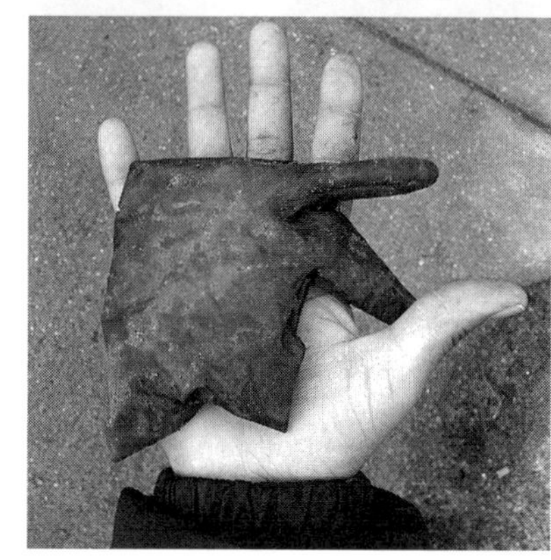
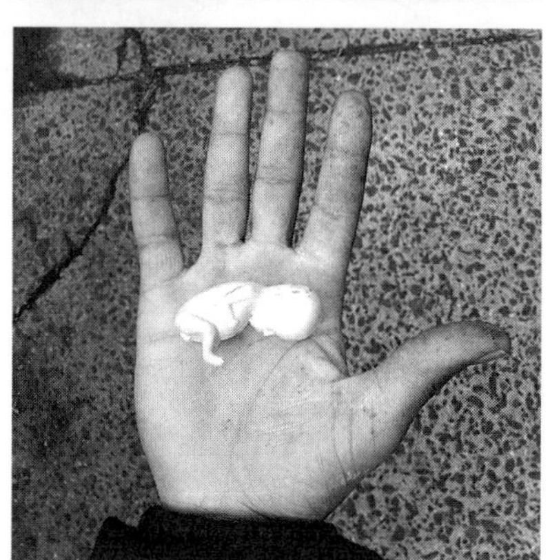

HARRELL FLETCHER, SOCRATES, 2004, stills from the video "Hello There Friend (Queens, New York)" with Raymond Denson / Videostills.

Solche absichtlichen «Pausen» und «technischen Probleme» bilden quasi Synapsen im Ablauf des Abends und geben Tracy die ungewöhnliche Möglichkeit, sich unmittelbar ans Publikum zu wenden und buchstäblich Platz zu schaffen für dessen Reaktionen und Teilnahme an ihrer Welt.

Kürzlich inszenierten *Tracy & the Plastics* in The Kitchen, New York, ihre erste Installation und abendfüllende Performance mit dem Titel ROOM (2005). Sie entstand unter Mitwirkung der Bildhauerin Fawn Krieger. Die Installation bestand aus einer Art «utopischem Wohnzimmer» aus billigem Spannteppich, Holz und Schaumstoff, das in gewisser Weise die *Lowtech*-Ästhetik der Videoprojektion widerspiegelte. Die Band trat in dieser Szenerie auf, die so beschaffen war, dass Musikerinnen und Publikum sich physisch im selben Raum aufhielten, aber gleichzeitig an die Art von Räumen erinnern sollte, in denen seit den 70er Jahren feministische Bewusstseinsbildungstreffen stattfanden. Das Projekt zeigte beispielhaft, wie Greenwood eine eigenwillige Post-*Seattle Slacker-* und Post-*Riot Grrrl*-Sensibilität mit einer in der Schwulen- und Punkbewegung wurzelnden politischen Grundhaltung und einer überraschenden Dosis popmusikalischer Virtuosität zu einer überaus fesselnden Erkundung von Dingen wie Sexualität, Gruppenzugehörigkeit, Gemeinschaft und Heimat zu verbinden weiss.

Mit einer ganz anderen Art von Kunst, in der das Handwerk jedoch ebenfalls eine Rolle spielt, wartet Christian Holstad auf. Er verwendet ästhetische Phänomene, die in den 60er Jahren populär waren, wie Psychedelik, Kitsch und *Camp*, sowie den *Glam*-Rock und verschiedene Disco-Stile der 70er Jahre, um aus unzähligen, ganz unterschiedlichen handgefertigten Objekten, Zeichnungen und Collagen verschwenderisch lebhafte Installationen zu schaffen. Holstads stark durch die Filme und Performances von Jack Smith beeinflussten Arbeiten sind vielfach leuchtende Denkmäler für bestimmte Personen oder erfundene Figuren, die aus wunderbar kompliziert gemusterten, handgenähten Quilts und weichen plastischen Elementen sowie Zeichnungen auf Zeitungspapier, pornographischen Collagen, Ballonen aus Papiermaché und verfremdeten *objets trouvés* bestehen.

Seine Installation im Whitney-Museum bestand zum Beispiel aus drei verschiedenen Arbeiten, die zusammen eine phantastische Toten-Mahnwache darstellten. Im Zentrum stand ein Lagerfeuer mit gesteppten Stoffscheiten und gehäkelten Flammen sowie ein «Begräbnis-Blumenkorb» im Stil der 30er Jahre, der hauptsächlich aus rezyklierten Rollschuhen und einer frivolen Garnitur aus symmetrisch angeordneten testikelähnlichen Formen bestand. Des Weiteren gehörten ein mit Venusfliegenfallen geschmückter Trauerkranz aus Wollfilz, Herrenunterwäsche aus Leder und absurd lange, rot-weiss-blaue Draperien aus Metallfolie dazu. Holstads Arbeit hatte mit ihrer – für den *Camp*-Stil typischen – Vereinigung von Gegensätzen paradoxerweise auch etwas Elegisches, da die Szenerie gleichzeitig eine gewisse Sentimentalität und eine Sehnsucht nach den verflossenen «Tagen des Disco», einer liberaleren Zeit der Befreiung, ausstrahlte. Die detailgenaue Theatralik der Installation war wohl eine Parodie auf überzogene Patriotismusbekundungen in jüngster Zeit, gleichzeitig aber auch ein feierliches Bekenntnis zur schwulen Sexualität, das laut Holstad auch als Würdigung des «rebellischen Geistes an allen Orten» zu verstehen sei.

Innerhalb eines breiten Spektrums repräsentieren Fletcher, Greenwood und Holstad unterschiedliche Facetten eines verbreiteten Trends unter jüngeren Künstlerinnen und Künstlern oder Künstlerkollektiven in New York und anderswo, die im Bemühen, neue Möglichkeiten zur gesellschaftlichen Veränderung zu eröffnen, dem ernsthaften, hoffnungsvollen gesellschaftlichen Engagement den Vorzug geben vor einer konfrontativen Protesthaltung. Ihre politische Einstellung ist quasi lyrisch, reich an grosszügigen Gesten und zutiefst optimistisch. In der heutigen Welt, in der Angst, Vorurteile und Gewalt allgegenwärtig sind, ist diese Haltung ohne Zweifel begrüssenswert und auf produktive Art erholsam.

(Übersetzung: Bram Opstelten)

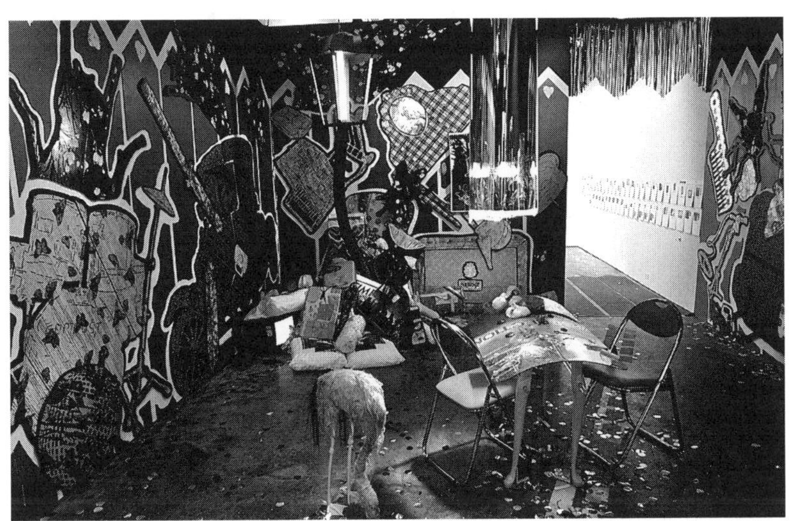

CHRISTIAN HOLSTAD, FEAR GIVES COURAGE WINGS, 2003, mixed media installation / ANGST VERLEIHT DEM MUT FLÜGEL. (PHOTO: DANIEL REICH GALLERY, NEW YORK)

CUMULUS

Aus Europa

IN JEDER AUSGABE VON PARKETT PEILT EINE CUMULUS-WOLKE AUS AMERIKA UND EINE AUS EUROPA DIE INTERESSIERTEN KUNSTFREUNDE AN. SIE TRÄGT PERSÖNLICHE RÜCKBLICKE, BEURTEILUNGEN UND DENKWÜRDIGE BEGEGNUNGEN MIT SICH – ALS JEWEILS GANZ EIGENE DARSTELLUNG EINER BERUFLICHEN AUSEINANDERSETZUNG.

IN DIESEM BAND ÄUSSERN SICH NATAŠA PETREŠIN, FREIE KURATORIN UND PUBLIZISTIN AUS LJUBLJANA, UND DEBRA SINGER, LEITERIN UND CHEFKURATORIN VON THE KITCHEN IN NEW YORK, VORMALS ASSOCIATE CURATOR AM WHITNEY MUSEUM OF AMERICAN ART.

WHAT TO DO WITH ALTERNATIVE/ ARTISTIC KNOWLEDGE?

NATAŠA PETREŠIN

The public relations bureaucracy's manipulative system of mediating the quasi-scientific facts and discoveries made by artistic research has become a necessary field to revisit within the discourse of contemporary art—especially after the notorious and ongoing case of Steve Kurtz' trial due to happen this year. Steve Kurtz—artist, activist, and founding member of Critical Art Ensemble—faces charges of mail and wire fraud for acquiring a harmless bacteria for one of the collective's artistic projects. Considering the right wing vertigo sweeping the EU and the US, empowered by neoconservative views about creativity, one cannot deny that art's position has once again been challenged, or changed.

If we are to question the role of the artist within the field of art, we should bear in mind a latter-day utopian desire to extend aesthetics into the outer world to provoke feedback and interaction. The echo of Beuys' visionary understanding of creativity can still be heard, and is very important in dealing with creativity as a right to expression that applies not only to the privileged artist but to everyone. Since Beuys, a notion of the artist as mediator or nomad, moving between different competencies has emerged, introducing the possibility for audience participation. Brian Holmes links this to the "alternative information ex-

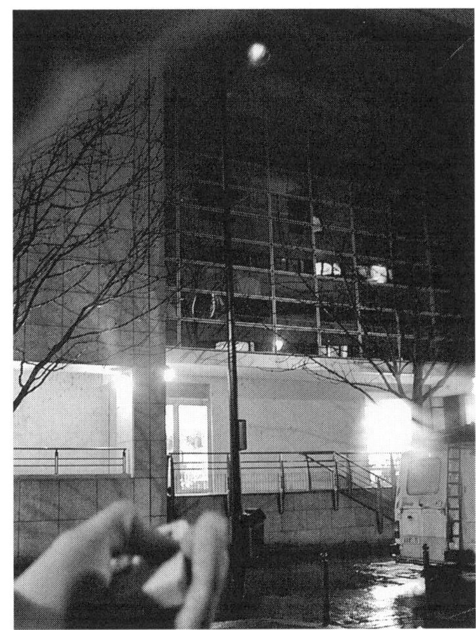

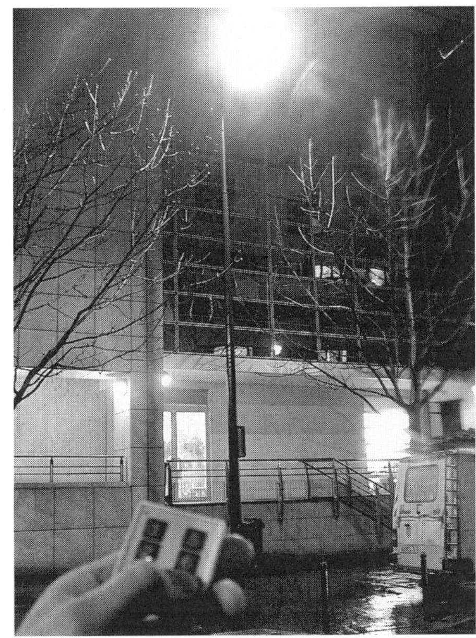

LEOPOLD KESSLER, PRIVATISIERT/PARIS, 2003, 3 Min.-20 Sek.-DVD / PRIVATIZED/PARIS, 3 min. 20 sec. DVD.

change, both semiotic and material ...," or to the "democratic debate about the exchange of ideas."[1] Alternative forms of journalism (also known as "citizen journalism"), scientific and scholarly knowledge, and the free software movement (its sharing of files, codes, and ideas) are all examples of an artistic striving for expression, ethics, and tolerant communication.

Reflecting on an artist's competency, and the notion of the artist as a public amateur discloses an interest in the tension between the potentiality and actuality of an act or a gesture, with particular focus on what potentiality carries within itself, and why we think of artists and art practices as potential agents of a change. Giorgio Agamben refers to Aristotle, and his understanding of all of the potential to be or to do something, as always being the potential to not-be or to not do something, without which potentiality would always already have passed into actuality and would be indistinguishable from it. This "potential not-to" is the cardinal secret of the Aristotelian doctrine of potentiality, which transforms every potentiality, in itself, into an impotentiality.[2] We can thus see artists as ethical figures who experience their own potentiality (of being their own possibility), and who further challenge the "evil that consists in the decision to remain in a deficit of existence, to appropriate the power to not-be as a substance and a foundation beyond existence; or to regard potentiality itself, which is the most proper mode of human existence, as a fault that must always be repressed."[3]

Consciously playing with the potentiality and functionality of an artistic (physical) work, German artist Leopold Kessler repairs, or reconfigures, public property. His interventions occur in hyper-regulated public space, which lacks a concrete renewal of obsolete or damaged objects, and which Kessler repairs or transforms. Subway signs, warning slogans on the banks of a river, or sign boards are made visible, changed, and repaired. Public lights get connected to a remote control by night and can be switched on and off according to the artist's specification—this switch is then, subsequently, transferred to the spectators, allowing them to play with the lights. With these gestures, Kessler sets the stage "for a discreet revolution against public authorities. In this way, he questions what he considers to be enforced limitations masquerading as protective measures for the citizenry."[4] Whenever he performs an action, Kessler wears a blue coat, symbolic of a repairman, and with some technical and mechanical ability, he solemnly operates in a field of appropriated and amateur knowledge.

Jakup Ferri, a young artist from Kosova, uses himself as the main protagonist of his videos, in which he establishes ironic distance from the issues of identity, history (cultural and family), and the role of the peripherally located artist. Ferri is extremely aware of how the visibility and invisibility of certain artistic practices and positions are produced, and how the breakthrough to the international scene is economically and politically defined by the centers of power. He and other artists from Eastern Europe or the Third World try to counteract the notion, imposed on them by the Western gaze, of having arrived late to all the art trends that the Western world established. In his video, THREE VIRGINS (2003), the artist screams his own name repeatedly over a recording of a performance by John Lennon and Yoko Ono, where they both continuously call each other's names. Thus he tries to surmount the impossibility (due to time lapse, but also contextual and geopolitical limits) of having been, at a crucial moment, at the place of the seminal happening. Another video, AN ARTIST WHO CANNOT SPEAK ENGLISH IS NO ARTIST (2003), is an homage to a 1992 work with the same title by the cult Croatian conceptualist Mladen Stilinović. Ferri, who in real life is not able to speak English, speaks broken English without pause for several minutes, thus creating a hilarious situation that slowly turns into introspective criticism when one realizes, burdened by Balkanism's discourse, the nature of this laughter-provoking problem.

The alternative knowledge produced by artists in the role of public amateurs also comes to us through the collaborative and participatory nature of the works themselves, or via the distribution oriented to new community nodes such as the Internet, chat rooms, public domains, and mailing lists. Pierre Lévy, in his essays on collective intelligence, has described the potential for reciprocal engagement between the

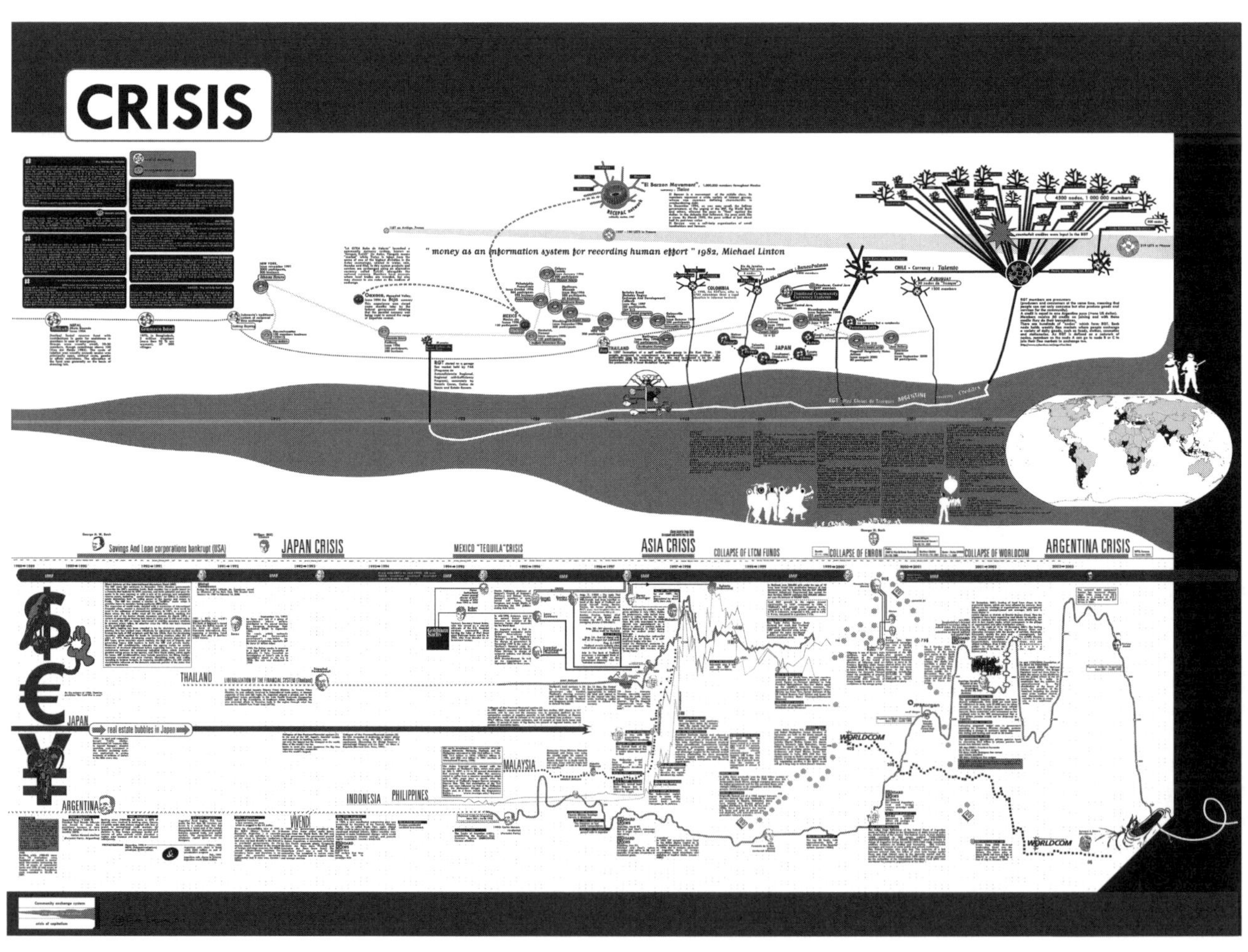

BUREAU D'ÉTUDES, CRISIS, 2004.

global audience and the artist: "Rather than distribute a message to recipients who are outside the process of creation and invited to give meaning to a work of art belatedly, the artist now attempts to construct an environment, a system of communication and production, a collective event that implies its recipients, transforms interpreters into actors, enables interpretation to enter the loop with collective action."[5]

Founded in 1998, the Paris-based Bureau d'études is an artist duo that promotes yet another level of artistic amateurism, one of researcher of world governance relations. Bureau d'études concentrates on mapping various issues of world governance (that is, networks of data-gathering systems, and bio war or global resistance movements) and addresses the notion of autonomous knowledge: "The being who brings autonomous knowledge and power into play is a potential being. S/he is not just there, frozen in a role or trained to seek or desire a particular, normalized possibility, or to choose among such possibilities. Her/his possibilities are not commodity-possibilities, controlled or rationalized by the capitalist system, but real chances, possible destinies brought into play by the activity of being."[6] Bureau d'études develops pictographic installations that visualize the distribution of power, in its various forms, on a global basis and show the interrelations between the different actors involved.

A different kind of mapping characterizes the work of EAST ART MAP (since 2003)—an ongoing research project by the Slovenian five-member artist group, Irwin. Following a so-called "retro principle" to utilize and combine different motifs, symbols, and signs from the fields of politics and art, they aim to transform historical meaning and content, and re-contextualize and deconstruct their related ideologies. Through EAST ART MAP (EAM), Irwin aims to critically (re)construct the history of art in Eastern Europe (from 1945 to the present) in an effort to transgress closed systems of interpretation and evaluation. Two hundred and fifty artists/events/projects, considered of major importance by twenty-four invited art critics, curators, and artists, have been identified so far. Most interestingly, EAM invites the public to provide data that might be likely to change the topography of the map that it is formulating. In this way, it is EAM's hope to accelerate the collection of data and democratize its organization.[7]

Yet another ongoing project that deals with democracy and governmentality was conceived and organized by the Finnish new-media artist Juha Huuskonen. PLAN *B FOR ARKADIANMÄKI (2005)[8] presents itself as an alternative Parliament that offers opportunities for citizens to voice their opinions and to experience the potential for governing. Several referenda (on sovereign microstates, forms of government, and non-objective media) and lectures aim to foster more online, as well as off-line, opinion sharing between Finnish and international audiences.

What is one to do with the knowledge that is mediated through these and many other artistic projects when today's politically and socially aware artists seem to only desire visibility, affect, and mobilization? They intend to adress responsibility in an economically and socially interdependent world. Globalized phenomena—like privacy/surveillance, intellectual property/copyleft, access/non-connectedness, and freedom of information/manipulation—are becoming concerns with which new media and contemporary artists are engaged; with it, they are obviously becoming of interest to policy makers, politicians, and lay citizens. Referring to Kurtz' case, Beatriz da Costa, the collective's long-term collaborator, gives us a clear answer: "Could CAE's work be perceived as a serious threat to an authoritarian capitalist system, which relies on public ignorance and knowledge distribution through controlled channels like the one reigning the US at this point in time? It could indeed."[9]

1) Brian Holmes, "Three Proposals for a Real Democracy. Information Sharing to a Different Tune," 2004, http://multitudes.samizdat.net/article.php3?id_article=1558.
2) Giorgio Agamben, *Potentialities: Collected Essays in Philosophy,* ed. and trans. by Daniel Heller-Roazen (Stanford: Stanford University Press, 2000).
3) Giorgio Agamben, *The Coming Community* (*Theory Out of Bounds,* vol. 1), trans. by Michael Hardt (Minneapolis: University of Minnesota Press, 2001), p. 45.
4) Leopold Kessler in *Manifesta 5* newspaper, ed. by Marta Kuzma, Massimiliano Gioni (San Sebastián, 2004), p. 17.
5) Pierre Lévy, *Collective Intelligence* (Paris: Editions La Découverte, 1997), p. 123, http://www.collectiveintelligence.info
6) Bureau d'études, "Autonomous Knowledge and Power," 2002, http://utangente.free.fr/anewpages/holmes.html
7) EAST ART MAP (EAM) (http://www.eastartmap.org) invites anyone to propose additions or modifications to any project or artwork included within EAM. Submitted proposals will be evaluated by a committee of six experts every two or three months.
8) For more information and documentation see http://www.publicopinion.fi
9) Beatriz da Costa, "Amateur Science, A Threat After All?," *Divanik, Conversations and Interviews About Media Art, Culture and Society* (Novi Sad: Kuda.org, 2004), appendix, p. 3.

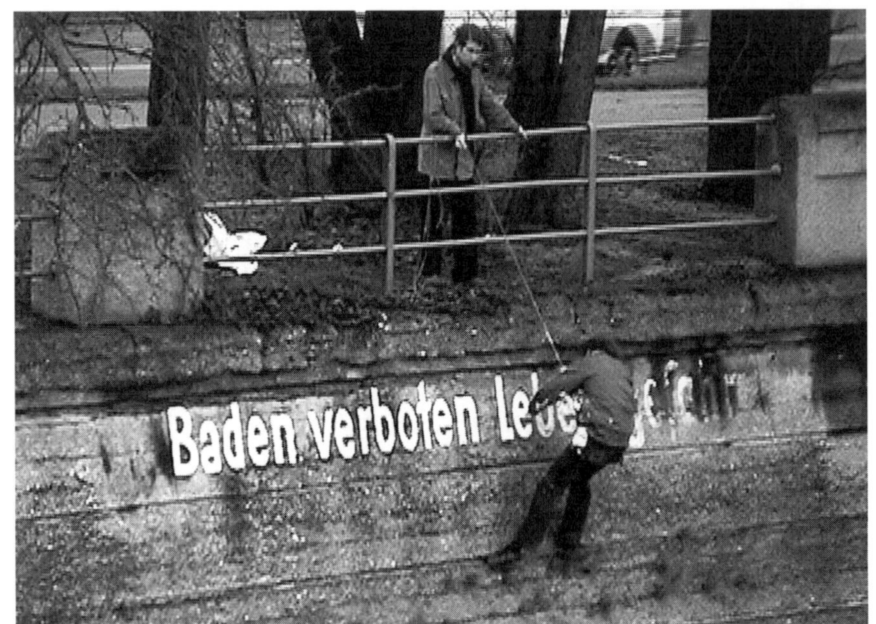

LEOPOLD KESSLER, BADEN VERBOTEN, 2003, 2 Min.-28 Sek.-DVD / NO SWIMMING, 2 min. 28 sec. DVD.

WAS TUN
MIT DEM ALTERNATIVEN WISSEN DER KUNST?

NATAŠA PETREŠIN

Das manipulative Instrumentarium, das die Public-Relations-Bürokratie zur Vermittlung von quasi-wissenschaftlichen Fakten und Resultaten aus dem künstlerischen Forschungsbereich verwendet, muss im Rahmen des zeitgenössischen Kunstdiskurses unbedingt noch einmal genauer unter die Lupe genommen werden – vor allem nach dem berüchtigten Fall von Steve Kurtz, der dieses Jahr vor Gericht verhandelt wird. Steve Kurtz – Künstler, Aktivist und Gründungsmitglied des *Critical Art Ensemble* – steht unter Anklage, weil er für eines der Projekte dieser Gruppe ein harmloses Bakterium erworben hat. Angesichts des kalten Windes von rechts, der derzeit durch Europa und die Vereinigten Staaten fegt, kräftig angefacht von neokonservativen Ansichten über Kreativität, lässt sich nicht bestreiten, dass die Stellung der Kunst erneut angefochten ist oder sich jedenfalls verändert hat.

Wenn die Rolle des Künstlers im Kunstbereich wiederum in Frage gestellt werden soll, so müssen wir den damit verbundenen utopischen Wunsch im Auge behalten, die Ästhetik in eine breitere Öffentlichkeit hineinzutragen, um Feedbacks und Reaktionen zu erhalten. Beuys' visionäres Kreativitätsverständnis liegt noch in der Luft und ist nach wie vor von grosser Bedeutung, wenn wir Kreativität als ein Recht des Ausdrucks für jedermann begreifen wollen und nicht nur als Vorrecht des Künstlers. Seit Beuys wird der Künstler zunehmend als Vermittler oder Nomade begriffen, der sich zwischen verschiedenen Kompetenzen hin und her bewegt, woraus sich auch die Möglichkeit zur Mitwirkung des Publikums ergibt. Brian Holmes bringt dies mit dem «alternativen Informationsaustausch, semiotischer und materieller Art» oder mit der «demokratischen Diskussion über den Ideenaustausch» in Verbindung.[1] Alternative Formen des Journalismus (auch «Bürger-Journalismus» genannt), des wissenschaftlichen und akademischen Wissens, aber auch die *Free Software*-Bewegung (das gemeinsame Nutzen von Dateien, Codes und Ideen) sind Beispiele für ein künstlerisches Bemühen um Ausdruck, ethisches Verhalten und tolerante Kommunikation.

Denken wir über die Fähigkeiten eines Künstlers nach, so verrät der Begriff des Künstlers als öffentlich auftretender Dilettant ein Interesse am Spannungsfeld zwischen Potenzialität und Aktualität einer Handlung oder Geste, insbesondere daran, was diese Potenzialität in sich birgt und warum wir Künstler und künstlerische Tätigkeiten als potenzielle Motoren der Veränderung betrachten. Giorgio Agamben verweist auf Aristoteles und dessen Lehre, dass die Möglichkeit, etwas zu sein oder zu tun, stets auch die Möglichkeit beinhaltet, etwas n i c h t zu sein oder n i c h t zu tun. Andernfalls wäre die Potenz immer schon Akt geworden und wäre daher von diesem nicht zu unterscheiden. Diese «Potenz-nicht-zu» ist das grundlegende Geheimnis der aristotelischen Lehre von der Potenz, das jedes Vermögen an sich in ein Unvermögen verwandelt.[2] Also können Künstler als ethische Figuren betrachtet werden, die ihre eigene Potenz erfahren (ihre eigene Möglichkeit zu sein) und ausserdem dem «Bösen» die Stirn bieten, «das einzig in der Entscheidung [besteht], in der Schuld der Existenz zu verbleiben, sich die Potenz-nicht-zu-sein als eine Substanz oder einen Grund jenseits der Existenz anzueignen, oder gar (und das ist das Schicksal der Moral) die Potenz, also den eigentlichsten Modus der menschlichen Existenz, als ein Verschulden zu betrachten, das es um jeden Preis zu unterdrücken gilt».[3]

Ganz bewusst mit Potenz und Funktion eines (physischen) Kunstwerks spielend, beschäftigt sich der deutsche Künstler Leopold Kessler damit, öffentliches Eigentum zu reparieren oder umzugestalten. Seine Interventionen finden im überregulierten öffentlichen Raum statt, in dem die konkrete Erneuerung überholter oder beschädigter Gegenstände gewöhnlich ausbleibt, bis Kessler eingreift und sie wieder instand setzt oder transformiert. U-Bahn-Symbole, warnende Hinweise am Flussufer oder Reklameschilder werden sichtbar gemacht, verändert und repariert. Strassenlaternen werden nachts mit einer Fernsteuerung versehen und können nach den Vorgaben des Künstlers ein- und ausgeschaltet werden – später überlässt er die Fernsteuerung dem Publikum, so dass es damit spielen kann. Mit diesen Gesten schafft Kessler «die Voraussetzungen für eine unauffällige Rebellion gegen öffentliche Instanzen. Auf diesem Weg stellt er die starken Einschränkungen in Frage, die seiner Ansicht nach den Bürgern unter dem Deckmantel von Schutzmassnahmen auferlegt werden.»[4] Bei seinen Aktionen trägt Kessler stets einen blauen Kittel, das typische Kennzeichen des Handwerkers, und betätigt sich feierlich, mit beachtlichem technischem

LEOPOLD KESSLER, REPARATUR, 2001–2002, 2 Min.-7 Sek.-DVD / REPAIRS 2 min. 7 sec. DVD.

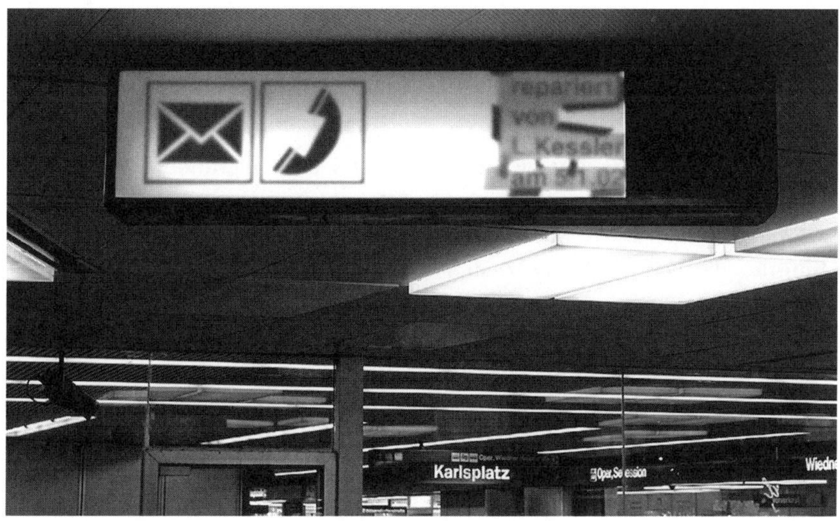

und mechanischem Geschick in einem Sachgebiet, mit dem er sich als Amateur vertraut gemacht hat.

Jakup Ferri, ein junger Künstler aus dem Kosovo, mimt in seinen Videos selbst den Hauptdarsteller. Er schafft darin eine ironische Distanz zu Themen wie Identität und Geschichte (kultureller und familiärer Art) und zur Rolle des Künstlers, der in einem kulturellen Randgebiet zuhause ist. Ferri weiss sehr genau, womit die Sichtbarkeit oder Unsichtbarkeit bestimmter künstlerischer Techniken und Positionen zusammenhängt und dass der internationale Erfolg von den wirtschaftlichen und politischen Machtzentren aus bestimmt wird. Er und andere Kunstschaffende aus Osteuropa und der Dritten Welt versuchen sich gegen die im Westen verbreitete Vorstellung zu wehren, dass sie sich mit Verspätung den etablierten Kunstrichtungen der westlichen Welt anschliessen. In seiner Videoarbeit THREE VIRGINS (Drei Jungfrauen, 2003) schreit der Künstler wiederholt seinen Namen über die Aufnahme einer Performance von John Lennon und Yoko Ono, in der beide unentwegt den Namen des jeweils anderen rufen. So versucht er die Tatsache zu überwinden, dass er (aus zeitlichen, aber auch kontextuellen und geopolitischen Gründen) im entscheidenden Moment unmöglich am Ort des Geschehens sein konnte. Ein anderes Video, AN ARTIST WHO CANNOT SPEAK ENGLISH IS NO ARTIST (Ein Künstler, der kein Englisch spricht, ist kein Künstler, 2003), ist eine Reverenz an das 1992 entstandene, gleichnamige Werk des kroatischen Kult-Konzeptkünstlers Mladen Stilinović. Ferri, der im richtigen Leben des Englischen nicht mächtig ist, radebrecht pausenlos mehrere Minuten lang auf Englisch. Dabei entsteht eine zum Schreien komische Situation, die langsam in eine nachdenkliche Selbstkritik übergeht, sobald man sich – die Balkanismus-Diskussion im Hinterkopf – bewusst wird, welcher Art das Problem eigentlich ist, das uns so zum Lachen bringt.

Das alternative Wissen, das von Künstlern in der Rolle öffentlich auftretender Dilettanten produziert wird, erreicht uns auch über die Kunstwerke selbst, da sie auf Zusammenarbeit und Mitwirkung ausgerichtet sind, oder aber durch deren Verbreitung über die Kanäle einer neuen Öffentlichkeit, wie Internet, Chatrooms, Public Domains und Mailing-Listen. Pierre Lévy beschreibt in seinen Aufsätzen zur kollektiven Intelligenz das Potenzial für den gegenseitigen Austausch zwischen einem globalen Publikum und dem Künstler wie folgt: «Statt eine Botschaft an einen Empfänger zu senden, der ausserhalb des kreativen Prozesses steht und dem Werk im Nachhinein Sinn verleiht, versucht der Künstler nun, eine Umgebung und Struktur für Kommunikation und Produktion zu schaffen, ein den Empfänger mit einschliessendes kollektives Ereignis, das den Hermeneuten zum Handelnden macht und Interpretation und kollektive Aktion in einer Schleife verbindet.» [5)]

Das 1998 gegründete *Bureau d'études* in Paris ist ein Künstlerduo, das den künstlerischen Dilettantismus auf einer anderen Stufe propagiert, nämlich zur Erforschung globaler Machtstrukturen. Das *Bureau d'études* konzentriert sich darauf, verschiedene Aspekte der Globalisierung (etwa die Vernetzung von Datensystemen und Widerstandsbewegungen gegen biologische Waffen oder die Globalisierung) zu kartographieren, und befasst sich mit der Idee des unabhängigen Wissens: «Ein Mensch, der sich auf unabhängiges Wissen und unabhängige Macht beruft, stellt ein Potenzial dar. So jemand steht nicht einfach da, in einer Rolle gefangen oder darauf konditioniert, eine bestimmte, genormte Möglichkeit zu suchen oder zu begehren, oder sich zwischen solchen Möglichkeiten zu entscheiden. Die Möglichkeiten solcher Menschen haben nicht einfach Warencharakter und können nicht durch das kapitalistische System kontrolliert oder rationalisiert werden, sondern es sind echte Chancen, mögliche Schicksale, die durch die Aktivität des Seins ins Spiel gebracht werden.» [6)] Das *Bureau d'études* entwickelt piktographische Installationen, welche die verschiedenen Formen der weltweiten Machtverteilung sichtbar machen und die Wechselbeziehungen zwischen den beteiligten Akteuren aufzeigen.

Eine andere Art der Kartographie findet sich in EAST ART MAP (seit 2003), einem laufenden Forschungsprojekt der fünfköpfigen slowenischen Künstlergruppe Irwin. Unter Berufung auf ein so genanntes «Retroprinzip» verwenden und kombinieren diese Künstler Motive, Symbole und Zeichen aus dem Bereich von Politik und Kunst, mit dem Ziel, historische Bedeutungen und Inhalte umzuwandeln und die damit verbundenen Ideologien in veränderten Kontexten zu sehen und zu dekonstruieren. Mit EAST ART MAP bezweckt Irwin eine kritische (Re-)Konstruktion der osteuropäischen Kunstgeschichte (von 1945 bis heute) und versucht geschlossene Interpretations- und Bewertungssysteme zu überwinden. Im Vorfeld wurden 250 Künstler, Events oder Projekte ausgewählt, die von vierundzwanzig eingeladenen Kunst-

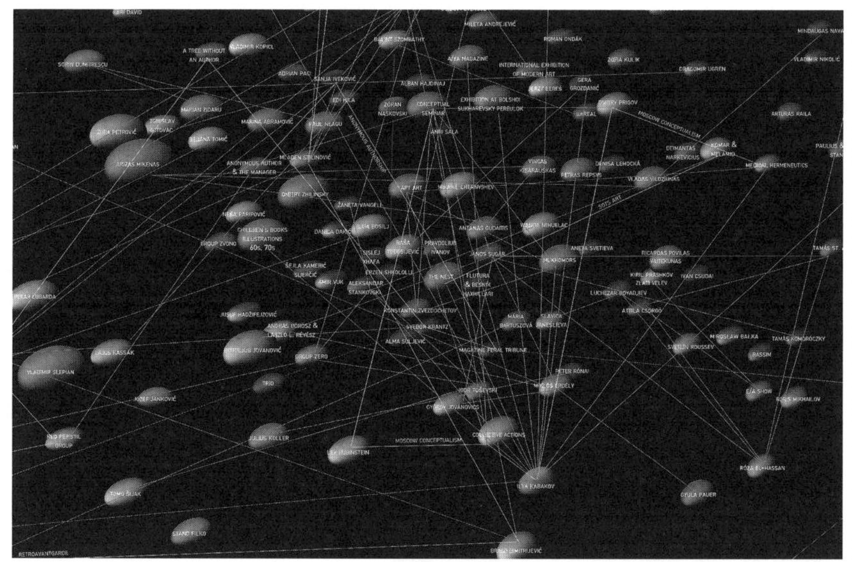

IRWIN, EAST ART MAP, A (RE)CONSTRUCTION OF THE HISTORY OF CONTEMPORARY ART IN EASTERN EUROPE, detail, ongoing project / EAST ART MAP, EINE (RE)KONSTRUKTION DER GESCHICHTE DER ZEITGENÖSSISCHEN KUNST IN OSTEUROPA, laufendes Projekt.

kritikern, Kuratoren und Künstlern als bedeutend eingestuft worden waren. Interessanterweise fordert EAST ART MAP die Öffentlichkeit auf, insbesondere Fakten zu liefern, welche die Topographie der entstehenden Karte verändern dürften. EAST ART MAP hofft auf diese Weise die Datensammlung zu beschleunigen und deren Organisation zu demokratisieren.[7)]

Ein weiteres laufendes Projekt zum Thema Demokratie und Regierung wurde vom finnischen Künstler Juha Huuskonen entwickelt und organisiert. Er arbeitet mit Neuen Medien: PLAN *B FOR ARKADIANMÄKI (2005)[8)] stellt sich als alternatives Parlament dar, das Bürgerinnen und Bürgern Gelegenheit bietet, ihre Meinung zu äussern und ihr eigenes Herrschaftspotenzial zu erfahren. Verschiedene Referenden (über souveräne Mikrostaaten, Regierungsformen und Parteimedien) sowie Vorträge sollen den Meinungsaustausch zwischen finnischem und internationalem Publikum fördern, und zwar sowohl on- wie offline.

Doch was soll dieses Wissen, das in solchen und anderen Kunstprojekten vermittelt wird, solange die heute politisch und gesellschaftlich engagierten Künstler ja anscheinend nur Transparenz, Betroffenheit und eine gewisse Mobilisierung erreichen wollen? Es geht ihnen darum, das Verantwortungsgefühl in einer Welt gegenseitiger wirtschaftlicher und sozialer Abhängigkeiten zu erhöhen. Neue Medien und zeitgenössische Künstler befassen sich immer häufiger mit globalen Phänomenen – Privatsphäre versus Überwachung; Urheberrecht versus Verzicht darauf; Zugang versus Nichtangeschlossensein; Informationsfreiheit versus Manipulation etcetera – Phänomene, die offensichtlich auch für Entscheidungsträger, Politiker und Normalbürger zunehmend von Interesse sind. Beatriz da Costa, langjähriges Mitglied des *Critical Art Ensemble*, gibt uns im Zusammenhang mit dem Fall Kurtz eine klare Antwort: «Könnte die Arbeit des CAE als ernsthafte Bedrohung für ein autoritäres kapitalistisches Regierungssystem aufgefasst werden, das auf der Ahnungslosigkeit der Bürger und der Kontrolle über alle wichtigen Informationskanäle beruht? Ein System also, wie es gegenwärtig in den USA herrscht? Allerdings.»[9)]

(Übersetzung: Irene Aeberli)

1) Brian Holmes, «Three Proposals for a Real Democracy. Information Sharing to a Different Tune», 2004, http://multitudes.samizdat.net/article.php3?id_article=1558
2) Vgl. Giorgio Agamben, *Potentialities: Collected Essays in Philosophy,* hg. und übers. v. Daniel Heller-Roazen, Stanford University Press, Stanford 2000.
3) Giorgio Agamben, *Die kommende Gemeinschaft,* Kap. 11: «Ethik», Merve Verlag, Berlin 2003, S. 45.
4) Leopold Kessler, in: *Manifesta 5 Newspaper,* hg. v. Marta Kuzma und Massimiliano Gioni, San Sebastián 2004, S. 17.
5) Pierre Lévy, *Die kollektive Intelligenz,* Bollman Verlag, Mannheim 1997, S. 129; http://www.collectiveintelligence.info
6) Bureau d'études, «Autonomous Knowledge and Power», 2002, http://utangente.free.fr/anewpages/holmes.html
7) EAST ART MAP (EAM) (http://www.eastartmap.org) fordert alle auf, Ergänzungen und Änderungsvorschläge zu den EAM-Projekten oder -Kunstwerken einzubringen. Die Vorschläge werden alle zwei bis drei Monate von einer aus sechs Experten bestehenden Kommission geprüft.
8) Vgl. dazu: http://www.publicopinion.fi
9) Beatriz da Costa, «Amateur Science, A Threat After All?», *Divanik, Conversations and Interviews about Media Art, Culture and Society,* Kuda.org, Novi Sad 2004, Anhang, S. 3.

BALKON

STEVEN PARRINO (1958–2005)

FABRICE STROUN

Radicality comes from content and not necessarily form. The forms are radical in memory by way of continuing the once radical, through extensions of its history. The avant-garde leaves a wake and, through mannerist force, continues forward. Even on the run, we sometimes look over our shoulders, approaching art with intuition rather than strategy. Art of this kind is more cult than culture.[1)]

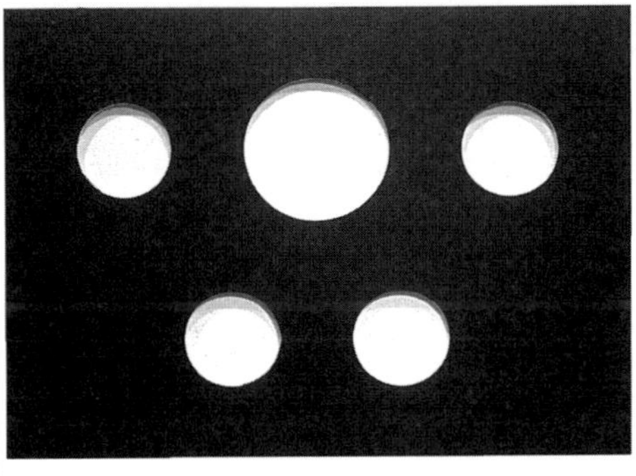

STEVEN PARRINO, UNTITLED (STOCKADE), 1988 acrylic on canvas, 76 x 104" / OHNE TITEL (BLOCKADE), Acryl auf Leinwand, 193 x 264 cm. (ALL PHOTOS: THE ESTATE OF STEVEN PARRINO)

The sudden loss of Steven Parrino to a motorcycle accident at the age of forty-six is made all the more infuriating by the fact that his work was in the process of a major reevaluation—one that did not come from the high spheres of the institution as much as from an emerging generation of artists, for whom Parrino represented an alive and vital link to the (supposedly obsolete) idea of "radicality." From the beginning, the production of this bond was at the heart of Parrino's many practices (art, music, writing).

Back in the early eighties, when the word on the street pronounced painting dead, rather than join the flock of mourners, Parrino took a shot at necrophilia. In his hands, appropriationist strategies became a kind of *black ops* technique, a means to convulsively incarnate the historical breakdown of avant-garde narratives. Not to provide a distanced, critically laden image of ideological collapse, but to produce a raw, visual materialization of its effects. Neither nostalgic, nor cynical, his "misshapen canvasses" and gutted monochrome paintings—a genre which in the late seventies and early eighties simultaneously held the promise of modern art's final teleological realization and the disillusionment of its post-modern addendum ("a painting of a painting")—owe more to Stella's *Black Paintings'* "what you see is what you see" credo than to any post-pop tradition of cultural intervention. And not just any Frank Stella *Black Painting*; but specifically: ARBEIT MACHT FREI (1958) and DIE FAHNE HOCH (1959). As far as Parrino was concerned, these works were not called "black" for nothing. If late modernism's conception of radicality is predicated on defining an object in the real world, in real time, and its post-modernist afterthought is the awareness that our perception of this "corporeal" condition is predicated on language and memory, why not just fold one over the other? One more title: "Swastika Girls," (1973) by Fripp & Eno, arguably Punk's first cut. The corpse is still warm. Make it twitch!

The "dumbness" of such literal gestures is to be taken at face value: "I always saw Europe as total poser weighed

---

FABRICE STROUN is an independent writer and curator based in Geneva.

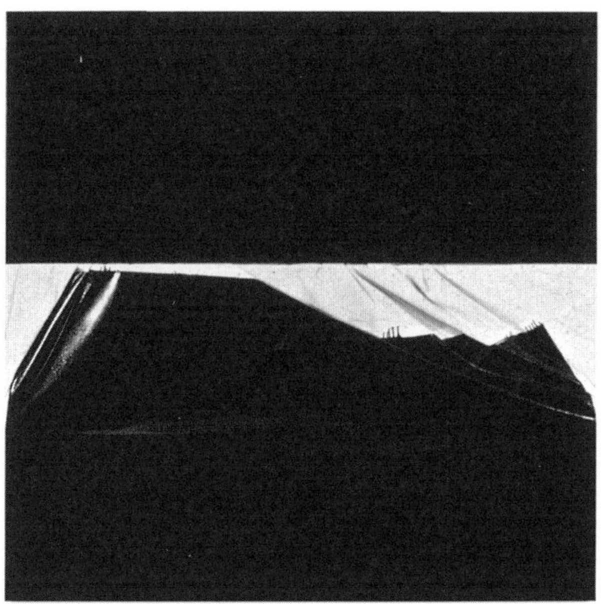

STEVEN PARRINO, KITTEN NATIVIDAD, 1991, enamel paint on canvas, 84 x 84" / Lackfarbe auf Leinwand, 213,4 x 213,4 cm.

down with history, and America as total substance with disposable history, even if American substance is violence, sex and stupidity."[2] Recently, Steven joked about the fact that in 1985 he was included in a group show titled "Smart Art"[3] and, in 1992, in another, titled "Dumb Painting,"[4] only to end up a few years later in "Ca-Ca-Poo-Poo."[5] Yet, even as he doused some of his paintings with a gooey silicon gel or chainsawed previous works into a pile of junk, the work had nothing to do with abjection, striving instead to reach a kind of stark necromantic elegance. Unlike Mike Kelley (alongside whom he exhibited in "Ca-Ca-Poo-Poo"), Parrino never claimed to unearth the repressed, psycho-cultural impulses of American culture. His exploitation of culture, whether high or low, was much less humanistic than that of his Californian counterparts. And much much more lively. Although his works made direct use of biker culture, Russ Meyer and George Romero anti-establishment cinema, and Ed "Big Daddy" Roth's Rat Fink, these references never have the function of erudite quotations. The inclusion of these images within his work was predicated on existential concerns rather than anthropological ones. Like the motifs of Warhol's *Death and Disaster* paintings, they are non-sites of an infinitely pliable, one-dimensional, "dumb" surface—a surface that Parrino strove to embody in his art as in his life, completely. "The idea of painting a painting is basically the same as painting a fender: simple and clean … Subjectivity is selection (the clean edit) and does not deal with the melodramas of fantasy, just the facts."[6]

Parrino's post-punk romanticism remained throughout the years, lean and mean. His pared-down living quarters/garage/studio on Manhattan Avenue in Brooklyn became a sanctuary for anyone trying to escape the "circus" of the art world. A place where career and money issues were made irrelevant, if only because its tenant had upheld, over a quarter-century, without remorse or regrets, an uncompromising relationship to both the art market and the institutional sphere. "Live free or die" was his motto, and although it may sound corny when taken out of context, for those who knew him, it was true.

In the words of Blair Thurman, an artist alongside whom he exhibited often since the early nineties, Steven Parrino was "the glue" between the United States and Europe most specifically through his friendships and collaborations with Olivier Mosset and Jutta Koether (another distortion junkie with whom Parrino made art and music). But, above all, Parrino was the glue between generations. Although he never held a formal teaching position his studio was always filled with (many) younger artists. Some just hung out there. Others, Parrino wrote on and exhibited with in group shows he curated. Others, still, like Amy Granat, were artists he collaborated with on a regular basis. With one or two exceptions, most of them were only marginally influenced by his aesthetic. What they got from him was a supreme DIY pride and, most importantly, a belief that art truly mattered. With Steven, art became an experiential and ethical posture that ran through everything he did, from painting a canvas to his relationships with other artists. Art was what stood in the face of mediocrity.

1) Steven Parrino, *The No Texts (1979–2003)* (New Jersey: Abaton Book Company, 2003), p. 46.
2) Steven Parrino, "The Road to Electrophia," ibid., p. 33.
3) Carpenter Center for the Arts, Harvard University, Cambridge, Mass., 1985.
4) Centraal Museum, Utrecht, 1992.
5) Kölnischer Kunstverein, Köln, 1998.
6) Steven Parrino, op. cit., p. 21.

STEVEN PARRINO (1958–2005)

FABRICE STROUN

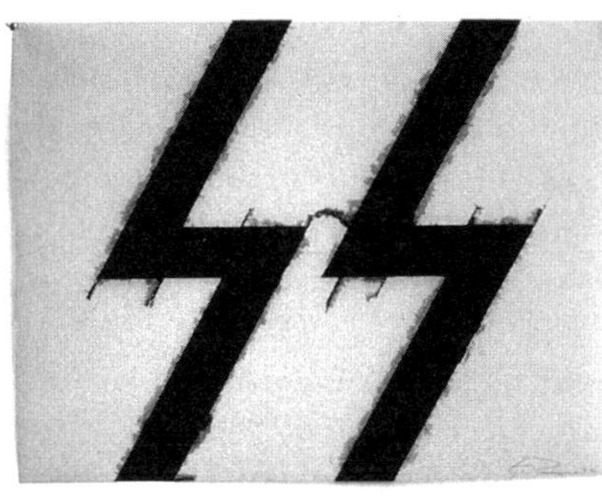

STEVEN PARRINO, UNTITLED, 1992, engine enamel spray on vellum / Maschinenlackspray auf Segeltuch.

Radikalität folgt aus dem Inhalt und nicht notwendig aus der Form. Die Formen sind in der Erinnerung radikal, indem sie das einst Radikale in seinen geschichtlichen Ausläufern fortsetzen. Die Avantgarde entwickelt in ihrem Kielwasser einen Sog und bewegt sich durch eine manieristische Kraft weiter vorwärts. Selbst wenn wir voranstürmen, werfen wir manchmal einen Blick über die Schulter zurück und nähern uns der Kunst mehr intuitiv als strategisch. Solche Kunst ist eher Kult denn Kultur. [1)]

Der plötzliche Verlust von Steven Parrino, der im Alter von sechsundvierzig Jahren bei einem Motorradunfall ums Leben kam, stimmt umso bitterer, als sein Werk gerade Gegenstand einer umfassenden Neueinschätzung war, und zwar weniger von höherer, institutioneller Seite als vielmehr seitens einer aufstrebenden Generation von Künstlerinnen und Künstlern, für die Parrino eine lebende und lebendige Verbindung zur (angeblich obsoleten) Idee der «Radikalität» darstellte. Dieses Band zu schmieden war von Anfang an ein zentrales Moment im vielseitigen künstlerischen (auch musikalischen und literarischen) Schaffen Parrinos.

In der ersten Hälfte der 80er Jahre, als die Malerei allgemein totgesagt wurde, verlegte sich Parrino auf die Nekrophilie, statt sich der Schar der Trauernden anzuschliessen. Unter seinen Händen wurden die Strategien der Appropriation zu einer Art «verdeckter Operation», einer Methode, die das historische Zusammenbrechen der Narrative der Avantgarde quasi konvulsivisch verkörperte. Es ging ihm nicht darum, ein distanziertes, kritisches Bild des ideologischen Kollapses zu zeichnen, sondern darum, dessen Folgen in einer rohen, ganz konkreten bildlichen Form sichtbar zu machen. Seine weder nostalgisch noch zynisch wirkenden «unförmigen Leinwände» und ausgeweideten monochromen Bilder – ein Genre, das Ende der 70er, Anfang der 80er Jahre sowohl das Versprechen der endgültigen teleologischen Erfüllung der modernen Kunst als auch die Enttäuschung durch ihre postmoderne Ergänzung («ein Bild eines Bildes») bereit hielt – sind eher den *Black Paintings* eines Frank Stella und deren Credo, «Was du siehst, ist was du siehst», verpflichtet als irgendeiner Post-Pop-Art-Tradition der kulturellen Intervention; allerdings nicht irgendeinem der *Black Paintings*, sondern ganz konkret den Bildern ARBEIT MACHT FREI (1958) und DIE FAHNE HOCH (1959). Was Parrino anging, wurden diese Bilder nicht umsonst «schwarz» genannt. Wenn die mit der Spätmoderne verbundene Idee der Radikalität darauf beruht, ein Objekt in der realen Welt und in der realen Zeit zu definieren, und die nachgeschobene Überlegung der Postmoderne in der Erkenntnis besteht, dass unsere Wahrnehmung dieser «körperlichen» Situation von der Sprache und Erinnerung abhängt, warum sollte man dann nicht einfach die eine über die andere stülpen? Noch so ein Titel: «Swastika Girls» (1973) von Fripp & Eno, der ersten Garnitur des Punk, wenn man so will: Die Leiche ist noch warm, bring sie zum Zucken!

Das «Dümmliche» solch konkreter Gesten ist für bare Münze zu nehmen: «Europa war für mich schon immer durch und durch Poseur, schwer gebückt unter der Last seiner Geschichte, und Amerika reine Substanz mit einer Geschichte zum Wegwerfen, selbst

FABRICE STROUN ist freier Autor und Kurator und lebt in Genf.

wenn diese Substanz aus Gewalt, Sex und Dummheit besteht.»[2] Es ist noch nicht lange her, da witzelte Steven, dass er 1985 in einer Gruppenausstellung mit dem Titel «Smart Art»[3] und 1992 in einer anderen mit dem Titel «Dumb Painting»[4] vertreten war, um wenige Jahre später bei «Ca-Ca-Poo-Poo»[5] zu landen. Doch selbst wenn er seine Bilder zum Teil mit klebrigem Silikon-Gel übergoss oder frühere Arbeiten mit einer Kettensäge zu Schrott sägte, hatte seine Kunst nichts mit dem «Abscheu» der *abject art* zu tun, sondern strebte vielmehr eine spröde, nekromantische Eleganz an. Im Unterschied zu Mike Kelley (der ebenfalls in «Ca-Ca-Poo-Poo» vertreten war) gab Parrino niemals vor, die verdrängten psychokulturellen Antriebe der amerikanischen Kultur freizulegen. Seine Ausbeutung der Kultur (ob anspruchsvoll oder trivial) war weniger humanistisch begründet als bei seinen kalifornischen Kollegen, dafür aber sehr viel lebendiger. Auch wenn seine Arbeiten unmittelbar auf die Bikerszene, an die gegen das Establishment gerichteten Filme eines Russ Meyer und George Romero, oder auf Ed «Big Daddy» Roths *Rat Fink* Bezug nehmen, haben diese Anleihen nie den Charakter «gebildeter» Zitate. Das Einbeziehen dieser Motive in sein Werk hatte seinen Grund in existenziellen, nicht in anthropologischen Anliegen. Wie bei den Sujets der *Death-and-Disaster*-Serie von Warhol handelt es sich um «Non-sites», um Nichtorte auf einer unendlich biegsamen, eindimensionalen, «nichts sagenden» Oberfläche – eine Oberfläche, die Parrino in seiner Kunst wie in seinem Leben voll und ganz zum Ausdruck bringen wollte. «Das Vorhaben ein Bild zu malen ist im Grunde dasselbe wie jenes, einen Kotflügel zu streichen: einfach und sauber ... Subjektivität heisst Auswahl (die Reinfassung) und gibt sich nicht mit den Melodramen der Phantasie ab, sondern nur mit den Tatsachen.»[6]

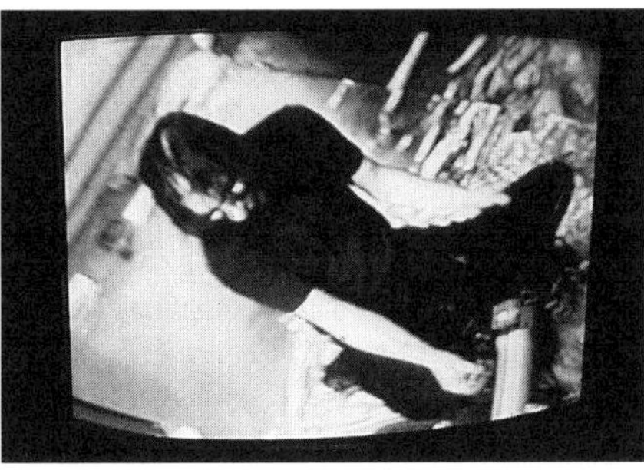

STEVEN PARRINO, GUITAR GRIND, 1995, video still / GITARRENSCHINDEREI, Videostill. (ALL PHOTOS: THE ESTATE OF STEVEN PARRINO)

Parrinos Post-Punk-Romantik blieb über die Jahre hinweg schlank und rank. Seine spartanische Unterkunft an der Manhattan Avenue in Brooklyn, die ihm Wohnung, Garage und Atelier zugleich war, wurde zum Zufluchtsort für Leute, die dem «Kunstzirkus» entfliehen wollten. Es war ein Ort, an dem Karriere- und Geldfragen jede Bedeutung verloren, und sei es nur, weil derjenige, der dort lebte, seit mehr als einem Vierteljahrhundert eine kompromisslos ablehnende Haltung gegenüber dem Kunstmarkt und den offiziellen Kunstinstituten vertreten hatte. «In Freiheit leben oder sterben», lautete sein Motto, und so abgedroschen dies aus dem Zusammenhang gerissen klingen mag, für die, die ihn kannten, brachte es die Sache auf den Punkt.

Laut Blair Thurman, einem Künstler, mit dem er seit Anfang der 90er Jahre häufig gemeinsam ausstellte, war Steven Parrino «der Kitt» zwischen der amerikanischen und europäischen Kunstszene, insbesondere durch seine Freundschaft und Zusammenarbeit mit Olivier Mosset und Jutta Koether (noch so eine nach Verzerrung Lechzende, mit der Parrino Kunst und Musik machte). Vor allem aber fungierte Parrino als Kitt zwischen den Generationen. Obwohl er nie eine offizielle Lehrstelle bekleidete, war sein Atelier stets Treffpunkt (zahlreicher) jüngerer Künstler. Manche hingen einfach nur so herum, über andere schrieb Parrino oder stellte gemeinsam mit ihnen (in von ihm kuratierten Ausstellungen) aus, und wieder mit anderen, etwa mit Amy Granat, arbeitete er regelmässig zusammen. Bis auf ein oder zwei Ausnahmen wurden sie nur am Rande von seiner Ästhetik beeinflusst. Was er ihnen jedoch vermittelte, war ein ausgeprägt hochgemutes Selbstvertrauen, die Dinge selbst in die Hand zu nehmen, und vor allem den Glauben, dass die Kunst von entscheidender Bedeutung war. Bei Steven wurde Kunst zu einer empirischen und ethischen Haltung, von der alles, was er tat, durchdrungen war, von seiner Malerei bis hin zu seinen Beziehungen mit anderen Künstlern. Kunst war, was sich dem Mittelmass widersetzte.

(Übersetzung: B. Opstelten / W. Parker)

1) Steven Parrino, *The No Texts (1979–2003)*, Abaton Book Company, New Jersey 2003, S. 46.
2) Steven Parrino, «The Road to Electrophia», ebenda, S. 33.
3) Carpenter Center for the Arts, Harvard University, Cambridge, Mass., 1985.
4) Centraal Museum, Utrecht 1992.
5) Kölnischer Kunstverein, Köln 1998.
6) Steven Parrino, op. cit., S. 21.

COMPLETE YOUR PARKETT LIBRARY
VERVOLLSTÄNDIGEN SIE IHRE PARKETT-BIBLIOTHEK

OUT OF PRINT / VERGRIFFEN: **NO. 1** ENZO CUCCHI, **2** SIGMAR POLKE, **3** MARTIN DISLER, **4** MERET OPPENHEIM, **5** ERIC FISCHL, **6** JANNIS KOUNELLIS, **7** BRICE MARDEN, **8** MARKUS RAETZ, **9** FRANCESCO CLEMENTE, **10** BRUCE NAUMAN, **12** ANDY WARHOL, **13** REBECCA HORN, **16** ROBERT WILSON, **17** FISCHLI/WEISS, **19** JEFF KOONS, MARTIN KIPPENBERGER, **20** TIM ROLLINS&K.O.S., **22** CHRISTIAN BOLTANSKI, JEFF WALL, **25** KATHARINA FRITSCH, **26** GÜNTHER FÖRG, PHILIP TAAFFE, JAMES TURRELL, **27** LOUISE BOURGEOIS, ROBERT GOBER, **29** CINDY SHERMAN, JOHN BALDESSARI, **30** SIGMAR POLKE, **31** DAVID HAMMONS, MIKE KELLEY, **35** GERHARD RICHTER, **38** ROSS BLECKNER, MARLENE DUMAS, **45** MATTHEW BARNEY, SARAH LUCAS, ROMAN SIGNER

For out-of-print issues you can register your name and address with Parkett and you will be notified, if your issue(s) become(s) available on the secondary market / Für vergriffene Bände nimmt der Verlag gerne Ihren Suchauftrag entgegen und macht Ihnen bei allfälliger Verfügbarkeit im Handel ein Angebot.

COLLABORATIONS

PARKETT – 20 YEARS OF ARTISTS' COLLABORATIONS
MIRJAM VARADINIS, ED.
KUNSTHAUS ZÜRICH
"A RARE BEHIND-THE-SCENES LOOK AT ONE OF THE ART WOLRD'S MOST RESPECTED ART MAGAZINES" (D.A.P., NEW YORK)
248 PAGES, 22 COLOR PAGES, 1 COLOR POSTER
248 SEITEN, DAVON 22 IN FARBE 1 FARBPOSTER
€ 32 / USA: **$ 39** / **CHF 45**
PLUS POSTAGE / ZZGL. VERSANDKOSTEN

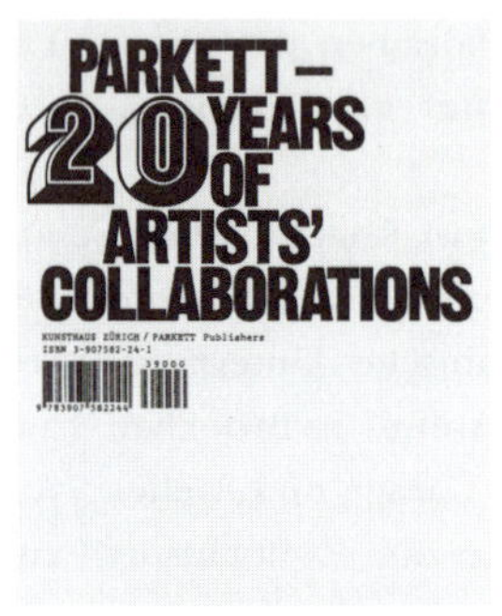

ISBN 3-907582-24-1

BERNARD FRIZE
KATHARINA GROSSE
RICHARD SERRA

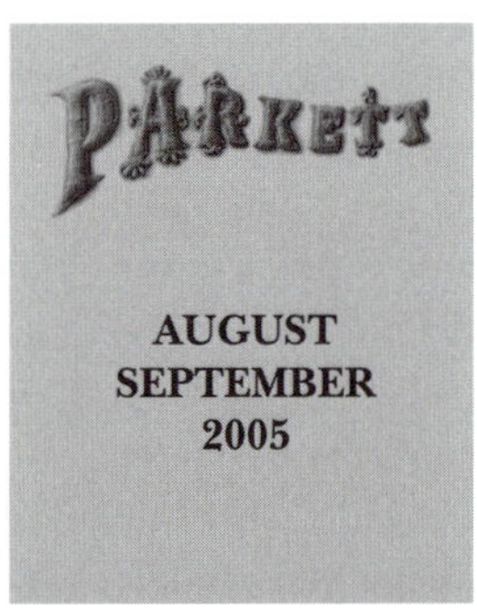

No. 74 - ISBN 3-907582-34-9

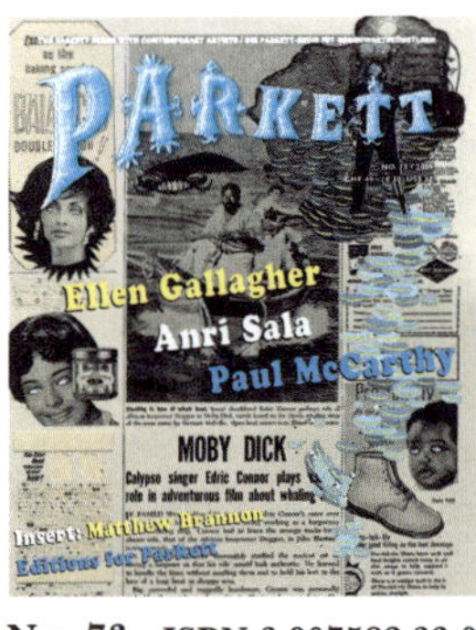

No. 73 - ISBN 3-907582-33-0

ELLEN GALLAGHER
ANRI SALA
PAUL McCARTHY
CLIFF, OKRI, NICHOLS GOODEVE
GODFREY, COOKE, VERWOERT
RELYEA, SIGLER & McCARTHY
INSERT: **MATTHEW BRANNON**
A. ROSENBERG: **JASON DODGE**
R. GOLDBERG: **TANIA BRUGUERA**
T. BEZZOLA: **HARALD SZEEMANN**
CUMULUS AMERICA: DEBRA SINGER
CUMULUS EUROPA: NATAŠA PETREŠIN
BALKON: F. STROUN ON **STEVEN PARRINO**

MONICA BONVICINI
URS FISCHER
RICHARD PRINCE
REBENTISCH, LERUP, HEISER
RICHARDSON, RUF, WEISSMAN
BLAIR, FOGLE, GINGERAS, PÉCOIL
INSERT: **LOREDANA SPERINI**
A. FRANKE: **MATTHEW BUCKINGHAM**
D. KURJAKOVIC: **SILVIE DEFRAOUI**
M. GLÖDE: **CHRISTIAN JANKOWSKI**
CUMULUS: S. SMITH, H. R. REUST
20 YEARS OF PARKETT: ESSAY BY BORIS GROYS
ARTISTS' PAGES, SPECIAL COLLABORATION: **ALEX KATZ** IN CONVERSATION WITH ENA SWANSEA & BRUCE HAINLEY

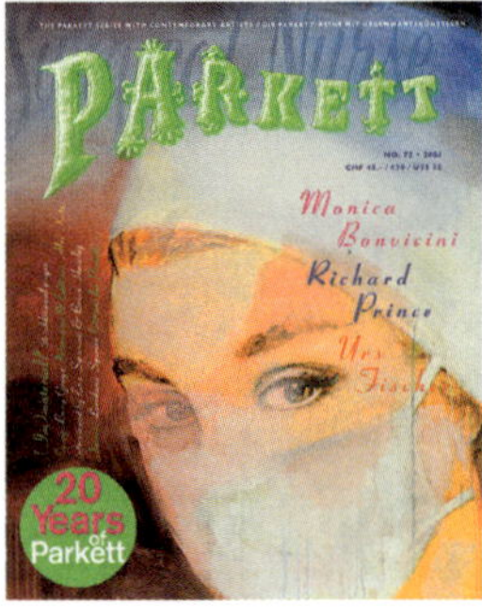

No. 72 - ISBN 3-907582-32-2

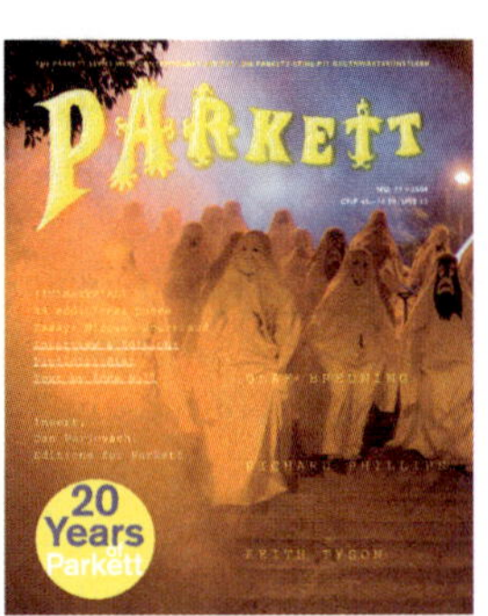

No. 71 - ISBN 3-907582-31-4

OLAF BREUNING
RICHARD PHILLIPS
KEITH TYSON
WAHLER, RODRIGUEZ, JETZER
DIEDERICHSEN, KOETHER, RATTEMEYER
ARCHER, WAGNER/TYSON, REUST
INSERT: **DAN PERJOVSCHI**
V. KATZ: **KIKI SMITH**, M. NICOL: **WALTER PFEIFFER**, F. McKEE: **FIONA BANNER**
CUMULUS: P. BIANCHI, W. BAERWALDT
BALKON: KLAUS THEWELEIT
20 YEARS OF PARKETT: ESSAY BY NICOLAS BOURRIAUD; ARTISTS' PAGES; SPECIAL COLLABORATION: **PIPILOTTI RIST**
ÄNNE SÖLL; CONVERSATION / GESPRÄCH

CHRISTIAN MARCLAY
WILHELM SASNAL
GILLIAN WEARING
SHERBURNE, SCHAFFNER, VERGNE
DAILEY, SZYMCZYK, JANSEN; CAMERON
BURN, WEARING/RABINOWITZ
INSERT: **NIC HESS**
GREG HILTY: **REBECCA WARREN**
D. VAN DEN BOOGERD: **AERNAUT MIK**
LES INFOS: C. WOOD ON **MARK LECKEY**
CUMULUS: C. THEA, G. SCHOR
BALKON: TINEKE REIJNDERS
20 YEARS OF PARKETT: ESSAY BY
JOHANNA BURTON, ARTISTS' PAGES
SPECIAL COLLABORATION: **FRANZ WEST**

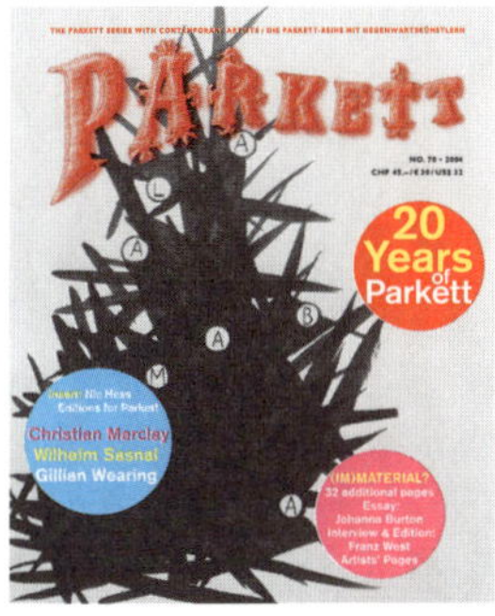

No. 70 - ISBN 3-907582-20-9

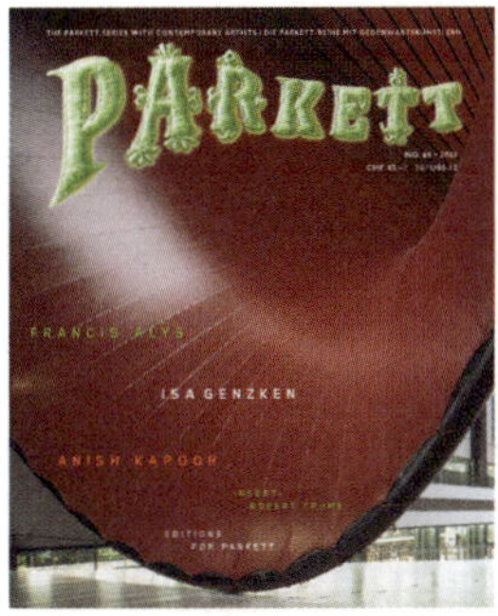

No. 69 - ISBN 3-907582-19-5

FRANCIS ALŸS
ISA GENZKEN
ANISH KAPOOR
SCOTT, ANTON, STORR, HEISER
LEE, KRAJEWSKI, BRYSON
FORSTER, WARNER
INSERT: **ROBERT CRUMB**
KAISER: **AMELIE VON WULFFEN**
COMER: **SWETLANA HEGER**
INQUIRY: CONSENSUS/KONSENS
CUMULUS AMERICA: J. PEARSON
CUMULUS EUROPE: E. TRONCY
BALKON: SERGIO RISALITI

FRANZ ACKERMANN
EIJA-LIISA AHTILA
DAN GRAHAM
FOGLE, DECTER, STANGE, ILES, ELFVING
KOCH, GUAGNINI/SCHNEIDER, MACDONALD
DI BARTOLOMEO, ROSENBERG MILLER
INSERT: **JONATHAN MONK**
D. KURJAKOVIC: **BOJAN SARCEVIC**
H. U. OBRIST: **BERNARD FRIZE**
G. JANSEN: **DIRK SKREBER**
LES INFOS: J. MURPHY
CUMULUS: C. RABINOWITZ, J. HOFFMANN
BALKON: HANS RUDOLF REUST

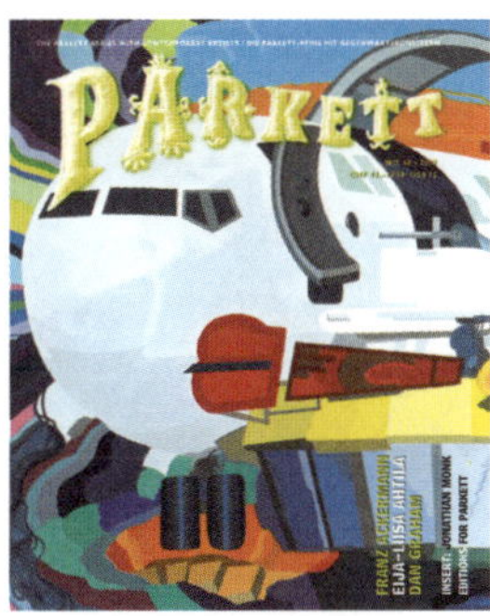

No. 68 - ISBN 3-907582-18-7

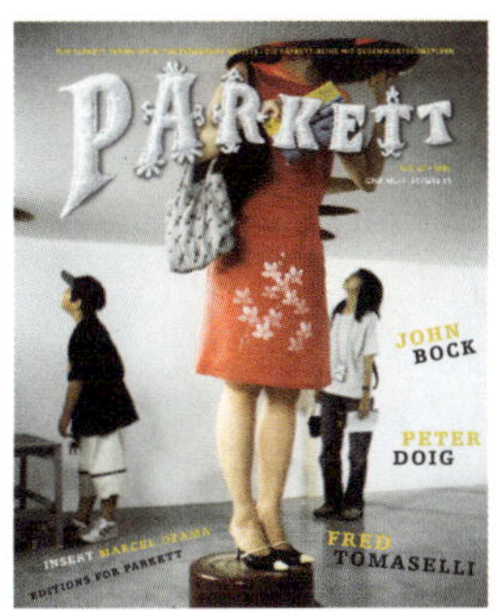

No. 67 - ISBN 3-907582-17-9

JOHN BOCK
PETER DOIG
FRED TOMASELLI
HOFFMANN, BIRNBAUM, AVGIKOS
BONAVENTURA, FUCHS, RUF
CAMERON, RONDEAU, PINCHBECK
INSERT: **MARCEL DZAMA**
T. SELVARATNAM: **SIMON STARLING**
S. OMLIN: **HANNE DARBOVEN**
VISCHER/HERZOG: SCHAULAGER BASEL
LES INFOS: H. BÖHME ON **WANG FU**
CUMULUS: FIRSTENBERG, KERSTING
BALKON: DANIELE MUSCIONICO

ANGELA BULLOCH
DANIEL BUREN
PIERRE HUYGHE
REBENTISCH, WILSON, PRINZHORN
RORIMER, GINGERAS, BUREN/HUYGHE
MILLAR, OBRIST, HOBBS
T. NICHOLS GOODEVE/G. BRUNO
E. DIMENDBERG: **ALLAN SEKULA**
LES INFOS: ROBERTO OHRT ON
MONICA BONVICINI
CUMULUS AMERICA: NATO THOMPSON
CUMULUS EUROPA: GREG HILTY

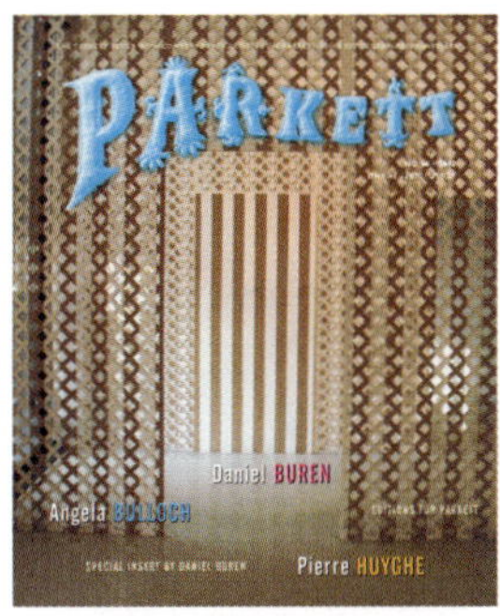

No. 66 - ISBN 3-907582-16-0

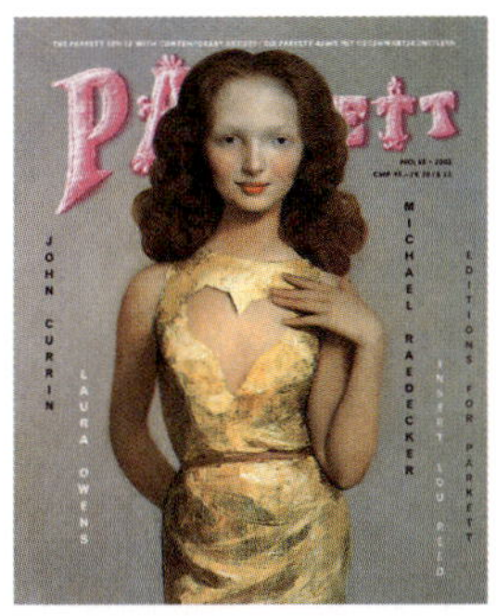

No. 65 - ISBN 3-907582-15-2

JOHN CURRIN
LAURA OWENS
MICHAEL RAEDECKER
SEWARD, VAN DE WALLE, BERG
FERGUSON, THOMSON, WEISSMAN
VERSCHAFFEL, MYERS, EGGERS
INSERT: **LOU REED**
KURT W. FORSTER: **JEFF WALL**
STORR: **DIETER ROTH & D. IANNONE**
K. BITTERLI: **HUBBARD/BIRCHLER**
LES INFOS: CHRISTINA VÉGH
CUMULUS: O. WESTPHALEN, T. HAHN
BALKON: SHEENA WAGSTAFF

OLAFUR ELIASSON
TOM FRIEDMAN
RODNEY GRAHAM
BLOM, MORGAN, CAMERON, MATSUI
WATERS/FRIEDMAN, COOKE, HALE
INSERT: **AMY SILLMAN**
VÉRONIQUE D'AUZAC:
XAVIER VEILHAN
INTERVIEW:
A.M. HOMES: **CHRIS VERENE**
HAKAN NILSSON: **ANNIKA LARSSON**
INQUIRY/UMFRAGE:
LEARNING FROM "DOCUMENTA"

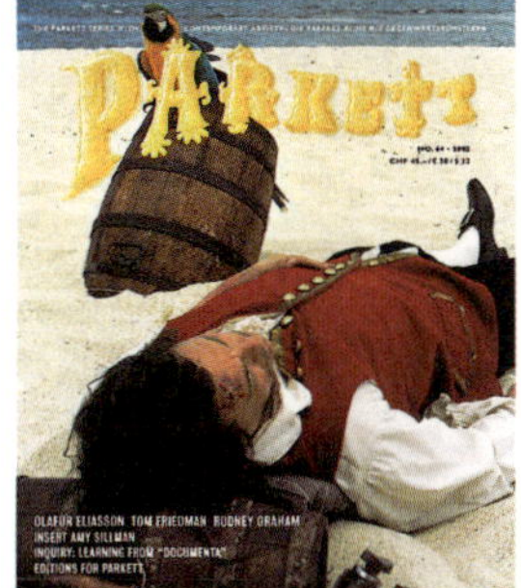

No. 64 - ISBN 3-907582-14-4

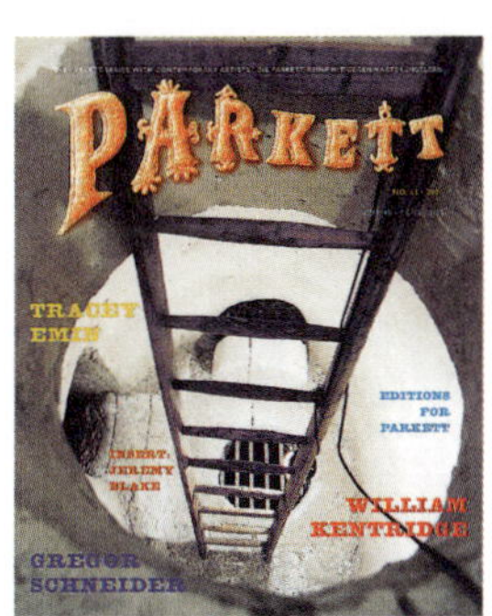

No. 63 - ISBN 3-907582-13-6

TRACEY EMIN
WILLIAM KENTRIDGE
GREGOR SCHNEIDER
BARBER, MUIR, PREECE
GUNNING, STEWART, GOLDBERG
PUVOGEL, LOOCK
INSERT: **JEREMY BLAKE**
CLAUDIA SPINELLI: **FABRICE GYGI**
RAINER FUCHS: **KATHARINA GROSSE**
ADRIAN DANNATT: **THE THREE**
CUMULUS: CHRISTIAN RATTEMEYER
DANIEL BIRNBAUM
BALKON: MICHAEL OPPITZ

JOHN WESLEY
TACITA DEAN
THOMAS DEMAND
MILLAR, CARABELL, SCHWARZ
NORDEN, KÖNIG/STOCKEBRAND
HAINLEY, SEARLE, RUBY, HEISER
INSERT: **G. STEINER & J. LENZLINGER**
PHILIP URSPRUNG: **ALLAN KAPROW**
RUSSELL FERGUSON: **GLEN WILSON**
EDWARD A. SCHEER: **MIKE PARR**
LES INFOS: DAVID GREENBERG
CUMULUS: G. CARMINE, S. DIETZ

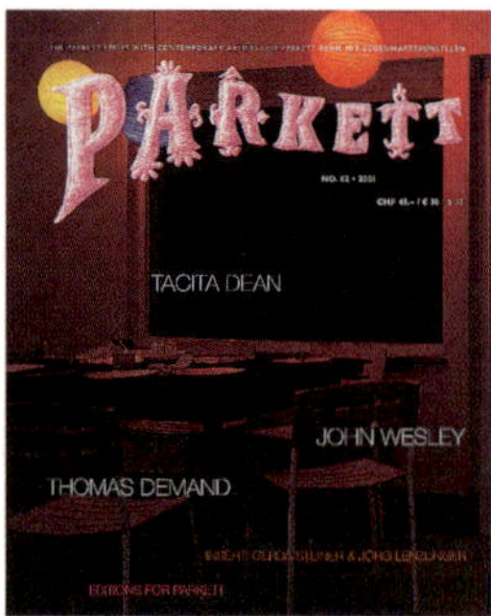

No. 62 - ISBN 3-907582-12-8

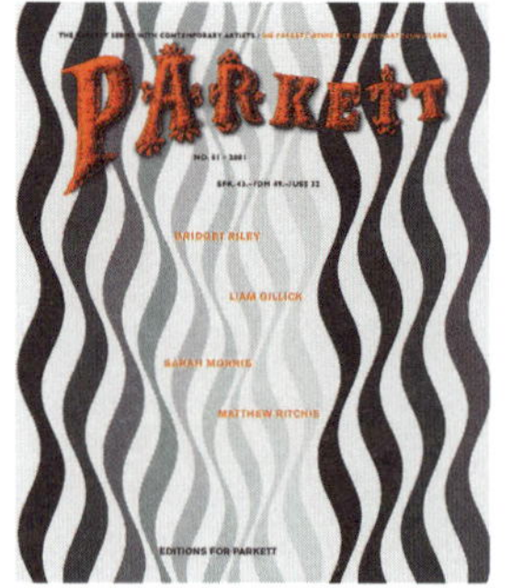

No. 61 - ISBN 3-907582-11-X

BRIDGET RILEY
LIAM GILLICK
SARAH MORRIS
MATTHEW RITCHIE
KUDIELKA, HICKEY
GILLICK, STEMMRICH, WOLLEN
NICHOLS GOODEVE, KLEIN
PRINZHORN, RABINOWITZ
GALISON/JONES, MARCUS
ELISABETH KLEY: **PAUL LINCOLN**
CUMULUS: O. ENWEZOR, M. WARNER
BALKON: STELLA ROLLIG

CHUCK CLOSE
DIANA THATER
LUC TUYMANS
PROSE, CLOSE/PEYTON, SHIFF
CLOSE/CURIGER, ARRHENIUS
HASLINGER, GILBERT-ROLFE
HOPTMAN, MOSQUERA, REUST
INSERT: **SHIRANA SHAHBAZI**
GREG HILTY: **JEREMY DELLER**
HOWARD SINGERMAN: **DAVID BUNN**
LES INFOS: T. DE DUVE—INTERVIEW
CUMULUS: F. WARD, H. U. RECK

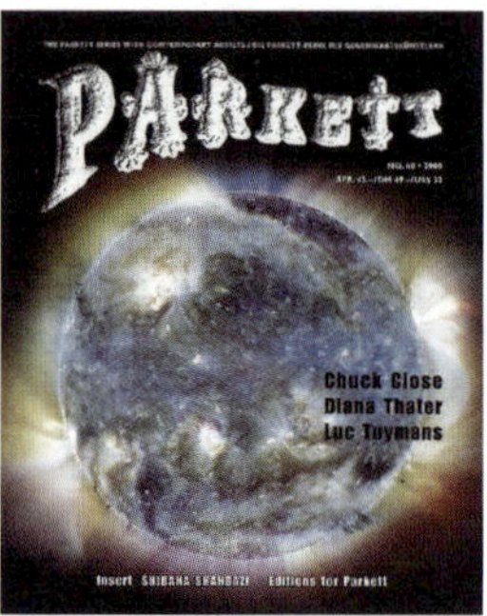

No. 60 - ISBN 3-907582-10-1

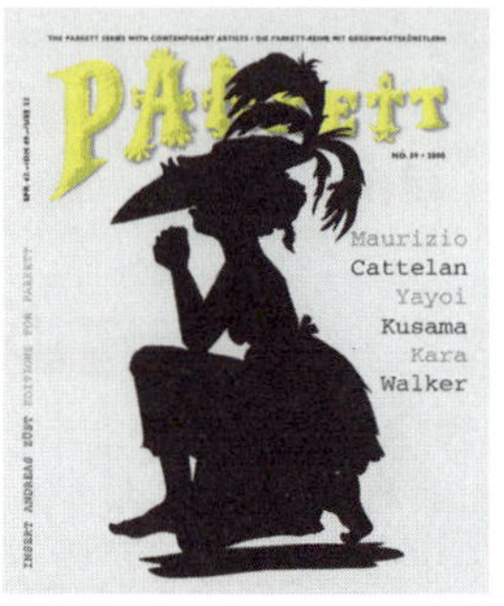

No. 59 - ISBN 3-907582-09-8

MAURIZIO CATTELAN
YAYOI KUSAMA
KARA WALKER
BOURRIAUD, GINGERAS, BONAMI
PANHANS-BÜHLER, MATSUI, POLLOCK
DUBOIS SHAW, JANUS, WALKER
INSERT: **ANDREAS ZÜST**
VINCENT KATZ
E. BRONFEN: **ANNETTE MESSAGER**
JAN AVGIKOS: **ANNA GASKELL**
LES INFOS: ALI SUBOTNICK
CUMULUS: M. ROWELL, L. FÖLDENYI
BALKON: MICHELLE NICOL

JAMES ROSENQUIST
SYLVIE FLEURY
JASON RHOADES
RUSSELL, KOONS/ROSENQUIST
HULTEN, FELIX, GLENN, LOBEL
DANNATT, RUF, KOETHER, FERGUSON
ORTH, SCHEIDEMANN/HERMANN
INSERT: **HENRY BOND**
G. WILLIAMS: **JANE & LOUISE WILSON**
S. ZIZEK, PAUL D. MILLER & CHRIS OFILI
LES INFOS: ANNA HELWING
CUMULUS: D. ROBBINS, H. TEERLINCK
BALKON: KNUT EBELING

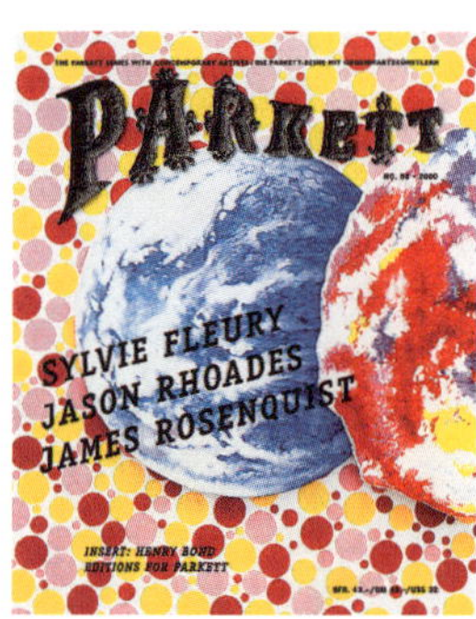

No. 58 - ISBN 3-907582-08-X

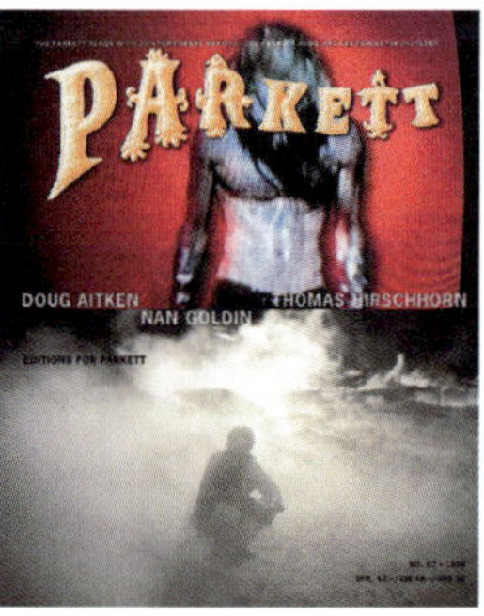

No. 57 - ISBN 3-907582-07-1

DOUG AITKEN
NAN GOLDIN
THOMAS HIRSCHHORN
ROBERTS, BONAMI, VAN ASSCHE
LEBOVICI, DANTO, LIEBMANN
FRIIS-HANSEN, HAKERT, EISENBERG
FLECK, GINGERAS, VERGNE, STEINWEG
D. GREENBERG: **DONALD BAECHLER**
ANDREA KROKSNES: **LOUISE LAWLER**
LIONEL BOVIER: **JOHN MILLER**
LES INFOS: RUDOLF SCHMITZ
CUMULUS: H.U. OBRIST, C. BUTLER
BALKON: J. STEINER/ANNELISE COSTE

ELLSWORTH KELLY
VANESSA BEECROFT
JORGE PARDO
KELLEIN, FER, MAURER, RIMANELLI
BRYSON, TAZZI, SEWARD, AVGIKOS
FERGUSON, VÉGH, VAN WINKEL
FRANGENBERG, BUSH
GREG HILTY: **CERITH WYN EVANS**
THOMAS Y. LEVIN: **CHRISTIAN MARCLAY**
LYNNE COOKE: **DIANA THATER**
LES INFOS: DIANE LEWIS
CUMULUS: A. DANNATT, P. NEDOMA

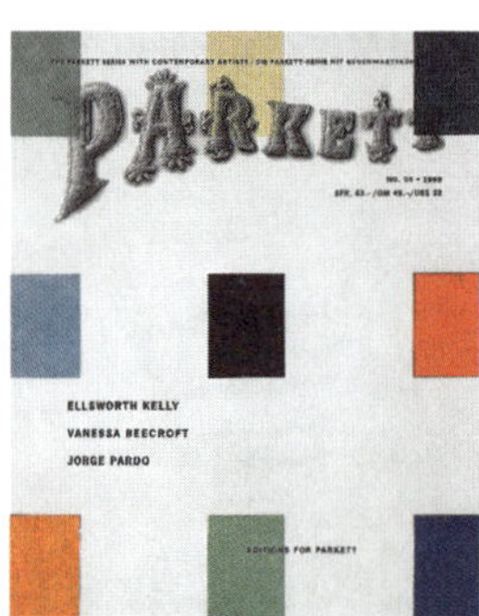

No. 56 - ISBN 3-907582-06-3

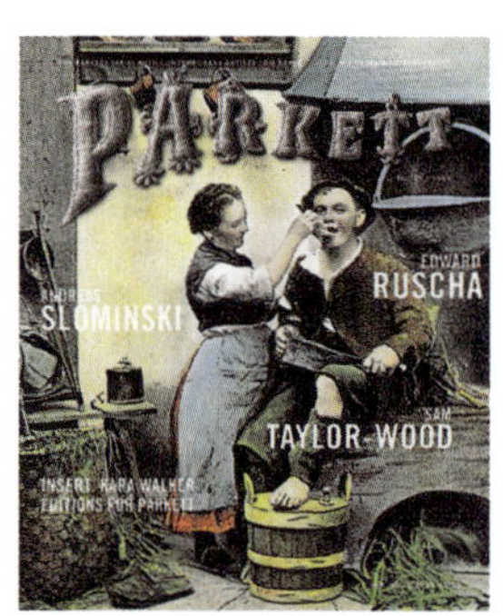

No. 55 - ISBN 3-907582-05-5

EDWARD RUSCHA
ANDREAS SLOMINSKI
SAM TAYLOR-WOOD
PERRONE, HIGGIE, SINGERMAN
SCHENKER, SCANLAN, SPECTOR, FREY
HEYNEN, GROYS/FUNCKE/HOFFMANN
BRONFEN, BONAMI, LAJER-BURCHARTH
INSERT: **KARA WALKER**
BORIS GROYS: **PAVEL PEPPERSTEIN**
RUDOLF SCHMITZ: **ALEXANDER KLUGE**
BEATRIX RUF: **EIJA-LIISA AHTILA**
CUMULUS: M. NICOL, S. ROLNIK

RONI HORN
MARIKO MORI
BEAT STREULI
SCHORR, GUNNARSSON, GOROVOY, LEWIS
SPECTOR, BRYSON, NAKAZAWA, NICHOLS
GOODEVE, STALS, DANTO, AMANO, SMITH
INSERT: **MATTHEW RITCHIE**
VINCENT KATZ: **ALEX KATZ**
H. BREDEKAMP: **STEPHAN VON HUENE**
PAUL D. MILLER: **SHIRIN NESHAT**
LES INFOS:
OKWUI ENWEZOR & WILLIAM KENTRIDGE
CUMULUS: VALÉRIA PICCOLI, MARIA LIND

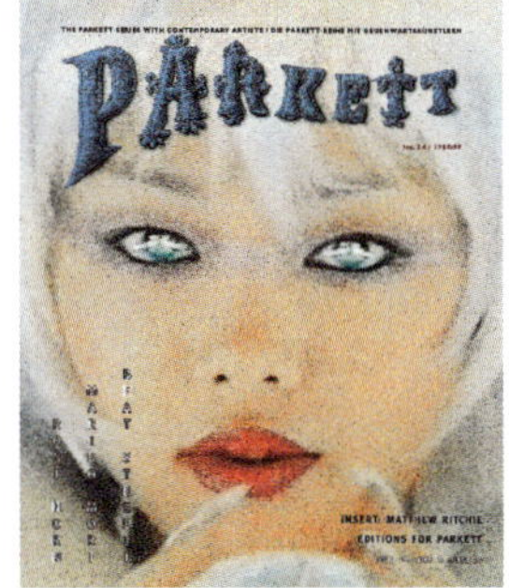

No. 54 - ISBN 3-907582-04-7

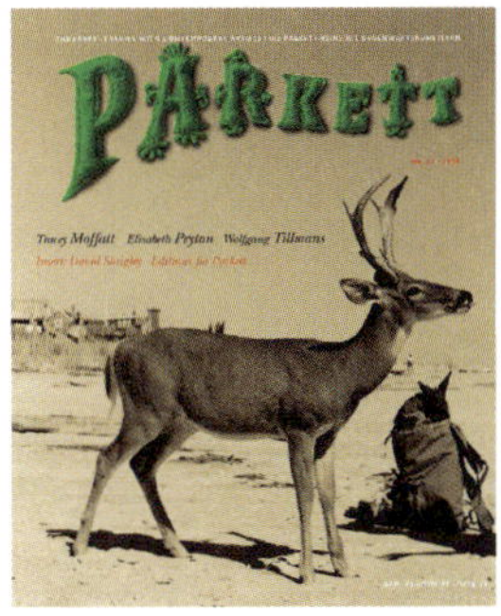

No. 53 - ISBN 3-907582-03-9

TRACEY MOFFATT
ELIZABETH PEYTON
WOLFGANG TILLMANS
MARTIN, LAJER-BURCHARTH, RIMANELLI
PILGRIM, URSPRUNG, LIEBMANN, MATSUI
WAKEFIELD, BUDNEY, NESBITT, ZIEGLER
INSERT: **DAVID SHRIGLEY**
C. BERNARD: **JOHAN GRIMONPREZ**
BERNARD MARCADÉ: **ROBERT GOBER**
LES INFOS DE L'ENFER: V. LIEBERMANN
CUMULUS: BLESSING, AUPETITALLOT
BALKON: STEINER/MAGNAGUAGNO

KAREN KILIMNIK
MALCOLM MORLEY
UGO RONDINONE
SCHORR, BÜRGI, JUNCOSA
MORLEY, LEBENSZTEJN, BONAMI
VERWOERT, HOPTMAN
INSERT: **THOMAS BAYRLE**
ED WHITE: **JEAN MICHEL OTHONIEL**
NEVILLE WAKEFIELD: **RICHARD SERRA**
GILDA WILLIAMS: **GILLIAN WEARING**
R. GRESKOVIC: **MERCE CUNNINGHAM**
CUMULUS: WALKER, KURZMEYER
BALKON: CECILIA VICUÑA

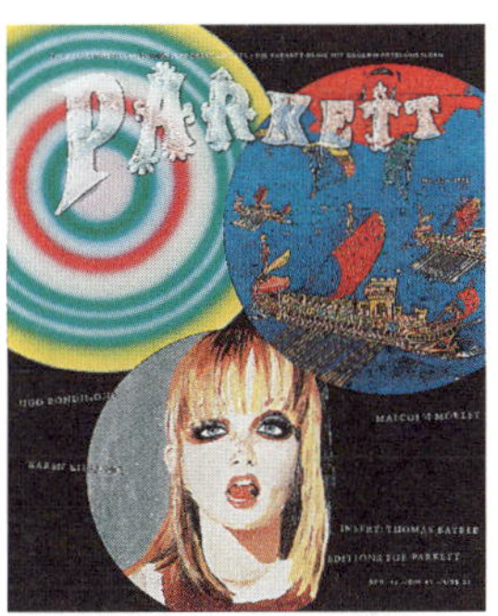

No. 52 - ISBN 3-907582-02-0

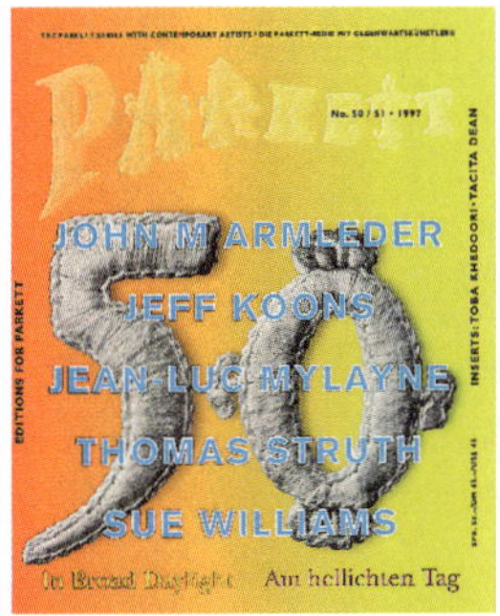

50/51 - ISBN 3-907582-00-4

JOHN M ARMLEDER, JEFF KOONS
JEAN-LUC MYLAYNE
THOMAS STRUTH, SUE WILLIAMS
DI PIETRANTONIO, BOVIER, MUNIZ
SEWARD, LOERS, NICHOLS GOODEVE
COOKE, DION, ARNAUDET, MYLAYNE
CURIGER, LINGWOOD,OKUTSU, BRYSON
SCHJELDAHL, NESBIT, DANNATT, CAMHI
INSERTS: **TOBA KHEDOORI, TACITA DEAN**
ONFRAY: **H. RIGAUD,** NICOL: **SAM SAMORE**
MURPHY, VAN DER WALLE, STEINER
KURT W. FORSTER: **FRANK GEHRY**
CUMULUS: COLEMAN, BIRNBAUM

LAURIE ANDERSON
DOUGLAS GORDON
JEFF WALL
FLOOD, BEZZOLA, FERGUSON
GILLICK/GORDON, BRYSON
PONTBRIAND, SCHORR, ANDERSON
BURCKHARDT, BUDNEY
INSERT: **SILVIA BÄCHLI**
COLIN DE LAND: **JOHN WATERS**
ROBERT STORR: **SEYDOU KEITA**
D. SALVIONI: **CLEGG & GUTTMANN**
CUMULUS: KITTELMANN, MEYER

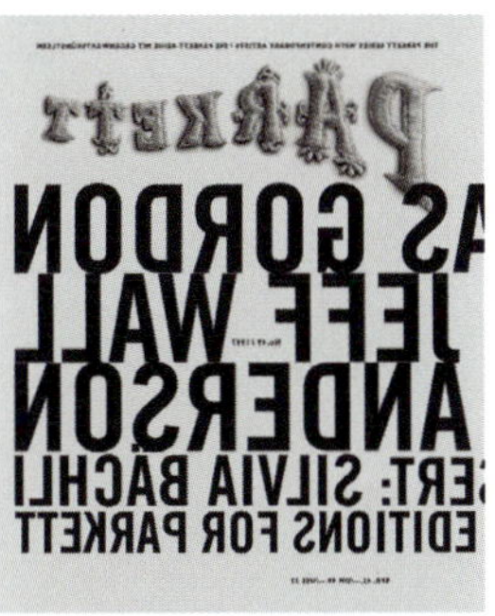

No. 49 - ISBN 3-907509-99-4

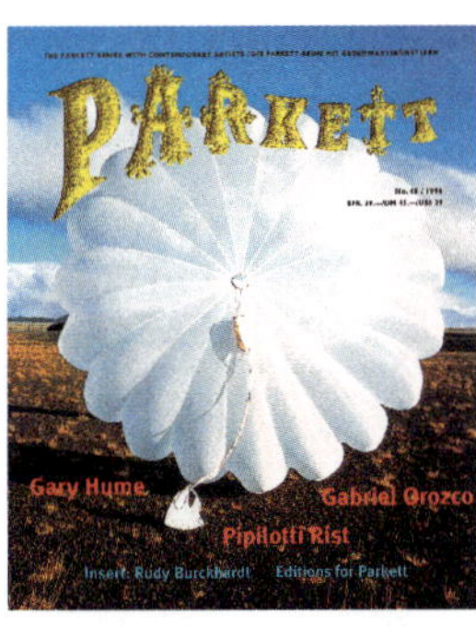

No. 48 - ISBN 3-907509-98-6

GARY HUME
GABRIEL OROZCO
PIPILOTTI RIST
BOVIER, MUIR, FOGLE, BONAMI
DE ZEGHER, SPECTOR, URSPRUNG
BABIAS, COLOMBO, ANDERSON
INSERT: **RUDY BURCKHARDT**
V. KATZ: **RUDY BURCKHARDT**
MARK VAN DER WALLE:
CHARLES LONG & STEREOLAB
FAYE HIRSCH: **BRUCE CONNER**
CH. DOSWALD: **IAN ANÜLL**
CUMULUS: LEGGAT, SCHNEIDER

TONY OURSLER
RAYMOND PETTIBON
THOMAS SCHÜTTE
COOKE, RICHARD, NERI
LEWIS, GROYS, ALS, RUGOFF
GOODEVE, SEARLE, MARI, REUST
WAKEFIELD, LOOCK, JANUS
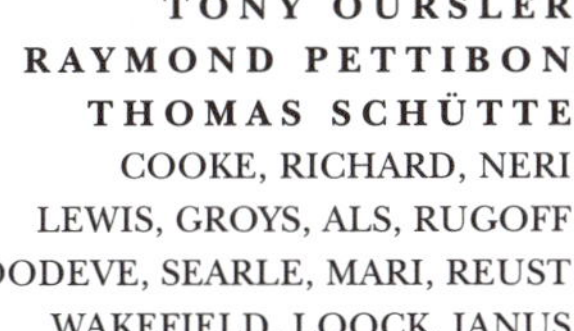
INSERT: **ZOE LEONARD & CHERYL DUNYE**
JURI STEINER: **EMMA KUNZ**
M. WECHSLER: **CHRISTOPH RÜTIMANN**
SUSAN MORGAN: **DIANE ARBUS**
CUMULUS: PRINCENTHAL, BOVIER/CHERIX

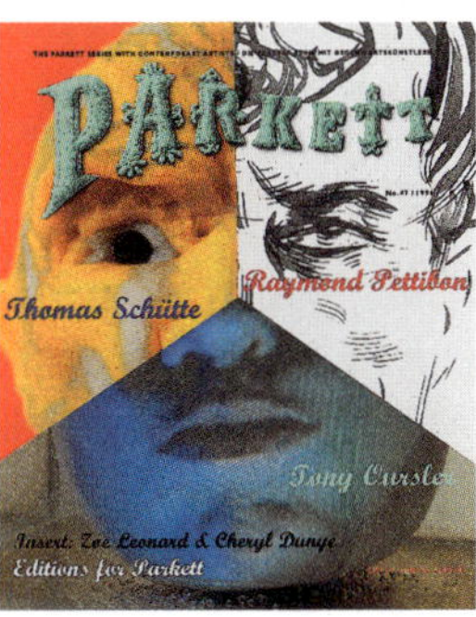

No. 47 - ISBN 3-907509-97-8

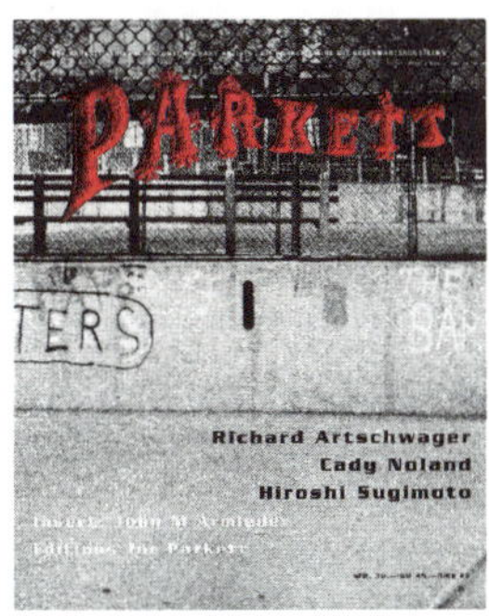

No. 46 - ISBN 3-907509-96-X

RICHARD ARTSCHWAGER
CADY NOLAND
HIROSHI SUGIMOTO
DEITCHER, SCHAFFNER, FORSTER
MUNIZ, ARMSTRONG, RELYEA
BOGDAN, GOODEVE, NICKAS
BRYSON, RUGOFF, DENSON
INSERT: **JOHN M ARMLEDER**
ROLAND WÄSPE: **ERWIN WURM**
D. BIRNBAUM: **ÖYVIND FAHLSTRÖM**
LES INFOS DU PARADIS: ROBERT FLECK
CUMULUS: MILLER, VETTESE
BALKON: MARTIN HELLER

VIJA CELMINS
ANDREAS GURSKY
RIRKRIT TIRAVANIJA
PRINCENTHAL, LEWIS, SILVERTHORNE
SHIFF, CRIQUI, BURCKHARDT, WAKEFIELD
SCHORR, MELO, GILLICK, FLOOD, STEINER
INSERT: **HANS DANUSER**
LES INFOS: LIAM GILLICK / DOUGLAS GORDON
LYNNE COOKE, DAVID DEITCHER
DANIEL KURJAKOVIC: **MARIE JOSÉ BURKI**
NAN GOLDIN: **PETER HUJAR**
NOEMI SMOLIK: **ANDREAS SLOMINSKI**
JASON SIMON: **MARK DION**
LUK LAMBRECHT: **MARK LUYTEN**

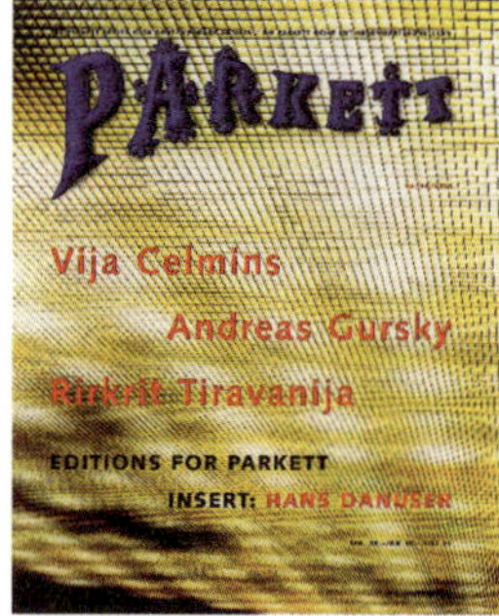

No. 44 - ISBN 3-907509-94-3

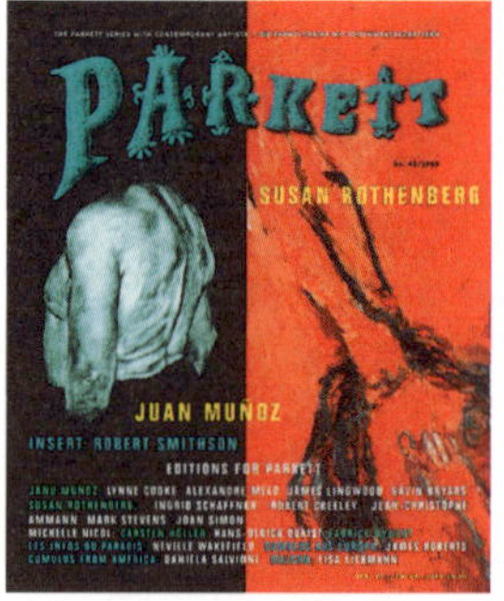

No. 43 - ISBN 3-907509-93-5

JUAN MUÑOZ
SUSAN ROTHENBERG
LYNNE COOKE, ALEXANDRE MELO
JAMES LINGWOOD, GAVIN BRYARS
ROBERT CREELEY, INGRID SCHAFFNER
JEAN-CHRISTOPHE AMMANN
MARK STEVENS, JOAN SIMON
INSERT: **ROBERT SMITHSON**
NEVILLE WAKEFIELD
MICHELLE NICOL: **CARSTEN HÖLLER**
H.U. OBRIST: **FABRICE HYBERT**

LAWRENCE WEINER
RACHEL WHITEREAD
B. ADAMS, F. RICHARD
D. SCHWARZ, D. SALVIONI
E. LEFFINGWELL, L. RELYEA
N. WAKEFIELD, R. SCHMITZ
T. FAIRBROTHER, S. WATNEY
INSERT: **NAN GOLDIN**
VINCE LEO: **ROBERT FRANK**
C. RITSCHARD: **MARKUS RAETZ**

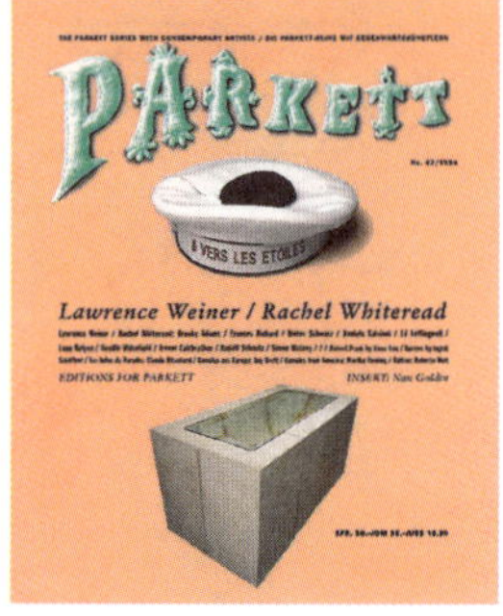

No. 42 - ISBN 3-907509-92-7

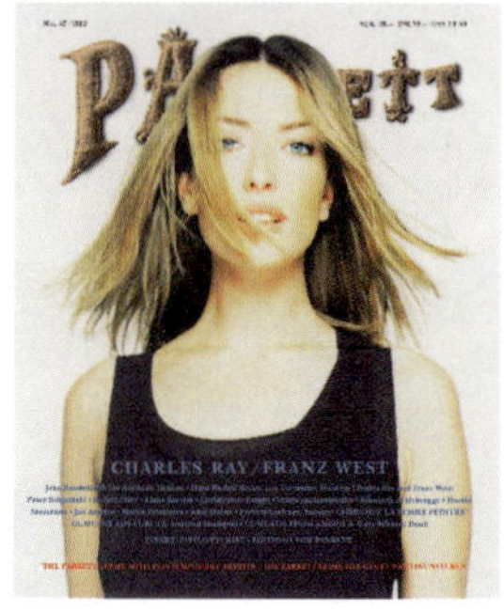

No. 37 - ISBN 3-907509-87-0

CHARLES RAY
FRANZ WEST
K. KERTESS, CH. KNIGHT
P. SCHJELDAHL, R. STORR
J. AVGIKOS, A. HUBER
M. PRINZHORN, E. SCHLEBRÜGGE
HARALD SZEEMANN
D. ZACHAROPOULOS
INSERT: **PIPILOTTI RIST**
JEAN BAUDRILLARD
HANS RUDOLF REUST: **LUC TUYMANS**
PARKETT INQUIRY:
CHERCHEZ LA FEMME PEINTRE

ILYA KABAKOV
RICHARD PRINCE
BORIS GROYS, ROBERT STORR
JAN THORN-PRIKKER
CLAUDIA JOLLES, EDMUND WHITE
SUSAN TALLMAN, DANIELA
SALVIONI, KATHY ACKER
INSERT: **TATSUO MIYAJIMA**
GUDRUN INBODEN: **ASTA GRÖTING**
LYNNE COOKE: **GARY HILL**
PATRICK McGRATH: **STEPHEN ELLIS**

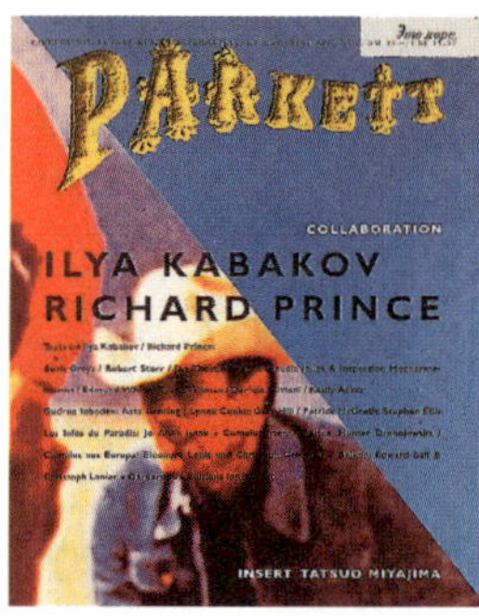

No. 34 - ISBN 3-907509-84-6

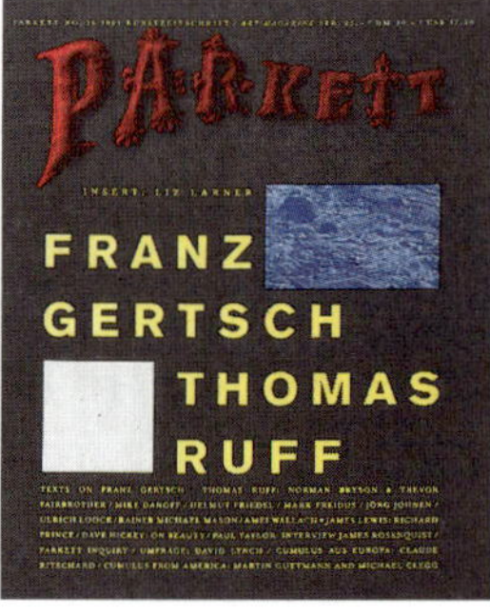

No. 28 - ISBN 3-907509-78-1

FRANZ GERTSCH
THOMAS RUFF
H. FRIEDEL, U. LOOCK
I. MICHAEL DANOFF
A. WALLACH. R. M. MASON
M. FREIDUS, J. JOHNEN
T. FAIRBROTHER/N. BRYSON
INSERT: **LIZ LARNER**
JAMES LEWIS: **RICHARD PRINCE**
DAVID HICKEY: **THE INVISIBLE DRAGON/DER UNSICHTBARE DRACHEN**
P. TAYLOR: **JAMES ROSENQUIST**

ALEX KATZ
JOHN RUSSELL, BROOKS ADAMS
DAVID RIMANELLI, FRANCESCO
CLEMENTE, MICHAEL KRÜGER
RICHARD FLOOD, PATRICK FREY
CARL STIGLIANO, BICE CURIGER
GLENN O'BRIEN
INSERT: **WILLIAM WEGMAN**
LISA LIEBMAN: **ROBERT GOBER**
JACQUELINE BURCKHARDT:
GIULIO ROMANO

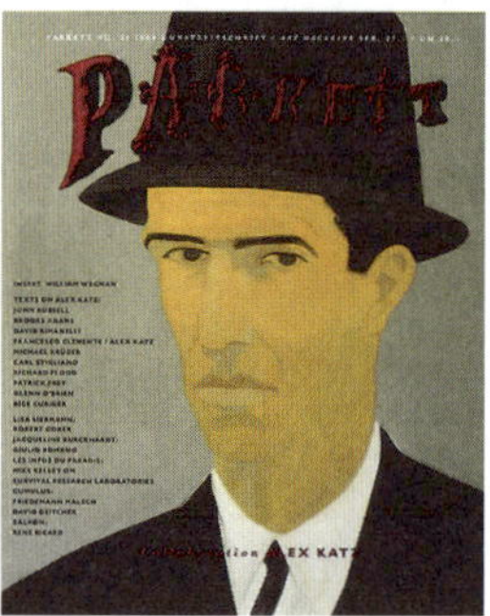

No. 21 - ISBN 3-907509-71-4

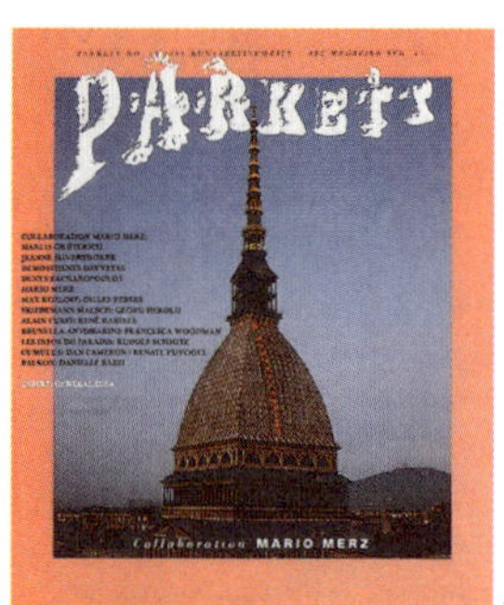

No. 15 - ISBN 3-907509-65-X

MARIO MERZ
MARLIS GRÜTERICH, JEANNE
SILVERTHORNE, DEMOSTHENES
DAVVETAS, HARALD SZEEMANN
DENYS ZACHAROPOULOS
INSERT: **GENERAL IDEA**
MAX KOZLOFF: **GILLES PERESS**
FRIEDEMANN MALSCH:
GEORG HEROLD
BRUNELLA ANTOMARINI:
FRANCESCA WOODMAN

Each volume of PARKETT is created in collaboration with artists, who contribute an original work specially made for the readers of PARKETT. The works are available in a signed and numbered Special Edition. Prices are subject to change. Postage is not included.

EDITIONS FOR PARKETT

Jeder PARKETT-Band entsteht in Collaboration mit Künstlern, die eigens für die Leser von PARKETT Originalbeiträge gestalten. Diese Vorzugsausgaben sind als nummerierte und signierte Editionen erhältlich. Preisänderungen vorbehalten. Versandkosten und MwSt. (Schweiz) nicht inbegriffen.

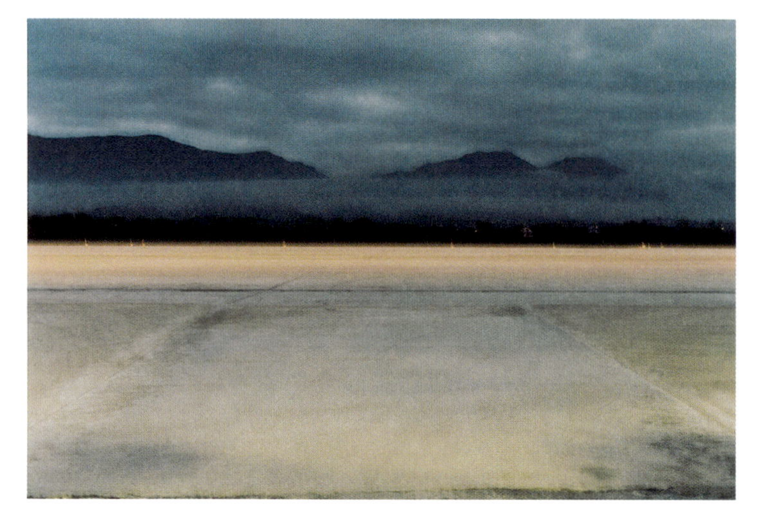

A BARREN PLACE AMONG PLACES: THE FACELESSNESS OF TECHNOLOGY VIES WITH THE ELOQUENCE OF DISTANT HILLS IN A DIVIDED UNIVERSE.

DER KARGE ORT ZWISCHEN DEN ORTEN: WINKEN NEUE HORIZONTE FERN UND BLAU, GERINNT DAS HIER UND JETZT ZUM BRACHEN FELD.

PARKETT 73

ANRI SALA

AIRPORT, 2005

C-print, paper size 20 1/2 x 27 9/16",
image size 16 1/2 x 23 5/8".
Edition of 60/XX, signed and numbered certificate
$ 1600 / € 1200

C-Print, Blattformat: 52 x 70 cm,
Bildformat: 42 x 60 cm.
Auflage: 60/XX, signiertes und nummeriertes Zertifikat.
CHF 1900 / € 1200

A BEEHIVE OF THOUGHTS BUZZING IN THE GULF BETWEEN WOMANHOOD AND SURVIVAL, PAST AND PRESENT, HUNGER AND SURFEIT, WORK AND PLAY...

WIE EIN BIENENSTOCK SUMMT DIESER KOPF ZWISCHEN EXISTENZNOT, WEIBLICHER MAGIE UND DER GELASSENHEIT DER LILIEN AUF DEM FELDE.

PARKETT 73

ELLEN GALLAGHER

RUBY DEE, 2005

Two-plate photogravure with aquatint and unique hand-shaped plasticine elements (in three colors) on multilayered laminated paper, framed.
Image size 6 x 4 x 1/8", with frame 9 1/4 x 7 1/4 x 1 1/4".
Produced by Two Palms Press, New York.
Edition of 30/XV, signed and numbered.
$ 3000 / € 2300

Photogravüre, Aquatinta und Knetmasse (dreifarbig, handgeformt), auf mehrschichtigem, laminiertem Papier, gerahmt.
Bildformat: 15,2 x 10,2 x 0,3 cm, mit Rahmen 23,5 x 18,4 x 3,8 cm.
Hergestellt bei Two Palms Press, New York.
Auflage: 30/XV, signiert und nummeriert.
CHF 3500 / € 2300

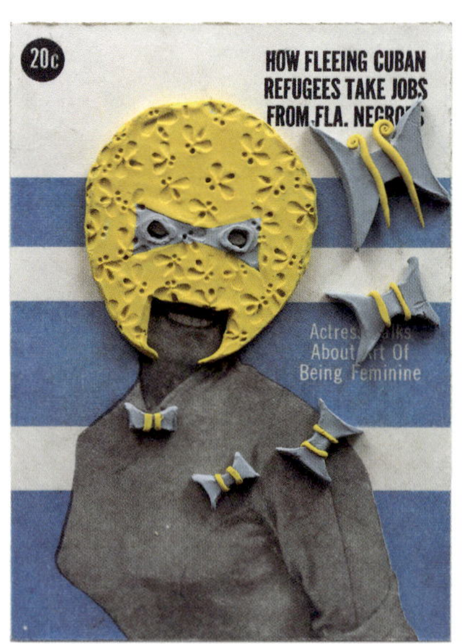

PARKETT 73

PAUL McCARTHY

PETER PAUL SKIN SAMPLE, 2005

15 color photographs (15 digital laser prints)
in cardboard box,
6 5/8 x 10" each.
Edition of 36/XII,
signed and numbered certificate.
$ 3300 / € 2500

15 Farbphotos (digitale Laserprints)
in Kartonschachtel,
je 16,8 x 25,4 cm.
Auflage: 36/XII,
signiertes und nummeriertes Zertifikat.
CHF 3800 / € 2500

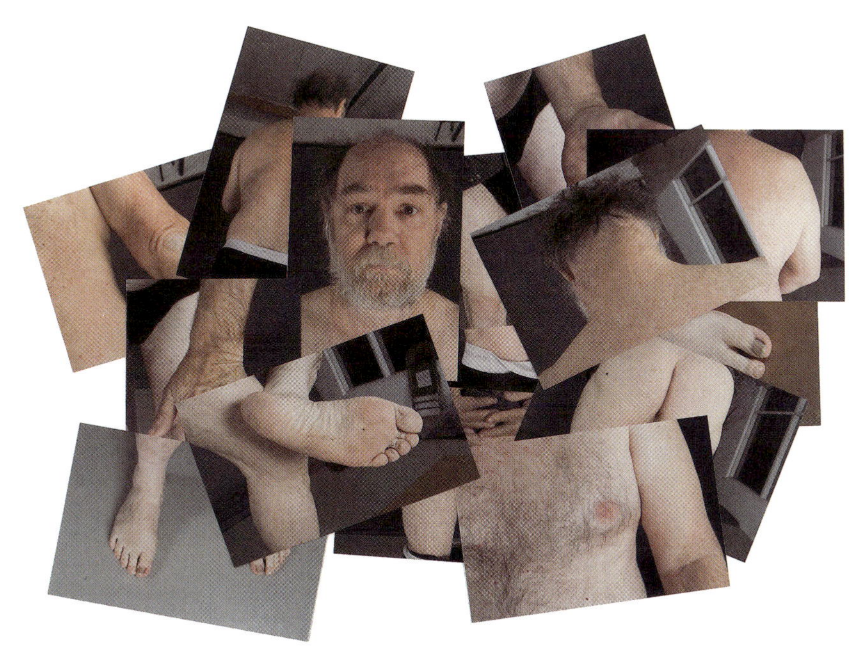

SKIN-DEEP FRAGMENTS GET UNDER YOUR SKIN IN THIS CANDIDLY UNINHIBITED AND TOUCHINGLY INTIMATE MEMENTO MORI.

FÜNFZEHN BILDSPLITTER DES (BEINAH) SPLITTERNACKTEN KÜNSTLERS – EIN KÜHNES UND BERÜHREND INTIMES MEMENTO MORI.

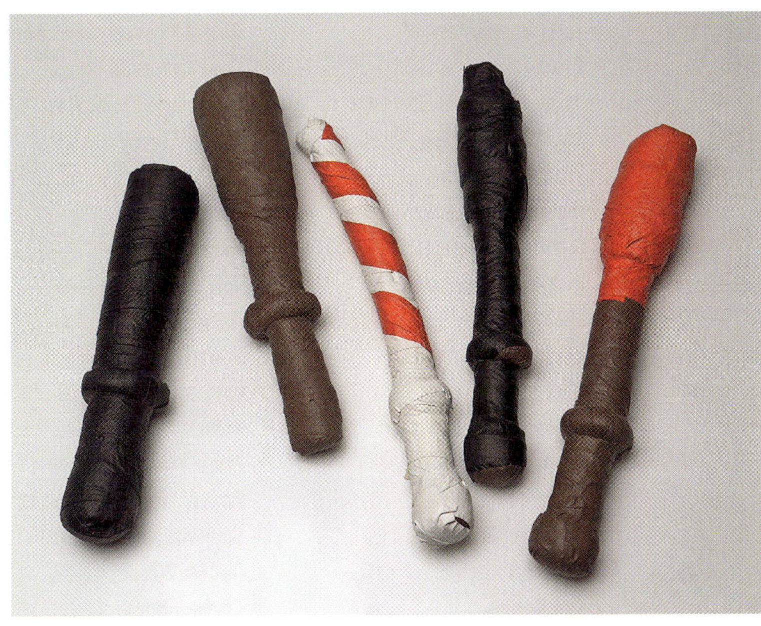

EMPTY THREATS? HYPERAGRESSION KEPT IN CHECK BY THE SOFT CORE OF ART.

LEERE DROHUNG? FURCHT EINFLÖSSENDER SCHLAGSTOCK MIT WEICHEM KERN.

PARKETT 73

PAUL McCARTHY

BILLY CLUB, 2005

Unique sculptural object, PVC, rubber foam, gaffers tape,
variable dimensions, ca. 20 x 4 x 4".
Edition of 36/XII, signed and numbered certificate.
$ 2000 / € 1600

Skulpturales Objekt, Unikat, PVC, Schaumstoff, Gaffers Tape,
unterschiedliche Grössen, ca. 55 x 10 x 10 cm.
Auflage: 36/XII, signiertes und nummeriertes Zertifikat.
CHF 2400 / € 1600

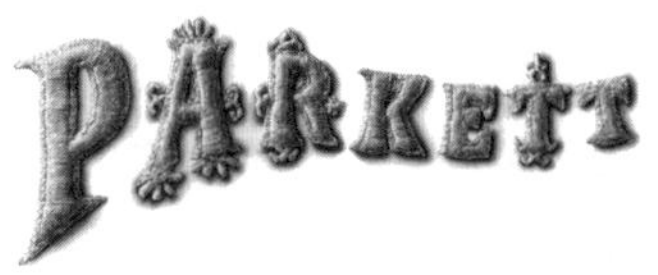

ARTISTS' MONOGRAPHS & EDITIONS / KÜNSTLERMONOGRAPHIEN & EDITIONEN

FOR AVAILABILITY SEE NEXT PAGE / LIEFERBARKEIT SIEHE FOLGENDE SEITE

Franz Ackermann, vol. 68
Eija-Liisa Ahtila, vol. 68
Doug Aitken, vol. 57
Francis Alÿs, vol. 69
Laurie Anderson, vol. 49
John Armleder, vol. 50/51
Richard Artschwager, vol. 23, vol. 46
John Baldessari, vol. 29
Stephan Balkenhol, vol. 36
Matthew Barney, vol. 45
Georg Baselitz, vol. 11
Vanessa Beecroft, vol. 56
Ross Bleckner, vol. 38
John Bock, vol. 67
Alighiero e Boetti, vol. 24
Christian Boltanski, vol. 22
Monica Bonvicini, vol. 72
Louise Bourgeois, vol. 27
Olaf Breuning, vol. 71
Angela Bulloch, vol. 66
Daniel Buren, vol. 66
Sophie Calle, vol. 36
Maurizio Cattelan, vol. 59
Vija Celmins, vol. 44
Francesco Clemente, vol. 9 & 40/41
Chuck Close, vol. 60
Enzo Cucchi, vol. 1
John Currin, vol. 65
Tacita Dean, vol. 62
Thomas Demand, vol. 62
Martin Disler, vol. 3
Peter Doig, vol. 67
Marlene Dumas, vol. 38
Olafur Eliasson, vol. 64
Tracey Emin, vol. 63
Urs Fischer, vol. 72
Eric Fischl, vol. 5
Peter Fischli / David Weiss, vol. 17, 40/41
Sylvie Fleury, vol. 58
Günther Förg, vol. 26 & 40/41
Tom Friedman, vol. 64
Katharina Fritsch, vol. 25
Bernard Frize, vol. 74
Ellen Gallagher, vol. 73
Isa Genzken, vol. 69
Franz Gertsch, vol. 28
Gilbert & George, vol. 14
Liam Gillick, vol. 61
Robert Gober, vol. 27
Nan Goldin, vol. 57
Felix Gonzalez-Torres, vol. 39
Douglas Gordon, vol. 49
Dan Graham, vol. 68
Rodney Graham, vol. 64
Katharina Grosse, vol. 74
Andreas Gursky, vol. 44
David Hammons, vol. 31
Thomas Hirschhorn, vol. 57
Damien Hirst, vol. 40/41
Jenny Holzer, vol. 40/41
Rebecca Horn, vol. 13 & 40/41
Roni Horn, vol. 54
Gary Hume, vol. 48
Pierre Huyghe, vol. 66
Ilya Kabakov, vol. 34
Anish Kapoor, vol. 69
Alex Katz, vol. 21, 72
Mike Kelley, vol. 31
Ellsworth Kelly, vol. 56
William Kentridge, vol. 63
Karen Kilimnik, vol. 52
Martin Kippenberger, vol. 19
Imi Knoebel, vol. 32
Jeff Koons, vol. 19, 50/51
Jannis Kounellis, vol. 6
Yayoi Kusama, vol. 59
Wolfgang Laib, vol. 39
Sherrie Levine, vol. 32
Sarah Lucas, vol. 45
Christian Marclay, vol. 70
Brice Marden, vol. 7
Paul McCarthy, vol. 73
Mario Merz, vol. 15
Tracey Moffatt, vol. 53
Mariko Mori, vol. 54
Malcolm Morley, vol. 52
Sarah Morris, vol. 61
Juan Muñoz, vol. 43
Jean-Luc Mylayne, vol. 50/51
Bruce Nauman, vol. 10
Cady Noland, vol. 46
Meret Oppenheim, vol. 4
Gabriel Orozco, vol. 48
Tony Oursler, vol. 47
Laura Owens, vol. 65
Jorge Pardo, vol. 56
Raymond Pettibon, vol. 47
Elizabeth Peyton, vol. 53
Richard Phillips, vol. 71
Sigmar Polke, vol. 2, 30 & 40/41
Richard Prince, vol. 34, 72
Michael Raedecker, vol. 65
Markus Raetz, vol. 8
Charles Ray, vol. 37
Jason Rhoades, vol. 58
Gerhard Richter, vol. 35
Bridget Riley, vol. 61
Pipilotti Rist, vol. 48, 71
Matthew Ritchie, vol. 61
Tim Rollins & K.O.S., vol. 20
Ugo Rondinone, vol. 52
James Rosenquist, vol. 58
Susan Rothenberg, vol. 43
Thomas Ruff, vol. 28
Edward Ruscha, vol. 18 & 55
Anri Sala, vol. 73
Wilhelm Sasnal, vol. 70
Gregor Schneider, vol. 63
Thomas Schütte, vol. 47
Richard Serra, vol. 74
Cindy Sherman, vol. 29
Roman Signer, vol. 45
Andreas Slominski, vol. 55
Beat Streuli, vol. 54
Thomas Struth, vol. 50/51
Hiroshi Sugimoto, vol. 46
Philip Taaffe, vol. 26
Sam Taylor-Wood, vol. 55
Diana Thater, vol. 60
Wolfgang Tillmans, vol. 53
Rirkrit Tiravanija, vol. 44
Fred Tomaselli, vol. 67
Rosemarie Trockel, vol. 33
James Turrell, vol. 25
Luc Tuymans, vol. 60
Keith Tyson, vol. 71
Kara Walker, vol. 59
Jeff Wall, vol. 22 & 49
Andy Warhol, vol. 12
Gillian Wearing, vol. 70
Lawrence Weiner, vol. 42
John Wesley, vol. 62
Franz West, vol. 37, 70
Rachel Whiteread, vol. 42
Sue Williams, vol 50/51
Robert Wilson, vol. 16
Christopher Wool, vol. 33

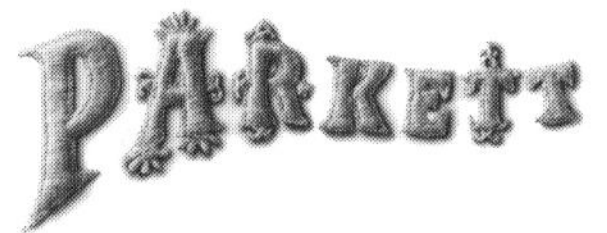

ARTISTS' EDITIONS FOR PARKETT SUBSCRIBERS
WWW.PARKETTART.COM

73

The PARKETT Series is created in collaboration with artists, who contribute an original work available exclusively to the subscribers in the form of a signed limited SPECIAL EDITION. The available works are also reproduced in each PARKETT issue.

Each SPECIAL EDITION is available by order from any one of our offices in New York or Zurich. Just fill in the details below and send this card to the office nearest you. Once your order has been processed, you will be issued with an invoice and your personal edition number. Upon receipt of payment, you will receive the SPECIAL EDITION. (Please note that supply is subject to availability. PARKETT does not assume responsibility for any delays in production of SPECIAL EDITIONS. Postage is not included.)

☐ As a subscriber to PARKETT, I would like to order the following Special Edition(s), signed and numbered by the artist.

PARKETT No.	ARTIST	NAME:
PARKETT No.	ARTIST	ADDRESS:
PARKETT No.	ARTIST	CITY:
PARKETT No.	ARTIST	STATE/ZIP:
PARKETT No.	ARTIST	COUNTRY:
PARKETT No.	ARTIST	PHONE:

☐ I have indicated my way of payment on the reverse side of this form.

Send this form to the PARKETT office nearest you:

PARKETT PUBLISHERS 155 AV. OF THE AMERICAS NEW YORK, NY 10013 PHONE (212) 673-2660 FAX (212) 271-0704

PARKETT VERLAG QUELLENSTRASSE 27 CH-8031 ZÜRICH TELEFON +41-1-271 81 40 FAX +41-1-272 43 01

Visit our website: www.parkettart.com

KÜNSTLEREDITIONEN FÜR PARKETT-ABONNENTEN
WWW.PARKETTART.COM

73

Die PARKETT-Buchreihe entsteht in Zusammenarbeit mit Künstlern, die eigens für die Abonnenten einen Originalbeitrag in Form einer limitierten und signierten EDITION gestalten. Diese Editionen sind auch in der Zeitschrift abgebildet und können mit dieser Bestellkarte in jedem unserer Büros in Zürich, Frankfurt oder New York bestellt werden. Sie erhalten dann Ihre persönliche Editionsnummer und eine Rechnung. Sobald wir Ihre Zahlung erhalten haben, schicken wir Ihnen Ihre Edition(en). Lieferung solange Vorrat. PARKETT übernimmt keine Verantwortung für allfällige Verzögerungen bei der Herstellung der Vorzugsausgaben. Versandkosten und MwSt (Schweiz) nicht inbegriffen.

☐ Ich bin PARKETT-Abonnent(in) und bestelle folgende EDITION(EN), nummeriert und vom Künstler signiert:

PARKETT Nr.	KÜNSTLER/IN	NAME:
PARKETT Nr.	KÜNSTLER/IN	STRASSE:
PARKETT Nr.	KÜNSTLER/IN	PLZ/STADT:
PARKETT Nr.	KÜNSTLER/IN	LAND:
PARKETT Nr.	KÜNSTLER/IN	TEL.:

☐ Meine Zahlungsweise habe ich auf der Rückseite angegeben.

Senden Sie die Bestellkarte an das PARKETT-Büro in Ihrer Nähe:

PARKETT VERLAG QUELLENSTRASSE 27 CH-8031 ZÜRICH TELEFON +41-1-271 81 40 FAX +41-1-272 43 01

PARKETT PUBLISHERS 155 AV. OF THE AMERICAS NEW YORK, NY 10013 PHONE (212) 673-2660 FAX (212) 271-0704

Besuchen Sie unsere Website: www.parkettart.com

PARKETT

SUBSCRIBE, COMPLETE OR SEND A GIFT SUBSCRIPTION TO THE BEST BOOK SERIES ON CONTEMPORARY ARTISTS – WWW.PARKETTART.COM

73

☐ I wish to subscribe to the PARKETT Series, starting with issue no. ______

☐ I wish to send a gift subscription, starting with issue no. ______ (a gift card in my name will be sent to the recipient):

☐ for 1 year (3 issues) at US $ 80 (USA/Canada), € 82 (Europe), € 98 (Rest of the World)

☐ for 2 years (6 issues) at US $ 145 (USA/Canada), € 150 (Europe), € 188 (Rest of the World)

☐ for 3 years (9 issues) at US $ 205 (USA/Canada), € 212 (Europe), € 278 (Rest of the World)

☐ for 1 year (3 issues) at the special student discount (US $ 65 for USA/Canada, € 67 for Europe). A copy of my student ID is enclosed. Postage included. All prices subject to change.

☐ I wish to complete my PARKETT library and order the following issue(s):

No. ______________________________

at € 30 each (up to no. 43: € 20; no. 44–48: € 28), postage not included. Within the USA & Canada $ 32 (up to no. 43: $ 22.50; no. 44–48: $ 29), add postage: $ 5 (USA), $ 10 (Canada). (Sold out: No. 1–10, 12, 13, 16, 17, 19, 22, 25, 26, 27, 29–31, 35, 36, 38, 45).

☐ I wish to order _____ copies of the PARKETT Postcard Set with Text Booklet on MoMA Show. 146 color postcards, booklet with 2 essays, color reproductions, 64 p., packed in a box, 6¼ x 4¾ x 2⅜", € 32 (USA $ 39) per set, plus postage.

☐ I wish to order _____ copies of "PARKETT – 20 Years of Artists' Collaborations," providing "a rare behind-the-scenes look at one of the art world's most respected art magazines." 248 p., 22 color pages, 1 color poster, € 32 (USA $ 39), plus postage.

NAME: ______________________________

ADDRESS: ______________________________

CITY: ______________________________

STATE/ZIP/COUNTRY: ______________________________

TEL.: ______________ FAX: ______________

E-MAIL: ______________________________

GIFT RECIPIENT: ______________________________

ADDRESS: ______________________________

CITY: ______________________________

STATE/ZIP: ______________________________

COUNTRY: ______________________________

☐ Charge my Visa Card ☐ Mastercard ☐ AMEX

Card No. ______________ Expiration date ________

☐ Payment enclosed (US check or money order) ☐ Bill me

DATE ______________________________

SIGNATURE ______________________________

Send this form to the PARKETT office nearest you:

PARKETT PUBLISHERS 155 AV. OF THE AMERICAS NEW YORK, NY 10013 PHONE (212) 673-2660 FAX (212) 271-0704

PARKETT VERLAG QUELLENSTRASSE 27 CH-8031 ZÜRICH TELEFON +41-1-271 81 40 FAX +41-1-272 43 01

Visit our website: www.parkettart.com

PARKETT

ABONNIEREN, VERVOLLSTÄNDIGEN ODER VERSCHENKEN SIE DIE UMFASSENDSTE BUCHREIHE ÜBER GEGENWARTSKÜNSTLER – WWW.PARKETTART.COM

73

☐ Ich abonniere die PARKETT-Reihe ab Nr. ______

☐ Ich verschenke ein PARKETT-Abonnement ab Nr. ______ (Der/die Beschenkte erhält eine Geschenkkarte in meinem Namen)

☐ für 1 Jahr (3 Bände) zu: € 78 (Deutschland), CHF 116.– (Schweiz), € 82 (übriges Europa)

☐ für 2 Jahre (6 Bände) zu: € 140 (Deutschland), CHF 216.– (Schweiz), € 150 (übriges Europa)

☐ für 3 Jahre (9 Bände) zu: € 200 (Deutschland), CHF 312.– (Schweiz), € 212 (übriges Europa)

☐ für 1 Jahr (3 Bände) zum Studenten-Sonderpreis (Deutschland: € 65 /Schweiz: CHF 96.– / übriges Europa: € 67). Eine Kopie meines gültigen Studentenausweises lege ich bei. Preise einschliesslich Versandkosten. Preisänderungen vorbehalten.

☐ Ich möchte meine PARKETT-Bibliothek vervollständigen und bestelle die folgenden noch erhältliche(n) Ausgabe(n):

Nr. ______________________________

zu je € 30 / CHF 45.– (bis Nr. 43: € 20 / CHF 30.–; Nr. 44–48: € 28 / CHF 39.–), zzgl. Versandkosten (vergriffen: Nr. 1–10, 12, 13, 16, 17, 19, 22, 25, 26, 27, 29–31, 35, 36, 38, 45).

☐ Ich bestelle _____ Ex. des aktualisierten PARKETT-Postkarten-Sets mit Textbüchlein zur MoMA-Ausstellung. 146 Farbpostkarten, Büchlein mit zwei Texten, Farbabb., 64 S., in bunter Schachtel, 16 x 12 x 6 cm. € 32 / CHF 45.– pro Set, zzgl. Versandkosten.

☐ Ich bestelle _____ Ex. «Parkett – 20 Years of Artists' Collaborations», das neue Buch, das «Einblick hinter die Kulissen der weltweit hoch geschätzten Kunstzeitschrift gewährt». 248 S., dt./engl., 22 Farbseiten, 1 Farbposter, € 32 / CHF 45.–, zzgl. Versandkosten.

NAME: ______________________________

STRASSE: ______________________________

PLZ/STADT: ______________________________

LAND: ______________________________

TEL.: ______________ FAX: ______________

E-MAIL: ______________________________

BESCHENKTE(R): ______________________________

STRASSE: ______________________________

PLZ/STADT: ______________________________

LAND: ______________________________

☐ Ich zahle mit Visa ☐ Eurocard/Mastercard ☐ AMEX

Karten Nr. ______________ Gültig bis ________

☐ Mein Scheck über CHF/€ ______________ liegt bei.

☐ Bitte senden Sie mir eine Rechnung.

DATUM ______________________________

UNTERSCHRIFT ______________________________

Senden Sie die Bestellkarte an das PARKETT-Büro in Ihrer Nähe:

PARKETT VERLAG QUELLENSTRASSE 27 CH-8031 ZÜRICH TELEFON +41-1-271 81 40 FAX +41-1-272 43 01

PARKETT PUBLISHERS 155 AV. OF THE AMERICAS NEW YORK, NY 10013 PHONE (212) 673-2660 FAX (212) 271-0704

Besuchen Sie unsere Website: www.parkettart.com

vol.	Collaboration		
74	Bernard Frize		
	Katharina Grosse		
	Richard Serra		
73	Ellen Gallagher	m	e
	Paul McCarthy	m	e
	Anri Sala	m	e
72	Monica Bonvicini	m	e
	Urs Fischer	m	
	Richard Prince	m	
71	Olaf Breuning	m	e
	Richard Phillips	m	e
	Keith Tyson	m	e
70	Christian Marclay	m	e
	Wilhelm Sasnal	m	e
	Gillian Wearing	m	e
69	Francis Alÿs	m	
	Isa Gentzken	m	e
	Anish Kapoor	m	
68	Franz Ackermann	m	e
	Eija-Liisa Ahtila	m	e
	Dan Graham	m	e
67	John Bock	m	e
	Peter Doig	m	e
	Fred Tomaselli	m	
66	Angela Bulloch	m	e
	Daniel Buren	m	e
	Pierre Huyghe	m	e
65	John Currin	m	
	Laura Owens	m	e
	Michael Raedecker	m	e
64	Olafur Eliasson	m	
	Tom Friedman	m	
	Rodney Graham	m	
63	Tracey Emin	m	e
	William Kentridge	m	
	Gregor Schneider	m	
62	Tacita Dean	m	e
	Thomas Demand	m	
	John Wesley	m	e
61	Liam Gillick	m	
	Sarah Morris	m	e
	Bridget Riley	m	
	Matthew Ritchie	m	e
60	Chuck Close	m	
	Diana Thater	m	e
	Luc Tuymans	m	e
59	Maurizio Cattelan	m	
	Yayoi Kusama	m	
	Kara Walker	m	
58	Sylvie Fleury	m	
	Jason Rhoades	m	
	James Rosenquist	m	
57	Doug Aitken	m	e

vol.	Collaboration		
57	Nan Goldin	m	
	Thomas Hirschhorn	m	
56	Vanessa Beecroft	m	
	Ellsworth Kelly	m	
	Jorge Pardo	m	e
55	Edward Ruscha	m	
	Andreas Slominski	m	
	Sam Taylor-Wood	m	
54	Roni Horn	m	e
	Mariko Mori	m	
	Beat Streuli	m	
53	Tracey Moffatt	m	
	Elizabeth Peyton	m	
	Wolfgang Tillmans	m	
52	Karen Kilimnik	m	e
	Malcolm Morley	m	e
	Ugo Rondinone	m	e
50/51	John Armleder	m	
	Jeff Koons	m	e
	Jean-Luc Mylayne	m	
	Thomas Struth	m	
	Sue Williams	m	
49	Laurie Anderson	m	e
	Douglas Gordon	m	
	Jeff Wall	m	
48	Gary Hume	m	
	Gabriel Orozco	m	
	Pipilotti Rist	m	
47	Tony Oursler	m	
	Raymond Pettibon	m	
	Thomas Schütte	m	e
46	Richard Artschwager	m	
	Cady Noland	m	
	Hiroshi Sugimoto	m	
45	Matthew Barney		
	Sarah Lucas		
	Roman Signer		e
44	Vija Celmins	m	
	Andreas Gursky	m	
	Rirkrit Tiravanija	m	e
43	Juan Muñoz	m	
	Susan Rothenberg	m	
42	Lawrence Weiner	m	e
	Rachel Whiteread	m	
40/41	Francesco Clemente	m	
	Fischli/Weiss	m	
	Günther Förg	m	
	Damien Hirst	m	
	Jenny Holzer	m	
	Rebecca Horn	m	
	Sigmar Polke	m	
39	Felix Gonzalez-Torres	m	
	Wolfgang Laib	m	

vol.	Collaboration		
38	Ross Bleckner		
	Marlene Dumas		
37	Charles Ray	m	
	Franz West	m	e
36	Stephan Balkenhol		
	Sophie Calle		
35	Gerhard Richter		
34	Ilya Kabakov	m	
	Richard Prince	m	
33	Rosemarie Trockel	m	
	Christopher Wool	m	
32	Imi Knoebel	m	
	Sherrie Levine	m	
31	David Hammons		
	Mike Kelley		
30	Sigmar Polke		
29	John Baldessari		
	Cindy Sherman		
28	Franz Gertsch	m	
	Thomas Ruff	m	
27	Louise Bourgeois		
	Robert Gober		
26	Günther Förg		
	Philip Taaffe		
25	Katharina Fritsch		e
	James Turrell		
24	Alighiero e Boetti	m	
23	Richard Artschwager	m	
22	Christian Boltanski		
	Jeff Wall		
21	Alex Katz	m	
20	Tim Rollins + K.O.S.	m	
19	Martin Kippenberger		
	Jeff Koons		
18	Ed Ruscha	m	
17	Fischli/Weiss		
16	Robert Wilson		
15	Mario Merz	m	
14	Gilbert & George	m	
13	Rebecca Horn		
12	Andy Warhol		
11	Georg Baselitz	m	
10	Bruce Nauman		
9	Francesco Clemente		
8	Markus Raetz		
7	Brice Marden		
6	Jannis Kounellis		
5	Eric Fischl		
4	Meret Oppenheim		
3	Martin Disler		
2	Sigmar Polke		
1	Enzo Cucchi		

m = available monograph / erhältliche Monographie, e = available edition / erhältliche Edition
Delivery subject to availability at time of order / Lieferung solange Vorrat

PARKETT IN BOOKSHOPS (Selection)

PARKETT IS AVAILABLE IN 500 LEADING ART BOOKSHOPS AROUND THE WORLD. FOR FURTHER INFORMATION CONTACT:
PARKETT GIBT ES IN 500 FÜHRENDEN KUNSTBUCHHANDLUNGEN AUF DER GANZEN WELT. FÜR WEITERE INFORMATIONEN WENDEN SIE SICH BITTE AN:
PARKETT VERLAG, QUELLENSTRASSE 27, CH-8031 ZÜRICH, TEL. +41-1 271 81 40, FAX 272 43 01, WWW.PARKETTART.COM;
PARKETT, 155, AVENUE OF THE AMERICAS, 2ND FLOOR, NEW YORK, N.Y. 10013, PHONE +1 (212) 673-2660, FAX 271-0704, WWW.PARKETTART.COM

NORTH & SOUTH AMERICA, ASIA, AUSTRALIA

DISTRIBUTOR / VERTRIEB
D.A.P. (DISTRIBUTED ART PUBLISHERS)
155 AVENUE OF THE AMERICAS,
2ND FLOOR,
NEW YORK, NY 10013

USA

AUSTIN, TX
BOOK PEOPLE
603 N. LAMAR

BEACON, NY
DIA: BEACON
3 BEEKMAN STREET

BERKELEY, CA
BERKELEY ART MUSEUM
2625 DURANT AVENUE

CODY'S BOOKS
2454 TELEGRAPHE AVENUE

BEVERLY HILLS, CA
RIZZOLI
9501 WILSHIRE BOULEVARD

BOSTON, MA
INSTITUTE OF CONTEMPORARY ART
955 BOYLSTON STREET

TRIDENT BOOKSELLERS
338 NEWBURY STREET

BUFFALO, NY
TALKING LEAVES
3158 MAIN STREET

CAMBRIDGE, MA
MIT PRESS BOOKSTORE
292 MAIN STREET

CHICAGO, IL
ART INSTITUTE OF CHICAGO
104 S. MICHIGAN

MUSEUM OF CONTEMPORARY ART
220 EAST CHICAGO AVENUE

QUIMBY'S
1854 W. NORTH AVENUE

SMART MUSEUM OF ART
5550 S. GREENWOOD AVENUE

CINCINNATI, OH
CONTEMPORARY ARTS CENTER
115 E. 5TH STREET

COLUMBUS, OH
COLUMBUS MUSEUM OF ART
372 COMMONS MALL

WEXNER CENTER BOOKSTORE
30 W. 15TH STREET

CORAL GABLES, FL
BOOKS & BOOKS
296 ARAGON ROAD

HOUSTON, TX
BRAZOS BOOKSTORE
2421 BISSONNET

CONTEMPORARY ARTS MUSEUM
5216 MONTROSE BOULEVARD

MENIL COLLECTION
1520 SUL ROSS

HUNTINGTON, WV
HUNTINGTON MUSEUM OF ART
2033 MCCOY ROAD

LOS ANGELES, CA
BOOK SOUP
8818 SUNSET BOULEVARD/
3333 BRISTOL ST.

MUSEUM OF CONTEMPORARY ART
250, S. GRAND

LOS ANGELES, CA
UCLA / ARMAND HAMMER MUSEUM OF ART
10899 WILSHIRE BOULEVARD

MIAMI, FL
BOOKS & BOOKS
296 ARAGON AVENUE, CORAL GABLES

MUSEUM OF CONTEMPORARY ART
770 N.E. 125TH STREET NORTH MIAMI

MIAMI BEACH, FL
BASE, 939, LINCOLN ROAD

MINNEAPOLIS, MN
THE WALKER ART CENTER BOOKSTORE
VINELAND PLACE

NEW YORK, NY
MUSEUM OF MODERN ART
11 WEST 53RD STREET

NEW MUSEUM OF CONTEMPORARY
ART STORE
556 WEST 22ND STREET

RIZZOLI
454 WEST BROADWAY

SAINT MARK'S BOOKSTORE
31 3RD AVENUE

COLISEUM BOOKS INC.
11 WEST 42ND STREET

OAKLAND, CA
DIESEL, A BOOKSTORE
5433 COLLEGE AVENUE

OAK PARK, MI
BOOK BEAT LTD.
26010 GREENFIELD

OMAHA, NE
JOSLYN ART MUSEUM
2200 DODGE STREET

PHILADELPHIA, PA
AVRIL 50
3406 SANSOM STREET

WATERSTONE BOOKSELLERS
2191 HORNIG ROAD

PITTSBURGH, PA
CARNEGIE INSTITUTE
4400 FORBES AVENUE

PORTLAND, OR
POWELL'S BOOKS
7 NW 9TH STREET

PROVIDENCE, NY
ACCIDENT OR DESIGN
128 N. MAIN STREET

RHODE ISLAND SCHOOL OF DESIGN
2 COLLEGE STREET, 1765

SAN ANTONIO, TX
SLOAN / HALL SAN ANTONIO
5930 BROADWAY

SAN FRANCISCO, CA
A CLEAN WELL LIGHTED PLACE
601 VAN NESS AVENUE

CITY LIGHTS BOOKSHOP
261 COLUMBUS AVENUE

SF MUSEUM OF MODERN ART,
MUSEUMBOOKS
151 3RD STREET, 1ST FLOOR

ST. LOUIS, MO
LEFT BANK BOOKS
399 NORTH EUCLID

SANTA MONICA, CA
ARCANA
1229 3RD STREET PROMENADE

BERGAMOT BOOKSTORE
2525 MICHIGAN AVENUE, G-5B

HENNESSEY & INGALLS BOOKS
214 WILSHIRE BLVD

ST. PAUL, MN
HUNGRY MIND BOOKSTORE
1648 GRAND AVENUE

SEATTLE, WA
UNIVERSITY BOOKSTORE
4326 UNIVERSITY WAY

WASHINGTON D.C.
NATIONAL GALLERY OF ART
6TH STREET & CONSTITUTION
AVENUE, NW

CANADA / KANADA

MONTREAL
OLIVIERI LIBRAIRIE BOOKSTORE
185 STREET CATHERINE WEST

TORONTO
ART GALLERY OF ONTARIO
317 DUNDAS STREET WEST

ART METROPOLE
788 KING STREET WEST

DAVID MIRVISH BOOKS ON ART
596 MARKHAM STREET

VANCOUVER
VANCOUVER ART GALLERY
750 HORNBY STREET

AUSTRALIA / AUSTRALIEN

DARLINGHURST
EAST SYDNEY BOOKSTORE
THE DOME, THE ELAN BUILDING
1 KINGS CROSS ROAD

SYDNEY
MUSEUM OF CONTEMPORARY ART
140 GEORGE STREET,
CIRCULAR QUAY NORTH

GLEE BOOKS
191 GLEBE POINT ROAD, GLEBE

NEW ZEALAND / NEUSEELAND

AUCKLAND
MAGAZZINO SUBSCRIPTION
P.O. BOX 905909

ASIA / ASIEN

JAPAN

TOKYO
AOYAMA BOOK CENTRE, SHIBUYA-KU
COSMOS AOYAMA GARDEN FLOOR B2F
5-53-97, JINGUMAE

ART & BOOKS
2-1-13-307
TAKANAWA, MINATO-KU

EOS ART BOOKS
DOMILE KITA 108
1-10-21 KICHIJOJI-KITAMACHI

SINGAPORE / SINGAPUR

PAGE ONE BOOKSTORE
20 KAKI BUKIT VIEW TECHPARK

CHINA

TAIPEI
ARTLAND BOOKS CO., LTD.
B1 122 JEN AI RD., SEC3

GREAT BRITAIN / GROSSBRITANNIEN

DISTRIBUTOR / VERTRIEB
CENTRAL BOOKS
99, WALLIS ROAD
LONDON E9 5LN

BRIMINGHAM
IKON GALLERY
1 OOZELLS SQUARE

BRIGHTON
BORDERS BOOKSHOP
CHURCHILL SQUARE SHOPPING CENTRE

BRISTOL
ARNOLFINI BOOKSHOP
16 NARROW QUAY

CARDIFF
CHAPTER ARTS CENTRE
MARKET ROAD

CARLISLE
CASTLE THE STORE
LONDON ROAD

LONDON
ARTWORDS BOOKSHOP
RIVINGTON STREET

BORDERS BOOKSHOP
120 CHARING CROSS ROAD

BORDERS BOOKSHOP
203–207 OXFORD STREET

BORDERS BOOKSHOP
N1 CENTRE ISLINGTON

CAMDEN ARTS CENTRE
ARKWRIGHT ROAD

HAYWARD GALLERY
SOUTH BANK

IAN SHIPLEY BOOKSHOP
70 CHARING CROSS ROAD

INSTITUTE OF CONTEMPORARY ARTS
12 CARLTON HOUSE TERRACE

THE MALL
SERPENTINE GALLERY
KENSINGTON GARDENS

TATE MODERN
BANKSIDE

WHITECHAPEL ART GALLERY
80 WHITECHAPEL HIGH STREET

OXFORD

MODERN ART OXFORD
30 PEMBROKE STREET

SCOTLAND / SCHOTTLAND

EDINBURGH

SCOTTISH GALLERY OF MODERN ART
75 BELFORD ROAD

IRELAND / IRLAND

CORK

LEWIS GLUCKSMAN GALLERY
UNIVERSITY COLLEGE

DUBLIN

DOUGLAS HYDE GALLERY
TRINITY COLLEGE

GERMANY / DEUTSCHLAND

DISTRIBUTOR / VERTRIEB

GVA VERLAGSSERVICE GÖTTINGEN
PF 2021
D-37010 GÖTTINGEN

BERLIN

BÜCHERBOGEN AM SAVIGNYPLATZ
STADTBAHNBOGEN 593

GALERIE 2000 KUNSTBUCHHANDLUNG
KNESEBECKSTRASSE 56/58

WIENS LADEN & VERLAG
LINIENSTRASSE 158 (HOF)

BIELEFELD

THALIA UNIVERSITÄTSBUCHHANDLUNG
FILIALE PHÖNIX, OBERNTORWALL 23

BREMEN

BEIM STEINERNEN KREUZ GMBH
BEIM STEINERNEN KREUZ 1

DRESDEN

WEISSLACK
LUISENSTRASSE 52

DÜSSELDORF

LITERATUR BEI RUDOLF MÜLLER
NEUSTRASSE 38

WALTHER KÖNIG BUCHHANDLUNG
HEINRICH-HEINE-ALLEE 15

FRANKFURT

KUNST-BUCH, KUNSTHALLE SCHIRN
RÖMERBERG 7

WALTHER KÖNIG BUCHHANDLUNG
DOMSTRASSE 6

HAMBURG

HELMUT VON DER HÖH BUCHHANDLUNG
GROSSE BLEICHEN 21

SAUTTER + LACKMANN BUCHHANDLUNG
ADMIRALITÄTSTRASSE 71/72

HANNOVER

MERZ KUNSTBUCHHANDLUNG
KURT-SCHWITTERS-PLATZ

HERFORD

PROVINZBUCHLADEN GMBH
HAEMMELINGER STRASSE 22

KARLSRUHE

HANS MENDE BUCHHANDLUNG
KARLSTRASSE 76

ZENTRUM FÜR KUNST &
MEDIENTECHNOLOGIE
MUSEUMSSHOP, LORENZSTRASSE 19

KÖLN

WALTHER KÖNIG BUCHHANDLUNG
EHRENSTRASSE 4

KIOSK-BUCH-EVENT GMBH
IM MEDIAPARK 7

MÜNCHEN

HANS GOLTZ BUCHHANDLUNG
FÜR BILDENDE KUNST
TÜRKENSTRASSE 54

ILKA KÖNIG BUCHHANDLUNG
MAXIMILIANSTRASSE 35

L. WERNER BUCHHANDLUNG
RESIDENZSTRASSE 18

NÜRNBERG

WALTHER KÖNIG BUCHHANDLUNG
LUITPOLDSTRASSE 5

STUTTGART

LIMACHER BUCHHANDLUNG
KÖNIGSTRASSE 28 / KÖNIGSBAU

SPAIN / SPANIEN

BARCELONA

LAIE – CAIXAFÒRUM
MARQUES DE COMILLAS 6–8

LAIE – CCCB (CENTRE DE CULTURA
CONTEMPORÀNIA DE BARCELONA)
MONTALEGRE 5

MADRID

MUSEO NACIONAL REINA SOFIA
C/ SANTA ISABEL, 52

FRANCE / FRANKREICH

PARIS

CENTRE POMPIDOU, FLAMMARION 4
26, RUE JACOB

GALERIE NATIONALE DU JEU DE PAUME
1, PLACE DE LA CONCORDE

LIBRAIRIE DU MUSÉE D'ART MODERNE
9, RUE GASTON DE SAINT-PAUL

CHRISTOPH DAVIET-THERY,
LIVRES & EDITIONS D'ARTISTES
10, RUE DUCHEFDELAVILLE

COLETTE
213, RUE SAINT-HONORÉ

ITALY / ITALIEN

MILANO

A&M BOOKSTORE
30, VIA TADINO

ROMA

GALLERIA NAZIONALE D'ARTE MODERNA
131, VIA DELLE BELLE ARTI

GALLERIA PRIMO PIANO
203, VIA PANISPERNA

NORWAY / NORWEGEN

OSLO

THE NATIONAL MUSEUM OF
CONTEMPORARY ART
BANKPLASSEN 4 / SKATTEFOG

PORTUGAL

LISBOA

MODULO CENTRO DIFUSOR DE ARTE
CALÇADA DOS MESTRES 34 A–B

PORTO

MODULO CENTRO DIFUSOR DE ARTE
AV. BOAVISTA 854

SWEDEN / SCHWEDEN

STOCKHOLM

KULTURHUSET KONSTIG
MEDIA & KONSTBOKHANDEL
SERGELS TORG 3

MODERNA MUSEET
SKEPPSHOLMEN

GÖTEBORG

GÖTEBORGS KONSTMUSEUM
GÖTAPLATSEN / AVENYN

TURKEY / TÜRKEI

ISTANBUL

ROBINSON CRUSOE BOOKS PUSULA
PRODUCTIONS
389 ISTIKAL CADDESI BEYOGLU

NETHERLANDS, BELGIUM AND LUXEMBURG

DISTRIBUTOR / VERTRIEB

IDEA BOOKS
NIEUWE HERENGRACHT 11
NL-1011 RK AMSTERDAM

NETHERLANDS / NIEDERLANDE

AMSTERDAM

ART BOOK
VAN BAERLESTRAAT 126

ATHENAEUM NIEUWSCENTRUM
SPUI 14–16

EINDHOVEN

MOTTA
BERGSTRAAT 35

GRONINGEN

SCHOLTENS / WRISTERS BOOKSHOP
FULDENSTRAAT 20

HAARLEM

ATHENAEUM
GED. OUDE GRACHT 70

HENGELO

BROEKHUIS
WEMENSTRAAT 45

MAASTRICHT

DE TRIBUNE
KAPOENSTRAAT 8

BELGIUM / BELGIEN

ANTWERPEN

COPYRIGHT BOOKSHOP
NATIONALSTRAAT 28A

BRUXELLES

PEINTURE FRAICHE
10, RUE DU TABELLON

TROPISMES LIBRAIRIES
GALERIE DES PRINCES 11

GENT

COPYRIGHT BOOKSHOP
JACOBIJNENSTRAAT 8

LUXEMBOURG / LUXEMBURG

LUXEMBOURG

CASINO LUXEMBOURG
41, RUE NOTRE-DAME

SWITZERLAND / SCHWEIZ

DISTRIBUTOR / VERTRIEB

SCHEIDEGGER & CO. C/O AVA
CENTRALWEG 16
CH-8910 AFFOLTERN A. A.

BASEL

FONDATION BEYELER
BASELSTRASSE 77, RIEHEN

GALERIE STAMPA
SPALENBERG 2

JÄGGI BUCHHANDLUNG
FREIE STRASSE 32

KUNSTHALLE BASEL
KLOSTERGASSE 5

BERN

STAUFFACHER BUCHHANDLUNG
IM KUNSTMUSEUM
HODLERSTR. 12

LUZERN

ORELL FÜSSLI / RÄBER BÜCHER & MEDIEN
FRANKENSTRASSE 7–9

GENÈVE

LIBRAIRIE PAYOT
5, RUE DE CHANTEPOULET

MENDRISIO

GABRIELE CAPELLI LIBRERIA
ARCHITETTURA
4, VIA NOBILI BOSIA

ST. GALLEN

RÖSSLITOR BÜCHER
WEBERGASSE 5

ZÜRICH

CALLIGRAMME BUCHHANDLUNG
HÄRINGSTRASSE 4

HOWEG BUCHHANDLUNG
WAFFENPLATZ 1

KUNSTGRIFF BUCHHANDLUNG
LIMMATSTRASSE 270

KUNSTHAUS ZÜRICH
HEIMPLATZ 1

KUNSTKIOSK
LIMMATQUAI 31

ORELL FÜSSLI KRAUTHAMMER
MARKTGASSE 12

ORELL FÜSSLI BUCHHANDLUNG
FÜSSLISTRASSE 4

SCALO BOOKS & LOOKS
LIMMATQUAI 18

SEC 52 BUCHHANDLUNG
JOSEFSTRASSE 52

E X H I B I T I O N S

ZÜRICH

GALERIE JUDIN AG	Lessingstrasse 5 8002 Zürich Tel. 043 422 88 88 www.galeriejudin.ch info@galeriejudin.ch	CARROLL DUNHAM A Survey of Drawings 1984–2004	**12.6.–16.7.2005**
ELISABETH KAUFMANN	Müllerstrasse 57 8004 Zürich Tel./Fax 043 322 01 15 elkauf@yahoo.com	YURI LEIDERMAN	**27.5.–9.7.2005**
		GEORGES ADÉAGBO, ERWIN BOHATSCH, WALTER DAHN	**ab 24.8.2005**
GALERIE LELONG	Predigerplatz 10–12 8001 Zürich Tel. 044 251 11 20 www.galerie-lelong.com galerie.lelong@dplanet.ch	JOAN MIRÓ	**4.6.–30.7.2005**
		ART 36 BASEL	**15.6.–20.6.2005**
		DAVID NASH	**8.9.–12.11.2005**
MAI 36 GALERIE	Rämistrasse 37 8001 Zürich Tel. 044 261 68 80 www.artgalleries.ch/mai36 mai36@artgalleries.ch	JOHN BALDESSARI	**11.6.–30.7.2005**
		ART 36 BASEL, Halle 2.1 Stand T4 ART Unlimited	**15.6.–20.6.2005**
MARK MÜLLER	Gessnerallee 36 8001 Zürich Tel. 044 211 81 55 www.markmueller.ch mark.mueller@dplanet.ch	JOSEPH MARIONI «Paintings» Room 3: DUANE ZALOUDEK «Nomad Song»	**11.6.–30.7.2005**
		ART 36 BASEL	**15.6.–20.6.2005**
		JUDY MILLAR «Paintings»	**25.8.–15.10.2005**
GALERIE RÖMERAPOTHEKE	Langstrasse 136 8004 Zürich Tel. 043 317 17 80 www.roemerapotheke.ch gallery@roemerapotheke.ch	SIMON ENGLISH	**28.5.–9.7.2005**
		JOHN PULE	**25.8.–22.10.2005**
BOB VAN ORSOUW	Limmatstrasse 270 Tel. 044 273 11 00 www.bobvanorsouw.ch mail@bobvanorsouw.ch	DAVID REED new paintings	**21.5.–23.7.2005**
		ERIK VAN LIESHOUT	**27.8.–1.10.2005**

E X H I B I T I O N S

ANNEMARIE VERNA	Neptunstrasse 45 8032 Zürich Tel. 044 262 38 20 www.annemarie-verna.ch office@annemarie-verna.ch	FRED SANDBACK (1943–2003) The Drawings (Catalogue available) ART 36 BASEL, Halle 2.0 Stand S1	 **23.4.–25.6.2005** **15.6.–20.6.2005**
NICOLA VON SENGER AG	Bleicherweg 45 8002 Zürich Tel. 044 201 88 10 www.nicolavonsenger.com info@nicolavonsenger.com	ERWIN WURM ART 36 BASEL, Halle 2.1 Stand K6 ART Unlimited – GIANNI MOTTI	**13.5.–16.7.2005** **15.6.–20.6.2005**
GALERIE JAMILEH WEBER	Waldmannstrasse 6 8001 Zürich Tel. 044 252 10 66 www.jamilehweber.com info@jamilehweber.com	ROBERT RAUSCHENBERG Spread and Scale JAHANGUIR – Paintings and Sculptures	 **20.5.–30.7.2005** **27.8.–8.10.2005**
BRIGITTE WEISS	Müllerstrasse 67 8004 Zürich Tel. 044 241 83 35 www.likeyou.com/brigitteweiss brigitteweiss@bluewin.ch	SAN KELLER GRAEME TODD	**bis 2.7.2005** **24.8.–29.10.2005**
		BASEL	
NICOLAS KRUPP	Erlenstrasse 15 4058 Basel Tel. 061 683 32 65 www.nicolaskrupp.com nic@nicolaskrupp.com	MARJETICA POTRC Voltashow Basel ATTA KWAMI	**28.5–9.7.2005** **14.6.–19.6.2005** **16.7.–27.8.2005**
		BERN	
KABINETT BERN	Gerechtigkeitsgasse 72–74 3011 Bern Tel. 031 312 35 01 www.kabinett.ch bern@kabinett.ch	CHRISTINA NIEDERBERGER	**13.5–27.6.2005**
		ST. GALLEN	
WILMA LOCK	Schmiedgasse 15 9000 St. Gallen Tel. 071 222 62 52 wilmalock@freesurf.ch	FRANZ ERHARD WALTHER Wortbilder Sommerpause nach Vereinbarung geöffnet	 **25.5.–16.7.2005**

12/06/05 >
28/08/05
hausderkunst

paul mccarthy
lala land
parodie paradies

haus der kunst
prinzregentenstrasse 1
d 80538 münchen
tel +49 89 21127-113
www.hausderkunst.de

T.M.

SENSATIONAL

S-T-R-E-T-C-H WIG

COOL LIGHT-N-AIRY VENTILATED CAP

With Built in SCALP That Looks Like SKIN

So natural — **LOOKS LIKE HAIR GROWING OUT OF HEAD.**
LOOKS LIKE YOU GREW IT YOURSELF

YOU WILL ENJOY THAT 100% NATURAL LOOK

BRUSH AND COMB TO ANY STYLE — ANY HAIRLINE INSTANTLY

6 WIGS IN ONE

STRETCHES for PERFECT FIT

OFF the FACE

ON the FACE

SIDE of FACE

FLIRTY BANGS

CENTER PART

SIDE PART

LIGHTWEIGHT COMFORTABLE PERMA-STYLED

WASH & WEAR

® VALMOR HAS A WIG YOU'VE NEVER SEEN BEFORE

NEW! DIFFERENT!

NEVER BEFORE A WIG LIKE THIS RETAINS STYLING

NEVER NEEDS SETTING

STYLE No. SK-129

PRICE ONLY $12.99

WAS $22.88

Worth Much More

SOLD BY OTHERS FOR MUCH MORE

The SKINATURAL STRETCH WIG

FABULOUS NEW WIG DESIGN

Has **Built in Scalp** that looks and feels like Skin. Right at the top where it's important. Every strand is hand-tied to the SKINATURAL Scalp which gives such natural appearance like living hair growing from the head. So truly natural, no one knows it's a wig. But most of all the SKINATURAL Scalp lets you comb or brush any style quickly with an ease you have always dreamed of. Because the Miracle fibres seem to grow straight out, wig can be styled or brushed in any direction. Never any more styling worries—a quick brushing is all it takes to create a dozen different styles:—**on the face, off the face, side of the face—comb lovely bangs or wear with center or side part.** Built-in simulated skin gives 100% natural appearance. **Special construction gives you instantly any hairline you want.** Never before a wig like this—Sensational—Amazing. Do anything you want with this fantastic **SKINATURAL** wig offered you by Valmor. Made from 100% **MIRACLE** Wash and Wear fibre. Just put on for Instant Beauty. Can be arranged in countless different styles just like you would your own hair. Save beauty parlor bills. More natural than any wig you can buy.

BUY A VALMOR® WIG. GET BEST VALUE FOR YOUR MONEY

Get **VERY BEST QUALITY** when you buy these **VERY BEST WIGS** and **HAIR PIECES** from **VALMOR.** All Stretch Wigs are pre-styled, pre-cut, Washable, Ready for Instant wear—Instant Beauty. No one knows you're wearing a wig or attachment. Gives you Exciting Sex appeal. **VALMOR** sells **FINEST** Quality at Lowest prices. Satisfaction Guaranteed on Delivery! Money refunded if not worn or altered.

COLORS: Black, Off-Black, Dark, Medium or Light Brown, Dark or Light Auburn, Blond, Platinum, Dark or Light Frosted or Mixed Gray. State color. Order now!

Order C.O.D.: Pay postman on delivery amount plus postage. If you send cash or money order company pays postage.

©1971

VALMOR HAIR STYLES Dept. 5125-SK129
2411 Prairie Ave. Chicago, Ill. 60616

Mail this ORDER COUPON Today

VALMOR HAIR STYLES DEPT. 5125-SK129
2411 PRAIRIE AVE., CHICAGO, ILL. 60616
PLEASE SEND ME THE FOLLOWING STYLES:

Style Number	Description	Price

Send C.O.D. I'll pay postman amount plus postage.
I enclose full amount—Company pays postage.

NAME ______ Box ______
Address ______ RFD ______
City ______ State ______ Zip ______

Check Color:
☐ Black ☐ Off Black
☐ Dark Brown
☐ Medium Brown
☐ Light Brown
☐ Dark Auburn ☐ Light Auburn
☐ Golden Blond ☐ Light Blond
☐ Honey Blond
☐ Platinum
☐ Light Frosted
☐ Dark Frosted
☐ Mixed Black & Gray
☐ Mixed Brown & Gray

DETAIL TAKEN FROM DeLuxe, 2004 A PORTFOLIO OF 60 ETCHINGS, EACH: 13 X 10 1/2 INCHES (33 X 26.7 CM)

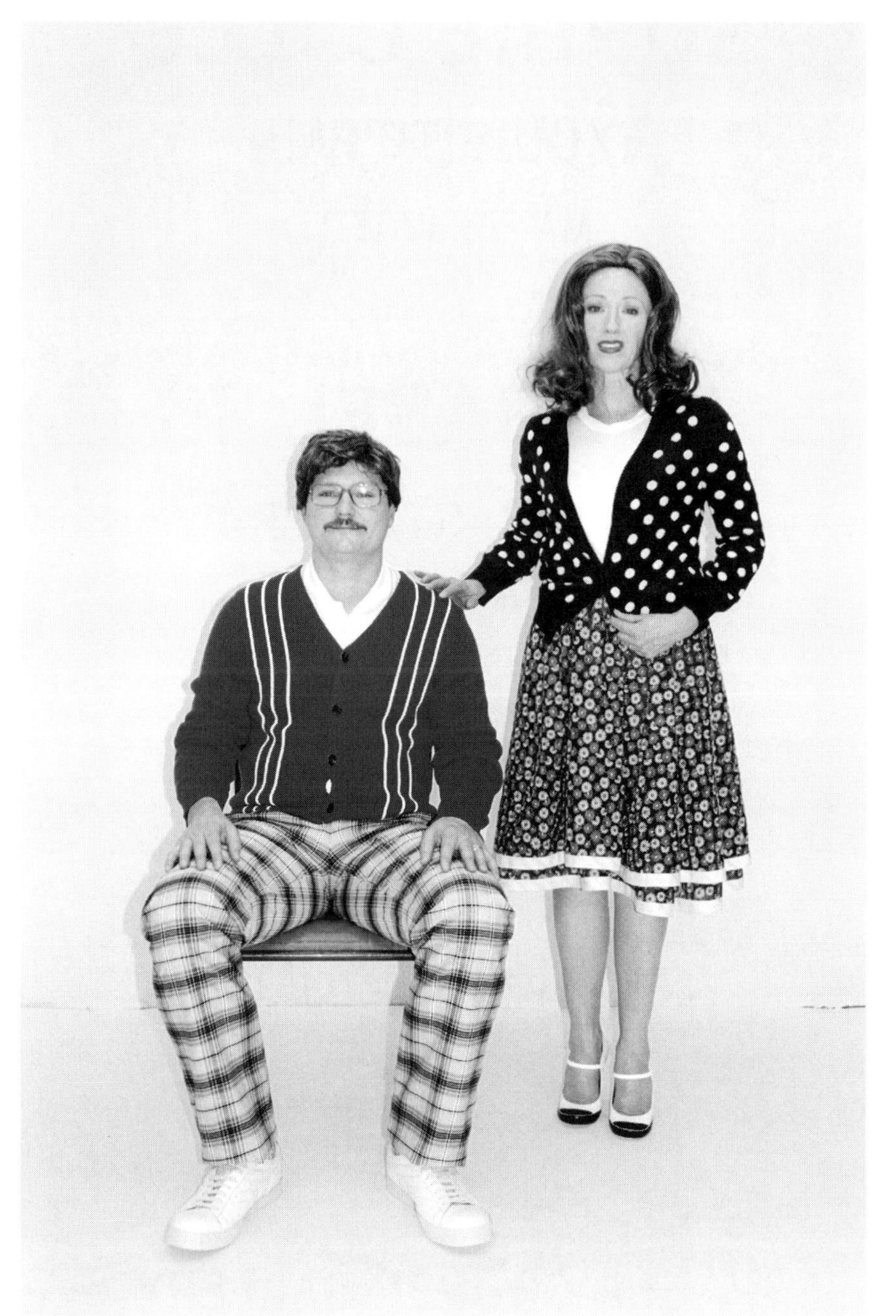

CINDY SHERMAN PHOTOGRAPHED BY JUERGEN TELLER

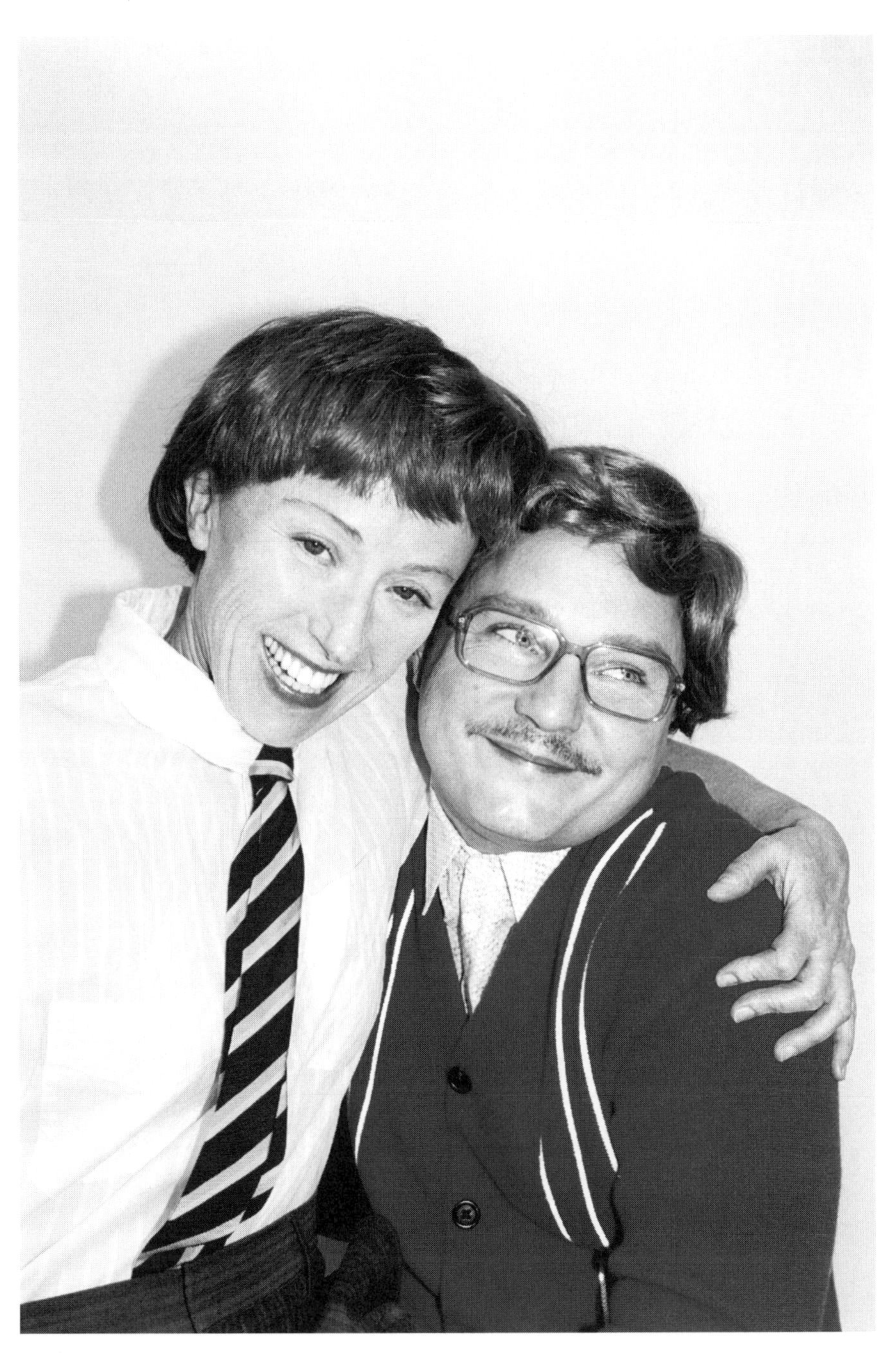

MARC JACOBS

12 June – 16 July 2005

CARROLL DUNHAM

A Survey of Drawings 1984 - 2004

A comprehensive catalogue will be available

SIGMAR POLKE

Vintage Photographs from a Private Collection

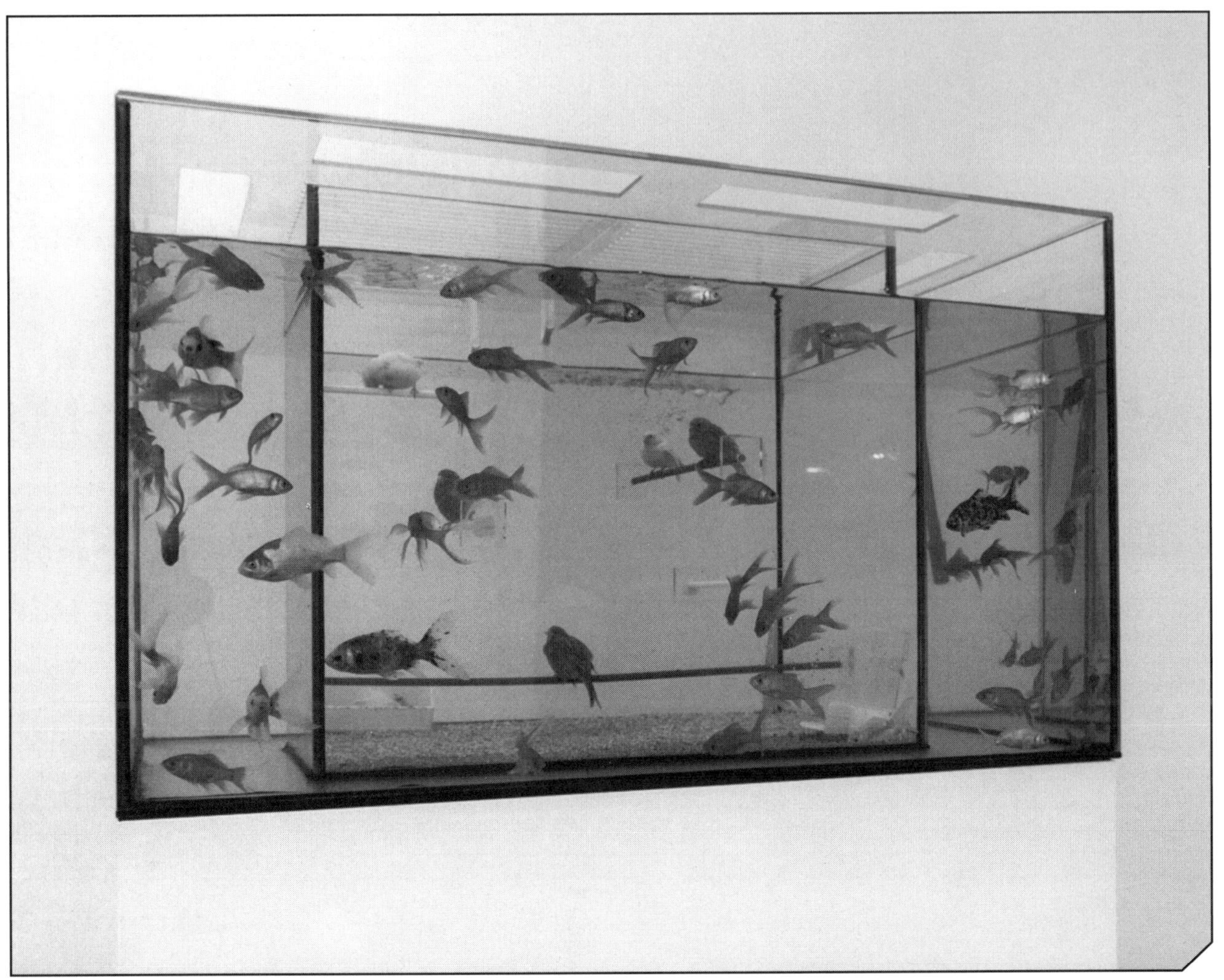

Robert Gligorov **DIVINA**

Galleria Pack - Milan / June - September '05

20 . 21

Galerie Edition Kunsthandel GmbH
Meisenburgstraße 169–173
45133 Essen
Tel. +49 (0)201 87100-0
Fax +49 (0)201 87100-10
info@2021art.com
www.2021art.com

Di–Fr 10–18 · Sa 11–16
und nach Vereinbarung

Otto Steinert: *Zwei Masken*, 1949
s/w Fotografie, Bromsilbergelatine, 28,5 x 37,5m
Vintage print

21|5–2|9|2005
Kabinette: Accrochage

Otto Steinert

Fotografien 1948–1973

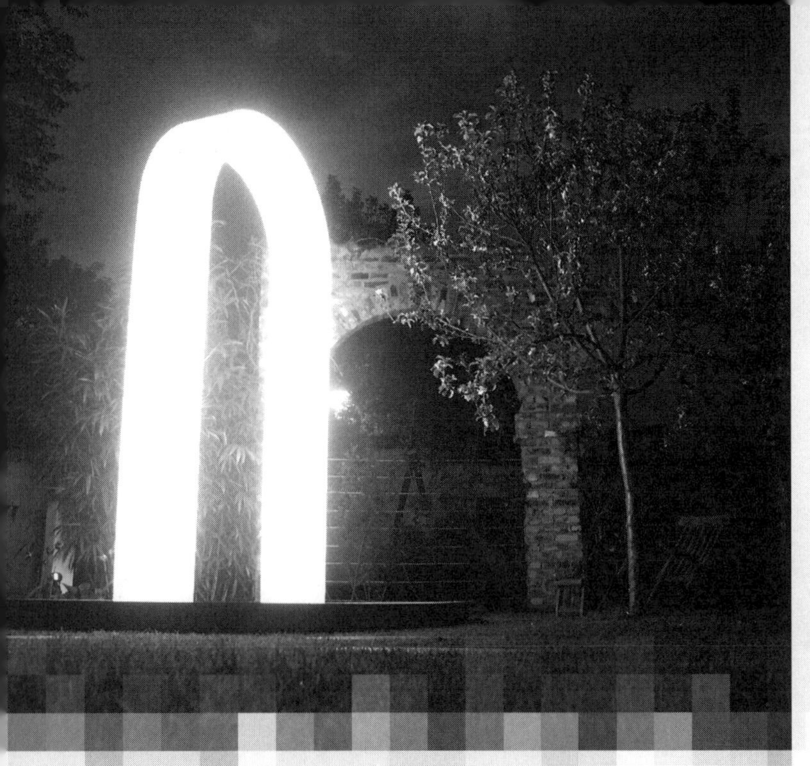

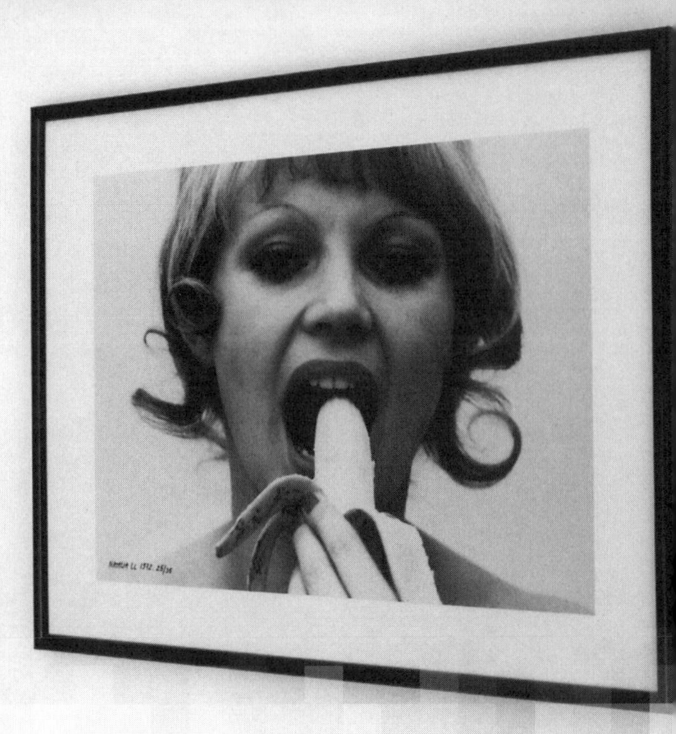

spiel.01 23.04. › 30.06.2005

Kinga Dunikowski

Knocking on Heaven's Door [installation, 2004]

Natalia LL

Consumer Art [photos, 1972]

brot.undspiele

brot.undspiele galerie | Gartenstraße 2 10115 Berlin | offen/open Di/Tue - Fr 11 - 13 & 15 - 18, Sa 14 - 18
http://brot.undspiele.com | info@brot.undspiele.com | Tel. +49 (0)177 388 38 76

JOSÉ MANUEL BALLESTER

SERGIO BELINCHÓN

MERLÍN CARPENTER

NAIA DEL CASTILLO

FILIPA CÉSAR

JOSÉ DAMASCENO

RICHARD DEACON

PIA FRIES

IÑAKI GRACENEA

ALEX HARTLEY

IGOR & SVETLANA KOPYSTIANSKY

GUILLERMO KUITCA

MAIDER LÓPEZ

JORGE MACCHI

MIQUEL MONT

FELICIDAD MORENO

MATTHIAS MÜLLER

JOAQUÍN PACHECO

FERNANDO RENES

JAMES RIELLY

RUI TOSCANO

DARIO URZAY

PETER ZIMMERMANN

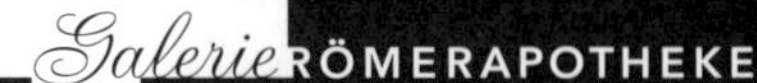

Galerie RÖMERAPOTHEKE

Langstrasse 136
8004 Zürich Switzerland
+41 (0)43 317 17 80
www.roemerapotheke.ch
gallery@roemerapotheke.ch

Mi–Fr 14–18.30 h, Sa 10–16 h

Simon English (GB)

28 May – 9 July 2005

John Pule (NZ)

25 August – 22 October 2005

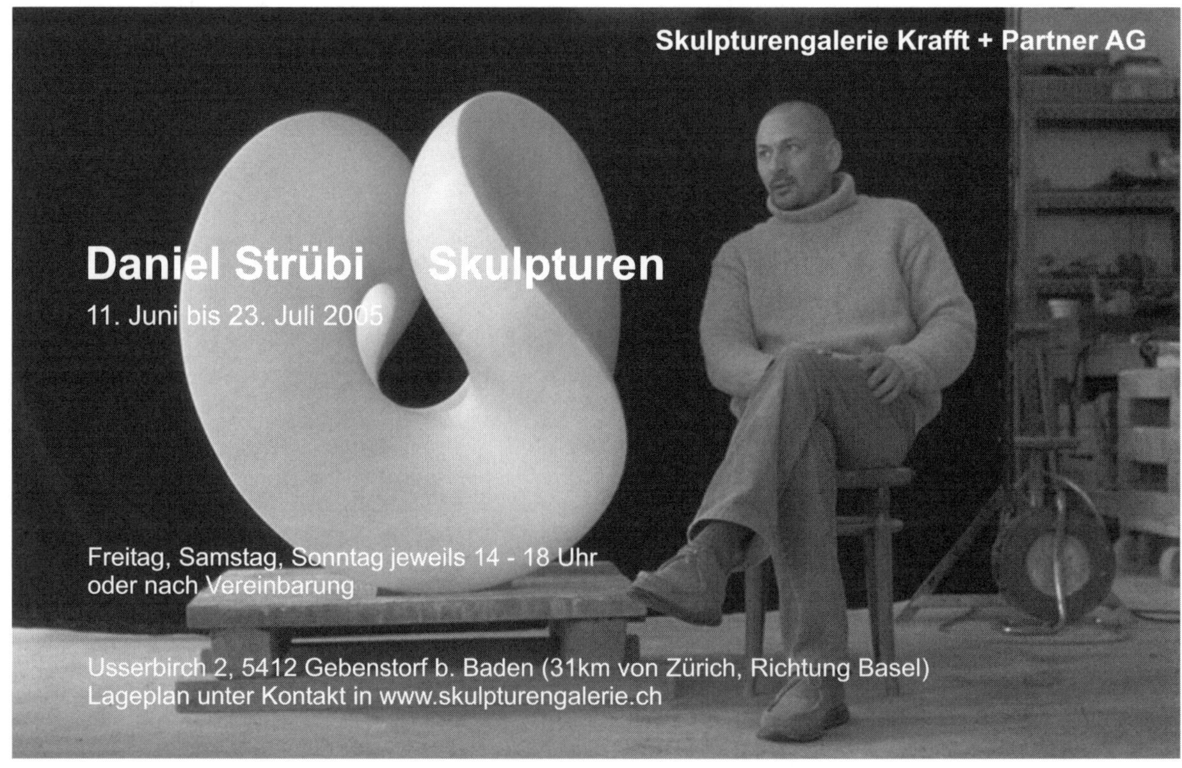

©GRRRR.NET

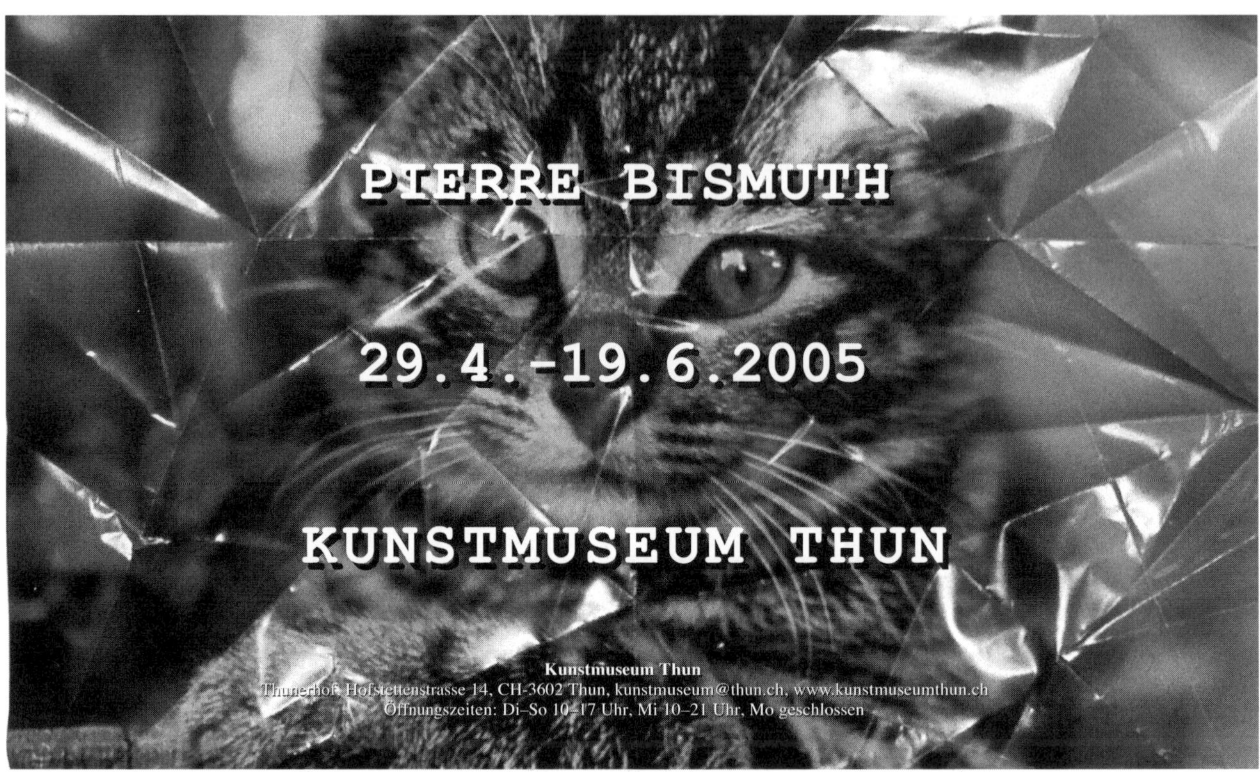
PIERRE BISMUTH
29.4.-19.6.2005
KUNSTMUSEUM THUN
Kunstmuseum Thun
Thunerhof, Hofstettenstrasse 14, CH-3602 Thun, kunstmuseum@thun.ch, www.kunstmuseumthun.ch
Öffnungszeiten: Di–So 10–17 Uhr, Mi 10–21 Uhr, Mo geschlossen

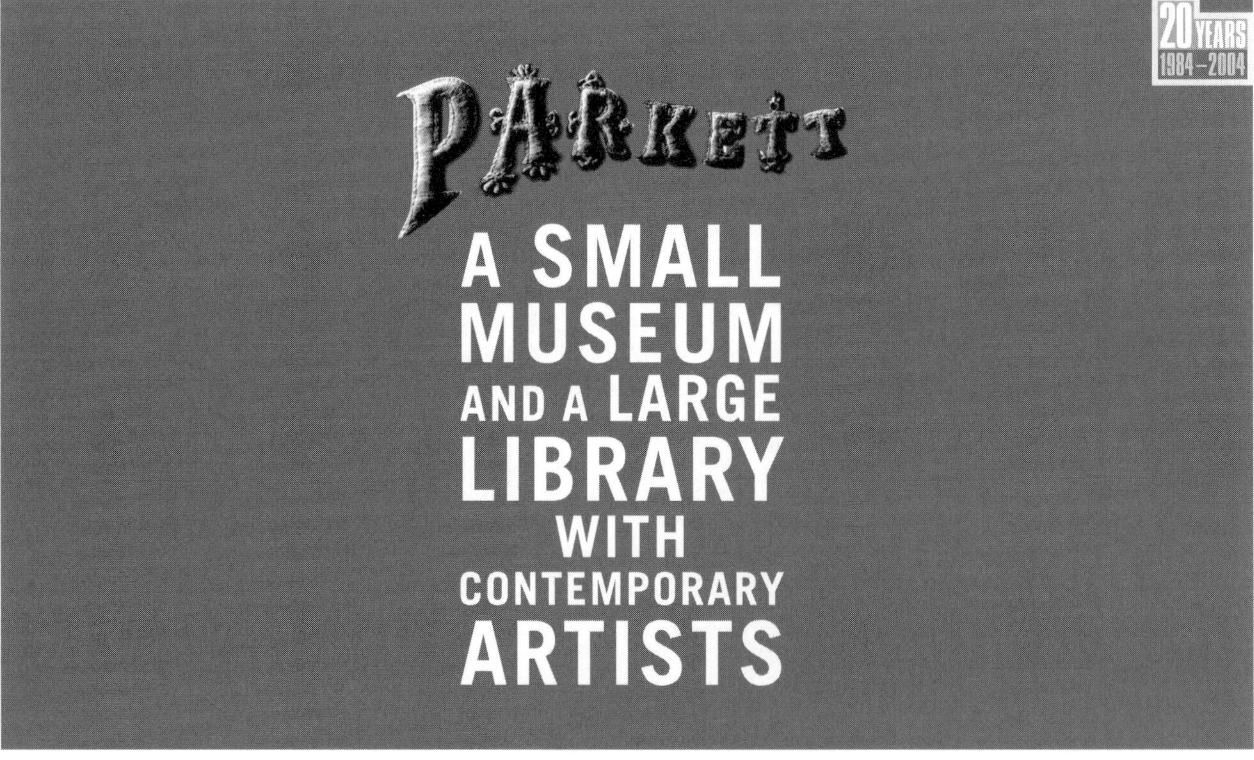
20 YEARS
1984–2004
PARKETT
A SMALL
MUSEUM
AND A LARGE
LIBRARY
WITH
CONTEMPORARY
ARTISTS

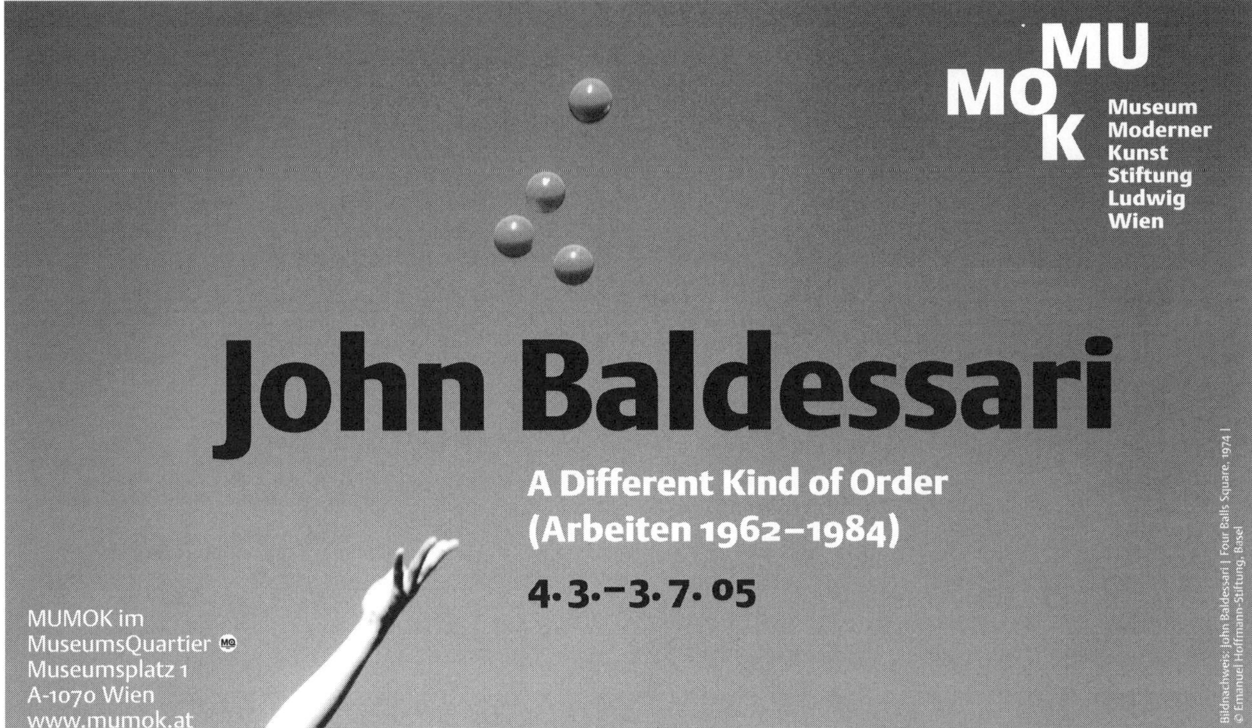
MU
MO
K
Museum
Moderner
Kunst
Stiftung
Ludwig
Wien
John Baldessari
A Different Kind of Order
(Arbeiten 1962–1984)
4.3.–3.7.05
MUMOK im
MuseumsQuartier
Museumsplatz 1
A-1070 Wien
www.mumok.at
Bildnachweis: John Baldessari | Four Balls Square, 1974 |
© Emanuel Hoffmann-Stiftung, Basel

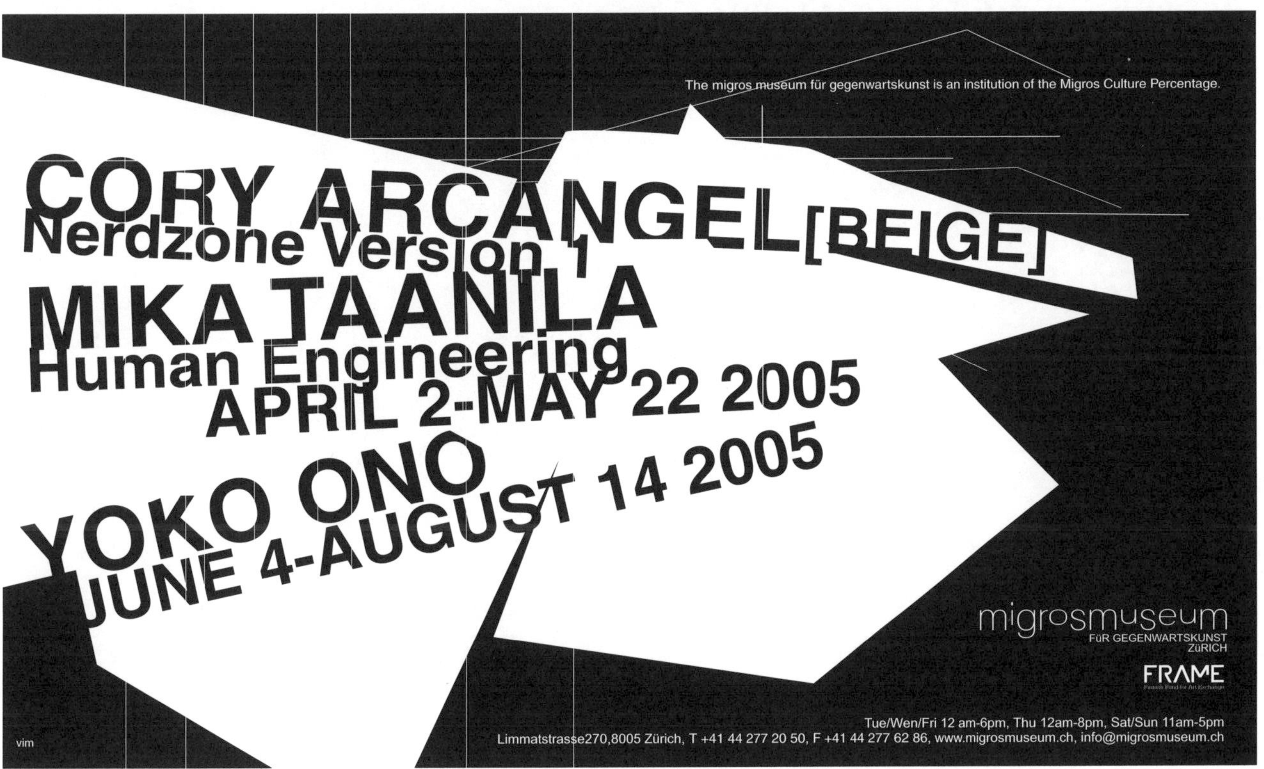
The migros museum für gegenwartskunst is an institution of the Migros Culture Percentage.
CORY ARCANGEL[BEIGE]
Nerdzone Version 1
MIKA TAANILA
Human Engineering
APRIL 2-MAY 22 2005
YOKO ONO
JUNE 4-AUGUST 14 2005
migrosmuseum
FüR GEGENWARTSKUNST
ZüRICH
FRAME
Tue/Wen/Fri 12 am-6pm, Thu 12am-8pm, Sat/Sun 11am-5pm
Limmatstrasse270,8005 Zürich, T +41 44 277 20 50, F +41 44 277 62 86, www.migrosmuseum.ch, info@migrosmuseum.ch
vim

RELAX (chiarenza & hauser & co) Die Belege / Les quittances / The Receipts 29 05–31 07 2005 Einzelausstellung / exposition personnelle

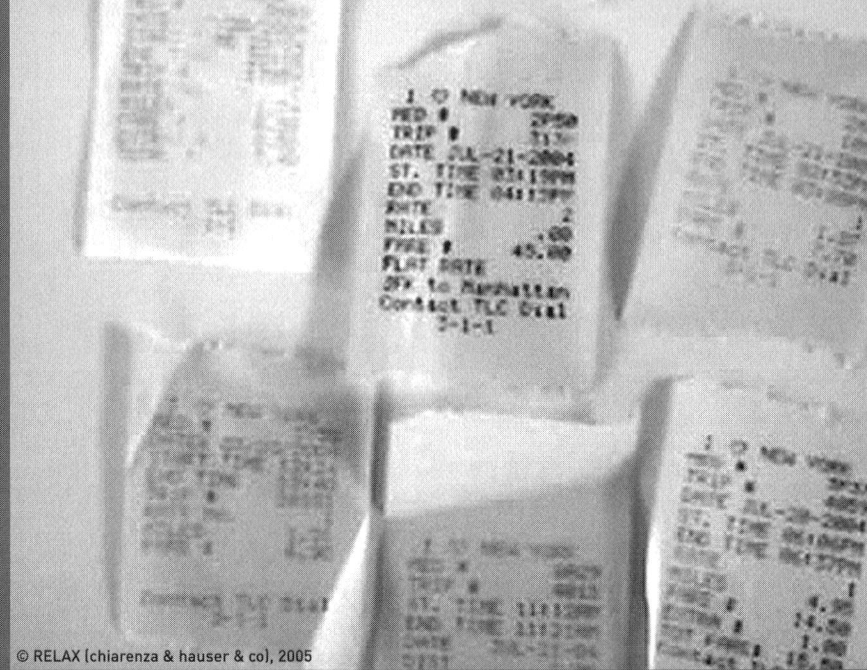

© RELAX (chiarenza & hauser & co), 2005

Eric Lanz 29 05–31 07 2005 Einzelausstellung / exposition personnelle

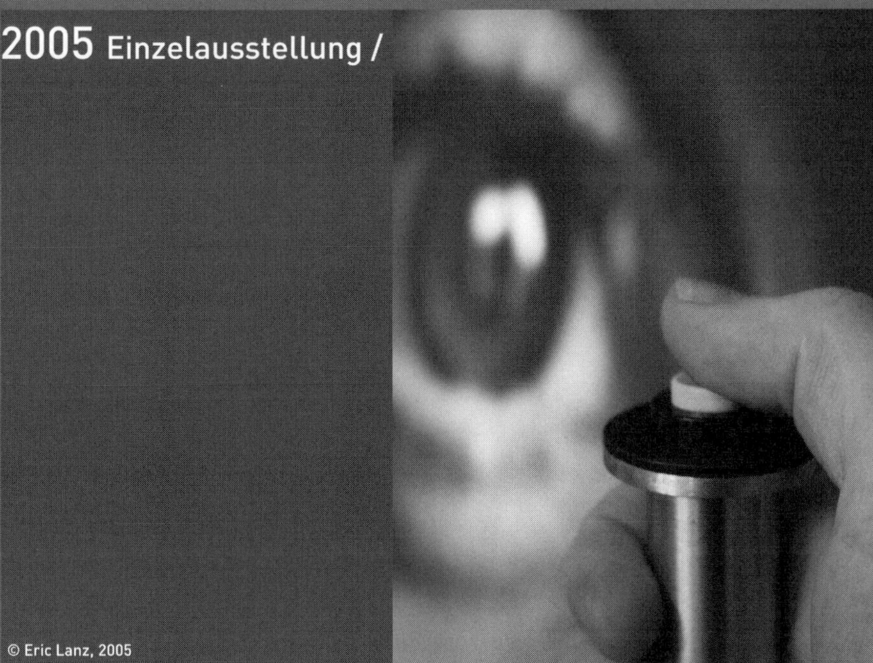

© Eric Lanz, 2005

CentrePasquArt Biel Bienne

CentrePasquArt Kunsthaus Centre d'art Seevorstadt 71-75 faubourg du Lac CH 2502 Biel Bienne T + 41 32 322 55 86 F +41 32 322 61 81 www.pasquart.ch info@pasquart.ch Öffnungszeiten heures d'ouverture Mi-Fr me-ve 14h-18h Sa-So sa-di 11h-18h Mo-Di geschlossen lu-ma fermé

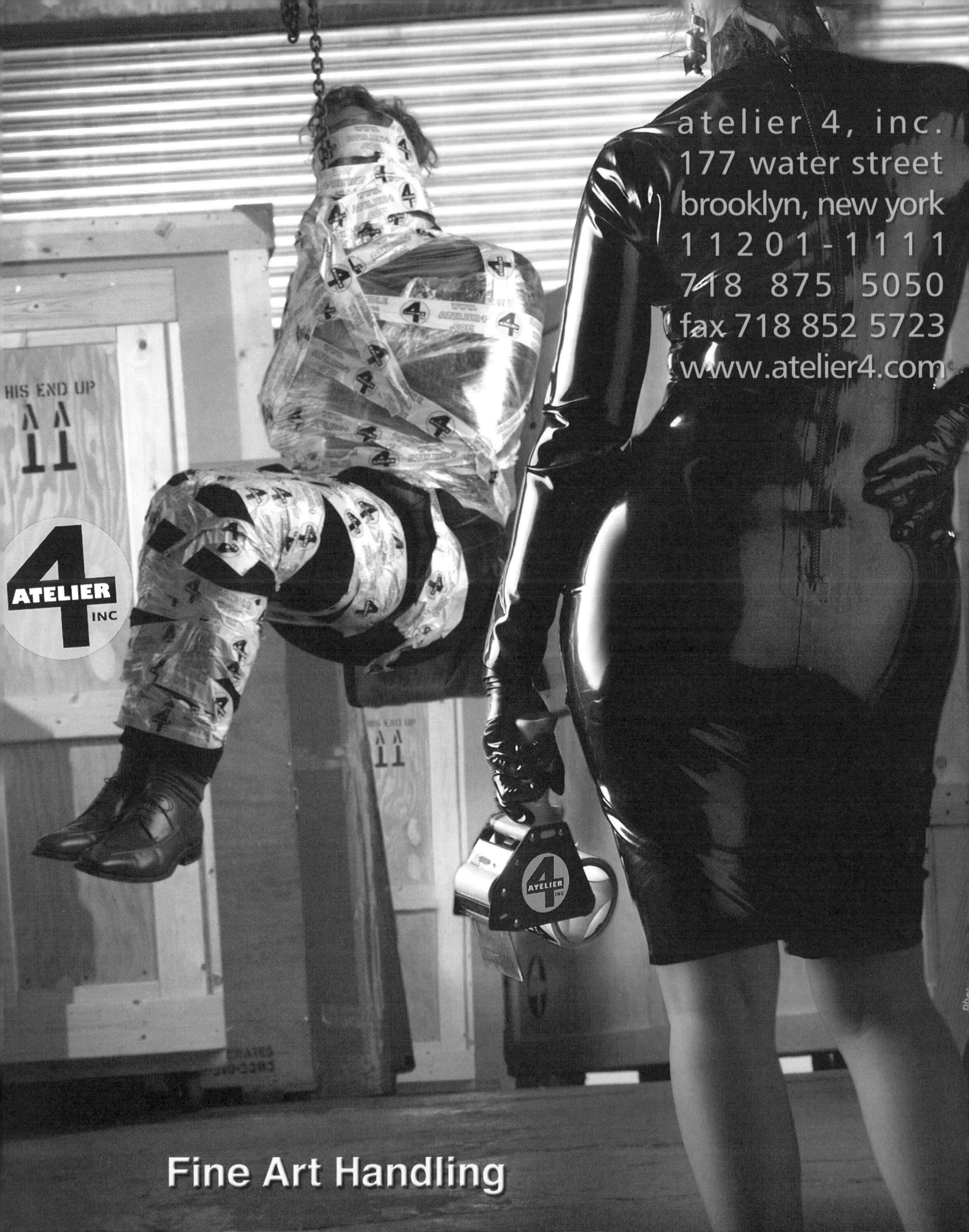
atelier 4, inc.
177 water street
brooklyn, new york
1 1 2 0 1 - 1 1 1 1
718 875 5050
fax 718 852 5723
www.atelier4.com
4 ATELIER INC
Fine Art Handling

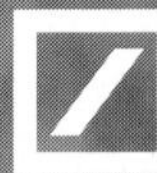

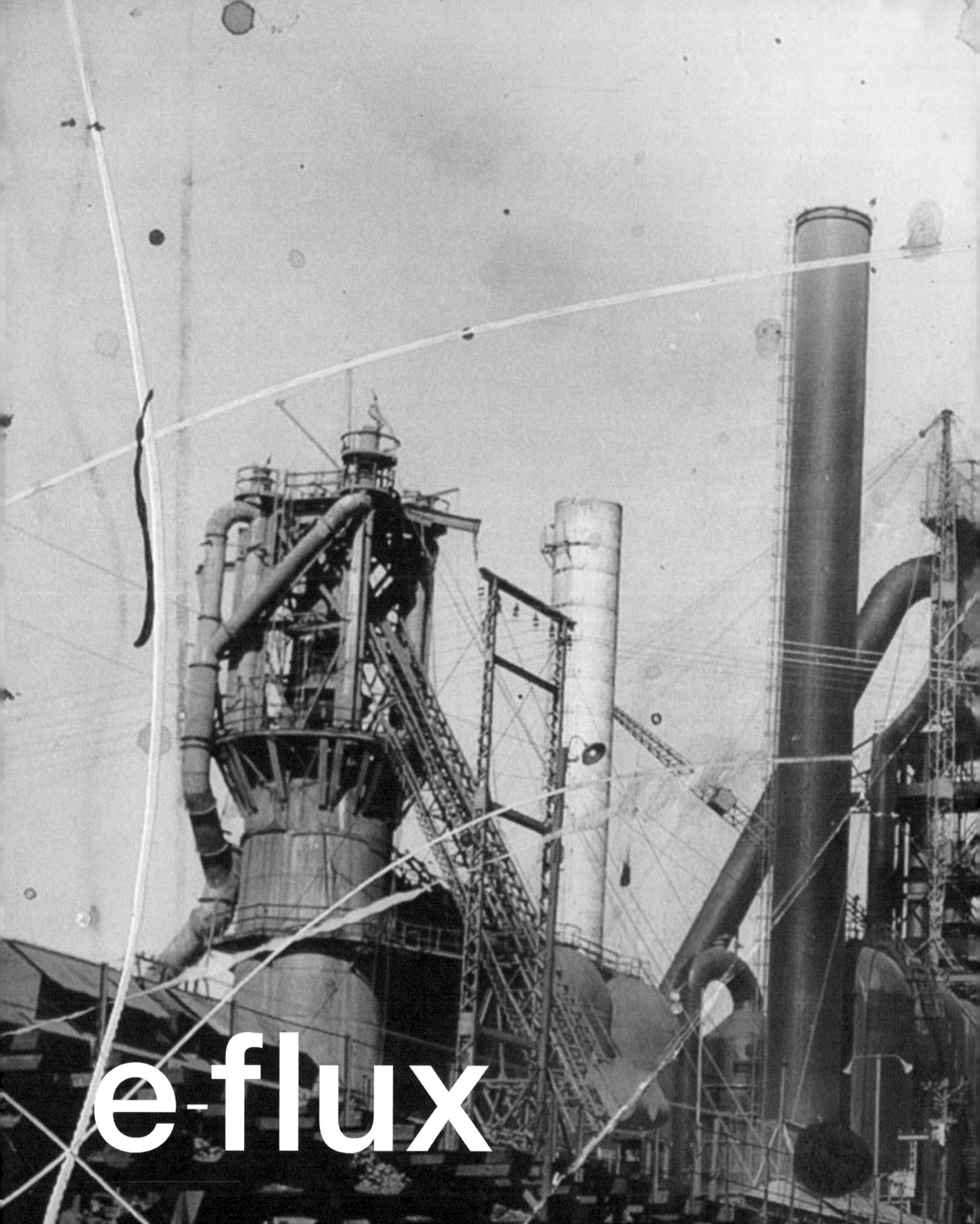
e-flux

FOR OUR 10 YEAR JUBILEE

WEEKDAY RODEO PACKAGE

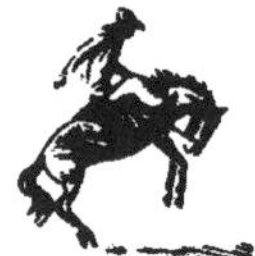

cut this out for two free tickets

Put Your Trust In Eyekon

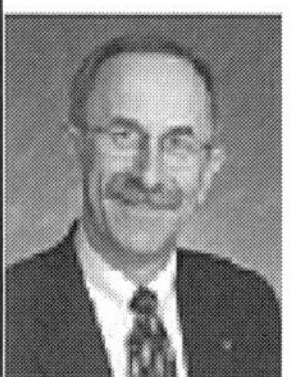

- CREATION*
- IT EXPERTISE*
- SOFTWARE PRODUCTS
- MAINTENANCE

Eyekon

Quellenstrasse 27 8005 Zürich Switzerland

*see website for details www.eyekon.ch

High Standard

COMMUNICATION Machines

- CLEAN THE VEHICLE
- CHECK THE FLUID
- ORGANISE YOUR MAINTENANCE RECORD

EYEKON

Quellenstrasse 27 8005 Zürich Switzerland

*see website for details www.eyekon.ch

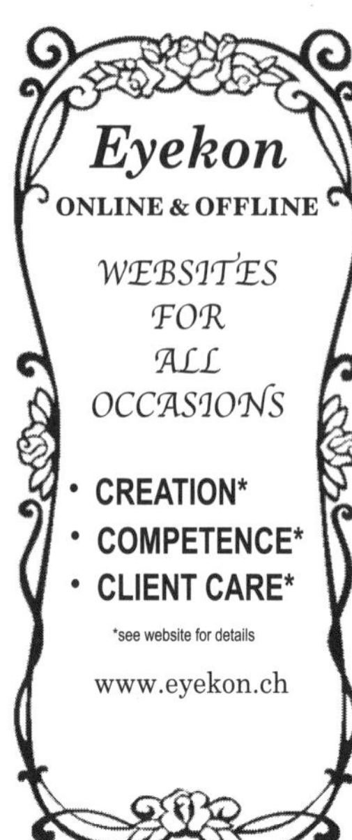

Eyekon

ONLINE & OFFLINE

WEBSITES FOR ALL OCCASIONS

- CREATION*
- COMPETENCE*
- CLIENT CARE*

*see website for details

www.eyekon.ch

call +41 043-444 77 77 or ignore us!

CLICK IT

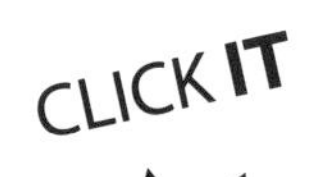

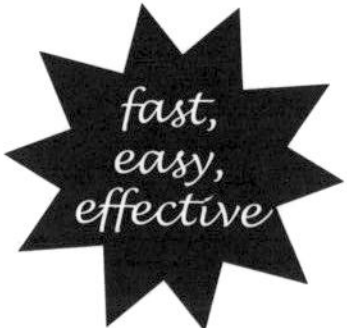

fast, easy, effective

FIND IT

www.eyekon.ch

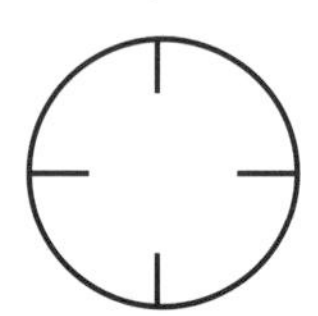

mention this ad for 10% off

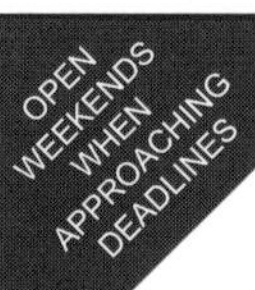

OPEN WEEKENDS WHEN APPROACHING DEADLINES

GET THE ATTENTION YOU NEED WITH..

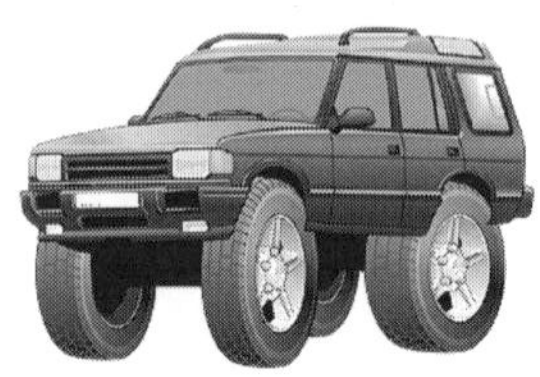

EYEKON

Quellenstrasse 27 8005 Zürich Switzerland www.eyekon.ch

EYEKON

KOMMUNIKATIOSMASCHINEN

- Kreation
- IT-Kompetenz
- Software Produkte
- Maintenance

www.eyekon.ch

Hauptrufummer

+41(0)43 444 77 77

Unverbindliche Offerte!

Kreation : Beratung/Konzeption, Kreation/Design,Projektmanagement, Texting/Redaktion

IT-Kompetenz : Software Entwicklung, Hosting

Software Produkte : Content Management System, Games & Social Software, Newsletter Tool

Maintenance : Website-Management, User- und Communitybetreuung, Text- und Bildredaktion, Webpublishing und Maintenance, Promotion, Schulung

preiswert UND zuverlässig

WE ARE user FRIENDLY

call us now +41 (0)43 444 77 77

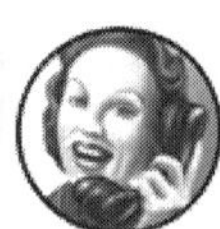

"All's Well That Ends Well"

at

Eyekon

integrating creation, technology and media.

Quellenstrasse 27 8005 Zürich Switzerland www.eyekon.ch

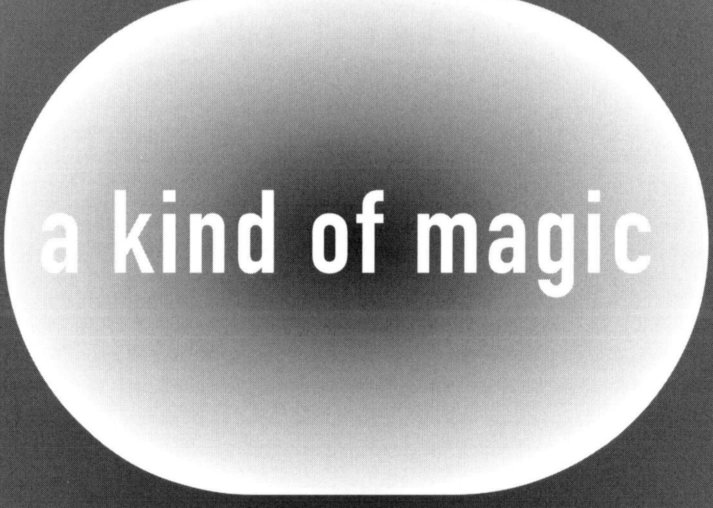

Kunstmuseum Luzern Museum of Art Lucerne
www. kunstmuseumluzern.ch

6 August – 27 November 2005

K|U|B

Kunsthaus **Bregenz**
Karl Tizian Platz
A-6900 Bregenz
Telefon +43-(0)5574-485 94-0
www.kunsthaus-bregenz.at

CLASSIC OF THE NEW

ROY LICHTENSTEIN

13|06–04|09|2005
täglich 10–21 Uhr

Roy Lichtenstein »Blonde Waiting« (Ausschnitt)|1964

ERIC HATTAN

www.hattan.ch

Au FRAC ALSACE
Fonds Régional d'Art Contemporain à Sélestat
"Vous êtes chez moi!"
Une exposition personnelle du 16 mai au 28 août 2005
www.culture-alsace.org

Au MAMCS
Musée d'Art moderne et contemporain de Strasbourg
"Le cri"
Une installation éphémère, octobre/novembre 2005
www.musee-strasbourg.org

Avec le CEAAC
Centre Européen d'Actions Artistiques Contemporaines à Strasbourg
"Le lampadaire"
Une proposition urbaine pour la commune de Lingolsheim
www.ceaac.org

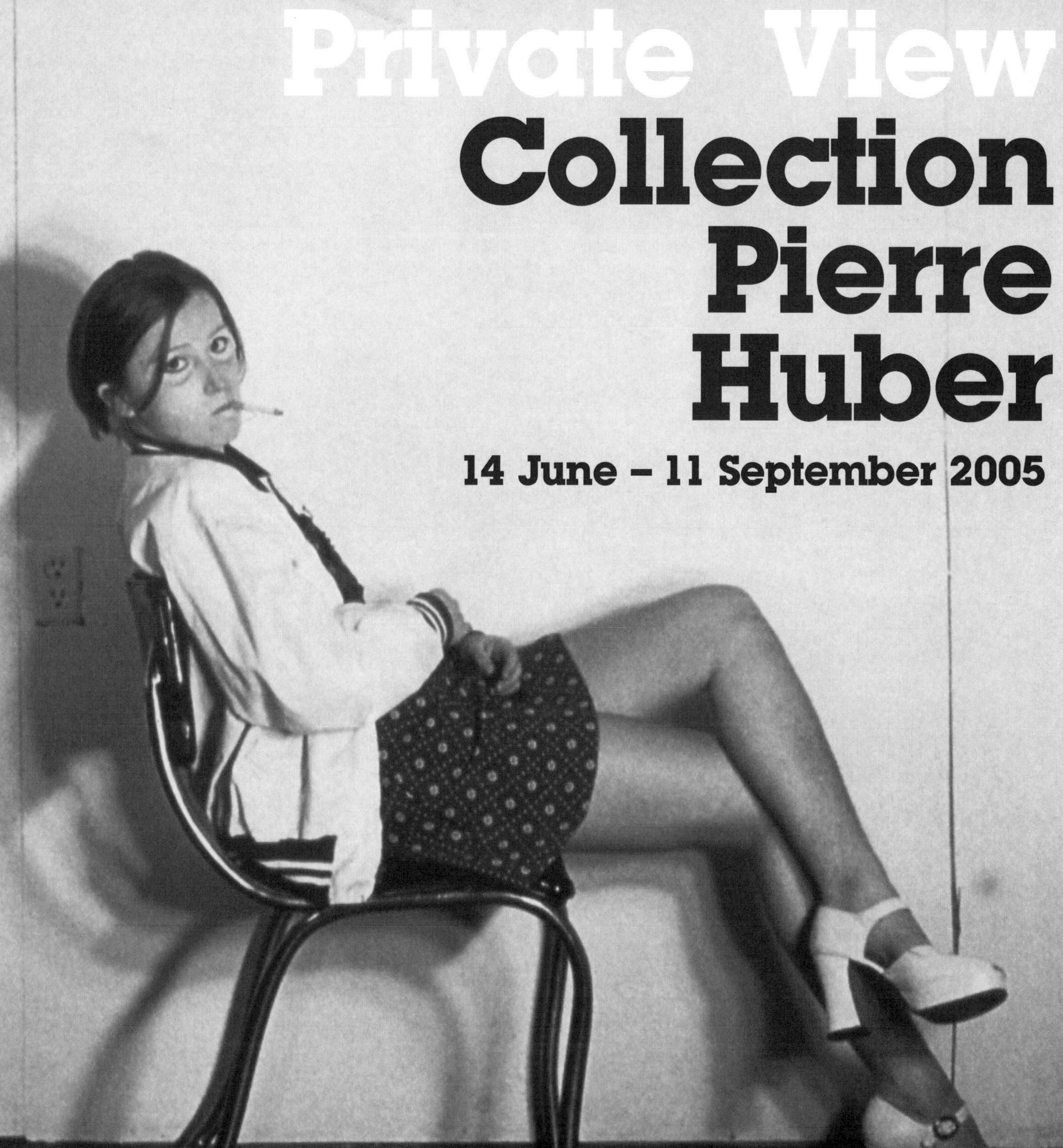

Musée cantonal des Beaux-Arts de Lausanne

Palais de Rumine Place de la Riponne 6 CH – 1014 Lausanne
T +41 (0)21 316 3445 F +41 (0)21 316 3446 info.beaux-arts@vd.ch www.beaux-arts.vd.ch

l'elac [l'espace lausannois d'art contemporain]
Rue de Genève 19 CH – 1003 Lausanne T +41 (0)21 311 2240 F +41 (0)21 311 2241

Catalogue available by JRP | Ringier [ISBN 2-940271-78-X]

et al.

the

fundamental

practice

NEW ZEALAND

AT THE 51ST VENICE BIENNALE

no no no no no no

si si si si si

go to --

Calle della Pietà
Off Riva degli Schiavoni
Behind S. Maria della Pietà (La Pietà)

An initiative of — In association with — Supported by

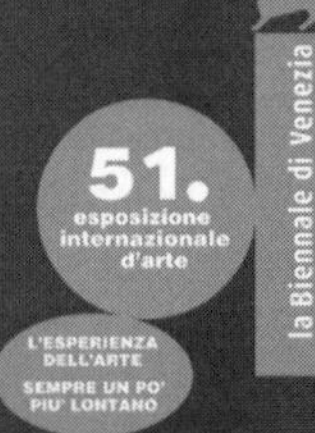
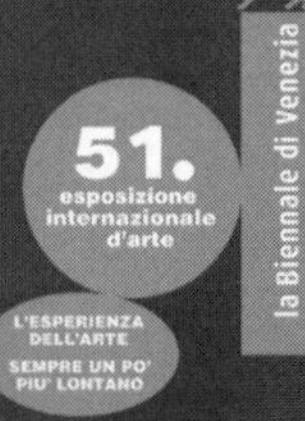

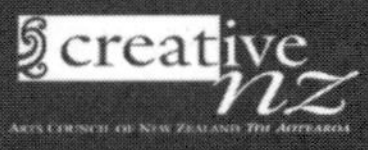

p.mule (dr), et al., APU / public projects Venice. original research output, 2004. Photo: Patrick Reynolds

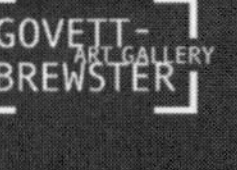

The Patrons of New Zealand at the Venice Biennale 2005

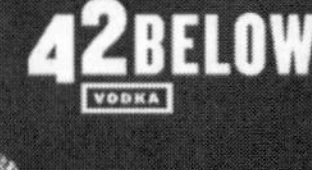

MONTANA RESERVE

LINDAUER Special Reserve

www.thefundamentalpractice.org

Arsenale
Piazza San Marco
Giardini

OK

OK AT THE S I : CHRISTIAN ANDERSSON / OLIVIER BLANCKART / VALENTIN CARRON / GABRIELE DI MATTEO / BOB GRAMSMA / LEOPOLD KESSLER / ADAM McEWEN / WERNER REITERER / BEN WOODESON /// CURATED BY MARC-OLIVIER WAHLER

APRIL 19 – JULY 16 2005

OKAY

OKAY AT THE GREY ART GALLERY NYU: CHRISTIAN ANDERSSON / VALENTIN CARRON / GABRIELE DI MATTEO / LARA FAVARETTO / LAURENT GRASSO / GRAHAM GUSSIN / LEOPOLD KESSLER / WERNER REITERER / NEDKO SOLAKOV / JEAN-LUC VERNA / BEN WOODESON /// CURATED BY MARC-OLIVIER WAHLER

APRIL 19 – JULY 16 2005

S I

SWISS INSTITUTE - CONTEMPORARY ART
495 Broadway / 3rd Floor / NEW YORK NY 10012

t (212) 925-2035 / f (212) 925-2040
info@swissinstitute.net / www.swissinstitute.net

GREY ART NYU GALLERY

GREY ART GALLERY, NEW YORK UNIVERSITY
100 Washington Square East, NYC 10003

t (212) 998-6780 / f (212) 995-4024
greygallery@nyu.edu / www.nyu.edu/greyart

OK / OKAY is made possible in part with public funds from the New York State Council on the Arts (NYSCA), a State agency; and with support from the Abby Weed Grey Trust; Pro Helvetia; *Étant Donnés*, the French-American Fund for Contemporary Art; the Danish Arts Council; Cultural Services of the French Embassy; Fundação Luso-Americano Para o Desenvolvimento; IASPIS; and Bundeskanzleramt Österreich Kunstsektion.

Leon Kossoff
Selected Paintings 1956–2000

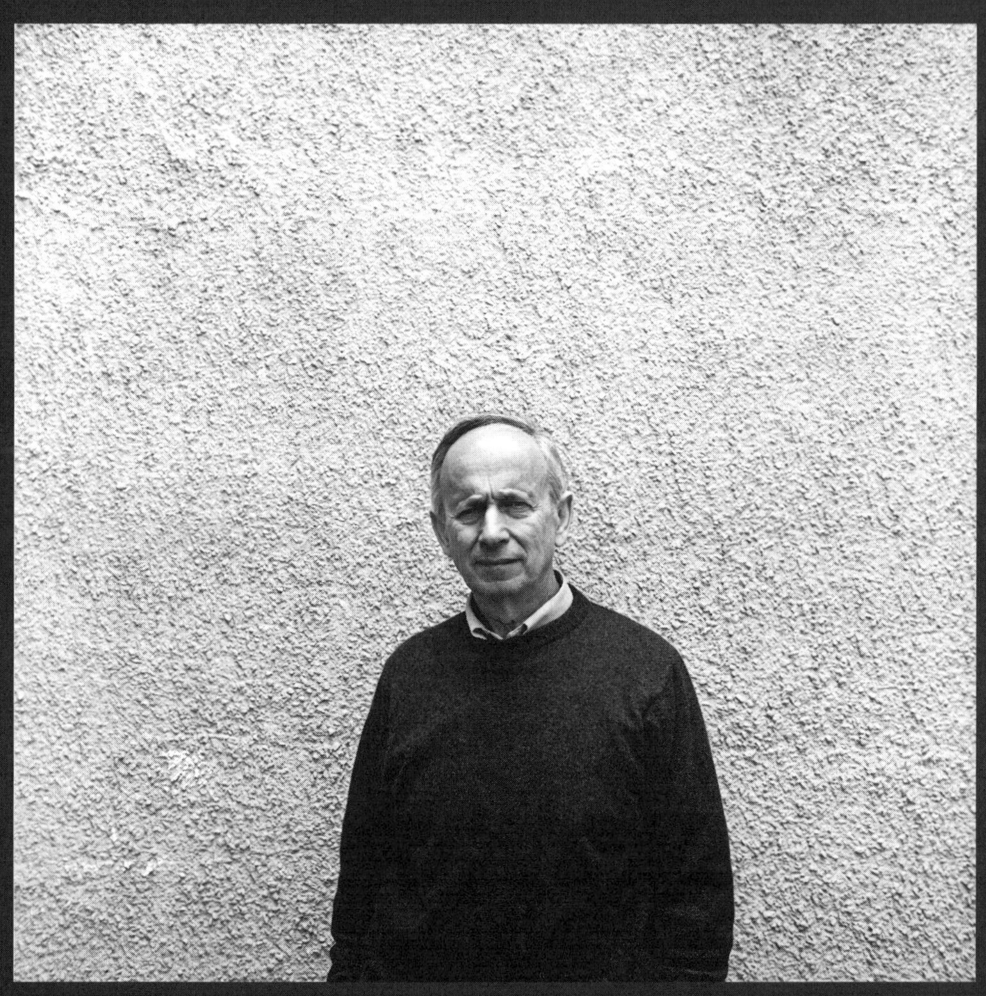

Kunstmuseum Luzern Museum of Art Lucerne
www. kunstmuseumluzern.ch

30 April – 24 July 2005

100 posters from
10 countries
designed
between
1958 and
1968

100 Plakate
aus 10 Ländern
entstanden
in der Zeit zwischen
1958 und
1968

—le spectacle dans la rue

a selection from
the celebrated exhibition
curated
by Antonio Boggeri
for Olivetti
in the late sixties

eine Auswahl aus
der berühmten Ausstellung
realisiert
von Antonio Boggeri
für Olivetti
Ende der Sechziger Jahre

31.5 – 3.9.2005

GALLERIAGOTTARDO

una fondazione per la cultura della
eine Kulturstiftung der
a cultural foundation of

BANCADEL GOTTARDO

Tuesday
2pm – 5pm
Wednesday – Saturday
11am – 5pm
Closed Sundays and Mondays

Dienstag
14.00 – 17.00 Uhr
Mittwoch bis Samstag
11.00 – 17.00 Uhr
Sonntag und Montag geschlossen

Institutional Patron
of the
Solomon R. Guggenh
Foundation

Viale Stefano Franscini 12
6900 Lugano
Switzerland

phone +41 91 808 1988
galleria@gottardo.com
www.galleria-gottardo.org

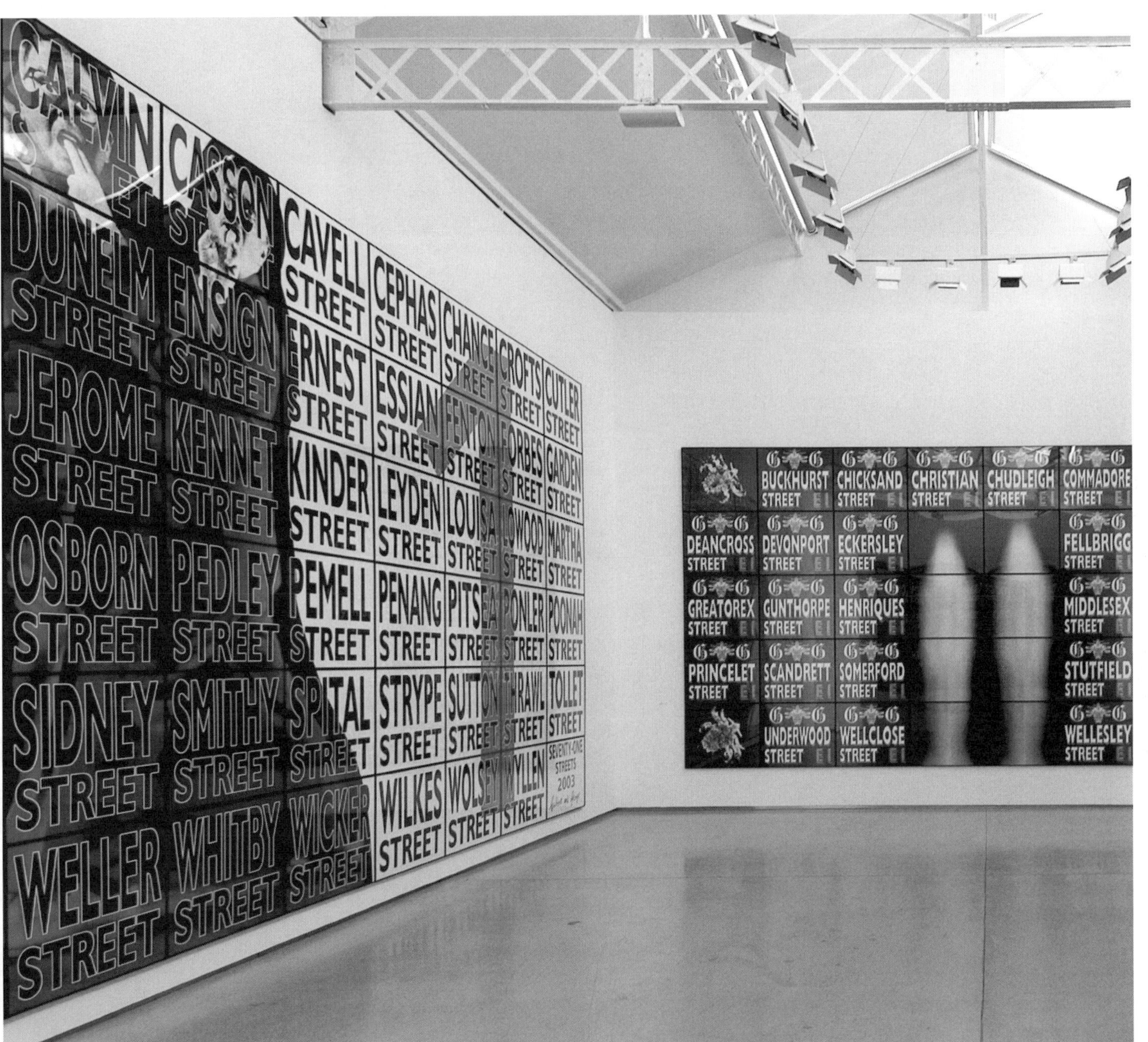
CALVIN
CASSON
DUNELM STREET
CAVELL STREET
CEPHAS STREET
ENSIGN STREET
ERNEST STREET
ESSIAN STREET
CROFTS STREET
CUTLER STREET
JEROME STREET
KENNET STREET
FENTON STREET
FORBES STREET
GARDEN STREET
KINDER STREET
LEYDEN STREET
LOWOOD STREET
MARTHA STREET
OSBORN STREET
PEDLEY STREET
PEMELL STREET
PENANG STREET
PONLER STREET
POONAH STREET
SIDNEY STREET
SMITHY STREET
SPITAL STREET
STRYPE STREET
SUTTON STREET
THRAWL STREET
TOLLET STREET
SEVENTY-ONE STREETS 2003
WELLER STREET
WHITBY STREET
WICKER STREET
WILKES STREET
WOLSEY STREET
WYLLEN STREET
BUCKHURST STREET
CHICKSAND STREET
CHRISTIAN STREET
CHUDLEIGH STREET
COMMADORE STREET
DEANCROSS STREET
DEVONPORT STREET
ECKERSLEY STREET
FELLBRIGG STREET
GREATOREX STREET
GUNTHORPE STREET
HENRIQUES STREET
MIDDLESEX STREET
PRINCELET STREET
SCANDRETT STREET
SOMERFORD STREET
STUTFIELD STREET
UNDERWOOD STREET
WELLCLOSE STREET
WELLESLEY STREET

EDITIONS

DEAR PARKETT SUBSCRIBER, DEAR READER,

It gives us great pleasure to present this latest survey of Parkett's currently available artists' editions. Following the exhibitions at the Museum of Modern Art, New York, at the Whitechapel Art Gallery, London, and at other venues, the Kunsthaus Zurich recently mounted "Parkett – 20 Years of Artists' Collaborations": the most complete presentation to date of all editions, prints, photographs, objects, multiples, and works made by artists especially for Parkett.

All of the artist's editions are documented in the new catalogue "Parkett – 20 Years of Artists'Collaborations" and also in our updated box containing color postcards of 146 editions and a booklet with two essays from the MoMA show (see images below). Visit our website www.parkettart.com.

Beatrice Fässler in Zurich (b.faessler@parkettart.com) or Monika Condrea in New York (m.condrea@parkettart.com) will be happy to answer any questions you may have regarding parkett's Musée en Appartement. Orders may be placed online (SSL secured) as well as by phone, fax or mail (see yellow order form in each issue). Prices are subject to change, postage and packaging are not indcluded; orders will be filled on a first-come first-serve basis.

SEHR GEEHRTE ABONNENTIN, SEHR GEEHRTER ABONNENT, LIEBE PARKETT-LESER,

Wir freuen uns, Ihnen diesen neuesten Überblick über die zurzeit erhältlichen Künstlereditionen zu präsentieren. Nach den Ausstellungen im Museum of Modern Art, New York, in der Whitechapel Art Gallery, London, und anderen Orten, zeigte das Kunsthaus Zürich diesen Winter die bisher vollständigste Übersicht aller von Künstlerinnen und Künstlern eigens für Parkett geschaffenen Editionen – Druckgraphik, Objekte, Photographien und Installationen.

Dokumentiert sind die Künstlereditionen im neuen Katalog "Parkett – 20 Years of Artists' Collaborations" und in der mit 146 Farbpostkarten neu komplettierten Postkartenbox (siehe Abb. unten), die auch ein Büchlein mit zwei Essays zur MoMA-Ausstellung enthält. Besuchen Sie auch unsere Webseite www.parkettart.com.

Für Fragen zu Parketts Musée en Appartement steht Ihnen Beatrice Fässler (b.faessler@parkettart.com) in Zürich jederzeit gerne zur Verfügung. Ihre Bestellung können Sie uns online (Site ist SSL-zertifiziert), per Telefon, Fax oder Post zukommen lassen (siehe gelben Antwortschein in jedem Parkettband). Preisänderungen bleiben vorbehalten. Versand, Verpackungskosten und MwSt. (Schweiz) sind nicht inbegriffen. Die Lieferung erfolgt in der Reihenfolge des Bestelleingangs solange Vorrat.

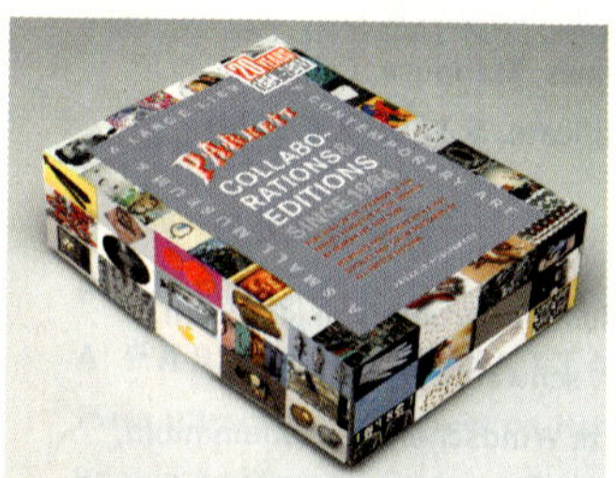

POSTCARD SET WITH
TEXT BOOKLET ON MOMA SHOW
146 color postcards,
booklet of 64 pages.
€ 32 / $ 39 / CHF 45
ISBN 3-907582-23-3

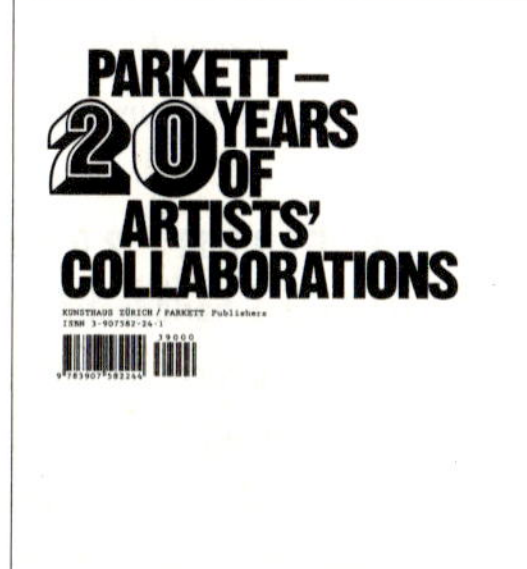

"A rare behind-the-scenes look"
Interviews, artists' sketches, photographs, and more, 248 p., color poster.
€ 32 / $ 39 / CHF 45

Yours sincerely / Mit freundlichen Grüssen

Dieter von Graffenried
Publisher/Verleger

Bice Curiger
Editor-in-Chief/Chefredaktorin

Parkett Verlag AG
Quellenstr. 27
8031 Zürich
Tel. +41-1-271 81 40
FAX +41-1-272 43 01

Parkett PUBLISHERS
155 AV. of the Americas
New York, NY 10013
phone (212)673-2660
FAX (212)271-0704
www.parkettart.com

FOR PARKETT

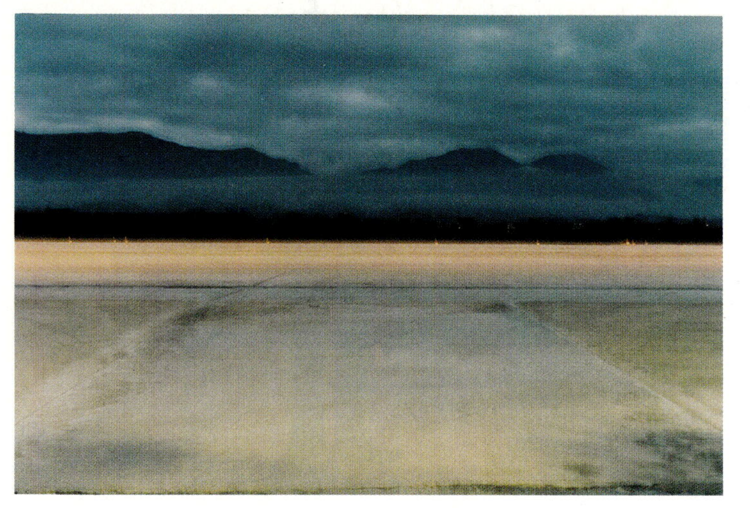

A BARREN PLACE AMONG PLACES: THE FACELESSNESS OF TECHNOLOGY VIES WITH THE ELOQUENCE OF DISTANT HILLS IN A DIVIDED UNIVERSE.

DER KARGE ORT ZWISCHEN DEN ORTEN: WINKEN NEUE HORIZONTE FERN UND BLAU, GERINNT DAS HIER UND JETZT ZUM BRACHEN FELD.

PARKETT 73

ANRI SALA

AIRPORT, 2005

C-print, paper size 20 1/2 x 27 9/16",
image size 16 1/2 x 23 5/8".
Edition of 60/XX, signed and numbered certificate
$ 1600 / € 1200

C-Print, Blattformat: 52 x 70 cm,
Bildformat: 42 x 60 cm.
Auflage: 60/XX, signiertes und nummeriertes Zertifikat.
CHF 1900 / € 1200

A BEEHIVE OF THOUGHTS BUZZING IN THE GULF BETWEEN WOMANHOOD AND SURVIVAL, PAST AND PRESENT, HUNGER AND SURFEIT, WORK AND PLAY...

WIE EIN BIENENSTOCK SUMMT DIESER KOPF ZWISCHEN EXISTENZNOT, WEIBLICHER MAGIE UND DER GELASSENHEIT DER LILIEN AUF DEM FELDE.

PARKETT 73

ELLEN GALLAGHER

RUBY DEE, 2005

Two-plate photogravure with aquatint and unique hand-shaped plasticine elements (in three colors) on multilayered laminated paper, framed.
Image size 6 x 4 x 1/8", with frame 9 1/4 x 7 1/4 x 1 1/4".
Produced by Two Palms Press, New York.
Edition of 30/XV, signed and numbered.
$ 3000 / € 2300

Photogravüre, Aquatinta und Knetmasse (dreifarbig, handgeformt), auf mehrschichtigem, laminiertem Papier, gerahmt.
Bildformat: 15,2 x 10,2 x 0,3 cm, mit Rahmen 23,5 x 18,4 x 3,8 cm.
Hergestellt bei Two Palms Press, New York.
Auflage: 30/XV, signiert und nummeriert.
CHF 3500 / € 2300

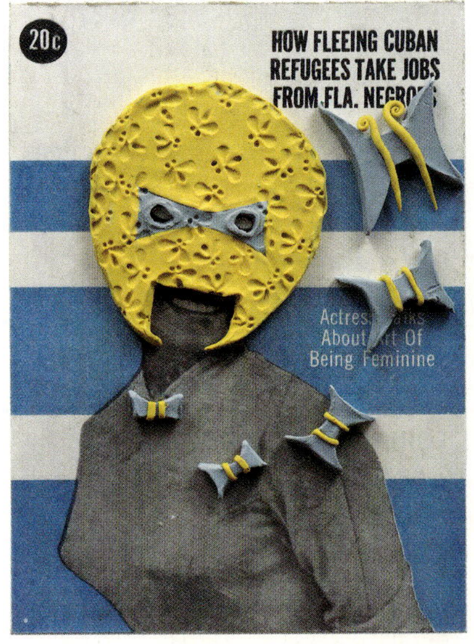